EXPLORER

Abu Dhabi
LIVE WORK EXPLORE

www.liveworkexplore.com

At Line Investments & Property, we are driven by the passion to lead that took us to scale new heights in developing the most sought after shopping malls in the region. Al Wahda Mall. Khalidiyah Mal , Al Raha Mall, Madinat Zayed Shopping Centre & Gold Centre, Mazyad Mall, Al Foah Mall and Mushrif Mall stand as a reigning glory to our promise of bringing the best overlooking the rest.

Abu Dhabi Explorer 2011/9th Edition
First Published 1999
2nd Edition 2002
3rd Edition 2003
4th Edition 2004
5th Edition 2006
6th Edition 2007
7th Edition 2009
8th Edition 2010
9th Edition 2011 ISBN 978-9948-450-17-7

Front Cover Photograph – Abu Dhabi Corniche – Pete Maloney

Printed and bound by Emirates Printing Press, Dubai, United Arab Emirates.

Explorer Publishing & Distribution
PO Box 34275, Dubai
United Arab Emirates
Phone +971 (0)4 340 8805
Fax +971 (0)4 340 8806
Email info@explorerpublishing.com
Web www.explorerpublishing.com

Welcome...

...to the all new **Abu Dhabi Explorer – Live Work Explore**, the ultimate insiders' guide to moving to, living in and loving one of the world's most exciting cities. Completely updated and written by local expats, this guide is brimming with inside information on how to make the most of your time in Abu Dhabi.

From red-tape to restaurants, housing to hobbies, entertainment to exploring, and shopping to socialising, we've got Abu Dhabi covered. Be sure to log on to www.liveworkexplore.com for more on the latest events, great competitions, and the chance to give us your insights on life in Abu Dhabi – whether it's a restaurant review or an expat experience.

And if all that wasn't enough, we also have our **lifestyle magazine** – *liveworkexplore* – available for sale on news stands around the UAE, or by subscribing online. A must-read, it includes travel features on far-off places, weekend breaks to the best of the GCC, real life issues on being an expat and the best of things to see and do in the Emirates.

And don't forget – whether it's dining out or driving off-road, shopping or snorkelling, working in the Gulf or whizzing off for a weekend break, Explorer has a guide for you. Check out all our guides, photography books and maps at www.explorerpublishing.com.

Happy exploring!

xxx

The Explorer Team

Contents

Contents

Contents

UAE: A Country Profile

UNITED ARAB EMIRATES

Located in the heart of the Middle East, the United Arab Emirates (UAE) is home to over 150 nationalities. While proud and protective of its Islamic culture, it is also one of the most progressive, cosmopolitan and open-minded countries in the region. From the desert wilderness of Abu Dhabi's Empty Quarter to the brash metropolis of Dubai and across to the rugged coastline of the country's east, its many landscapes lie waiting to be explored. Whether you're new to this remarkable land or have been living here for years, there's always something new to discover.

Location

Located on the eastern side of the Arabian Peninsula, the UAE borders Saudi Arabia and the Sultanate of Oman, with coastlines on both the Arabian Gulf and the Gulf of Oman. The country comprises seven emirates: Abu Dhabi, Ajman, Dubai, Fujairah, Ras Al Khaimah, Sharjah and Umm Al Quwain. Abu Dhabi is by far the largest emirate, occupying over 80% of the country; the emirate of Dubai is second largest, although Abu Dhabi and Dubai share similar population sizes (p.9).

The country is perhaps best known for the modern, rapidly expanding metropolises of Abu Dhabi and Dubai, but visitors may be surprised by the variety of landscapes when they venture beyond the cities. The coast is littered with coral reefs and more than 200 islands, most of which are uninhabited. The interior of the country is characterised by sabkha (salt flats), stretches of gravel plain, and vast areas of sand desert. To the east rise the Hajar Mountains ('hajar' is Arabic for 'rock') which, lying close to the Gulf of Oman, form a backbone through the country, from the Musandam Peninsula in the north, through the eastern UAE and into Oman.

Abu Dhabi Theatre

UAE Fact Box

Coordinates: 24°00' North 54°00' East
Total land area: approx. 83,600 sq km
Total coastline: 1,318km
Highest point: 1,527m
Abu Dhabi total land area: 67,340 sq km

The highest point is Jebel Yibir at 1,527 metres. The Rub Al Khali, or Empty Quarter, occupies a large part of the south of the country. Stretching into Saudi Arabia, Oman and Yemen, it's the largest sand desert in the world, covering an area roughly the same size as France, Belgium and the Netherlands. This stark desert is interrupted only by salt flats and occasional oases, and its spectacular sand dunes rise to more than 300 metres.

Climate

The UAE has a subtropical and arid climate. Sunny blue skies and high temperatures can be expected for most of the year. Rain falls on an average of only 25 days per year, mainly in winter (December to March). In the UAE, it rarely rains very heavily or for long periods. However, in the Hajar Mountains, the amount of rainfall can be much higher and flash floods in the wadis are not unheard of.

Although infrequent, when it comes, heavy rainfall can really take its toll on the city of Abu Dhabi within a relatively short period. Not all roads have adequate drainage and even those that do are not designed for massive downpours, so drains get blocked by sand. In addition, many of Abu Dhabi's drivers are not accustomed to wet conditions and tend to respond by putting their hazard lights on, which can be confusing for other drivers. Heavy rain, although infrequent, can quickly lead to flooding and disruption to business; schools and companies have had to close due to impassable roads in the past.

During winter, there are occasional sandstorms when the sand is whipped up off the desert. This is not to be confused with a shamal, a north-westerly wind that comes off the Arabian Gulf and can cool temperatures down. Sandstorms cover anything left outside in gardens or on balconies and can even blow inside, so make sure your doors and windows are shut.

Temperatures range from a low of around 10°C (50°F) in winter to a high of 48°C (118°F) in summer. The mean daily maximum is 24°C (75°F) in January, rising to 41°C (106°F) in August.

Humidity is usually between 50% and 65%. However, when combined with the high summer temperatures, even 60% humidity can produce extremely uncomfortable conditions. The most pleasant time to visit the UAE is in the cooler winter months, when temperatures are perfect for comfortable days on the beach and long, lingering evenings outside. For up-to-date weather reports, log on to www.adiamet.gov.ae or www.das.ae, or call Abu Dhabi International Airport Meteorological Department forecaster on 02 575 7326.

HISTORY

Abu Dhabi's early existence is closely linked to the arrival and development of Islam in the greater Middle East region. Islam developed in modern-day Saudi Arabia at the beginning of the seventh century AD with the revelations of the Quran being received by the Prophet Muhammad. Military conquests of the Middle East and North Africa enabled the Arab empire to spread the teachings of Islam from Mecca and Medina to the local Bedouin tribes inhabiting the surrounding areas. This unifying foundation enabled the Arab empire to expand further into the Middle East and North Africa.

Emirs Or Sheikhs?

While the term emirate comes from the ruling title of 'emir', the rulers of the UAE are called 'sheikhs'.

Periods of dominance from other empires followed over the centuries, with the Turks, Mongols and Ottomans all exerting their influence over the region. In the early 19th century, the British and Portuguese dipped their oars into Arabian waters. They were attracted by the strategic advantages of the area's

UAE TIMELINE

Stone Age	Modern human settlement in the UAE dates back to ca.7000BC
Bronze Age	Archaeological evidence of human settlements; the domestication of the camel boosts trade
Iron Age	The invention of *falaj*, an irrigation technology, takes place somewhere between 1300-300BC
630	Envoys from the Prophet Muhammad arrive, heralding the conversion of local people to Islam
1761	The Baniyas tribe discovers fresh water in Abu Dhabi and settles on the island; leading to the construction of Qasr Al Hosn
1790s	The pearl trade is booming off the coast of Abu Dhabi
1835	Maritime Truce signed between the Trucial States and Britain
1930s	The first oil concession in Abu Dhabi is granted to Trucial Coast Oil Development Company
1950s	Oil is discovered in the UAE, exports begin in 1962
1966	HH Sheikh Zayed bin Sultan Al Nahyan becomes ruler of Abu Dhabi
1971	Britain withdraws from the Gulf and The UAE is established, with HH Sheikh Zayed bin Sultan Al Nahyan of Abu Dhabi as the leader. The UAE joins the Arab League
1972	Ras Al Khaimah joins the UAE
1973	The UAE launches a single currency, the UAE dirham
1981	The Gulf Cooperation Council is formed, with the UAE as a founding member
1985	Emirates Airline is founded
1999	The doors of the Burj Al Arab, the tallest hotel in the world, open for the first time in Dubai
2001	Construction starts on Dubai's Palm Jumeirah
2003	Etihad Airways is founded
2004	Sheikh Zayed bin Sultan Al Nahyan dies and is succeeded as leader of the UAE by his son, Sheikh Khalifa bin Zayed Al Nahyan
2005	Emirates Palace, billed as the world's most expensive hotel, opens to the public
2007	The Sheikh Zayed Mosque, the eighth largest mosque in the world, opens during Ramadan. Work also begins on Yas Island and Saadiyat Island
2008	In the wake of global economic crisis, much of the UAE's property market crashes
2009	Abu Dhabi hosts its inaugural Formula 1 Grand Prix at Yas Marina Circuit; the Sheikh Khalifa Bridge opens, linking the new areas of Abu Dhabi directly to the Corniche; Dubai Metro, the region's first public mass-transit system, is launched
2010	The tallest building in the world, the Burj Khalifa, opens; Ferrari World Abu Dhabi, the world's largest indoor theme park, opens

position between Europe and India, and keen to quash the rise of piracy in the local waters. By 1820, the British had exerted their authority and a general treaty was agreed by the local rulers, denouncing piracy. The following years witnessed a series of maritime truces, with Abu Dhabi and the other emirates accepting British protection in 1892. In Europe, the area became known as the Trucial Coast, a name it retained until the departure of the British in 1971.

Girl Power

Following elections back in 2007, a number of women were voted in to government positions. Today, over 40% of government employees are women, one of the highest rates in the world.

Despite opportunities for fishing and grazing, it was not until the discovery of freshwater, in 1761, that the ruling Al Nahyan family moved from the Liwa Oasis to Abu Dhabi island. By the 1800s, the town had developed considerably and, during the second half of the 19th century, led by Sheikh Zayed bin Khalifa (or 'Zayed the Great'), Abu Dhabi became the most powerful emirate along the western coast of the Arabian Peninsula. It was under Zayed's rule and great influence that Abu Dhabi and the northern emirates accepted the protection of Britain.

When Britain announced its withdrawal from the region, in 1968, the ruling sheikhs of Bahrain, Qatar and the Trucial Coast realised that, by uniting forces as a single state, they would have a stronger voice in the wider Middle East region. Negotiations collapsed when Bahrain and Qatar chose independence; however, the Trucial Coast remained committed to forming an alliance and, in 1971, the federation of the United Arab Emirates was born. The new state comprised the emirates of Abu Dhabi, Dubai, Ajman, Fujairah, Sharjah, Umm Al Quwain and, by 1972, Ras Al Khaimah. Under the agreement, the individual emirates each retained a certain degree of autonomy, with Abu Dhabi and Dubai providing the most input into the federation. The leaders of the new federation elected the ruler of Abu Dhabi, His Highness Sheikh Zayed bin Sultan Al Nahyan, to be their president of the newly-founded country. The well-liked and much-respected Sheikh held this position until he passed away on 2 November, 2004.

His eldest son, His Highness Sheikh Khalifa bin Zayed Al Nahyan, was then elected to take over the presidency. Despite the unification of the seven emirates, boundary disputes have caused a few problems. At the end of Sheikh Zayed's first term as president, in 1976, he threatened to resign if the other rulers didn't settle the demarcation of their borders. The threat proved an effective way of ensuring cooperation. The formation of the UAE came after the discovery of huge oil reserves in Abu Dhabi in 1958 (Abu Dhabi has an incredible 10% of the world's known oil reserves). This discovery dramatically transformed the emirate. In 1966, Dubai, which was already a relatively wealthy trading centre, also discovered oil.

GOVERNMENT & RULING FAMILY

The Supreme Council of Rulers is the highest authority in the UAE, comprising the hereditary rulers of the seven emirates. Since the country is governed by hereditary rule, there is little distinction between

ABU DHABI RULING FAMILY TREE

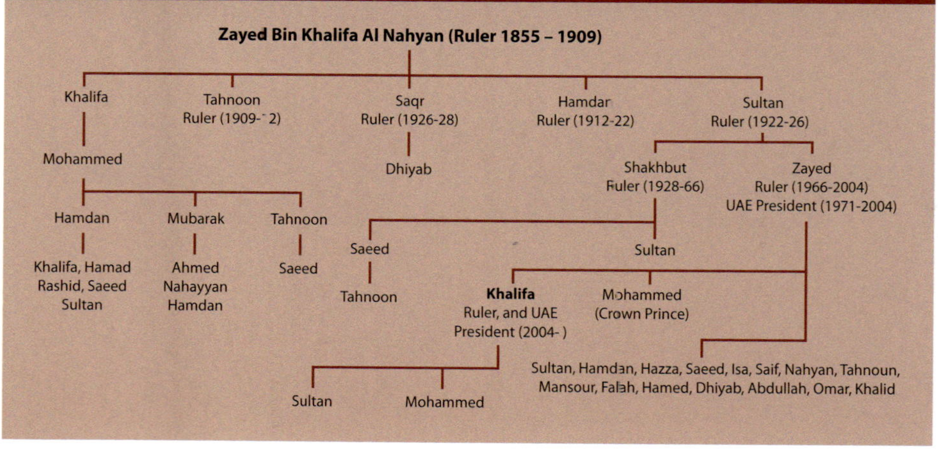

Abu Dhabi Corniche

the royal families and the government. The Supreme Council is responsible for general policy involving education, defence, foreign affairs, communications and development, and for ratifying federal laws. Each Emirate has one single vote, and the rulers of Abu Dhabi and Dubai have power of veto over decisions.

Modern UAE

Trade and commerce are still the cornerstones of the economy, with the traditional manufacturing and distribution industries now joined by finance, construction, media, IT and telecoms. With so many world-class hotels, leisure and entertainment options, the UAE is becoming an increasingly popular and important tourist and sporting destination.

The Supreme Council elects the chief of state (the president) from among its seven members. The current president is the ruler of Abu Dhabi, Sheikh Khalifa bin Zayed Al Nahyan. He took over the post in November 2004 from his late father, Sheikh Zayed bin Sultan Al Nahyan. The Supreme Council also elects the vice president of the UAE, currently Sheikh Mohammed bin Rashid Al Maktoum, ruler of Dubai. The president and vice president are elected and appointed for five-year terms, although they are often re-elected time after time, as was the case with Sheikh Zayed. The president appoints the prime minister (currently Sheikh Mohammed bin Rashid Al Maktoum) and the deputy prime ministers (currently Sheikh Saif bin Zayed Al Nahyan and Sheikh Mansour bin Zayed Al Nahyan).

The Federal National Council (FNC) reports to the Supreme Council. It has executive authority to initiate and implement laws and is a consultative assembly of 40 representatives, half of whom are chosen for the post in the FNC Elections. In 2011, nearly 130,000 Emiratis are eligible to run and vote in the elections. The Council monitors and debates government policy but has no power of veto.

The individual emirates have some degree of autonomy and laws that affect everyday life vary between them. For instance, if you buy a car in one emirate and need to register it in a different emirate, you will have to export and then re-import it.

INTERNATIONAL RELATIONS

The UAE remains open in its foreign relations and firmly supports Arab unity. HH Sheikh Khalifa bin Zayed Al Nahyan is very generous with the country's wealth when it comes to helping Arab nations and communities that are in need of aid.

The UAE became a member of the United Nations and the Arab League in 1971. It is a member of the International Monetary Fund (IMF), the Organisation of Petroleum Exporting Countries (Opec), the World Trade Organisation (WTO) and other international and Arab organisations. It is also a member of the Arab Gulf Cooperation Council (AGCC, also known as the GCC), whose other members are Bahrain, Kuwait, Oman, Qatar and Saudi Arabia.

All major embassies and consulates are represented either in Abu Dhabi or Dubai, or both. See Embassies & Consulates on the last page of this book.

SHEIKH KHALIFA: A PROFILE

Sheikh Khalifa bin Zayed Al Nahyan is the president of the UAE and ruler of Abu Dhabi. Upon the death of his father, Sheikh Zayed bin Sultan Al Nahyan, in 2004, Sheikh Khalifa took over as Abu Dhabi's ruler and was quickly and unanimously elected by the seven members of the Supreme Council as the president of the country.

Sheikh Khalifa was born in Al Ain in 1948, the eldest son of Sheikh Zayed, and he was named Crown Prince of Abu Dhabi in 1969. Since then, he has held a number of high government positions and worked closely with Sheikh Zayed throughout his father's presidency in the development of infrastructure and basic human needs for the citizens of the UAE.

Sheikh Zayed is still enormously revered in the UAE and, so far, under his son, Sheikh Khalifa's leadership, the country, and especially Abu Dhabi, has witnessed astonishing growth. With his focus on the continuing development of the country's infrastructure, economic health and cultural contributions, he has laid the foundations for a prosperous UAE without sacrificing his goals of ensuring the country's security, furthering its international relations, safeguarding its environment, and promoting its heritage.

Recently, the Burj Khalifa, the world's tallest building, located in Dubai, was named after Sheikh Khalifa and he has remained generous with Abu Dhabi's oil wealth, ensuring that the other emirates aren't left behind. The most significant loan, of course, was the recent US $10 billion loan to Dubai, but Sheikh Khalifa is also known for his philanthropic commitments, such as the major gift in 2007 to Johns Hopkins Medicine, in honour of the late Sheikh Zayed.

FACTS & FIGURES

Population

The UAE population has grown rapidly in recent years as expat arrivals, robust economic expansion and high birth rates have continued to push up the total number. According to the World Bank, the UAE's population stood at 4.6 million in 2009 and, according to Abu Dhabi Statistics Centre, the capital's population stood at 1.64 million in that year.

In early 2011, the UAE Statistics Bureau estimated that the country's population has shot up by 65% in four years to reach 8.26 million. However, the official census has been delayed from the scheduled April 2010 date and it is unlikely that the results will be published before mid-2012 at the earliest. Nearly nine out of ten UAE residents are expats, with Emiratis accounting for 11.5% of the population.

World's Richest City

In 2007, *Fortune Magazine* named Abu Dhabi the world's richest city. The emirate has 10% of the world's oil reserves and has invested its sovereign wealth wisely to create a healthy economy. Its global profile has increased in recent years as the emirate has become an economic powerhouse.

Local Time

The UAE is four hours ahead of UTC (Universal Coordinated Time – formerly known as GMT). Clocks are not altered for daylight saving in the summer, so when Europe and North America gain an hour, the time in the UAE stays the same. During this period the time difference is one hour less, so when it is 12:00 in the UAE it is 09:00 in the UK instead of 08:00, as it is during the winter. The table shows time differences between the UAE and various cities around the world (not allowing for any daylight savings in those cities).

Time Zones

Amman	-2	**Los Angeles**	-12
Athens	-2	**Manama**	-1
Auckland	+8	**Mexico City/Dallas**	-10
Bangkok	+3	**Moscow**	-1
Beijing	+4	**Mumbai**	+1.5
Beirut	-2	**Munich**	-3
Canberra	+6	**Muscat**	0
Colombo	+2	**New York**	-9
Damascus	-2	**Paris**	-3
Denver	-11	**Perth**	+4
Doha	-1	**Prague**	-3
Dublin	-4	**Riyadh**	-1
Hong Kong	+4	**Rome**	-3
Johannesburg	-2	**Singapore**	+4
Karachi	+1	**Sydney**	+6
Kuwait City	-1	**Tokyo**	+5
London	-4	**Toronto**	-9
		Wellington	+8

Social & Business Hours, Weekends

Working hours differ greatly in the UAE, with much of the private sector working a straight shift (usually from 08:00 to 17:00 or 09:00 to 18:00, with an hour for lunch), while a minority work a split shift (working from 09:00 to 13:00, then taking a long lunch break before returning to work from 16:00 to 19:00). It's not uncommon for working hours in private companies in the UAE to be longer than in other countries.

Emirates Palace

UAE: Facts & Figures

The UAE, and Abu Dhabi in particular, have witnessed huge growth as commerce, industry and tourism take a hold. Take a look at the main numbers affecting the country and its capital city.

UAE Free Zones

There are more than 30 free zones in the UAE. Designed to encourage investments from overseas, free zones allow 100% foreign ownership, 100% repatriation of profit and 0% tax.

Abu Dhabi GDP By Sector

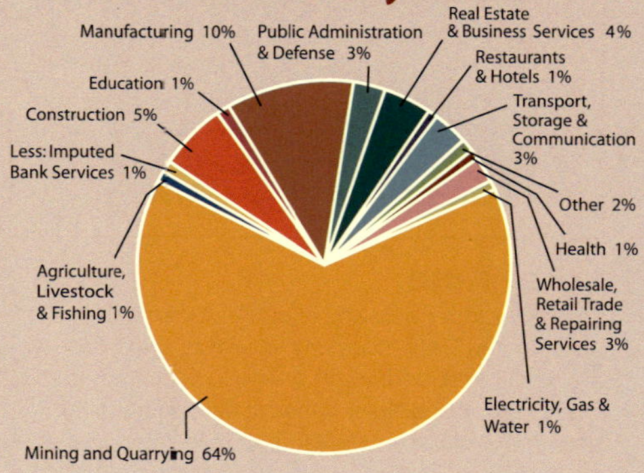

Source: Statistics Center – Abu Dhabi

UAE GDP By Emirate

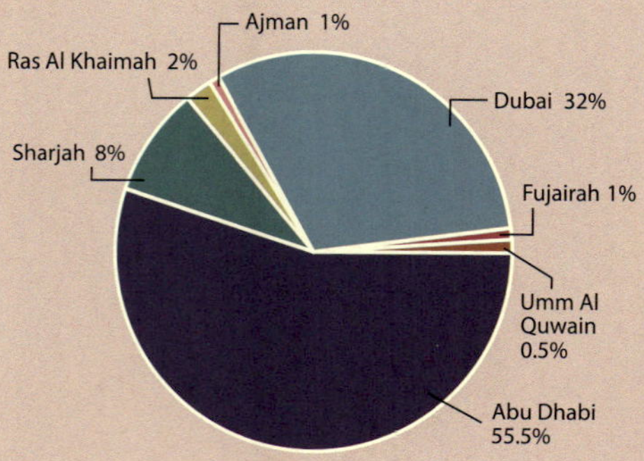

Source: Ministry of Economy

UAE GDP By Sector

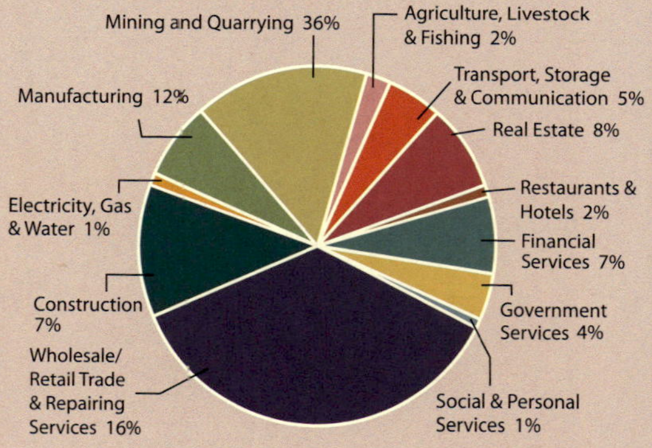

Source: UAE Yearbook 2010

Temperature & Humidity

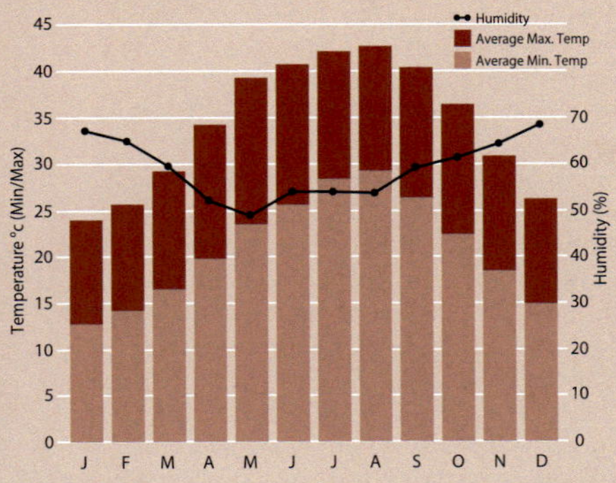

Rainfall

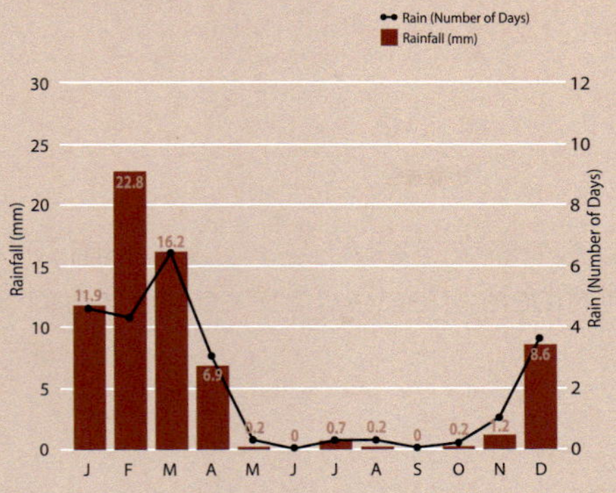

Source: Meteorological Department, Abu Dhabi International Airport & National Center of Meteorology and Seismology

Population By Emirate

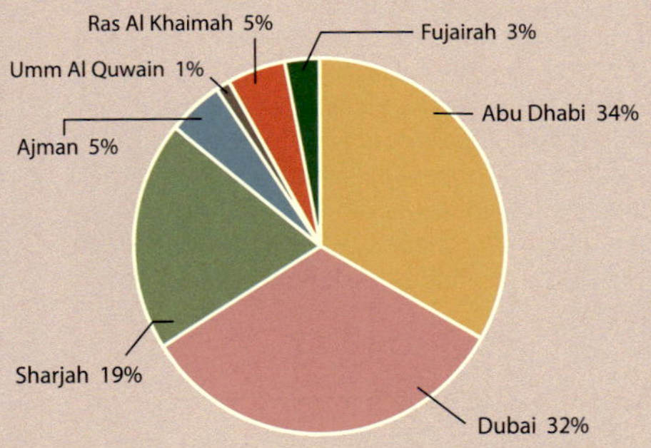

Source: Ministry of Economy

Education Levels

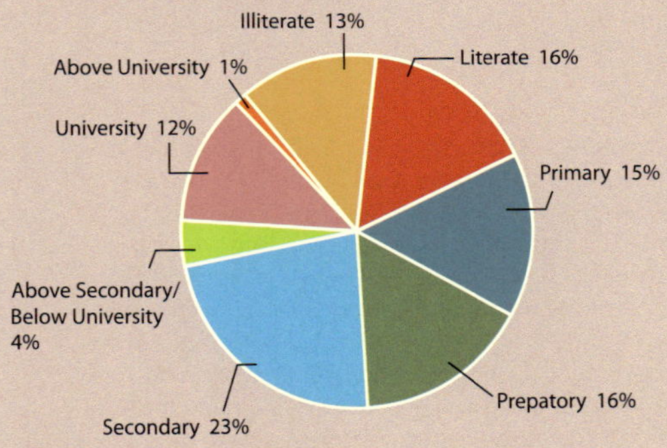

Source: Statistics Center – Abu Dhabi

Abu Dhabi Population Age Breakdown

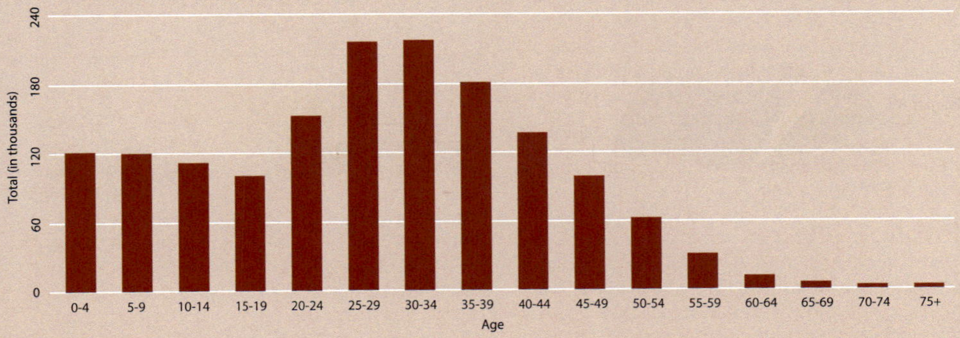

Source: Statistics Center – Abu Dhabi

Government offices are generally open from 07:30 to 14:30, Sunday to Thursday. Embassies and consulates operate similar hours, but may designate specific times and days for certain tasks (such as passport applications), so it's best to call before you go. Most embassies take a Friday/Saturday weekend. All will have an emergency number on their answering service, website or on their office doors.

The majority of larger shops and shopping centres are open throughout the day and into the evening, generally closing at 22:00 or midnight. Traditional shops and smaller street traders often operate under split shift timings, closing for three or four hours in the afternoon. Some food outlets and petrol stations are open 24 hours a day.

Friday is the Islamic holy day and therefore a universal day off for offices and schools; most companies and schools have a two-day weekend over Friday and Saturday. Some companies still require a six-day week from their staff, while others operate on a five-and-a-half-day system. Consumer demand means that the hospitality and retail industries are open seven days a week.

Ramadan Hours

According to the labour laws, all companies are obliged to shorten the working day by two hours during Ramadan. Even though this is to assist Muslim employees who are fasting, the law makes no distinction in this regard between Muslim and non-Muslim employees. So, technically, even expats are entitled to a shorter working day. However, many international companies do not follow this principle and labour lawyers would advise you not to make a fuss if you are not given a shorter working day during Ramadan. Some lucky expats do get to work shorter hours during Ramadan and many businesses, schools and shops change their hours slightly during this special period of the year.

Abu Dhabi's traffic has a totally different pattern during Ramadan; instead of being gridlocked in the mornings and quiet in the afternoons, the mornings are almost jam-free and you'll sail through any usual trouble spots, while in the afternoons the roads tend to get busy and sometimes totally clogged. Night-time activity increases during Ramadan, with many shops staying open later (until midnight or even 01:00) and the city's many shisha cafes and some restaurants stay open until the early hours.

Public Holidays

The Islamic calendar starts from the year 622AD, the year of Prophet Muhammad's migration (Hijra) from Mecca to Al Madinah. Hence the Islamic year is called the Hijri year and dates are followed by AH (AH stands for Anno Hegirae, meaning 'after the year of the Hijra').

As some holidays are based on the sighting of the moon and do not have fixed dates on the Hijri calendar, Islamic holidays are more often than not confirmed less than 24 hours ahead of time. Most companies send an email to employees the day before, notifying them of the confirmed holiday date in advance.

Some non-religious holidays are fixed according to the Gregorian calendar. It should be noted that the public sector often gets additional days off or holidays where the private sector may not (for example on National Day the public sector gets two days of official holiday, whereas private sector companies take only one day). This can be a problem for working parents, as schools fall under the public sector and therefore get the extended holidays, so your children will usually have more days off than you do. No problem if you have full-time home help, but if not then you may have to take a day's leave.

Below is a list of the holidays and the number of days they typically last. The listed number of days (the length of holiday) applies mainly to the public sector, so if you work in the private sector you may get fewer days per holiday. The main Muslim festivals are Eid Al Fitr (the festival of the breaking of the fast, which marks the end of Ramadan) and Eid Al Adha (the festival of the sacrifice, which marks the end of the pilgrimage to Mecca). Mawlid Al Nabee is the holiday celebrating the Prophet Muhammad's birthday, and Lailat Al Mi'raj celebrates the Prophet's ascension into heaven.

Lunar Calendar

The Hijri calendar is based on lunar months; there are 354 or 355 days in the Hijri year, which is divided into 12 lunar months, and is thus 11 days shorter than the Gregorian year. There are plenty of websites with Gregorian/Hijri calendar conversion tools, so you can find the equivalent Hijri date for any Gregorian date and vice versa. Try www.rabiah.com/convert.

Public Holidays

Eid Al Adha (3)	6 Nov 2011 (Moon)
Islamic New Year's Day (1)	26 Nov 2011 (Moon)
UAE National Day (2)	2 Dec 2011 (Fixed)
New Year (1)	1 Jan 2012 (Fixed)
Mawlid Al Nabee	4 Feb 2012 (Moon)
Lailat Al Mi'raj (1)	17 Jun 2012 (Moon)
Eid Al Fitr (3)	19 Aug 2012 (Moon)
Eid Al Adha (3)	25 Oct 2012 (Moon)
Islamic New Year's Day (1)	15 Nov 2012 (Moon)
UAE National Day (2)	2 Dec 2012 (Fixed)
New Year (1)	1 Jan 2013 (Fixed)

Currency

The monetary unit is the dirham (Dhs.), which is divided into 100 fils. The currency is also referred to as AED (Arab Emirate dirham). Notes come in denominations of Dhs.5 (brown), Dhs.10 (green), Dhs.20 (light blue), Dhs.50 (purple), Dhs.100 (pink), Dhs.200 (yellowy-brown), Dhs.500 (blue) and Dhs.1,000 (browny-purple). The denominations are indicated on the notes in both Arabic and English. To see examples of the UAE's banknotes, visit the website of the Central Bank of the UAE (www.centralbank.ae) and click on 'currency' on the left. There are a total of six coins in circulation, but you typically only come across the three largest denominations: the Dhs.1, 50 fils and 25 fils. Distinguishing between the coins is tricky if you are not an Arabic speaker – the amount is written in Arabic only. The Dhs.1 coin is the largest, the 50 fils is smaller but seven-sided, and the 25 fils is of a similar size to the 50 fils but is circular. All are silver in colour. The dirham has been pegged to the US dollar since 1980, at a mid rate of $1 to Dhs.3.6725.

Exchange Rates

Foreign Currency	1 Unit FC = x Dhs	Dhs1 = xFC
Australia Dollars (AUD)	3.89	0.26
Bahrain Dinars (BHD)	9.74	0.10
Bangladesh Taka (BDT)	0.05	20.07
Canada Dollars (CAD)	3.72	0.27
Denmark Kroner (DKK)	0.70	1.43
Euro (EUR)	5.20	0.19
Hong Kong Dollars (HKD)	0.47	2.12
India Rupees (INR)	0.08	12.51
Japan Yen (JPY)	0.05	20.89
Jordan Dinars (JOD)	5.17	0.19
Kuwait Dinars (KWD)	13.46	0.07
Malaysia Ringgits (MYR)	1.24	0.81
New Zealand Dollars (NZD)	3.10	0.32
Oman Rials (OMR)	9.54	0.10
Pakistan Rupees (PKR)	0.04	23.77
Philippines Pesos (PHP)	0.09	11.49
Qatar Riyals (QAR)	1.01	0.99
Saudi Arabia Riyals (SAR)	0.98	1.02
Singapore Dollars (SGD)	3.04	0.33
South Africa Rand (ZAR)	0.52	1.93
Sri Lanka Rupees (LKR)	0.03	29.97
Sweden Kronor (SEK)	0.57	1.75
Switzerland Francs (CHF)	4.66	0.21
Thailand Baht (THB)	0.12	8.15
United Kingdom Pounds (GBP)	5.94	0.17
United States Dollars (USD)	3.67	0.27

Source: www.xe.com September 2011

Exchange Centres

Al Ansari Exchange 02 610 8888, *www.alansariuae.com*
Al Fardan Exchange 02 622 3222, *www.alfardanexchange.com*
Al Rostamani International Exchange Company 02 643 0643, *www.alrostamaniexchange.com*
Habib Exchange Company 02 627 2656, *www.habibexchange.com*
Lari Money Exchange 02 622 3225
UAE Exchange 02 610 5555, *www.uaeexchange.com*

ENVIRONMENT

Flora & Fauna

While the variety of flora and fauna in the UAE is not as extensive as in some parts of the world, a number of plants and animals have managed to adapt to life in arid conditions. In addition, the Abu Dhabi Municipality has an extensive greening programme in place and areas along the roads are unusually colourful for a desert environment, with grass, palm trees and flowers being constantly maintained by an army of workers and round-the-clock watering. The city also boasts a large number of well-kept parks (see p.211).

The region has about 3,500 native plants, which is perhaps surprising considering the high salinity of the soil and the harsh environment. The most famous is, of course, the date palm, which is also the most flourishing of the indigenous flora. In mountainous regions, flat-topped acacia trees and wild grasses create scenery not unlike that of an African savannah. The deserts are unexpectedly green in places, even during the dry summer months, but it takes an experienced botanist to get the most out of the area.

Indigenous fauna include the Arabian leopard and the ibex, but sightings are extremely rare. Realistically, the only large animals you will see are camels and goats (often roaming dangerously close to roads). Other desert life includes sand cats, sand foxes, desert hares, gerbils, hedgehogs, snakes and geckos.

Recent studies have shown that the number of species of birds is rising each year, due in part to concerted greening efforts. This is most apparent in the parks, especially in spring and autumn, as the country lies on the route for birds migrating between central Asia and east Africa. Al Wathba lake, some 30km south of Abu Dhabi city, attracts numerous species of birds, but is currently inaccessible. The Ajban area to the city's north attracts twitchers (p.273) for its variety of bird species, while you can see flamingos at the Ras Al Khor Wildlife Sanctuary at the southern end of Dubai Creek.

Off the coast of the UAE, the seas contain a rich abundance of marine life, including tropical fish, jellyfish, coral, the dugong ('sea cow') and sharks. Eight species of whale and seven species of dolphin have been recorded in UAE waters. Various breeds of turtle are also indigenous to the region including the loggerhead, green and hawksbill turtles, all of which are under threat. Sightings by snorkellers and divers off both coasts are not uncommon, particularly at places such as Snoopy Island (p.259) and Khor Kalba (p.258) on the East Coast.

Bu Tinah, a tiny archipelago which lies in Abu Dhabi waters, has received much attention of late. Its rich natural habitat of coral, seagrass, mangroves, flamingos, osprey, dolphins, hawksbill turtles and dugong saw Bu Tinah nominated as one of the seven wonders of the natural world; however the area is protected and not open to visitors.

Environmental Issues

Environmental Initiatives & Organisations

On the positive side, the UAE government and local municipalities have started making significant efforts towards reducing waste and consumption and raising environmental awareness. Masdar City (www.masdarcity.ae), a cutting edge development in Abu Dhabi, is at the forefront of the Emirate's efforts to emerge as a global leader in green technologies and sustainable development. Once completed, Masdar City will be the world's first waste-free, carbon-neutral development; already operational is the Masdar Institute of Science and Technology (p.149). By 2013, plastic carrier bags will have been phased out across the country. In 2011, Abu Dhabi Corniche won the international Blue Flag award, given to beaches that meet strict environmental criteria and water quality. Other programmes are in place to revitalise the coral reefs off the coast.

See Them For Yourself

Beyond the city, you'll find hardy creatures that survive in the sand dunes, mountains and wadis, despite harsh conditions. If you're camping in the desert, look out for trails on the dunes in the morning left by gerbils, camels, dung beetles and the elusive sand skink.

The government effort is being accelerated by various environmental organisations which aim to protect the environment, as well as to educate the population on the importance of environmental issues. The Environment Agency Abu Dhabi (www.ead.ae) assists the Abu Dhabi government in the conservation and management of the emirate's natural environment, resources, wildlife and biological diversity.

Sir Bani Yas Island, part of Abu Dhabi emirate, is home to an internationally acclaimed breeding

Abu Dhabi marina

Girls Gone Green

Abu Dhabi Eco-Chicks is a group of 'educated, empowered and eco-minded' ladies who get together to make a difference. Their website, http://abudhabiecochicks.wordpress.com, is a great resource for all the latest issues and campaigns affecting the environment and Abu Dhabi.

programme for endangered wildlife. Created as a private wildlife sanctuary by the late Sheikh Zayed, it is now an exclusive eco-resort (02 801 5400, www.anantara.com). Emirates Wildlife Society is a national environmental NGO that operates in association with the WWF (www.panda.org/uae). In addition, The Breeding Centre for Endangered Arabian Wildlife (06 531 1212) at Sharjah Desert Park, has a successful breeding programme for wildlife under threat, particularly the Arabian leopard. Al Ain Wildlife Park & Resort (p.236) has been equally instrumental in conserving species; its Arabian oryx breeding programme has been particularly successful. See also Environmental Groups (p.281).

Water Usage & Desalination

Abu Dhabi, naturally surrounded by saltwater, sand and not much else, seems an unlikely place to experience such rapid growth. The city has risen from the dunes in just over 50 years. Of course, this has taken a toll on the environment and, according to the WWF's Living Planet Report 2008, the UAE has the highest ecological footprint per person in the world, narrowly edging out perennial offender, the USA. Even more surprising, water usage in the UAE is the highest per capita in the world and the fresh water supply is being decimated by the ever-increasing population. This has forced the country to rely more and more on desalination and, in the next few years, production will need to be drastically ramped up to meet demand. Pair this with a negligible amount of arable land (meaning more imports) and a population of expats who invest less into the community than a long-term resident or citizen would, and the UAE will be hard-pressed to improve upon its poor environmental track record in the near future.

However, the late Sheikh Zayed was visionary in his respect for the environment, seeking to balance its health with that of the country's population and, with increasing awareness, Abu Dhabi is attempting

Green Abu Dhabi

to become a better steward to life, land and water. The construction of the carbon-neutral Masdar City is an attempt to show what can be accomplished with human ingenuity and ambition, and Masdar's research university is constantly striving for and developing new green technology to combat business as usual.

Water Way To Save

As part of its water conservation initiatives, Abu Dhabi has recently launched a campaign to install water saving devices free of charge in every household in the emirate. The initiative will notably reduce residents' water bills and save as much as 75 billion litres of water annually. The 'Watersavers' campaign will be rolled out over the next few years. See www.watersavers.ae for more information.

In addition, there are a number of environmentally friendly initiatives and government-backed education programmes, such as Heroes of the UAE (www.heroesoftheuae.com). Its website outlines how individuals, schools and businesses can help to overcome the challenges the country faces.

Water Retention **Habiba Al Marashi** chairperson, Emirates Environmental Group

There is an urgent need for all sectors to save water. The solutions vary from simple to complicated ones like checking for leaks, turning taps off, using a pail of water for washing cars, using water saving fixtures and recycling water to name a few. However, saving water requires a conscious effort on all our parts to ensure that we are saving a precious and expensive resource.

Going Green

If everyone in the world was to live like the average UAE resident, calculations suggest that 4.5 planets would be needed to provide the natural resources. Indisputably, the UAE is living beyond its ecological means and habits have to change.

Responsibility

Perhaps it is a result of living in a nation inhabited by a huge number of expatriates, but the average UAE resident seems to feel very little responsibility towards their new country's environment. Expats from countries where 'green' initiatives, such as household recycling, are commonplace may be surprised by the lack of awareness and facilities for similar schemes in the UAE. Government efforts, such as the ban on plastic carrier bags, are firm steps in the right direction but they are slow to take effect. In the meantime, there is a pressing need for all residents to start making a personal contribution to reduce the impact of their presence.

Recycling

On the recycling front, UAE residents are becoming more proactive. The Emirates Environmental Group (p.116), for example, has reported a large increase in its school, corporate and community recycling drives which collect paper, plastic, glass, aluminium and toner cartridges. Equally, mobile phones, broken computers and all kinds of electronic equipment can now be recycled through the EnviroFone campaign (www.enviroserve.ae/envirofone) or even at your nearest Plug-ins store (800 758 4467). Abu Dhabi National Energy Company (www.taqa.ae) has a programme which aims to place recycling centres into key areas, such as Al Hosn University and the American International School (see p.145). If your area doesn't have a recycling scheme, it can involve rather a lot of administrative wrangling with the developer or community management company, but it's worth bringing the issue to the attention of your residents' committee to try to build support and put pressure on the developers. In the meantime, you can always take your own waste to the recycling bins which are dotted around Abu Dhabi.

Abu Dhabi has many parks

Consider the three Rs – reduce, reuse and recycle. Look for a positive and practical change that you can make to a routine and make it a habit. Once you've done that, don't rest on your laurels – find the next change that you can make, and the next.

Small Efforts For Big Changes

The first step towards a greener life in the UAE is simply to consider the three Rs – reduce, reuse and recycle. Look for a positive and practical change that you can make to a routine – like switching off the lights when you leave a room – and make it a habit. Once you've done that, don't rest on your laurels – find the next change that you can make, and the next. You'll soon find that looking for ways to use the three Rs becomes habit in itself, influencing buying decisions, product consumption and usage levels. Changing the world may be a lofty goal, but changing yours and your family's personal habits is extremely achievable, makes a difference and sets an example. Here are a few suggestions to help get you started...

Getting Started

- The average UAE resident consumes more than double the amount of energy of citizens in France and the UK; more even than America, traditionally the worst ecological offender. Simple actions, such as turning air conditioning up a few degrees or using energy efficient light bulbs can have a big impact. A simple Watersaver device can save 550 litres a day per household. Find more ideas at www.heroesoftheuae.ae.
- Invest in reusable water bottles rather than buying bottled water for all your drinking needs, which sends a tremendous amount of waste to landfills. If you can't imagine drinking from the tap, invest in a water cooler and buy the big five-gallon containers.
- Take the bus or organise a carpool. When you drive to the shops, combine it with other errands to cut down on carbon emissions.
- Cover your pool in the summer. An uncovered pool loses up to 3,785 litres of water per month through evaporation.
- Unplug you phone charger. As much as 95% of the energy used by phone chargers is wastage caused by leaving them continually plugged in.
- Create your own desert oasis and choose native plants for your back garden to cut down on the volumes needed for daily watering.
- You often have to rip away several layers of bags and wrapping to get to your take-out order. Prepare your own meals more often to do away with the middlemen.
- Make the most of Abu Dhabi's arid climate and dry your laundry in the open air rather than using the tumble dryer.
- Plastic bags will be phased out by 2013; stay ahead of the trend by using reusable carriers or jute bags and help cut down on the millions of plastic bags that go into landfills every year.
- According to the Centre of Waste Management, recycling will soon be mandatory in the UAE capital. In the meantime, there are already workplace recycling programmes (contact the Environment Agency Abu Dhabi at customerservice@ead.ae for more details) and a few drop-off sites for individuals conveniently located at Spinney's supermarkets.
- If you're a thrift store junkie, check out the UAE's second-hand stores and markets (see Shopping, p.303), such as the thrift shop in the St. Andrew's Church compound (www.standrewauh.org).

BUSINESS & COMMERCE

Overview

The UAE is considered the second richest Arab country, after Qatar, on a per capita basis. The country has just under 10% of the world's proven oil reserves (most of it within Abu Dhabi emirate) and the fourth largest natural gas reserves.

The UAE GDP was growing at a rate of over 7% per year prior to the crash of 2009 and, after a temporary blip in that year, the economy reverted back to positive territory by registering 3.2% growth in 2010 (www.cia.gov). At an estimated$246.8 billion in 2010, the UAE economy is the second largest in the Gulf, after Saudi Arabia. Successful economic diversification means that the UAE's wealth is no longer solely reliant on oil revenue; services alone already account for more than half of the GDP. In mid-2011, the International Monetary Fund forecasted that the UAE's non-oil sector would accelerate to 3.3% growth, up from 2.1% in the year before. Boosting Abu Dhabi's infrastructure and manufacturing sector is central to the UAE's plans to wean its economy off oil. The government aims to boost growth by creating jobs, lowering the costs of running businesses and by attracting more foreign investment.

Abu Dhabi Investment Authority (ADIA)

The Abu Dhabi Economic Vision 2030 is a blueprint, created by Abu Dhabi Council for Economic Development, the Department of Planning and Economy and the General Secretariat of the Executive Council, that aims to lead the emirate's economy into a highly diversified future, focused on acquisitions, aerospace, energy and industry, healthcare, infrastructure, real estate and hospitality, communications and service ventures. Across the country, these sectors are playing an increasingly important part in the national economy. Other sectors, such as publishing, recruitment, advertising and IT, while not as developed in terms of size, have been steadily growing in Abu Dhabi and Dubai, aided in part by the various free zones.

However, don't be fooled by the high national income into thinking that the average expat coming to work in Abu Dhabi will automatically be on a huge salary. The wealth isn't spread evenly and, even before the financial crisis, the salaries for most types of jobs, with the exception of highly skilled professionals, were dropping. This downward trend is attributed in part to the willingness of workers to accept a position at a lower wage. While the UAE GDP per capita income stands at around Dhs.95,000, this figure includes all sections of the community and the average labourer, of whom there are many, can expect to earn as little as Dhs.600 ($165) per month.

While the unemployment level of the national population in the UAE is lower than that of many other Arab states, there are still a significant number of Emiratis out of work (over 30,000, according to some estimates). This is partly due to a preference for public sector work and partly because of qualifications and salary expectations not matching the skills required in the private sector. However, the government is trying to reverse this scenario and reduce unemployment in the local sector with a 'Nationalisation' or 'Emiratisation' programme (which is common to countries throughout the region). The eventual goal is to rely less on an expat workforce, which will be achieved by improving vocational training and by making it compulsory for certain types of companies, such as banks, to hire a set percentage of Emiratis.

Trade

Abu Dhabi has come a long way since the days when the pearling industry was its primary source of trade. Now, with roughly one-tenth of the world's oil reserves, as well as vast natural gas assets, it has become a major international player. But with a trade policy based on economic openness and liberalisation, both emirate and country continue to diversify, as non-oil and gas exports steadily rise. Even in light of the economic downturn of 2009, Abu Dhabi's foreign trade has grown significantly, including non-oil exports with particular emphasis on re-exports.

Abu Dhabi has also made significant efforts over the past few years to attract foreign investment in order to increase opportunities for development and prosperity. With flexible and investor-friendly laws, availability of raw materials and funds, tax exemptions and low tariffs, the investment climate in the UAE, and Abu Dhabi in particular, is an ideal one for foreign investment. Qatar, Saudi Arabia, Japan, South Korea and the US are among the UAE's biggest trade partners for exports, while the US, China, India and Germany top the list of major import sources.

Tourism

The UAE is well ahead of many other countries in the Middle East in terms of travel and tourism. Boosting tourism plays a central part in the government's economic diversification plans and is a major driving force behind the array of record-breaking infrastructure and hospitality developments announced over the past few years. In Dubai, work on key tourism developments is going ahead, despite gloomy economic conditions and, in the past couple of years, major projects such as Dubai Metro (p.54), the Burj Khalifa (p.6) and the Meydan racecourse (www.meydan.ae) have been completed. Others have fallen victim of the credit crunch and are either delayed, cancelled or on indefinite hold.

Abu Dhabi was previously viewed by many as Dubai's lesser-known sibling but, in recent years, the capital has set itself up to become a major tourist destination in its own right. The city has recently witnessed an unprecedented boom in both plans for and construction of new hotels, amusement and theme parks, shopping malls, sports and recreational facilities, and art galleries and museums. Luxurious tourist resorts, including the Emirates Palace hotel (p.201), have put Abu Dhabi on the global tourism map and outside the city, there's now a handful of classy resort hotels and attractions, such as Al Ain Wildlife Park, being developed to widen the offering. Other mega-projects include Saadiyat Island, which will be home to the Sheikh Zayed National Museum, the Louvre Abu Dhabi and the Guggenheim – all three are slated to open in 2013. Until then, neighbouring Yas Island will continue to hog most of the limelight with its brand new hotels, its annual Formula 1 Grand Prix, big-name concerts and the splendours of Ferrari World, the world's largest indoor theme park.

Even during the global downturn of 2009, Abu Dhabi experienced an 8% growth in its tourism sector. A year later, Abu Dhabi attracted more than 1.8 million visitors, and with several new hotels scheduled for completion in 2011, the emirate is on track to welcome over two million visitors that year.

But it's not just leisure travel that the emirate is going for. The Abu Dhabi National Exhibition Centre (ADNEC), which opened in 2007, has contributed greatly to the number of business events held in town. The centre now welcomes over one million visitors per year and in addition to trade fairs that attract an international audience, large-scale popular events like the Abu Dhabi International Book Fair (see p.27) and The Bride Show Abu Dhabi (see p.27), help keep the local public involved too.

Everyday there is news of upcoming events in the city and the Abu Dhabi Tourism Authority wants the world to know about it, working to attract more tourists to the emirate with a multimillion-dollar worldwide advertising campaign and initiatives.

Economic Growth

Abu Dhabi has undergone tremendous growth since the discovery of oil and the late Sheikh Zayed bin Sultan Al Nahyan took over as ruler of the emirate. However, compared to the Dubai of the late 1990s and early 2000s, Abu Dhabi grew at a snail's pace. That all changed at the beginning of Sheikh Khalifa's rule. Thanks to relaxed real estate laws and new free zones, foreign money started pouring in and driving a boom that lasted a good five years, bringing the luxurious Emirates Palace, the transformation of Yas Island (p.196) and Saadiyat Island (p.197), as well as huge residential construction projects on Reem Island (p.87).

Really Tax Free?

Do taxes exist in the UAE? Yes and no. You don't pay income or sales tax, except when you purchase alcohol from a licensed liquor store – when you'll be hit with a steep 30% tax. The main tax that you will come across is the municipality tax of 5% on rent and 10% on food, beverages and rooms in hotels. The rest are hidden taxes in the form of 'fees', such as your car registration renewal, visa/permit fees and Dubai's Salik (road toll).

Abu Dhabi has undergone tremendous growth over the past decade. Huge development projects are either on the way or have been finished. However, despite its immense wealth and impressive progress, Abu Dhabi did not remain completely untouched by the financial crisis of 2009; progress on some of the most significant projects in Abu Dhabi slowed, and other projects were scaled back. Nevertheless, Abu Dhabi's oil wealth meant that the capital could afford to ride out the storm (and even extend Dubai a $10 billion loan to fight off its own creditors) before returning to growth in 2010. The outlook is positive: the International Monetary Fund (www.imf.org) has outlined expectations of steady economic growth through to 2016. With its sizable government-led projects and ambitious expansion plans, Abu Dhabi is positioned to benefit greatly as its transformation into an increasingly significant global hub continues.

CULTURE & LIFESTYLE

Culture

The UAE manages what some Arab cities fail to achieve: a healthy balance between western influences and eastern traditions. Its culture is still very much rooted in the Islamic customs that deeply penetrate the Arabian Peninsula and beyond. However, the country's effort to become modern and cosmopolitan is proof of an open-minded and liberal outlook.

Islam is more than just a religion; it is a way of life that governs even mundane everyday events, from what to wear to what to eat and drink. Therefore, the culture and heritage of the UAE is closely linked to its religion. However, the UAE is tolerant and welcoming; foreigners are free to practise their own religion, alcohol is served in hotels and the dress code is liberal. Women face little discrimination and, contrary to the policies of neighbouring Saudi Arabia, are able to drive and walk around uncovered and unescorted.

The rapid economic development over the last 30 years has changed life in the United Arab Emirates beyond recognition. However, the country's rulers are committed to safeguarding their heritage. They are therefore keen to promote cultural and sporting events that are representative of their traditions, such as falconry, camel racing and traditional dhow sailing. Arabic culture in poetry, dancing, songs and traditional art and craftsmanship is encouraged.

Courtesy and hospitality are the most highly prized virtues, and visitors are likely to experience the genuine warmth and friendliness of the Emirati people. Luckily, the negative view of Islam that has affected many Muslims living abroad has not had an impact on Abu Dhabi, where you'll find people of various nationalities and religions working and living side by side without conflict. In Islam, the family unit is very important and elders are respected for their experience and wisdom. It's common for several generations to live together in the same house. Polygamy is practised in the UAE, with Islam allowing a man to have up to four wives at one time, providing he has the financial and physical means to treat each of them equally. However, a Muslim man taking more than one wife is more the exception than the norm, and most Muslim families resemble the traditional western family unit: mum, dad and kids.

Weddings are important cultural occasions; the men and women celebrate separately with feasting and music. They are usually very large affairs; however, the government has placed a ceiling of Dhs.50,000 on dowries, and overly lavish weddings can result in a prison sentence or Dhs.500,000 fine. The government-sponsored Marriage Fund, based in Abu Dhabi, assists Emiratis with marriage, from counselling and financial assistance (long term loans of up to Dhs.70,000 for a UAE national man marrying a UAE national woman) to organising group weddings to keep costs down. With so many UAE Nationals studying abroad, and so many expats in Abu Dhabi and Dubai, inter-cultural marriages are increasingly common. The Marriage Fund strongly encourages nationals to marry fellow nationals (in an effort to preserve the culture and reduce the number of UAE spinsters), but it is easier for a national man to marry a non-national woman than it is for a national woman to marry a non-national man.

When you first arrive, you may find many aspects of the local culture seem very strange to you. Take time to observe and understand before you pass judgement; you'll soon realise that the many different nationalities living here make Abu Dhabi a sometimes-frustrating but ultimately fascinating city.

Race Relations

Abu Dhabi is a diverse, multicultural society with many different nationalities living side by side. Even though most of the time this is a harmonious arrangement, there are times when where you come from does seem to be an important factor. For example, some job advertisements are very forthcoming about their racial requirements, asking for 'western candidates' or 'fluent Arabic'. And salaries in the city definitely reflect nationality, with employees from Asia sometimes getting paid less than their western colleagues, even when doing similar jobs. Unfortunately, this kind of racism spreads to other areas too – it is becoming increasingly common for landlords to refuse tenants of certain nationalities, and certain bars and nightclubs have been accused in the past of having racist door policies (usually strenuously denied by those outlets, of course).

Language

Arabic is the official language of the UAE, although English, Hindi, Malayalam and Urdu are all commonly spoken throughout the country.

Arabic is the official business language, but English is so widely used that you could conduct business here for years without learning a single word of Arabic. Most road signs, shop signs and restaurant menus are in both languages. The further out of town you go, the more you will find just Arabic, both spoken and on street and shop signs.

Arabic isn't the easiest language to pick up, or to pronounce. But if you can throw in a couple of words here and there, you're more likely to receive a warmer welcome or at least a smile – even if your pronunciation is terrible. See the opposite page for a list of useful Arabic phrases, and p.152 for Arabic language courses.

Religion

Islam is the official religion of the UAE, and is widely practised throughout the country. The Islamic holy day is Friday. The basis of Islam is the belief that there is only one God and that Prophet Muhammad is his messenger. The faith shares a common ancestry with Christianity and many of the prophets before Muhammad can be found in Christian as well as Muslim writings. There are five pillars of Islam which all Muslims must follow: the Profession of Faith, Prayer, Charity, Fasting and Pilgrimage. Every Muslim is expected, at least once in his or her lifetime, to make the pilgrimage (Hajj) to the holy city of Mecca (also spelt Makkah) in Saudi Arabia.

Additionally, a Muslim is required to pray (facing Mecca) five times a day. Times vary according to the sun's position. Most people pray at a mosque, but it's not unusual to see people kneeling by the side of the road if they are not near a place of worship. It is considered impolite to stare at people praying or to walk over prayer mats. The modern-day call to prayer, transmitted through loudspeakers on the minarets, ensures that everyone knows it's time to pray.

Islam is the principle religion, but the UAE is tolerant of other denominations; the ruling family has, in the past, donated land for the building of churches. There is a vibrant Christian community in Abu Dhabi while there is even a Hindu temple in Dubai.

BASIC ARABIC

General

Yes	*na'am*
No	*la*
Please	*min fadlak (m)* / *min fadlik (f)*
Thank you	*shukran*
Please (in offering)	*tafaddal (m)* / *tafaddali (f)*
Praise be to God	*al-hamdu l-illah*
God willing	*in shaa'a l-laah*

Greetings

Greeting (peace be upon you)	*as-salaamu alaykom*
Greeting (in reply)	*wa alaykom is salaam*
Good morning	*sabah il-khayr*
Good morning (in reply)	*sabah in-nuwr*
Good evening	*masa il-khayr*
Good evening (in reply)	*masa in-nuwr*
Hello	*marhaba*
Hello (in reply)	*marhabtayn*
How are you?	*kayf haalak (m) / kayf haalik (f)*
Fine, thank you	*zayn, shukran (m)* / *zayna, shukran (f)*
Welcome	*ahlan wa sahlan*
Welcome (in reply)	*ahlan fiyk (m) / ahlan fiyki (f)*
Goodbye	*ma is-salaama*

Introductions

My name is...	*ismiy...*
What is your name?	*shuw ismak (m) / shuw ismik (f)*
Where are you from?	*min wayn inta (m) / min wayn inti (f)*
I am from...	*anaa min...*
America	*ameriki*
Britain	*braitani*
Europe	*oropi*
India	*al hindi*

Questions

How many / much?	*kam?*
Where?	*wayn?*
When?	*mataa?*
Which?	*ayy?*
How?	*kayf?*
What?	*shuw?*
Why?	*laysh?*
Who?	*miyn?*
To/for	*ila*
In/at	*fee*
From	*min*
And	*wa*
Also	*kamaan*
There isn't	*maa fee*

Taxi Or Car Related

Is this the road to...	*hadaa al tariyq ila...*
Stop	*kuf*
Right	*yamiyn*
Left	*yassar*
Straight ahead	*siydaa*
North	*shamaal*
South	*januwb*
East	*sharq*
West	*garb*
Turning	*mafraq*
First	*awwal*
Second	*thaaniy*
Road	*tariyq*
Street	*shaaria*
Roundabout	*duwwaar*
Signals	*ishaara*
Close to	*qarib min*
Petrol station	*mahattat betrol*
Sea/beach	*il bahar*
Mountain/s	*jabal/jibaal*
Desert	*al sahraa*
Airport	*mataar*
Hotel	*funduq*
Restaurant	*mata'am*
Slow Down	*schway schway*

Accidents & Emergencies

Police	*al shurtaa*
Permit/licence	*rukhsaa*
Accident	*haadith*
Papers	*waraq*
Insurance	*ta'miyn*
Sorry	*aasif (m) / aasifa (f)*

Numbers

Zero	*sifr*
One	*waahad*
Two	*ithnayn*
Three	*thalatha*
Four	*arba'a*
Five	*khamsa*
Six	*sitta*
Seven	*saba'a*
Eight	*thamaanya*
Nine	*tiss'a*
Ten	*ashara*
Hundred	*miya*
Thousand	*alf*

Arabic Family Names

Arabic names have a formal structure that traditionally indicates the person's family and tribe. Names are usually taken from an important person in the Quran or from the tribe. This is followed by the word bin (son of) for a boy or bint (daughter of) for a girl, and then the name of the child's father. The last name indicates the person's tribe or family. For prominent families, this has Al, the Arabic word for 'the', immediately before it. For instance, the President of the UAE is His Highness Sheikh Khalifa bin Zayed Al Nahyan. When women get married, they do not change their name.

National Dress

On the whole, Emiratis wear traditional dress in public. For men, this is the dishdasha or khandura: a white, full length shirt dress, which is worn with a white or red checked headdress, known as a gutra or sifrah. This is secured with a black cord (agal). Sheikhs and important businessmen may also wear a thin black or brown robe (known as a bisht), over their dishdasha at important events, which is equivalent to the dinner jacket in western culture. In public, women wear the black abaya: a long, loose black robe that covers their normal clothes, plus a headscarf called a sheyla. The abaya is often of sheer, flowing fabric and may be open at the front. Some women also wear a thin black veil hiding their face, and gloves. Older women sometimes still wear a leather mask, known as a burkha, which covers the nose, brow and cheekbones. Underneath, women traditionally wear a long tunic over loose, flowing trousers (sirwall), which are often heavily embroidered and fitted at the wrists and ankles. However, these are used more by the older generation and modern women will often wear the latest fashions under their abayas.

Dressing Down

Abu Dhabi is less strict than many of its regional neighbours. Women are not required to cover their hair, but you should avoid wearing anything too tight or revealing. In public, both men and women should wear garments that cover shoulders and knees. It's fine to wear shorts at sports clubs and swimwear at the pool or beach but don't forget hats and sunscreen. You'll quickly get a feel for what is and isn't acceptable, and it differs from emirate to emirate. Dubai is more liberal still, while Sharjah is a touch more conservative.

Food & Drink

The food in Abu Dhabi reflects the diversity of its culture so pretty much every type of international cuisine imaginable is on offer. Regardless of the size of your budget, you can eat good food from virtually any part of the world. The many hotels have different internationally themed restaurants and the standard of the cuisine is what you'd expect from a top notch establishment. From modern European to Asian fusion or Mexican, you can get pretty much anything you fancy. While restaurants located in hotels are licensed to serve alcohol (see Alcohol, p.307), some of the best places to eat are the small streetside cafeterias around town, where you can feast on a tasty meal for two and still get change from Dhs.50. All of the main fastfood chains have branches here, so you won't have to venture too far to find a McDonalds, Burger King or KFC.

In terms of food shopping there are several large supermarkets (p.330) that stock a variety of international brands. The largest is probably Carrefour (p.330) at Marina Mall which is reasonably priced and its shelves stock a variety of products from around the world. Spinneys (p.331) and Abela (p.330) are more expensive but sell an excellent range of British, South African and American foods. Australia's jones the grocer (p.331) caters to gourmet tastes and there's now an increasingly good offering of organic food too (see p.321). There are co-operative societies in virtually every central district of the city; some are open 24 hours and offer great value. For local fresh fish and produce, the fish market down at Port Zayed (p.192) is definitely worth a visit but get there early for the freshest catch straight off the boat.

Arabic Cuisine

Arabic cuisine is very meat orientated and, with the exception of mezze, there is not much on the vegetarian menu. While modern Arabic cuisine comes from a blend of Moroccan, Tunisian, Iranian and Egyptian cooking styles, the term invariably refers to Lebanese food. Takeaway outlets selling shawarma (lamb or chicken sliced from a spit and served in pita bread with salad and tahina) and falafel (mashed chickpeas and sesame seeds, rolled into balls and deep fried) are worth a visit at least once. Mezze is a selection of dishes often served with Arabic bread, a green salad and pickles. Dishes can include hummus (a creamy dip made from ground chickpeas, olive oil and garlic), tabouleh (finely chopped parsley, mint and cracked wheat salad), fatoush (lettuce and tomato with small pieces of fried Arabic bread), and fattayer (small pastries filled with cottage cheese and spinach).

Charcoal grilling of meat and fish is popular. Khouzi is a Ramadan favourite (whole lamb served on a bed of rice, mixed with nuts), an authentic local dish also served at the mansaf, a traditional, formal Bedouin dinner with dishes placed on the floor in the centre of a ring of seated guests. Other typical dishes include kibbeh (deep fried mince, pine nuts and bulgur) and a variety of kebabs.

A traditional minaret

The Grand Mosque

Men praying

Sheikh Zayed Mosque

The meal ends with Lebanese sweets, which can be extremely sweet, but delicious. The most widely known are baklava (filo pastry layered with honey and pistachio nuts) and Umm Ali, a dessert with layers of milk, bread, raisins and nuts. And to accompany your meal, you must sample the extensive variety of fresh juices.

Emirati Cuisine

There are also opportunities to sample the local Emirati food. The legacy of the UAE's trading past means that local cuisine uses a blend of ingredients imported from around Asia and the Middle East. Spices such as cinnamon, saffron and turmeric along with nuts (almonds or pistachios), limes and dried fruit add interesting flavours to Emirati dishes.

Dried limes are a common ingredient in Arabic cuisine, reflecting a Persian influence. They are dried in the sun and are used to flavour dishes, either whole or ground in a spice mill. They impart a distinctively musty, tangy, sour flavour to soups and stews.

Pork

Pork is taboo in Islam. Muslims should not eat, prepare or even serve pork. In order for a restaurant to serve pork on its menu, it should have a separate fridge, preparation equipment and cooking area. In restaurants, where bacon appears on a menu, you will usually be served beef or veal bacon. Supermarkets are also required to sell pork in a separate area and Spinneys and Choithram both have screened-off pork sections. As pork is not locally produced you will find that it's more expensive than many other meats. All meat products for Muslim consumption have to be halal, which refers to the method of slaughter.

Alcohol

Alcohol is only served in licensed outlets associated with hotels (restaurants and bars), plus a few leisure clubs (such as golf clubs and sports clubs) and associations. Restaurants outside of hotels that are not part of a club or association are not permitted to serve alcohol. Nevertheless, permanent residents who are non-Muslims can get a liquor licence (p.44) which allows them to obtain alcohol for consumption at home.

Shisha

Smoking the traditional shisha (water pipe) is a popular and relaxing pastime enjoyed throughout the Middle East region. It is usually savoured in a local cafe while chatting with friends. They are also known as hookah pipes, hubbly bubbly or nargile. Shisha pipes can be smoked with a variety of aromatic flavours, such as strawberry, grape, mint or apple. Unlike a normal cigarette or cigar, the smoke is softened by the water, creating a more soothing effect, although it still causes smoking-related health problems. Plans are being considered to ban shisha cafes in Abu Dhabi's residential areas, due to increasing awareness about the dangers of passive smoking and to ensure young people aren't being encouraged to take up smoking.

Even so, smoking shisha is one of those things that should be tried at least once during your time in the UAE, especially during Ramadan, when tents are erected throughout the city and filled with people of all nationalities. You can buy your very own shisha pipe from souvenir shops or from supermarkets, and once you get to grips with putting it all together you can enjoy the unique flavour anytime you want.

For the best shisha experience, try Mirage Marine (p.379) or Ma Wa Weel (02 639 1333).

Dates

One of the very few crops that thrive naturally across the Middle East, date palms have been cultivated for around 5,000 years. It's said that in some countries the Bedouin way of life was sustained primarily by dates and camel milk up until as recently as the mid 20th century. High in energy, fibre, potassium, vitamins, magnesium and iron, with negligible quantities of fat, cholesterol and salt, dates are a cheap and healthy snack. Just five dates per day provide enough nutrition for one recommended daily portion of fruit or vegetables.

Tipping

It is entirely up to the individual whether to tip for services and it is not a fixed expectation as you may find in other countries. Some people in Abu Dhabi choose not to tip at all, but for those who feel that the service was worth recognising, the usual amount is 10% and tips are greatly appreciated. An increasing number of restaurants now also include a service charge on the bill, although it's not clear whether this ever sees the inside of your waiter's pockets, so some people add a little extra. Tips in restaurants and bars are often shared with other staff. See Going Out for more information (p.345).

For taxi drivers, it is regular practice to round up your fare as a tip, but this is not compulsory, so feel free to pay just the fare, especially if his driving standards were poor. For tipping when collecting your valet-parked car at hotels, around Dhs.5 is average. At petrol stations, especially when you get your windows cleaned, it's common practice to give a few dirhams as a tip. In beauty salons, spas and hairdressers, tipping is at your discretion but around 10% of the treatment price is an acceptable amount.

Cultural Dos & Don'ts

You'll find that, in general, people in the UAE are patient when it comes to cultural etiquette and are keen to explain their customs to you. However, there are a few cultural dos and don'ts that you should be aware of to avoid causing offence to others.

PDAs

Not a reference to the latest handheld gadget but to public displays of affection: these are a no-no in the UAE and anything more than an innocent peck on the cheek will at best earn you disapproving looks from passers by.

Appropriate Attire

While beachwear is fine on the beach, you should dress a little more conservatively when out and about in public places. If in doubt, ensuring that your shoulders and knees are covered is a safe bet. That said, when out at bars and clubs in the evening, pretty much anything goes. A pashmina is always useful for the journey home or in case the air conditioning is set to 'deep freeze'.

Photography

Abu Dhabi is full of snap-worthy sights and normal tourist photography is fine. Like anywhere in the Arab world, it is courteous to ask permission before photographing people, particularly women. In general, photographs of government and military buildings should not be taken.

Arabic Coffee

It's likely that you'll be served traditional Arabic coffee (kahwa) during formal business meetings. This is an important social ritual in the Middle East so be polite and drink some when offered. Cups should be taken in the right hand and if there is a waiter standing by, replenishing your cup, the signal to say that you have had enough is to gently shake the cup from side to side.

Meeting People

Long handshakes, kisses and warm greetings are common when meeting people in the Middle East. It's normal to shake hands with people when you are introduced to them, although if you are meeting someone of the opposite sex, be aware that a handshake may not always be welcome. It's best to take your cue from the other person and not offer your hand unless they first offer theirs. It's polite to send greetings to a person's family, but can be considered rude to enquire directly about someone's wife, sister or daughter. You may see men greeting each other with a nose kiss; this is a customary greeting in the Gulf region but is only used between close friends and associates and you should not attempt to greet someone in this way.

Out On The Town

Abu Dhabi has a good variety of nightlife and alcohol is widely available in hotel bars, pubs and clubs (see Going Out, p.345). Remember, however, that you're in a Muslim country and drunken or lewd behaviour is not only disrespectful but can lead to arrest and detention.

Business Etiquette

Business meetings in the region will usually start with introductions and small talk before you get down to business. Business cards will be exchanged – you should treat them with respect; as an extension of the person who gave them. Punctuality to meetings is important and arriving late is considered to be very bad mannered. Do not assume, however, that your meeting will start at the appointed time or that once started it will not be interrupted.

Home Values

When visiting an Emirati home it is customary to remove your shoes; however, it's best to take your cue from your host. Traditionally, men and women dine separately and meals are eaten while seated on floor cushions. When you sit, be carefully not to point your feet at anyone or to show the soles of your feet. Mealtimes are long and leisurely and as a guest your plate will be heaped high. Try everything offered but if you're not sure you'll like something, take a small amount that you can finish. If you invite a Muslim to your home, you should not offer pork or alcohol, as this may cause offence.

LOCAL MEDIA

Newspapers & Magazines

The UAE has a number of daily English language broadsheets. The cream of the crop is definitely Abu Dhabi's *The National*, arguably the region's first national newspaper offering quality journalism, intelligent editorial and meaty lifestyle pieces. Other titles include *Gulf News, Khaleej Times* and *Gulf Today*.

In most areas of Abu Dhabi, you can also pick up a free copy of *7Days*, a tabloid-size newspaper published five days a week that features local and international news, business and entertainment news, and a sports section. Whichever country you're from, chances are you'll be able to find copies of your favourite home paper in Abu Dhabi's supermarkets.

There are plenty of local magazines, including a range of Middle Eastern editions of international titles that are produced here (examples include *OK!, Grazia, Harpers Bazaar, Men's Fitness* and *Stuff*). Keep an eye out for expat titles like *liveworkexplore* (Explorer's monthly lifestyle magazine targeted directly at expats), *Connector* and *Aquarius*, as well as for listings magazines such as *TimeOut Abu Dhabi* and *What's On*.

Censorship

International magazines are available in bookshops and supermarkets, at inflated prices. All titles are examined and, where necessary, censored to ensure that they don't offend the country's moral codes. You'll find much the same is true of international films and TV shows, the vast majority of which make it over to the UAE, although they are assessed before they hit cinema screens or are shown on TV.

Radio

The UAE has a number of commercial radio stations that broadcast in a wide range of languages. The leading English language stations operate 24 hours a day and, while most are physically based in Dubai, they can usually be picked up with a good reception throughout Abu Dhabi:

Dubai 92: current music, competitions and popular DJs, 92.00FM, www.dubai92.com

Dubai Eye: quality talk radio, 103.8FM, www.dubaieye1038.com

Virgin Radio: Hit music along the lines of Virgin Radio in other cities, 104.4FM, www.virginradiodubai.com

Channel 4: contemporary music for a younger audience, 104.8FM, www.channel4FM.com

The Coast: Middle of the road and classic hits throughout the day, 103.2FM, www.1032thecoast.com

Radio 1: hit music broadcast across the country, 104.1FM, www.gulfnews.com/radio1

Radio 2: contemporary music broadcast throughout the UAE, 99.3FM, www.gulfnews.com/radio2

The BBC World Service can also be picked up in Abu Dhabi on 90.3FM.

Satellite Radio

Depending on your satellite TV provider, you may get some radio stations through your decoder. Various channels are available, including Virgin Radio from the UK and the BBC World Service. You can also access a variety of music channels – from country to pop. You can get around 20 music channels on Orbit Showtime.

Television

Local TV is in a state of continuous improvement – gone are the days when all you could watch was early episodes of ER and Mad About You, with all the kissing scenes cut out. Channels like Dubai One and MBC4, despite being free-to-air, are doing a good job of securing the rights to some fairly mainstream international shows, and Fox Movies, also free-to-air, has often been the first Middle Eastern TV channel to screen major Hollywood movies.

Satellite or cable TV is a staple in most expat homes – although it can be a bit hit and miss when judged by international standards. Some shows are aired just a few days later than they are in the US or UK, while others are delayed by a few months.

Always On The Box

Orbit Showtime offers a Showbox service, with which you can pause live television and record your favourite shows on a digital box. You can also watch special previews of forthcoming movies, or virtual 'boxsets' of popular series. See www.osn.com for more info.

Internet & Directory Of Useful Websites

When compared to other Middle-East nations, the UAE is near the top for internet connectivity, but when you bring Europe and the US into the picture the country's offerings aren't exactly the best value in the world. That said, it's relatively easy to get hooked up if you live in the established areas of Abu Dhabi city.

Right away, you will probably find that using the internet while in Abu Dhabi has a few quirks that can take some getting used to, not least the much-despised proxy that blocks access to any sites deemed offensive. What is or isn't offensive is up to the Telecommunication Regulatory Authority (TRA), which

supposedly applies the same rules to both Etisalat and du subscribers (See p.98) for how to get hooked up).

While living in a Muslim community, you can certainly expect sites containing pornography or dubious religious content to be blocked, but until recently VoIP (Voice over Internet Protocol) access was blocked. Regulators finally authorised VoIP phone in March 2010, but only existing licence-holders may offer VoIP, thus excluding popular services such as Skype. The TRA said it was making it legal for people to place international calls through the internet, but would allow only licensed operators to run such services; the four companies licensed to offer international VoIP services are Etisalat, du and the satellite firms Yahsat and Thuraya.

For consumers, that means the prices of any international internet calls will be set by those companies and it is not yet clear whether this will result in substantial cost savings. So, if you do want to speak to friends and family abroad, you either have to use the actual telephone, use authorised VoIP services (when they're made available), or try the voice options offered through instant messaging services, such as Windows Messenger or Google Chat. Of course, you can access Skype and other blocked sites with the help of a proxy blocker, but then you're technically breaking the law.

It's a frustrating conundrum, made even more so by the lack of any reasons other than financial, but rules are rules. Other sites that you will not be able to access include online dating sites, sites dealing with gambling or drugs, and, oddly, some photo-sharing sites as well.

UAE CALENDAR 2011-12

The UAE hosts a wide variety of public events. Whether you choose to chill out to tunes from world music, swot up at annual art fairs, raise money for charity or watch as the world's greatest golfers fight it out for titles and prize money, the UAE offers some unforgettable experiences.

Abu Dhabi HSBC Golf Championship — January

Abu Dhabi Golf Club Madinat Khalifa A (Khalifa City A)
www.abudhabigolfchampionship.com

With US $2 million in prize money and some of the biggest names in golf appearing, the Abu Dhabi Golf Championship is one of the biggest sporting events.

Standard Chartered Dubai Marathon — January

Dubai Media City Dubai **04 433 5669**
www.dubaimarathon.org

This event attracts runners aiming to fundraise or work off that festive winter tummy in either the 10km road race or 3km charity run, as well as the more daring and elite marathon runners who take on the full 42km.

Volvo Ocean Race — January

Nr Marina Mall Breakwater
www.abudhabivolvooceanrace.ae

The first ever Middle Eastern leg of the Volvo Ocean Race stops in Abu Dhabi in 2012. A brand new Destination Village will welcome the race, coinciding with a festival of events across the country.

USEFUL WEBSITES

Abu Dhabi Information

www.abudhabi.ae	Abu Dhabi government portal with tons of information
www.visitabudhabi.com	Abu Dhabi tourism site
www.abudhabitourism.ae	Abu Dhabi Tourism Authority
www.adach.ae	Abu Dhabi Authority for Culture and Heritage
www.adnec.ae	Abu Dhabi National Exhibition Centre
www.adpolice.gov.ae	Abu Dhabi Police
www.dubizzle.com	Great website for classifieds and community, Dubai and Abu Dhabi
www.liveworkexplore.com	Essential info on living in the UAE from Explorer Publishing
www.sheikhzayed.com	Site dedicated to the life of the late UAE President
www.thenational.ae	Local newspaper
www.abudhabiwoman.com	Forums and advice for women living in Abu Dhabi

UAE Information

www.7days.ae	Local newspaper
www.gulfnews.com	Local newspaper
www.khaleejtimes.com	Local newspaper
www.ameinfo.com	Middle East business news
www.government.ae	UAE Government 'e-portal
www.adiamet.gov.ae	Weather information from the Department of Atmostpheric Studies

Al Ain Aerobatic Show

Dubai Shopping Festival January – February
04 2235 444
www.dubaievents.ae
The month-long shopping extravaganza is a great time to visit the city for bargain-hunters.

Abu Dhabi Yacht Show February
Yas Marina Yas Island West **800 44763**
www.abudhabiyachtshow.com
The three-day event sees more than 150 yacht manufacturers, brokers, services and accessories attract thousands of sea loving guests to Yas Marina.

Al Ain Aerobatic Show February
Al Ain Intl Airport Al Ain **800 555**
www.alainaerobaticshow.com
A five-day annual air show which sees flying daredevils from around the world performing aerobatic stunts and displays that truly wow the crowds. The 2012 show may temporarily take place in December, check the website for details.

The Bride Show Abu Dhabi February
Abu Dhabi National Exhibition Centre (ADNEC)
Al Safarat
www.thebrideshow.com
This show brings the whole wedding industry together, showcasing dresses, entertainment, honeymoon destinations and wedding organisers.

Dubai Duty Free Tennis Championships February
The Aviation Club Dubai **04 282 4122**
www.dubaidutyfreetennischampionships.com
Firmly established on the ATP and WTP circuits, this US $1 million tournament attracts the world's top men's and women's seeds.

Omega Dubai Desert Classic February
Emirates Golf Club Dubai **04 380 2112**
www.dubaidesertclassic.com
This longstanding PGA European Tour fixture has been won by legends such as Ernie Els and Tiger Woods, and is a popular event among the golfing community of the UAE.

Terry Fox Run February
The Corniche
www.terryfoxrun.org
Each year, thousands of individuals run, jog, walk, cycle and rollerblade their way around an 8.5km course for charity. The proceeds go to cancer research programmes at approved institutions around the world. For more information, email abudhabiterryfoxrun@gmail.com.

Abu Dhabi Desert Challenge March
Various Locations **02 296 1122**
www.abudhabidesertchallenge.ae
Over 20 years old, this high profile motorsport event attracts some of the world's top rally drivers and bikers to race on the Empty Quarter's challenging desert routes and take on its steepest dunes.

Abu Dhabi International Book Fair March
Abu Dhabi National Exhibition Centre (ADNEC)
Al Safarat **02 657 6180**
www.adbookfair.com
A joint venture between Frankfurt Book Fair and the Abu Dhabi Authority for Culture and Heritage, the Abu Dhabi International Book Fair is the Middle East's largest book fair, attracting authors and publishing professionals from all over the world.

Abu Dhabi International Triathlon March
Al Ras Al Akhdar
www.abudhabitriathlon.com
With a prize purse of $250,000, the Abu Dhabi International Triathlon is one of the world's richest triathlons, attracting talent from all over the world.

UAE National Day

Every 2 December, the country turns green, black, red and white all over. In fact, the flag becomes as ubiquitous as traffic jams as residents throughout the Emirates celebrate the birth of the UAE. Cars, trucks and taxis are decorated with flags and pictures of the country's rulers to show their patriotism. And, especially along the Corniche and in public parks and markets, military bands and folklore exhibitions entertain the crowds. It wouldn't be an independence celebration without fireworks, and Emirates Palace hotel holds the city's biggest display, set to music.

Art Dubai
March

Madinat Jumeirah Dubai 04 384 2000
www.artdubai.ae

Art Dubai has grown into a truly international art exhibition, with over 70 galleries from 30 countries around the world now represented in the programme. Running alongside the exhibition is the Global Art Forum, a lecture and discussion board programme.

Dubai World Cup
March

Meydan Racecourse, Meydan Rd Dubai 04 327 0077
www.dubaiworldcup.com

Billed as the world's richest horse race, the Dubai World Cup has certainly become one of the premier thoroughbred races of the year, and the new Meydan course and hotel are destinations in their own right. One of the biggest events in the UAE sporting and social calendar.

Emirates Airline Festival Of Literature
March

Dubai 04 342 0060
www.eaifl.com

In its short history, this literary festival has grown to host more than 80 authors, with such heavyweights as Amit Chadhuri, Yann Martel, Martin Amis and Michael Palin having appeared to discuss their works to an international audience. On slate are readings, debates, panels and various workshops for adults and kids alike.

Skywards Dubai International Jazz Festival
March

Dubai Media City Dubai 04 391 1196
www.dubaijazzfest.com

The Jazz Festival attracts a broad range of artists from all around the world to a chilled and pleasant setting in Dubai Media City. Macy Gray, the Brand New Heavies and James Blunt have all taken to the stage in previous years.

Wakestock Abu Dhabi
March

The Corniche Al Khubeirah
www.wakestock.ae

A three-day competition and the first stop of the WWA Wakeboard World Series is capped off each night by rock, pop and DJ concerts. In addition, free wakeboarding lessons are offered for those interested in taking up the sport.

Abu Dhabi Festival
March – April

Emirates Palace Al Ras Al Akhdar 02 651 0300
www.abudhabifestival.ae

The festival hosts an impressive lineup of recognised musicians and orchestras from around the world. It is a strong advocate of cross-cultural understanding, playing a major role in reviving art and culture across the Middle East.

Al Ain Classics Festival
March – April

Al Ain www.aacf.ae

Now in its second decade, the Al Ain Classics hosts some of the most distinguished musicians in their fields; the festival attempts to showcase music from both the Arab and Western worlds.

Al Gharbia Watersports Festival
April

Mirfa Public Beach, Al Gharbia 02 404 4000
www.algharbiafestivals.com

From kiteboards and surf ski kayaks among the waves to chilled-out camping and concerts on shore, the annual Al Gharbia Watersports Festival has it all for UAE's water lovers.

Exhibitions

With a steely focus on increasing MICE (meetings, incentives, conferences and exhibitions) tourism, Abu Dhabi has invested heavily in its state-of-the-art exhibition space, ADNEC (www.adnec.ae). The exhibition centre is also the venue for numerous musical and cultural events, as well as meetings and exhibitions, and has a number of outlets. The Aloft Hotel at ADNEC is already open while a Hyatt hotel will open soon in Capital Gate – the world's 'most leaning' building.

Dubai Dragon Boat Festival
April

www.dubaidragonboat.com

Open to social, school and corporate groups, this fun, competitive and sociable team-building event takes place each spring.

Gulf Film Festival
April

04 391 0069
www.gulffilmfest.com

Promoting the work of filmmakers from the GCC, the week-long festival also showcases a number of international movies and a competition for Emirati short films.

Red Bull Air Race
April

The Corniche Al Khubeirah
www.redbullairrace.com

Abu Dhabi is the starting fixture of the Red Bull Air Race World Series. Spectators can view the action close up from the Corniche as the planes rip through the air just metres above the water.

WOMAD Abu Dhabi
April

www.womadabudhabi.ae

Co-founded by Peter Gabriel, the three-day World of Music, Arts and Dance festival attracts nearly 100,000 spectators for the music and dance acts, art installations, workshops and food stalls from all over the globe.

Summer in Abu Dhabi
July – August

Various Locations **02 444 0444**
www.summerinabudhabi.ae

A family carnival held away from the sizzling streets in the air conditioned comfort of ADNEC. The exhibition halls are home to a host of games, sports and educational experiences to keep kids busy and active during the summer months.

Abu Dhabi Film Festival
October

Various Locations **02 556 4000**
www.abudhabifilmfestival.ae

Headed by Peter Scarlet since 2009, the festival has gone from strength to strength to become the region's premier film event. The last two years have seen a stellar line-up and, with more films, more grants and awards, and more film stars and celebrities making appearances, the future looks promising.

Dubai Fashion Week
October

Dubai World Trade Centre Dubai **04 334 4930**
www.dfw.ae

One of the glitziest events on the annual calendar, in which regional fashion designers present their collections to the world's fashion media.

Abu Dhabi Classics
October – May

www.abudhabiclassics.com

A series of classical music concerts by international artists and orchestras which takes placed at venues across the capital and at Al Jahili Fort in Al Ain. The festival runs from October to May and gets bigger, lasts longer, and becomes more adventurous every year.

Dubai World Championship
November

Jumeirah Golf Estates Dubai
www.dubaiworldchampionship.com

The world's best golfers converge on Dubai for the final fixture of the PGA European Golf Tour and a shot at a share of the multi-million prize fund.

Formula 1 Etihad Airways Abu Dhabi Grand Prix
November

Yas Marina Circuit
www.formula1.com

Racing fans delight in this big weekend in November; as this is one of the last races of the F1 season, excitement is guaranteed and the event usually features a number of big name entertainers to top off the experience.

Emirates Airlines Dubai Rugby Sevens
November – December

The Sevens Dubai **04 321 0008**
www.dubairugby7s.com

Over 130,000 spectators descend on The 7evens stadium over the course of three days to watch top international teams compete for the coveted 7s trophy, while Gulf teams go head to head with local competition, all of which tends to keep the party atmosphere going into the wee hours.

Abu Dhabi Art
November – February

Saadiyat Cultural District Sadiyat Island
www.abudhabiartfair.ae

This art fair boasts an impressively full programme of exhibitions, lectures, debates and workshops.

Abu Dhabi Adventure Challenge
December

www.abudhabi-adventure.com

The Abu Dhabi Adventure Challenge is a multi-sport endurance test with six consecutive days of racing. The disciplines include sea kayaking, camel hiking, mountain biking and adventure running.

Creamfields Abu Dhabi
December

Yas Arena Yas Island West
www.creamfields.ae

Abu Dhabi hosts the Creamfields festival which offers up some of the world's most renowned and sought-after dance DJs performing across multiple arenas and stages to a crowd of thousands.

Mubadala World Tennis Championship
December

Zayed Sports City Al Safarat
www.mubadalawtc.com

After three years of hosting the world's number one and two seeds and attracting record crowds of up to 15,000 fans, this three-day tournament has quickly become a stellar way to kick off each sporting year in Abu Dhabi. In 2011, the final takes place on New Year's Eve. In addition to the matches, a series of tennis-based activities and tournaments are organised in the run-up to the event, including the popular Community Cup.

Abu Dhabi's golf scene is thriving

Abu Dhabi: Becoming A Resident

CITY PROFILE

Half a century ago, Abu Dhabi was small and undeveloped with no sealed roads and only a handful of permanent buildings. The economy was based around pearl diving, fishing and date palm cultivation; until the discovery of oil in 1958 which brought about a radical change.

And In 83rd Place...

Abu Dhabi ranked number 83 in the Mercer's 2010 Quality of Living Survey (www.mercer.com) and was the third ranking city in the Middle East and Africa region after Dubai (75) and Port Louis (82).

While it's become cliched to talk about Abu Dhabi as a sleepy coastal village that transformed into a modern metropolis, tax-free expat haven and headquarters for luxury living, the truth is that, behind these cliches, Abu Dhabi is, for most people, a wonderful place to live with excellent career opportunities, a readily available network of social contacts, some unique activities and, apart from a few sweaty months in summer, brilliant weather.

Most expats will tell you that their standard of living is better here than it was back home; they can travel more, spend more time with family, enjoy outdoor living and make more friends.

This chapter is here to help you, whether you are making the decision to move or not, you've just arrived and don't know where to start, or you find yourself faced with an overwhelming amount of red tape. Just remember, procedures and laws do change regularly, sometimes in quite major ways. While these changes are generally announced in newspapers, they are often implemented quickly so it's a good idea to be prepared for the unexpected.

ABU DHABI'S ECONOMY & TRADE

In 2008, when the rest of the world saw economies crumble, Abu Dhabi's GDP actually rose by 30% and, after a temporary slow-down in 2009, the city's fortunes were one again on the up in 2010. Thanks to newly-rising oil prices, the economy looks set to receive another boost in 2011; although the service sector has grown rapidly following the city's transformation into a modern metropolis, oil is still a significant contributor to Abu Dhabi's economy, accounting for around half of the annual GDP.

But, knowing the oil will eventually run out, the ruling family and government has ploughed great sums into other industries and of particular note is the investment in tourism. This is best demonstrated by the developments on Saadiyat Island and Yas Island, which now includes the F1 circuit, The Yas Hotel, the Ferrari World theme park and several other hotels. The construction, commercial and financial sectors are now also significant contributors to the economy.

While Abu Dhabi hasn't been completely immune to the globally challenging economic climate of late, a full blown recession was averted thanks mainly to the property market. While neighbouring emirates, Dubai in particular, were hit hard by the crisis, with real estate plummeting by up to 50%, demand remained high in the Abu Dhabi property market with certain areas of the city boasting some of the highest rents per square metre of any city in the world.

While many Abu Dhabi residents could feel as if the recession never really hit, certain projects did fall victim, resulting in redundancies and a noted departure of professionals from the construction sector in particular. Almost all the projects shelved or put on hold were still in the planning phase and there are still a large number of large, high profile developments going ahead.

Drinking In Abu Dhabi

While drinking alcohol is forbidden for Muslims, it is served in the many bars, clubs and restaurants throughout Abu Dhabi. You won't find a booze aisle in your local supermarket, although some people have made the mistake of stocking up on the 0% alcohol beers that line the shelves. To buy alcoholic beverages from specialist liquor stores, you'll need a licence to apply for a license (see p.44).

Major Developments

Al Bateen Wharf

A complete regeneration of Abu Dhabi's oldest district to complement the heritage buildings and old dhow boatyards, the new Al Bateen Wharf (www.tdic.ae) will be a total facelift and include a fisherman's village, with a 400 room twin tower hotel, a boardwalk flanked by cafes and restaurants, and a marina complex which will feature dry stacking. It will also have health clubs, spa facilities, a business centre and a range of apartments.

Arzanah

Arzanah (www.arzanah.ae) is a 1.4 million square metre mixed-use development being constructed around Zayed Sports City at the eastern end of the island. There will be a range of apartments and villas located amid a network of landscaped gardens complete with footpaths and cycle paths, although property cannot be bought by expatriates. Amenities for residents and visitors will include a two-kilometre stretch of beach and a canal, around which will be

City centre

The Corniche

Zayed Shopping Centre

The dhowyards

A city centre mosque

hotels, indoor and outdoor retail areas, a Carrefour hypermarket, restaurants and cafes, sports facilities including bowling, tennis and an ice rink, and an aquatic centre.

Central Market

One of the city's landmarks, the redevelopment of the Central Market (www.centralmarket.ae) area has at its core three, silver blade-like towers thrusting into the sky. Designed by architects Foster & Partners, the project houses an Arabian Souk, shopping boutiques and a choice of eateries; later a string of offices, tower apartments and a number of luxury hotels will open their doors. Following the 2011 opening of the Souk Central Market (p.324), this development has already begun to revitalise the downtown area of the city.

Transport Projects

Abu Dhabi International Airport has grown with the city and the latest addition was Etihad's Terminal 3; now work is underway on the Midfield Terminal Complex, which will deliver a new passenger terminal and increase the airport's capacity to 40 million passengers per year. Initial work has also begun on a metro system which will run 131km throughout the city, with sections both above and below ground. The Abu Dhabi Metro is due for completion in 2016.

Masdar City

Masdar City (www.masdarcity.ae) will be a dream eco-city in the desert: a zero-carbon, zero-waste $20 million city powered by renewable energy sources. The seven-year sustainable development project will be built in phases, and hopes to attract companies, scientists and entrepreneurs from around the world to live and work there. The high-density city will be car free, with no one living more than 200 metres from local public transport – light rail transit (LRT) and personal rapid transit (PRT) – and will be connected to Abu Dhabi by high-speed rail links. Currently the retail area includes an organic grocery store (p.331), cafes, a travel agency, bank outlets and a monthly community market.

Qasr Al Hosn & Cultural Foundation

Qasr Al Hosn is the oldest building in the city, dating back more than 200 years. The Abu Dhabi Authority for Cultural Heritage (www.adach.ae) is working on an ambitious programme of conservation for Qasr Al Hosn and the neighbouring Abu Dhabi Cultural Foundation. The site will then be fully accessible to visitors as the nation's prime memorial and its principal historical site. The exhibits will include monuments, artefacts and antiquities belonging to the ruling family, and the site will also be home to the Natural History Museum, housing exhibits from the region.

The Souk Central Market

Saadiyat Island

Abu Dhabi's principal development, Saadiyat Island (www.saadiyat.ae), which translates as 'island of happiness', is being developed over this decade at a multi-billion cost. Once complete, Saadiyat Island will feature major cultural attractions, numerous hotels and stretches of pristine beach. The Cultural District will be the hub of the project with several museums and arts centres, including the Sheikh Zayed National Museum, the Guggenheim museum and a Louvre art museum. Two bridges and a tunnel will link Saadiyat with Abu Dhabi island. The island will eventually be home to over 145,000 residents and a number of venues have already opened to visitors. The Manarat Al Saadiyat houses an excellent art exhibition space and a Saadiyat Island visitor centre, as well as a restaurant, while the Monte Carlo Beach Club will open its doors in September 2011 and golfers can take to the green at the Saadiyat Beach Golf Club.

Shams Abu Dhabi

Shams Abu Dhabi (www.sorouh.com), a self-contained development, will include commercial and entertainment districts, a five-star hotel, a marina, and a residential area for 55,000 people, all surrounded by mangrove forests and the sea. Connected to the mainland by two bridges, the partially opened residential area is bisected by canals and pedestrian walkways. At the entrance to the development, The Gate District will be a breathtaking arch of eight towers.

Stare Wars

As annoying and infuriating as it is to have someone blatantly stare at you, it happens here. The good news is that these stares are not really sexual or predatory in nature – they are more the result of curiosity. The bad news is that there is little you can do to stop this strange little quirk of living in the region. Your best defence is to avoid wearing tight or revealing clothing, particularly in certain areas such as Al Meena.

CONSIDERING THE CITY

Sunny days, great shopping, outdoor living and tax-free salaries sum up the Abu Dhabi dream. Of course, there are red-tape hassles and everyday annoyances, but for many expats these are far outweighed by the positives.

Costs of living in Abu Dhabi reached a peak towards the end of 2008, when rents were sky-high, and prices for everything were increasing as a result. If there has been any positive side to the global recession, it's that prices have stabilised a little and, as long as your job is secure, you're actually better off now than you were before. While the rental market is still more expensive than other emirates, supply is finally catching up with demand. Housing options to suit different lifestyles and incomes are becoming increasingly available, with tenants even gaining some negotiating opportunities for cheaper rents and multiple cheque payments. The job market is still growing in most sectors, but before you jump on the first plane, make sure you test the waters by contacting potential employers, monitoring newspaper appointments pages and scouring international recruitment websites.

You should also consider how you will enter the city and stay here. To stay in Abu Dhabi long-term, you need a residency visa, and for this you need a 'sponsor'. Your sponsor is usually your company, or your spouse if you are not working (see p.38). If you don't have work lined up, you can enter on a visit visa, but will only be allowed to stay for a limited time (p.36).

BEFORE YOU ARRIVE

If you're coming to Abu Dhabi to work, or even just to look for work, you should have any qualification certificates and important documents (such as your marriage certificate, birth certificate and educational degrees) attested in your home country. This can be quite a lengthy process, and can involve solicitors and the UAE foreign embassy.

Property owners may consider selling up before the move, but don't be hasty. It may be wise to wait and give yourself a year before you commit long-term – although many people have come intending to stay 'for a year or two' and are still in the country five or ten years later.

You also need to get your financial affairs in order, such as telling banks and building societies, and the tax office – tax rules differ from country to country, so check whether you have to inform the tax office in your home country of any earnings you accrue while in Abu Dhabi. Speak to your pension company too (see Work, p.110).

If you've got kids, you should start researching schools as soon as possible. There are fortunately a lot more schools in Abu Dhabi today than there were a few years ago, although it can still be very tough to get a guaranteed place at the school of your choice. The earlier you get your child's name on the waiting list, the better.

When it comes to choosing an area of Abu Dhabi to live in, you should take your time to explore the different residential areas (see p.84 for a head start). It's a good idea to arrange temporary accommodation for when you first arrive (try to negotiate this with your employer), so that you can look for your perfect home. Speak to shipping companies (p.88) about bringing your stuff over, and try to book as far in advance as you possibly can.

If you're coming to Abu Dhabi on a 'look-see', do your homework before you arrive. Contact recruitment agencies in advance, sign up with online job sites, and visit agencies in your home country that specialise in overseas recruitment. Check also that your qualifications or industry experience are in demand here. See Work (p.106) for more information.

WHEN YOU ARRIVE

As you would expect during an international move to any new city, you're likely to arrive to find a long 'to-do' list waiting for you in Abu Dhabi. You'll be doing a lot of driving around, plenty of form filling, and a healthy smattering of waiting in queues in government departments. Just keep your sense of humour handy and soon all the boring red tape will be a distant memory.

eGate Card

The eGate service allows UAE and GCC nationals, as well as expats with a valid residence permit, to pass through both the departures and arrivals halls of Abu Dhabi International Airport (as well as those of Dubai and Al Ain International Airports) without a passport. Swipe your smart card through an electronic gate and through you go, saving a great deal of time otherwise spent in long queues. Applications for a card are processed within minutes at Abu Dhabi International Airport. The eGate card costs Dhs.200 and is valid for two years. You'll need your passport containing the valid residence permit and you will be fingerprinted and photographed. Payment can be made by cash or credit card. For further information, see www.abudhabi.ae.

The first thing you'll probably need to sort out is visas – you may be lucky enough to have a company PRO (personnel relations officer) who does this all for you; if not, see p.39.

House-hunting will also be high up on your agenda – see p.68 for advice on finding your ideal home, and then dealing with all those tricky extras, like electricity, water, phones and furniture.

You're almost certainly going to need a car and while the bad news is that driving here can be a little scary at first, the good news is that cars and their upkeep are cheap. See Driving, p.56.

As for paperwork, you're going to need to get a driving licence, of course, but also the less obvious liquor licence if you're planning on buying alcohol to drink at home. See p.44.

And once you've got the administrative stuff out of the way, it's time to put your feelers out and start meeting your fellow expats – a task which some find challenging, but most find easier than expected.

See How To Make Friends, p.42.

GETTING STARTED

Entry Visa

Visa requirements for entering Abu Dhabi vary greatly between different nationalities, and regulations should always be checked before travelling, since details can change with little or no warning. GCC nationals (Bahrain, Kuwait, Qatar, Oman and Saudi Arabia) do not need a visa to enter Abu Dhabi. Citizens from many other countries (including the UK, USA, Australia and many EU countries) get an automatic visa upon arrival at the airport (p.38). The entry visa is valid for 30 days, although you can renew for a further 30 days at a cost of Dhs.620.

Expats with residency in other GCC countries, who do not belong to one of the 33 visa on arrival nationalities but who do meet certain criteria (professions such as managers, doctors and engineers), can get a non-renewable 30 day visa on arrival – check with your airline before flying.

People of certain nationalities who are visiting the Sultanate of Oman may also enter the UAE on a free-of-charge entry permit. The same criteria and facilities apply to UAE visitors entering Oman (although if you have Abu Dhabi residency you will pay a small charge).

All other nationalities can get a 30 day tourist visa sponsored by a local entity, such as a hotel or tour operator, before entry. The fee is Dhs.100, and the visa can be renewed for a further 30 days for Dhs.620.

Customs

Before you fly into Abu Dhabi, be aware that several prescription medications are banned, especially anything containing codeine or temazepam. The UAE maintains a zero-tolerance policy on recreational drugs, and even microscopic amounts could land you in jail. Your bags will be scanned on arrival to ensure you have no offending magazines or DVDs. Each passenger is allowed 2,000 cigarettes, 400 cigars or two kilograms of tobacco. Non-Muslims are also allowed four 'units' of alcohol; a unit is either one bottle of wine, one bottle of liqueur or spirits, or half a case of beer.

Citizens of eastern European countries, countries that belonged to the former Soviet Union, China and South Africa can get a 30 day, non-renewable tourist visa sponsored by a local entity, such as a hotel, before entry into the UAE. The fee is Dhs.100.

Other visitors can apply for an entry service permit (exclusive of arrival/departure days), valid for use within 14 days of the date of issue and non-renewable. Once this visa expires, the visitor must remain out of the country for 30 days before re-entering on a new visit visa. The application fee for this visa is Dhs.120, plus an additional Dhs.20 delivery charge.

Visa On Arrival

Citizens of the following countries receive an automatic visit visa on arrival: Andorra, Australia, Austria, Belgium, Brunei, Cyprus, Denmark, Finland, France, Germany, Greece, Hong Kong, Iceland, Ireland, Italy, Japan, Liechtenstein, Luxembourg, Malaysia, Malta, Monaco, Netherlands, New Zealand, Norway, Portugal, San Marino, Singapore, South Korea, Spain, Sweden, Switzerland, United Kingdom, United States of America and Vatican City.

For those travelling onwards to a destination other than that of the original departure, a special transit visa (up to 96 hours) may be obtained free of charge through certain airlines operating in the UAE.

A multiple-entry visa is available to visitors who have a relationship with a local business, meaning they have to visit that business regularly. It is valid for visits of a maximum of 14 days each time, for six months from date of issue. It costs Dhs.1,000 and should be applied for after entering the UAE on a visit visa. For an additional Dhs.200, a multiple entry visa holder is eligible for the eGate service (see p.36). Many travel companies will be able to arrange visas on your behalf against small processing charges.

Fully Fledged Resident

After entering Abu Dhabi on an employment or residency visa, you have 60 days to complete all of the procedures involved in becoming a resident – although it's unlikely to take anywhere near that long. If you need to leave the country again before the process is completed, you should be able to do so as long as you have the entry visa that was stamped in your passport when you first entered. It's probably best though that you avoid booking any holidays in those first few weeks.

Residence Permit

In order to live in Abu Dhabi, you need to have a residence permit. There are two types of permit, both of which require the individual to be sponsored: one is for those sponsored for employment, and the other is for residence only (for example when you are sponsored by a family member who is already sponsored by an employer). There was a property-owner visa issued for a while which fell into the latter category, with the developer acting as sponsor, but without employment rights. However, this law ceased to exist in 2008, meaning buying a property no longer entitles you to a residency permit – although certain property owners are still able to apply for investor-based residency and are entitled to a multiple entry visa (renewable for Dhs.2,000 provided the owner leaves and then re-enters the country within a fixed time frame).

The residency permits used to be valid for three years but, following a new ruling in late 2010, are now only valid for two years at a time, after which you are eligible to apply for renewal. To keep your residency valid, you cannot leave the UAE for a period of more than six months at any one time.

Embassy Insight **Yacoob Abba Omar,** South African ambassador to the UAE

The main role of the embassy is to promote South Africa to our host country. Aside from consular services, we also deal with signing agreements, arranging for various delegations to visit SA, and meeting with industry and government representatives.

Despite the current economic climate, the business ties between South Africa and the UAE have been growing from strength to strength, with bilateral trade between the two countries reaching Dhs.6.14 billion in 2008. I believe that we will be seeing more South African initiatives in the future, as South African businesses are resilient and innovative and have the reputation of adhering to high standards and quality.

We encourage South African citizens to register with the Embassy. This would come in handy especially during emergencies, but we also connect citizens with the South Africa Business Council so they can network with fellow South Africans.

Our flagship event is the Freedom Day celebration on 27 April, which is aimed at key contacts of the Embassy. We also support SABCo in hosting the South Africa Family Day, which the South African community attends in droves to celebrate Freedom Day. My advice to first timers is to begin by learning some of the culture and traditions of our host country. Use the opportunity of being here to visit many countries in the region.

For a full list of embassies in Abu Dhabi, see the last page of this book.

This is particularly relevant to women going back home to give birth, or children studying abroad. If the residency is cancelled, the original sponsor can visit the Immigration Department and pay Dhs.100 for a temporary entry permit which will waive the cancellation and allow the person to re-enter the UAE. You'll need their passport copy, and will have to fax them a copy of the permit before they fly back.

Employer Sponsorship

If you have moved to Abu Dhabi to take up a job, your employer is obliged to sponsor you. Your new company's PRO should handle all the paperwork, meaning you probably won't have to visit the Immigration Department yourself. They will take your passport, employment visa (with entry stamp), medical test results, attested education certificates, copies of your company's establishment immigration card and trade licence, and three passport photos. For a fee of Dhs.300 (plus typing fees) the Immigration Department will process everything and affix and stamp the residency permit in the passport. This may take up to 10 days, during which time you'll be without your passport, but for an extra Dhs.100 they can do it on the same day. Your company must pay these fees for you. When arranging your residency, the company will apply directly for your labour card (see right). The Ministry of Labour website (www.mol.gov.ae) has a facility for companies to process applications and transactions online.

PROs & NOCs

In Abu Dhabi, a PRO is your company's 'man who can' – he liaises with various government departments and carries out admin procedures. The PRO will take care of all visa, residency, health card and labour card applications. An NOC is a no objection certificate, and is essentially a letter stating that the person in question permits you to carry out a particular procedure. You'll find you need one of these in a variety of situations, whether it's from your employer, allowing you to switch jobs, or your own NOC permitting a family member to work.

To be accepted by the authorities here, your education certificates must be verified by the issuing institution, a solicitor or public notary in your home country, and then by your foreign office to verify the solicitor as bona fide, and finally by the UAE embassy. It's a good idea to have this done before you come to Abu Dhabi, but Empost does offer a verification service at a cost of Dhs.500 per degree. The minimum turnaround time you can expect for this service is two weeks.

Family Sponsorship

If you are sponsored and resident in Abu Dhabi, you should be able to sponsor your family members, allowing them to stay in the country as long as you are here. To sponsor your wife or children, you will need a minimum monthly salary of Dhs.3,000 plus accommodation, or a minimum all-inclusive salary of Dhs.4,000, although there are rumours that this amount may rise to as high as Dhs.10,000 – see www.abudhabi.ae for the latest regulations. Only what is printed on your labour contract will be accepted as proof of your earnings, so make sure you're happy with this before starting the job.

Labour Card

Once you have your residency permit, either through your employer or family sponsor, you need a Labour Card for work. If you are on a family residency and decide to work, your employer, not your visa sponsor (usually your husband), will need to apply for a labour card. You'll need to give your employer the usual documents including a letter of no objection (NOC) from your sponsor (husband/father), your passport with residency stamp, attested certificates, passport photos, and a photocopy of your sponsor's passport. The Labour Card will cost your employer Dhs.1,000, and must be renewed annually. See Work, (p.104).

To apply for residency visas for your family, you will need to take your passport, the passports of all your family members, and your labour contract to the Family Entry Permit counter at the Immigration Department (02 446 2244, 600 522 222). Your company PRO may help you with this process, but in most cases you will need to do it (and pay for it) on your own. After submitting all the relevant documents, you will be told to return after a couple of days to collect the visas. Once the visas are processed, your family members must apply for a health card and take the medical test.

With the medical test out of the way, you then return to the Immigration Department with all the essential documents as before, plus the medical test result and the attested birth certificate (if sponsoring a child) or attested marriage certificate (if sponsoring your spouse).

For Dhs.300 (plus typing) the application will be processed and, around five days later, the passport – with the residency permit attached – will be ready for collection (for an additional Dhs.100, you can have the process completed on the same day).

If the family member is already in the UAE on a visit visa, you can still apply for residency as above. Once processed, the family member must, however, exit the country and re-enter with the correct visa,

Sponsoring A Maid

To sponsor a maid you must have a salary above Dhs.6,000 per month and be able to provide the maid with housing, medical insurance and the usual benefits, which include an airfare back to their home country at least once every two years. The process is very similar to sponsoring a family member (see p.39), the main differences being the additional costs involved – you have to pay a 'maid tax' of around Dhs.5,200 per year.

When you are processing a health card for a maid, driver or cook, you will need to pay an additional fee (Dhs.60 – Dhs.100) to have him or her vaccinated against hepatitis. There will also be a small typing fee (see Domestic Help, p.99).

or, alternatively, you can pay Dhs.500 to have the visa swapped. If you have family sponsorship and then get a job, you don't need to change to employer sponsorship, but the company will need to apply for a labour card on your behalf. It is common to hear that women can't sponsor their husbands unless they are doctors, nurses or teachers. While this used to be the rule, today it is possible for working women to sponsor their husbands and children, provided that they meet the minimum salary requirements (usually Dhs.10,000 per month). If you are in this situation you should speak to the Immigration Department and present your case. The main disadvantage of a wife sponsoring her husband is that the spouse's visa must be renewed annually, while, on the other hand, if a husband sponsors his wife, the spouse's visa only needs to be renewed every three years.

Older Children

For parents sponsoring children, difficulties arise when sons (not daughters) turn 18. Unless they are enrolled in full-time education in the UAE, they must transfer their visa to an employer. Alternatively, parents can pay a Dhs.5,000 security deposit (one-off payment) and apply for an annual visa. Daughters can stay on their father's sponsorship until they get married.

There are constraints when UAE residents want to sponsor their parents – a special committee reviews each case individually. Usually, the committee considers the age and projected health requirements of the parents and will also need proof that you will be fully providing for them, that your accommodation is suitable for housing them. In addition, you will need to pay a deposit of around Dhs.5,000 per parent. They will need medical insurance and the visas will only be issued on an annual basis.

Sheikh Khalifa Medical City

Medical Test

You need to take a medical test to get your residence visa – you will be tested for communicable diseases such as tuberculosis and HIV. Food handlers and domestic workers may require extra tests and vaccinations. To take your test, you will need the test form filled out in Arabic (there are typing offices near the screening centres that can do this for you for around Dhs.20), a valid passport copy and a copy of your entry visa, and the test fee of Dhs.250, plus Dhs.50 for immunisation costs.

Screening Centres

There are three screening centres in Abu Dhabi. Mubadala's brand new Capital Health Screening Centre (02 496 9666) is located on Muroor Road at the Al Jazira Sports Stadium. Another facility is located on Airport Road near Sheikh Khalifa Medical City (02 633 1300), while the third one is located in the Musaffah area (02 552 8371).

Blood will be taken and, if your tests are positive for HIV, you will be deported. Therefore, if you are at all nervous about the possibility of testing positive, it may be a good idea to get tested by your doctor in your home country. You will also need to undergo a chest x-ray to test for TB, while female domestic workers are usually subject to a pregnancy test.

There are just four screening centres to serve the emirate, so you will likely find the government testing centres chaotic, which can be a little bit scary if it's your first experience of Abu Dhabi's healthcare system. Rest assured that, despite appearances, medical hygiene standards are followed and test results are processed efficiently.

How To Make Friends

Getting to know new people is one of the most important things you can do to help you settle in when you move to a new city – here are just a few ways to get connected.

Whether you are a social butterfly who usually flits from social group to social group, or someone who is more likely to keep themselves to themselves, it is very easy to make friends in Abu Dhabi. Meeting new people early on is one of the keys to dealing with culture shock and beginning the whole settling-in process. Remember, the vast majority of people living in Abu Dhabi are in the same boat. Most people are far from their friends and family, and the transient nature of the city means that even those who have been here a long time are keen to meet new people as other friends will have left. The best advice is to dive right in and make an effort to get involved in anything that interests you. Whether this be plucking up the courage to start a conversation in the supermarket or writing a post on a forum arranging an outing, everybody has to start somewhere. To help you get started, there are numerous nationality-based, sporting and social groups in Abu Dhabi, and these are handy for broadening your network of acquaintances and, ultimately, your circle of friends.

Social groups

Royal Society of St George: A society dedicated to raising money for charities through organising events and social evenings. www.rssgauh.com

Abu Dhabi Irish Society: The Abu Dhabi Irish Society is open to all Irish people and anyone wanting a taste of Irish culture in Abu Dhabi. Regular events include society outings, social evenings, Irish dancing classes and Gaelic games. The society also hosts the Irish Business Forum meetings. www.irishsocietyabudhabi.com

Scottish St Andrew's Society of Abu Dhabi: This group of expat Scots, joined by more than a few 'foreigners', enjoys getting together for social gatherings and Scottish cultural activities, including the Burns supper in January. www.adscots.com

Aussies Abroad: An organisation dedicated to the promotion of Australian culture in the UAE. Social and recreational events include regular drinks nights, annual Anzac Day functions and balls. www.aussiesabroad-abudhabi.com

St David's Society: Formed by a group of enthusiastic Welsh expats, the youngest of the British tribal societies now has over 120 members. A regular newsletter keeps members informed of monthly events, such as dhow trips, quiz evenings, weekend breaks or social gatherings. www.stdavidssocietyabudhabi.blogspot.com

The UAE has a liberal attitude to other religions. Even if you are not a regular church-goer, churches can act as good community hubs.

American Women's Networks: The goal of this informal group of women is to offer an informative and welcoming atmosphere to newcomers, and help connect them to local resources and interests. Although mainly for North Americans, they also welcome women with links to America. www.awnabudhabi.com

Leisure

A new start is the perfect opportunity to get involved with a new hobby or skill, while meeting like-minded people.

Duplays: A web-based sports network that lists all the teams for all the sports available in the city. If sport is your thing, then joining a team is one way of immediately meeting a whole bunch of like-minded people. www.duplays.com

Abu Dhabi Country Club: A popular choice for aerobics and fitness classes. Check the website for an up-to-date timetable. www.adhfc.com

Networking

Networking is one of the easiest ways to make new business contacts, so it makes sense that it is a good way to increase your social circle too. With strict laws against dating and matchmaking services here in Abu Dhabi, these social networking groups are purely for meeting like-minded people in a friendly, social setting. See Work, p.108, for details of business networking groups.

Meet-Up: www.meetup.com is a popular forum for finding friends with similar hobbies where you can arrange times for sessions in an easy-going manner, rather than having to stick to a rigid routine.

Women's Groups: There are many organisations set up purely for women to meet other women and make new friends. It may be daunting going along to your first coffee morning but within minutes you'll be surrounded by people who have all been in your shoes before and who will be willing to lend a hand. They also organise day trips and have online forums with updates on events, accommodation advice, furniture for sale and even job opportunities. Visit www.abudhabiwoman.com and www.expatwoman.com.

Mum's The Word: Abu Dhabi Mums is a non-profit social group for mums with pre-school children. It is open to anyone who is expecting or has children up to the age of 5 years. Members receive discounts at various retail outlets in the city and Christmas and Easter parties are organised. www.abudhabimums.ae

Churches

The UAE has a liberal and welcoming attitude to other religions. For example, there are several active churches established across Abu Dhabi. Even if you are not a regular church-goer, the churches here tend to also act as good community hubs, so it might be worth checking out any scheduled events or activities.

Arab Evangelical Church
Airport Road, 02 445 5188

Evangelical Community Church
Airport Rd, 02 446 4563

St Andrew's Church Abu Dhabi
Airport Rd, 02 446 1631

St George's Orthodox Cathedral
Airport Rd, 02 446 4564

St Joseph's Cathedral Abu Dhabi
Airport Rd, 02 446 1929

St. Mary's Catholic Church
Al Ain, 03 721 4417

ID Card

The UAE is in the process of implementing an ambitious countrywide ID card programme, which, when complete, will require all nationals and residents to register for and carry the card. So far, the project has had some major hiccups, including various deadline delays, low turnouts for registering, and administrative problems.

To date, several deadlines for all expats to apply for their UAE ID card have already passed, but only a small number of people can actually say that they are ID card carriers. In early 2011, it was announced that the card scheme would be linked to obtaining a residence permit and by mid-2011, Emirates Identity Authority said that it had sent over two million SMS messages relating to the processing of applications in that year alone. The final deadline for registration has been moved several times, but here's what you need to know:

All residents, both nationals and expats, must be in possession of a UAE ID card, the purpose of which is to secure personal identities and cut down on fraud and identity theft. The card will eventually replace all other cards, such as health cards, labour cards and even driving licences. UAE Nationals must pay Dhs.100 for their ID cards; expat residents should pay a fee that is linked to the validity of their residence visa, paying Dhs.100 per year of validity left (so, for example, if your residence visa expires in two years, you will pay Dhs.200 for your ID card) and a small delivery fee. ID cards for children under the age of 15 are necessary and are half the cost of adults' cards. To register for your card, take your passport to an authorised typing centre to get the forms processed. You will then receive a SMS confirmation of your appointment to get your fingerprints and photograph taken, with your ID card delivery following a few weeks later.

You can find more up-to-date information, as well as a list of registration centres, at www.emiratesid.ae.

Driving Licence

If you are in Abu Dhabi on a visit visa and wish to drive a hire car, you need a valid international licence (although you can only do this if your nationality is on the transfer list on the right).

If you want to drive a private vehicle, you will need to get a temporary or permanent Abu Dhabi driving licence (except for GCC nationals who are allowed to drive on their existing GCC licences). You are not allowed to drive a privately owned Abu Dhabi car on just an international driving licence. As soon as your residence visa comes through, then you will need to switch to an Abu Dhabi driving licence, which is valid for 10 years. If you are not a citizen of one of the licence transfer countries, you will need to take a driving test. Obtaining a motorcycle licence follows the same procedure.

Tests

When submitting the necessary documents to the Traffic Police Licensing Department (www.adpolice.gov.ae), you will be required to take an eye test and will also have to provide proof of your blood group.

Automatic Licence Transfer

Citizens with licences from the following countries are eligible for automatic driving licence transfer: Australia, Austria, Belgium, Canada, Denmark, Finland, France, Germany, Greece, Ireland, Italy, Japan, Netherlands, New Zealand, Norway, Poland, South Africa, South Korea, Spain, Sweden, Switzerland, Turkey, United Kingdom, United States.

To apply for the licence transfer, you will need to bring your original passport along with a copy of it; three recent passport photos; your foreign licence (which needs to be issued by the same country as your passport) along with a copy; a translation of the licence; and a letter from your employer. Finally, you will need to take an eye sight test and provide information on your blood group.

Traffic Police

Traffic & Patrols Departments – 02 419 6666
Traffic & Licensing Department – 02 419 5555

Liquor Licence

Abu Dhabi has a relatively liberal attitude towards alcohol. You can't buy alcohol in supermarkets, but you can buy it from licensed liquor shops for home consumption, if you have a liquor licence. Only hotels and sports clubs are allowed to serve alcoholic drinks in their bars and restaurants. Independent restaurants do not serve alcohol. To drink in a bar or restaurant you need to be 21 or older.

Applying for a liquor licence is straightforward, as long as you are non-Muslim and a resident of Abu Dhabi. Pick up an application form from any branch of A&E, Spinneys Liquor, GMP, ADMMI or High Spirits. You will need to return to the store with a completed form (employees at the stores should be able to complete the Arabic translation for you), a letter of no objection from your company/sponsor or your contract of employment (which must include salary information), a copy of your passport showing the visa resident page, and payment. Your monthly allowance is usually 10% of your monthly salary and the licence fee is usually 20% of that figure. However, several stores insist on a maximum permitted allowance of Dhs.2,000, making the fee Dhs.400. Many of the companies have special offers whereby they give you back the value of the licence fee in vouchers to spend in their outlets.

The liquor store will then process your application through the police on your behalf. Once approved, you will get a specified amount (based on your monthly salary, and determined at the discretion of the police) to spend on alcohol each month. The limit is usually enough to last you a month, although if you've got a big party planned you might need to stockpile over a few months, since you can't overspend on your limit. It should take around 10 days to process your licence.

Once you have your licence, you can buy alcohol from any branch of A&E, Spinneys Liquor, GMP, ADMMI or High Spirits throughout Abu Dhabi. However, it can work out expensive, even though there is no additional tax at the till like in Dubai. The range and service, however, is excellent. You can also buy alcohol from shops in several neighbouring emirates, such as the Al Hamra Cellar in Ras Al Khaimah, the 'hole in the wall' near the Ajman Kempinski, and the Barracuda Beach Resort in Umm Al Quwain, which are usually much cheaper than the licensed stores. To buy from these shops you do not need to show your liquor licence, but you do need to have a licence on you when transporting alcohol. It is also illegal to buy alcohol for home consumption unless you have a licence, so it is wise to keep your licence updated, even if you only ever buy your alcohol from 'non-licence' shops.

BEFORE YOU LEAVE

Leaving already? Whether your time in Abu Dhabi lasts months, years, or longer, there are some things you should take care of before jumping on the plane. In the wake of the global recession, the past few years have seen tales of expats fleeing debts, abandoning cars at airports and walking away from unmanageable negative property equity. Things are now on the up, with the improving economy, so such incidences should hopefully be history. However, here's what you need to take into consideration when going home.

Ideally, when you leave, you should have wrapped up your financial affairs so you don't end up 'doing a runner'. Other things you will probably need to take care of include:

Getting electricity, water and other utilities disconnected – remember that most providers (ADDC and Etisalat) will need at least two days' notice to take a final reading and return any security deposits you have paid. You'll need to settle the final bill before you get your deposit, and make sure you keep hold of the original deposit receipt to smooth the process.

You'll also need to go through the official channels to close any bank accounts you have here. Banks (p.118) have been known to freeze an individual's account once they have been informed by the sponsor of a visa cancellation, so it's a good idea to get your finances in order first.

Settle your debts – you can get into serious trouble if you try to leave the country without paying off all your loans and outstanding bills, so be sure to keep on top of payments to avoid large sums complicating your exit.

Cancelling Your Visa

Your visa and how you cancel it will depend on the type of document you have. If you're on a residence visa that has been sponsored by your employer, as soon as your employment ends, so does your privilege to a work visa. Just as your employer would have been responsible for sorting out your paperwork, it is their responsibility to cancel it.

There's not much paperwork involved. You'll have to submit your passport and sometimes sign a waiver or a memorandum of understanding clarifying that you have received all monies owed to you. Once your visa has been cancelled, you have a grace period of 30 days to leave the country, after which time you will be fined at a rate of Dhs.25 per day for the first 6 months, Dhs.50 per day for the next 6 months, and Dhs.100 per day after that.

If you are in Abu Dhabi on a spousal visa, and have, for example, separated or just need to leave, you will need the help of your husband or wife to cancel your status. The whole process takes about five days, whichever visa you happen to be on, and is reasonably smooth.

Leaving rented accommodation, make sure the place is spick and span so you can reclaim your entire security deposit. The landlord may also require a clearance certificate from ADDC to show you've paid all your bills, so leave enough time for all the red tape. If you own property, you may choose to either sell or rent out – see Housing, p.80, for more information.

Sell your car – this has been tricky recently, with many people owing more than they can sell the car for, but persevere and be prepared to take a financial hit if you need to offload to a dealer quickly. See p.62 for useful addresses.

Organise your shipping – shop around for good rates and give as much notice as possible to the shipping company. See p.88.

Sell the stuff you're not taking – have a garage sale, list items in supermarkets or on www.dubizzle.com or www.expatwoman.com, or check if a second-hand dealer will give you a fair price.

If you have pets – if you are taking them with you, you need to make sure their vaccinations are up to date, particularly the rabies vaccination. There are other procedures to be followed when exporting pets (p.138), and ideally you need around six months to prepare. If you can't take your pets with you, you should rehome them with a new family.

New Horizons

Even for the most laid-back of people, moving to a new country and new continent can be as strange as it is exciting.

Moving to a new country will likely turn out to be a wonderful experience which will broaden your mind in the years to come. In the beginning, however, it may take some time to settle into life in any new destination. For some, it's culture shock; for others, it's simply daily frustration. As you prepare to make the move, the prospect of weekly manicures and pedicures, remaining cool in an air conditioned 4WD while someone else stands at the petrol pump and refuels your car, and doing it all in a country of malls brimming with designer boutiques can be invigorating.

However, upon arriving, the reality is often different and, while many come to discover a higher quality of living, a taste for adventure and to take advantage of opportunities to experience things they never would have done in their home countries, there's no doubt that the first few weeks can be a little tricky for even the most stoic of expats.

Fortunately, there's plenty of help, advice and resources on hand to smooth the transition, and you'll even find many unexpected home comforts. While bright skies and endless sand ought to be enough to tell you that you're in the Middle East, the expat havens of restaurants serving up pork and bars pouring pint after pint could quickly have you forgetting. There's nothing wrong with enjoying these slices of home but bear in mind that, no matter how tolerant the UAE may be, you're in a Muslim country and need to behave accordingly.

Not that you should be scared to engage with the local Emiratis. You'll find comfort in discovering that most speak exceptional English, are extremely well educated and are keen to engage in conversation, particularly about sports and music. Take heed of a couple of cultural quirks and then dive into the local culture.

Women will encounter few problems, although you may sometimes struggle with a little unwanted interest if dressed in a revealing way. The best advice is to dress a bit more conservatively than you usually would, and you should avoid any problems.

Both expat men and women may attract extra looks or the occasional attempt to negotiate a higher cab fare, but this type of behaviour has grown increasingly rare in Abu Dhabi.

In fact, for most expats, the greatest culture shocks and frustrations come not from living in an Islamic country, but from living somewhere with a different pace and attitude to life: namely, for most new expats, the driving and the bureaucracy.

Although the situation is constantly improving, a popular topic of office discussion in the morning is the persistent lack of car parking in some parts of the city. The government is aware of this and trying to remedy the congestion. Parking is continually improving due to the Mawaqif paid parking programme but in heavily congested areas, such as Hamdan Street and Tourist Club Area, it may still be best to leave your car at home and catch a cheap taxi to save yourself a headache.

Adding to the frustrations, the driving standards of some residents leave a lot to be desired. Motorists drive fast, while tailgating and overtaking in the hard shoulder is a common sight on Abu Dhabi's highways, although the recent installation of frequent speed cameras has had a notable effect for the better. The best advice is to stay calm and alert, and drive within the recommended speed limits.

If the traffic is fast and busy, the opposite is true of the multitude of seemingly simple administrative tasks, such as visa processing, licences and contracts that you face in your first few weeks in the UAE.

Yes, many government offices, medical centres and banks are heaving with people, but unfortunately that can mean just long queues rather than fast action. Allow a lengthy timeframe to avoid disappointment. It is prudent to regularly (and politely) chase up the status of your pending paperwork, as it's not altogether rare for documents to go astray or be forgotten about, but if you allow each setback and delay to get to you, you might not make it past the first few weeks.

Above all, however, be patient and accept that things may not be done exactly the same way as in your home country. Remember that you have arrived in a new country as a guest, and try to make the most of every opportunity to understand and appreciate another culture as you will ultimately end up learning a lot from it.

If homesickness does kick in, just imagine what you would be doing had you not made the move, which probably includes an umbrella, trashy TV and dreaming about your next holiday in the sun. Keep your free time packed, meet lots of new people, join lots of clubs and revel in the climate, conditions and even all the idiosyncrasies that make your new life so different. You'll soon be at ease with the new pace of life and, every now and then, an efficient process may even surprise and delight you.

Waterside living

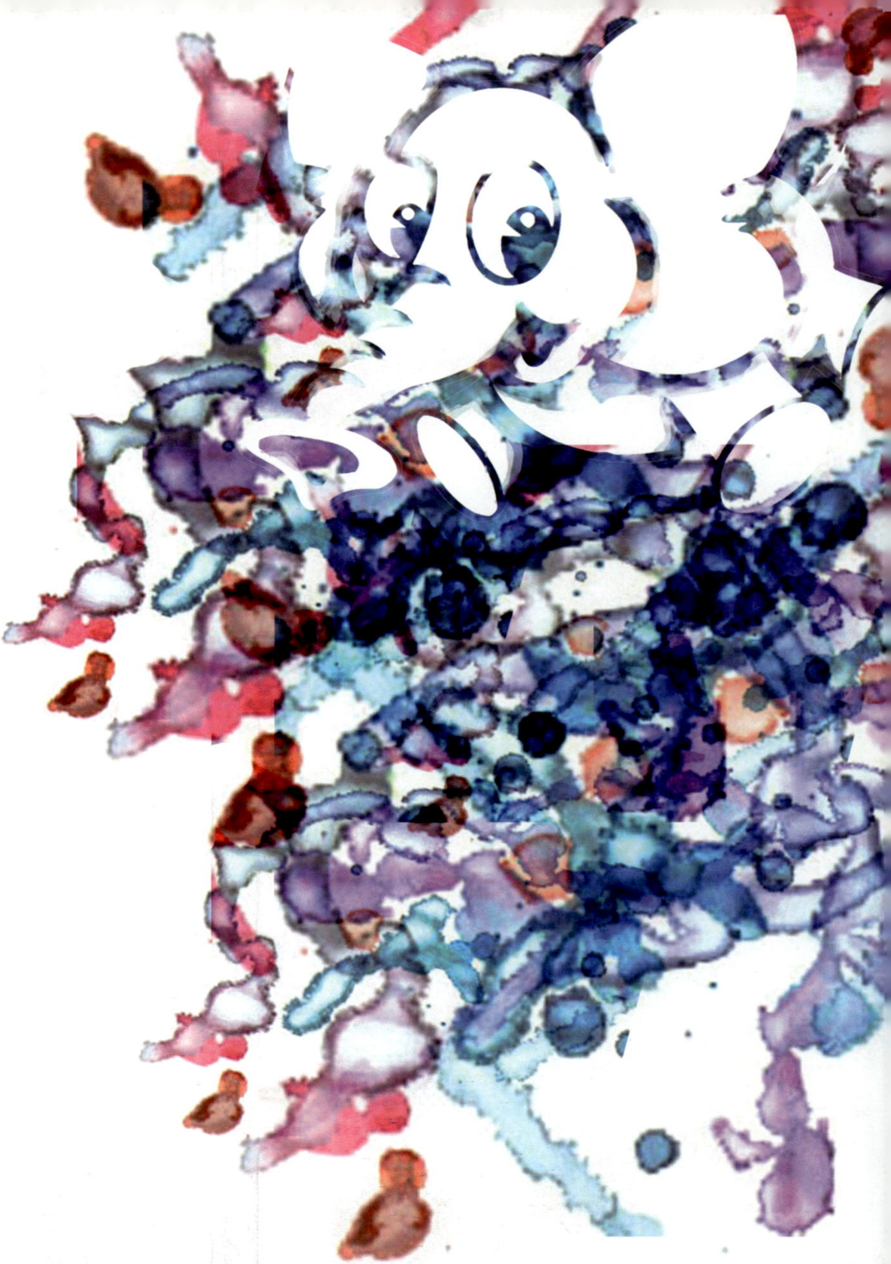

Getting Around

GETTING AROUND IN ABU DHABI

Private cars and taxis have long been the primary means of transportation for many of Abu Dhabi's residents and the government has made great strides in improving the city's infrastructure to accommodate all of the drivers. Traffic is still a major problem, but improvements such as the Sheikh Khalifa Highway have eased congestion a little. Abu Dhabi's public transportation options are also slowly getting better.

Many residents of Abu Dhabi are crazy about their cars and you'll see just about every make and model imaginable cruising down the wide highways. Buying, insuring, registering and maintaining your car is fairly easy and straightforward, but getting a driving licence can be a drawn-out nightmare for some. Abu Dhabi's roads can also be dangerous if you're not careful, but if you avoid speeding, pay attention at all times and learn how to drive a little defensively you will gain confidence in no time.

Abu Dhabi Road Network

Abu Dhabi's road network is excellent, and most main roads have at least three lanes. Streets are generally well-signposted with bilingual blue or green signs indicating the main areas or roads in and out of the city. Visitors should find Abu Dhabi's streets relatively easy to negotiate.

Abu Dhabi city is linked to the mainland by three bridges: Al Maqtaa Bridge, Mussafah Bridge and Sheikh Zayed Bridge. In addition, the Sheikh Khalifa Bridge and Expressway provide an alternative route to and from the city through Saadiyat and Yas Islands.

The streets on the main island are built on a grid system. Al Khaleej Al Arabi Street and Al Salam Street flank either side of the city, while Airport Road (2nd Street) runs in the middle from the Corniche to Al Maqtaa Bridge.

People often rely on landmarks to give directions; there is an official street name and numbering system, but the streets are often referred to by their colloquial names. For example, Sheikh Zayed the First Street is also known as Seventh Street, but the eastern section is popularly called Electra Street. Other confusing street names include: Al Bateen St (officially Hazaa bin Zayed The First St); Coast Rd (Al Khaleej Al Arabi St); New Airport Rd (East St); Nadja St (Bani Yas St); Eastern Ring Road (Al Salam St); Defence Rd (Hazaa bin Zayed The First St); Old Airport Rd (Shk Rashid bin Saeed Al Maktoum St) and Khalidiyah St (Sultan bin Zayed St).

Traffic Regulations

While the driving infrastructure is very good, the general standard of driving is variable. As a result, it is important that you pay extra attention and take a cautious approach. It is even more important to remember that you drive on the right side of the road in Abu Dhabi – and throughout the United Arab Emirates, of course – so a highway's right-hand lane is its slow lane and you should overtake on the left. People sometimes ignore this rule and drift into the centre lane or overtake on either side. If you are caught doing this, however, you could receive a traffic fine (see p.58).

Speed limits are usually between 60km/h and 80km/h around town, while on main roads and roads to other emirates they are 100 to 120km/h. The speed limit is clearly indicated on road signs. The number of fixed and mobile radar traps has increased in Abu Dhabi and the fines are hefty, so exercise caution. If you see the flash of the radar camera, you've been caught and will have to go online (www.abudhabipolice.ae) to check the amount of the fine, which will be due when you renew your registration (or sell your car).

Maps

With new roads popping up on a weekly basis, finding your way around Abu Dhabi can be difficult. Explorer Publishing produces several of the most up to date street maps available, including the fully indexed *Abu Dhabi Street Atlas* and the pocket-sized *Abu Dhabi Mini Map*.

Parking

In most cities of the UAE, parking is readily available and people rarely have to walk too far because of the oppressive heat during the summer months. In Abu Dhabi, the parking situation is improving, but it continues to be quite a big problem in the city centre. Over the last few years, more underground pay-parking areas have appeared, particularly in the business district, and there are several more under construction. There is usually a small charge, but it is worth paying to return to a cool car – and to avoid driving around small, crowded street parking lots, trapped in a one way system for hours, waiting for a space to become available.

In order to improve the situation, the Department of Transport has introduced pay and display meters (see Mawaqif, p.51). The meters, which are all solar powered, have garnered a mixed response from residents and workers alike. All of the major shopping malls have ample car parking spaces and the new office and residential buildings springing up all over the city seem to have parking intelligently factored into their design plans.

If you are looking for a space on the street, don't be tempted to park illegally, as the police are quick to hand out tickets, which will set you back Dhs.200.

Road Signs

Signposting in Abu Dhabi is generally very good once you understand the system. Blue or green signs indicate the roads, exits or locations out of the city, while brown signs show heritage sites, places of interest and hospitals. Abu Dhabi's signage system now relies more heavily on street names and numbers, compared to the older system which relied more on local area names.

Mawaqif

The integrated parking management system, Mawaqif, has been introduced to ease parking in the city. Although it varies by neighbourhood, Mawaqif charges (Dhs2-3 per hour) are generally not levied between 22:00 and 07:00. Fridays and official holidays are also exempt.

Residential permits are also available, allowing residents to park in any available standard parking bay in the area where they live. The annual fee for parking permits is Dhs.800 for the first vehicle and Dhs.1,200 for the second vehicle. To apply, you need a passport copy with residency visa, a lease or ownership contract, your last electricity bill and vehicle ownership documents. Verification and processing of resident permits takes a minimum of three working days.

For more information visit www.mawaqif.ae or visit the Customer Service Centre on the corner of Hamad Bin Mohamed Street and Al Salam Street (open 07:00-21:00 Sat to Thurs and 17:00-21:00 Fri), although you may want to catch a cab there as parking is a nightmare!

If the signage gets confusing, remember that Al Maqtaa, Al Mussafah, and Sheikh Zayed bridges all lie at one end of the island, while following any sign for the Corniche will lead you to the other end of the island; finally, look out for signs for Yas Island and you'll get onto the Sheikh Khalifa Highway, the giant ringroad that joins the Corniche with the Abu Dhabi-Dubai Road to the city's north.

Once you do get off the island, simply put, Dubai means north, Al Ain means east, and Tarif, Al Gharbia and Madinat Zayed all mean south.

Address System

All roads are numbered to aid navigation but, in general, numbers are being phased out and replaced with official road names. In the meantime, remember that the odd numbered streets run eastwards from First Street (the Corniche) to 31st Street, while the even numbered streets run south from Eighth Street (Al Salaam Street) down to Second Street and then suddenly from 22nd Street down to 32nd Street. All of which is pretty confusing. Although all roads in the capital city have an official name or number (or, in most cases, both), many roads are actually referred to by a different moniker by both individuals and companies. This lack of consistency makes locating an address difficult (post is delivered to PO Box numbers and not individual letterboxes, so official addresses don't really exist in the UAE).

You will find that companies often only list their building name, road and nearest landmark when giving their address. Hotels, mosques, shopping centres, parks and monuments, all of which are littered throughout the length of Abu Dhabi island, make useful reference points if you're trying to find a location or give directions to someone else. After a little time, you'll also get used to all the names given to roads and areas.

Explorer's *Abu Dhabi Street Atlas* makes locating particular buildings much easier with an index of almost 5,000 roads and buildings.

Cycling

Abu Dhabi is not the most bike friendly of places but, if you're willing to brave some crazy drivers, there are some areas where you can ride, including the Corniche which has cycle paths. Away from summer, exploring on two wheels is a good way of getting to know the city, especially its parks and some of the newer residential areas that have fewer cars and wide footpaths. Cycling does require a lot of care and a helmet is a must. Commuting by bike is extremely rare, especially once you factor in sweating, plus there are no lock-ups outside buildings and offices.

The Abu Dhabi government plans to make cycle lanes a key component of its new transport master plan, but the soaring summer temperatures are likely to prevent cycling from becoming the popular form of transport it is in European cities.

Walking

Cities in the UAE are generally very car oriented and not designed to encourage walking. Additionally, summer temperatures of over 45°C are not conducive to spending any length of time walking through the city. The winter months, however, make walking a comfortable way to get around and people can be found strolling through the streets, especially in the evenings. The relative compactness of Abu Dhabi's main commercial area makes walking a pleasant way of getting around at these times and, in general, the pavements are in good condition, although it can be quite a drop from the pavement to the road.

The biggest hindrance is haphazard parking, which can occasionally completely cover downtown pavements. Areas of construction or roadworks are marked, and those areas are best avoided, especially where they are demolishing older buildings. There are pedestrian crossings, although drivers tend to ignore them and will seldom slow down. Crossing a main road anywhere but on a marked crossing is illegal and there are fines for jaywalking. Special pedestrian underpasses have been built under some major roads. Those along the Corniche are worth a visit just to see the beautiful mosaics covering the subway walls.

Strolling along the Corniche and Breakwater is a popular pastime, even more so in the winter months when temperatures are perfect for enjoying the outdoors. There you will find retail kiosks, outdoor cafes and the new public beach, which are all best explored on foot.

For other great places to meander in the city, see p.299 for the best parks and other recommended walking routes.

People With Disabilities

Most of Abu Dhabi's four and five-star hotels have adequate wheelchair facilities and the Abu Dhabi International Airport is well equipped for physically challenged travellers with a special check-in gate that has direct access from the car park, dedicated lifts and a meet and greet service. The service is known as 'Golden Class' (02 575 7466). Please note that it's always advisable to contact your airline prior to travel if you need a wheelchair on arrival.

In the rest of the city, in general, facilities for physically challenged people are limited, particularly at tourist attractions where wheelchair slopes are often little more than steeply angled delivery ramps. Accessibility in pedestrian areas is also of varying standards, but there is some good news for Abu Dhabi residents with disabilities – things are starting to get better, with a few development initiatives currently underway across the city:

Abu Dhabi Municipality has pledged to install lifts on all the pedestrian bridges throughout the Salam Street and Tourist Club areas in order to assist children, the elderly and the physically challenged to cross those busy roads more safely.

In addition, Abu Dhabi recently saw the launch of a fleet of limited mobility accessible buses and Tawasul Transport (02 673 4444) provides wheelchair accessible taxis on request. The UAE capital may be a little behind western cities in this regard but, to its credit, the municipality is determined to catch up – new hotels and offices now have to incorporate ramps and braille into their designs thanks to the recent tightening of construction legislation for public buildings, so the city is becoming much more accessible to those who have special needs.

There are specially designated parking spaces in most shopping malls and supermarkets – to use these spaces you will need to obtain a special parking permit from the Abu Dhabi General Police Directorate (02 446 1461).

PUBLIC TRANSPORT

Abu Dhabi's government is currently working on overhauling the city's entire transport network to cater for the escalating number of both visitors and residents. The Surface Transport Master Plan (STMP) has been created as part of 'Plan Abu Dhabi 2030' and will eventually include an integrated rail, metro, tram, bus and ferry system along with an improved road network and special pavements and lanes for pedestrians and bicycles.

Meanwhile, however, the car is still the most popular and practical method of getting around Abu Dhabi. With the lack of trains and trams, and walking and cycling limited due to the searing summer heat, the population that uses public transport relies on the city's public bus service.

Air Travel

Abu Dhabi's location at the crossroads of Africa, Asia, and Europe makes it a popular hub and therefore an easily accessible destination from many corners of the world. London is less than seven hours away; Frankfurt, six; Hong Kong, eight; and Nairobi, four. Most European capitals and other major cities have direct flights to Abu Dhabi, many with a choice of operator.

The Abu Dhabi International Airport (code: AUH) is currently undergoing renovations as part of a multi-billion expansion plan. Upon completion of the Midfield Terminal, scheduled for 2014, the airport will have 58 gates, over 20,000 square metres for food and retail, and be equipped to handle upwards of 20 million passengers annually, with the potential to further increase capacity. For more information on the airport go to www.abudhabiairport.ae or contact the customer service desk (02 575 7818) or flight information line (02 575 7500).

Opened in 2009, Terminal 3 is exclusively for Etihad Airways, the national and award-winning airline of the UAE that is based in Abu Dhabi. Etihad is one of the fastest-growing airlines in the world, flying to 50 international destinations, including non-stop flights to London, New York, Hong Kong and Sydney.

On leaving the airport, you'll find that taxis are freely available outside the terminal. There is also an hourly round-the-clock bus service between the airport and Abu Dhabi's central bus station. It costs just Dhs.3 each way. Etihad also runs its own private bus service, which is free for those with a boarding pass and makes the journey between Abu Dhabi International Airport and Dubai.

Terminals 1 and 2 (Terminal 3 is adjacent to Terminal 1) have short and mid-stay parking, as well as a SKYPARK, while Terminal 2 has long-stay parking and a free shuttle bus to all other terminals. See www.abudhabiairport.ae for rates.

For those departing Abu Dhabi and looking to check luggage and select seats ahead of time, there are two options for early check-in. Passengers can check into the City Terminal, located in the Tourist Club Area, up to 24 hours before a scheduled flight, depending on the airline. ADNEC, the Abu Dhabi National Exhibitions Company, also offers round-the-clock check-in services. Contact the City Terminal (02 644 8434) or ADNEC (02 444 9671) to see if you're eligible for early check-in.

Pack Carefully

When you arrive in Abu Dhabi, your bags are x-rayed. Be aware of any materials – books, DVDs, magazines, etc – that could be deemed as immoral, sexually explicit, religious propaganda or potentially offensive, as they are strictly prohibited and will be confiscated if found. All narcotics (and even certain prescription and over-the-counter drugs containing codeine or temazepam) are banned and possession could result in an immediate jail term. Contact drugcl.csc@moh.gov.ae or call the Ministry of Health and Drug Control on 02 611 7240 before you travel to check if your medication is on the controlled list.

Al Ain has its own international airport (code AAN), which is about 20km west of the city centre. While the number of airlines operating out of here is not huge, the introduction of this airport has certainly eased the pressure on Abu Dhabi International Airport by redirecting some of the air traffic – particularly cargo planes. Most flights go to Mumbai, Karachi, Dhaka and Colombo. For more information on flights to and from the Garden City, contact the airport's customer service desk (03 855 555).

The UAE's biggest airport is Dubai International Airport (code: DXB) which welcomes more than 150 airlines operating to and from nearly 200 destinations. Dubai's official airline, Emirates (www.emirates.com), operates scheduled services to almost 100 destinations in over 50 countries. Dubai-based low-cost carrier flydubai (www.flydubai.com), flies to 13 mainly regional destinations. All three Dubai terminals have both short and long-term parking facilities, as well as busy taxi ranks. There are Metro stations at both Terminal 1 and Terminal 3, and Terminal 2 is accessible from a newly-opened station on the Green Line.

The vast new Al Maktoum Airport (also known as Dubai World Central, www.dwc.ae), located in the Jebel Ali area of Dubai, recently began freighter operations. It is likely that construction will continue until 2022, with passenger services gradually added. Upon completion, it will be capable of handling upwards of 100 million passengers annually.

In addition to the aforementioned, two more airlines are based in the UAE. Low-cost carrier Air Arabia is based in Sharjah and RAK Airways is the national operator of Ras Al Khaimah, a northern emirate (see Out Of The City, p.234).

Airlines

Air Arabia 06 508 8888, *www.airarabia.com*
Air Blue 02 645 4050, *www.airblue.com*
Air France 800 23823, *www.airfrance.ae*
Air India Express 02 632 2300, *www.airindiaexpress.in*
Bahrain Air 02 633 4466, *www.bahrainair.net*
British Airways 800 0441 3322, *www.britishairways.com*
Cathay Pacific 02 622 4586, *www.cathaypacific.com*
China Southern Airlines 04 221 8888, *www.flychinasouthern.com*
Egypt Air 02 621 4230, *www.egyptair.com*
Emirates 04 214 4444, *www.emirates.com*
Etihad Airways 02 511 0000, *www.etihadairways.com*
flydubai 04 301 0800, *www.flydubai.com*
Gulf Air 02 651 6888, *www.gulfair.com*
Jazeera Airways 04 209 5555, *www.jazeeraairways.com*
Kish Air 04 272 0006, *www.kishairline.com*
KLM 02 403 8600, *www.klm.com*
Kuwait Airways 02 631 2230, *www.kuwait-airways.com*
Lufthansa 02 639 4640, *www.lufthansa.com*
Middle East Airlines 02 622 6300, *www.mea.com*
Pakistan International Airlines 02 635 2600, *www.piac.com.pk*
Qatar Airways 02 621 0007, *www.qatarairways.com*
RAK Airways 07 233 8673, *www.rakairways.com*
Royal Jet Group 02 575 7000, *www.royaljetgroup.com*
Royal Jordanian 02 627 5084, *www.rj.com*
Saudi Airlines 02 635 1400, *www.saudiairlines.com*
Shaheen Air International 02 626 5111, *www.shaheenair.com*
Singapore Airlines 02 622 1110, *www.singaporeair.com*
Sri Lankan Airlines 02 633 7125, *www.srilankan.lk*
Sudan Airways 02 833 3967, *www.sudanair.com*
Turkish Airlines 02 626 1010, *www.turkishairlines.com*

Boat

Despite being located on an island, opportunities for getting around by boat in Abu Dhabi are limited and there are currently no scheduled passenger services from Abu Dhabi to other countries or even to Dubai. Boat trips for the public are mainly in the form of tours and sightseeing day trips rather than for commuter travel and various companies offer popular trips by dhow or motorboat to explore the islands off the coast (see Tours and Sightseeing, p.226).

If you know your bow from your stern, you could try hiring a fishing boat privately. Moreover, if you fancy being the captain of your own vessel, you could join the many expats here in Abu Dhabi who invest in a boat for regular weekend jaunts to one of the 200 different islands that are scattered offshore (see more information on The Islands, p 197). The ideal climate makes boating a popular hobby; check out www.uaeboats4sale.com for boat bargains.

Dhow Do You Do?

The Bateen shipyards are among the oldest areas of Abu Dhabi and there you can see craftsmen practicing the ancient Arabian art of dhow building. As well as traditional working boats, racing dhows are built and stored here too.

Bus

The Abu Dhabi Department of Transport responded to the increasing need for public transport services by launching a two year bus initiative in 2008, and by the end of 2011, the Transport Department expects to have 123 routes in operation.

With bus routes all over the emirate, as well as interurban buses on the island, the service runs more or less around the clock and fares are inexpensive, costing as little as Dhs.1 for travel within the capital.

'Ojra' bus passes can be purchased at the central bus station next to Al Wahda Mall or at any Red Crescent kiosk on the island. An interurban pass costs Dhs.40 for one month of unlimited use. For more information on Ojra call 800 55555 or visit www.ojra.ae where comprehensive bus route maps can be found and easily downloaded in PDF format. Those without passes can simply deposit a Dhs.1 in the silver box upon entering the inter-urban bus; drivers can't provide change, so be sure to have a coin handy. Buses are gender segregated with a special ladies' section in the front.

Big Bus Tour

If you're new to the city, try hopping onto a Big Bus Tour bus. Operating between 09:00 and 17:00 every day, tickets cost Dhs.200 for adults and Dhs.100 for under 15s, and are valid for 24 hours. The tour circumnavigates Abu Dhabi island and is ideal for learning where landmarks such as the Meena souks, the Corniche, Emirates Palace, ADNEC, Sheikh Zayed Mosque and Abu Dhabi Mall are all located before taking on the roads on your own.

The main bus station in Abu Dhabi is on Hazza bin Zayed Road next to Al Wahda Mall and there are clearly marked bus stops on nearly every major road on the island. There are currently 80 air-conditioned bus shelters in the city, and plans are underway to more than triple the number by 2013.

The Abu Dhabi-Dubai Emirates Express is operated jointly by the Abu Dhabi and Dubai municipalities. The 150km route along Sheikh Zayed Road takes around two hours by bus. The route operates reliably every 30 minutes between 06:30 and 21:30 at the central bus station in Abu Dhabi. Return buses leave Dubai's Al Ghubaibah station from 06:00 until 21:00. The cost per person has recently increased to Dhs.20 for a one way ticket. Bus routes to Al Ain as well as the Western Region are also available at similarly inexpensive fares, if you don't mind spending a bit more time getting there as you would by your own car.

Metro

Work is underway on Abu Dhabi's own metro system, but, for the moment, you can't go on the rails in the UAE capital. If you take a trip to Dubai, however, why not avoid all that stressful traffic, park up at Jebel Ali or Ibn Batutta and jump on the Dhs.28 billion Dubai Metro. Almost all of the Red Line stations are now open, so you can get on in the south of the city and travel all the way along Sheikh Zayed Road, passing Dubai Marina, Mall of the Emirates, the Burj Khalifa and Dubai Mall, the old areas of Bur Dubai and Deira, before ending up just past the airport in Rashidiyah. The Green Line opened in September 2011, running generally parallel to the Dubai Creek on both sides through Deira and Bur Dubai and sharing two interchanges with the Red Line. Trains run from around 06:00 to 24:00 every day except Friday (14:00 to 01:00) and Saturday (until 01:00) at intervals of 3 to 4 minutes at peak times. Each train has a section for women and children only, and a first or 'Gold' class cabin. One way fares in regular class start at Dhs.1.80 and go up to Dhs.5.80 – if you're hopping on and off all day, don't worry as the maximum daily fare is Dhs.14 by using the NOL card.

Taxi

If you don't have a car, taxis are the most common method of getting around and they are reasonably priced and plentiful. The city has a 7,000 strong taxi fleet that is overseen by TransAD (the centre for regulation of transport for hire cars, www.transad.ae). TransAD was established in 2007 to regulate the taxi service and establish an internationally recognised public transportation system in Abu Dhabi. It allows a few companies to run as franchise operations but has been regulating all taxi operations since the rather radical overhaul began.

TransAD imposes stringent rules on drivers, regularly fining those who commit offences such as demanding a fare higher than that on the meter, or even refusing to stop when hailed (all Dhs.500 fines). Some drivers will try to negotiate their fare with you,

An Abu Dhabi taxi

Parking in the city

Road sign

Central bus station

but keep in mind that this is totally illegal and you are within your rights to insist on the meter. Taxi drivers' English skills vary and, infuriatingly, they are often not familiar with street names or places, so it really helps to know where you are going. If you're new to the city, it's a good idea to take the phone number of your destination and a pocket map (such as Explorer's *Abu Dhabi Mini Map*) in case you get lost.

Pretty In Pink

TransAD also operates a fleet of 70 women-only taxis. With pink roof lights and purple logos, they are driven by female taxi drivers and charge exactly the same fares as standard Abu Dhabi cabs.

Taxis can either be flagged down at the roadside or booked by phone. If you're struggling to flag a cab your best bet is to get to a mall or a main hotel, as this is where you'll tend to find large groups of them.

All taxi companies service the airport and there are also specially registered airport taxis there; the journey into town costs Dhs.70-80.

The street taxis (which are being phased out) are easily recognizable thanks to their white and gold livery, as well as the green taxi sign on the roof. Those with silver livery and a yellow sign on the roof are the newer taxis.

Dodgy Cabs

Finding a taxi in busy areas can be frustrating and many people turn to illegal cabs, particularly at the airport. Be warned that these unlicensed vehicles don't have to meet the safety standards that official taxis do – and if you're involved in an accident you may find yourself dragged into court. They are difficult to trace, and there have even been a few cases where drivers have been the victims or perpetrators of crimes.

Daytime (06:00-22:00) metered fares in the city start at Dhs.3 and increase by an additional Dhs.1 for every subsequent kilometre of a journey. Most trips around the city shouldn't cost more than Dhs.15. Nighttime fares are slightly more, with the starting fare at Dhs.3.60 and increasing by Dhs.1.20 per kilometre. The fare chart must be in plain view inside every taxi and whilst tips are welcome, it's illegal for a driver to demand one. If you have any problems with a taxi driver call 600 535 353 – as part of its development, TransAD welcomes feedback.

Passenger Rights

Taxi drivers are obliged to accept any fare, no matter the distance. They are also obliged to drive in a safe manner, so don't be timid about asking them to slow down. If a driver refuses to pick you up because of your destination or refuses to drive responsibly, you can call TransAD and report the driver.

Taxi Companies

Al Arabia Taxi 02 558 8099
Al Ghazal Taxis Abu Dhabi 02 444 7787
Al Ghazal Taxis Al Ain 03 751 6565
CARS Taxi 02 551 6164
National Taxi 600 543 322
Q-Link Taxi 02 448 8864
Tawasul Taxi Abu Dhabi 02 673 4444
Tawasul Taxi Al Ain 03 782 5553
TransAD 02 417 3888, *www.transad.ae*

DRIVING

Getting A Driving Licence

Visitors, and people waiting for their residency permit to be processed, can apply for a temporary licence which is valid for six months and is issued by the Traffic Police Licensing Department (www.adpolice.gov.ae). To obtain one you will need to fill out the application form and take your essential documents along, including your full driving licence (paper counterpart and card if you're British). The licence is processed within a couple of minutes and costs Dhs.110. If you don't have a licence from your own country, then you will have to take a test. For further information, contact the Abu Dhabi Licensing Department (02 419 5555).

Once you have your residence visa you may apply for a permanent UAE licence. Nationals of countries listed on p.57 can automatically transfer their driving licences, as long as the original licence is valid. To apply for a permanent driving licence, submit the necessary documents (your existing foreign licence, passport with visa page, letter of no objection from your employer or sponsor and a passport photo with Dhs.200) to the Traffic Police Licensing Department, where you will be required to take an eye test and will also have to provide proof of your blood group. Legal translation of your original licence may also be required; contact the Licensing Department for further information based on your home country.

The licence is produced within minutes and is valid for 10 years, with renewal a straightforward process. Holding a passport and license from separate countries can cause problems so, if possible, ensure that both are from the same issuing country before you arrive.

If you are from a country that falls under the automatic licence transfer list, but your licence has expired, you will have to sit the full driving test. The alternative is to return home, renew your licence, and save yourself the hassle. Citizens of other GCC countries do not need to apply for the licence transfer.

Always carry your licence when driving. If you fail to produce it during a police spot check, you will be fined. You should also ensure you have the car's registration card in the car.

Automatic Licence Transfer

Citizens with licences from the following countries are eligible for automatic driving licence transfer: Australia, Austria, Belgium, Canada, Denmark, Finland, France, Germany, Greece, Ireland, Italy, Japan, Netherlands, New Zealand, Norway, Poland*, South Africa, South Korea*, Spain, Sweden, Switzerland, Turkey, United Kingdom, United States.

Replacement is only available for compact car.

If your nationality is not on the automatic transfer list, you will need to sit a UAE driving test to be eligible to drive in Abu Dhabi, regardless of whether you hold a valid driving licence from your home country or not. If you haven't driven in your country of origin and need to get a driving licence, the following information will apply to you as well.

The first step is to get a learning permit – start by picking up an application form from the Traffic Police. You will need your essential documents, the driving licence documents and Dhs.40. You will be given an eye test at the Traffic Police Department.

The Emirates Driving Company (02 551 1911, www.edcad.ae), a semi-governmental organisation part-owned by the Abu Dhabi Traffic Police, is the only government backed company providing driving lessons in Abu Dhabi. You can find a list of independent instructors on the website of the Abu Dhabi Chamber of Commerce (www.abudhabichamber.ae) and some of them will be recommended by The Emirates Driving Company. The list changes regularly, so the best thing to do is contact them directly and ask for up to date advice.

Traffic Jam Session

Avoid getting stuck in annoying traffic jams for hours on end by tuning into any of the following radio channels, which provide regular updates about the Abu Dhabi traffic situation throughout the day.

Radio 1 – 100.5FM
Radio 2 – 106.0FM
Abu Dhabi FM – 90.0FM

Some driving institutions insist that you pay for a set of pre-booked lessons and, in some cases, that package extends to 52 lessons and can cost as much as Dhs.3,000. The lessons must be taken on consecutive days and usually last 30-45 minutes.

Other companies offer lessons on an hourly basis, as and when you like, for about Dhs.35 per hour. Women are traditionally required to take lessons with a female instructor at a cost of Dhs.65 per hour. If a woman wants to take lessons with a male instructor, she must first obtain an NOC from her husband or sponsor and the Traffic Police.

When your instructor feels that you are ready to take your test, you will be issued with a letter to that effect and can apply for a test date. You will need to fill out the necessary application form at the Traffic Police and to also hand in your essential documents, driving licence documents, and Dhs.35. The wait between submitting your application and the test date can be as much as two or three months.

The test actually consists of three different tests on different dates. One is a Highway Code test, another an 'internal' test, which includes parking and manoeuvres, and the third is a road test. When you have passed all three, you will be issued with a certificate within about five days. You take this to the Traffic Police (www.adpolice.gov.ae) to apply for your permanent licence.

The rules for riding a motorbike in the UAE are similar to those of driving a car, and if you have a transferable licence from your home country, you can get either a six-month temporary licence or a 10 year permanent one (see the list of nationalities).

The Abu Dhabi Traffic Police Licensing Department (02 419 5555) is located on 23rd Street in Muroor, between Eastern Ring Road (Eighth Street) and New Airport Road (Second Street).

More information can be found on the Abu Dhabi Police website, www.adpolice.gov.ae.

Busy interchange

Driving Schools

Al Harbi Driving School Nr Bank of Umm Al Quwain, Tourist Club Area, 02 671 6177

Delma Driving School Delma Island, 02 878 1838

Emirates Driving Company Mussafah, 02 551 1911, *www.edcad.ae*

Renewing A Driving Licence

This follows much the same procedure as the initial licence transfer. When it's time to renew your licence, you will need to go to the Traffic Police Licensing Department with your expired licence, a letter of no objection from your employer or sponsor, a passport photograph and another form of ID (soon, this will have to be your UAE ID card). You'll take another eye test and receive your new licence promptly.

Car Pooling

There is no official car pooling organisation in Abu Dhabi; however you may be able to find people to share journeys with. Try the community section of Dubizzle Abu Dhabi or one of the chat forums on www.abudhabiwoman.com or www.expatwoman.com.

Safe Driver

If you've had a drink, don't even think about getting behind the wheel of your car. Dubai's Safer Driver (04 268 8797, www.saferdriver.ae). currently does not have an internal Abu Dhabi service, but will send a driver to pick you up from either Dubai or Abu Dhabi and drive you and your car back to either other city for you. Rates vary depending on distance, but the minimum charge is Dhs.475. Money well spent.

Road Toll

Abu Dhabi doesn't levy an official road tax or toll for using its roads, although there is a car registration fee of approx Dhs.200 payable annually at which time your vehicle is inspected for safety and road worthiness (see Registering A Vehicle, p.63).

Dubai, however, has an automated toll system with four gates strategically placed around the city, known as Salik. Abu Dhabi residents need to be prepared for this when they visit Dubai so as not to incur the Dhs.50 fine each time they pass through a toll gate. Stickers, which can be purchased at most major Dubai petrol stations and registered online, are attached to the windscreen and read by radio frequency as you pass the toll spots. It's easy to top up your balance; see www.salik.ae or call 800 72545 (800 SALIK) for more information.

Traffic Fines & Offences

If you are pulled over by the police or are involved in an accident and don't have your licence with you, you could be fined there and then. You will be given a 24 hour grace period in which to present your licence to the police station; if you fail to do so, you risk having your car impounded and facing a court appearance.

Driving is on the right hand side of the road and it is mandatory to wear seatbelts in the front seats and advisable in the back. Children under 10 years old are no longer allowed to sit in the front of a car, although you may still see this happening. The ban is now countrywide and fines and penalties are issued to any one caught, including points on your licence. The maximum number of points which can be added to a licence before it is revoked is 24.

Understandably, many people choose to block out the sun's glare by getting their windows tinted. The legal limit for window tint is 30% for both expats and locals alike, but you will find that exceptions are often made for Emiratis whose vehicles far exceed this limit.

Speed limits are usually 60-80km per hour around town, while on major roads they are 100-120km per hour. The speed is usually indicated on road signs, which are dotted at regular intervals along all main roads. There is no leeway for breaking the speed limit and there are a growing number of police-controlled speed traps, both fixed and mobile radar cameras, around Abu Dhabi with more popping up due to the recent police initiatives. The fine for speeding starts at Dhs.400 and increases depending on speed increments. The police also have discretionary power to confiscate vehicles and occasionally this does happen.

Keep Your Cool

Rude gestures and even small expressions of 'road rage' towards other motorists can get you into hot water leading to fines, imprisonment and even deportation – so it really is in your own best interest to remain calm at all times. Swearing is considered an extremely offensive act and you could be prosecuted. Of course it goes without saying, but you should exercise particular caution when dealing with police and officials.

You do not receive any notification when you are caught on camera, so it can be quite a shock when you re-register your car and collect all the fines in one go. Keep a check on the number of fines against your vehicle by visiting www.adpolice.gov.ae and entering your vehicle registration. If you do, you can even pay online using a credit card. Fines can also be paid in the Traffic Fines section of the Traffic Police office.

Breakdowns

In the event of a breakdown, you will usually find that passing police cars stop to help, or at least to check your documents. Traffic Police recommendations are that you should pull your car over to a safe spot but, if you are on the hard shoulder of a highway, it is suggested that you pull your car as far away from the yellow line as possible and step away from the road until help arrives.

The Arabian Automobile Association (800 4900) offers a 24 hour roadside breakdown service for an annual charge. This includes help for minor mechanical repairs, battery boosting, if you run out of petrol, get a flat tyre or lock yourself out. The more advanced service includes off-road recovery, vehicle registration and a rent a car service. It's a similar concept to the AA in Britain or AAA in the States. For more information go to www.aaauae.com.

In The Event Of An Emergency

Make sure, no matter how short your journey, that your mobile phone is with you and charged, and that you have a bottle of water in the car along with the number of a recovery service, your car registration documents and a blanket.

Other useful breakdown or recovery services include Abrat Al Sahraa Transport and Recovery (02 555 5848), Dana Auto Recovery Service (02 555 5555), International Automobile & Touring Club (02 632 4400) and Lucky Car Recovery (02 555 5522). Some dealers offer a free breakdown service for the first few years after buying a new, or even used, car. Be sure to ask the dealership about this option when purchasing a vehicle.

Traffic Accidents

All accidents must be reported to the police. In the city of Abu Dhabi, for minor collisions that do not require emergency services, call 02 446 2462 and wait for the police to arrive. For more serious accidents, dial 999 for emergency help. In other areas of the emirate, use 999 for all accidents, regardless of their severity. If there is only minor damage to the vehicles involved, the instruction from the Traffic Police (and a recent advertising campaign) is for drivers to move their vehicle to the side of the road. Once the police arrive, they will assess the accident and apportion blame.

Zero Tolerance

If you've had any alcohol at all, don't even consider driving. Abu Dhabi has a 100% zero tolerance policy and it will be straight to jail and in many cases deportation if you're caught by the police. There are plenty of taxis available so there's never any excuse to risk it.

If you disagree with their judgement, it's tough luck. The police then document the necessary details and give you a copy of the accident report. Submit the paper to your insurance company to get the vehicle repaired. In Abu Dhabi a white accident report means you are at fault, and pink means you are not to blame. You will also have to pay Dhs.500 if you get the white slip.

Saeed

Saeed is a private organisation assisting the police. It responds to non-fatal traffic accidents in Abu Dhabi. In operation since 2008, Saeed staff are on the scene quickly in their three wheeled electric operated vehicles and they are now the first to respond to the majority of 999 traffic related calls. While usually much faster than the police, there is a Dhs.500 charge attached to Saeed's service, payable by the party at fault.

The police may, in some circumstances, retain your driving licence until you obtain the necessary documentation from the insurance company saying the claim is being processed. Your insurers will then give you a paper that entitles you to retrieve your licence from the police.

Stray animals can be another hazard to avoid on the roads in the UAE. If an animal hits your vehicle and causes damage or injury, the animal's owner should pay compensation. However, if you are found to have been speeding or driving recklessly, you must compensate the owner of the animal, which can be expensive.

Petrol Stations

Petrol stations in Abu Dhabi are run by the Abu Dhabi National Oil Company's distribution division, ADNOC-FOD, and are usually open around the clock. There are plenty of stations on the main roads around Abu Dhabi emirate, but the ones on the island itself are mostly tucked away and can be difficult to find, though they are often signposted. Most offer extra services, such as car washing or shops selling all those necessities that you forgot to buy at the supermarket, and all ADNOC petrol stations now accept credit card payment for petrol.

Pumps are managed by an attendant, who often cleans your windscreen while you're filling up; although the price of petrol has fluctuated in comparison with other countries, and is expensive compared to other Gulf countries, most expats should still find it very cheap as compared to their home countries. For example, you would expect to pay around Dhs.70 to fill up a small car, such as a Toyota Yaris, with unleaded petrol. Petrol stations in the other emirates are numerous and run by the companies Emarat, EPPCO and ENOC. Pumps are also managed by attendants in the rest of the UAE but many stations will only accept cash.

GETTING A CAR

Hiring A Car

New arrivals to Abu Dhabi often find that they have no other option than to hire a vehicle until their residency papers go through. Others are perhaps unsure of how long they plan to stay in the UAE or simply prefer the relatively hassle-free option of renting over buying a vehicle. Most leasing companies include the following in their rates: registration, maintenance, replacement, 24 hour assistance and insurance.

All the main international car rental companies, plus a few extra, can be found in the UAE. It is best to shop around as the rates vary considerably. The larger, reputable firms generally have more reliable vehicles and a greater capacity to help in an emergency (an important factor when dealing with the aftermath of an accident). Find out which car hire agent your company uses, as you might qualify for a corporate rate. But do beware if you travel regularly to Dubai, as most rental companies will keep track of how many times you pass through the Salik toll gates (p.58) and charge you at the end of the month, along with a Salik service charge. If you are commuting between emirates also be aware that more companies are implementing a monthly mileage limit.

Leasing is generally available on a weekly, monthly or yearly basis. Monthly leasing prices start at around Dhs.1,500 for a small vehicle, such as a Toyota Yaris, and go up from there. As the lease period increases, the price decreases. So, if you're considering keeping the car for a long period, it may not work out that much more expensive than buying.

Before you take possession of your leased car, do a thorough check for any dents or bumps. To hire any vehicle, you will need to provide a passport copy, credit card (not debit card) and a valid driving licence. Those with a residence visa must have a UAE driving licence to drive a hired car, while those on a visit visa can use a licence from their home country as long as it is at least one year old. Comprehensive insurance is essential; make sure that it includes personal accident coverage, and perhaps Oman cover if you're planning on exploring.

Car Hire Companies

Al Ghazal Transport Co 02 634 2200, *www.adnh.com*
Al Raeed Rent A Car 02 446 9915, *www.alraeeduae.com*
Avis Rent A Car 02 575 7180, *www.avis.com*
Budget Rent A Car > ***p.61*** 02 443 8430, *www.budget-uae.com*
Diamond Lease 02 622 2028, *www.diamondlease.com*
Dollar Rent A Car 02 641 9002, *www.dollaruae.com*
Europcar 02 626 1441, *www.europcar-middleeast.com*
Eurostar 02 645 5855, *www.eurostarrental.com*
FAST Limo 02 555 1441
Fast Rent A Car 02 632 4000, *www.fastuae.com*
Hertz Rent A Car 02 672 0060, *www.hertzuae.com*
National Car Rental 800 3130, *www.national-me.com*
Sahab Rent A Car 02 633 4200, *www.sahabuae.com*
Sixt Rent A Car 02 550 3929, *www.sixt.com*
Thrifty Car Rental 02 634 5663, *www.thriftyuae.com*
United Car Rentals 02 642 7278, *www.unitedcarrentals.com*

Buying A Car

Aside from the at-times horrendous traffic, the UAE is something of a motorist's dream. Petrol is cheap, big engines are considered cool and the wide highways stretching across the country are smooth and perfect for weekend drives. Buying a car is unlikely to cause a major headache either: the vast majority of the major car manufacturers are available through franchised dealerships in Abu Dhabi and more are expected to join in once the Motor World Abu Dhabi development is completed (the first phase is scheduled for completion in October 2011). Expat buyers are often pleasantly surprised by the low cost of new cars compared to prices in their home countries. For many, this lower initial cost, coupled with much cheaper fuel and maintenance costs, means they can afford something a little more extravagant than they might drive at home. The chaotic traffic, teamed with the open desert that covers most of the country, can be enough to persuade expats to turn to a 4WD or SUV – the extra bulk and height certainly makes you feel better protected.

There is a large second-hand car market in the UAE. Dealers are scattered around town, but the best area to start in is Mussafah, while Airport Road also has a decent selection of used car dealers. Expect to pay a premium of between Dhs.5,000 and Dhs.10,000 for buying through a dealer (as opposed to buying from a private seller), since they also offer a limited warranty, insurance, finance and registration. Some Abu Dhabi residents venture up to Dubai to purchase second-hand cars from the Dubai Municipality Used Car Complex at Ras Al Khor, where all the cars have been thoroughly checked by EPPCO's Tasjeel service. It is certainly possible to find a bargain but be aware of the additional hassle involved when you try to register a vehicle from another emirate (see p. 62, Importing A Car). This area is also home to Golden Bell Auctions (04 333 3647, www.goldenbellauctions.com), with sales held every Wednesday evening. All cars up for auction have to undergo a test at the nearby EPPCO/Tasjeel garage, and all outstanding fines will have been cleared.

If you decide to buy a vehicle privately, check out the classifieds in *Gulf News* and *Khaleej Times*, or on the noticeboards at Abela and Spinneys supermarkets, St Andrew's Church and many of the sports clubs. You can also pick up a copy of *Auto Trader UAE,* which has

a huge number of new and used cars advertised for sale. There are a number of websites which are worth searching too: Dubizzle (www.dubizzle.com) now has a very good Abu Dhabi site, while Expat Woman (www.expatwomanabudhabi.com) has all kinds of classifieds specific to Abu Dhabi and Al Ain; www.autodealer.ae is a used car website which covers all of the Emirates, and www.souq.com is an auction site which includes cars in its listings.

Get A Check Up

Before buying a used car, it is advisable to have it checked by a reputable garage. This is especially necessary with 4WDs, which may have been driven off-road a lot. This service will set you back around Dhs.400, and it is best to book in advance. The major garages in Abu Dhabi are located out of the city, in Mussafah. To get to Mussafah, take the Coast Road out of the city over Mussafah Bridge and keep going.

Importing A Car

It is possible to import or export your car, but be prepared for paperwork, paperwork and a bit more paperwork. Furthermore, given the amount of choice available locally, it hardly makes sense. Indeed, most people tend to take advantage of the bustling second-hand market available locally when they arrive and leave the region; however, if you're keen to hang onto your chosen four wheels, the best thing to do is to contact a car dealership who should be able to advise and assist you through the process. You could also contact Kanoo Shipping (02 672 0939, www.kanooshipping.com) or Khalidia International Shipping (02 627 2272, www.khalidiashipping.com) for more details. If you buy a car in one of the other emirates and want to register it in Abu Dhabi, then you have to officially export and import it. Exporting means going to the traffic department in the emirate in which the car is registered with copies of your passport and driving licence, along with around Dhs.450 to cover your export licence, export insurance and export plates, which are usually blue.

Tinted Windows

Currently, the government allows you to avoid the sun somewhat by tinting your vehicle's windows up to 30%. Some areas have facilities where you can get your car windows tinted, but don't get carried away – remember to stick to the limit. Random checks take place and fines are handed out to those caught in the dark. Tinting in Sharjah is allowed for a fee of Dhs.100 per year and Ajman residents may tint for Dhs.200 per annum, but only if they are women.

On arrival in Abu Dhabi, you should register the vehicle as normal (see Registering A Vehicle, p.63). You usually have two days in which to complete this process. One catch to be aware of is that you're not supposed to drive the car between emirates – it should be transported.

New Car Dealers

Abu Dhabi Motors BMW 02 507 5800, *www.bmw-abudhabi.com*
Al Futtaim Motors Lexus 02 419 9888, *www.alfuttaimmotors.com*
Al Futtaim Motors Toyota 02 419 9999, *www.alfuttaimmotors.com*
Al Habtoor Motors Aston Martin, Bentley, Mitsubishi 02 678 8400, *www.alhabtoor-motors.com*
Al Masaood Automobiles Nissan 02 677 2000, *www.nissan-almasaoodautomobiles.com*
Al Nuaimi Cars Est Toyota, 02 446 2297
Al Otaiba Group Chevrolet 02 558 8777, *www.otaibagroup.com*
Al Yousuf Motors Daihatsu 02 558 8890, *www.aym.ae*
Ali & Sons Audi 02 665 8000, *www.audiabudhabi.com*
Ali & Sons Volkswagen 02 681 7770, *www.volkswagen-abu-dhabi.com*
Bin Hamoodah Automotive Chevrolet 02 444 8888, *www.binhamoodah.ae*
Central Motors Fiat, Mercedes-Benz, Jeep 02 554 6333, *www.alfahim.com*
Citroen Emirates Citroen 02 446 7786, *www.citroenemirates.com*
Elite Motors Mitsubishi 02 642 3686
Emirates Motor Company Mercedes-Benz 02 656 7777, *www.mercedes-benz.com*
Galadari Automobiles Mazda 02 677 3030, *www.mazdauae.com*
Habtoor Royal Car Showroom Aston Martin, Bentley, Mitsubishi 02 642 3114, *www.habtoormotors.com*
Juma Al Majid Est Hyundai 02 644 0233, *www.hyundai-ae.com*
Liberty Abu Dhabi Automobiles Cadillac, Hummer 02 551 5858, *www.libertyautos.com*
Omeir Bin Youssef Group Peugeot 02 622 7777
Peugeot Peugeot 02 635 1901
Premier Motors Ford, Jaguar, Land Rover, Ferrari, Masserati 02 558 8344, *www.premier-motors.ae*
Western Motors Jeep 02 667 6000, *www.jeepabudhabi.com, www.fiatuae.com*

Used Car Dealers

501 Cars 02 445 9997, *www.501cars.com*
Al Ain Class Motors 03 763 3333, *www.alainclass.com*
Al Futtaim Automall 02 673 3504, *www.automalluae.com*
Al Hilal Auto 02 417 4720, *www.alhilalbank.ae*
Ali & Sons 02 681 7770, *www.volkswagen-abu-dhabi.com*
Ali & Sons 02 665 8000, *www.audiabudhabi.com*

Prestige Cars 02 681 0111, *www.prestigecars.ae*
Princess Car 02 558 5050, *www.princesscar.com*
Reem Automobile Showroom 02 446 3343, *www.reemauto.com*

Gulf Spec

When buying a car – used and European or American marques in particular – check that it is 'Gulf Spec'. This means that the manufacturer has done things to reinforce the vehicle against the harsh climate, such as an electric fan over oil coolers, enlarged radiators, enlarged AC condensers and air filters better suited to dealing with the sand in the air.

Vehicle Finance

Many new and second-hand car dealers will be able to arrange auto finance for you, often through a deal with their preferred banking partner. Previously, this involved writing out years and years worth of post-dated cheques, but most official dealers and main financial establishments will now be able to set up monthly automatic transactions for you.

Always ask about the rates and terms of the auto loan, and then consider going directly to one of the banks to see if they can offer you a better deal. It is often easier to get financing through the bank that receives your salary. Also, the interest rates on personal loans are often a little lower than those on car loans. Ask your bank if you qualify for a personal loan.

Vehicle Insurance

Before you can register your car, you must have adequate insurance. Insurers will need to know the usual details, such as year of manufacture, value and chassis number. If you got a real bargain of a car and feel it's worth much more than you paid, make sure you instruct the insurance company to cover it at the market value. Take copies of your UAE driving licence, passport and the existing vehicle registration card.

Blood Money

As the law currently stands, the family of a pedestrian killed in a road accident is entitled to Dhs.200,000 diya (blood) money. The money is usually paid by the insurance company unless there's any evidence of the driver having been under the influence of alcohol. However, an amendment to the law is being considered to put a stop to the terrible trend among desperate lower-income workers of killing themselves to provide for their family. This will mean blood money is not automatically due if the victim was walking across a road not intended for use by pedestrians, such as the Abu Dhabi-Dubai Road.

Annual insurance policies cover a 13 month period (this allows for a one-month grace period when your registration expires). Rates depend on the age and model of your car and your previous insurance history, but very few companies will recognise any no-claims bonuses you have accrued in your home country. Rates are generally 4-7% of the vehicle value, or a flat 5% for cars over five years old. Fully comprehensive cover with personal accident insurance is highly advisable, and you are strongly advised to make sure the policy covers you for 'blood money'. For more adventurous 4WD drivers, insurance for off-roading accidents is also recommended. Young or new drivers might need to call a few insurance companies before finding one that is willing to insure them, especially if they own a sports car. If you have no claims for three years, you will probably qualify for a reduction in your insurance rates.

Transferring Ownership

All transactions must be directed through the Traffic Police (see p.44). A Dhs.3,000 fine is imposed on both buyer and seller for cars sold unofficially. To register a used car in your name, you must transfer vehicle ownership. You will need to collect an application form from the Traffic Police (see p.56) and submit it, along with a no objection letter from the finance company, the original licence plates, the valid registration card, the insurance certificate and Dhs.20. The previous owner must also be present to sign the form.

Car Insurance Companies

Abu Dhabi National Insurance Company (ADNIC) 02 408 0100, *www.adnic.ae*
Abu Dhabi National Takaful Company 02 410 7700, *www.takaful.ae*
Al Ain Ahlia Insurance 02 445 9900, *www.alaininsurance.com*
Al Khazna Insurance 02 676 7000, *www.alkhazna.com*
Alliance Insurance 02 632 6067, *www.alliance-uae.com*
Arab Orient 02 676 3222, *www.araborient.com*
AXA Insurance (Gulf) > ***p.65*** 02 495 7999, *www.axa-gulf.com*
Emirates Insurance Company 02 644 0400, *www.eminsco.com*
Gargash Insurance 02 671 7100, *www.gargashinsurance.com*
Nasco Karaoglan 02 642 2255, *www.nascodubai.com*
National General Insurance 02 667 8783, *www.ngi.ae*
Oman Insurance 02 612 8444, *www.tameen.ae*
RSA Abu Dhabi 02 635 1800, *www.rsagroup.ae*

Registering a Vehicle

All cars must be registered annually with the Traffic Police. Allow plenty of time; expect to be pushed from counter to counter, filling in form after form.

City life in Abu Dhabi

Before starting the registration procedure, check you do not have any traffic offences and fines against your car number because the registration procedure cannot be completed until these have been settled.

There is a one month grace period after your registration has expired during which time you can re-register your vehicle (hence, the 13 month insurance period). You must have your valid insurance papers ready before registering or re-registering your car.

In order to obtain licence plates for the vehicle, it must first be tested and then registered with the Traffic Police. If you have purchased your vehicle brand new from a dealer, they will probably do the registration for you; otherwise you will have to get it done yourself. A new vehicle does not need to be tested for the first two years, though it must be re-registered after the first year. Re-registration costs Dhs.100 plus Dhs.5 for a sticker which is placed onto your number plate. The test involves a technical inspection, checking lights, bodywork, fire extinguisher and emissions.

Once the car has been passed, you will receive a certification document. This will cost between Dhs.60 and Dhs.80. Once your vehicle is insured, you must submit the insurance documents (valid for 13 months), the proof of purchasing agreement and the vehicle 'passing' certificate to the Traffic Police, along with the essential documents and Dhs.360.

Pimp Your Ride?

The area between Al Salam and Al Falah Streets is the place to head for accessories. Small workshops can provide everything from new tyres and alloys to custom car covers and window tinting – you can even get your car seats reupholstered.

Vehicle Repairs & Maintenance

By law, no vehicle can be accepted for major 'collision' repairs without an accident report from the Traffic Police, although minor dents can be repaired without a report. Your insurance company will usually have an agreement with a particular garage to which they will refer you. The garage will carry out the repair work and the insurance company will settle the claim. Generally, there is Dhs.500 deductible for all claims, but check with your insurance company for details of your policy.

If you purchase a new vehicle, your insurance should cover you for 'agency repairs' – repairs at the workshop of the dealer selling the car – although this is not a guarantee and you may have to pay a premium. It's worth it though, as your car's warranty (two to three years) may be invalid if you have non-agency repairs done on it. Even if you buy a fairly new second-hand car (less than three years old) it may be beneficial to opt for agency repairs to protect the value of the car. When buying a used car, many shoppers like to see a history of agency maintenance, especially for relatively new vehicles. It may seem ridiculous to have an oil change at the dealership every 5,000km, but it often pays off when selling.

Besides accidents and bumps, common problems in this part of the world include the air-conditioning malfunctioning, batteries suddenly giving up and tyres blowing out. The aircon is likely just to need topping up, which is fairly straightforward. Car batteries don't tend to last too long in the hot conditions, and you may not get much warning (one day your car just won't start), so it's always handy to keep a set of jump leads in the boot.

If you get your car started, it's worth a trip to Mussafah, where there's a concentration of small workshops. Haggle hard for repairs, spares and even a new battery.

To Oman And Back

It is wise to check whether your insurance covers you for the Sultanate of Oman as, within the Emirates, you may find yourself driving through small Omani enclaves (especially if you are off-road, near Hatta, through Wadi Bih and on the East Coast in Dibba). Insurance for a visit to Oman can be arranged on a short-term basis, usually for no extra cost.

Vehicle Repairs

ADM Abu Dhabi Motors 02 558 8000, *www.bmw-abudhabi.com*
Al Habtoor 02 555 3344
Al Mazroui & Clevy Auto Services 02 555 4589
Ali & Sons 02 555 3363, *www.ali-sons.com*
Elite Motors Workshop 02 558 3441
Trading Enterprises 02 555 4246

Managed by:
LINE
MADINAT ZAYED SHOPPING CENTRE

Housing

HOUSING

Apart from securing your new job, getting your accommodation satisfactorily sorted out is probably the most crucial factor in making your move to Abu Dhabi a success. The first thing to decide is what type of accommodation you want (and can afford) to live in, and in what part of town. This chapter provides a detailed roundup on the different residential areas in Abu Dhabi (p.84), focusing on the type of accommodation available, the amenities, and the general pros and cons. There are sections on the procedures and practicalities involved in both the rental (p.70) and owning (p.74) markets too, discussing what you need to do to secure your dream pad. Once you've found somewhere to live, this chapter also tells you how to get settled in, covering everything from getting your TV and electricity connected to sprucing up the garden. Happy house hunting.

ACCOMMODATION OPTIONS

Hotel & Serviced Apartments

Hotel apartments are ideal if you require temporary, furnished accommodation, although they are a relatively expensive option. Apartments can be rented on a daily, weekly, monthly or yearly basis. They come fully furnished and serviced (with maid service), and usually have satellite TV and excellent leisure facilities. Water, electricity and sometimes internet are included in the rent. Rates vary hugely according to the area and facilities provided. They can also fluctuate depending on the time of year, but usually, if you take a yearly lease, your rate will be fixed for that year.

Al Diar Palm Hotel Apartments Muroor St, Nr Al Salat Plaza, Madinat Zayed, 02 642 0900, *www.aldiarhotels.com*
Al Maha Arjaan By Rotana Sheikh Hamdan Bin Mohammed St, Al Markaziyah, 02 610 6666, *www.rotana.com*
Al Manzel Hotel Apartments Sheikh Zayed First St, Tourist Club Area, 02 644 8000, *www.almanzel-hotelapartments.ae*
Al Rawda Arjaan By Rotana Old Airport Rd, Nr Al Wahda Sports Club, Al Wahdah, 02 403 5000, *www.rotana.com*
Beach Rotana Abu Dhabi Liwa St, Nr Abu Dhabi Mall, Tourist Club Area, 02 697 9000, *www.rotana.com*
Cassells Hotel Apartments Sheikh Zayed Second St, Al Markaziyah, 02 610 7777, *www.cassellshotelapartments.ae*
Century Hotel Apartments Al Salam St, Al Markaziyah, 02 644 7665, *www.aldiarhotels.com*
Corniche Towers Hotel Apartments Corniche Rd, Nr Volkswagen Service Center, Al Khalidiyah, 02 681 0088
Euro Hotel Apartments East Rd, Al Dhafrah, 02 641 3111, *www.ramee-group.com*
Fortune Hotel Apartments Al Salam St, Tourist Club Area, 02 645 0666, *www.fortune-hotels.net*
Hilton Baynunah Corniche Road East, Markaziya West, 02 632 7777, *www.hilton.com*
Hilton Corniche Hotel Apartments Corniche Rd, Al Markaziyah, 02 627 6000, *www.hilton.com*
Ivory Hotel Apartments Nr KIA Motor Showroom, Tourist Club Area, 02 644 7644, *www.ivoryhotelapts.ae*
Mourouj Hotel Apartments East Rd, Nr Madinat Zayed Shopping Mall, Al Dhafrah, 02 641 3555, *www.mouroujhotelapartments.ae*
Murjan Asfar Hotel Apartments Sheikh Rashid Bin Saeed Al Maktoum Rd, Nr ADNEC, Al Musalla, 02 643 3330, *www.asfarhotels.com*
Platinum Residence Khaled Bin Alwaleed St, Al Khalidiyah, 02 634 4463, *www.phauae.com*
Rainbow Hotel Apartment Sheikh Hamdan St, Nr Crowne Plaza, Markaziya East, 02 632 6333, *www.rainbowauh.com*
Ramee Guestline Hotel Apartments I Hamdan St, Nr Al Salama Hospital, Tourist Club Area, 02 674 7000, *www.rameehotels.com*
Ramee Hotel Apartments East Rd, Nr Al Falah Plaza, Al Muroor, 02 642 2696, *www.rameehotels.com*
Royal Regency Hotel Apartment Sheikh Hamdan Bin Mohammed St, Al Markaziyah, 02 626 6566
Sahara Hotel Apartments Sheikh Zayed Second St, Al Markaziyah, 02 631 9000, *www.saharahotelapartments.com*
Staybridge Suites Yas Island Golf Plaza, Yas Island East, 02 656 3333, *www.staybridge.com*
Vision Hotel Apartments Old Mazda Rd, Tourist Club Area, 02 699 2666, *www.visionhotel.net*

Owning A Property

Since 2005, foreigners have been allowed to purchase freehold property in certain areas of Abu Dhabi. With new developments such as Saadiyat and Al Reef coming to the market, there is an increasing amount of choice at different price levels. Property prices soared for a few years and, while everything came crashing down in neighbouring Dubai, a shortage of supply coupled with consistent demand insulated Abu Dhabi from the worst. Prices have levelled out a little and, although they remain high, buying a house is a viable option for people planning on staying in Abu Dhabi for the long term. It's not a decision to be taken lightly though, and it pays to really do your research. For more information on the procedures and pitfalls involved in buying a property, see p.74.

Standard Apartments

Abu Dhabi apartments come in various sizes, from studio to four-bedroom, with widely varying rents (and conditions) to match. Newer apartments usually have centralised air conditioning (C A/C) and older ones have noisier air conditioning units built into the wall. C A/C is normally more expensive, although in some apartment buildings, your air-conditioning costs are included in the rent. Many of the newest developments utilise district cooling, a system in which all of the buildings within an area receive cold water from a central cooling plant. Residents living in apartments with district cooling will need to sign an agreement with the local cooling company and pay that company monthly. The cost of chilled water can also creep up during the hotter months.

Top-of-the-range apartments often come semi-furnished (with a cooker, fridge and washing machine), and have 24 hour security, covered parking, a private gym and a swimming pool.

One downside to apartment living is that you'l have to do with less privacy than in a villa and will be at the mercy of your neighbour to a certain extent. Also, depending on the area, parking may be a problem too: some apartments do not have dedicated parking and others might come with just one dedicated space – check to see if you get a space with your apartment.

Villas

The villa lifestyle is attractive, but it doesn't come cheap, and smart villas are snapped up pretty quickly. The good news is that, if you look hard enough and use the grapevine, you might find the perfect villa that won't break the budget. Depending on the location, size and age of the property, a villa may be cheaper than some apartments, but be aware that air-conditioning costs will be higher. Villas differ greatly in quality and facilities. Independent ones often have bigger gardens, while compound villas are usually newer and may have shared facilities like a pool or gym.

No Place To Park?

Many apartments charge an additional rental fee for covered or underground parking. In some areas, this is essential, as finding parking outside your apartment can be nearly impossible, particularly if you live in the city centre although the Mawaqif paid parking programme is slowly easing this problem.

Villa Sharing

Sharing a large villa is a popular option with young professionals for economic and lifestyle reasons. The downside is the lack of privacy and the chore of

Corniche high-rises

finding new housemates when someone moves out. If you're looking to share an abode, www.dubizzle.com is the best place to start. See right for information on the legality of accommodation sharing.

RENTING A HOME

Employers are legally obliged to provide accommodation or an accommodation allowance, although no guidelines are given as to how much this should be. Some large organisations, like ADNOC, have their own compounds or residential complexes. Other companies have arrangements with particular apartment buildings or compounds and reserve a percentage of the properties for their employees. Your contract may offer you the option of choosing company facilities, or taking a cash amount. Accepting company facilities will save you a great deal of time, effort, and stress in finding a place to live, and it will probably be well-maintained. Some expats use the company facilities for the first year, until they are settled, and then look for something they are happier with.

In general, the rent for most property is paid annually, in advance. Some landlords may accept payment in more than one cheque, meaning that you provide them with an agreed number of post-dated cheques that will be cashed on their due date. Some employers will arrange to pay your rent payments directly from your salary, which can save a lot of hassle.

Rents in Abu Dhabi have been astronomically high in the last few years with supply vastly outstripping demand. The good news is that, the situation is getting much better for tenants as more housing stock is being released onto the market, increasing rental options and decreasing rents.

Finding A Rental Home

There are a number of ways to find suitable accommodation, the most obvious of which is via a real estate agent (see p.74). The advantage of an agent is that he or she will do the work for you. The downside, of course, is that agents charge a fee, usually 5% of the yearly rent or Dhs.5,000, whichever is higher. Agents will be able to show you several properties, but if that agent also represents the landlord, they might not have your best interests in mind. If you have the time, it is worth checking classified ads in local newspapers, although this works better when trying to find shared accommodation. Dubizzle (www.dubizzle.com) is another good option when looking for a place to call home (see p.71).

Sometimes an even better bet is to drive around a few areas and look out for 'To Let' signs displayed on vacant villas; these will display the phone number of either the landlord or the letting agent.

If you find a particularly attractive apartment building, try asking the security guard on duty if there are any vacant properties. Often this extra effort when looking for a home can result in a 'real find' and many proud barbecues to come. It also helps to ask colleagues and friends to keep an eye out for vacancies in shared villas.

Sharing

Sharing an apartment is an easy way to save money, but renters should be aware that groups of people living together in certain areas (for example, near schools and in areas deemed for families only) is frowned upon, and may even be illegal. The number of apartment and room sharing adverts pasted all over town implies that authorities have accepted it as a necessary part of growth and development, but the legality of sharing remains hazy. While the law clearly stipulates that it is illegal for unmarried men and women to live together, it's doubtful that the Abu Dhabi authorities would come knocking on doors to check the marital status of tenants, as they

HOUSING ABBREVIATIONS

When looking for property to rent in newspaper classifieds or online, there's a whole new language to learn. Here's our guide to some of the most common abbreviations:

BR	Bedroom
C A/C	Centralised air conditioning (sometimes included in the rent)
C/port	Car port (usual in compounds)
D/S	Double-storey villa
Eff	Efficiency
Ensuite	Bedroom has private bathroom
Ext S/Q	Servants' quarters located outside the villa
Fully fitted	Includes appliances (oven, kitchen, refrigerator, washing machine)
Hall flat	Apartment has an entrance hall
HWS	Hot water system
L/D	Living/dining room area
M/a	Mature age (either you or the building)
Ns/prof	Non-smoking professional
OSP	Off-street parking
PWK	Per week
S/S	Single-storey villa
Shared pool	Pool is communal for all villas on compound
Spac	Spacious
W A/C	Window air conditioning (often indicates an older building)
W/robes	Built-in wardrobes (closets)

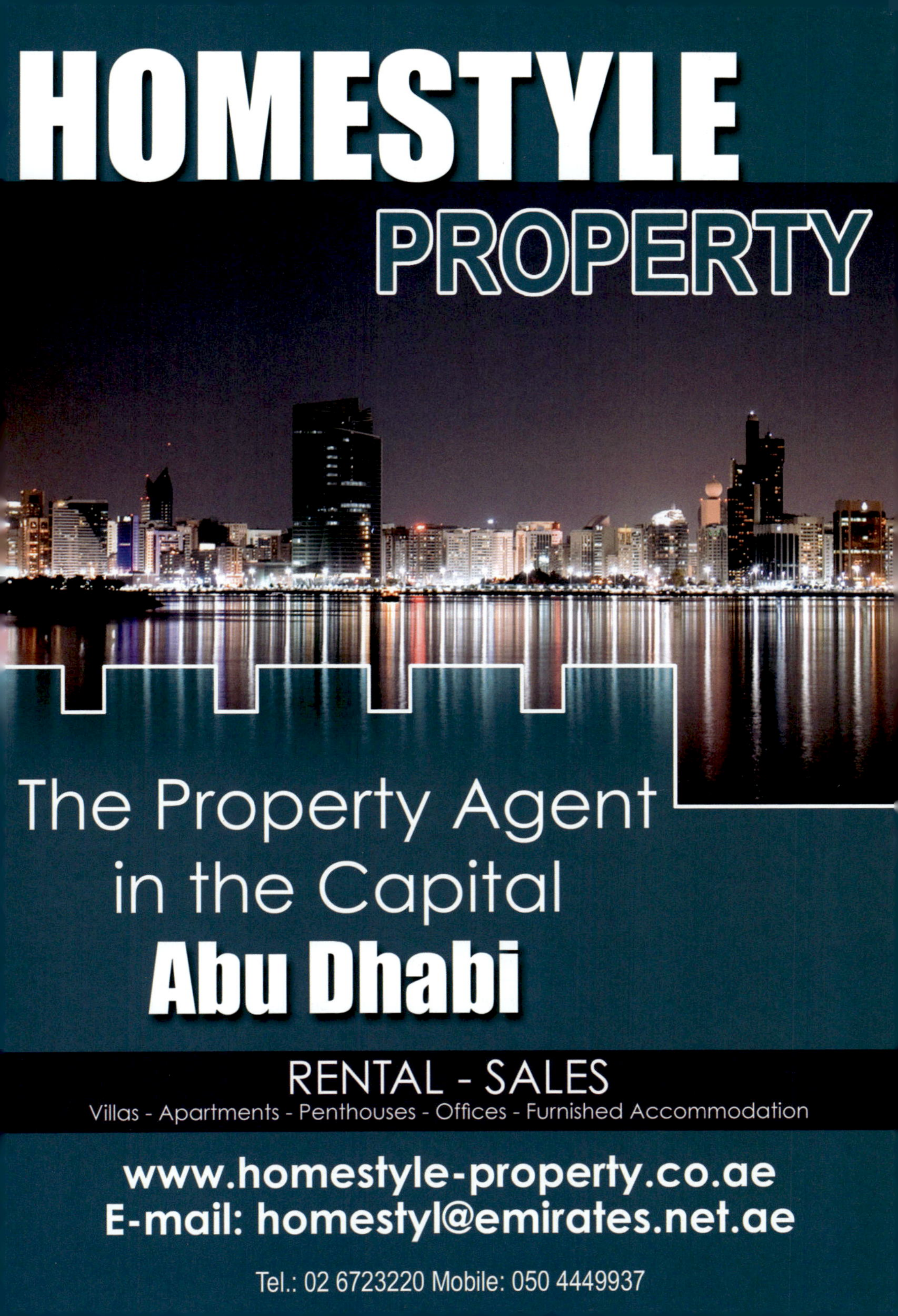
HOMESTYLE
PROPERTY
The Property Agent
in the Capital
Abu Dhabi
RENTAL - SALES
Villas - Apartments - Penthouses - Offices - Furnished Accommodation
www.homestyle-property.co.ae
E-mail: homestyl@emirates.net.ae
Tel.: 02 6723220 Mobile: 050 4449937

did in Sharjah in 2010. It is generally understood that unrelated singles of the same sex are allowed to share as long as it's not in a neighbourhood designated for families and the home is not overcrowded. Sharing should be approached with caution as the local laws are subject to change at any time.

Dubizzle

Dubizzle (www.dubizzle.com) is a good starting point for house hunting. The site features listings by various real estate agents and private individuals alike and whether you're looking to buy or rent, browsing the ads will quickly give you an idea as to the current market prices. You can also find second hand furniture at bargain prices here.

The Lease

In order to process the lease for a rental, the estate agent will need a copy of your passport and visa, and a rent cheque. To rent through your company, you will need a copy of the company's trade licence, a photocopy of the passport of whoever is signing the rent cheque, and the cheque itself.

In addition to the financial terms, your lease will state what you are liable for in terms of maintenance and what your landlord's responsibilities are. Given that expenses such as water and electricity can quickly add up, it is important that you read the contract and discuss any points of contention before you sign on the dotted line.

You should check for the following:

- **Rent payment** – do you have to pay a whole year upfront or in regular instalments? If you can afford to provide fewer cheques, you can use that as a bargaining chip to lower the rent.
- **Maintenance** – who is responsible for day to day maintenance and repairs? Some rents may be fully inclusive of all maintenance and repairs, or you may be able to negotiate a cheaper rent if you carry them out yourself.
- **Water and electricity** – are these included? If not, will they be billed separately? Some apartments have a standard fee for electricity.
- **Parking** – landlords do not have to provide parking, so check first to see if there is an additional charge for underground or covered parking.
- **Security deposit** – is one required and if so, how much (usually between Dhs.3,000 and Dhs.5,000)?
- **Home improvements** – are DIY or decorating permitted?
- **Pets** – are they permitted and are there any restrictions on type of pet? In some apartments, cats are permitted but dogs are not; there are seldom such restrictions in villas.

Other Rental Costs

Extra costs to be considered when renting a home include:

- Water and electricity deposit of Dhs.1,000 paid to Abu Dhabi Distribution Company (ADDC).
- A one-off, fully refundable security deposit (usually between 2% and 5% of the annual rent, although some landlords stipulate a fixed amount of around Dhs.5,000).
- Real estate commission – 5% of annual rent (one-off payment).

If you are renting a villa, don't forget that you may have to maintain a garden and pay for extra water. With the arid climate, your water bill will quickly add up – especially in the parching summer months. To avoid massive water bills at the end of every month, some people choose to get a well dug in their garden for all that necessary plant and grass watering. Expect to pay around Dhs.1,500 to Dhs.3,000 to have a well dug and a pump installed.

Early Termination Penalties

Most leases are usually fixed for one year. If you leave before the year is up, you will probably have to pay a penalty. Rent is usually paid annually, although some landlords allow you to pay in two or three instalments (with post-dated cheques). If you really want to get out of your lease, you may be able to sublet it to new tenants, but this can only be done with your landlord's consent.

RERA & The Rent Committee

The Abu Dhabi Committee for Settlement of Rent Disputes (02 651 3606) was created to oversee rent disagreements between landlords and tenants. The committee also oversees rental prices and, where necessary, can impose increase caps.

Any tenant that has a dispute regarding rent increases, eviction and breaches of contract, can take their case to the committee; in many cases, the committee rules in favour of the tenant.

If the case goes to court, the Arabic copy of your lease will be the version referred to, so make sure you get it translated before you sign your lease agreement, in case there are any hidden extras.

Full details about settling rental disputes are available on the Abu Dhabi Government's website www.abudhabi.ae (under 'Land Transactions') or you can call the committee directly.

Alternatively, if your property is managed by Abu Dhabi Commercial Properties (www.adcp.ae) – and a surprisingly high percentage are – you can lodge a complaint with them.

YOU ARE WELCOME!
You are different. That's why we have created luxurious, inspirationally designed, fully serviced residences.
Introducing the serviced residences within Jumeirah at Etihad Towers, Abu Dhabi.
STAY DIFFERENT™ at Jumeirah Hotels & Resorts.
For enquiries please contact JADinfo@ jumeirah.com
Jumeirah
at ETIHAD TOWERS
ABU DHABI
DUBAI / FRANKFURT / LONDON / MALDIVES / NEW YORK / SHANGHAI
OPENING SOON: ABU DHABI / AZERBAIJAN / KUWAIT / MALLORCA

Real Estate Agents

Al Jar Properties Nr National Bank of Abu Dhabi, ICAD 1, Mussafah, 800 5527, *www.aljarproperties.com*
Asteco Property Management Al Ghaith Tower, Nr Shk Hamdan St, 02 626 2660, *www.astecoproperty.com*
Aztec Properties 050 681 9914, *www.aztecproperties.ae*
Better Homes Delma Street, Villa #416, Al Markaziyah, 02 667 8722,*www.bhomes.com*
Cassells Real Estate Various Locations, 02 681 7666, *www.cassellsrealestate.org*
Cluttons Al Mamoura Bldg B, East Rd, Al Nahyan, 02 659 4001, *www.cluttons.com/abudhabi*
Finders & Keepers > ***p.IBC*** Bainunah St, Al Batin Business Centre, 02 406 9428, *www.findersnkeepers.com*
Future View Real Estate 02 627 2992, *www.futureviewproperty.com*
Hayatt Real Estate > ***p.75*** East Rd9, Al Muroor, 02 448 0518, *www.hayattrealestate.com*
Homestyle Property > ***p.71*** 02 672 3220, *www.homestyle-property.co.ae*
LLJ Property 02 495 0500, *www.lljproperty.com*
Sherwoods Nr Al Noor Hospital, Gibca Tower, Sheikh Khalifa St, 02 626 6887, *www.sherwoodsproperty.com*
Silver Lake Property Management Off Hamdan St, Seven Star Rent A Car Bldg, Al Markaziyah, 02 676 2465, *www.silverlakeuae.com*

BUYING A HOME

Buying property in Abu Dhabi can be a little confusing at first. This is predominantly because owning a property in Abu Dhabi is a relatively new concept for non-GCC expatriates and, therefore, real estate laws are new and constantly changing. It was only in 2005 that Sheikh Khalifa passed the law that enables expatriates to buy property within designated investment areas of the city.

Non-GCC nationals are not permitted to own land, but they can purchase properties on developed land on a 99 year leasehold basis (known as an Usufruct lease). Expats can also lease and build on undeveloped land on a 50 year development lease (known as a Musatahah lease), but it is very uncommon for individual expatriates to do as so few undeveloped land plots are ever released for private ownership/leasing.

Abu Dhabi's Urban Planning Council (www.upc.gov.ae) has identified the following areas in which expats can currently invest in property: Sowwah Island, Reem Island, Raha Beach, Lulu Island, Al Reef, Yas Island, Saih as Sidirah, Saadiyat Island, Hydra Village and Masdar.

However, within these areas, most of the properties for sale are part of ongoing projects like Shams Abu Dhabi and Marina Square (both on Reem Island), Al Bandar (Raha Beach) and Al Reef Villas. Indeed, Al Reef was the first of these developments to be inhabited with the first villas handed over to buyers in late 2009 and with most stages scheduled for completion by the end of 2011.

Residential Developments

Despite a handful of developments open to foreign purchases reaching completion, the main buying option for non-GCC expats at present is an off-plan purchase, bought directly from the developer. Abu Dhabi is undergoing massive growth and the main developers are taking a key role in the emirate's transformation.

Although the financial crisis slowed progress on some major developments, it hasn't caused problems to the same extent that it has in Dubai, and 2011 and 2012 will see a number of large-scale projects reach completion, such as on Reem Island, Sowwah Island and Raha Beach. Abu Dhabi's developers are generally extremely reputable, but the level of finish and facilities management capability will vary from development to development. When considering buying, it is essential to research the development company thoroughly before jumping in and making a binding commitment.

The major developers in Abu Dhabi are:

Aldar Properties (www.aldar.com). Projects include Yas Island, Al Raha Beach, Central Market, the iconic HQ building, Al Gurm Resort and Al Raha Gardens.

Tourism Development & Investment Company (TDIC) (www.tdic.ae). Responsible for many of Saadiyat Island's cultural, residential, commercial and tourism projects, developer of Sir Bani Yas and Dalma islands, plus a number of Abu Dhabi's hotels and resorts.

Ask The Experts Duncan Pickering, partner, DLA Piper Middle East LLP

At present, the real estate market is largely unregulated and, whilst there are many very reputable developers, there are some less reputable ones out there too. It is important that buyers have a lawyer with local experience to review all of the documents and background information before any contractual commitment is signed. Buyers should be aware of all of the laws, what they are actually buying and what the future costs (such as service charges) may be. Buyers must also have properly documented financing arrangements in place to ensure that they have all of the funds required to complete – otherwise, they risk losing their deposits.

Sorouh (www.sorouh.com). Developer for Shams Abu Dhabi – one of the biggest developments on the capital's horizon. The company also has big plans for Lulu Island.

Mubadala Development Company (www.mubadala.ae). Owned by the Abu Dhabi government, this company is developing Sowwah Island, which will be part of the capital's central business district, and has impressive blueprints for Arzanah and the Mina Zayed Waterfront.

Tamouh (www.tamouh.com). Marine Square on Reem Island is a huge project; Tamouh is also involved with Danet Gateway and Meena Plaza.

Manazel Real Estate (www.manazel-re.com). Manazel's Al Reef Villas are nearly fully occupied, and its first properties in Mussafah are due to reach completion in phases from 2011 through to 2016.

Islamic Mortgages

Shariah-compliant or Islamic mortgages are alternative financing options that are available to non-Muslims. The term 'home finance' is used as opposed to mortgages. Complying with Islamic beliefs, the bank purchases the asset on behalf of the buyer who then effectively leases it back from the institution at a marked-up price, but with zero interest. The bank owns the title deeds of the purchased property until the full amount is repaid.

Legal Issues

By law, there may be no requirement to have a solicitor act for you when buying property in Abu Dhabi, but doing so provides extra peace of mind. Inheritance laws should be considered before buying in Abu Dhabi and it is strongly advised that you have a local will in place (see Inheritance Law, p.124).

Lending A Hand

A mortgage consultancy or broker will conduct all the legwork for you. Upon assessing your circumstances, choice of property and financial eligibility, they will gain pre-approval on your behalf, cutting out the middlemen banks and all the running around that goes with dealing with them, essentially holding your hand until the keys are handed over. Your fee to the mortgage broker is either a percentage of the purchase price (approximately 0.5%) or a set price agreed at the outset.

House Hunting

Despite the recent slowdown, real estate is still big business in Abu Dhabi, so it's no surprise that the capital is crawling with agents. And because there are, on the whole, only a few developments offering properties to expatriate buyers, an agent can be indispensable when finding your dream home. The list of real estate agents on p.74 is a good starting point, but often it's just a case going through the property listings in Gulf News (www.gnads4u.com) or on www.dubizzle.com to find out which properties are listed with which agent.

There is currently no governing body for real estate agents in Abu Dhabi and your experience with a particular company may come down to the specific person that you deal with. In many cases, it can help to ask for friends' and colleagues' recommendations. If you're already in touch with a real estate lawyer concerning potential property purchases, it might be worth asking for names of trustworthy agents.

In general, expect to pay a flat fee to the agent, usually 2% – 5% of the purchase price, upon completion of the sale. Always ask for full explanations

Homes in Qasr El Bahr

of the fees and associated costs of sale. Don't feel too shy to ask if there are hidden costs.

Going It Alone

Private sales are not very common in Abu Dhabi. It is extremely rare to see properties for private sale advertised and the majority of private sales are transacted between family, friends or business associates. Of course, there's nothing to stop you looking for a private sale as a way of cutting out the middleman and saving you agency fees. When they do crop up, private sales are usually advertised via notice boards in community centres or local supermarkets, listed as classified adverts in Gulf News, or featured online at www.dubizzle.com or www.gnads4u.com.

Maintenance Fees

Maintenance fees are payable by the owner and cover the developer's cost of maintaining all the facilities and communal areas. Fees are typically paid annually, although some developers are now accepting quarterly payments.

Potential purchasers should factor in maintenance fees when deciding where to buy. Not only do fees vary from developer to developer but also from one development to the next. These fees are rarely mentioned in any of the developers' contracts and, if they are, the fine print will nearly always read 'subject to change.'

If you live in an apartment, communal facilities may include a gym, changing areas, tennis courts, playground facilities and a swimming pool. Fulltime security and cleaning personnel will also be employed to service communal areas. In a villa, communal responsibility will extend to security personnel manning the way to gated communities and all communal landscaping. Both will include rubbish collection, and villa communities may also enjoy pools and tennis courts.

Mortgages

The UAE mortgage industry is still in its relative infancy compared to other countries. The country is home to many of the world's international finance houses, as well as local banks and lenders, but although familiar names such as HSBC, Lloyds TSB, Barclays, Standard Chartered and Citibank sit alongside local entities, sophisticated borrowing structures are difficult to secure and can take longer to complete than in other parts of the world.

The financial crisis that began in late 2008 also saw a lot of banks in the region suspend or severely curtail their mortgage lending activities. Some banks began to lend again in 2009, but on a much more cautious basis than in the gung-ho pre-recession days.

When considering buying property, you should be aware that many banks and lenders only provide

Buildings in Tourist Club Area

mortgages for select developments, which vary from institution to institution. Additionally, each bank and lender has different acceptance criteria and mortgage processes, which change frequently.

Interest rates vary massively from approximately 6.5% up to 9.5%, which is significantly higher than in some parts of the world, and many lenders will insist on life insurance being taken on the loan amount. This is often a stumbling block if overlooked and not addressed before the transfer date. In addition, many lenders will only finance up to a maximum of 85% – and often less – of the property price (100% finance mortgages do not currently exist in the UAE and are unlikely to appear anytime soon). The amount financed by the lender also varies and depends on whether the property is a villa or an apartment and where they are and who built them.

Equity release and mortgage transfers have recently been introduced to the market, offering investors the opportunity to release equity and secure better rates. To combat price sensitive customers moving their loans, most banks have introduced exit fees but there are still completely flexible mortgages available. New innovations also include international mortgages, which offer loans in currency denominations other than dirhams. This offers clients the ability to structure their loan in a preferred currency, with the ability to switch.

Mortgage Application

It is possible for prospective buyers to seek a mortgage pre-approval before beginning their property search, which can give the buyer confidence when entering the market. For a mortgage application, you need your passport plus copies, six months of bank statements, salary confirmation from your employer and six months of salary slips.

Buyer's Confidence

The property market may not be the get-rich-quick scheme it once was, but there are still plenty of reasons to own a home in the UAE. If you decide to take the plunge and snap up a home in the Emirates, just how do you go about it?

Location, Location, Location

The first step is choosing your location which, while always a major factor, becomes even more significant in the UAE.

First and foremost, which emirate do you want to buy in? This may sound a little broad and ridiculous but it's not as ludicrous a consideration as you may think. Dubai and Abu Dhabi are, for obvious reasons, the most popular options but Ajman is marketing itself as a Dubai commuter destination, with properties far cheaper than you'll find in the larger emirates. Due to high prices and limited availability in Abu Dhabi, many working in the capital have chosen to set up home in Dubai, with a property in Dubai Marina just an hour's drive from the Abu Dhabi office.

The question of freehold or leasehold also impacts hugely upon your location. 'Freehold gives non-GCC nationals the opportunity to own entirely, while leasehold offers a lease on the property which would usually run from a period between 30 and 99 years. Leasehold means that the land or the property is never entirely owned by the client in full,' explains Landmark Properties director of sales and leasing, Michael Michael.

Traditionally, non-GCC nationals could only buy on a leasehold basis but, since 2002, Dubai has introduced freehold property rights within designated zones. Now, the majority of purpose-built, community style developments in Dubai boast freehold units, with many in Abu Dhabi now following suit.

That dealt with, buyers should consider the usual property purchasing factors and bear in mind that, unless your budget knows no bounds, willingness to compromise is a must. Think about your circumstances and lifestyle. How long will it take to get to work, do you have a young family that requires nearby schools and play areas, or is access to public transport a factor? Just as important is to have a firm top figure in mind and to not exceed it; if you see somewhere that will need some work, how much will that cost and do property and renovations come in on budget?

Another major consideration in this part of the world is whether you want to buy a pre-owned property, a brand new property, or even an off-plan property. 'Off-plan is a non-ready property that was a popular option for investors and end-users in Dubai during the pre-crash upswing, as it offered spread payment plans and affordable prices giving buyers an opportunity to get on the property ladder,' continues Michael.

The off-plan option still has certain advantages, but Michael adds that buying habits are changing. 'We are now noticing that clients are demanding completed to near-completed properties in freehold areas as they want to see the finished product before purchasing, to make sure the specifications are to their liking.

'Knowing they can move into their properties or rent them almost immediately is a massive draw, while buying in a freehold area also gives peace of mind for easier re-sale opportunities in the future.'

Securing Finance

Securing finance is one of the most worrying aspects of buying a property in the UAE as the process differs a little from those in most people's home countries. 'Rates are variable and, unfortunately, there aren't any fixed rate options like you find in Europe or the US,' explains Tamweel senior financial consultant, Dean Biddulph. 'Also, banks here have far fewer mortgage products on offer compared to many other locations around the world.'

The reality is that buyers have the choice between a refinance or equity-release mortgage for completed properties, or a new mortgage product for a complete or under-construction property. If buying directly from the developer, they'll often have a partner on board who can offer favourable rates and terms.

'Mortgages are available for both freehold and leasehold properties,' continues Biddulph, 'with up to 85% finance available on completed units and between 75% and 80% on properties still under construction. Interest rates typically range from 6.5% to 8.5% depending on the finance type, lender, project and your down payment, and the maximum loan tenor is up to 25 years.'

Before You Sign

Property found, offer accepted, mortgage secured… in most countries, that would be the end of the story, but there's a whole other area that you should consider before signing on the dotted line. As your dream pad is almost certain to be in a larger development or community, even if you have bought a freehold property, you can't do just anything you like with it, and there will still be several costs that need paying.

Service charges can differ greatly from one property to another, warns Place Strata Management's Jim O'Hare. 'That can affect re-sale chances and property values if there's little or no reserve cash in the sinking fund, or if service charges are considered too high.'

Dubai is leading the way in real estate regulation, such as Strata Law which governs responsibilities over common facilities among other things, and the other emirates, Abu Dhabi and Ajman in particular, are already hatching plans to follow suit with similar systems to the Dubai model.

As a final point, there is no requirement to have a solicitor act on your behalf to buy a property in the UAE, although – for peace of mind, at least – you may wish to run any contracts past a real estate legal specialist.

There are certain issues not directly related to the buying process but important nonetheless – inheritance, for example – that can be legal minefields in the UAE and differ according to a whole range of factors.

So while the property buying process in the UAE differs from other places in the world and warrants careful planning and the consideration of several key elements, all involved in the industry are now subject to much more stringent rules regarding transparency, thanks in part to the economic downturn.

A mortgage 'approval in principle' should only take up to four working days to come through upon submitting the correct paperwork. Generally, employed applicants can borrow a higher percentage of income than self-employed. Most lenders offer mortgages of up to 50% of disposable monthly income, based on the applicant's debt burden ratio – your realistic ability to service the monthly payments from your income, minus your other financial commitments. The larger the deposit placed, the better your terms are likely to be. Mortgage terms are usually for 25 years. Age restrictions are in place and vary, but lenders will normally finance individuals up to 65 years of age.

The next step is for the lender to provide an unconditional approval on the basis that any conditions noted in the pre-approval are satisfied. This is to assure you that no further requirements need to be fulfilled in order for you to get your mortgage. Finally, you can start house hunting. Once you've found your dream home, the lender will issue an offer letter, followed by the mortgage documentation, which states the terms and conditions of the mortgage. Once the paperwork is signed and sent back to the lender, the settlement process can begin. This is when the lender transfers the mortgage payment to either the seller or to the existing lender who has the first charge over the property. This usually occurs on the day of transfer or as per the conditions of the lender. Then it's time to collect your keys and call the removal van.

Tourist Club Area

Other Purchase Costs

In addition to the purchase cost and deposit required, the charges incurred by the property purchaser securing a home with a mortgage are as follows:

- Real estate agents/brokers fee: 2% – 5% of the purchase price.
- Mortgage arranged via bank or lender: 1% to 1.25% mortgage processing fee based on value of loan.
- Land registry (see below): 1% of the purchase price.

Optional Costs

You are not legally required to engage a lawyer for property transactions in the UAE, but you may wish to employ legal help to see you through the process. Legal costs vary depending on whose services you use. See p.124 for a listing of law firms. If employing the services of a mortgage consultancy or broker, the typical cost is 0.5% of the property price.

Valuation

Your mortgage lender will arrange a valuation of your chosen property via an independent source. This is in order to determine the market worth against the selling price and the lenders loan to you. The cost to the buyer is between Dhs.2,500 and Dhs.3,000. Additional obligatory costs to the mortgaged property buyer equate to approximately an extra 6% on top of the purchase price, not including any cash deposit required.

Land Registry

The government of Abu Dhabi's Department of Municipal Affairs (www.dma.ae, 02 678 5555) is the emirate's land registry and transactions agency. Upon completion of a sale, a land registry fee is due (1% of the property price). Registering the property establishes legal ownership and provides the new owner with a title deed, safeguarding against future disputes.

Selling A Home

When selling your property, your first and most important task is to find yourself a preferred agent. Some real estate agencies charge 'marketing' fees of 1% to 2% of the sale price, so be careful. For a list of popular estate agents, see p.74. You can, of course, try to market and sell your property privately to avoid real estate fees. Advertising online is an increasingly common route to find buyers, but be prepared for plenty of calls from bargain hunters offering significantly below the asking price. There is no legal need for a property survey, assessment or solicitor, so all of these fees are negated, although if you decide to go it alone, think carefully about engaging a solicitor.

Al Mushrif

A city mosque

Khalifa City

Apartment living

Villa living

Residential Areas Map

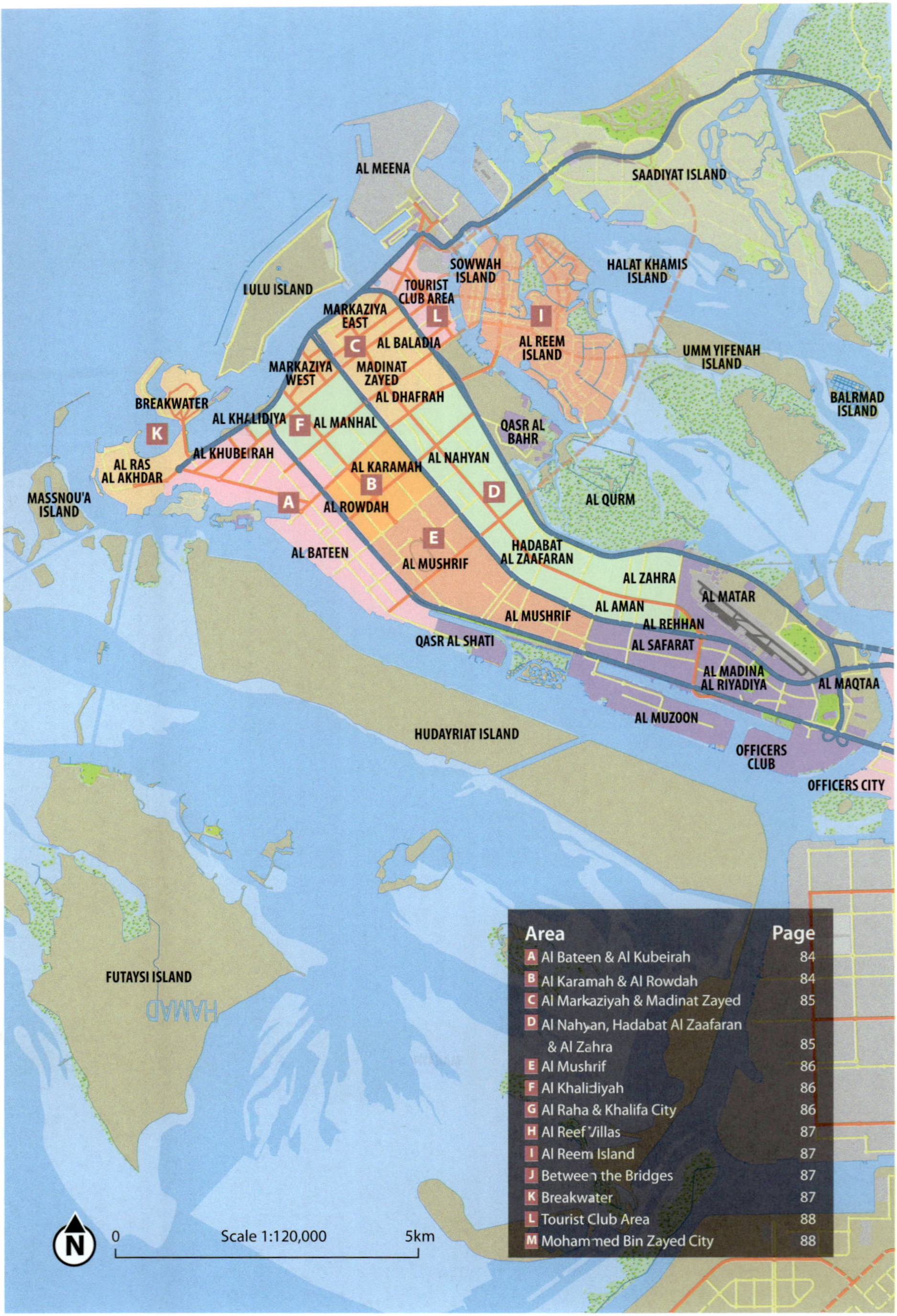

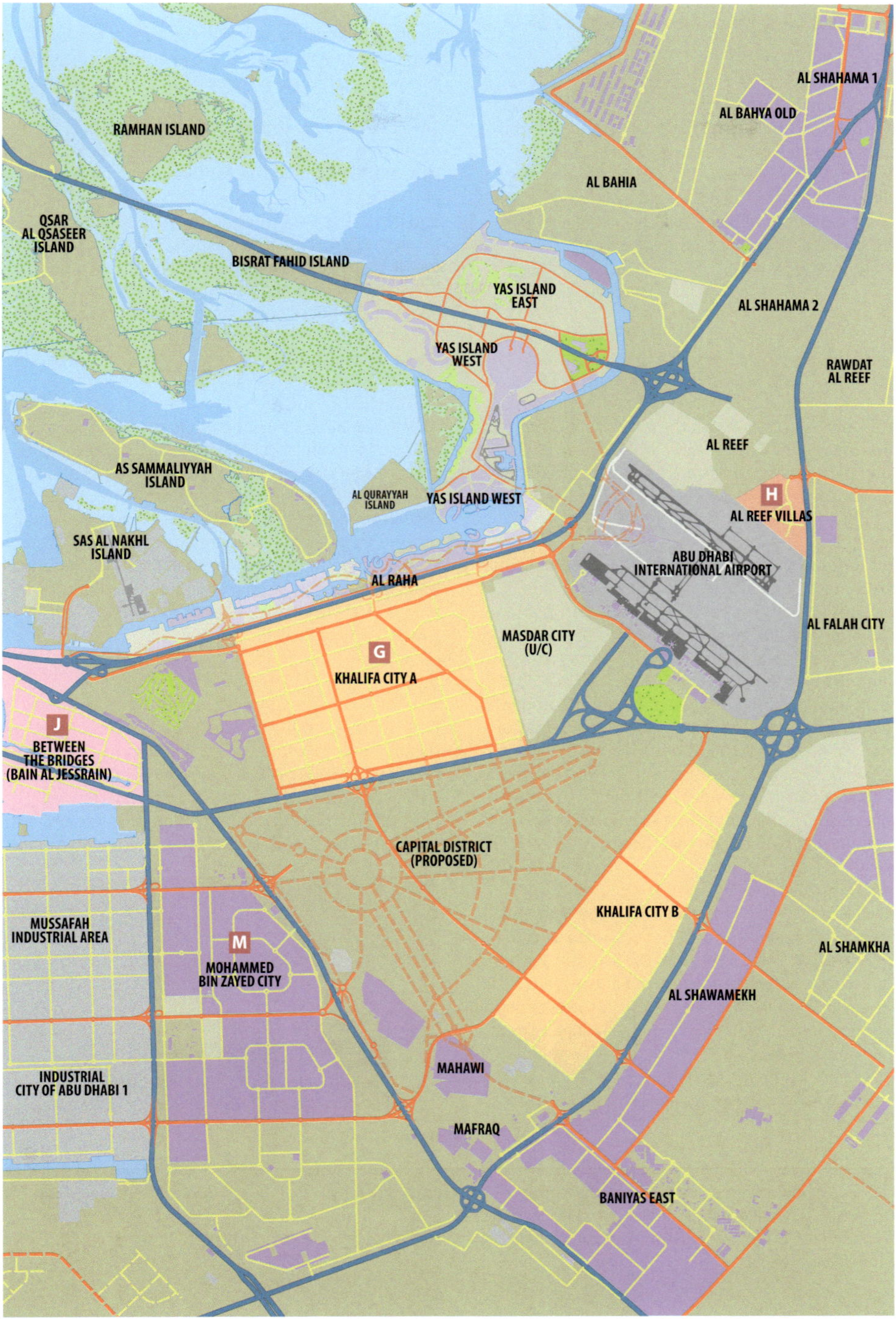
RAMHAN ISLAND
QSAR AL QSASEER ISLAND
BISRAT FAHID ISLAND
AL SHAHAMA 1
AL BAHYA OLD
AL BAHIA
YAS ISLAND EAST
YAS ISLAND WEST
AL SHAHAMA 2
RAWDAT AL REEF
AL REEF
AS SAMMALIYYAH ISLAND
AL QURAYYAH ISLAND
YAS ISLAND WEST
H
AL REEF VILLAS
SAS AL NAKHL ISLAND
ABU DHABI INTERNATIONAL AIRPORT
AL RAHA
AL FALAH CITY
MASDAR CITY (U/C)
G
KHALIFA CITY A
J
BETWEEN THE BRIDGES (BAIN AL JESSRAIN)
CAPITAL DISTRICT (PROPOSED)
MUSSAFAH INDUSTRIAL AREA
KHALIFA CITY B
M
MOHAMMED BIN ZAYED CITY
AL SHAMKHA
AL SHAWAMEKH
INDUSTRIAL CITY OF ABU DHABI 1
MAHAWI
MAFRAQ
BANIYAS EAST

RESIDENTIAL AREAS

Al Bateen & Al Kubeirah

A large and highly sought-after area of the island, occupied mostly by UAE nationals, complete with palaces, walled properties, decorative fountains and beautiful streetscaping. It's a quiet area, popular with families, and the tone is set by Baynunah Street, which runs from Al Bateen to the Corniche and is easily one of the most picturesque and well-kept roads in Abu Dhabi.

Accommodation

Even with a drop in rental prices throughout the city, rents remain expensive here. Expect to pay anything from Dhs.75,000 per year for the smallest of flats, to Dhs.400,000 and above for multi-bedroom villas. Most of the housing takes the form of villas, but there are some larger flats available in Al Kubeirah, which tend to get snapped up very quickly thanks to their relative affordability.

Shopping & Leisure

Residents of the northern third of the area can enjoy the Corniche and all that goes with it – running, cycling and hanging out at the beach. For shopping, Al Bateen Mall (02 666 1222) provides the basics but, for those wanting more, there's a branch of Spinneys in Al Kubeirah and Marina Mall (p.338) is a short drive away in Breakwater. The InterContinental (p.202) and Hilton Al Kubeirah offer a wide array of licensed establishments and the Marina Al Bateen Resort (p.194), with its restaurant and Waves Lounge Bar (02 665 0144), provides other options. For the big spenders, Emirates Palace (p.201) is close by and guarantees treatment fit for a sheikh.

Healthcare & Education

Healthcare facilities in the area are good with both the popular Gulf Diagnostic Center Hospital (p.164) on Khaleej Al Arabi Street, and the Swedish Medical Centre (p.159) firmly entrenched. For teeth, the American Dental Clinic (p.171) on 13th Street and the Modern German Dental Centre on Baynunah Street have the area covered. The American Community School of Abu Dhabi (p.145) and the Al Bateen Science School, a private Arabic school, are both in the area.

Al Karamah & Al Rowdah

There's not very much to differentiate between these two areas, both of which have quiet, unassuming streets lined by date palms and leafy trees. These areas do offer a suburban lifestyle and are quite popular with western expats.

Accommodation

Housing options are mainly in the form of large, single-family villas and low-rise apartments, including two well-established compounds in Al Karamah, which are predominantly occupied by expat families. The closer you get to downtown, the easier it is to find relatively inexpensive flats – some even dipping under Dhs.100,000. That said, prices tend to fluctuate a lot, and villas can go for anywhere between Dhs.250,000 and Dhs.350,000 for three and four bedroom properties, and between Dhs.400,000 to Dhs.550,000 for seven, eight and nine bedroom places. The area's size and the age of different dwellings makes for large variations in prices, so it's worth viewing properties in different areas and price ranges to get an idea of what works best to your budget.

Shopping & Leisure

Al Wahda Mall (p.336) is the prime shopping spot with a Lulu hypermarket (p.331) and an extensive selection of name brand stores. There is also an Abu Dhabi Co-op (p.330) on the corner of Al Nahyan Street and Al Bateen Street. As is common all over the capital, small grocery shops and tiny restaurants and cafeterias are scattered about. The new Grand Millennium Al Wahda hotel (p.201) offers several dining options but other than that, there's not a whole lot to do in the area – which is a draw in itself for many.

Healthcare & Education

The best bet for healthcare is Sheikh Khalifa Medical City (p.166) just off 11th Street, which incorporates the old Central Hospital, but Gulf Diagnostic Center Hospital (p.159) is relatively close by over in Al Bateen. As for education, the Sheikh Zayed Private Academy (02 446 9777, www.szpag.com) is an exclusive and prestigious girls' school offering an international

Al Karamah

curriculum. Abu Dhabi International Private School in Al Karamah (p.145) is an International Baccalaureate school, and closer still are Abu Dhabi Women's College (www.adwc.hct.ac.ae) and the relatively new Pearl Primary School (p.148).

Al Markaziyah & Madinat Zayed

The area boxed in by the Corniche, Al Salam Street, Al Falah Street and Old Airport Road is regarded as Abu Dhabi's downtown. This is the place for those looking to live in the heart of the city; virtually everything the capital has to offer can be found here, except possibly a parking spot. The traffic is generally terrible and the slow changing traffic lights can mean that even short journeys seem to take forever. With the exception of the border along Salam Street, the area is not subject to the inconveniences of the ongoing construction of the nearby Tourist Club Area.

Accommodation

Demand and location mean that this is some of the most expensive real estate around. However, the financial crisis, coupled with substantially increased supply, has brought the rents down significantly. One and two bedroom places are available for under Dhs.150,000, while the closer an apartment is to the Corniche, the higher the price. A three bedroom penthouse with a sea view goes for a solid Dhs.300,000.

Shopping & Leisure

With hotels like Le Royal Meridien (p.202) and the Millennium (p.203) overlooking the Corniche, and the Crowne Plaza (p.203) on Hamdan Street, there's no shortage of licensed restaurants and bars in the area, and the array of small, independent restaurants offer almost everything else a person could hope for. There's a cinema in Al Mariah Mall (p.339) and, close by, the National (02 671 1700) and El Dorado (02 676 3555) cinemas specialise in Bollywood and other Indian flicks. In addition, there's a Lulu Centre on Al Salam Street, plus the Liwa (p.342) and Hamdan Centre (p.340) both on Hamdan Street. The Madinat Zayed Shopping Centre and Gold Centre (p.342) is a somewhat eclectic affair with stores selling everything from high-priced gold jewellery and kitschy desert-themed souvenirs to bedroom suites and home accessories.

Healthcare & Education

The area's high concentration of medical facilities offers plenty of choice to residents. The New Medical Centre Specialty Hospital (p.165) is just off Airport Rd and 7th Street, while Lifeline Hospital (p.165) is at the corner of 4th and 7th streets. The Dar Al Shifa Hospital (p.164) is on 11th Street, and Al Noor Hospital (p.161) is between Hamdan and 3rd streets, close to 4th Street. Also nearby, at the Corniche end of 4th Street, is the Hospital Franco-Emirien (p.165). Schools are a little less profuse, but there are a couple of options nearby. The GEMS American Academy (p.146) is located on Najda Street, just beyond Al Falah Street, and Al Muna Primary School (www.almunaprimary.sch.ae), which follows the British curriculum, is between Hamdan and 7th streets and is located behind the Liwa Center.

Al Nahyan, Hanabat Al Zaafaran & Al Zahra

Sandwiched between Muroor Road and the Eastern Ring Road, this area runs all the way from 11th Street down to Al Bateen Airport. Encompassing primarily low-rise residential and single-family housing in old villas, with new villa compounds such as Al Maqtaa village, the area has a decent mix of expats and locals and, in many parts, there's a nice community feel. The freshly revamped Eastern Ring Road now provides easy access.

Accommodation

As one might imagine, rental prices vary quite a bit over such a large area. Many of the villas are old or rundown, so there are some bargains available; however, if you want a nicely maintained two-bedroom flat, expect to pay Dhs.100,000 to Dhs.150,000, and for villas with three bedrooms and up, Dhs.200,000 marks the low end. Expect to pay more with reputable agents and in closer proximity to downtown. The best deals are to be found in Al Zahra, closest to Al Bateen Airport.

Shopping & Leisure

The northern end of Al Nahyan is close to Al Wahda Mall (p.336), and there are a couple of grocery stores dotted around the area; the nearby Carrefour (p.330) on Airport Road offers relief for those in Muroor. The Eastern Corniche (p.197) runs along the Eastern Ring Road and is a great place to jog, cycle and picnic, while the eastern mangroves are perfect for canoeing and kayaking. Sheikh Khalifa Park, south of Al Bateen Airport, is a large patch of greenery, complete with playground equipment. As far as restaurants go, there are endless options within easy reach by heading north to downtown or south to the Park Rotana (p.203) and the hotels and cafes around Souk Qaryat Al Beri (p.342).

Healthcare & Education

The Middle East Specialized Medical Centre (p.168) is in Hadabat Al Zaafaran and provides general medical and dental services. Heading north to 11th Street takes you to the Dar Al Shifa Hospital (p.164) and the Sheikh Khalifa Medical City (p.166). In terms of schools, American International School (p.145) and the Lycée Louis Massignon (02 444 8085 www.llm.ae) are both on 29th Street, just beyond Al Zahra. Abu Dhabi Indian School (02 448 8025 www.adisuae.com) is in the centre of Hadabat Al Zaafaran.

Al Mushrif

A sleepy area in the very centre of the island, Al Mushrif consists mainly of villas, which range from the palatial to the abandoned. It's close to the Churches Area, home to various Christian congregations, which goes some way to explaining why it's popular with many expats. There are definitely deals to be had, with two bedrooms starting at about Dhs.110,000 and three-bedroom villas starting at Dhs.150,000. Bigger places start from around Dhs.350,000 and go up significantly higher for the largest villas with seven bedrooms or more. Except for in the small shops along Airport Road, there's not a whole lot of shopping to be done in the area, but Abu Dhabi Equestrian Club (p.288) and the newly renamed Abu Dhabi Country Club (p.179 formerly Abu Dhabi Health and Fitness Centre) offer some leisure reprieve. As for education, the British School – Al Khubairat (p.146) in the Church Area is one of the most popular schools for expats in the city.

Al Khalidiyah

Definitely one of the most popular and upscale areas of the city, and in high demand for its proximity to the Corniche, Khalidiyah Garden and plentiful shopping opportunities. With such leisure destinations in easy reach, it's a very pedestrian friendly area. It's an attractive area for expats but there's a good mix of residents with lots of Arab expats and locals too. There's always plenty to do, but in a quiet, refined sort of way.

Accommodation

There are lots of options to choose from here, from luxury apartments overlooking the water, to inland compound villas. You might be able to find a bargain studio for under Dhs.60,000, but more common are two and three bedroom apartments that go for rents ranging from just under Dhs.150,000 to Dhs.200,000. Khalidiyah Village is a compound of about 150 villas and apartments; a three bedroom apartment here will set you back Dhs.180,000, while a six bedroom villa goes for up to Dhs.400,000. The area's popularity means that everything tends to get snapped up quickly.

Shopping & Leisure

Abela (p.330) and Choithram (p.330) are the main supermarkets in the area, both with hefty stocks of western brands. There's a Lulu (p.331) hypermarket in the Khalidiyah Mall (p.337), in addition to dozens of big name stores and a Cine Royal cinema (p.350). There's also the Khalidiya Centre that has a branch of Paris Gallery and a handful of smaller stores. As far as entertainment goes, there are a number of restaurants in the Sheraton Khalidiya (p.204), as well as plenty of options just minutes away in Al Khubeira or, in the other direction, Madinat Zayed. For the active Abu Dhabian, there are cycling and jogging tracks along the Corniche, and volleyball nets on the public beaches.

Healthcare & Education

The Khalidiya Urgent Care Centre (p.165) is located next to Khalidiyah Mall on 26th Street but, for more extensive services, head to Sheikh Khalifa Medical City (p.166). The Gulf Diagnostic Center Hospital (p.159) is not far away in Al Bateen. With very few schools in this area, the closest options, like the American Community School (p.145), are in Al Bateen as well.

Al Raha & Khalifa City

These areas are either for those who want the quiet life, those who are planning on putting down long-term roots or, increasingly, those who are drawn by the more affordable housing costs. Non-GCC expats are eligible to buy property in Al Raha, which is a long beachfront development with big plans. The Khalifa Cities (A and B) are inland with less going on, but more facilities are being opened including the new Raha Gardens retail village with cafes, a salon, pharmacy, money exchange and pet shop. The recent opening of the Al Forsan leisure complex is an additional draw for many.

Accommodation

Al Raha is one of the few places in Abu Dhabi where villas and apartments are for sale to non-GCC residents. However, the units get snapped up quickly. Two bedroom apartments go for Dhs.1.5 million and above, while four bedroom villas typically go for between Dhs.3 million and Dhs.4 million. Three bedroom townhouses start at around Dhs.190,000. Khalifa A is more affordable, with a four bedroom villa going for around Dhs.170,000. Khalifa B, meanwhile, offers some of the city's cheapest accommodation, with two and three bedroom apartments going for between Dhs.70,000 and Dhs.125,000.

Shopping & Leisure

Beyond the dining and shopping options at Al Raha Mall (p.339), there's an Abela and a recently opened Spinneys supermarket in the area; Etihad Plaza also

Living In Khalifa City **Rosana Salamey,** Khalifa City resident of one year

Khalifa City is a great place to live for those looking to escape the crowded city life. Although the area is still partially under construction, the daily necessities are easily available at any of the nearby markets. Moreover, it's only a 10 minute drive away from Yas Island and Al Raha Beach, so there's always something to do if you're looking for a night out.'

has a couple of cafes, but otherwise there's not too much going on here. Al Raha Beach Hotel and the 'between the bridges' hotels (the Shangri-La Qaryat Al Beri, Traders Hotel and the Fairmont Bab Al Bahr) are the best bets for entertainment, while Yas Island (p.196), with its clutch of hotels and growing entertainment venues, is a short drive away. For leisure pursuits, Abu Dhabi Golf Club (p.286) is located in Madinat Khalifa A, and the recently opened Al Forsan International Sports Resort (p.288) offers members pool, gym, shooting, equestrian, cable watersports, paintball and go-karting facilities.

Healthcare & Education

There are no real medical facilities in the area yet, but there are certainly some good schools with Raha International (p.148), Al Yasmina (p.145) and the Canadian International School (p.146) adding some decent alternatives to Abu Dhabi island's offerings. A GEMS American Academy school is due to open in late 2011.

Al Reef Villas

Al Reef Villas is one of the areas in which expatriates can buy property on a 99 year leasehold basis. Most villas quickly sold out when they first went on sale four years ago and, for any properties that become available, expect to pay in excess of Dhs.1 million for two bedrooms (perhaps even up to Dhs.1.3 million), and Dhs.1.6 million plus for a four bedroom. Located out in the desert beyond the airport, there's not much in the way of amenities or entertainment, but options are expanding dramatically on Yas Island, and the Sheikh Khalifa Highway offers a quick and direct route to Al Meena, the Tourist Club Area and the Corniche. Al Reef Villas also offer some of the best value rentals in Abu Dhabi, with prices for three bedroom starting from around Dhs.120,000.

Al Reem Island

With Tala Tower having already opened in summer 2010, and the Sun and Sky Towers in Shams Abu Dhabi due to welcome their first residents by the end of 2011, Al Reem Island will soon be open for business. This mega-project suffered a number of setbacks caused by the financial crisis and, in the case of Tala Tower, a fire. One-bedroom apartments are for sale to expats in Marina Square, starting from Dhs.1 million, while two-bedroom apartments in Shams Abu Dhabi cost more than Dhs.2 million. Rents for one bedroom flats start around Dhs.100,000, while two bedrooms will set you back around Dhs.150,000 a year. Other than the Paris-Sorbonne University Abu Dhabi (p.150), there are few amenities, but big promises have been made, with schools, parks, restaurants and medical centres on the way.

Between the Bridges

Besides the Shangri-La Residences, which are prohibitively expensive, the only other places to live in are Golf Gardens, Sas Al Nakhl Village and Officers' City with its Mangrove Village and Seashore Villas compounds. You'll need a good amount of luck in finding a place and, if any do become available, expect to pay between Dhs.220,000 to Dhs.350,000 a year for a four to six bedroom villa. Residents of the area enjoy the quiet, family-friendly atmosphere and the built-in conveniences – a branch of Spinneys (p.331), plus gyms, pools and beach access, are all within reach of each compound. Also, with the Shangri-La Qaryat Al Beri (p.342), the Traders' Hotel (p.204) and the Fairmont Bab Al Bahr (p.201) nearby, there are plenty of restaurants and nightspots to bring a buzz to the otherwise quiet lifestyle. As far as healthcare is concerned, the closest facilities are the Mussafah Clinic (02 552 0777) and the New National Medical Centre (p.165), both in Mussafah. Again, you'll have to travel a little way to find schools; Raha International (p.148) and Al Yasmina (p.145) are in Al Raha, the Canadian International School (p.146) is in Khalifa City A, and the GEMS Cambridge High School (p.146) is in Mussafah.

Breakwater

Established in 2006, Marina Village is an exclusive development offering the only residential properties in the Breakwater area. The view is inspiring, but the prices, at upwards of Dhs.500,000 for a four bedroom villa, are among the city's most expensive. However, for the well-to-do, this is a nice, quiet little corner of the island which comes with gyms and private pools as part of the deal. There's the new Mirage Marine (p.376) restaurant complex in the area and Marina Mall (p.338) is right next door. Also, Emirates Palace is a quick spin (or swim) away for a night of fine dining.

The Busy Buzz Of The Tourist Club Area

Sorcha Grisewood Tourist Club Area resident of two years

The unattractive, noisy, congested and overcrowded heart of downtown Abu Dhabi is a good location if you enjoy being close to hotels, shops and restaurants. Abu Dhabi Mall, Le Meridien Abu Dhabi and the Beach Rotana are all in walking distance, and there are several expat haunts in the area like The Captain's Arms, Brauhaus, and Trader Vic's. I love the huge variety of cheap Indian, Filipino and Lebanese restaurants, but I hate the parking situation – if you're new, expect to spend lots of time driving around trying to find a space until you become familiar with the area.

For both medical facilities and schools, the most convenient options are in Al Bateen (p.84).

Mohammed Bin Zayed City

Mohammed Bin Zayed City lies opposite Khalifa City B near Mussafah and is also becoming extremely popular with residents looking for a bit more space for their money. The area still has a lot of building work underway and some streets have the appearance of construction sites, but it is well serviced with the Delma and Mazyad Malls including Carrefour and LuLu supermarkets close by. Three bedroom apartments can be commonly found for under Dhs.90,000 and four bedroom villas with a private garden can be snapped up for Dhs.150,000.

Tourist Club Area

Busy, noisy, lively and hectic, the Tourist Club Area is a good place to live if you want to be close to all the action. The location in the city centre is astonishing and there's a great mix of nationalities living here, providing a great initiation for those new to Abu Dhabi. With several hotels within walking distance, there's never a shortage of things to do and the Corniche is nearby too. However, you will have to be willing to trade all the benefits off against Al Salam Street's construction and crawl-pace traffic until works are completed at the end of 2011.

Accommodation

This is mainly a high-rise neighbourhood where prices range from Dhs.50,000 for a slightly questionable studio right up to around Dhs.150,000 for a three bedroom flat. The high concentration of people here and quick turnover means that you can usually find something here, even if it's not your dream home.

Shopping & Leisure

With Abu Dhabi Mall (p.334), countless supermarkets and grocery stores, a couple of liquor stores and the old Abu Dhabi Co-op (p.339), shopping options are abundant. The restaurant choices seem infinite too. From hole-in-the-wall joints to the high-end offerings of five-star hotels, there are plenty of options, taking in everything from a Dhs.10 biryani to a thick porterhouse steak and bottle of cabernet. In terms of leisure activities, there are hotel health clubs, tennis courts and gyms, plus there's a bowling alley and the Grand Abu Dhabi cinema (p.350) at Abu Dhabi Mall.

Health & Education

Al Salama Hospital (p.164) is on Hamdan Street and the city's main maternity hospital, Corniche Hospital (p.164), is next to the Sheraton Hotel (p.204). Abu Dhabi Grammar School Canada (02 666 2900, www.agsgrmmr.sch.ae) is the only school in the area.

SETTING UP HOME

Moving Services

When hiring from abroad, Abu Dhabi employers sometimes offer help (such as a shipping allowance or furniture allowance) but the city is also well served by relocation specialists. There are two options if you are looking to move your furniture and personal effects to or from Abu Dhabi: air freight and sea freight. Air freighting is fast but expensive, so it's a good option if you're only moving smaller amounts. If you have a larger consignment, sea freight will take longer (on average, six weeks from the UK to Abu Dhabi) but is comparatively cheap.

If you decide to send your additional belongings by air, you can enquire with the airline you are flying with. Gulf Air (www.gfcargo.com) and Etihad (www.etihadcrystalcargo.com) have dedicated cargo handling departments and fly direct to Abu Dhabi from multiple destinations around the globe.

If you have more goods than can reasonably, or affordably, be flown on the same plane as you, you will need to call in the services of a removal company. Companies with a wide international network are usually the best and safest option but, more importantly, it will mean you have a local contact in both your departure and arrival destinations. It's important to check that any removals company is not only competent in the country of origin, but that they have reliable agents in the country to which you are shipping your personal belongings, if they don't handle this part of the move themselves. Most removal companies offer free consultations plus advice and samples of packing materials. It's worth contacting a number of companies as quotes can vary widely.

Once your belongings have arrived in Abu Dhabi and are ready for collection, you'll be notified by phone or letter. Some agencies carry out the customs clearing process for you, but with others you have to handle this part yourself.

Even if your agency handles your paperwork, you may be called to be present while the customs officers open your boxes to ensure nothing illegal or inappropriate (such as banned DVDs or books) is being brought into the country.

One Stop Shops

The larger international removals companies, such as Allied Pickfords (www.alliedpickfords.ae), Bishop's Move (www.bishopsmove.com) and Writer Relocations (www.writercorporation.com) can take a lot of the stress out of moving to Abu Dhabi. In addition to packing, shipping and storing your possessions (and even your car, if you're particularly attached to it), some firms can help speed up the visa process, find you rental accommodation in advance, organise travel for your pets and even find suitable schools for your children.

After this, depending on the agreement you have with the removal company, either their representative in Abu Dhabi will help you transport the boxes to your new home or you can make the arrangements locally.

You can find small removal companies advertised in the classifieds section of the newspapers. However, for a cheaper option, head for the Central Post Office in Madinat Zayed. In the car park next door, you will find a number of small trucks and drivers who will transport your goods for a fee (be sure to negotiate). You will need to pack the goods yourself. These drivers don't provide any insurance, so pack fragile items very carefully or transport them yourself.

When it's time to move on from Abu Dhabi, just carry out the process in reverse: weed out the things you no longer want or need, sell them or give them to charity, then call the removal company and have them ship everything home – don't forget the insurance. The cargo section of Omeir Travel (02 628 0323, www.omeir.com/cargo) handles local freight and is a good place to start.

Relocation experts offer additional services to help you settle in quickly. Practical help ranges from finding accommodation and schools to getting your phone connected and sourcing medical care. In addition, a good relocation specialist can also put you in touch with social networks to help you get established.

Relocation & Removal Companies

Abu Dhabi Shipping Agency Salem Saif Saqer Al Mehairbi Bldg, 8th St, Tourist Club Area, 02 644 9100, *www.adsa.ae*

Allied Pickfords > *p.89* Tower Bldg, Hamdan St, Hadabat Al Zaafaran, 02 677 9765, *www.alliedpickfords.com*

Crown Relocations > *p.37* Mina Centre, Al Meena, 02 673 3076, *www.crownrelo.com*

Delight Movers 02 643 4733, *www.delightmovers.com*

Gulf Agency Abu Dhabi (GAC) Airport Rd, 02 673 0500, *www.gacworld.com*

Writer Relocations > *p.93* 050 640 1706, *www.writercorporation.com*

Furnishing Accommodation

Most properties, including rentals, are unfurnished, and don't even have basic white goods such as a cooker or fridge. Not all villas have fitted cupboards and wardrobes. However, Abu Dhabi is home to many furniture shops, ranging from Swedish simplicity at IKEA (p.318) to modern design at THE One (p.318), so you should have your new pad kitted out and feeling like home in no time. See p.318 for more information on where to buy furniture, and for white goods.

Smooth Moves

- Get more than one quote – some companies will match lower quotes to get the job.
- Make sure that all items are covered by insurance.
- Ensure you have a copy of the inventory and that each item is listed.
- Don't be shy about requesting packers to repack items if you are not satisfied.
- Take photos of the packing process to use for evidence if you need to make a claim.
- Carry customs restricted goods (DVDs, videos or books) with you: it's easier to open a suitcase in the airport than empty a box outside in the sun.

Second-Hand Furniture

To save a little money, second-hand furniture is definitely an option, and Abu Dhabi has a wealth of used furniture and upholstery shops. Many of these are located in the Tanker Mai community, just off Muroor Road between 15th Street and Delma Street. In addition, it seems that on almost every corner, there's a skilled carpenter that will make furniture to order, often at very reasonable rates. With so many people constantly arriving and leaving Abu Dhabi, there is a busy trade in second-hand goods among the expat community. Check the busy listings and classifieds at www.dubizzle.com, www.websouq.com and www.expatwoman.com. Also check the message boards at supermarkets like Spinneys and Abela and newspaper classifieds for garage and carboot sales as many expats hold their own 'everything-must-go' sales when it's time to pack up and move on.

EXPLORER
live work explore
UAE
your guide to living in and loving the Emirates
GROWING UP IN THE SUN
WHY KIDS LOVE THE UAE
OMANI ROAD TRIP
MODERN MUSCAT TO ANCIENT BAHLA
PLUS...
DUBAI WORLD CUP
MARINA PAVILION
ART DUBAI
PADDY'S DAY
MAKING A SPLASH
THE UAE'S BEST WATERSPORTS TRIED AND TESTED
THERE'S
MORE TO
LIFE THAN
BRUNCH
Information and
inspiration every month
www.liveworkexplore.com
EXPLORER

Furniture Leasing

If you're only planning to be in Abu Dhabi for a short time, acquiring all that furniture and all those appliances only to get rid of them in a couple of years, may not make sense in terms of hassle and cost. Furniture leasing is an alternative option. Some real estate companies, especially during the downturn, started branching out and offering newer services, so it's worth asking (see Real Estate Agents, p.74). Indigo Living (p.92) in Dubai offers short and long term leasing options across the UAE.

Curtains & Blinds

Year-round sunshine is a draw for many expats coming to Abu Dhabi, but not everyone can sleep with the sun beating through the window. Some properties have windows built to standard sizes, which means you can buy ready-made options from shops such as IKEA (p.318) or Pan Emirates (p.318). If these don't measure up though, there are several companies that will tailor and install curtains and blinds to fit your property, though usually for a higher price than the pre-made ones. IKEA also has a fabric section and offers a tailoring service for basic curtains and roman blinds at very reasonable prices. Alternatively, most tailors will be happy to run up a simple pair of curtains for you. Community notice boards and even online classifieds have adverts for second-hand blinds or curtains that were specially made to fit the strange window sizes found in many freehold developments.

Al Hijad Furniture & Curtains Sheikh Hamdan Bin Mohammed St, Al Markaziyah, 02 678 0057
Areeca Furniture & Curtains Mina Rd, Nr Al Diar Capital Hotel, Al Meena, 02 679 0010, *www.areeca.com*
Avenue Home Design Center Al Raha Mall, Al Raha, 02 556 6100, *www.avenueinterior.com*
Bin Husain Curtains & Decor Al Falah St, Mussafah, 02 555 1520, *www.binhusain.net*
Dubai Blinds Fairmont Dubai, Dubai, 04 312 4086, *www.dubaiblinds.com*
Gemaco Interiors Gemaco Bldg, Sheikh Rashid Bin Saeed Al Maktoum Rd, Madinat Zayed, 02 633 9100, *www.gemaco-uae.com*
Royal Blinds Sheikh Zayed First St, Nr ADCB Bank, Markaziya East, 02 678 9877, *www.royalblinds.com*
Sedar Sheikh Zayed First St, Tourist Club Area, 02 633 4477, *www.sedaremirates.com*

Interior Design

Moving into a new, empty apartment can be a hassle if you've arrived without any furnishings – but starting with a blank canvas can also be a great opportunity to create a home from scratch. Whether you need help with choosing colours for the walls, decorative art to hang on them, or the furnishings throughout, there are an increasing number of specialists just a phone call away. The possibilities are endless and an interior designer's job is to sort out what fits you and your life best. It's a great option to help you get settled.

Areeca Furniture & Curtains

Mina Rd, Nr Al Diar Capital Hotel Al Meena
02 679 0010
www.areeca.com
Map **2 R3**
Offering high-end, bespoke soft furnishings, upholstery, furniture, plus full interior design services.

Gemaco Interiors

Gemaco Bldg, Sheikh Rashid Bin Saeed Al Maktoum Rd Madinat Zayed **02 633 9100**
www.gemaco-uae.com
Map **2 L5**
Specialist in modern, international furnishings with a track record for excellent customer service.

Indigo Living

Mall Of The Emirates Dubai **04 323 3370**
www.indigo-living.com
Map Metro **Mall of the Emirates**
Along with interior design consulting, this Dubai-based store offers furniture rentals. Also has a branch on The Walk in Dubai Marina (04 428 1350) and in Al Quoz Industrial Area 1 (04 341 6305).

Saraya Interior Design

Sheikh Khalifa Bin Zayed St, Nr Hamdan Post Office Markaziya East
02 674 7433
www.sarayaid.ae
Map **2 P3**
An international firm with experience kitting out everything from homes to hotels.

Household Insurance

Though household theft is relatively uncommon in Abu Dhabi, insurance is the best way to guarantee your valuables are protected. There are a number of local and internationally recognised insurance companies operating in the UAE that offer coverage against theft, fire, natural disasters and water damage. To apply, you will need to submit a declaration estimating the value of your household contents. In the event of a claim, the provision of receipts is necessary. Good coverage will include periods while you are away, though insurers may stipulate minimum security requirements in the policy.

Abu Dhabi National Insurance Company ADNIC Bldg, Sheikh Khalifa Bin Zayed St, Markaziya East, 02 408 0100, *www.adnic.ae*
Arab Orient Insurance 02 676 3222, *www.araborient.com*

AXA Insurance (Gulf) > *p.65* National Consultative Council Complex, Delma St, Al Nahyan, 02 495 7999, *www.axa-gulf.com*
Emirates Insurance Company Tourist Club Area, 02 644 0400, *www.eminsco.com*
Gargash Insurance Al Yasat Tower, Nr Raha Hospital, Bani Yas St, Al Raha, 02 671 7100, *www.gargashinsurance.com*
Guardian Insurance Brokers 02 677 7116, *www.gib-uae.com*
National General Insurance Al Sahel Tower, Old Passport Rd, Al Khalidiyah, 02 667 8783, *www.ngi.ae*
RSA Abu Dhabi Habib Bank Bldg, Sheikh Hamdan Bin Mohammed St, Markaziya East, 02 635 1800, *www.rsagroup.ae*

UTILITIES & SERVICES

Electricity & Water

Electricity and water services are provided by the government and run by Abu Dhabi Distribution Company (ADDC). The service is excellent, and power cuts and water stoppages are rare. When you register, there is a deposit of Dhs.1,000. If the property has been leased through your company, they may arrange the deposits and settle the bills for you.

Water and electricity deposits, as well as monthly bills, can be paid at any ADDC outlet, online (www.addc.ae, 800 2332) or through various banks. Those offering this service are listed on the reverse side of the bill. ADDC charges a standard rate per unit, currently 15 fils a unit for electricity, 0.2 fils per unit for water for expatriates . Your bills will fluctuate quite significantly depending on the time of year; your electricity bill is higher in the summer when the air conditioning is on around the clock. If you have a garden, the sprinklers will also need to be on more frequently during the hotter months.

Electricity

The electricity supply in Abu Dhabi is 220/240 volts and 50 cycles. The socket type is identical to the three-point British system but most appliances here are sold with two-pin plugs. However, adaptors can be purchased at any grocery or hardware store.

Water

The tap water is desalinated seawater: it is safe to drink but not always as pleasant to taste as bottled mineral water. Residents and visitors generally drink bottled water, which is widely available. Bottled water is usually served in hotels and restaurants. Instead of buying 1.5 litre bottles of water for use at home, you can invest in a water cooler or stand and have five gallon bottles delivered to your door.

> **In Hot Water**
>
> The water in your cold taps can get so hot in summer that you have to turn off your water heaters – in fact this is often the only way to get cooler water, since your hot water unit is usually inside the house, away from the sun's glare. You know winter's coming when you have to turn the water heater on again.

The deposit for each bottle is around Dhs.30, and each refill is around Dhs.9. A decent water cooler will set you back about Dhs.300, and can dispense hot and cold water. Alternatively, at most hypermarkets you can buy a simple stand, which doesn't use any electricity, for around Dhs.30. Water suppliers will deliver refill bottles to your door. Some provide prepaid coupons, so you don't have to be at home when they deliver – you can just leave the empty bottles and coupons outside your door.

Water Suppliers

Awafi Mineral Water Nr Toyota Building, Mussafah, 02 555 5762, *www.awafiwater.com*
Masafi 800 5455, *www.masafi.com*
Nestle Pure Water Dubai, 800 4404, *www.nestlewaters.ae*
Oasis Water Abu Dhabi Various Locations, 02 558 2030, *www.oasiscome2life.com*

> **Apartments Are Cool**
>
> You can expect a significantly higher A/C bill in a villa – not only are most villas bigger than your average apartment, but many apartment buildings include air conditioning costs in the rent.

Gas

There is no mains gas supply in Abu Dhabi. Some newer apartment buildings supply gas for cooking from central storage tanks situated on the roof or underground, but for residents of older buildings and those living in villas, it is common to buy gas canisters for cooking. These generally cost Dhs.250 for a new canister from most local 'corner' shops. Each refill costs around Dhs.75, depending on the size of the canister.

If you live away from the centre of town, you can hear the gas delivery van's bell ringing in the morning and afternoon, as it goes on its rounds. Two companies that deliver are Al Ruwais Industrial Gases (02 555 9295) and Tarish Ateeq Al Qubaisi Gas (02 559 9477).

Sewerage

The Mafraq Wastewater Treatment Works receives and treats the sewage and waste water from both industry and the municipality, for Abu Dhabi city and

the surrounding areas. The treated water is reused for irrigation, landscaping and agricultural activities. This is part of the city's efforts to protect the environment from pollution. The sewage is collected on a regular basis from septic tanks by sewage trucks. It is then pumped to the plant through more than 15 pumping stations. The sewage undergoes complex treatments to free the water from bacteria and it is regularly tested by the Environment Agency (www.ead.ae).

Rubbish Disposal

If you live in an apartment, your rubbish will generally be disposed of down a garbage chute accessible from each floor. The rubbish is then transferred to a skip or dumpster. You will also find dumpsters by the roadside in residential areas, and all rubbish needs to be put inside them. They are emptied by the municipality on a regular basis and taken to a landfill in the Mussafah industrial area.

While dumpsters are emptied regularly (generally every night) they can be a bit of a nuisance, particularly if they don't have lids. They tend to attract street cats and the occasional rat. If you have a problem with your dumpster, a call to the municipality (800 555) will ensure it is taken care of – or call Feline Friends (p.282) if the cats are troubling you.

The number of recycling collection points throughout the city is increasing. You'll find collection points near government buildings, at supermarkets and at large hotels. Also, once a year there is a big can-collecting competition between all the schools. This is organised by the Environment Agency. Abu Dhabi Municipality has recently distributed recycling bins to many households as the start of an ongoing domestic waste recycling programme. The Emirates Environmental Group (www.eeg-uae.org) is an active organisation and is always looking for volunteers to help with clean-ups.

Telephone

There are two telecom companies operating in the UAE, du (www.du.ae) and Etisalat (www.etisalat.ae). Both service providers offer mobile packages while at the moment, Etisalat is the sole provider of landline services in Abu Dhabi.

To install a landline you must apply directly to Etisalat with a completed application form, a copy of your passport and residence visa, a no-objection letter from your sponsor and Dhs.245. Once the application is submitted, it is wise to maintain close follow up on progress with polite enquiries to Etisalat. Connection installation times vary widely from an efficient three days to several (frustrating) weeks. Quarterly rental for a standard landline (for all sockets) is Dhs.45. You then have to choose which Etisalat package you want for calls.

Etisalat building

With Etisalat, all calls made locally (within the city) from one landline to another are free. Calls to anywhere else in the UAE cost between Dhs.0.12 and Dhs.0.24 per minute; calls to mobiles cost Dhs.018 per minute at off-peak times and Dhs.024 at peak times. For international calls, the tariffs vary from country to country. Etisalat's off-peak timings for national calls are 14:00 to 16:00 and 19:00 to 07:00, Saturday to Wednesday; and at weekends from 14:00 on Thursday to 07:00 on Saturday. Discounted long distance rates are available all day Friday and on public holidays. See ww.etisalat.ae for full details.

Codes & Prefixes

Abu Dhabi	02	**Jebel Ali**	04
Ajman	06	**Ras Al Khaimah**	07
Al Ain	03	**Sharjah**	06
Dubai	04	**Umm Al Quwain**	06
Fujairah	09	**UAE**	
Hatta	04	**Country Code**	971

du offers a range of packages, but to route your call through the du network on your Etisalat landline, you need to dial the prefix 08888 before the number. To apply for a package, visit the du shop on Khalifa Street (02 622 0109), taking your passport and a copy of your tenancy contract. There is a Dhs.25 activation fee but there is no longer a monthly fee for the service. du charges for calls by the second, rather than per minute. Calls to other national landlines are 0.25 fils per second; calls to mobiles cost 0.5 fils per second. du offers round-the-clock off-peak international rates but tariffs vary depending on destination; calling the US is currently charged at 2.28 fils per second, while calling the UK will cost 3.18 fils per second. For national calls, off-peak timings are 14:00 to 16:00 and 19:00 to 07:00, Saturday to Wednesday; and at weekends from 14:00 Thursday to 07:00 Saturday. du also offers a prepaid service whereby customers buy pay-as-you-go recharge cards and top up the credit on their landlines, rather than being billed monthly.

Cheap Calls Not Allowed

Downloading certain voice over internet protocol (VoIP) services, such as Skype, can be difficult within the UAE due to sites being blocked here. However, if you have downloaded the software in a different country, or within an area where the restriction is lifted, such as in certain free zones, it will still work when calling another computer but not when calling landlines or mobiles. See also Internet, p.98.

Public payphones are all over the city; a few accept coins, but most require phone cards, which are widely available from many shops and supermarkets. They come in denominations of Dhs.30, but for international calls, beware... the units vanish at a truly amazing rate.

Mobile Phones

Mobile phone users can choose between du (prefix 055) and Etisalat (prefix 050 or 056). Both providers offer monthly or pay-as-you-go packages. You can register for a pay-as-you-go SIM card for either Etisalat or du from any of the company kiosks located in malls, or from any of the many mobile phone shops scattered throughout the city. To get a line, you will need your passport with residency visa. A du pay-as-you-go line costs Dhs.55 and this includes Dhs.10 credit. An Etisalat pay-as-you-go line costs Dhs.165 and also includes Dhs.10 credit. Both du and Etisalat require you to renew your line every year. The renewal fee for a du line is Dhs.55 and Dhs.100 for an Etisalat line, although both frequently have special offers including free credit when you renew.

Both companies also offer monthly post-paid services. To sign up for a post-paid plan through du, you will need to take your passport and residency visa as well as either a UAE credit card, a recent utility bill with your physical address, your tenancy agreement, or a salary certificate that shows a minimum salary of Dhs.2,500 per month. For an Etisalat post-paid mobile line you will need to take your passport with residency visa as well as a salary certificate showing a minimum salary of Dhs.2,500 per month. A new du post-paid line costs Dhs.62 plus a Dhs.30 service charge every month, while an Etisalat line costs Dhs.125 plus Dhs.20 every month.

Missing Mobile?

Lost your mobile? For Etisalat, call 101, or du customer care 055 567 8155, to temporarily disconnect your number (you will need to know your passport number for security). Your SIM card can be replaced and you can keep the same number, but you'll lose all the numbers you had saved in your phone's memory. To replace the SIM, go to a branch of Etisalat or du with your essential documents and a fee of Dhs.50. If you need to cancel your mobile number permanently, you will need to fill in the cancellation forms.

Television

The local media in the UAE is improving dramatically and television is no exception. There are a number of free channels but non-Arabic speakers are limited in the number of channels they can actually understand.

Because of this, many expats opt for paid TV programming from one of the satellite services like the Orbit Showtime Network (OSN). However, if you don't fancy having a satellite dish installed or your rental arrangement doesn't allow it, Etisalat's E-Vision cable service has a number of packages that include channels from most satellite and paid providers in the area. For added convenience, Etisalat offers customers phone, internet and television bundles, and Yahsat (www.yahsat.ae), a satellite subsidiary of Mubadala Development, plans to offer the same three-way bundle across satellite connections by late 2011.

VoIP

Regulators finally authorised VoIP (Voice over Internet Protocol) phone service in 2010, but only existing licence-holders may offer it. This means popular services such as Skype are excluded from the deal. Those companies that are licensed are Etisalat, du and the satellite firms Yahsat and Thuraya. However, if Skype is already downloaded to your computer, you can still use it to call other computers, and if you have a Virtual Private Network or some other type of proxy blocker, you can use it to call other phones. Just be aware that this is technically breaking the law. See also Internet, p.98.

Safety Net

Abu Dhabi Police's website (www.adpolice.gov.ae) has a guidance section that offers excellent advice for surfing the internet safely, covering everything from online shopping and wireless network security, to online safety for children.

There are an increasing number of HD channels launching in the UAE, including Abu Dhabi HD which shows sport and entertainment programmes, and OSN Movies & GE HD which broadcasts a 'best of' selection of OSN shows and movies. OSN customers can purchase a Showbox (a recordable digital receiver), with which users can pause live television and record favourite shows. The box also allows viewers to watch special previews of forthcoming movies or virtual 'boxsets' of popular series. See www.osnetwork.com for more info.

ART Dubai, 04 806 1111, *www.artonline.tv*
E-Vision Airport Rd, *www.evision.ae*
Eurostar Nr Zania Blg, Electra St, 02 634 7357, *www.eurostargroup.com*
Firstnet Jebel Ali Free Zone, Dubai, 04 806 1222, *www.firstnettv.net*
Global Direct Television Electra St, 02 621 8382, *www.gdtvuae.ae*
Orbit Showtime Network > *p.25* Dubai Media City, Dubai, 04 367 7777, *www.osn.com*

Spoilt For Choice

Far from being a TV backwater, you'll find most major series and films show on local satellite networks although they will generally be a month or two behind the UK or USA. Orbit Showtime, for example, shows Desperate Housewives, Lost, Flash Forward, Glee and Grey's Anatomy. Abu Dhabi Media Company has the rights for Premier League football, and shows all 380 games a season live via a set-top box and Internet Protocol TV.

Internet

All internet usage is regulated by the Telecommunications Regulatory Authority (TRA). This means that many sites that are deemed to be offensive, either religiously, culturally or politically, are blocked and can't be accessed.

Although both Etisalat and du provide internet services in the UAE, only Etisalat provides internet in Abu Dhabi at present. Prices start at Dhs.79 a month for dial-up internet and steadily rise for faster service, topping out at the 'Superior' service for Dhs.699 a month for 30Mbps broadband. There is a Dhs.200 installation fee, plus a one off payment for the modem. Etisalat also has wi-fi hotspots around the city. You can purchase prepaid access cards that provide different increments of time depending on how much is spent. Etisalat also offers plans for unlimited access, and sell a number of different USB Wi-Fi modems that allow users to access the internet anywhere that mobile signals are available. Go to www.etisalat.ae for more details.

Dial & Surf

This facility allows you to surf without subscribing to the full Etisalat internet service. All that's required is a computer with a modem and a regular Etisalat phone line – no account number or password is required. In theory, you then simply dial 500 5555 to gain access. However, in practice it may not be quite so straightforward, since there are different set-ups depending on your software. If you have difficulties, contact the helpdesk (800 5244). The charge of 12 fils per minute is made for the connection and billed to the telephone line from which the call is made.

Postal Services

There is currently no postal delivery service to home addresses, and everyone has their mail delivered to a PO box. Mail is first delivered to the Central Post Office and then distributed to clusters of PO boxes in various areas. To get your own PO box, fill in the application form at your nearest post office and pay the annual fee (Dhs.150); you will be given a set of keys (Dhs.10 per key) to access your own box. Empost will send you notification by email when you receive registered mail or parcels in your PO box. For an extra Dhs.9 you can have the item delivered to your door. However, you might have to pay customs charges on international packages. Many people have mail delivered to their company's PO box instead of arranging a private one.

Letters and packages do occasionally go missing and, if the item has not been registered, there's little that you can do apart from wait – some turn up months after they are expected.

Gift Express

If you would rather not chance the post, Gift Express provides a selection of gifts that can be sent to most countries (www.giftexpressinternational.com).

Empost offers a courier service for both local and international deliveries. Delivery times are guaranteed and packages can be tracked. Registered mail is a relatively inexpensive alternative, and can also be tracked via a reference number. All of the major international courier services deliver to Abu Dhabi, including DHL (800 4004), FedEx (800 3339), UPS (800 4774) and Aramex (02 555 1911), and all of them will deliver to your door. If you are expecting a package, make sure the person sending it has included the correct phone number, as that is often the only way for the courier to find your location.

Carpet Cleaners & Laundry Services

Wall-to-wall carpets are rare in this part of the world, but loose rugs and carpets are commonplace. When they're looking a bit grubby, the companies listed below can pay you a visit, give you a quote, and take the carpets away to be cleaned, returning them a couple of days later. All of the carpet services listed below will also come to your house to clean upholstery.

There are no self-service launderettes, but laundry shops are everywhere. As well as dry cleaning and laundry, they all offer ironing services. If you have specific instructions, make sure these are noted when you drop off your laundry – creases in trousers are standard, so if you don't want them, speak up.

Compensation policies for lost or damaged items vary, but losses are rare, even in the places that look most disorganised. Larger chains, such as Champion Cleaners (050 105 4972), normally have a free pick-up and delivery service. Expect to pay Dhs.12 for a shirt, Dhs.45 for a suit and Dhs.40 for a quilt.

Aroma Cleaning Hamdan St, Mussafah, 02 671 5330
Delight Cleaning Services Al Salam St, Nr Camp Trading, Salam St, 02 678 9216, *www.delightclean.com*
Modern Cleaning Methods 02 645 2825, *www.modernmethodsco.com*

Domestic Help

Domestic help is readily available in Abu Dhabi, on both a full or part-time basis, and the affordability is likely to be better than in most expats' home countries. If you are looking for a bit of help on the home front, there are a number of options. Legally, a housemaid may only be employed by the individual who sponsors her, but in practice many maids take on cleaning or babysitting for other families; if caught, you can face a hefty fine, but the law is rarely enforced and it is a fairly common practice. If you are looking for someone part-time, but want to stay within the law, there are many companies and agencies in Abu Dhabi that provide daily, weekly or monthly cleaning service and maids on an hourly basis, and for around Dhs.20 to Dhs.30 per hour they'll take care of all your sweeping, mopping, dusting, washing, and ironing. Most companies stipulate a minimum number of hours, usually two or three per visit.

Abu Dhabi Maids 050 926 4074, *www.abudhabi-maids.com*
Exiles Maid Service 02 559 0748, *www.exilesmaidservice.ae*

HOME IMPROVEMENTS

Maintenance

Whether you're a home owner or live in rental property, and whether you are responsible for your property's general maintenance or have an assigned company to take care of it, housing in Abu Dhabi requires constant maintenance – not in small part thanks to the climate. Air conditioning units can be temperamental and need regular servicing, plumbing problems aren't uncommon, electrics can go haywire and creepy crawlies like to pay a visit

Most homeowners employ the services of a maintenance company. Annual contracts don't come cheap, but the benefit is that it will cover you for most of your maintenance needs. The contract should include regular scheduled servicing of air conditioning units and boilers, seasonal pest control protection, basic masonry works and 24 hour emergency call out services. Most companies offer extra services such as swimming pool maintenance and gardening for an add-on fee.

Typical costs for such maintenance contracts go from Dhs.7,000 up to Dhs.11,000 per year. If you are renting, check whether your landlord has such a maintenance contract in place before hiring anyone. It's also worth checking if the development company responsible for your accommodation already employs maintenance services, and a recent trend has been for developers to branch out into maintenance themselves.

If it's up to you to get a problem fixed, there are plenty of companies around to help you. It's advisable to listen to the suggestions of friends and co-workers, especially if they have had positive experiences in the past with a particular company. Dubai-based company Home Safe (04 323 8511, www.homesafe.ae) offers complete maintenance packages as well as odd jobs on everything from masonry and painting to AC and pool services, and the company operates a weekly Abu Dhabi service. For A/C problems, you can also try York Air Conditioning and Refrigeration Inc (02 641 4277) or Prime Central Air (02 672 4648). For pest control, try National Pest Control (02 563 1680). However, for any of these services, there are dozens of options, and it's always good to do your research before you decide.

If you live in a community development, your developer will have standard rules and regulations relating to noise, parking, and general upkeep of your property. These will be detailed on the developers' website and local security guards perform regular checks. If you live in a villa, a dirty or messy garage may be frowned upon, and you could be fined for such things as parking on the street rather than in a designated bay, so it's worth making yourself aware of what is required of you as either a tenant or homeowner.

Builders

As with so many of Abu Dhabi's property laws, alterations are a hazy issue. The first expats to own property in Abu Dhabi have only recently been given the keys to their finished homes and nascent laws are still changing regularly; even people involved in real estate law aren't always sure of specifics.

As an expatriate, any place of your own will be in a new development. If you wish to make alterations to your property, your first step would be to approach the developer to find out the changes they will allow. In master developments, for instance, there are strict rules regarding the consistency between properties, and any changes may have to remain within the general layout and design.

In Dubai, where the expat property market is slightly more mature, permission applications for alterations are submitted to the master developer, who must approve the plans and receive a deposit of Dhs.5,000 before any building work can start. An inspector makes a site visit during the works and carries out a final assessment on completion, after which your deposit is returned if you have met all the guidelines. Developers determine the colour of the paint you may use on the exterior of your property and the design and style of any doors, gates or decorative iron fencing. It's likely that a similar system will become the norm in Abu Dhabi in due course.

Many developers employ maintenance companies, contractors and subcontractors, so it's likely that, if you are given permission to carry out your alterations, you may be required to use one of the companies that your developer already works with. Often, for smaller projects, the contractor you hire can arrange approval itself, saving time and effort on your part. Just make sure you've got a reputable contractor on your side. Ask people you trust for references or start with these options: Dwellings Group (02 412 4149) and Abu Mohison General Maintenance & Contracting (02 552 2775).

Painters

Once you own a property, you are free to decorate the inside any style you choose. If you rent, the likelihood is that your landlord will not mind you painting or decorating as you please on the basis that he has your deposit, and will be happy to keep hold of it should you not leave the villa or apartment in its original state. It's often the case that landlords don't need much of a reason to hold back security deposits, so it's worth checking and getting something in writing before you get the roller out.

Breakwater villa with garden

An excellent range of paints and associated implements can be found at Jotun Paints (02 551 0300) and Ace Hardware (02 673 1665). Companies like Evershine (02 553 1851) offer painting services. The cost of internally painting a whole villa can vary between Dhs.3,000 and Dhs.8,000, depending on size, materials and contractor.

Gardens

Abu Dhabi, though not exactly blessed with ample yearly rainfall, has somehow managed to turn, and keep, its parks and lawns green. Irrigation is the city's saving grace, and anyone wanting a green garden must copy that blueprint. Lushness requires due diligence and, in the hot summer months, many plants will require watering as much as twice a day. If you're not up to watering by hand, it's worth considering hiring a gardener or even having a simple irrigation system installed.

If maintaining a grassy garden seems like too much hassle which, especially if you're only renting, is understandable, you can always opt for astroturf. Fake lawns are increasingly popular; they stay green throughout the year and need no watering (although you do need to hose them down every few weeks). You can buy astroturf (in varying degrees of quality) in Ace Hardware, while Clearview (www.clearview.ae) installs fake lawns. Another option is to go for block paving or decking. Again, you can purchase decking in Ace Hardware (www.aceuae.com), while Alomi (www.alomirealwoodflooringllc.com) is a wood merchant that has carpenters with experience in laying decks.

If you are buying a brand new house, the developers may have left you with no more than a sandpit plot, so you will need to start your garden from scratch, and landlords are not obliged to landscape the gardens of new villas before they rent them to you either.

To cut down on watering bills, you could have a borehole dug, but because expats do not enjoy land rights, this will involve you getting permission from the landowner. In any case, the general rule of thumb is the further away from the sea you are, the deeper you will have to drill. On the other hand, the further you get from the sea, the less you have to worry about the salinity of the water. It's also worth planting hardy native species as this will greatly cut down on the quantities of water required.

Whatever greenery you decide to plant, the plant souk at Meena Port is the perfect starting point. It sells a wide array of plant types, ranging from lush and thirsty to the most desert-hardened, and there's plenty to inspire even the most amateur of gardeners. Many of the stores in the souk offer landscaping services at very reasonable rates as well. A more upmarket alternative is Exotica (02 644 4416, www.exoticaemirates.com) in the Tourist Club Area. In

Al Karamah villas

addition to a healthy selection of plants, it offers landscaping and irrigation services. Other places that sell plants are IKEA (p.318), Carrefour (p.330), Spinneys (p.331) and even the Abu Dhabi Co-op (p.339). All these stores also sell small selections of gardening tools, outdoor furniture and hoses, but to properly 'tool up' for large outdoor jobs, head to Ace Hardware (www.aceuae.com), which stocks almost anything you could ever need for sprouting an oasis in this desert. For information on buying garden furniture, see Shopping, p.304.

Swimming Pools

A lot of properties in Abu Dhabi have private pools or at least access to a shared development pool. If you don't have one in your villa, you can always pay to have one installed – but it doesn't come cheap. Another option is to have a custom-made, free-form fibre glass and ceramic tiled pool fitted. As tough and durable as a concrete version, these pools are effectively portable. Delivery of one of these usually takes around four weeks, with an on-site installation period of approximately 10 days. Prices for such a pool start at around Dhs.110,000, which does include all labour costs, pumps and filtration. Try Pools by Design (050 754 6852) or, if you want a more traditional pool, speak to Absolute Pools (www.absolute-pools.com).

Aside from cleaning, your pool will also need the water to be changed and chemical levels checked and balanced on a regular basis. Those Pool Guys (www.thosepoolguys.com) and Falcon Crest (www.fcstswimming.com) are both well-established in the UAE and can take care of maintenance. Most pool maintenance companies will also be able to perform standard repairs to things such as broken lights and filters.

Work, Finance & The Law

WORKING IN THE UAE

Expat workers come to Abu Dhabi for a number of reasons: to advance their career, for a higher standard of living, to take advantage of new opportunities or, most commonly, for the lifestyle and the experience of living and working in a new culture. Whatever the reason, there are various advantages to working here.

While the biggest bonus of working in Abu Dhabi may seem to be tax-free salaries, the cost of living (or your newly acquired lifestyle) can somewhat balance out this benefit.

In addition, the instability of the world's economy has had an effect on the job market in the UAE, and there has been a shift from the fervent recruitment drive of past years, with many previously employed in Dubai taking advantage of Abu Dhabi's increased stability and looking for work in the country's capital.

However, the situation is constantly changing. At the very senior end of the scale, there remain some idyllic opportunities and huge packages that attract the big players, predominantly in the construction, aviation and finance industries.

For less senior positions, the image of a cushy expat life in the Gulf is changing, with much more competition in all areas of the market and an increasing number of people looking for work in Abu Dhabi. Not so long ago, foreign expats could walk into jobs that they could only dream of back home, but these days the market is much more competitive, not least because of the effects of the global economic downturn. All-inclusive packages with accommodation and education allowances are also not as common, although basic benefits still apply (such as annual flights home and 30 calendar days leave).

Work-wise, Abu Dhabi is still a land of opportunities for skilled professionals. It is easier to change industries, as skill sets are less pigeonholed than in other countries and jobs in certain industries (such as construction) are more available.

One of the main differences about working in Abu Dhabi, as opposed to your country of origin, is that you or your spouse need to be sponsored (see p.39) by an employer, which often leaves people feeling tied or uncomfortably obligated to their employer. If you leave the company, your current visa will be cancelled and you will have to go through the hassle of getting a new residency permit (for you and your family, if they are on your sponsorship).

Labour Card

To work in the private sector in the UAE, you are legally required to have a valid labour card. The labour card can only be applied for once you have residency and is usually organised by the company PRO (see p.39). If you are recruited from your home country, your company will have to get approval from the Ministry of Labour. You will then enter on an employment visa, get a health card, take the medical test, and get the residency stamp in your passport. The company PRO then takes all of the relevant paperwork to the Ministry of Labour where the actual labour card will be issued (even though it has 'work permit' printed on the back).

The card features your photo and details of your employer. You're supposed to carry the card with you at all times but it is highly unlikely that you will ever be asked to produce it. The process can also be quite slow, and it's possible you may not receive your card for a few weeks, or sometimes even months, after starting work. The labour card costs Dhs.1,000 (paid by your company). Its expiration is linked to that of your residence visa, and is currently valid for two years. It must be renewed within 50 days of expiry. Failure to do so will result in a fine (which your company will be liable for) of Dhs.5,000 for each year the card has expired.

If your employer is arranging your residency, you will need to sign your labour contract before the labour card is issued. This contract is printed in both Arabic and English. It's not necessarily your agreed 'contract' as such – most employees will sign a more comprehensive contract. Unless you read Arabic, it may be advisable to have a translation made of your details, since the Arabic is the official version in any dispute. However, if there is any discrepancy, the judge would want to know why your company got the details wrong in the first place (see Employment Contracts, p.108).

Working Hours

Working hours differ dramatically between companies; straight shifts vary from 07:30 to 14:30 for government organisations to the common 09:00 to 18:00 for private companies. Most retail outlets tend to be open from 10:00 to 22:00 but often operate shifts. Teachers start early, at around 07:30, and classes finish around 14:00, although their hours aren't as predetermined as other roles.

Although less common nowadays, some offices and shops operate split shifts, which allow for a longer break in the afternoon (hours are usually 08:00 to 13:00 and 16:00 to 19:00).

The maximum number of hours permitted per week according to UAE Labour Law is 48, although some industries, such as hospitality and retail, have longer stipulated hours. Annual holiday allowance starts at one calendar month per year, or roughly 22 working days. Some employees, especially those in management, have more than this and long service usually adds to holiday allowance.

Friday is the Islamic holy day and, therefore, a universal day off for offices and schools. Consumer demand means that the hospitality and retail industries are open seven days a week, although most smaller shops will not open until Friday evening. Saturday is the second day of the weekend; some companies work five and a half days a week and some operate a six-day week, taking only Friday as a rest day.

Public holidays (see p.10) are set by the government, while the timing of religious holidays depends on the sighting of the moon. This can mean that it is difficult to plan holidays, as confirmation of public holidays can come just days before the event. The labour law states that all employees (even non-Muslims) are entitled to a shorter working day during Ramadan, although labour lawyers would advise you not to insist on this if you are non-Muslim or not fasting.

Business Culture

Like anywhere in the world, doing business in the UAE has its idiosyncrasies. Even if you work for a western company, the chances are that some of your business transactions will be with Emiratis, whether on a customer or client basis. While you're likely to find that Emiratis are open to different styles of business and are generally keen to explain their customs, understanding some of the local business etiquette can help you keep one step ahead of the competition.

It's a good idea to dress conservatively for meetings, particularly if you are female, and it is advisable to cover your knees and arms. You may also have a meeting with a woman wearing a *hijab* (a veil which leaves the face uncovered), or some women choose to wear a *niqab* which covers the full face. Don't be surprised if greetings are more tactile in the UAE than in your home country; long handshakes, kisses and effusive compliments are common. While it's normal to shake hands with people of the same sex, if you are meeting someone of the opposite sex, it's best to take your cue from the other person and not offer your hand unless they offer theirs.

It's polite to send greetings to a person's family, but can be considered rude to enquire directly about someone's wife, sister or daughter. A nose kiss is a customary greeting in the Gulf region but is only used between close friends and associates and you should not attempt to greet someone in this way.

Business meetings will usually start with numerous greetings and an exchange of business cards – you should take the time to read the card as a sign of respect. Punctuality is important and arriving late to meetings is considered very impolite – however, don't assume that your meeting will start at the appointed time or that it will not be interrupted. If you're attending a business meeting at an Arab-

Aldar HQ

owned company, it's likely that you'll be served traditional Arabic coffee, or *kahwa*. Sharing coffee is an important social ritual in the Middle East so you should drink some when offered. Cups should be taken in the right hand and, if there is a waiter standing by replenishing your cup, there are two ways to signal that you have had enough: either leave a small amount of coffee in the bottom of your cup or gently tip the cup from side to side.

While not so much a matter of etiquette, patience is the ultimate virtue when doing business in the UAE. Things often move more slowly and decisions take longer than you may be used to. Keeping in regular contact with your clients and customers helps to maintain genial relations and picking up the phone rather than relying on email can make the world of difference.

Finding Work

Until the financial crisis hit, Abu Dhabi's economy was booming and, therefore, the recruitment market was more than buoyant. But even at the height of the crisis in 2009, Abu Dhabi suffered less than its neighbouring Dubai, for example. By 2010, things were looking up once more and in 2011, there were reports of increased recruitment across the UAE. The newly rising oil prices are adding to the economic upturn and are as such likely to boost the job market too. However, the competition for good positions is greater which means there is a stronger focus on what skills employees will bring to the table.

There are numerous recruitment agencies in Abu Dhabi but employers also use local newspapers and headhunters to advertise job opportunities. It is undoubtedly easier to look for a job once you are in Abu Dhabi. Your first step should be to get your hands on the Gulf News appointments supplement (www.gnads4u.com), published daily except Fridays and Saturdays, or the Khaleej Times' Appointments (www.khaleejtimes.com) everyday except Friday – also available online. The National has a careers section that is available to those who subscribe online.

It is also beneficial to check listings on online versions of international newspapers as companies within the UAE often post jobs on these sites. Websites for The Guardian (www.guardian.co.uk) and The Times (www.timesonline.co.uk) newspapers in the UK and The Washington Post (www.washingtonpost.com) in the US are often a good resource. You can also upload your CV to sites like www.monstergulf.com, www.naukrigulf.com, www.bayt.com and www.gulftalent.com. Job advertisements are also posted on Dubizzle (www.dubizzle.com).

It is a good idea to register with a recruitment agency and to contact companies directly and start networking (p.42). Networking sites like www.linkedin.com can be useful too. Thanks to Abu Dhabi's relatively small size, the more people you meet, the more likely you are to bump into someone who just happens to work somewhere that has a vacant position that you might be able to fill. Many larger Abu Dhabi-based companies have vacancy listings on their websites, so if you have a company in mind, it's up to you to keep checking its site for updated listings. Advertisements in Abu Dhabi can be more direct than in other countries and, while it isn't always acceptable to specify candidate requirements like nationality in other countries, advertisements here will often detail whether they are looking for a 'western applicant', for example.

Hiring Again

According to a 2011 survey by HSBC Holdings, the economy in the Emirates is picking up again, with new orders increasing sharply and job creation rising for several consecutive months.

Most recruitment agencies accept CVs via email, but you can check whether they accept walk-ins. The agency will then set up an interview where you are usually required to fill out a form summarising your CV, you will also need a few passport photos. The agency takes its fee from the registered company once the position has been filled. It is illegal for a recruitment company to levy fees on candidates for this service, although some might try.

Headhunters (also known as executive search companies) will usually contact desirable candidates directly to discuss opportunities, but this is normally for more senior positions.

Should you be suitable for a job, a recruitment agency will mediate between you and the employer and arrange all interviews. However, don't rely too heavily on the agency finding a job for you. More often than not, agencies depend on candidates spotting one of their advertised vacancies. You can sign up with more than one agency but they may both try to put you forward for the same job. In this case, it is at your discretion which agency you want to represent you. Below is a list of recruitment agencies based in the UAE. Some of these agencies specialise in certain industries so do your research and register accordingly.

For additional information and tips n finding work in Abu Dhabi, grab a copy of *Working in the Gulf*, a career guide to all GCC countries with country and city-specific chapters and listings for recruitment firms, ministries of labour and more.

Recruitment Agencies

ABC Recruitment Arabian Business & General Services, Lulu Center Bldg, Salam St, Markaziya East, 02 676 8558, *www.abcrecruitment.ae*

BAC Middle East Nr Lamcy Plaza, Sultan Business Centre, Dubai, 04 337 5747, *www.bacme.com*

Charterhouse > *p.109* Regus Al Bateen Business Centre, 34 Bainunah St , Al Bateen, 02 406 9819, *www.charterhouseme.ae*
Executive Appointments Arjaan Tower, Dubai Media City, Dubai, 04 453 5300, *www.exec-appointments.com*
IMG IMG Bldg, Corniche St, Markaziya East, 02 626 8885, *www.imgrec.com*
Jobscan Executive Search Nr KFC, Sheikh Hamdan Bin Mohammed St, Markaziya East, 02 627 5592, *www.jobscan.ae*
Manpower Professional (Clarendon Parker) Dubai Internet City, Dubai, 04 323 3723, *www.manpower-me.com*
Specialist Services Resources National Bank of Abu Dhabi Bldg, Salam St, Tourist Club Area, 02 644 2868, *www.specserve.com*
Talent Partners Villa 31, Villa Garden City, Al Khalidiyah, 02 667 2535, *www.talent2.com*
WTS Energy 202 Al Ferdous Tower, Salam St, Markaziya East, 02 676 0950, *www.worldwideworker.com*

Networking & Events

With Abu Dhabi still a relatively small city, made up of real business areas that are smaller still, networking is critical, even across industries. Everyone seems to know everyone and getting in with the corporate 'in-crowd' definitely has its plus points. Business acumen here can, at times, be more important than specific industry knowledge, so it pays to attend business events and trade shows. Make friends in government departments and this will often land you in the front line for opportunities. Likewise, bad news is rarely made public here, so staying in tune through the grapevine can help prevent wrong decisions. Social networking sites like LinkedIn (www.linkedin.com) and Xing (www.xing.com/net/lewa) are great resources when looking for new jobs or contacts. There are specific sub-groups within this sites for business professionals based in the UAE.

Business Councils

Abu Dhabi Business Women Council Abu Dhabi Chamber of Commerce & Industry, Markaziya West, 02 617 7526, *www.adbusinesswomen.ae*
Abu Dhabi Chamber Of Commerce & Industry Corniche Rd, Markaziya West, 02 621 4000, *www.abudhabichamber.ae*
AmCham Abu Dhabi 02 631 3604, *www.amchamabudhabi.org*
Australian Business Group Abu Dhabi Green Tower, Sheikh Khalifa Bin Zayed St, Markaziya East, 050 264 1134, *www.ausbg.net*
British Business Group Cert Technology Park, East Rd, Al Nahyan, 02 445 7234, *www.britishbusiness.org*
Canadian Business Council Abu Dhabi Cert Technology Park, East Rd , Al Nahyan, 02 446 7223, *www.cbcabudhabi.com*
French Business Group Nr Al Diar Regency Hotel, Al Salam St, Tourist Club Area, 02 674 1137, *www.fbgabudhabi.com*
German Emirati Joint Council For Industry & Commerce (AHK) Abu Dhabi Mall, Tourist Club Area, 02 645 5200, *www.ahk.de*
Iraq Business Council Abu Dhabi Green Tower, Sheikh Khalifa Bin Zayed St , Markaziya East, 02 627 1570, *www.ibcad.com*
Lebanese Business Council Green Tower, Sheikh Khalifa Bin Zayed St, Markaziya East, 02 626 6204, *www.lbc-uae.com*
Philippine Business Council Of Abu Dhabi (PBC-AD) Nr Eldorado Cinema, Sheikh Zayed The First St, Tourist Club Area, 02 672 0288, *www.philippinebusiness.org*
South African Business Council Various Locations, 050 237 0812, *www.sabco-uae.org*
Swiss Business Council Inovex Office, Building 343 (MAFCO), Muroor Rd, Al Nahyan, 02 445 8265, *www.swissbcuae.com*
Trade Representative Of The Netherlands Netherlands Embassy, Al Masood Tower, Sheikh Hamdan Bin Mohammed St, Markaziya East, 02 695 8000, *www.netherlands.ae*

Employment Contracts

An employment contract should list the full details of your employment, including the name of the employer, details of your salary and a breakdown of your responsibilities. Accepting an expat posting can have its pitfalls, so before you sign your contract pay special attention to things such as probation periods, accommodation, annual leave, education allowance, travel entitlements, medical and dental cover, notice periods, and repatriation entitlements.

Sowwah Island

Sowwah Island, located adjacent to the Tourist Club Area, is set to become Abu Dhabi's new central business district. Its commercial heart, Sowwah Square, will be home to the new HQ of Abu Dhabi Securities Exchange, slated to open in late 2011. For more info, visit www.mubadala.ae.

There is often confusion over the offer letter and the contract. An offer letter should give details of the terms of the job you are being offered, such as salary, leave, hours and other benefits; if you accept the terms of this offer, it then becomes a legally binding contract. You may be asked to sign an additional Ministry of Labour contract that accompanies your residency application, but the initial offer letter remains, in effect, your contract. If you receive your employment contract in both English and Arabic, it is a good idea to have the Arabic version translated to ensure they match – the Arabic version will prevail in the UAE courts.

The UAE Labour Law mandates an end-of-service gratuity payment for employees to compensate for the lack of a pension system. The rules are a bit convoluted, but basically, an employee on a fixed-term contract, who has completed one or more years of continuous service, will be entitled to 21 days' pay for each of the first five years of service, and 30 days' pay for every additional year, to a maximum of two full years' pay. If the employee is on an 'unlimited duration' (open-ended) contract and terminates it of his own accord, he will get a third of the gratuity for a service period of between one and three years, two thirds for three to five years, and the full amount if service exceeds five years.

Leaving before the end of your fixed-term contract, or being fired for breaking the UAE Labour Law, could result in the loss of your gratuity payment. Gratuity payments are worked out according to your basic salary. Bear in mind that your total monthly remuneration will be split into various categories (basic salary, plus housing, transport and utilities allowances). You will still get the same cash salary at the end of every month, but because your basic salary is much lower than your total salary, your gratuity payment is lower. Although employees are entitled to gratuity, companies in financial trouble have in the past not been able to pay the money out of their operating budgets, and the government is currently considering restructuring the gratuity system or introducing a pension plan.

The UAE Labour Law states that probation periods can be set for a maximum of six months, although three months is more common. Some companies may delay the residency process illegally until the probation period is up, which can make settling in difficult – no residency means you can't sponsor family members, buy a car or get a bank loan.

By law, employees are not entitled to paid sick leave during their probation period and most companies do not permit annual leave to be taken during this time – you will continue to accrue annual leave over the course of the year. Discuss these matters with your future employer before signing your contract.

Free Zones

Free Trade Zones (FTZ) have been set up in Abu Dhabi to attract more investment from foreign companies. An independent Free Zone Authority governs each individual zone, and the major advantages for companies establishing themselves in a free zone is that they may have 100% foreign ownership, pay no corporate taxes for 15 years (renewable for additional years), are allowed 100% repatriation of capital and profits, plus there are no personal income taxes, and no currency restrictions.

For employees working in a free zone, one of the big advantages is the lack of red tape if you move jobs to another free zone company. This is because the free zone is your sponsor rather than the individual company, so if you change your employer, you won't actually be switching sponsors.

The free zones in the capital all have easy access to the main transit hubs, business districts and sea transport routes. The Industrial City of Abu Dhabi (ICAD I, II and III) is located off the island at Mussafah, next to Mussafah Industrial Area. Development is underway at the Khalifa Industrial Zone of Abu Dhabi (Kizad), which, upon its completion scheduled for late 2012, will be two-thirds the size of Singapore and eventually function as the primary port for the capital. In addition, the Abu Dhabi Airports Company is building Abu Dhabi Airport Free Zone at Abu Dhabi International Airport, Masdar City will be an environmental and scientific free zone, and plans exist to set up a free zone that will act as an international financial hub.

Labour Law

The UAE Federal Law Number 8 for 1980 on regulation of labour relations (otherwise known as the UAE Labour Law) outlines information on employee entitlements, employment contracts and disciplinary rules. The law is employer friendly, but it also clearly outlines employee rights. You can download a copy of the document from the Ministry of Labour website (www.mol.gov.ae); the document has not been fully updated for some time but amendments and additions are often posted on the site.

Maternity Leave

Under UAE Labour Law, women are entitled to 45 days' maternity leave, on full pay, once they've completed one year of continuous service – fathers are not yet entitled to paternity leave.

Maternity leave can only be used directly before and after the birth. Those who have been with their employer for less than a year can claim 45 days on half pay (see p.131 for more information).

Labour unions and strikes are illegal, although there have been some protests by labourers in the past. The labourers achieved some results and the employers concerned were forced to pay wages immediately or remedy living conditions, and a hotline was set up for other unpaid workers to report their employers. If you find yourself in the situation where you have not been paid, you can file a case with the UAE Labour Department who will take the necessary action. You could also get a lawyer to deal with the claim on your behalf (see p.124 for a list of law firms). Although lawyers are expensive in Abu Dhabi, the employer will have to bear the cost if the case is settled in your favour.

Changing Jobs

Until recently, anyone leaving a job and cancelling their visa faced the possibility of being 'banned' for six months. Fortunately, the banning rules have been relaxed, and effective January 2011, anyone on an unlimited contract who has completed at least two years of service with their employer can transfer to a new job without having to get a no-objection certificate or NOC. Should you have less than two years under your belt and looking to change jobs, there may still well be the possibility of negotiating with your current employer to arrange a transfer, particularly if you are leaving on good terms.

It is important to review whether a non-compete clause was added to your contract, particularly if your new role is with a direct competitor to your current employer. This clause could mean that you are restricted to taking an unrelated role before returning to your current field. However, in practice this can be a tricky one for your employer to enforce, certainly if you have worked for the same firm for two years or more. To change sponsors, pick up the relevant forms from the Ministry of Labour and get them typed in Arabic. Get the forms signed and stamped by both your previous and new employers, and submit them along with the trade licence and establishment card of your new company. Everything goes to the Immigration Department who will amend your visa. In most cases, your new employer will take care of this procedure for you.

There are some exceptions where you can transfer your sponsorship without the approval of your current sponsor, such as death of your sponsor, change of company ownership, company closure and cancellation of your company's trade licence. If your company has closed, it is important to note that you will receive an automatic labour ban unless the company has cancelled its trade licence.

Regulations differ in the free zones, as you are technically sponsored by the free zone authority (FZA) rather than the company. Therefore, if you move to another company within the free zone, there is no need to transfer your visa.

Banning

The notorious 'ban' is a topic of frequent discussion in Abu Dhabi, however, the details of when and for how long you can be banned change from case to case. There are two types of ban: an employment ban that restricts employment for a period (usually six months to a year), or a visa ban (which restricts entry or departure from Abu Dhabi).

A visa ban is often imposed if you have committed a serious criminal offence, or you have absconded. Theoretically, it is possible for your employer to ban you from working with another company for a short period of time, even if you have served the correct notice period and have left on good terms. However, this is less likely since a new fee was introduced and employers now have to pay to ban an employee.

A six-month employment ban can also be imposed by the Ministry of Labour, with no instruction from your previous employers, but this is indeterminate and can often be resolved. If you do receive a ban, all is not lost, it may be possible to pay for your ban to be lifted.

The laws regarding banning change frequently and revisions are occasionally posted online without any announcements to the general public; check the Ministry of Labour website (www.mol.gov.ae).

NOC

A No-Objection Certificate was once required to work for another employer, though laws were recently amended so that you won't need an NOC if you have spent at least two years with a current employer. If you're considering switching jobs, check with the Ministry of Labour or a lawyer to see whether you should seek an NOC.

Exhibitionist Tendencies

With financial uncertainty still rocking businesses, but exhibitions still in the work diary, should you keep putting yourself out there? Is it better to conserve cash or continue to showcase?

The Middle East is becoming a hub for international conferences, trade shows and exhibitions. The economic shockwaves of the last couple of years, however, have prompted many local companies to question the merits of intense marketing. Budgets were slashed across the board, from in-house advertising costs and PR contracts to international travel and salaries, but could exhibiting be the outlay that brings the most worthwhile returns?

Exhibitions offer opportunities for businesses to interact with, talk (and listen) to new prospects, demonstrate products and services in real life instead of in a catalogue and check out the competition. By meeting a high volume of contacts in a short amount of time, exhibitions are actually a cost-effective way of boosting trade – providing you follow up on those many business cards you accumulate. Even better, with hotel occupancy down and airlines reducing prices, there are travel deals to be had; by sending more company representatives to attend, opportunities can be maximised further. If you can dominate in these times, you can prosper at the expense of competitors. If contacts are in place, your brand remains strong and you manage to retain staff, then you could be ideally placed to capitalise once the market shows signs of upturn. A recent survey by industry research company Exhibit Surveys Inc. revealed that up to 66% of trade show visitors plan to purchase one or more products as a result of attending an exhibition. Exhibiting may thus be the wisest spend in securing both long and short-term business goals.

Alex Heuff, PALME exhibitions director at IIR Middle East explains: 'Trade shows are still the most cost-effective root to market for local and international firms. In times of financial constraint, for companies big and small, taking part in a trade-related exhibition or event remains the best way of using tighter resources to stay directly in front of customers. I expect the events sector to play a critical role as the catalyst to stimulate the investment climate and boost economic growth, while playing a major role in driving up visitor traffic in the region. Some sectors will always do well in an economic downturn, such as IIR's Arab Health Show, Middle East Electricity and PALME, where secondary shows targeting hobbies and lifestyle may not weather the storm and personal buying habits shift. When times are good you should exhibit, when times are bad, you must exhibit.'

As many European trade shows and conferences shift their attention – and budgets – to Asia and emerging markets such as India, China and Russia, the Middle East is often the location of choice. Thanks to its unique position, excellent conference facilities, transport links, and the potential for a few, post-exhibition, relaxing days on the beach to celebrate a deal being done, the UAE finds itself in a prime position and is pushing to capitalise on this trend.

Major Exhibitions In Abu Dhabi & Dubai

January
Arab Health
www.arabhealthonline.com
World Future Energy Summit
www.worldfutureenergysummit.com

February
Big Boys Toys
www.bigboystoysuae.com
The Bride Show Abu Dhabi
www.thebrideshow.com
Gulf Education Supply Show
www.gesseducation.com
Offshore Arabia
www.offshorearabia.ae

March
Abu Dhabi International Book Fair
www.adbookfair.com
Careers UAE
www.careersuae.ae
Gulf Incentive, Business Travel & Meetings Exhibition
www.gibtm.com
WETEX
www.wetex.ae

April
Cityscape Abu Dhabi
www.cityscapeabudhabi.com
Map Middle East
www.mapmiddleeast.org

May
Arabian Travel Market
www.arabiantravelmarket.com
The Hotel Show
www.thehotelshow.com
MECOM
www.mecomexpo.com

June
Beautyworld Middle East
www.beautyworldme.com

September
Gifts & Premiums
www.premium-dubai.com
International Hunting & Equestrian Exhibition Abu Dhabi
www.adihex.net
Cityscape
www.cityscape.ae
Chic Lady Show
www.chiclady.al-hader.com

October
Abu Dhabi Medical Congress
www.abudhabimed.com
Business Travel Show
www.businesstravelshowdubai.com
GITEX Computer Shopper & Home Electronics
www.gitexshopperdubai.com
GITEX Technology Week
www.gitex.com
International Automobile Show
www.int-autoshow.com
Sweets Middle East
www.sweetsmiddleeast.com
International Jewellery and Watch Show Abu Dhabi
www.jws.ae
BETT Middle East
www.bettmiddleeast.com

November
Sharjah World Book Fair
www.sharjahbookfair.com
Big Five Exhibition
www.thebig5exhibition.com
Dubai World Game Expo
www.gameexpo.ae
Holiday & Travel Show
www.al-hader.com
Middle East Manufacturing Exhibition
www.memexnews.com
HomeStyle
www.homestyleshows.com

December
International Real Estate & Investment Show
www.realestateshow.ae
Abu Dhabi International Motor Show
www.admotorshow.com
Middle East Business Aviation
www.meba.aero
World Green Tourism
www.worldgreentourism.ae
The National Exhibition for Small & Medium Enterprises
www.sme.al-hader.com

Absconding

Anyone leaving the country without cancelling their residence visa with their sponsor will be classed as 'absconding' and may receive a ban, though employers have to wait six months to report absconders who have left the country. Anyone who leaves their employment and remains in the country without notifying their employer can be reported as having absconded after a period of seven days. Absconders are reported to the Ministry of Labour, who then pass information on to Immigration and the police.

Under Article 120 of the Labour Law, if you leave the country or are unaccountable for seven days in a row or 20 days in total, your company can terminate your employment contract without awarding you gratuity pay or any outstanding benefits.

During the economic downturn, there were reports of residents leaving the city at short notice to avoid the ramifications of defaults on bank loans and debts. If you default on a loan and the bank files a case against you, you could receive a visa ban which restricts you from either entering or leaving the country. Details of this claim are filed with the Immigration Department, the police and the Ministry of Labour, which means you could be identified and detained when your visa is scanned at the airport on departure or arrival.

NOC

A No-Objection Certificate is a letter of confirmation awarded by your former employer or the Ministry of Labour giving you permission to work for another employer. If you have an NOC from your previous employer, and the Ministry of Labour approves the move, your visa transfer should be hassle-free. But this is one area where laws change frequently so it's best to check with the Labour Department or a lawyer first.

Redundancy

Redundancy can be a serious blow in a city like Abu Dhabi where you may only stay as long as you have a job. If you are made redundant, try not to dwell on feelings of self doubt about your performance or likeability and instead focus on the financial ramifications. Firstly, discuss with your employer whether they could be flexible with your visa status. If you have a good relationship, you should have room to negotiate the terms under which you leave, and it's worth requesting a few months' leeway so you have the opportunity to find a new employer and sponsor. If your company wishes to cancel your visa immediately, you have a 30 day grace period in which to leave the country or find new employment before incurring any fines for overstaying your visa. Similarly, if you're in company accommodation, negotiate

Abu Dhabi National Exhibition Centre

Flying Solo

With the gradually improving economy, more expats are taking the plunge to go into business on their own in the Emirates. If you'd like to try your hand at business, freelancing may be the way forward.

During the financial crisis, becoming a freelancer was often out of necessity rather than choice. Now, with the economy once more growing, choosing to go freelance can help you explore business opportunities created by the new upturn – while enjoying the other benefits of flying solo.

For some, like digital media professional Russell, the advantages of freelancing are clear: 'Freelancing offers freedom and the chance to earn a better living. You get to concentrate on work you enjoy and can pick and choose jobs once you're established.'

But it's not always easy: not knowing where your next pay cheque is coming from can be a source of anxiety, made worse by continual invoice chasing with unreliable clients.

Also, benefits such as medical insurance and holiday pay are funded from your own pocket, and there's no cover if you are sick or unable to work.

Solid contacts are important wherever you are in the world, so good networking skills are indispensable. They are even more vital in the UAE, says Russell, where being granted a contract or even just an opportunity to pitch 'really is all about who you know.'

Networking groups and business councils are both excellent places to widen your professional network, but it would be foolhardy to simply start freelancing without having at least one regular, reliable client already lined up.

It goes without saying that word of mouth can either make or break your reputation, so tread carefully and make sure you act professionally at all times. This is especially important in the UAE, where everyone seems to know everyone, and where social functions often double as professional networking opportunities and vice versa.

If you do decide to freelance, there are currently really only two options, both of which only cover media industries.

Dubai Media City (www.dubaimediacity.com) and spin-offs such as Studio City are the first and there is no issue with an Abu Dhabi resident setting up in a Dubai free zone.

- Only media professionals of the following categories are eligible: artists, editors, directors, writers, engineers, producers, photographers, camera operators and technicians in the fields of film, TV, music, radio or print media.
- The permit includes a residence visa, access to 10 shared work stations, and a shared PO Box address and fax line.
- A minimum of three hours per week and no more than three hours per day must be spent at the hot desk.
- A business plan, CV, bank reference letter and portfolio must be submitted along with your application.

- Costs at DMC include:
- Dhs.5,000 security deposit (refundable)
- Dhs.5,000 joining fee (one-off payment)
- Dhs.8,000 annual permit fee
- Dhs.4,000 annual membership fee.

Alternatively, Abu Dhabi's twofour54 could be a possibility.

- Only media professionals of the following categories are eligible: broadcast graphic designers, post production sound editors, video editors, set designers, set riggers, camera operators, camera assistants, floor managers, gaffers, lighting operators, lighting assistants, production engineers, production sound engineers, production sound assistants, special effects technicians, vision mixers, gallery operators, grips, hairdressers, make-up artists and TV production stylists.
- The permit includes a residence visa
- A CV, high resolution passport photo and colour passport scan must be submitted along with your application.

- Costs at twofour54 include:
- Dhs.2,500 annual licence fee.
- Dhs.2,200 visa fee.
- Dhs.5,000 security deposit, refundable upon termination of the licence.
- On top of these, you'll also need to take desk or office space at twofour54 – there are various solutions available.

when you need to move out. If the company has paid upfront, they may let you stay for a fixed period. As there are no overdraft facilities in Abu Dhabi, it is a good idea to plan for every eventuality and put money aside as a buffer should you lose your job; this money can help pay for key bills like rent and car loans.

Company Closure

Employees faced with the unfortunate situation of company bankruptcy or closure are entitled, under UAE Labour Law, to their gratuity payments and holiday pay, but you will need to speak to the Labour Department for the proper process as it is complex. An employee of a firm that has been closed can transfer sponsorship to a new employer if they find a new job, but, if not, their visa will be cancelled and they will have to leave the country.

To transfer the visa they'll need an attested certificate of closure, issued by the court and submitted to the Ministry of Labour & Social Affairs (02 681 1890). If your company closes without cancelling its trade licence, you may receive a short time ban from taking a new role with a new employer. Consult the appropriate government offices to get your paperwork right, or invest in the services of a lawyer (p.124) who specialises in labour issues.

Voluntary & Charity Work

There are a number of opportunities to do voluntary or charity work in the UAE with groups always looking for committed volunteers. If it's environmental voluntary work you're after, the Emirates Environmental Group (www.eeg-uae.org) runs regular campaigns. If you're unsure which group you'd like to support, check www.volunteerinabudhabi.com.

Volunteer Organisations

All As One
Dubai **04 311 6707**
www.aaodubai.org
The Dubai branch of an international charity and NGO that raises money for housing, caring for, treating and educating orphaned children in Sierra Leone.

Environmental Agency – Abu Dhabi
Al Mamoura Bldg, Muroor Rd Al Nahyan **02 445 4777**
www.ead.ae
Map **2 M8**
Always keen for volunteers who are willing to get involved, particularly in work related to education.

Ewaa Shelters For Women & Children
Various Locations **050 558 4812**
www.shwc.ae
A non-profit, non-governmental organisation operated under the UAE Red Crescent, Ewa'a Shelters help female victims of human trafficking and exploitation. Volunteers can help provide education, health, and entertainment services.

Feline Friends
Various Locations **050 582 2916**
www.felinefriendsuae.com
Helps cats in the UAE. Volunteers rescue and re-home stray cats and kittens, promote street cat control and provide care to sick and injured cats.

Gulf For Good
Dubai Humanitarian City Dubai **04 368 0222**
www.gulf4good.org
Organises challenges – from climbing Kilimanjaro to cycling, hiking and kayaking through the wilderness of Borneo – with challengers' sponsorship going to local charities based in the countries where the challenges take place.

Make A Wish Foundation UAE
Dubai Humanitarian City Dubai **04 368 0217**
www.makeawish.ae
This foundation gives children with life-threatening illnesses and their families magical experiences to help them cope with their battles.

Médecins Sans Frontières > *p.95*
Villa # 4/1, Nr Madinat Zayed Complex, Al Muroor St Al Nahyan **02 631 7645**
www.msf-me.org
Map **2 N4**
This is an international and independent non-profit organisation that provides emergency medical relief around the world and relies on volunteers to provide aid in any way possible. Volunteers can become involved locally, mainly through organising fundraising events or participating in awareness campaigns.

Red Crescent Society
Nr Abu Dhabi Bus Station, Al Muroor Rd Al Nahyan **02 641 9000**
www.rcuae.ae
Map **2 M8**
The Abu Dhabi branch of the wide-reaching charity helps provide medical and educational assistance, responds to aid appeals and also provides sponsorship for orphans.

Special Care Centre
Nr Al Wahda Mall Al Dhafrah **02 641 8418**
www.donateabrick.org
Map **2 M7**
A non-profit organisation which supports children with special needs. The centre is always in need of volunteers to help with activities and events. Register by filling in a form at the centre.

Strays Of Abu Dhabi (SAD)

Various Locations **050 130 7392**
www.straysofabudhabi.com

Dealing primarily with the rehoming of stray and abandoned dogs, Strays of Abu Dhabi also assists with other animals in genuine need of help. The organisation needs volunteers to walk dogs, provide weekend foster homes and to raise funds.

Working As A Freelancer/ Contractor

The opportunities for freelance or contract work in Abu Dhabi have in the past been limited as, generally speaking, you could not legally work without a residence visa and a labour card, and you could not work for anyone who is not your sponsor. Due to the new part-time labour laws, however, the possibilities of working freelance or contract work seem to be expanding, as you can now accept such work if you are sponsored by your spouse.

It is also possible to work on a contract or consultancy basis for short-term contracts by being employed by a company or agency which then sub-contracts you to another firm. As yet, there is no proper Abu Dhabi equivalent of the 'freelance visa' available at Dubai's Media City, however media professionals can set up as freelancers at twofour54 (see Flying Solo, p.115.) Other professions can work in a Free Trade Zone (FTZ) where you are sponsored by the particular FTZ and so can move around within the zone (see Free Trade Zones, p.110); as an individual freelancer however, the cost of setting up and maintaining a presence in a free zone can be prohibitive.

Working Part-time

The laws governing part-time work were amended in early 2011, and while it's still a bit nebulous as the UAE government irons out the details, there are several important changes. Those sponsored by a husband or wife can seek part-time employment without the need for a permit. If you're looking to secure a part-time position, written permission from your sponsor spouse is all that's required. In effect, this frees housewives or husbands to have greater flexibility and options when seeking a position, as they are already sponsored by their working spouse. There's good news for parents looking to get the teens out of the house, too; those on student sponsorship visas are permitted a one-year part-time work permit, as are teenagers between the ages of 15 and 18. The jobs available to teens are restricted to occupations not requiring heavy manual labour and working hours are limited to six daily, so you might want to rethink sending the kids off to work a summer in the oilfields.

The new labour laws stipulate that employers should give priority to UAE and GCC citizens, although it's unclear exactly how that will be enforced. Check with the Ministry of Labour (www.mol.gov.ae or 800 665) for further information.

Setting Up A Small Business

The business climate in the UAE has made a rapid recovery from the global downturn of 2009. Although the pre-crisis levels of absolute optimism are unlikely to be repeated any time soon, there certainly are opportunities for savvy entrepreneurs.

Starting a business requires meticulous market research, a strict, realistic business plan and responsive action to take advantage of fleeting openings in the market. Several high-profile cases have also made it clear that there are serious risks involved in doing business in the country; bankruptcy laws are not as defined as in other countries and mismanagement of funds could result in harsh repercussions, including deportation or even jail time.

The government and ruling families have passed legislation and formed organisations that aid the start-up process in the UAE. In August 2009, the UAE Ministry of Economy removed the minimum capital requirements for new businesses, which used to be Dhs.300,000.

One of the major hesitations that entrepreneurs have about starting a business here in the UAE is the requirement of having a local sponsor control a majority stake of the company. The increasing number of free zones (p.110) in the region, however, eliminate that rule and allow for full private foreign ownership. The licensing process for opening a business in a free zone is also more streamlined and helped by the free zone organisation.

Government and private sector-sponsored initiatives are also helping to spur growth and educate potential business owners. Abu Dhabi University (www.adu.ac.ae) has a Centre of Excellence for Innovation and Entrepreneurship which enables and supports Emiratis, while the Khalifa Fund to Support and Develop Small & Medium Enterprises (www.khalifafund.gov.ae) encourages local business people with training and development. The annual Abu Dhabi Forum on Entrepreneurship provides discussion and ideas.

There are various business groups in Abu Dhabi that help facilitate investments and provide opportunities for networking with others in the community. Some business groups and councils (p.108) provide information on trade with their respective countries, as well as on business opportunities both in Abu Dhabi and internationally. Most also arrange social and networking events on a regular basis.

Before you set up, contact the Abu Dhabi Chamber of Commerce & Industry (www.abudhabichamber.ae) and the Ministry of Economy (www.economy.ae). Both can offer some excellent advice. Embassies or consulates can also be a good business resource and may be able to offer contact lists for the UAE.

FINANCIAL AFFAIRS

Bank Accounts

There are several reputable banks in Abu Dhabi, including names well-known globally, such as HSBC, Citibank, Barclays Bank and Lloyds TSB Bank. However, banks that operate internationally rarely actually have connections with their counterparts in other parts of the world, so you won't be able to view or manage accounts held in other countries through your Abu Dhabi account.

Safe Keeping

The National Bank of Abu Dhabi (www.nbad.ae, 800 2211) offers its account holders subsidised safety deposit boxes at five of its city branches for the safekeeping of precious or valuable items. Contact the bank directly for more details.

Most banks offer online banking, so you can check your balance, transfer money and pay bills online. There are plenty of ATMs (cash points) around Abu Dhabi and most cards are compatible with the Central Bank network (some also offer global access links). You may pay a small fee for using another bank's ATM but it should never be more than a few dirhams.

To open an account in most banks, you need a residence visa or to have your residency application underway. To apply, you will need to submit your original passport, copies of your passport (personal details and visa) and an NOC from your sponsor. Some banks set a minimum account limit – this can be around Dhs.2,000 for a deposit account and as much as Dhs.10,000 for a current account. This means that, at some point in each month, your account balance must be above the minimum limit; many people avoid this complication by having their monthly wage deposited into their accounts.

If you don't have a residence visa, meBANK (an offshoot of Emirates Bank) will open an account for you and provide an ATM card, but not a chequebook. meBANK also allows you to apply online for an account (www.me.ae).

Although credit cards are widely available, banks are currently still exercising more caution than they have been in the past, due to the recent global credit crisis, particularly where loans are concerned.

A number of laws have been introduced to combat money laundering. The UAE Central Bank monitors all incoming and outgoing transfers, and banks and currency exchanges are required to report transfers over a certain limit. Additionally, if you need to send more than Dhs.2,000 by international transfer you may have to show a valid passport.

Main Banks

Abu Dhabi Commercial Bank (ADCB) Al Salam St, Tourist Club Area, 02 696 2222, *www.adcb.com*
Abu Dhabi Islamic Bank 02 610 0600, *www.adib.ae*
Al Hilal Bank 02 499 4444, *www.alhilalbank.ae*
Al Masraf Al Masraf Tower, Sheikh Hamdan Bin Mohammed St, Tourist Club Area, 02 672 1900, *www.arbift.com*
Bank Of Sharjah Al Mina St, Tourist Club Area, 02 679 5555, *www.bankofsharjah.com*
Barclays Bank Al Jazeera Tower, Sheikh Hamdan Bin Mohammed St, Markaziya East, 02 495 8555, *www.barclays.ae*
Citibank Corniche Plaza Bldg, Al Salam St, Markaziya East, 02 698 2206, *www.citibank.com*
Commercial Bank Interantional (CBI) Shk Srour Bldg, Corniche Rd, Al Khalidiyah, 02 681 8448, *www.cbiuae.com*
Commercial Bank Of Dubai Baniyas Tower, Corniche St, Markaziya East, 02 626 8400, *www.cbd.ae*
Crédit Agricole Corporate and Investment Bank Al Muhairy Centre, Al Manhal, 02 631 2400, *www.ca-privatebank.com*
Dubai Bank IMG Bldg, Corniche Rd, Markaziya East, 02 800 5555, *www.dubaibank.ae*
Dubai Islamic Bank Nr Etisalat, Sheikh Rashid Bin Saeed Al Maktoum St, Madinat Zayed, 02 634 6600, *www.alislami.ae*
Emirates Islamic Bank Sheikh Rashid Bin Saeed Al Maktoum St, Al Musalla, 02 446 4000, *www.emiratesislamicbank.ae*
Emirates NBD Al Baluchi Tower, Sheikh Zayed The Second St, Tourist Club Area, 02 60054 0000, *www.emiratesnbd.com*
First Gulf Bank Sheikh Zayed The First St, Al Khubeirah, 02 60052 5500, *www.fgb.ae*
HSBC Omeir Bin Yousuf Bldg, Nr Etisalat Bldg, Sheikh Rashid Bin Saeed Al Maktoum St, Madinat Zayed, 02 60055 4722, *www.hsbc.ae*
Mashreq Bank Blue Tower,Sheikh Khalifa Bin Zayed St, Markaziya East, 02 612 7248, *www.mashreqbank.com*
National Bank Of Abu Dhabi Nr Sheikh Khalifa & Baniyas Sts, Markaziya East, 02 611 1111, *www.nbad.com*
RAK Bank Nr Abu Dhabi Mall, Tourist Club Area, 02 644 8227, *www.rakbank.ae*

Bank Opening Hours

Banking hours are generally 08:00 to 13:30, Saturday to Wednesday, and 08:00 to 12:00 on Thursday. Some branches, especially those in malls, remain open later in the evenings, even as late as 22:00; all banks are closed on Fridays.

The Royal Bank Of Scotland 235 Sheikh Rashid Bin Saeed Al Maktoum St, Al Karamah, 02 800 2030, *www.rbsbank.ae*
Standard Chartered Crystal Tower, Khalidiyah Financial Centre, Sheikh Zayed The First St, Al Khalidiyah, 02 60052 2288, *www.standardchartered.ae*
Union National Bank UNB Bldg, Salam St, Markaziya East, 02 674 1600, *www.unb.co.ae*

Financial Advice

There seems to be overabundance of financial advisers in the city who may contact you over the phone and advertise their services. Most advisers won't ask for money initially, however they may ask you for contact details of your friends and family members so that they can continue to spread the word.

Financial Planning

Many expats are attracted to Abu Dhabi for the tax-free salary and the opportunity to put a little something away for the future. However, Abu Dhabi's alluring lifestyle can quickly steer you away from your sensible goals. It is often necessary for residents to get credit cards and bank loans to finance their life and lifestyle – especially as start-up costs such as accommodation (often paid a year upfront) and buying a vehicle kick in quite soon after arrival – and it is easy to slip into debt.

You'll find there is little or no support if you do (see Debt, p.124). It is therefore extremely important to plan your finances straight from the off, and arrange a safeguard in case your finances take a turn for the worse or you're hit by an unexpected cost or setback. Expenses as innocuous as home or vehicle repairs, dental or medical treatments, or even unforeseen flights home can very quickly put a strain on the bank account.

When choosing a financial planner in Abu Dhabi, you should ensure that they are licensed by the Central Bank of the UAE (04 665 2220, www.centralbank.ae), so that you have some recourse in the event of a dispute. You should also consider the company's international presence – you'll still want the same access to advice, information and your investments if you return home. It may also be better to use an independent company or adviser who is not tied to a specific bank or savings company and, therefore, will objectively offer you the full range of savings products on the market.

Before leaving your home country, you should contact the tax authorities to ensure that you are complying with the financial laws there. Most countries will consider you not liable for income tax once you have proven that you are a UAE resident (a contract of employment is normally a good starting point). However, you may still have to fulfil certain criteria, so do some research before you arrive (if you are already here, check with your embassy). You may still be liable for tax on any income you receive from your home country (for example, if you have rented out your property).

If you have a pension scheme in your home country, it may not be worth continuing your contributions once you come to Abu Dhabi, but rather to set up a tax-free, offshore savings plan. It is always advisable to speak to your financial adviser about such matters before you make any big move.

Financial Advisers

DeVere & Partners (PIC) PIC. Middle East, Al Qubaissi Tower, Sheikh Hamdan Bin Mohammed St, 02 676 5588, *www.pic-uae.com*
Holborn Assets Level 15, Al Shafar Tower, Dubai, 04 457 3800, *www.holbornassets.com*
KPMG Level 32, Emirates Towers Offices, Dubai, 04 403 0300, *www.kpmg.com*
Mondial (Dubai) Suite 110, Pinnacle Bldg, Sheikh Zayed Rd, Dubai, 04 399 6601, *www.mondialdubai.com*
Prosperity Offshore Investment Consultants Fairmont Tower, Sheikh Zayed Rd, Dubai, 04 312 4334, *www.prosperity-uae.com*

Staying In The Black Graham Bentley PIC de Vere Group

Abu Dhabi is one of the best places to be right now, financially speaking. There are amazing opportunities for getting out of debt, staying out of debt and saving for your future, providing you know how. You need to get organised, make a list of all your monthly repayments and prioritise them. Get rid of the credit cards with the extortionate interest rates first. Work out how much you need to spend on debt repayments each month, then half of what you have left over you should be saving, and the other half for living on. It may not sound feasible but this is why it is important to speak to a financial adviser; together you can look at how to offset certain debts by finding ways of making your money work harder for you, which is a lot easier than it sounds in a tax-free environment. The most important thing is to live within your means. Don't get sucked into the expensive lifestyle, make going for a meal in an expensive restaurant a treat rather than the norm. It's easy to fall down the slippery slope and end up in more debt than when you first arrived, just remember to stay level-headed.

Abu Dhabi Commercial Bank

Credit Cards

The process for obtaining a credit card is fairly straightforward and is usually offered by the bank connected to your payroll account. If you are eligible, you'll often receive phone calls from your bank offering credit cards – if you opt for one, a representative will usually offer to meet you to set up the account. Banks will normally ask that you have a minimum salary (dependent on the credit amount), a salary certificate, which details your earnings (this should be provided by your employer), and a copy of your passport with your residence visa and work permit.

Most shops, hotels and restaurants accept the major credit cards (American Express, Diners Club, MasterCard and Visa). Smaller retailers are sometimes less likely to accept credit cards, often charging additional fees in the past. Effective July 2011, however, the Supreme Committee for Consumer Protection passed a resolution prohibiting extra processing fees. Check www.economy.ae for details or to report a violation. If you are paying in cash, you may sometimes be allowed a discount – it's certainly worth enquiring.

Cash For Gas

Although credit cards are accepted at Abu Dhabi petrol stations, strangely, you are no longer able to use your credit card to buy petrol at garages in most the other emirates. Garages in Dubai and Fujairah, for example, only accept cash at the petrol pumps and some at their convenience stores too, so make sure you have cash at hand.

If you lose your credit or debit card, you must contact the bank as soon as possible and report the missing card. Once you have reported the loss, it is highly unlikely that you will be held liable for any further transactions made on the card. As a consequence of ATM fraud, banks have now set a limit on the amount of cash you can withdraw per day in order to limit the financial damage of stolen credit cards (the amount varies from card to card). In addition to these measures, banks also advise the public on how to prevent credit card crime. A frequent problem is that people do not change their pin when they get the card. This is vital for secrecy, and banks also suggest you continue to change your pin on a regular basis.

Offshore Accounts

While offshore banking used to be associated with the very wealthy or the highly shady, most expats now take advantage of tax efficient plans.

An offshore account works in much the same way as a conventional account, but it can be adjusted specifically for you. Money can be moved where it will produce the best rewards, and cash accessed whenever and wherever you need it, in your desired currency. Offshore accounts allow for management through the internet and over the phone, in a range of currencies (most commonly in US dollars, euros or pounds sterling).

If you are travelling outside the UAE, try to make sure that your account comes with 24 hour banking, internationally recognised debit cards, and the ability to write cheques in your preferred currency. To open an account, there is usually a minimum balance of at least $10,000. Do some thorough research before opening an account, and check the potential tax implications in your home country.

It is important to seek independent financial advice, and not just the opinion of the bank offering you an account. Lloyds TSB (www.lloydstsb.ae) and HSBC (www.hsbc.ae) both offer good offshore services but will, of course, only advise on their own products. To open your account, you may have to produce certain reports or documents from your chosen country. However, for those willing to do the research and undertake the admin, offshore banking can prove to be a lucrative investment.

Taxation

The UAE levies no personal income taxes or withholding taxes, but there are rumours that income tax and VAT may be introduced in the future. There are no firm dates for implementation at present, and it would no doubt be unpopular and possibly hamper attempts to attract foreign investment, but the IMF is advising Middle Eastern governments to introduce tax reforms in order to diversify their resources.

The only noticeable taxes you pay as an expat are a 5% municipality tax on rental accommodation, a 30% tax on alcohol bought at licensed liquor stores and 50% tax on tobacco (although cigarettes are still comparatively cheap). The municipality tax is included in your ADWEC bill, and if you don't pay, your utilities will be cut off.

There is also a 6% Abu Dhabi Tourism Authority tax and a 10% service charge in hotel food and beverage outlets; sometimes this is included in the display price, but be sure to read the small print at the bottom of the menu to avoid any surprises. Independent food and beverage outlets will not charge the Tourism Authority tax, but may still have the service charge.

Taxing Issue

You may need to register your residency in the UAE with the government in your home country to avoid paying income tax or capital gains tax. It's best to check with your consulate for exact details. There are also rumours that income tax will be introduced in the UAE, however, at present, nothing concrete has been announced by the government.

Top Tips For Healthy Personal Finance

Don't Neglect Your Credit Cards: They are great to bail you out in emergencies, but unless you are disciplined when using them, credit cards can land you in trouble. Leave them in a secure place at home where you won't be tempted and always make the minimum repayments on time to avoid late fees.

Try To Live Off Half Your Salary: Really examine your expenses and be brutal when it comes to deciding what you can live without – manicures, double lattes, fancy restaurants and gym memberships are all luxuries, and cutting them out of your budget could mean surprising savings at the end of the month.

Entertain At Home: Eating out in Abu Dhabi's lavish restaurants is so alluring, but it doesn't come cheap. In tough financial times, master the art of 'cocooning' – staying in and inviting friends round for dinner or a movie night.

Shop Smart: Certain supermarkets may be convenient and stock all your favourites from back home, but they are much more expensive than other, more basic supermarkets. You'll save more if you buy your everyday items from a larger hypermarket (p.330). Decide on a grocery budget at the beginning of the month, and make it last.

Don't Pay Full Price For Anything: Shops in the city regularly offer promotions, sales and buy-one-get-one free promotions. Shop around to find the best bargains; you'll be amazed at what you can save.

Get Packing: There's no such thing as a free lunch, but packing your own sandwiches is the next best thing. It's healthier and the savings you'll make do add up at the end of the month.

Take Advantage Of Exchange Rates: Certain items can work out much cheaper when buying from Amazon, even when you factor in the shipping, simply because of the exchange rate. You can get a current CD for over Dhs.10 cheaper than what you'd pay in a retail outlet here – so if you're ordering a few, you could save a bundle. If you've got visitors coming over, get your Amazon order delivered to them (most orders ship free locally), and get them to bring it with them.

Buy Second-hand: Visit Sarah's Flea Market in Officer's City (www.fleamarketuae.com) for a browse through other people's unwanted items or try the Safa Park Flea Market in Dubai (it is held indoors at Safa School Hall from June to September; www.dubai-fleamarket.com). Supermarket noticeboards are cluttered with great pre-owned items looking for new homes, as is the Abu Dhabi section of Dubizzle (www.dubizzle.com).

Reduce Costs Over Summer: If you are planning to be away for some time over the summer, look into downgrading your satellite TV and internet packages for a few months. That way, you can usually upgrade again come September without having to pay any reconnection fees. Better yet, if you only have satellite TV so you can watch the Premier League football, cancel it completely over summer. You can always re-subscribe when the season kicks off again.

Cost Of Living

Bottle of wine (off-licence)	Dhs.40
Burger (takeaway)	Dhs.12
Can of soft drink	Dhs.1.5
Car rental (per day)	Dhs.100
Cigarettes (pack of 20)	Dhs.7
Cinema ticket	Dhs.30
Cleaner (per hour)	Dhs.25
Dozen eggs	Dhs.8
House wine (glass)	Dhs.25-40
Loaf of bread	Dhs.4.5
Milk (1 litre)	Dhs.5.5
Mobile to mobile call (local, per minute)	30 fils
New release DVD	Dhs.85
Newspaper (international)	Dhs.15
Petrol (gallon)	Dhs.6.25
Pint of beer	Dhs.20
Six-pack of beer (off-licence)	Dhs.25
Taxi (10km journey)	Dhs.20
Text message (local)	18 fils
Water 1.5 litres (supermarket)	Dhs.1.5

Cheques

Cheques aren't commonly used as a method of payment in Abu Dhabi and most residents will only have to organise them when handing over post-dated cheques for rental agreements. The most important thing to remember is that issuing a cheque when you have insufficient funds in your account to cover the amount is considered a criminal offence. If your cheques bounce and a complaint is filed with the authorities, you could be arrested. When writing a post-dated cheque, it is important that you are sure of your finances; you should also encourage the beneficiary to deposit the cheques as soon as possible (if that is best). A cheque cannot be cancelled, unless it is mislaid or stolen, so a cheque you wrote several months ago could land you in big trouble, if cashed unexpectedly.

Debt

In a city that seems to run on credit cards and post-dated cheques, it can be quite a shock (and a major inconvenience) to find that severe penalties are dealt out for late or missed payments. While you may be forced to take large loans to purchase vehicles or for annual rent, it is important to note that, if you are suddenly made redundant and your finances spiral out of control, there is no safety net.

Unlike some countries, where you will receive several reminders for missed payments, if you are late paying for basic household bills such as electricity or water, your services may be disconnected without much warning – even if you regularly pay your bills. Missed payments on credit cards bills will often incur fines or restrictions to services, and it is also considered a criminal offence to write a cheque when you have insufficient funds to cover the balance (see Cheques). In some cases, failure to meet payments can lead to prosecution, a visa ban (p.111) and jail time.

The economic downturn of 2009 highlighted this issue when several residents, who were made redundant, made a swift departure from the UAE to avoid prosecution. Banks are subsequently more cautious about who they offer loans to. There are also rumours that debt collectors are increasingly being employed to recover outstanding debts from residents who have returned back to their home countries.The best way to avoid any unpleasant situations is avoid getting into debt in the first place – plan well, and always keep some money in reserve.

Don't Bank On It

There are no bankruptcy laws in the UAE, so individuals who fall into financial difficulties are fully liable for their debt. If you are unable to keep up with repayments for your bank loans and your bank files a complaint against you, you may be faced with a visa ban or an extended term in jail.

LEGAL ISSUES

Shariah Law

The country's constitution permits each emirate to have its own legislative body and judicial authority. Abu Dhabi has retained its own judicial system, including appellate courts (courts of appeal), which are not part of the UAE federal system. There are three primary sources of UAE law, namely federal laws and decrees (applicable in all emirates), local laws (laws and regulations enacted by the individual emirates), and Shariah (Islamic law). Generally, when a court is determining a commercial issue, it gives initial consideration to any applicable federal and local laws. If these do not address the issue, Shariah may be applied. Moreover, Shariah generally applies to family law matters, particularly when involving Muslims.

Afridi & Angell Al Ghaith Tower, Sheikh Hamdan Bin Mohammed St, Markaziya East, 02 627 5134, *www.afridi-angell.com*

Al Tamimi & Company Arab Tower, Sheikh Hamdan Bin Mohammed St, Markaziya East, 02 674 4535, *www.tamimi.com*

Clyde & Co West Tower, Abu Dhabi Mall, Tourist Club Area, 02 644 6633, *www.clydeco.co.uk*

Consolidated Consultants – Jafar Tukan & Partners Nr City Terminal & Saba Hotel, Tourist Club Area, 02 644 2955, *www.ccjo.com*

DLA Piper Middle East LLP Penthouse C2 Bldg, Al Bateen, 02 494 1500, *www.dlapiper.com*

Emirates Advocates Abu Dhabi Islamic Bank, Baniyas St, Markaziya East, 02 639 4446, *www.emiratesadvocates.com*

Habib Al Mulla & Company Alia Tower, Sheikh Khalifa Bin Zayed St, Markaziya East, 02 676 6003, *www.habibalmulla.com*

Hadef & Partners Blue Tower, Sheikh Khalifa Bin Zayed St, Markaziya East, 02 627 6622, *www.hadefpartners.com*

International Advocates & Legal Consultants Bin Hayai Bldg, Sheikh Zayed the First St , Al Khalidiyah, 02 633 5000, *www.alalamyalawyers.com*

Kudsi Law Firm Falcon Tower, Al Nasr St, Markaziya West, 02 633 6500, *www.kudsilawfirm.ae*

Reed Smith Golden Falcon Tower, Sheikh Hamdan Bin Mohammed St, Markaziya East, 02 622 2636, *www.reedsmith.com*

Simmons & Simmons ADNIC Bldg, Sheikh Khalifa Bin Zayed St, Markaziya East, 02 651 9200, *www.simmons-simmons.com*

SNR Denton Al Ghaith Tower, Sheikh Hamdan Bin Mohammed St, Markaziya East, 02 626 6180, *www.snrdenton.com*

Trowers & Hamlins Tower C1, Al Bateen Towers, Bainuna St, Al Bateen, 02 410 7600, *www.trowers.com*

Wills & Estate Law

Having a valid will in place is one of those essential things that everybody should do. It is especially important to seek legal advice when drawing up your will if you become a property owner in Abu Dhabi. This is one area where the law is rather complicated – under Shariah law, the basic rules for who inherits property after someone's death differ from those in other countries. For example, in the event of your death, it may be the case that your sons (or brother, if you don't have any sons) are first in line for inheritance and your wife could end up with nothing. Therefore, it is better to make sure that you have a clear last will and testament in place. An Abu Dhabi-based lawyer will be able to assist you with a locally viable will. See the table on p.124 for a list of law firms, or contact Just Wills (www.just-wills.net), part of a UK-based estate planning organisation that has a presence in the UAE.

Family Law

In accordance with the constitution of the UAE, family law (which governs matrimonial matters such as divorce) will either be governed by UAE law – which is Shariah law – or by the laws of the individuals' originating country. If the parties are from different countries, the law applicable will be the law under which their marriage was solemnised.

Normally, the court will look into the possibility of reconciliation before granting a divorce. This means that, before filing for divorce, you can approach the Family Guidance and Reformation Centre which functions under the Abu Dhabi Judicial Department (02 651 2222, www.adjd.gov.ae). Anyone experiencing marital problems or any family dispute is able to approach this organisation. The other party in the dispute will be called in and the counsellors will try to help you reach an amicable settlement. If the matter is not resolved, the Guidance Centre may refer the matter to the court for legal proceedings to take place.

In deciding on the custody of children, the court's paramount concern will be the child's welfare. In Shariah law and most other laws, the custody of the child will be the mother's right while the child is a minor, unless there are compelling reasons to decide otherwise. For more information on divorce, see p.132.

Crime

Abu Dhabi is known for having a low crime rate – in fact, for many expats, it is one of the key benefits of living here. However, it would be naive to think that there is no crime, as there are cases of theft, rape and even murder, but these occur on such a small scale that they rarely affect the quality of life of the average expat. The most common reason for expats getting on the wrong side of the law is driving under the influence of alcohol. In the UAE, there is a zero-tolerance policy toward drinking and driving. If even a sip of alcohol has passed your lips, you are not allowed to drive. While there are few spot checks, if you have an accident, even a minor one in which you were not at fault, you might be breathalysed and the consequences can be serious. Driving the morning after a heavy night is risky, since you will still have alcohol in your system. You will be arrested, and the usual penalty is a minimum 30 days in prison, although it can vary from case to case. You should bear in mind too that your insurance company is likely to refuse to pay the claim if you were in an accident, even if you were not to blame. It's just not worth the risk – cabs are cheap and there are plenty of them.

It also pays to keep your cool if you are involved in any altercation; obscene gestures can result in a prison sentence or a fine and even deportation. Even using profane language on the phone can lead you in serious trouble, so if you feel yourself getting frustrated, it's probably best to hang up. The bottom line is that harming others, whether verbally or physically, will get you into trouble. If the other party is injured, a jail term may be in order, though if the victim chooses to drop the charges then you will be released. If you are detained for being drunk and disorderly, you may spend a night in the cells but, if you are abusive, you could be looking at a fine or longer sentence.

In 2010, two vacationing Britons were sentenced to a month in prison followed by deportation after an Emirati woman alleged they kissed and embraced in a restaurant. This high-profile case should serve as a reminder that the authorities may extend the full arm of the law if you are caught breaking it.

Police

Abu Dhabi has a large, active, and highly respected police force who take community involvement seriously. The uniforms are easily identifiable: the standard uniform is ash-grey but traffic police wear white sleeves and a white belt to differentiate themselves. Police vehicles are generally red and white with blue and red lights on the roof, but you will also see brown SUVs and pick-ups, as well as some unmarked vehicles. The police are approachable; most speak some English and they are generally helpful if you need to ask simple questions or for directions. They will also respond promptly if there is a problem.

Jaywalking

In an attempt to cut pedestrian casualties on Abu Dhabi roads, the police are cracking down on jaywalkers. Crossing the street at an unauthorised point could land you a Dhs.200 fine, so do the smart thing and cross only at marked intersections, bridges, or subways.

The emergency telephone number is 999 and you can use it if you are involved in a traffic accident or to report a crime or criminal behaviour.

In the event of a road accident, call 999 immediately. In the case of non-serious accidents, if no one is hurt and vehicle damage is minor, drivers are recommended to move their vehicles to the side of the road to avoid blocking traffic. In some cases, the first vehicle to respond may not be a police vehicle but one of a new group of vehicles that is white with black and orange markings from Saeed (see p.59).

If the accident is serious, the vehicles should not be moved. When the police arrive, have your vehicle registration card, driver's licence and insurance papers ready for them and follow their instructions. They will ask for your opinion of what happened and then decide who was at fault. If the police decide you were at fault, you will be given a pink form. If the police determine you are not at fault, you will be given a green form. The form allows you to have your vehicle repaired. A garage cannot repair accident damage without a form.

Rather than dismissing minor crimes, the police deal quickly with 'nuisance' problems, such as rowdy neighbours and the harassment of women. They can also direct other emergency services (fire, ambulance and rescue), though the fire department can also be called directly on 997. Community policing has been found to be very successful and is being expanded to other regions. The Abu Dhabi police website has plenty of useful information.

If You Are Arrested

If you are arrested, you will be taken to a police station and questioned. If it is decided that you must go to court, the police will pass the case to the public prosecutor who will then set a date for a court hearing. If the offence is a minor one, you may get bail and the police will keep your passport and often the passport of another UAE resident who is willing to vouch for you. Police stations have holding cells, so, if you don't get bail, you'll be held until the hearing. All court proceedings are conducted in Arabic, so you should try to make sure you have secured the services of a translator. If sentenced, you'll go straight from court to jail.

Upon being arrested, you are advised to contact your embassy or consulate (see inside back cover for contact details) as soon as possible. They will be able to liaise with family, advise on local legal procedures and provide a list of lawyers, but they will not pay your legal fees. The consulate will try to ensure that you are not denied your basic human rights, but they cannot act as lawyers, investigators, secure bail, or get you released. Also worth remembering is the fact that anyone arrested and detained on a Thursday evening will languish in a cell until the courts reopen after the weekend – if it's a holiday (such as Eid) you'll be inside even longer. The main prison is in Al Watba, between Abu Dhabi and Dubai, and there is a small local prison located at the police station in Khalidiyah.

Victim Support

There are some support services available to those who have been victims of crime. Women and children, who are victims of domestic violence, can contact the Family Development Foundation (02 409 0111, www.fdf.ae) which is in the process of setting up a shelter for family violence victims; the organisation also offers counselling and advice for women and their partners. The UAE Red Crescent also operates the EWAA women's shelters in Sharjah, Ras al Khaimah, and Abu Dhabi.

The National Committee to Combat Human Trafficking (02 404 1000, www.nccht.gov.ae) assists those who are victims of sexual abuse. Its website also provides information on other support services in the UAE. Abu Dhabi Police (www.adpolice.gov.ae) offers a social support centre.

Prohibited Items

Taking illegal narcotics is an absolute no-no – even the smallest amounts of marijuana or hashish could earn you a prison sentence of four years or more, which would almost certainly be followed by deportation. Even airport passengers in transit with drug residue on clothing or luggage can face stiff penalties. If you're found guilty of dealing or smuggling, you could be looking at a life sentence, or even the death penalty (although this is uncommon).

Some medications that are legal in your home country, such as codeine, Temazepam and Prozac, may be banned here – check with the UAE embassy in your home country before leaving and, if you are in any doubt, try to find an alternative. If you must bring the medication with you, keep a copy of the prescription and obtain a medical report from your doctor – this may help explain your case if you are questioned. There is a list of approved drugs on the Ministry of Health website (www.moh.gov.ae) but it is not known how frequently this list is updated or how reliable it is.

Tips For Women

The following general tips are useful for women in Abu Dhabi:

- Stick to the dress code; tight, revealing clothing equals unwanted attention.
- Be careful when out alone at night, especially after a few drinks.
- Never get into an unmetered taxi; and always take down the taxi number.
- As long as you exercise due care and attention, Abu Dhabi is a safe place for women.

Laws To Remember

Licence To Drink: There are several places you can go to buy alcohol if you don't have a liquor licence, but the fact of the matter is that, if you want to enjoy a few drinks in Abu Dhabi, you should really have a 'little black book'. The good news is that it is relatively easy to get a licence: just head down to any bottle shop, grab the application form and then follow the instructions on p.44.

Crimes Of Cohabitation: You would have to be pretty unlucky to get pulled up on this – especially given just how many people disregard this rule – but the UAE law states that men and women who are not related to each other can not live together If you are worried about the risk, however low it may be, the choice is to get married, or live apart.

Illegitimate Bumps: Getting pregnant if you are not married is a big no-no here. If you are having your prenatal check-ups at a government hospital, you will be asked for your marriage certificate when you register. If you are at a private clinic, you won't have to show your marriage certificate until the baby is born. Either way, you need to have that crucial piece of paper before giving birth here, or you could be looking at a spot of bother that transcends sleepless nights and dirty nappies.

Remain Orderly: Drinking in public view (unless you are at a licensed venue or event), is illegal. Being drunk and disorderly in public is against the law, no matter where you are. Be careful when you are ordering that seventh cocktail – if that's the one that's going to make you lose your decorum, think about the consequences and make sure there is someone responsible for getting you home safely (apart from the taxi driver).

Keep The PDAs In Check: Holding hands won't land you in any trouble, but think twice before kissing, hugging and other public displays of affection. It may be acceptable in some places (like in airport lounges), but it has been known to get people into trouble, particularly if the kissing and hugging is on the more amorous side. Beware in nightclubs: a seemingly innocent kiss, even between married couples, can result in a bouncer giving you a rather firm warning.

Bounce Into Jail: It is a criminal offence to bounce a cheque in the UAE and can result in jail time, so make sure you have enough money in your account to honour it. And don't rely on post-dating here: there are many reports of funds being cleared from your account long before the date that is written on the cheque.

Don't Have One For The Road: It goes without saying that drinking and driving is illegal. But what many people fail to understand is that there is no such thing as a safe, legal limit when it comes to drinking and driving here. Even a sip of wine or a strong brandy pudding can put you over the limit, because the limit is zero. If you are driving, you should stick to soft drinks, and only soft drinks, all night. If you are drinking, it's best to leave the car keys at home and get a cab.

Over The Counter But Outside The Law: Codeine is widely available in over-the-counter medications in countries like the UK, and Temazepam is a commonly prescribed sleep aid. However, they are illegal substances in the UAE, and possessing them could result in arrest. You can't buy them here, and it's a good idea to tell your overseas visitors not to stock up on the Tylenol or Restoril before they arrive. If they do need these medications, they should carry a doctor's prescription, translated into Arabic if possible.

Respect Ramadan: In the UAE, it is illegal to eat, drink or smoke in public view during Ramadan fasting hours. 'In public view' includes your car, the beach, and even the gym. You should not chew gum either. Many restaurants have closed off sections where you can eat lunch out of sight, and most offices set up a little area where non-Muslims can eat and drink during the day. If these options are not available to you, then you should wait for Iftar (the breaking of the fast) before eating, drinking or smoking.

Look Mum, No Hands: It's one of the most widely flouted laws in the history of the legal system, but it is absolutely illegal to drive while talking on your mobile handset. Apart from being dangerous, not just for you but for your fellow road users, it is punishable with hefty fines and black points. Invest in a hands-free kit, or better yet, switch your phone off while driving – it may be one of your few opportunities to enjoy some peace and quiet in the midst of a typical busy day.

Family & Education

FAMILY

Family is a huge part of life in Abu Dhabi, as well as an integral part of Emirati culture. From birth to higher education, bringing up your family here is a rewarding and enjoyable experience. The facilities, from the practical to the pleasurable, are world-class and Abu Dhabi has so much to offer families of all nationalities. However, while the nurseries, play centres and facilities for babies and toddlers are very good, and the primary and secondary schools of extremely high standard, older children may have more of a struggle settling into life in the Emirates.

With improved education facilities, especially at university level, and an ever-expanding leisure industry, teens have a lot to keep them occupied, but the challenge is often transport. An overhauled bus system and cheap taxis have to be relied upon as driving your teenagers to and from malls can be a bit of a chore. Also, chores need to be enforced for older kids in order to avoid 'expat brat' syndrome – unfortunately, there are few options for Saturday jobs in Abu Dhabi, so you may want to encourage your older children to volunteer (p.116).

Children are rarely expected to be seen and not heard in Abu Dhabi and many restaurants are abuzz with kids running around. There are, however, places where kids will be less welcome, so you should always call before you turn up. Cinemas also seem to have a pretty open-door policy – although often to the annoyance of other patrons. Parks (p.211), beaches (p.212) and amusements centres (p.214) keep families happy and childcare options are available, although more in the form of paid babysitters than parent-run babysitting circles.

Whether you come with your family or have a family here, Abu Dhabi is a great place to call home.

Getting Married

Many expats choose to return to their country of origin in order to get married; however, it is possible to get married in Abu Dhabi, as long as you adhere to certain legal criteria.

Shotgun Weddings

It's illegal to have a baby out of wedlock in the UAE. If you are unmarried and fall pregnant, you have two choices: get married quickly or leave the country. You'll be asked for your marriage certificate when you give birth and if there is a significant discrepancy in your dates you will face many questions and a lot more paperwork.

To marry before a Shariah court in Abu Dhabi, the man must be a Muslim while the woman can be a non-Muslim. A Muslim woman cannot marry a non-Muslim man in the emirate. Even if you get married at the Shariah court, the church or a temple, you will still need to register your wedding in your home country.

Weddings aren't limited to churches and embassies; many people choose to get married in one of the hotels but you could also consider a beach wedding or a ceremony aboard a yacht.

There are plenty of hotels (see p.198) to choose from for your reception and your chosen venue will be able to assist you with everything from layout to music, menus to recommended florists. For those with limitless budgets, you could marry on the beach in front of the Emirates Palace (p.201) or in the stunning ballroom at the Park Rotana (p.203). If you fancy having the Grand Mosque as your photo backdrop, you can't beat the Shangri-La hotel (p.203) and, for an environmentally friendly do, check out the Millennium Hotel (p.203), winner of the Best Environment Hotel at the MENA Awards 2009. The eco-conscious creative team will come up with globe-friendly concepts for your special day.

Tailor-Made

There are many talented tailors in Abu Dhabi (p.306) and you may wish to have your wedding dress tailor-made. The off-the-rack selection is limited, but you may find what you want at the recently opened boutique store Alice Temperly in Marina Mall (p.338). If you can't find what you're looking for here, many of Abu Dhabi's brides and couples choose to scoot up the road to Dubai where the choice is more expansive.

You may find that a wedding planner is just what you need, especially when your family support network is miles away. C'est La Vie (www.clvweddings.com), Wedding.ae (www.wedding.ae) or Fonoon (www.fonoon-uae.com) are good options.

Wedding photographers Lisa Lundqvist (www.lisalundqvistweddingphotography.com) and Jonathan Gibbons (www.jgibbonsphotography.com) are both based in Abu Dhabi, while local florists Exotica (02 644 4416) and Petals (02 443 9880) pride themselves on their spectacular wedding arrangements. Most spas (p.181) offer special services for brides and Lina of www.linasmakeup.com promises to make you feel like a princess on the day. For further inspiration, visiting the Abu Dhabi Bride Show (see p.27) is a must. This annual exhibition covers the full spectrum of what you'll need for your big day.

The Paperwork

While bright sunshine on your Abu Dhabi wedding day is almost guaranteed, rules and regulations are not; they often vary between venues so it's best to do plenty of research to ensure you know what to expect.

As a Muslim marrying another Muslim, for example, you should apply at the marriage section of the Shariah Court, Sheikh Zayed Court. For further information, the Shariah Court can advise (800 2353). You'll need two male witnesses and the bride should ensure that either her father or brother attends as a witness. In terms of paperwork, you must hold a valid residence visa, plus you'll need your passports along with copies, proof that the groom is Muslim and the Dhs.50 fee.

If you are not Muslim, you must contact your embassy for advice and all couples, regardless of where they get married, must register the marriage with their embassy afterwards. In all cases, you need to produce an original or legalised birth certificate, and a certificate of marital status. In most cases, a marriage performed in Abu Dhabi is legally recognised worldwide, but it's best to check with your embassy; the passport division will also be able to assist you with changing your name after you are married.

Christians can choose to marry at one of the churches in Abu Dhabi. The cost of the ceremony and church fees for an Anglican ceremony (Anglican Church of St Andrews, 02 446 1631, www.standrewauh.org) is Dhs.1,500, while marrying at the Catholic St Joseph's Cathedral (02 446 1929, www.stjosephsabudhabi.org) costs Dhs.200, and before you start on your table plan, you should first contact the chaplain of your particular denomination for a prenuptial enquiry appointment.

Each denomination's requirements differ, although it's worth noting here that if you're not concerned about sticking to a particular doctrine but would like a church wedding, the Anglican ceremony is somewhat simpler to arrange than the Catholic equivalent. For ceremonies in hotels or unusual venues, contact the Evangelical Community Church for advice, www.eccad.org.

Filipino citizens are required to contact their embassy before the court will authenticate the marriage certificate and Hindus can be married through the Indian embassy (further information can be found on the Indian Embassy website, www.indembassyuae.org).

Having A Baby

In many ways, having a baby while you are living in Abu Dhabi as an expat is very easy. The standard of maternity healthcare, whether you choose to go private or government, is excellent and, as long as you have insurance or the means to pay for healthcare, there is absolutely no reason to return to your home country to give birth (more on maternity healthcare on p.169).

There is a better chance that you can get away with one income in Abu Dhabi, meaning that one parent (in practice, usually the mother) has the opportunity to stay at home after having a baby rather than having to return to work for financial reasons. And you will have access to cheap childcare and babysitting services here, so you may find that you can be a little more independent than your counterparts back home.

Of course, there are some disadvantages too. If you are pregnant and working, then you've got some pretty paltry maternity leave to look forward to: just 45 days' paid leave and absolutely nothing for dads. You can take another month unpaid, as long as your employer agrees; and, if you need some extra time for medical reasons, you can take up to 100 days, although this is only granted upon production of a medical certificate from your doctor. Having an understanding employer can obviously result in these maternity leave rules being slightly more flexible.

Another disadvantage to living here and having a baby is the absence of the family support network you may have had back home – grandparents and other family members, who would normally muck in to help you with mundane tasks like cooking, cleaning and babysitting are now thousands of miles away. Fortunately, there are strong networks of other parents who meet up regularly and offer plenty of support to each other; for example, www.abudhabimums.ae.

Pregnant Out Of Wedlock

If you fall pregnant but are not married, then there is no reason to panic, but there are several decisions that you will need to make fairly quickly. It is illegal to

Planning The Big Day Suzie Jackson, 26, newlywed

The events team at the Hilton Abu Dhabi assisted us with pretty much all the organising and created a package deal for us which was really useful. I met with them monthly in the run up and they kindly threw in lots of free added extras for us, including extra dishes on the buffet, a free wedding cake and even the honeymoon suite! The ceremony took place in the Hilton's garden by the lake and was just beautiful. We kept out of the sun by starting everything at 16:30. Finding cravats and waistcoats for the guy's outfits proved impossible, so my sister brought them from the UK and I managed to get my whole outfit, dress, veil, the lot, from The Wedding Shop in Dubai. On the day, we gave everyone little Arabic scrolls printed with the order of service as our wedding favours and, to keep our budget from spiralling out of control, we saved on printing by emailing our invites, used a photographer buddy of ours to take the pictures, and our friends kindly loaned us their cars.

have a baby out of wedlock while you are a resident in the UAE and if you deliver your baby at any hospital here, private or public, and can't produce a marriage certificate, you will most likely face a prison sentence. Therefore, as soon as you see the blue lines on the pregnancy test, you need to sort a few things out. The easiest solution is to have a quick wedding, after which you can go on to have antenatal care in a government or private hospital without any fear of punishment. If this is not an option, you can stay in Abu Dhabi until a reasonable time before you are due to give birth, and even have your antenatal check-ups in a private hospital, but you will need to ensure that you return to your home country to actually deliver the baby. Once you have delivered, you can return to Abu Dhabi with the baby: there are no rules against being a single mother here (see p.133 for more information on single parents).

Babies Born Back Home

Babies born abroad to expatriate mums with UAE residency are required to have a residence visa or a visit visa before entering the UAE. The application should be filed by the father or family provider, along with the essential documents, a salary certificate (for the provider, not the baby) and a copy of the birth certificate.

Birth Certificate & Registration

The hospital that delivers the baby will prepare a 'notification of birth' (which will be in Arabic) upon receipt of hospital records, photocopies of both parents' passports, your marriage certificate, and a fee of Dhs.50.

Take the notification certificate for translation into English at the Preventative Medicine Department of Sheikh Khalifa Medical City (p.166) or Al Ain Hospital (p.161), where you will be issued with an application form. The certificate then needs to be attested at the Ministry of Health (Dhs.20) and the Ministry of Justice & Foreign Affairs (Dhs.150) – procedures for which the baby's father must be present.

Every expat child born in the UAE should be registered with their parents' embassy. If parents are from different countries, you will probably be able to choose which nationality your child adopts and, in some cases, they may be able to take on dual nationality. Check with your embassy for further details. Remember, your baby needs a UAE residence visa within 120 days of birth and to do this, you need to have received his or her passport, so you should start the process as soon as possible. If you don't get the residency within that time, you will be fined Dhs.100 for every day you go over the limit. If you feel like you've got enough on your plate with your new arrival, MEDI-Express (www.mediexpress.ae) offers a service, for a fee, that will take much of the administration and hassle out of arranging the birth certificate for your baby.

More Maternity?

The UAE's Federal National Council is considering plans that will see maternity leave for the country's working mothers increase to 100 days, with the possibility of reducing the working day by two hours for up to four months after delivery.

Adoption

While you can't adopt a UAE National baby, many couples in Abu Dhabi adopt children from Africa, Asia and the Far East. Adoption regulations vary according to which country the child is from, but once you clear the requirements of that country and complete the adoption process, you'll have no problems bringing your new child into the UAE on your sponsorship. Check with your embassy about the procedure for applying for citizenship of your home country for your new child. If you're considering adoption, a good place to start is the Adoption Support Group (p.136).

Getting Divorced

Statistics show that the UAE has one of the highest divorce rates in the Arab world. To counter this, bodies such as the State Marriage Fund have launched

Baby No. 3 **Jenny McDougall, 38,** housewife

This is the third baby I've had abroad. Being pregnant overseas can be nerve-racking with the obvious communication challenges combined with confusion over where the best place to go for appointments is, but it's perfectly possible and the Corniche Hospital has some of the best expertise I've come across in Abu Dhabi. However, there were some operational struggles – it would sometimes take six hours to complete a 20 minute appointment due to the backlog of people waiting. When I discovered the new Al Noor Hospital, I went there for my check-ups – their expertise was fine and the turnaround was so much more efficient. My advice to anyone having a baby here is never be afraid to ask for a second opinion and to build up your support network group ASAP. You'll need friends who understand what you're going through when the baby is born. I'd highly recommend investing in the help of a doula – you'll find their support absolutely invaluable.

schemes offering education and counselling services to National couples. Expats can get divorced in Abu Dhabi and, in some cases, the procedure can be relatively straightforward.

However, expat couples wishing to divorce may also be governed by the laws of their home country (if the couple has mixed nationalities, the home country of the husband applies), so it is advisable to seek legal advice. A husband who sponsors his wife has the right to have her residence visa cancelled in the event of divorce. See p.124 for a list of law firms.

It can be challenging getting divorced while living abroad, especially if the situation isn't amicable. If you are the one filing for divorce and you have legal representation in your home country, it is likely that you will also need a solicitor here to serve the divorce papers to your spouse. In addition, whilst you may be living in Abu Dhabi and, therefore, think custodial issues are not relevant, it may still be a good idea to arrange for a residence and access order or similar through the courts in your home country in order to clarify your parental rights for when you do intend to return. If the relationship between you and your spouse has deteriorated, it is a good idea to try and meet with a mediator. You can approach the Family Guidance and Reformation Centre which functions under the Abu Dhabi Judicial Department (800 2353, www.adjd.gov.ae).

Single Parents

It is possible to live in Abu Dhabi and sponsor your children as a single parent here. There will be extra requirements that you need to meet, including a minimum salary level and a letter of no objection from the other parent (or a death certificate, in the case of a deceased spouse). You may also need to show your divorce certificate, but it is best to visit the Immigration Department to find out the exact requirements, as these may change from time to time.

Being a working single parent in Abu Dhabi may seem daunting for a number of reasons. Firstly, as an expat, your support system may not be as great as back home, where friends and family can help out and, secondly, in a country where marriage and family are so important, you may feel a little like the 'odd one out'. However, once you get used to people enquiring where your husband is (if you have a child with you people assume you're married), there are actually lots of advantages of living in Abu Dhabi as a working single parent.

The nurseries (p.140) in Abu Dhabi are very good and a few offer full day care, plus they are generally much more affordable than in your home country. There is also the option of having a live-in nanny (see Sponsoring a Maid, p.40), which means that you can not only work as a single parent but you can maintain a social life.

Babysitting & Childcare

Although there is no registered network of childminders in Abu Dhabi, there are quite a few options. Many parents hire a full-time maid who will clean and cook along with taking on babysitting duties but, if you do choose this option, be very clear about any childcare expectations from the very beginning. A few local domestic help agencies offer babysitting services but may not wish to look after very young babies. Exiles (www.exilesmaidservice.ae), a maid service available in Khalifa City and Al Raha Gardens, for example, provides childcare services to their existing clients. Bear in mind that First Aid and childcare qualifications are not legally required for babysitters or childcare workers, but you can always request that a suitable person be found. If you are unsure, always ask to interview the babysitter beforehand.

Do You Doula?

A doula can be hired to provide support and advice during pregnancy, childbirth and after the birth of your child. This can be vital as there is very little in the way of post-partum care in Abu Dhabi. Fully trained, they can help take a lot of the stress out of the experience, for mothers in particular. Visit www.expatdoula.com or www.dubaidoulas.com.

If you're looking for a live-in nanny, try Majestic Nannies (www.majesticnannies.com, 02 665 5056), established in Abu Dhabi in 2003. The company specialises in providing qualified, internationally trained and experienced childcare staff for 'discerning' parents.

Networking and word-of-mouth can pay huge dividends, as many parents with young children will be in the same boat as you. Abu Dhabi Mums (www.abudhabimums.ae) provides a wide variety of activities and services and, whilst they don't specifically offer childcare services, becoming involved with their activities is a great way to build up your network. It is likely that you will meet another parent who is willing to take care of your child for a fee or perhaps, at least, trade evenings.

Most four and five star hotels will happily organise childcare for guests and there are plenty of creche facilities around Abu Dhabi but be warned that they are of varying standards. You'll need to investigate further in order to find one you're comfortable with and you can expect to pay anything between Dhs.15 to Dhs.40 per hour (See Nurseries and Preschools, p.140).

Activities For Kids

Abu Dhabi is a veritable playground for kids with so many different activities on offer. In the cooler months, take advantage of the great outdoors with a trip to the kid-friendly parks (p.211) that are great for running, playing and eating alfresco. You could also try playing Frisbee on the beach (see p.212) or get them learning how to sail (see p.293). It's a good idea to keep an eye on the local press as, most months, there's something going on for kids, from a roaming theatre group to a visiting circus and, as the weather heats up, you'll find that there's still plenty to keep them occupied with everything from pottery to yoga, bowling, ice skating and martial arts – all of which are on offer all year round.

There are plenty of well-equipped indoor play centres around town offering all sorts of fun play and learning opportunities and many of these centres are conveniently placed within shopping malls. Check out Fun City at Marina Mall (p.338), Kidoos at Abu Dhabi Mall (p.334), Sparky's at Khalidiyah Mall (p.337) and My Playground (02 634 0035) which can be found on the first floor of the Marks & Spencer building in Al Markaziyah and hosts great facilities, such as a bouncy castle, cinema, library, sandpit and maze to keep the younger kids occupied.

There are various other clubs that run after-school activities (p.136) and summer camps (p.135), with most hobbies covered.

Abu Dhabi International Sailing School

Abu Dhabi International Marine Sports Club
Breakwater **02 681 3446**
www.adimsc.ae
Map **2 E1**

Children must be confident swimmers to join this school which offers sailing lessons for children over 8 years old. Children are taught the basic techniques by professional instructors.

Abu Dhabi Pottery

16th Street, Nr Khalidiya Garden Al Khalidiyah
02 666 7079
www.abudhabipottery.com
Map **2 G4**

Classes are available for adults and children over 5 years old, giving you the chance to try hand building and the wheel technique. Classes cost Dhs.150 for adults and Dhs.85 for children; there are supportive, knowledgeable instructors on hand who can help your child create something original to take home.

Noah's Ark Art & Music Institute

Villa 7/3, Sheikh Rashid Bin Saeed Al Maktoum St
Markaziya West **02 641 9793**
www.noahsarkjingles.com
Map **2 L4**

This school has been offering classes for adults and children since 2008. A wide range of art and music classes are available, from Singing Juniors (for kids aged between 3.5 years to 6 years) to Jingles instrument lessons (piano, guitar, drums, keyboard) Classes cost Dhs.150

Royal Institute Of Music & Arts

Markaziya East, Khalifa St 02 622 5410
Map **2 L3**

Classes of varying level are on offer here, from theory to practical coaching by experienced and certified music teachers in guitar, piano, keyboard, drums, violin, and vocals. The institute is recognised by the Ministry of Education and it also prepares students for the music examinations conducted by Trinity Guildhall and ABRSM Colleges of Music, London.

Edutainment & Fun Zones

Just about every mall in the capital has play areas for kids. Some are little more than glorified video game arcades while others have small rollercoasters and other rides. Marina Mall's Fun City (p.216) is one of the largest. Likewise, Sparky's (p.216) in Khalidiya Mall boasts room to move and plenty of options. FunZone (p.216), Kidoos (p.216) and Wanasa Land (p.216) are all sure to get the kiddies worked up in a frenzy of excitement. See also Discover Abu Dhabi, p.187.

Whiz Kidz

Jumbo Electronics Bldg, Defence Rd, Nr Dar Al Shifaa Hospital Al Dhafrah **02 641 7450**
Map **2 P7**

Whiz Kidz offers a range of activities, including classes on drawing, cooking, painting, arithmetic training, calligraphy, public speaking and etiquette. The monthly fee to join the kids' club costs Dhs.200 to Dhs.600. The club opens from 9:00 to 18:00 every day except on Fridays.

Yoga Tree & Soma Pilates Studios

Villa 405/1, Al Khaleej Al Arabi St & Hazaa Bin Zayed The First Sts Al Bateen **02 667 6579**
www.yogatree.ae
Map **2 G6**

Offering a variety of classes for adults and children, Yoga Tree provides a good opportunity for kids to be introduced to yoga in a fun and relaxed environment. The classes run for 30 minutes and a package of four classes can be purchased for Dhs.140.

The Young Musician Music Institute

Nr Vegetable Market Madinat Zayed **02 556 2080**
www.theyoungmusician.com
Map **2 M5**

For the budding rock guitarist or concert pianist in the family, The Young Musician Music Institute offers music lessons, including guitar, piano, and voice tuition. The Institute works with the Trinity College of London curriculum, and examinations and certificates are available twice a year. There is also a branch at Al Raha Mall.

Mother & Toddler Activities

There is very much a community spirit among expat mums in Abu Dhabi that is well worth tapping into. A number of mother and baby or toddler groups offer support and camaraderie for new mums feeling a million miles from friends and family. It's quite unusual to find a stay-at-home dad here, as they tend to be the primary earner in Abu Dhabi, but most groups should also welcome dads to the fold. Abu Dhabi Mums (www.abudhabimums.ae) is a fantastic resource and lists a variety of mother and toddler activities available in the emirate including day outings, music groups and various arts and crafts. It also organises regular social activities for its members, provides information on useful services and allows members access to its toy library and stock of baby equipment.

As a new mother, you will find that a group like this is an invaluable way to meet other mums and it's an easy way to quickly establish a much needed support network.

Summer Camps

The summer holidays are longer in the UAE than in many other countries and, due to the hot weather, children can find themselves cooped up indoors for the majority of their holidays. Fortunately, Abu Dhabi has a good variety of activities to keep children occupied over the sticky summer months. For starters, there are summer camps run by various organisations, while several nurseries also offer summer day care for younger children. You'll likely find that it is necessary to book in advance, as places for the best summer schemes tend to fill up quite quickly.

Family Festival

Abu Dhabi Tourism Authority hosts an annual festival of family activities (www.summerinabudhabi.ae) at the Abu Dhabi National Exhibition Centre (p.192) and shopping malls right across the city. Shows, sporting events and educational activities are organised to keep both kids and parents entertained.

Little Smarties (p.143) in Khalifa City and The Butterfly Montessori (p.142) both offer summer day care for preschoolers. For slightly older kids, Libra Summer Camps (www.libra-uae.com, 055 922 8362) is a professionally run company that prides itself on only using highly experienced and qualified coaches or teachers, all of whom have been fully screened. Run by British expats, it provides a varied, fun and educational experience in a safe environment with an emphasis on team sports, crafts and music. Camps are

Urban Park

run at multiple venues across Abu Dhabi and cater for children aged 5 to 14.

Some hotels in Abu Dhabi also cater for the kids during the holidays. The Sheraton Abu Dhabi (p.204) and Beach Rotana Abu Dhabi (p.200), for example, both run fun-packed summer programmes that include swimming lessons, ball games, treasure hunts, island trips and tournaments.

As ever, word-of-mouth is usually the best way to find out about new camps and activities in the emirate and learn which one might best suit you and your kids – for updates, check out forums on sites such as www.expatwoman.com and www.abudhabiwoman.com.

Dib Dib

Brownies, Guides, Cubs and Scouts Groups are all well established in the region, having been in Abu Dhabi since 1967. All children, from 5 year olds through to 18 year olds and older, can join the groups, which are based on the UK Guide and Scout movements. Parents who want to get more involved should feel free to volunteer as they're always looking for adults to help run the units. For more information on Brownies and Guides, contact abudhabi.dc.bgifc@gmail.com; for more information on Cubs and Scouts contact Geir Johnsen, Group Scout Leader (geirkj@broadpark.no, 050 613 3912) or Ade Waite, Group Scout Leader (adewaite@hotmail.com, 050 815 6537).

After-School Activities

Most schools pride themselves on offering a broad spectrum of after-school activities in addition to their set academic curriculum and they often see these extracurricular activities as important parts of a child's overall development. Activities vary but they can include anything from sports teams, drama and computer clubs to dance lessons, singing or even gardening classes.

Local sports clubs in Abu Dhabi also provide a range of children-friendly activities and, whether your kid dreams of bending it like Beckham at the Abu Dhabi Football Academy or your little one fancies taking centre stage at Turning Pointe (p.279), you will find plenty to keep them occupied; check the Activities Finder on p.271 to see which sports are on offer in the capital. The Libra Group (www.libra-uae.com) also runs a wide range of exciting after-school activities around and throughout Abu Dhabi – with academies in swimming, football, rugby, basketball, tennis and martial arts offering training to young athletes.

Support Groups

Life in Abu Dhabi can sometimes be challenging, and with many residents leaving behind loved ones, there is often a lack of the family support network that many people are used to. Making the first step of reaching out for help can be tough, however, there are groups out there that are more than willing to help ease you through the difficult patches.

Check out the list below, or look for updates of support groups in Explorer's monthly magazine *liveworkexplore* (www.liveworkexplore.com), or in any of the monthly health magazines such as *Connector* or *Aquarius*. Online forum Abu Dhabi Woman (www.abudhabiwoman.com) may also provide fruitful leads: there are discussions covering all aspects of life in the UAE, and various informal support groups and coffee groups can also be found here.

Be aware that, if a suitable support group does not exist in Abu Dhabi, you're more than likely to find it in Dubai.

If possible, follow personal recommendations as standards can vary enormously, especially if a group or workshop is linked to a business. Be wise and use your discretion.

Abu Dhabi Ladies

Various Locations **050 886 3841**
www.abudhabiladies.ae

A support group open to ladies of all ages who want to find new friends. The group offers lots of activities on an informal basis. Abu Dhabi Ladies meet every Wednesday at the Hilton Hotel Jazz Bar between 10:00 and 12:00.

Abu Dhabi Mums

Various Locations
www.abudhabimums.ae

A voluntary but well-run organisation that provides support and offers a range of activities for parents and children. It also arranges events and member discounts, while supplying vital information to the capital's mothers.

Adoption Support Group

Dubai **04 360 8113**
www.groups.yahoo.com/group/asgdubai

Meetings are held once a month for parents who have adopted children or who are considering adoption. For more information on the meetings, call Carol on the number listed above.

Alcoholics Anonymous

Various Locations **056 788 1416**
www.aaarabia.org

Anyone needing help can contact this organisation 24 hours a day for advice. Meetings are held every Saturday, Monday and Wednesday at the St Andrew's Centre at 20:00, and Fridays at Le Meridien at 10:00. Al Ain meetings are held at the Hilton on Saturdays at 20:15 and at the Oasis Hospital on Tuesdays at 20:15.

Dubai Dyslexia Support Group

Dubai **04 344 6657**

This group holds occasional meetings for people with dyslexia and may be able to assist you if you suspect that your child is suffering from the condition.

Future Centre For Special Needs

Villa 250, Baynunah St Al Bateen **02 666 9625**

www.future-centre.com

Map **2 E6**

A non-profit organisation that educates and supports people with special needs as well as carrying out research. The centre offers therapy-based sessions to those who do not attend classes or who are awaiting placement.

Ladies Of Courage

Sheikh Khalifa Medical City Al Dhafrah

02 819 4495

www.skmc.ae

Map **2 K7**

A breast cancer support group that meets every third Thursday of the month at Sheikh Khalifa Medical City. Meetings are organised by staff at the centre and are open to everyone – call for timings.

Multiplied UAE

Various Locations **050 295 6235**

www.multiplieduae.com

This is an online support group offering a forum for parents of multiples to exchange advice and ask questions. Also, many parents get together for play dates and activities with their children.

Narcotics Anonymous UAE

ECC Offices, Villa 8/2, 8th Street, Nr Al Khubairat School Al Mushrif

050 131 0055

www.nainarabia.com

Map **2 L13**

A non-profit organisation which offers advice and support for those suffering from drug addiction. Classes are conducted in both English and Arabic. Narcotics Anonymous holds weekly meetings on Fridays at 19:00 at the Al Mushrif centre. Call Lisa (050 416 2857) or Wessam (050 268 7890) for directions or further information.

Overeaters Anonymous

Dubai **050 249 4650**

www.oaindubai.net

An organisation that helps individuals deal with the emotional and physical stress of varioius compulsive eating disorders. Meetings are organised on Tuesdays at 17:30 – call Sally for more information on the location and how to join.

Stillbirth & Neonatal Death Society

Dubai **055 393 2804**

www.dubai-sands.org

This is a UK-based charity for those families experiencing pregnancy loss, either through stillbirth, neonatal death or late miscarriage. Contact Angela on 04 382 2801 or Anita on 050 644 7903. SANDS also offers hospital and home visits.

Death

In the event of the death of a friend or relative, the first thing to do is to notify the police by dialling 999. The police will fill out a report and the body will be taken to a hospital where a doctor will determine the cause of death and produce a report. The authorities will need to see the deceased's passport and visa details. Abu Dhabi Police will investigate in the case of an accidental or suspicious death, and it's likely that an autopsy will be performed at a government hospital. If you're unhappy with the outcome of an investigation, you could hire a private investigator, but this is a bit of a grey area so seek advice from your embassy or consulate (see the last page of this book).

Certificates & Registration

The Abu Dhabi authorities will also need to see the deceased's passport and visa details. The hospital will issue a death certificate declaration on receipt of the doctor's report, for a fee of Dhs.50. Make sure that the actual cause of death is stated, then take the declaration of death and original passport to the Al Asima police station, next to the Spinneys in Al Khalidiya. The police will give permission to release the body in a letter which, along with the death declaration, original passport and copies, should be taken to the Department of Preventative Medicine. In Abu Dhabi, this is at Sheikh Khalifa Medical City (p.166); in Al Ain, you will need to go to the Al Ain Hospital (p.161). The actual death certificate will be issued here for a small fee. If you are sending the deceased home, you should also request a death certificate in English or have the certificate translated into the appropriate language. Then take the certificate to the Ministry of Health and the Ministry of Foreign Affairs for registration. Notify the relevant embassy or consulate of the death so it can be registered in the deceased's country of origin. Although this is not always obligatory, for legal purposes, a death certificate from the home country, or a consular report of death, may be mandatory. They will also issue their own death certificate which could cost up to Dhs.700. You will need to take the original passport and death certificate along for the passport to be cancelled. The deceased's visa must also be cancelled by the Immigration Department. You should take with you the local death certificate, original cancelled passport and the consulate death certificate.

Returning The Deceased To Their Country Of Origin

To return the deceased to their country of origin, contact the cargo section of Omeir Travel Agency (www.omeir.com, 02 612 3456). The company has experience in making such arrangements and will give you all the necessary information, along with the procedure to follow. The body will also need to be embalmed, for which you must get a letter from the police. Embalming can be arranged through the Sheikh Khalifa Medical City for Dhs.1,000, which includes the embalming certificate (there should be no charge if a copy of the deceased's medical card is supplied). The body must be identified before and after embalming. The following documents should accompany the deceased overseas: the local death certificate, a translation of the death certificate, the embalming certificate, NOC from the police, the consulate death certificate and NOC, and the cancelled passport.

Local Burial Or Cremation

More often than not, the deceased is repatriated to their country of origin, however, Abu Dhabi does have mortuary, cremation and burial sites all equipped with modern and proper facilities. Cremation is available only to Abu Dhabi residents and, for more information, you should contact New Medical Centre (02 633 2255). Further details and assistance can be obtained from consular officials at your embassy. Local burial is also possible in Abu Dhabi and takes place at the Abu Dhabi Christian Cemetery with all arrangements for the funeral made with St Andrew's Church (02 446 1631).

Middle East Funeral Services, a company based in Dubai but operating throughout the UAE, can handle all funeral-related procedures in Abu Dhabi offering guidance wherever needed. More information can be found on its website, www.mefs.ae, or you can phone 04 273 0313 (available 24 hours a day).

Pets

The attitude towards pets in Abu Dhabi is mixed so it is sensible to keep your pet under control at all times. Pets are prohibited from parks and beaches, and there aren't many places where you can walk your dog, other than the streets in your area. Even in these areas, dogs must always be on a lead and certain breeds (call 800 555 for complete details of which breeds) must be muzzled. You should check with your landlord what their pet policy is before you move in. It is almost always stated in contracts that pets are not allowed but, if you talk to the landlord, there may be some leeway. If your landlord seems unreliable, it is definitely worth having your contract amended.

Be sure to keep your pet indoors or within your garden to avoid contact with strays or nervous neighbours. Abu Dhabi has a significant problem with strays, although Feline Friends (p.116), Strays of Abu Dhabi (p.117) and K9 Friends (p.282) are hard-working animal charities that take in as many as they can. The Abu Dhabi Municipality is also hard at work solving the problem of strays.

> **Sleek Salukis**
>
> The saluki is the breed of dog most commonly associated with the region; they are used in traditional forms of hunting. The Arabian Saluki Centre (www.arabiansaluki.ae) offers a wealth of information and if you'd like your own desert dog, contact K9 Friends (p.282) or Strays (p.117).

You should inoculate your pet annually against rabies and register it with the municipality who will microchip cats and dogs, and provide plastic neck tags. If the municipality picks up an animal without a tag and microchip, it is treated as a stray and will be kept for a short time before being put down. Vets will not provide treatment for your cat or dog if it has not been microchipped. While rare, there have been reports of dogs being stolen, either to be sold to unscrupulous pet shops, or for dog fighting. Ensure your garden is secure and don't let your dog roam around on the street.

> **Looking For A Pet?**
>
> Open since 2010, the Abu Dhabi Animal Shelter (www.abudhabianimalshelter.com) houses stray dogs and cats looking for a new home. Check the website for details on the adoption process.

Bringing Your Pet To Abu Dhabi

Pets may be brought into the UAE without quarantine as long as they are microchipped and vaccinated with verifying documentation, including a government health certificate from the country of origin. Pets must also have an import permit and an additional RNATT (rabies) blood test is required for pets entering the UAE from many countries. However, you cannot import cats and dogs under 4 months old and all pets must arrive as cargo. Bear in mind also that rabies injections must have been done more than 21 days prior to applying for the import permit. The companies mentioned in Taking Your Pets Home also deal with importing pets. To find out more, check out http://petimport.moew.gov.ae and create an account.

Taking Your Pet Home

The regulations for 'exporting' your pet depend on the rules of the country to which it is going. Basic requirements are a valid rabies vaccination, not older than one year but not less than 30 days old, and a health certificate that can be obtained from the

Ministry of Environment & Water (cost Dhs.100, www.moew.gov.ae). It is normally issued one week before departure. You'll also need an export certificate and a travel box, normally wooden or fibreglass, which meets the airline regulations.

Animal Hospital

The Falcon Hospital near the Abu Dhabi Airport has a pet care centre which was opened in July 2007 and boasts a cat and dog 'hotel' facility with 100 large, air-conditioned rooms. Smaller animals such as parrots, rabbits and turtles are looked after too. The centre also features a dog-training area, a cat and dog-grooming salon and a pet clinic, but the facility often gets booked up quickly. You can find out more about its services on p.214.

Your local vet or the airline you are travelling on can inform you of specific regulations pertaining to your destination, such as blood tests and quarantine. The UK, for example, requires a rabies blood test (RNATT) to be done six months in advance of departure in order to avoid quarantine.

The British Veterinary Centre (p.140), American Veterinary Clinic (p.140), the German Veterinary Clinic (p.140) and Dubai Kennels and Cattery (p.140) all provide complete international travel services, and can assist with importing and exporting your pet.

Pet Grooming & Training

Standards of care at Abu Dhabi's veterinary clinics are reasonably high, and prices do not vary dramatically.

Kennels are generally of a good standard, although spaces are limited during peak times (summer and Christmas). An alternative is to use an at-home pet-sitting service – someone will come into your house at least once a day to feed and exercise your pet for a reasonable fee (for a bit extra, they might even water your plants). Try forums such as www.abudhabiwoman.com to be pointed in the direction of someone who can help.

In terms of grooming, there are a number of companies that offer everything from basic shampooing, medicated baths and nail clipping to more indulgent options such as pet fashion.

Pet Boarding

There is very little in the way of niche offerings for pet lovers in Abu Dhabi, therefore it's extremely likely that once you find a vet that you like, you'll use the company for boarding and grooming too. All of the establishments below offer veterinary services, as well as having kennels and catteries, and offer full grooming services for your all precious pets.

Abu Dhabi Falcon Hospital *> p.vii,139, 215* Nr Abu Dhabi International Airport, Al Shamkha, 02 575 5155, *www.falconhospital.com*

American Veterinary Clinic Al Falah 9th Street, Al Khalidiyah, 02 665 5044, *www.americanvet.ae*

The British Veterinary Centre Khaleej Al Arabi St, Al Khalidiyah, 02 665 0085, *www.britvet.com*

Dubai Kennels & Cattery *> p.141* Street 34, Dubai, 04 285 1646, *www.dkc.ae*

German Veterinary Clinic 39th Street, Madinat Khalifa A (Khalifa City A), 02 556 2024, *www.germanvet.ae*

Mrs. Doolittle's Various Locations, 050 125 3705, *www.mrsdoolittlespetservices.net*

National Veterinary Hospital Al Mushrif, 02 446 1628, *www.nationalvet.com*

New Veterinary Clinic Al Raffedeeyam Laundry Bldg, Baniyas St, Tourist Club Area, 02 672 5955

EDUCATION

There is no cause for concern that your child's education will suffer as a result of going to school in Abu Dhabi; on the contrary, many parents report satisfaction with the way a multicultural upbringing results in well-rounded, worldly wise children Something you can't escape, unfortunately, is paying high school fees – as an expat, your child will have to go to private school, and it will cost you a pretty penny. So, before you hand over wads of your hard-earned cash, it is really worth doing your research and picking a school that best suits the needs of your child. Have a chat with other parents for word-of-mouth recommendations, or ask your company's HR departments which schools they are used to dealing with. And as Abu Dhabi traffic can be a nightmare, it makes sense to look at schools near your home or office as a starting point.

School terms run to a similar calendar to education systems in the UK and USA, with the academic year starting in September after a long summer holiday.

Nurseries & Pre-Schools

Some nurseries accept babies from as young as 3 months, although most prefer to take on children who have started walking (around 12 months). Fees and timings vary dramatically, so it's best to call around and visit a few nurseries to get an idea of what's available. As a general rule of thumb, most nurseries are open for four or five hours in the morning and charge anything from Dhs.3,000 to Dhs.12,000 per term.

The more popular nurseries have long waiting lists, so if you're after a particular establishment, it may be necessary to enrol your child before he or she is even born to ensure a spot.

Some of the bigger primary schools also have nursery sections – if you've got a primary school in

mind for your child, it is worth checking to see if they have a nursery, as this may help you secure a place in the school itself a few years down the line.

There are a number of factors to consider when you are looking for a nursery and it is always a good idea to take your time to visit several schools to get a hands-on feel of the place and the quality of the facilities and training before making a decision.

Try to drop in during the day so that you can have a look at the facilities while there are children around. Many of the nurseries in Abu Dhabi operate morning hours which may rule them out if you are working full time. However, many will also run late classes for an extra fee and a number of them have early-bird drop-offs. They may also organise sessions during the holiday periods.

Another factor worth thinking about when selecting your child's nursery is whether or not they provides meals – having to make a packed lunch every morning when you're trying to get ready for work may not be suitable for you.

Bright Beginnings Nursery

30th Street, Al Mehairba Al Bateen **02 445 5339**
www.brightbeginnings.ae
Map **2 F11**

Bright Beginnings accepts children from just 8 weeks old, and follows a broad-based curriculum that will prepare children for both the American and British school systems. It has a lovely covered outdoor play area that includes a splash pond, and excellent art and learning facilities. Parents can opt for a two, three or five-day week. It is also open during the summer, while an afternoon programme is available at an additional cost. Another branch operates in Al Mushrif (02 449 2840).

Busy Bees Nursery

12th Street Madinat Zayed **02 621 9492**
www.busybeesnursery.org
Map **2 M5**

Formerly known as Sesame Street Private Nursery, Busy Bees Nursery follows an American curriculum. Its focus is on learning through social play. English is spoken by all teachers and a 30 minute Arabic lesson is given daily. Busy Bees is open from 08:00 until 13:00. Age: 18 months to 4 years old.

Butterfly Montessori Pre-School

28th Street Al Bateen **02 665 8611**
www.admont.ae
Map **2 H6**

Butterfly Montessori Pre-School follows an American nursery curriculum and uses the Montessori education method, encouraging learning through exploration, expression and play. It is open daily between 07:15 and 13:00. Age: 6 months to 4 years.

First Steps School & Nursery

Al Karama St Al Karamah **02 446 0960**
www.firststeps.ae
Map **2 K8**

A popular nursery and pre-school, the atmosphere is extremely friendly and the excellent staff combine fun and creativity with expression. Its classes are based on the British curriculum and it also features a basic introduction to Arabic. Both three-day and five-day weeks are offered. Age: 1 to 5 years old.

Giggles English Nursery

Al Meena Rd Tourist Club Area **02 673 4226**
Map **2 S2**

Giggles was established in 1987 and welcomes all nationalities although it follows the British curriculum. A first aid expert is on site, and bus transport is available at an additional cost. Two nurseries are in operation: one on Meena Road and one at Giggles English School on Airport Road (02 641 6255). Age: 18 months to 4 years old (Al Meena Road); kindergarten to grade six (Airport Road).

Humpty Dumpty

Villa 3, 11th Street Al Bateen **02 666 3277**
www.humptynursery.com
Map **2 F8**

There are two Humpty Dumpty nurseries in Abu Dhabi, one in Al Bateen and one in Madinat Khalifa A (02 556 1068). The nurseries teach children to learn through play, social interaction, self discovery and self expression. They have 'ready beds' for children's rest and relaxation. They are open from 07:30 to 14:00, Sunday to Thursday; there is also an afternoon club which runs from 14:00 to 15:00. Age: 1 to 4 years.

International Montessori Nursery

Off 31st Street Al Rehhan **02 449 4680**
www.imn.ae
Map **1 H7**

The Montessori system promotes learning through experience and interaction, and as such, the classes at the International Montessori Nursery are mixed in age with a high teacher to child ratio. It offers a flexible drop-off and pick-up system, between 07:15 and 08:30 and 12:00 and 14:00. Children can attend two, three or five days a week. Age: 18 months to 5 years old.

Jigsaw Nursery & Creche

Cnr Karama St & Delma St Al Karamah **02 445 5222**
www.jigsawnurseryad.com
Map **2 K9**

Based on a British curriculum for the full age range of preschoolers, Jigsaw Nursery and Creche promotes balanced development. Infants are well catered for, while older children can receive regular music lessons and Arabic lessons. Age: 12 months to 4.5 years.

Kotwals Nursery

Villa 79A, 63rd Street, Nr Mazyad Mall Mohammed Bin Zayed City **02 559 0068**
Map **1 Q11**
This is a Montessori nursery which has created a 'school within a house' approach. Its dedicated programme uses an innovative approach to learning using linguistics, non-competitive study and encourages children to make their own decisions. It also offers afternoon care and other care programmes. Age: 4 months to 4 years old.

Leens Nursery

Al Falah St, Nr Al Falah Plaza Al Dhafrah **02 642 2350**
Map **2 N6**
This long-established nursery school for kids has been teaching the Indian curriculum for 35 years. Age: 18 months to 4 years old.

The Montessori Way

Montessori is a popular teaching method that encourages a more flexible approach to learning than a strict academic curriculum. Children are encouraged to discover new things through imaginative play, social interaction and physical activity. The method is also used to help children to develop their own instinct to learn and is a good foundation for the International Baccalaureate curriculum. Several nurseries mentioned in this chapter offer Montessori based teaching methods including: International Montessori Nursery, Butterfly Montessori, Radiant Montessori Nursery, Kotwals Nursery and all four Stepping Stones nurseries.

Little Smarties Nursery School

21st Street Madinat Khalifa A (Khalifa City A)
02 556 5500
www.littlesmartiesnursery.com
Map **1 R7**
Located in Madinat Khalifa A, Little Smarties is an international nursery that prepares students for the British school system. The applied curriculum is based on Letterland and Jolly Phonics. The nursery's priority is to create a safe environment where children's confidence, creativity and curiosity can be nurtured. Hours are 08:00 to 14:00 daily. Age: 12 months to 4 years old.

Noah's Ark Nursery

Al Najda St Madinat Zayed **02 635 1035**
www.noahsarknurseryad.com
Map **2 P4**
For infants aged between 20 months and 4 years, this bright and friendly nursery and day care centre is open 07:00 to 18:30, Sunday to Thursday and 07:00 to 13:30 on Saturdays. Its curriculum takes a 'learning through play' approach. Also has a branch in Musaffah (same contact number as above).

Radiant Montessori Nursery

Nr Gate B Sheikh Zayed University Al Nahyan
02 445 5576
www.rmn4me.com
Map **2 M9**
This school provides a Montessori nursery education to children for three, four or five days per week. It also has optional afternoon sessions and transport is available. Facilities are varied and of a good standard. Age: 3 months to 5 years old.

Stepping Stones Nursery

13th Street, Nr American Community School
Al Bateen **02 681 5583**
www.steppingstones.ae
Map **2 D5**
Stepping Stones encourages children to learn through play, themed activities, crafts, cooking and 'pretend play'. Options are available for three-day or five-day weeks. The school has three branches, with Al Rawda (02 445 2260) and Bain Al Jasrain (02 558 8318) offering the British curriculum, and Al Bateen following the American curriculum; both include aspects of the Montessori learning system. There is a late class until 13:15. Age: 18 months to 4 years.

Teddy Bear American Nursery

Nr Civil Defence Madinat Khalifa A (Khalifa City A)
02 556 8566
www.teddybearnursery.net
Map **1 R7**
Excellently equipped American nursery with a curriculum based on intellectual, physical, social, moral and emotional development of children. The nursery offers plenty of creative activities and also runs a summer camp. Age: 14 months to 4 years.

Tweety Nursery & Creche

Muroor Rd, Nr Aramex Al Nahyan **02 443 9892**
Map **2 N8**
With a good range of facilities and experienced staff, Tweety Nursery & Creche focuses on providing a well-rounded learning environment that promotes positive social interaction and confidence in children. The creche is open 07:00 to 19:00, while the nursery's opening hours are 08:15 to 12.45, Sunday to Thursday. Age: 7 months (creche), 1 to 4 years (nursery).

Primary & Secondary Schools

As an expatriate in Abu Dhabi, you most likely have no choice but to enrol your child in private education – although expat kids can attend government schools provided there is space, they must speak Arabic and you'll most likely end up paying tuition fees too. In practice, private schools are pretty much the only option for most expat families.

When planning your child's education, there are several golden rules that will help ease the process: firstly, if you have a school in mind, get your child's name on the waiting list as soon as possible, since the demand for spaces at the more popular schools is high. Secondly, consider the 'school run' when choosing your school – Abu Dhabi's rush-hour traffic can turn a short journey into a tedious hour-long trek every morning. Thirdly, pick a school that offers the best curriculum for your child: if you are British and are planning to return home after a couple of years, it might be best to find a school that offers the English National Curriculum; similarly, if you think you might end up elsewhere on another expat assignment after you leave Abu Dhabi, it might be better to choose the International Curriculum, which will help your child slot into a wide range of curriculums.

School Rehaul

In mid-2011, Abu Dhabi Education Council (ADEC) announced a major rehaul of the schooling system. Part of the Abu Dhabi 2030 vision, ADEC said that 40 schools will be merged, 23 new will open, 11 will be renovated and 19 relocated. ADEC also announced the closure of six villa schools, and plans to set up three affordable private schools. None of the schools listed in this guide are subject to the rehaul, which is predominantly aimed at improving the public schooling sector.

Kids here start school as early as 3 years old (in schools that offer a foundation or reception year), and usually graduate from secondary school at around 18 years. Most schools are open from 08:00 to 13:00 or 15:00, from Sunday to Thursday. Ramadan hours are shorter – usually starting an hour or so later and finishing an hour earlier.

School fees are a contentious issue: private education doesn't come cheap. For a good school, you can expect to pay Dhs.25,000 plus per year for KG years, Dhs.30,000 and up for the middle primary years, and as much as Dhs.60,000 per year for secondary school. Ouch! If you're lucky, your company may offer school fees as part of your package. On top of this, you will usually need to pay around Dhs.500 to put your child's name on a school's waiting list, and a registration fee (around Dhs.2,000), which comes off your fees.

Be prepared to accept that there are a lot of school holidays here in Abu Dhabi. The summer holidays stretch for 10 long weeks over the hottest months of July and August, when many kids return to their home countries for extended holidays, or attend summer camps. There are also holidays in April and December. Schools close for at least a week twice a year for Eid Al Fitr and Eid Al Adha, and will most likely also open for reduced hours during the month of Ramadan. If one of you is a stay-at-home parent, then this poses few problems in terms of childcare; however, if both of you work, you will need to make sure that you have alternative arrangements for childcare during school holidays and random days off.

School Inspections

Education standards in private schools are high and it is controlled and maintained by the Abu Dhabi Education Council (www.adec.ae). Visit ADEC's website to see the criteria by which the council judges private schools. In addition to quality inspections, ADEC also regulates school fees; all annual increases must be pre-approved and are currently capped at 20%.

Which Curriculum?

Choosing the right curriculum for your child can be obvious – for example, if you're planning on being in Abu Dhabi for a year or two before returning to your home country, it makes sense to pick the curriculum that is offered back home, such as the English National Curriculum or the American Curriculum. However, if you are not sure what your future plans are, you may want to consider the International Baccalaureate Programme (IB), which is compatible with most curriculums worldwide.

There are distinct differences between each curriculum; it is a good idea to do plenty of research before deciding which one is best for your child.

School Uniforms

Most private schools in Abu Dhabi will insist on students wearing the official school uniform. Each school will use a particular uniform supply shop and this will be the only place where you can buy official school items. Before heading out and spending a fortune on uniforms, check with the school and with other parents which items are compulsory and which are not: a sturdy pair of black school shoes and a pair of non-marking trainers are usually essential items, whereas a branded school bag is often not.

School Transport

If, for whatever reason, you are not able to do the school run every morning and afternoon, you can make use of the bus services offered by most schools. The advantages are that the bus driver will get to deal with the traffic every day and, since school transport has to abide by some strict regulations, you can rest assured that your child will reach school safely. The disadvantages are that it can be a very expensive option: you will pay the same fee whether you live 500 metres or 10 kilometres from the school. Also, if your child is one of the first on the pick-up roster, it will mean a very early start and then a very long ride on the bus as it drives round to pick up all the other kids headed for the same facility – followed by the same all over again in the afternoon.

Still, for parents who work or don't drive, school transport is a godsend given the limited public transportation options. You should speak to your school directly about the costs and arrangements.

Abu Dhabi International Private School

Al Karamah St Al Rowdha **02 443 4433**
www.aisuae.com
Map **2 J8**
Abu Dhabi International Private School follows an excellent international programme that allows students to graduate with the relevant American, British or International Baccalaureate qualifications. It has a capacity for 900 co-ed students ranging in age from kindergarten to grade 12, with a set percentage of slots reserved for children with special needs. The multinational staff are predominantly native speakers from various English-speaking countries. The school offers sports and activities such as soccer, volleyball, basketball, badminton, tennis, hockey, cooking, arts and crafts, and dance.

Al Rabeeh School

21th Street Madinat Khalifa A (Khalifa City A)
02 448 2856
www.alrabeeh.sch.ae
Map **1 F6**
Well-established junior school educating 600 co-ed students between the ages of 3 and 11. The curriculum is a varied international one, and all classes are given in English.

Abu Dhabi's family focus

Al Yasmina School

Al Dhafrah **02 501 4888**
www.alyasmina.sch.ae
Map **1 P7**
This is a large international school catering mainly to families living off the island. Al Yasmina has a capacity for 1,800 students, ranging from kindergarten to 16 years old and it follows the English National Curriculum. It will eventually offer A-levels. The school has excellent facilities and a comprehensive extra-curricular programme.

The Club Creche

Open to pre-schoolers, The Club's (p.179) very own creche is open between 08:00 and 12:30 every day. Members can attend a fitness class, sunbathe by the pool or play tennis safe in the knowledge that their children are being fully and expertly supervised.

American Community School

Off Sultan bin Zayed St, Nr BMW Showroom
Al Bateen **02 681 5115**
www.acs.sch.ae
Map **2 F5**
The American Community School serves nearly 1,000 students of many nationalities. It offers the American curriculum, although it also offers the International Baccalaureate (IB) curriculum as well. Learning is encouraged through a diverse mix of activities, and there is a full extracurricular programme available. With a kindergarten, elementary school, middle school and high school, students from 4 years to grade 12 (usually age 18) are accepted.

American International School

29th Street, Off Airport Rd Al Rehhan **02 444 4333**
www.aisa.sch.ae
Map **1 H7**
This school is one of the largest in Abu Dhabi, with over 1,000 students, from pre-school to grade 12 (typically, age 4 to 18). It was founded in 1995 and serves both expat and local children. The school offers both the American and IB curriculums. Facilities include a library, music rooms, art rooms, science labs, computer labs and a gym.

The Australian School Of Abu Dhabi

Btn Streets 32 & 40 Madinat Khalifa B (Khalifa City B)
02 586 6980
www.aia.vic.edu.au
Map **1 V12**
Open in Khalifa City A since 2007, the school caters for a full range of students from kindergarten through to year 12 (17 or 18 year olds). Its curriculum is based on Australian and International Baccalaureate

programmes, with Arabic language and Islamic classes also available to Muslim students. Sports and extracurricular activities are a major part of school life; there are football fields, a 25-metre swimming pool, a gym and basketball courts.

Brighton College Abu Dhabi

Bloom Gardens, Diplomatic Quarter Al Matar **02 441 8513**
www.brightoncollegeabudhabi.net
Map **1 J7**

New to the city in 2011, Brighton College Abu Dhabi is an offshoot of the very successful Brighton College in the UK; it follows the British Curriculum and accepts enrolment requests for children aged between 3 and 14 – classes for older students are expected to be added in 2012.

Developing The Future

The Pearl, Al Yasmina and Al Muna schools have all been developed and are being run by Aldar Academies, a recent subsidiary of the developers behind Yas Island. Aldar also plans to open its first secondary school in Al Bateen in September 2011 and says it hopes to open many more schools across the UAE capital in the years to come. Schools currently operate from the British International Curriculum and there are plans to also introduce the International Baccalaureate. See www.aldaracademies.com.

The British International School

Nr Abu Dhabi University Madinat Khalifa A (Khalifa City A) **02 510 0100**
www.bisabudhabi.com
Map **1 Q11**

The British International School offers the English National Curriculum and caters for students from 3 to 18 years of age. The impressive purpose-built site has state-of-the-art facilities for sport, technology, culture and the arts. At capacity, the school will have 2,000 students (it is currently 'growing through' to the last few year groups), but it promises small class sizes and low student-teacher ratios. The school is operated by Nord Anglia Education.

The British School Al Khubairat

Off Airport Rd Al Mushrif **02 446 2280**
www.britishschool.sch.ae
Map **2 K12**

This popular, not-for-profit school was established in 1971 and is one of the best-known schools in Abu Dhabi. It follows the British curriculum, which is taught by multinational teachers. Children aged 3 to 18 can attend the school. Facilities include an auditorium, sports pitch, libraries and a swimming pool.

The Cambridge High School

86th Street Mohammed Bin Zayed City **02 552 1621**
www.gemscis-abudhabi.com
Map **1 N12**

Another school based on the British curriculum, Cambridge High School educates children between kindergarten and year 13, guiding them through GCSEs, AS Levels and A levels. The school has playgrounds, a swimming pool, science lab, multimedia labs, music and art studios, a library and courts for various sports. Extracurricular activities play an important role in school life. It also has a fleet of school buses picking up and dropping off all over Abu Dhabi.

Canadian International School

Off 20th Street Madinat Khalifa A (Khalifa City A) **02 556 4206**
www.cisabudhabi.com
Map **1 T8**

The Canadian International School is a new school located in Madinat Khalifa A. It follows the Alberta programme of study and inquiry-based learning. All teachers are educated and certified in Canada. Boasting all-new facilities, including a new 25 metre pool, primary and secondary students are based in two different buildings on the property, with classes available for KG1 through to grade 12.

Emirates National Schools

Mohammed Bin Zayed City **800 2008**
www.ens.sch.ae
Map **2 N9**

Emirates International is a multicultural school for students from KG1 through to grade 12 (around 18 years old), offering American diploma and International Baccalaureate programmes. English is the main language, although Arabic children are offered language and culture lessons, while western children have the opportunity to learn Arabic and French. Sports and arts play important roles. There is also an Al Nahyan Campus (02 642 5993) covering KG and primary, and it has a girl's school. A primary and a girl's school are located at its other campus in Al Ain (03 761 6888).

GEMS American Academy

Najda St Al Dhafrah **02 641 6333**
www.gemsaa-abudhabi.com
Map **2 P6**

GEMS American Academy used to be located in the heart of Abu Dhabi, but as of September 2011, the school is scheduled to operate from a new location in Khalifa City A. While fees are on the expensive side, they include textbooks and supplementary materials. The school also operates a bus service for an additional cost.

The Glenelg School Of Abu Dhabi

Nr Petroleum Institute & Abu Dhabi Golf Club
Umm Al Nar **02 599 2001**
www.gsad.sch.ae
Map **1 M8**

Run by the Glenelg School of the US, this branch follows the American school curriculum. English is the main language of teaching, but both Arabic and Islam arguably play a more significant role here than at several of the other international schools. Arabic language and social studies, Islamic studies and world languages are all offered. The school caters for the full age range from KG1 to grade 12.

Homeschooling

One of the main reasons for homeschooling in the UAE is to avoid the hefty private school fees. K12 (www.k12.com/int/arabian_gulf) in Dubai's Knowledge Village offers some online courses, but schools in your home country will be able to provide you with the curriculum, materials and online testing, for a fee. For excellent additional support and organised group outings, log on to the Abu Dhabi Home Schoolers Association website (www.abudhabihomeschoolers.org), where you'll find information on membership and homeschooling resources. The Ministry of Education do offer homeschooling for all nationalities but the curriculum is only in Arabic. Many expats who have multiple children find that, whilst nurseries tend to be more affordable than in their home countries; when it comes to schooling, it makes more financial sense to return home where education is often offered by the government for no fee.

Our Own English High School

Al Salam St, Nr Harley Davidson Bldg Al Dhafrah
02 642 5990
www.gemsoo-abudhabi.com
Map **2 Q7**

Operated by global school giant GEMS, the curriculum comes from the National Council of Educational Research and Training, New Delhi. It covers the full range of age groups, and has excellent educational, artistic and sporting facilities, as well as a full extracurricular programme.

The Pearl Primary School

Btn 4th & 11th Streets, Nr New Airport Rd
Al Dhafrah **02 641 8887**
www.pearlprimary.sch.ae
Map **2 N7**

Offers studies based on the UK's Whole School Curriculum Plan. The Pearl is part of the Aldar Academies umbrella, providing classes from foundation stage (kindergarten) to Year 6 (usually aged 10 to 11). It is a fairly new school with top-class facilities that include a 25 metre swimming pool, grass playing fields, a library and a technology lab.

Raha International School *> p.147*

Al Raha Gardens, Off 3rd Street Madinat Khalifa A (Khalifa City A) **02 556 1567**
www.ris.ae
Map **1 R7**

Raha International School offers the International Baccalaureate organisation's Primary Years Programme and Middle Years Programme. Facilities include a swimming pool, a learning pool, a large sports hall, a library and an art and design studio. For those interested in sports, there are tennis courts, sports fields and recreation play areas.

Horizon Private School Nr Canadian International School, Madinat Khalifa A (Khalifa City A), 02 556 0811, *www.horizonprivateschool.com*
The International School Of Choueifat Mohd Bin Khalifa St, Al Mushrif, 02 446 1444, *www.iscad-sabis.net*

University & Higher Education

In the past, the vast majority of expat teenagers have returned to their home countries when moving from secondary to tertiary education. However, a growing number of institutions within Abu Dhabi and the other emirates now entice more people into studying in the UAE. Degrees and diplomas are now offered in the arts, sciences, business and management, and engineering and technology. Furthermore, there are a number of government projects underway to improve and expand Abu Dhabi's higher education facilities. Zayed University will be upgraded and relocated, and there will be a new University City constructed in the next couple of years. The Abu Dhabi Vocational Education and Training Institute (p.149) opened in late 2007, providing vocational training and qualifications in industry sectors such as health, law and tourism. The New York Film Academy Abu Dhabi (p.149) opened in 2008, offering both two-year and shorter term courses and workshops in acting and film making, while the Masdar Institute of Science & Technology now provides cutting-edge programmes within sustainable development.

Destination Education

With the growing number of leading education providers now based in Abu Dhabi, more and more students will find a suitable degree on offer close to home. Should you wish to broaden your options, Dubai's Knowledge Village (www.kv.ae) and Academic City (www.diacedu.ae) both offer a number of other options for further study. Knowledge Village groups a number of leading international universities and colleges together in the same area and encourages students and faculty members to interact, creating a unique learning environment. In addition, it provides access to student housing and a number of other useful services.

Current academic options include American University in the Emirates (www.aue.ae), Birla Institute of Technology and Science (www.bitsdubai.com), Cambridge College International Dubai (www.cambridgecollegeinternational.nsw.edu.au), Esmod Dubai French Fashion University (www.french-fashion-university.com), Heriot-Watt University Dubai (www.hw.ac.uk/dubai), Mahatma Gandhi University (www.mgudxboc.com), Manchester Business School (www.dubai.mbs.ac.uk), The British University in Dubai (www.buid.ac.ae), University of Wollongong in Dubai (www.uowdubai.ac.ae), European University College Brussels, Royal College of Surgeons in Ireland (www.rcsileadership.org) and the Canadian University of Dubai (www.cud.ac.ae).

Some universities, including several of the ones listed above, offer students the opportunity to study part-time, or via e-learning. International correspondence courses are also available. The UK-based Open University (www.open.ac.uk) is popular, as is the South African-based UNISA (University of South Africa). UNISA recently opened an office in Dubai (www.unisa.ac.za). Gulf News' classifieds section carries adverts for the numerous other study options for short courses.

Abu Dhabi University

Khalifa St Madinat Khalifa A (Khalifa City A) **800 23968**
www.adu.ac.ae
Map **1 Q11**

The Abu Dhabi University has campuses in both Abu Dhabi and Al Ain. Any student, regardless of nationality, is encouraged to apply. Its courses include business administration, computer science and information technology, and education. Contact the admissions office for more information.

Abu Dhabi Vocational Education & Training Institute

Nr Al Maqta Park Al Maqtaa **800 8600**
www.veti.ac.ae
Map **1 M8**

Abu Dhabi Vocational Education and Training Institute (VETI) opened at the start of the 2008/2009 academic year. It provides vocational diplomas in areas such as information technology, fashion design, finance, hotel management, property development, paralegal studies and graphic design. Facilities include smart board technology, Wi-Fi and a sports hall. Other campuses are located in Al Ain (800 8100) and Al Gharbia (800 8450).

Centre Of Excellence For Applied Research & Training

CERT Technology Park Al Nahyan **02 404 8501**
www.certonline.com
Map **2 N12**

This establishment offers courses in a variety of fields, including engineering, business and health sciences, some of which are through online tuition. Specialised courses such as advanced diplomas in professional training, business English, food inspection and highway maintenance, and the University of Strathclyde MBA, are also available.

Emirates College Of Technology

Millennium Tower, Sheikh Hamdan St Markaziya East **02 626 6010**
www.ectuae.com
Map **2 N2**

There are two locations in Abu Dhabi, its male-only campus on Hamdan Street and a campus for women (02 642 0420) on Defence Street. Emirates College of Technology offers diplomas in business administration and computer information systems, HR management, e-commerce and marketing, banking and finance, accounting, computer design and animation, and mass communication and Public Relations.

European International College

5th Street Al Matar **02 449 1450**
www.eic.ac.ae
Map **1 J7**

An institution which is focused on hotel management and tourism – however, several courses are on offer under this umbrella including a bachelor's degree in hospitality. The college is affiliated with prestigious western hospitality institutions, and offers a full and diverse student experience.

Masdar Institute of Science & Technology

Nr Abu Dhabi Airport, Masdar City **02 810 9333**
www.masdar.ac.ae
Map **1 U7**

Open since 2009, Masdar Institute of Science & Technology provides cutting-edge education and research into renewable energy solutions, advanced technologies and sustainable development. The 2009 intake consisted of 88 graduate students and by 2010, the institute had 170 students. Eight two-year long, graduate level degrees are currently on offer.

New York Film Academy Abu Dhabi

Muroor Rd Al Nahyan **02 446 6442**
www.abudhabifilmschool.com
Map **2 M9**

A joint venture from ADACH (see p.207) and the New York Film Academy, this film school offers full-time and part-time courses in everything from on-camera acting to documentary and feature filmmaking. The courses cover a broad range of necessary disciplines, including writing, directing, editing and cinematography; which should be perfect for any budding Spielbergs.

New York Institute Of Technology

Centre Of Excellence For Applied Research & Training Al Nahyan **02 404 8523**
www.nyit.edu
Map **2 N12**

This is the Abu Dhabi branch of this well-known higher education institute. Principal academic offerings are in architecture and design, the arts, science, engineering, and computer science. Students also have the chance to spend time studying at one of its other locations which include Canada, China, Jordan and, of course, Manhattan.

Education UK Exhibition

Organised annually by the British Council, the Education UK exhibition is part of an initiative to enhance educational relations between the UK and the UAE. Students from across the UAE can attend the event in order to gather information on British universities, whether they have campuses here in the UAE or in the UK. The 2010 event was held in January and took place in both Abu Dhabi and Dubai. Check www.britishcouncil.org for details of future events.

New York University Abu Dhabi

Off Al Nasr St, Nr ADIA Tower Markaziya West **02 628 4000**
www.nyuad.nyu.edu
Map **2 L3**

The relatively new branch of this well-regarded American institution is primarily a research university, with a liberal arts and science college. Undergraduate education here is based on a vast and varied curriculum which results in full NYU degrees. Appealing to international students, the university is looking to give students the full, traditional college experience, including an exceptional extracurricular and sporting proramme.

Paris-Sorbonne University Abu Dhabi

Shk Rashid Bin Saeed Al Maktoum St Al Reem Island **02 656 9555**
www.sorbonne.ae
Map **1 G4**

The legendary Sorbonne arrived in Abu Dhabi in 2006. Having grown from 100 students to 600 over the first five years in the emirate, the university is based in a cutting-edge educational campus on Al Reem, offering top facilities and teaching for undergraduate and masters degrees in law, business, languages, philosophy, history of art and more. New masters' programmes for the academic year starting in October 2011 include human resource management, performing arts management, tourism, banking and finance, and multimedia publishing.

The Petroleum Institute

Airport Rd Al Maqtaa **02 607 5100**
www.pi.ac.ae
Map **1 M8**

This institute is dedicated to education and research in areas significant to the engineering, geoscience and general oil and gas industries. The institute is supported by many of the world's biggest oil-producing companies. There's a wide portfolio of undergraduate and graduate programmes available.

Zayed University

Nr Defence & 4th Street Al Nahyan **02 599 3111**
www.zu.ac.ae
Map **2 M9**

This is a massive university complex with separate colleges offering arts, science, business science, communication & media, education studies, languages and information technology. Postgraduate study is also offered here and students can enroll for a master's degree and a range of business and management courses.

Special Needs Education

The available support for children with special needs is increasing by the year in Abu Dhabi. Some of the establishments based in the city are listed below; turn to p.154 for more information.

Abu Dhabi Autism Center

Nr Al Mafraq Hospital Mafraq **02 582 1621**
Map **1 T13**

Largest centre of its kind in the UAE, the non-profit organisation helps autistic children and their families. It deals with the medical side of the condition in terms of diagnosis, therapy, psychiatry and neurology, while also working on a holistic approach to increasing children's comfort and social interaction.

Al Noor Speech, Hearing & Development Centre

Nr Fatima Bin Mubarak School Al Zahra **02 449 3844**
Map **1 H6**

Run partially as a charity, this centre takes in young students who cannot afford to go to other centres in the UAE. Students of all ages and all types of disabilities are accepted, with the centre providing both formal and informal education, as well as vocational training. The aim is for students to become fully self-dependent.

British Institute For Learning Development > *p.128*

22nd Street Madinat Khalifa A (Khalifa City A)
02 556 6078
www.british-ild.com
Map **1 S8**

Specialist school for children with sensory deprivation and learning difficulties. Run by British experts and supported by St Andrew's College International, the school takes a thorough approach encompassing speech therapy, educational psychology, reading development, play therapy, therapeutic listening and an 'astronaut programme' which aims to increase learning capacity and intelligence.

Future Centre For Special Needs

Villa 250, Baynunah St Al Bateen **02 666 9625**
www.future-centre.com
Map **2 E6**

A non-profit institution for youths between the ages of 3 and 20. Classes cater to those with ADHD and behavioural disorders, Down's syndrome, cerebral palsy and traumatic brain injury; there's also an autism unit. The combination of education, therapy and care enables specialised and holistic services to be offered to children and young adults with complex needs, degenerative conditions and additional sensory impairments, while also supporting their families.

Teaching English

If you're interested in a career move, would like to expand your skill set or are just looking to earn a little extra cash on the side, you might like to consider a TEFL (Teaching English as a Foreign Language) or TESOL (Teaching English to Speakers of Other Languages) course. Abu Dhabi Men's College (www.admc.hct.ac.ae) offers courses, as do the British Council (www.britishcouncil.org/me) and Abu Dhabi Higher Colleges of Technology (www.hct.ac.ae). If you can't find anything to suit in Abu Dhabi, plenty of institutions within Dubai's Knowledge Village (www.kv.ae) also offer courses. The four-week courses cost around Dhs.9,000.

Language Courses

The Mother Tongue Arabic Language Center

Bin Fardan Bldg, Zayed the First St Al Khalidiyah
02 639 3838
www.mothertongue.ae
Map **2 G4**

A centre that specialises in teaching Arabic to non-Arabic speakers at levels from absolute beginner to advanced. The highly-acclaimed courses typically run for around 12 weeks with three classroom hours per week at a cost of Dhs.1,800 per course. Both the facilities and teachers are of excellent quality.

Alliance Francaise Choithram Bldg, Al Khalidiyah, 02 666 6232, *www.af-abudhabi.net*
American Language Center Shk Hamdan Bin Mohd St, Nr Hamdan Centre, 02 627 2779, *www.alcuae.com*
Berlitz Bin Haiyai Bldg, Sheikh Zayed First St, Al Khalidiyah, 02 667 2287, *www.berlitz.ae*
British Council Al Nasr St, Al Khalidiyah, 02 691 0600, *www.britishcouncil.org/me*
Circolo Italiano 02 643 9626, *www.cicer-abudhabi.com*
ELS Language Centers > *p.153* Villa 9, Al Najda St, Nr Dar Al Shifa Hospital, Al Dhafrah, 02 642 6640, *www.elsmea.com*
Goethe-Institut Gulf Region Electra St 2nd St, Tourist Club Area, 02 672 7920, *www.goethe.de*
International English Institute For Language Studies Defence Rd, Al Nahyan, 02 642 2407

Libraries

The National Library, established in 1981, carries over 300,00 titles in Arabic and around 100,000 in foreign languages. A separate children's library was established in 1996, with 15,000 kids' volumes available, predominantly in Arabic, French and English. In addition, several private establishments and associations run libraries at their facilities.

Alliance Francaise Choithram Bldg, Al Khalidiyah, 02 666 6232, *www.af-aboudabi.net*
The Club > *p.297* Al Meena, 02 673 1111, *www.the-club.com*
Daly Community Library St Andrew's Church Abu Dhabi, Al Mushrif, 02 446 4752, *www.standrewauh.org*
National Library 02 621 5300, *www.adach.ae*

Learning Arabic

Special Needs & Learning Support

The UAE boasts an excellent private school system for expats; however, it is sometimes more difficult to find quality education for children with special needs.

If your child has physical or learning difficulties, there are several organisations that can help. In 2009, it was announced by the Ministry of Education that private schools in the UAE would be required, by law, to provide adequate facilities for children with special needs. While it remains to be seen when or how this ruling will be implemented in full, recognising that less able children deserve the same quality of education as other children can surely be seen as a positive step, and one which is long overdue.

There are schools that seem to be leading the way in terms of opening doors to children with special needs. The American Community School in Sharjah boasts a state-of-the-art campus and actively addresses the needs of students with various learning difficulties. Certain other private schools in Dubai and Abu Dhabi will offer places to children with mild dyslexia or Down's syndrome.

Dr Lesley P Stagg, principal of Greenfield Community School, believes that as long as the school is able to meet the specific needs of a particular child in terms of facilities, curriculum and staffing, then there is no reason to turn away a child with special needs. 'We assess each case individually, and our main decider is whether the child will benefit from being educated at our school,' says Dr Stagg. 'In terms of special facilities and services, we offer in-class and withdrawal support, we have a therapy room where visiting therapists can work with students with special needs, and we request parents to employ personal assistants ('shadows') in cases where this helps the child remain focused in the classroom.'

Delice Scotto, principal at the Al Mizhar American Academy for Girls, implements a similarly broad-minded approach. 'All children who require learning support work in small groups and individually with learning support teachers according to Individualised Education Plans (IEPs),' she explains. 'With these support systems in place, learning support students at our school can be successfully integrated into mainstream school activities. 'Students are assessed at the admissions stage, and undergo a psycho-educational evaluation,' continues Scotto. 'Out of this assessment come recommendations that serve as a basis for that child's IEP, and as long as that child's needs are able to be met by our learning support department, they will be offered a place.'

There are currently three full-time learning support teachers at the Academy, all of who have master's degrees in special education from the United States, as well as extensive experience in dealing with students with a variety of special needs, from dyslexia and ADHD to emotional disabilities and the Autism spectrum. At Greenfield Community School, there is a similarly progressive approach to ensuring staff can meet the needs of all children: 'several of our teachers have specialist training in all aspects of special educational needs, including gifted and talented children, and we offer ongoing professional development to raise skills further,' says Dr Stagg.

Dubai Dyslexia Support Group, a non-profit support group that holds regular meetings for families affected by dyslexia, are also a great resource outside of the schooling system. The group is run by Anita Singhal, who

is well aware of the difficulties facing such families here: 'not all schools offer support,' she says. 'The main problem is finding a school with a learning support unit or specialist help, and unfortunately, awareness is lacking in many schools.'

However, it's not all bad news – according to Singhal, nearly all dyslexic children, bar those with severe dyslexia, can integrate fully into mainstream education with the correct support. And parents have a huge role to play in helping their children overcome learning challenges. 'One of the key things a parent can do is to develop a dyslexic child's self esteem,' says Singhal. 'Never compare them with other siblings or their peers, and encourage their strengths rather than focusing on weaknesses'.

Unfortunately, the picture is not so bright for children with more severe learning difficulties or special needs. While in an ideal world it may be desirable for these children to attend 'normal' schools, the truth is that the majority of private schools in the UAE do not have sufficient facilities or support to cope with severe disabilities or meet the special needs of some children. While this may result in, for example, a child with a physical disability not being able to attend a mainstream school despite not having any cognitive impairment, some parents feel that there is little point pushing the issue.

Children with Down's syndrome are among those who find inclusion in mainstream schools a challenge. Although more and more schools are opening their doors to children with Down's syndrome, there are still many schools and nurseries that refuse to allocate places to these children, according to Ingeborg Kroese, co-ordinator 0-5 years, All 4 Down Syndrome Support Group. 'Even those children with Down's Syndrome who are in mainstream schools require part-time or full-time learning support assistants who help them access the curriculum,' she says. 'These learning support assistants are funded by the parents, and so financial constraints are a very real problem.' One of the key mandates of the All 4 Down Syndrome group is to encourage early intervention activities (physiotherapy, speech and language therapy and occupational therapy), which can stimulate development of children with Down's syndrome under the age of 5. The group also holds regular talks with Dubai's Knowledge and Human Development Authority (KHDA) to discuss ways to increase inclusion of less able children in mainstream education organisations.

Organisations such as the British Institute for Learning Development aim to bridge a gap between private schools that may lack adequate facilities and more extreme solutions in the form of centres for children with severe disabilities. Although it focuses more on learning support and sensory therapy than on helping children with physical disabilities, the institute seeks to address children's learning and behavioural problems through occupational therapy and neuro-developmental therapy (Sensory Integration). Students are supported through work with speech therapists, psychologists and specially qualified teachers. With this approach, Dr Chris Reynolds, who established the institute in 2002, believes that both 'slow learners' and 'gifted learners' can make great progress.

See the list of Special Needs schools and groups on p.150.

Health, Fitness & Well-Being

HEALTH

Both private and public healthcare services are available in the UAE. General standards are very high, with English-speaking and internationally trained medical staff in most facilities but, as in most countries, private healthcare is seen as preferable as you are much more likely to experience shorter waiting times and generally more comfortable inpatient facilities.

Under UAE Labour Law, an employer must provide access to healthcare for all of its employees. This can take one of two forms: either the employer pays for a private medical insurance policy, or it pays contributions towards government healthcare and covers the costs of obtaining a health card for each employee (p.158).

Government Healthcare

The Health Authority of Abu Dhabi (www.haac.ae) runs the following hospitals through its healthcare services company SEHA (www.seha.ae): Al Mafraq, Sheikh Khalifa Medical City, Corniche and Al Rahba. In Al Ain, SEHA also operates Al Ain Hopsital and Tawam Hospital. In the Western Region, SEHA is responsible for the Al Gharbia Hospitals umbrella, which covers smaller primary healthcare providers, such as those in Madinat Zayed, Ghiathy, Marfa, Al Sila, Delma and Liwa.

With the exception of emergency care, which is available for free unless you require any follow-up treatment, you will need a health card to access government health services (see below). In order to see a doctor, you will need to present your health card and a form of ID (ID card, labour card, driving licence or passport) and will be charged a nominal fee (usually Dhs.50) for a consultation. Additional charges may apply for further tests, treatment and medication.

Health Card

Employers in Abu Dhabi must pay for health cover for all of their employees. An employer can decide whether to provide health cards for its staff or pay for a private insurance policy. If your employer provides you with a health card, you are entitled to subsidised healthcare at government-run hospitals and clinics.

The health card must be renewed each year, but you only need to take a new medical test when your residence visa is due for renewal.

Your employer should start the process for you, by telling you which of the city's three Disease Prevention and Screening Centres to go to (there are two more in Al Ain and the Western Region).

The process requires you to complete blood tests and a chest x-ray for prevention of communicable diseases; see Becoming A Resident, p.32 for details of the process.

Accidents & Emergencies

Sheikh Khalifa Medical City (p.166) and off-island Al Rahba Hospital (p.161) have the best equipped accident and emergency (A&E) departments in Abu Dhabi, although Al Mafraq (p.161) and Al Noor Hospitals (p.161) also have good, general A&E departments. Part of Sheikh Khalifa Medical City, the Khalidiyah Urgent Care Center (p.165) in the heart of the city treats minor emergencies, such as abdominal pains, cold and flu, minor bone breaks, ear, nose and throat issues, asthma attacks, rashes, vomiting and diarrhoea.

In Al Ain, Al Ain Hospital (p.161) deals with general accidents and emergencies, while Tawam Hospital (p.168) specialises in emergency trauma cases. The A&E departments at both these hospitals are very efficiently managed and, even if you have a relatively minor injury, you rarely have to wait very long to see a doctor.

While finding a place to get emergency treatment is easy, getting there can be more problematic as Abu Dhabi's paramedic services have only just started to develop. Abu Dhabi Police receives all 999 calls, although you can dial 998 to be put straight through to ambulance services. An ambulance will be dispatched to take the patient to the relevant hospital depending on the type of medical emergency. Private medical firms, such as NMC (www.nmc.ae, 02 633 2255), also run fleets of ambulances, although be warned that you'll need to subscribe to the services or pay for one-off use.

General Medical Care

For general non-emergency medical care, there are a few different options available. Most hospitals have a walk-in clinic where you can simply turn up, present your health or insurance card, register and queue to see a general practitioner. It's common to be seen by a triage nurse who will take down the details of your medical history and ailment before you see a doctor. These departments usually operate on a first-come-first-served basis, so waiting times can vary dramatically. Early evening, at the end of the working day, is generally a busy time and best avoided, if possible. It's advisable to call the hospital prior to visiting to make sure that they operate a walk-in service and to check opening times. If you are on a private healthcare plan, make sure in advance that the hospital is on your insurer's network.

Most hospitals and smaller clinics offer family medicine as part of their outpatient services. You can usually call to make an appointment, but there's no guarantee that you'll get an appointment on the same day. If your usual family medicine department has no available appointments but you need immediate non-emergency medical care, they may admit you through the A&E department, but they will advise you of this when you call.

Finding A General Practitioner

While some people prefer the convenience of walk-in clinics, others would prefer to register with a practice where they are familiar with the administrative procedures and they can see the same doctor on return visits. There are a number of clinics in Abu Dhabi which offer general practice and family medicine, and it's worth asking friends and colleagues for recommendations. Most areas of the city have a local medical centre, so if proximity to your home or place of work is important, you should be able to find something nearby.

Stay Calm, Act Fast

In the event that you're faced with a medical emergency, try to stay calm, call for an ambulance and, while waiting, follow these instructions:

- Clear a path to the patient – move furniture and unlock doors.
- If possible, have someone waiting to meet the ambulance, especially if your villa or apartment number is not clearly visible from the street.
- Do not move the patient unless their life is threatened by external factors, such as fire, falling debris or electricity.
- Be prepared to answer the following questions related to the patient's condition: are they conscious; are they breathing; are they bleeding?

Al Aahed Medical Centre Suhail Salam Al Khaily Bldg, Hilton Rd, Al Ain, 03 764 2791
Al Dhahery Clinic Saeed Hillal Abdulla Al Kuwaiti Bldg, Main St, Al Ain, 03 765 6882
Dawn Medical Centre Sheikh Hamdan Bin Mohammed St, 02 621 6900
Dr McCulloch Clinic Al Noor Hospital, Markaziya East, 02 626 2677, *www.dr-mcculloch.com*
Family Medical Clinic Al Ain Hospital, Al Ain, 03 763 5200, *www.alain-hospital.com*
Gulf Diagnostic Center Hospital Al Khaleej Al Arabi St, Al Bateen, 02 665 8090, *www.gdc-hospital.com*
Hamdan Medical Centre Khaleej Pharmacy Bld, Hilton St, Al Ain, 03 765 4797
Ibn Sina Medical Centre Shk Zayed The Second St, Al Khalidiyah, 02 681 6400, *www.ibnsinauae.com*
New Al Ain Medical Clinic 225 Main St, Mina Bazaar, Al Ain, 03 764 1448
Swedish Medical Centre Khalidiya St, Al Bateen, 02 681 1122

Private Healthcare

Private healthcare facilities in Abu Dhabi are expanding dramatically and standards are very high. Many employers opt to provide their staff with private insurance policies which gives access to a network of private hospitals and clinics. Waiting times are generally shorter in private clinics.

If you have private health insurance, it's worth checking what you are entitled to as levels of cover vary depending on the policy. Dental care, maternity and screening tests aren't usually covered as standard, and you may need to have been on the policy for a year before you can receive maternity cover. Before making an appointment to see a healthcare professional, always check whether the clinic or hospital is part of your insurer's network to avoid being landed with the full costs yourself. Your insurer will also provide details about its payment policy; some companies offer direct billing, which means the insurer pays the hospital or clinic directly and you only pay a nominal fee each time you access medical services, while others require you to pay the cost of the consultation, treatment and medication upfront and then file a claim to the insurer.

If your employer is paying for your medical insurance, your employment contract will state whether your spouse and dependants are included in the policy. If you plan to cover the cost of insuring your family yourself, you may need to purchase a separate policy for them as it's not always possible to extend existing policies.

Medical Insurance Companies

Abu Dhabi National Insurance Company ADNIC Bldg, Sheikh Khalifa Bin Zayed St, Markaziya East, 02 408 0100, *www.adnic.ae*
Alliance Insurance Ghanam Al Mazroui Bldg, Madinat Zayed, 02 632 6067, *www.alliance-uae.com*
Allianz Risk Transfer AG Dubai International Financial Centre (DIFC), Dubai, 04 702 6666, *www.allianz.com*
AXA Insurance (Gulf) > *p.65* Delma St, Al Nahyan, 02 495 7999, *www.axa-gulf.com*

Quick & Easy **Stuart Griffiths,** British expat, 61

I've been living in the UAE for over 20 years, and have visited doctors and specialists on a number of occasions and noticed big improvements in recent years. There are some good doctors and clinics, and some that are not so good. It's really down to trial and error to find one you like, as different doctors and practices suit different people. You can get access to health professionals very quickly and easily, and you'll find getting tests done and results back is a much quicker process in the UAE than some other countries; in the UK, for example, it can take a long time, but here you can often walk in off the street and have tests done straight away, with the results back in a day or two. Seeing a specialist is also easier.

BUPA International Khalid Al-Attar Towers, Sheikh Zayed Rd, Dubai, 04 331 8688, *www.bupa-intl.com*
Daman National Health Insurance Company Millennium Tower, Nr Hamdan Centre, Shk Hamdan Bin Mohd St, Markaziya East, 02 614 9555, *www.damanhealth.ae*
Gargash Insurance Al Yasat Tower, Nr Raha Hospital, Bani Yas St, Al Raha, 02 671 7100, *www.gargashinsurance.com*
Greenshield Insurance Al Musalla Towers, Khalid Bin Al Waleed Rd, Dubai, 04 397 4464, *www.greenshield.ae*
Lifecare International Khalid Al-Attar Towers, Sheikh Zayed Rd, Dubai, 04 331 8688, *www.lifecareinternational.com*
MedNet UAE Dubai Internet City, Dubai, 04 390 0710, *www.mednet-uae.com*
MetLife Alico Dubai International Financial Centre (DIFC), Dubai, 04 360 0555, *www.metlifealico.ae*
Nasco Karaoglan Al Muroor, 02 642 2255, *www.nascodubai.com*
National General Insurance Al Sahel Tower, Old Passport Rd, Al Khalidiyah, 02 667 8783, *www.ngi.ae*
Nextcare UAE Business Avenue Bldg, Sheikh Rashid Rd, Dubai, 04 605 6800, *www.nextcare.ae*
Oman Insurance Blue Tower, Shk Khalifa Bin Zayed St, Markaziya East, 02 612 8444, *www.tameen.ae*
RSA Abu Dhabi Habib Bank Bldg, Sheikh Hamdan Bin Mohammed St, Markaziya East, 02 635 1800, *www.rsagroup.ae*

Your History

It's worth requesting a copy of your medical history from your doctor in your home country and giving it to your new clinic to ensure your medical background is taken into consideration when you seek medical advice. Most insurance policies don't cover holiday vaccinations, so if you plan to travel beyond the UAE, you can save yourself a lot of money and needles if you have a record of which jabs you've already had.

Pharmacies & Medication

The UAE has a more relaxed policy on prescription drugs than many other countries and most can be bought over the counter. If you know what you need, it cuts out the hassle of having to see a doctor just so that you can get a prescription. Pharmacists are willing to offer advice, but bear in mind that they don't know your medical history. Always tell the pharmacist if you have any pre-existing conditions and allergies or are taking other medications, and make sure that you understand the administration instructions in case these aren't available in English.

You might find it frustrating that certain common medications from your home country are not available here (such as Gaviscon for infants and Pepto Bismol); you can however bring these into the country for your own personal use and often you can find a locally available equivalent. You may find that there are similar products (such as Infacol instead of infant Gaviscon) so it is worth taking the medications to the pharmacy and asking if they have something that does the same thing.

There are pharmacies all over the city and a number are open 24 hours a day, such as Urban Pharmacy (02 445 8584), Lifeline (02 633 2255), Al Noor (02 613 9101) and Al Ain Pharmacy (03 765 5120). Supermarkets and petrol station convenience stores sell basic medications and first aid equipment. It's worth checking if your local pharmacy offers deliveries as this is often an unadvertised service. Deliveries can be handy if you need regular medication, such as blood pressure medication or diabetic supplies, and can be useful for those days when you wake up feeling too poorly to get out of bed. There is not normally a delivery charge but be sure to tip the driver.

Prohibited Medications

Certain medications do require a prescription, and some medications (such as codeine, Diazepam and temazepam) are banned in the UAE, even though they are widely available in other countries. It's a crime to have these medicines in your possession, unless you can produce an official prescription from your doctor in your home country, but even then you might end up at the police station while it is translated into Arabic. Unless it is absolutely necessary and there's no locally available alternative, it's best to avoid medications that are banned in the UAE. The list of banned drugs changes regularly, so it's best to check with the Registration & Drug Control Department at the Ministry of Health (www.moh.gov.ae) before travelling with any medication.

Main Hospitals

In general, both private and government hospitals deliver high standards of care in Abu Dhabi. Most hospitals offer a comprehensive range of inpatient and outpatient facilities, so if you like a particular hospital but need to see a specific specialist, the chances are the hospital will be able to cater to your needs. Once you have registered with one hospital it is easier to return there for further treatment.

For very specialist treatment, you'll be referred to somewhere else in the city. Many of the services offered in hospitals are also offered in clinics and small practices, so if you have a hospital phobia, then this might be a better option for non-emergency treatment. See Specialist Clinics & Practitioners, p.168.

It is worth having a look around the main hospitals before deciding which one suits you – especially if you are intending to have a baby in Abu Dhabi. For more information on having a baby in Abu Dhabi, see p.131.

Ahalia Hospital

Nr Liwa Centre, Sheikh Hamdan Bin Mohammed St Markaziya East **02 626 2666**
www.ahaliagroup.com
Map **2 M3**

The flagship facility of the large Ahalia private medical care group, the Ahalia Hospital is a state-of-the-art facility and has 24 hour casualty and ambulance services, along with specialists in cardiology, homeopathy, neurology, radiology and many other medical disciplines. The Ahalia Group specialises in corporate services and provides medical care to the staff of a large number of Abu Dhabi companies.

Al Ain Hospital

Sheika Bood Ibn Sultan St Al Ain **03 763 5888**
www.alain-hospital.ae
Map **4 D2**

One of the two major government-run hospitals in the city of Al Ain (the other being Tawam Hospital), the Al Ain Hospital has 30 different departments, including cardiology, orthopaedics, paediatrics, urology and ENT. This 412 bed hospital offers specialist and general surgery, although its main focus is on emergency and acute care.

Al Mafraq Hospital

Sheikh Rashid Bin Saeed Al Maktoum Rd, Al Mafraq Airport Area **02 582 3100**
www.haad.ae
Map **1 T13**

One of the UAE's biggest and busiest hospitals, the Al Mafraq government hospital is located some 35 kilometres from the city centre. It has more than 500 beds, a broad 36 clinical and non-clinical departments, as well as a whole host of tertiary medical facilities. In the UAE, Al Mafraq is best known for its expertise in complex surgery, its advanced ophthalmology department, the specialist burns unit and the specialist paediatrics department. It also has a well-equipped emergency department. Al Mafraq hospital is the closest hospital option for residents of Raha Gardens, Khalifa City A and B.

Al Noor Hospital

Sheikh Khalifa Bin Zayed St Markaziya East **02 626 5265**
www.alnoorhospital.com
Map **2 N3**

One of Abu Dhabi's best known private hospitals, with a number of off-shoot branches in Al Ain, Beda Zayed and Mussafah, Al Noor has excellent emergency medical facilities, as well as specialists in cardiology, gynaecology, paediatrics, dermatology, dental and more. There are even departments dealing with slightly less traditional treatments, such as the Chinese medicine clinic, a Lasik centre and a sleep laboratory.

Round-the-clock healthcare

Visiting doctors can treat anything from sports injuries and spinal problems to vascular diseases and rheumatology. Another branch is located on Airport Road (02 444 6655); working in conjunction with the Al Markaziya branch, this purpose-built hospital offers a wide range of medical services including the first private renal dialysis unit in Abu Dhabi.

Al Raha Hospital

Hyper Market Bldg, Bani Yas St Madinat Zayed **02 633 0440**
www.alrahahospital.com
Map **2 P4**

A private general hospital in the centre of the island, which has grown consistently over the past decade or so, Al Raha has excellent, state-of-the-art facilities covering urology, gynaecology, ENT, dentistry, internal medicine, paediatrics, anaesthesia, radiology and pathology disciplines.

Al Rahba Hospital

Abu Dhabi-Dubai Rd Al Rahba **02 506 4101**
www.alrahba.ae
Map **3 D2**

Another of Abu Dhabi's principal government hospitals, Al Rahba is located just off the island on the Abu Dhabi-Dubai highway. A 163 bed hospital, it has an extensive set of outpatient departments that include dermatology, diabetic education, dialysis, ENT, endocrinology, nephrology, neurosurgery, obstetrics and gynaecology. The hospital runs a number of specialist programmes, covering areas such as back pain, smoking cessation, travel preparation and women's health initiatives. Al Rahba also has a neonatal intensive care unit.

To Your Health

While you're likely to enjoy a generous slice of the good life in Abu Dhabi, all-you-can-eat brunches and the party lifestyle will eventually take their toll. Living in hot, dry, dusty conditions can also have an effect on your well-being. Here are some of the common health complaints you should be aware of.

Piling On The Pounds

While many people in Abu Dhabi spend the greater portion of their time in outdoor pursuits during the winter months, the heat of the summer means that, for four months of the year, it's easy to fall into lazy ways. In general, people have a more sedentary lifestyle here, and the city's car culture, all-you-can-eat-and-drink brunches and fastfood outlets at every turn see many new expats gaining a few extra pounds. Fortunately, there are a number of weight loss groups and nutritionists on hand to help (p.176), as well as ample fitness centres and gyms (p.178) and opportunities to take part in sports (see Activity Finder, p.272) to keep you active and help shift the extra weight.

Diabetes

Obesity is also a major contributing factor to the UAE's high incidence of diabetes. Recent figures from the Imperial College London Diabetes Centre in Abu Dhabi (www.icldc.ae) show that nearly 20% of the UAE's population suffer from diabetes, with the majority of them being Type 2, a preventable form of diabetes which is strongly linked to lifestyle and eating habits. The government is aggressively promoting awareness campaigns headed by organisations, such as the Imperial College London Diabetes Centre in Abu Dhabi itself, to educate the population about preventive measures, healthy eating and the benefits of an active lifestyle. If you suffer from diabetes or think you may be at risk, you can speak to your doctor or contact a specialist diabetes clinic. There are also a number of nutritionists who can help you manage Type 2 diabetes through diet (see Nutritionists & Slimming, p.176).

New Germs

The UAE is a transitory place and, with so many people coming and going and bringing new germs with them, you may find that bugs and colds are more common. With the stresses involved in moving to a new place, you may also find that your immune system is impaired for a while and you are not as resilient to germs as you normally are. Generally speaking though, if you maintain an active lifestyle and a good diet, your immune system will fight off any unwanted allergies before you even know about it. It's worth keeping a closer eye on your kids and if any strange symptoms appear, a trip to the doctors is best, even if it's just to put your mind at rest.

Sun Safety

It goes without saying that extra sun care needs to be taken when out and about in the UAE. The hot sun and high temperatures are recipes for sunburn and heat stroke if you are not prepared. Sun block is widely available in supermarkets and pharmacies. Sun hats, light, loose clothing that covers your limbs, sunglasses and seeking shade are recommended when out and about in the hotter parts of the day and during the summer months. With high temperatures throughout the year, you should also ensure that you drink enough water to remain hydrated; this is particularly important when you exercise and during the summer months. It's wise to keep a couple of bottles of water in the car in case of emergencies. If you have a breakdown in busy traffic during the summer, you may be faced with an uncomfortable wait while the police or recovery truck comes to the rescue. You should also be aware of any changes to your skin, such as new moles or ones that change shape, colour or bleed. Contact your doctor or a dermatologist if you have any concerns.

Other Ailments

If you suffer from asthma, you may find that the dusty outdoor environment and the dry, air-conditioned indoors aggravate your symptoms and you may need to rely on your inhaler more often than you would at home. A number of medical practices offer asthma clinics, including NMC (www.nmc.ae). Sinusitis can also be triggered by the dust, although this is more common among people who have lived in the city for a number of years. Ear, nose and throat (ENT) specialists can advise the best course of treatment and arrange surgery if necessary (see Specialist Clinics, p.168). The average working week in the UAE is longer than in many other countries. Spending longer hours in the office can take its toll on your body, making you more susceptible to bugs and colds; it can also make you prone to suffering from stress injuries such as repetitive strain syndrome.

Mosquito Prevention

Finally, while the WHO declared the UAE malaria-free in 2007, mosquitoes are common at the beginning and end of winter, particularly around the water, and the perfect alfresco evening can be ruined by bites from these tiny critters. Mild mosquito-repellant sprays and lotions are usually effective enough to keep the mozzies at bay, so you shouldn't need to resort to DEET-based or tropical strength products. If you prefer natural remedies, citronella oil is reportedly an effective mosquito-repellant and is available in health food stores (p.321). To save yourself from being bitten while you sleep, plug-in mosquito repellers are available from most supermarkets (p.330) and pharmacies (p.160).

Al Reef International Hospital

Emirates General Market Bldg, Sheikh Zayed The First St Madinat Zayed **02 632 8000**
Map **2 P4**
A recently renovated, mid-sized, private hospital offering general surgery, paediatrics, neonatology, endoscopic surgery, dermatology, radiology and imaging, gynaecology and obstetrics. It has emergency services, as well as inpatient and outpatient facilities.

Al Salama Hospital

Sheikh Hamdan Bin Mohammed St
Tourist Club Area **02 671 1220**
www.alsalamahospital.com
Map **2 R3**
With more than 30 years of experience, this private hospital is located in the Tourist Club Area and provides inpatient and outpatient treatments in obstetrics, infertility, cardiology, neurosurgery, pathology, sports medicine and physical therapy.

Behavioral Sciences Pavilion

Sheikh Khalifa Medical City Al Dhafrah **02 610 4962**
www.skmc.gov.ae
Map **2 K7**
This government-run specialist psychiatric hospital, located within Sheikh Khalifa Medical City, provides across-the-board psychiatric diagnosis, treatment and support for adults, adolescents and children.

Corniche Hospital

Nr Corniche Rd Markaziya East **02 672 4900**
Map **2 Q2**
The government-owned Corniche Hospital is a purpose-built obstetrics and gynaecology facility that is also home to the largest maternity department in the city, boasting 253 beds,14 birthing rooms, 174 cots and 50 neonatal intensive care cots. The hospital is run by the renowned Johns Hopkins Medicine group.

Dar Al Shifaa Hospital

Bani Yas St Al Dhafrah **02 641 6999**
www.daralshifaa.net
Map **2 P7**
The extensive facilities at this private hospital include: emergency, neonatal intensive care, paediatric and neonatology, obstetrics and gynaecology, maternity and delivery, ENT, urology and lithotripsy, dermatology, internal medicine, cardiology, and physical medicine and rehabilitation.

Delma Island Hospital

Delma Island, Western Region
02 878 1888
Map **3 A2**
Small government facility providing emergency services, internal medicine, paediatrics, obstetrics and gynaecology, general surgery, and dialysis to residents and tourists on the 45 square kilometre island off the coast of Al Gharbia.

Emergency healthcare

Emirates International Hospital

Nr Al Ain Civic Centre Al Ain **03 763 7777**
Map **4 D2**
This private facility in Al Ain has specialist departments including accident and emergency, physiotherapy, dermatology, venereology, cardiology, cardiovascular, ENT, internal medicine, obstetrics and gynaecology, ophthalmology, general surgery, laparoscopy and urology, plus extensive maternity facilities, including a special care baby unit. The separate male and female wards both have VIP suites for inpatients.

Ghayathi Hospital

Silla Rd, Ghayathi Ruwais **02 874 1666**
Map **3 B3**
Government-run Ghayathi Hospital provides basic medical services for people in the small towns of Ghiathy, Bida Mutawa and Seer Bani Yas, located in the far west of the emirate.

Gulf Diagnostic Center Hospital

Al Khaleej Al Arabi St Al Bateen **02 665 8090**
www.gdc-hospital.com
Map **2 G10**
This well-established private hospital in Al Bateen offers much more than diagnostics; in addition to specialist areas including tropical medicine, pathology, psychology and a range of surgeries, the hospital offers a full range of outpatient medical services including general practice and dentistry. Inpatient facilities include comfortable en-suite rooms, VIP suites and a relatives' lounge for visitors.

Hospital Franco-Emirien

Nahda Tower, Corniche Rd Markaziya East
02 626 5722
www.hfe.ae
Map **2 N3**
Surgeons at the large, private Hospital Franco-Emirien specialise in abdominal, orthopaedic and gynaecological operations. The hospital also has a maternity ward and a delivery suite, in addition to an outpatient clinic, an emergency ward and a large dental centre.

Khalidiya Urgent Care Center

Nr Khalidiyah Mall Al Khalidiyah **02 665 3475**
www.skmc.gov.ae
Map **2 H5**
A 24/7 emergency care centre linked to Sheikh Khalifa Medical City. The centre takes some of the strain off SKMC's A&E facility, by dealing with minor emergencies such as cold and flu symptoms, vomiting and diarrhoea, minor breaks and sprains, ENT problems and rashes.

Lifeline Hospital

Sheikh Zayed The Second St Markaziya East
02 633 5522
www.lifelineauh.ae
Map **2 N4**
A top-class and extremely well-equipped private hospital in the city centre, Lifeline Hospital offers a 24 hour emergency department (with ambulance service), a diagnostics clinic, maternity ward and an in-house pharmacy, plus specialist MRI and mammography departments.

Madinat Zayed Hospital

Tariq Rd Madinat Zayed **02 884 4444**
Map **3 C3**
A mid-sized 25 bed government hospital in the Al Gharbia western region of Abu Dhabi emirate, this facility offers surprisingly extensive medical services that include an emergency department, general medicine and an advanced ophthalmology department, plus it is the frequent home to a wide range of visiting specialists.

National Hospital

Al Salam St, Off Sheikh Zayed the Second St
Madinat Zayed **02 671 1000**
www.nmc.ae
Map **2 P5**
This state-of-the-art, private hospital offers general medicine and surgery, in addition to a wide range of specialised medical disciplines including IVF treatment, sports physiotherapy and holistic health (which incorporates complementary and alternative health therapies).

NMC Specialty Hospital Al Ain

Hamdan Bin Mohd St Al Ain **03 755 5999**
www.nmc.ae
Map **4 D2**
The latest private facility from the NMC Group, the Al Ain branch of this hospital has extensive outpatient facilities with inpatient care to be added to its capabilities shortly. There are also several family doctors based out of the hospital, as well as a dental surgery, an in-house pharmacy and a state-of-the-art diagnostics centre.

NMC Specialty Hospital Abu Dhabi

Sheikh Zayed The Second St Madinat Zayed
02 633 2255
www.nmc.ae
Map **2 M4**
As one of the UAE capital's largest private facilities, NMC Specialty Hospital offers a fairly comprehensive range of medical services, plus a general outpatient unit which operates 24 hours a day. The NMC group runs house visits from doctors, while a private ambulance service is also available. Specialist departments at the hospital include paediatrics, cardiology, orthopaedics, dentistry, neurology, gastroenterology, urology, eye care, psychiatry, dermatology and ENT.

Lifeline Hospital

Oasis Hospital

Sanaiya Al Ain **03 722 1251**
www.oasishospital.org
Map **4 D2**

A small, private hospital in Al Ain, which is locally renowned for its maternity and specialist baby care units. Outpatient services include a diabetes clinic, physiotherapy, infectious diseases and pre-natal care.

Sheikh Khalifa Medical City

Al Karamah St Al Dhafrah **02 610 2000**
www.skmc.gov.ae
Map **2 K7**

Encompassing several 'Centres of Excellence', Sheikh Khalifa Medical City (SKMC) is the flagship institution for Abu Dhabi's public health system. Sheikh Khalifa Medical City consists of a 568 bed acute care hospital, 14 specialised outpatient clinics and the blood bank, which is accredited by the Joint Commission International. SKMC also manages a 125 bed behavioural sciences pavilion, six family medicine clinics, two walk-in clinics, an urgent care centre, and two dental centres within Abu Dhabi. SKMC operates under the management of Cleveland Clinic of the USA, and is owned by the Abu Dhabi Health Services Company (also known as SEHA), which oversees operations of all public hospitals within the emirate.

Specialized Medical Care Hospital

Main St Al Ain **03 755 2291**
Map **3 C4**

A private facility in the Al Jahili area, the Specialized Medical Care Hospital offers 24 hour hospital care with a particular emphasis on minor and one-day surgical procedures, plus an outpatient care manifesto that includes paediatrics, dentistry, cardiology, obstetrics and gynaecology.

Dubai Healthcare City

There are plans to create a medical district for Abu Dhabi but, until then, Dubai Healthcare City adds plenty of facilities to the UAE. The aim of the development is to create a global hub for medical treatment, prevention and research. City Hospital (www.ehl.ae) and a range of private clinics and research institutes are already open, including Boston University Institute for Dental Research & Education Dubai (www.budubai.ae), American Academy of Cosmetic Surgery Hospital (www.aacsh.com), Dubai Gynaecology & Fertility Centre (www.dgfc.ae), Dubai Bone & Joint Center (www.dbaj.ae), Imperial Healthcare Institute (www.imperialhealth.org) and Moorfields Eye Hospital Dubai (www.moorfields.ae). See www.dhcc.ae.

Sheikh Khalifa Medical City

Serious Medical Conditions

Medical facilities for chronic medical conditions are continually improving in Abu Dhabi. Here's the lowdown on the most prevalent serious illnesses in the UAE and where to go to receive treatment for them.

If you suffer from a serious medical condition, you'll find a good range of services available in Abu Dhabi and most clinics will help you seek treatment overseas or in your home country if services aren't available here.

Heart Disease

Heart disease is the highest cause of death in the UAE with over 40% of UAE fatalities linked to heart problems, according to Ministry of Health figures. The MoH promotes heart disease awareness with regular campaigns to educate people about contributing factors such as smoking, obesity, stress, high blood pressure, diabetes and sedentary lifestyles, most of which have an above-average prevalence in the UAE. Care for heart disease patients has improved dramatically in recent years thanks to Sheikh Khalifa Medical City (p.166) which, in 2010, held its first Cardiac and Vascular Disease Conference.

Stroke

Stroke is the third biggest killer in the UAE, after heart disease and accidents and, worldwide, is the most common cause of lifelong disability. Most major hospitals have a neurosciences department offering neurological screening, treatment and rehabilitation; Al Ain Hospital (p.161) has a dedicated stroke unit, as does the Neuro Spinal Hospital (www.nshdubai.com) in Dubai.

Cancer

Tawam Hospital (p.168), in Al Ain, runs a cancer care centre and maintains the UAE's only cancer registry. On occasion, the hospital runs campaigns offering women free breast cancer check-ups. It also has a full oncology department, offering radiotherapy, chemotherapy, haematology, counselling and diagnostics. American Hospital (www.ahdubai.com), in Dubai, has both a cancer care centre and a paediatric oncology unit. Safe & Sound (www.safeandsound.ae) is a UAE-wide breast cancer awareness campaign and its website is packed with information on the disease, self examination and fund-raising activities. Life Diagnostic Centre (p.168), among others, has a dedicated breast cancer clinic.

Early Detection & Prevention

With all chronic diseases and serious illnesses, it is imperative to seek medical attention as early as possible to improve the chances of survival and minimise any lasting effects. Some insurance policies do not cover pre-existing or chronic medical conditions, so check your paperwork carefully and consider taking out additional cover if you have a family history of a disease or are particularly at risk through contributing factors.

Tawam Hospital

Khalifa Ibn Zayed St, Al Ain **03 767 7444**
www.tawamhospital.ae
Map **4 B3**
This private hospital is best-known for its expert maternity clinic. The hospital is affiliated with the prestigious American Johns Hopkins Medicine group and offers specialised clinics that include an oncology department, an emergency trauma department, a diabetes centre, an infertility clinic providing treatments such as IVF, and a pain clinic which attempts to deliver a range of pain-relief treatments, such as acupuncture.

First Aid

Abu Dhabi presents the perfect opportunity to try outdoor pursuits such as dune bashing, stand-up paddle boarding and other activities that you might not have considered at home. With new physical activities comes the potential for injury, often a long way from medical access. If your first aid skills are non-existent or rusty, you can brush up on your general CPR and other techniques in a short course or even attend a tailor-made paediatric first aid course for parents and nannies. Licensed medics at LifeStartME (050 702 0236) can arrange training.

Specialist Clinics & Practitioners

Whatever your ailment, the chances are you will find a relevant specialist at one of the many hospitals or medical clinics. At most, you can make appointments without referral, but it is recommended that you discuss your condition with your doctor before seeking specialist help, as they will be able to offer advice on who the best specialist is for your particular ailment. Most places will advise you over the phone or by email to save you the hassle of making an appointment, but a face-to-face consultation is recommended to ensure you get the best possible advice. Most hospitals also offer a range of outpatient medical specialities; the NMC Speciality Hospital (p.165) prides itself on providing the highest possible care for an extensive range of medical conditions. If you prefer a more personal environment, there are numerous small specialist practices dotted throughout the capital, offering diagnosis and treatment of a range of medical conditions. In addition, many general practice clinics have resident specialists; Dr McCulloch's general practice clinic (p.159), for example, offers a maternity clinic, screening for childhood diseases, treatment for acute illness and occupational medicine (specialising in aviation), and are specialists in medical care for divers. It is worth checking at your local clinic (see p.159) before seeking specialist services elsewhere.

Advanced Cure Diagnostic Center

Nr Al Bateen Mall Al Bateen **02 667 5050**
www.cure.ae
Map **2 F6**
Diagnosis and treatment for a wide spectrum of illnesses, with specialists covering cardiology, ENT, hepatology, obstetrics and gynaecology, paediatrics, immunology, pulmonary care, critical care, sleep medicine, neurology, orthopaedics and dermatology.

Al Rawdah German Medical Center > *p.vi*

Nr Abu Dhabi International Private School, Al Karamah St Al Karamah **02 652 0200**
www.argmc-uae.com
Map **2 J8**
Cutting-edge centre for paediatrics, physiotherapy, radiology, osteopathy, dermatology and diabetology.

Freedom Medical Clinic

Nr Lifeline Hospital , East Rd Markaziya East **02 633 6744**
Map **2 N4**
A well-respected general medicine practice with medical, laboratory, radiology and ultrasound facilities.

Golden Sands Medical Center

Sands Pharmacy Bldg, Al Falah St Madinat Zayed **02 642 7171**
www.gsmconline.com
Map **2 N6**
General medicine, ophthalmology and radiology are available at this clinic.

Imperial College London Diabetes Centre

Nr Zayed Military Hospital, Al Khaleej Al Arabi St Al Safarat **02 404 0800**
www.icldc.ae
Map **1 G8**
The world-renowned specialist centre for research, training, diagnostics and treatment. Offers diabetes management including dietetics, podiatry, radiology, endocrinology, non-invasive cardiology, metabolic and endocrine disorder management.

Life Diagnostic Centre

Lulu St Markaziya East **02 633 2300**
Map **2 N4**
This clinic houses a specialist breast cancer and mammography department.

Middle East Specialised Medical Centre (MESMC)

Nr Emirates Media, East Rd Al Nahyan **02 446 7446**
www.mesmc.com
Map **2 M9**
Private city centre facility with doctors dealing with general and internal medicine, dentistry and ENT.

New National Medical Centre

Nr Cambridge School Mussafah **02 552 0100**
www.nmc.ae
Map **1 N12**
The centre's departments include a 24 hour emergency unit, internal medicine, paediatrics, gynaecology, obstetrics, dermatology, ENT, ophthalmology and urology. An ambulance and house-call service are also available.

Skin Sense

The strong sun in Abu Dhabi means you should be especially wary of any new moles or irregular marks that appear on your skin, or if existing moles change or grow in size. Dermatologist clinics specialise in looking after your skin, including Dr Menon's Laser Med Clinic (www.drsmenon.com) and Dr Ahmed Kamel Clinic (02 626 0040).

Obstetrics & Gynaecology

Most hospitals and general practice clinics in Abu Dhabi offer gynaecologic and obstetric medical services. In your home country, you may be used to receiving reminders from your doctor when you are due for a smear test or mammogram; in the UAE, however, you will need to be more proactive, and while a gynaecologist can advise you on how frequently you should have check-ups, it will be up to you to remember when you are due for a test and to schedule an appointment. If you are looking for a long-term gynaecologist, then it's worth checking out some of the specialist clinics listed below. 'Well Woman' check-ups can be done on a regular basis (usually annually) and offer the chance to get your regular check-ups out of the way in one go, at the same time as having a general health check.

The majority of contraceptives are available in Abu Dhabi (although the morning-after pill is not) and a gynaecologist will be able to advise you on the most suitable form of contraception for you. If you take oral contraceptives, a variety of brands are available over the counter in pharmacies without prescription. Because of the risk of thrombosis, you should make a point of going to your doctor to have your blood pressure checked every six months, just to make sure everything is ok. It's worth noting that, although rarely enforced, the law states you should be married in order to be prescribed or purchase contraceptives.

Maternity Care

If you are having a baby, the level of maternity care in Abu Dhabi is very good. Among expats, the most popular maternity hospitals are Al Noor and Corniche (see Main Hospitals, p.160). Before you decide on a government hospital, it's worth checking their policy regarding husbands and family members being present in the labour ward. Certain hospitals may not allow your husband to be with you in the labour ward, although he can be present at delivery if it is not by caesarean; if you are persuasive and there are no local ladies admitted, your husband may be allowed access to the ward. However, if this is a deal-breaker, it's best to know upfront.

All government hospitals now charge expatriates for maternity services, and delivery and costs vary quite notably according to the package you choose. Private hospitals will be more expensive, although, if you shop around a little and speak to friends who have been through it all before, you may be surprised to find that, in some cases, the difference between government and private maternity care is not as great as you might think. No matter which you opt for, if you have medical insurance, check that it covers maternity costs – some have a limitation clause (you may need to have been with the insurer for at least 12 months prior to conception) and some may not cover any costs at all. Some insurers also require prior written advice of your expected delivery date and method as well as the last scan before birth: for hassle-free reimbursement, it is best to check your insurer's requirements well before your due date.

Most private hospitals offer tailored maternity packages that include prenatal care, delivery and postnatal care for you and the baby. Be aware that the price the hospital quotes is for the most basic 'best

Mum's The Word **Jennifer Simon** 37, mother of two

There are lots of options for paediatric care in Abu Dhabi and the doctors are generally very friendly and helpful. I've taken my daughters to a few different places. Doctors in general here seem to be quick to prescribe medication, and this is true for paediatric care as well. I think it's important to shop around a bit until you find a paediatrician that you like, feel confident taking advice from and who will not prescribe drugs unnecessarily, to ensure you get the best possible care and attention for your child. The Gulf Diagnostic Center Hospital is good, but can get very busy at times. The Advanced Cure Diagnostic Centre also provides a good service – you don't need a referral from your regular doctor to see a specialist paediatrician, but you are supposed to make an appointment in advance. If your child becomes ill suddenly, you can turn up and see a doctor quite quickly, although you may have to wait a while if your child isn't seriously ill.

case scenario' delivery, and if you have any additional requirements, such as an epidural or an assisted delivery, you will be charged extra.

If you give birth by caesarean section, the cost is usually significantly higher and the hospital stay is also longer. If you go to an independent gynaecologist for your prenatal care, you will usually be offered a choice of hospitals and delivery packages, where your doctor can attend for the birth.

Waterbirths are now possible at the Al Ain Cromwell Hospital (www.alaincromwell.com), a brand-new facility specialising in services for women and children.

Corniche (p.164), Al Rahba (p.161) and Dar Al Shifa (p.164) hospitals all have neonatal intensive care units and Oasis Hospital (p.166) has a special care baby unit.

For more information on having a baby in Abu Dhabi see Having A Baby, p.131.

Obstetric & Gynaecology Clinics

Prenatal care and maternity services are offered at many main hospitals (p.160) and specialist clinics (p.168); the medical facilities and practitioners listed below are those which exclusively offer or specialise in obstetrics, gynaecology and pre and postnatal care. In addition, B4Baby and Beyond is the first and only private midwife clinic in Abu Dhabi and offers antenatal care, lactation advice and a well-baby clinic. The clinic is located in the Swedish Medical Centre (02 681 11220) which also has an on-site obstetrician and gynaecologist. A number of gynaecology clinics offer fertility testing, but only a few clinics offer assisted reproductive technology and IVF treatment; National Hospital (p.165) and Tawam Hospital (p.168) are two of the few facilities that offer IVF.

British Clinic

Sheikh Zayed The Second St Tourist Club Area
02 677 1252
www.thebritishclinic.net
Map **2 R4**

A specialised clinic offering fertility techniques and minimally invasive therapy, as well as general obstetric services, maternity care and antenatal counselling.

Dr Amal Al Biely

Damas Jewellery Bldg, Khaled Bin Al Walid St
Markaziya East **02 632 4934**
Map **2 M4**

Well-regarded, independent gynaecology and obstetrics specialist.

Dr Wafa

Al Noor Hospital Markaziya East **02 626 9444**
www.alnoorhospital.com
Map **2 N3**

A very highly-regarded private specialist based at – although not associated with – Al Noor Hospital.

HealthPlus Women's Health Center

Hazaa Bin Zayed The First St Al Karamah
02 643 3494
www.hplus.ae
Map **2 J8**

A newly opened centre of excellence covering general obstetrics and gynaecology, maternal-foetal medicine, minimally invasive surgery, urogynaecology and reproductive medicine. It is the first of 20 such centres set to open across the emirate.

Paediatrics

The majority of the government and private hospitals and general medical centres have full-time paediatricians. A growing number of these hospitals have devoted paediatric departments (see Main Hospitals, p.160 and General Practice Clinics p.159). Abu Dhabi is quite well-served for neonatal care with the Corniche (p.164), Al Rahba (p.161), Dar Al Shifaa (p.164) and Oasis (p.166) hospitals all having facilities to care for newborns with health problems but, for issues occurring after the newborn stage, you will need to find another paediatrician.

Your kids deserve the best, so don't be afraid to ask questions to determine the best choice. Call around and request the experience and qualifications you need, or you think your child may need. Ask other parents for recommendations. Dr McCulloch Clinic (p.159), Gulf Diagnostic Center Hospital (p.164) and Advanced Cure Diagnostic Center (p.168) are all popular with expat parents. There are also specialists, such as paediatric surgeons and neurodevelopment therapists, and doctors that care for children with special needs and learning difficulties. Your paediatrician should be able to give appropriate referrals.

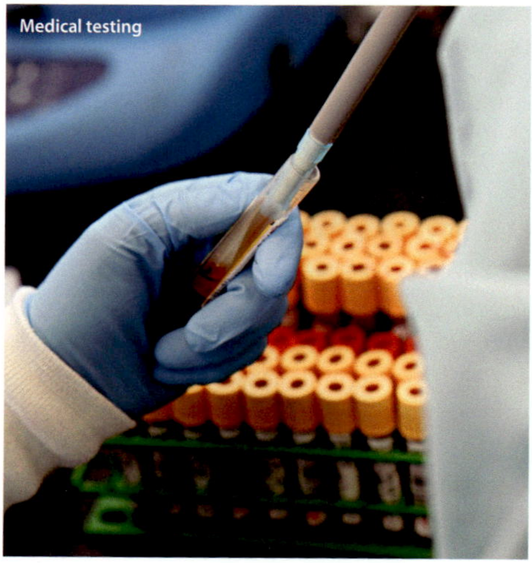
Medical testing

Dr Abdullah Azzam Paediatric Clinic

Sheikh Zayed The First St Al Khalidiyah **02 634 4185**
Map **2 K4**
An independent paediatrics clinic in Al Khalidiyah.

Dr Ahmed Al Hilfi Clinic

City Seasons Hotel & Apartments, Sheikh Zayed The Second St Markaziya East **02 674 4438**
Map **2 P4**
A friendly and professional independent outfit in the city centre. Dr Al Hilfi specialises in paediatric surgery.

Troubled Minds

If your child is having trouble adjusting to life in Abu Dhabi, finding it hard to fit in at a new school or missing friends and family back home, an outside perspective can sometimes help. The American Center For Psychology and Neurology offers child counselling and psychology services which are useful for children with emotional difficulties and can help kids cope with family issues, such as parents going through divorce. The NMC Specialty Hospital (p.165) deals with psychiatric disorders in children and offers a range of therapies, including counselling and family therapy.

Dr Ghiath Sandouk

Gulf Diagnostic Center Hospital Al Bateen
02 665 8090
www.gdc-hospital.com
Map **2 G10**
A paediatric allergist based at Gulf Diagnostic Center Hospital.

Dr Jazia

Gulf Diagnostic Center Hospital Al Bateen **02 665 8090**
www.gdc-hospital.com
Map **2 G10**
A popular privately practicing paediatrician.

Dr Raad Al Khayyat

Aster Medical Centre Tourist Club Area **02 645 6100**
Map **2 R4**
An independent general paediatrician.

Dr Sami Kanderian Clinic

City Seasons Hotel & Apartments, Sheikh Zayed The Second St Markaziya East **02 678 7846**
Map **2 P4**
A general paediatrics clinic.

Ghaleb Khalayli Paediatric Clinic

Al Hamiri Bldg, Sheikh Khalifa Bin Zayed St, Aflaj Hazza Al Ain **03 766 3998**
Map **4 D3**
A general paediatrics clinic in Al Ain.

Dentists & Orthodontists

Dentistry in Abu Dhabi is, like most other medical services, of a very high standard but with prices to match. Standard health insurance packages generally do not cover dentistry, unless it's for emergency treatment brought about by an accident. You may be able to pay an additional premium to cover dentistry, but the insurer may first want proof that you've had regular, six-monthly check-ups for the previous two or three years.

If you have a health card, you're entitled to dentistry at your assigned hospital and, if your hospital does not have a dental section, it will refer you to another public hospital that does. Service is generally very good, but the rates may not actually be any lower than those of a private dental clinic. It is well worth speaking to friends, neighbours and colleagues to find a dentist that provides good service at reasonable prices, as a standard filling could set you back anywhere between Dhs.50 and Dhs.1,000. If it is root canal treatment that you need, expect to part with anything from Dhs.600 to Dhs.3,000.

As well as routine and surgical dental treatment, cosmetic dentistry is also big business in Abu Dhabi, so if you're looking for a smile makeover, there is plenty of choice. The clinics listed below are specialist dental clinics. For a wider choice, many general practice clinics (p.159), specialist clinics (p.168) and main hospitals (p.160) also offer dental services.

Advanced American Dental Clinic

Nr American Community School Al Bateen
02 681 2921
www.americandentalclinic.com
Map **2 E5**
With busy branches in both Abu Dhabi and Dubai, this is a well-known dental practice that offers everything from orthodontic dentistry and periodontal treatments to endodontic treatments, teeth whitening, neuromuscular dentistry and cosmetic dentistry.

Al Ain International Dental Clinic

Commercial Bank Of Dubai Bldg Al Ain **03 751 1660**
www.alainden.ae
Map **4 D2**
Established in 1997, this Swedish-run dental clinic offers laser dentistry, preventive treatment, child and adolescent dental care, cosmetic dentistry and prevention of gum and jaw disease.

Barbara Dental Clinic

Al Manara Pharmacy Bldg, Shk Khalifa Bin Zayed St Markaziya East **02 626 9898**
www.barbaradc.ae
Map **2 N3**
Well-known practice with GP, implants and orthodontics.

British Dental Clinic

Shk Hamdan Bin Mohammed St Markaziya East
02 677 3308
Map **2 Q3**
Expert dental surgeons provide emergency, preventative, general dental care and cosmetic dentistry at this friendly, well-known clinic.

Canadian Dental Clinic

Sheikh Khalifa Bin Zayed St Al Ain **03 766 6696**
Map **4 D2**
Experienced dentists offer full range of procedures.

City Dental & Medical Centre

Main St Al Ain **03 764 2252**
Map **4 C2**
Provides a full range of dental procedures and treatments.

Dr Elisabeth Dental Clinic

Hilton Corniche Hotel Apartments, Shk Khalifa Bin Zayed St Markaziya East **02 626 7822**
Map **2 N3**
General dentistry and dental care in a friendly city centre environment.

Dr Firas Dental Clinic

Marina Mall Breakwater **02 633 5990**
www.drfirasclinic.com
Map **2 D1**
Offers everything from cosmetic dentistry, veneers, fillings, crowns and bridges, to root canals, gum treatment, teeth cleaning, extractions and emergency care to patients of all ages.

Gulf Dental Clinic

Nr Al Ain Oasis Al Ain **03 765 4373**
Map **4 D2**
A general dental and orthodontic clinic which is popular and well-regarded among expats living in Al Ain.

International Dental Clinic

Arabian Home Pharmacy Bldg, Sheikh Rashid Bin Saeed Al Maktoum Rd Al Manhal **02 633 3444**
Map **2 L6**
High quality dental clinic providing all general dentistry services.

Maher Medical Centre

Mercedez Benz Bldg, West Corniche Rd
Al Khalidiyah **02 666 3588**
Map **2 H4**
Part of a larger general medicine facility, the dental clinic provides a full spectrum of dental check-ups and treatments.

Modern German Dental Center

C6 Tower, Bainuna St Al Bateen **02 667 3235**
Map **2 D6**
Specialists in general dentistry, with dentists specialising in outpatient surgery, such as root canal treatment, tooth bleaching, poophyla crowns and implants.

Child Health In The UAE

Dr Maurice Khoury, paediatrician, Advanced Cure Diagnostics

Abu Dhabi does not have a Child Health Record like the one available in the UK or France, which gives advice and guidance to parents and includes compulsory check-ups at specific ages. Paediatricians in Abu Dhabi do, however, perform these check-ups as part of routine early-years examinations. Close follow-up is recommended during the first year, with monthly examinations for the first six months, then every two to three months until 12 months, then every three to six months until your child is 4 years old. After then, a yearly check-up is a minimum recommendation. Check-ups will assess growth and psychomotor development and a quick exam of major systems – ears, neurological, eyes, mouth and teeth, heart sounds and breathing, abdomen, genital inspection and skin assessment.

The Ministry of Health in the UAE follows an immunisation calendar which is based mainly on the US calendar. Immunisations in the first year of life are actually almost identical in all countries around the world. The main difference is with the timings of the different shots and the number required for full immunity. Any child immunised in the UAE will be fully compliant with the UK or the US schedule when they reach 18 months.

The UAE still recommends immunisation for tuberculosis (BCG) at birth, although the routine use of this vaccine in Western Europe and North America has been discontinued. Exposure, however, might be higher in the UAE. The country is a travel hub and this definitely increases risk of exposure.

Children growing up in the UAE are not at a higher risk of contracting any particular 'exotic' diseases; however there is a notably higher incidence of allergy-related disease, especially asthma, which is probably due to the combination of local climate factors in association with individual predisposition. No specific measures of prevention need be taken. If your child should be diagnosed with asthma, proper treatment can be given to allow for a normal active lifestyle.

Paris Dental Clinic

Abu Dhabi Coop Bldg, Shk Hamdan Bin Mohammed St Markaziya East **02 677 3373**
www.pdc.ae
Map **2 R3**
A well-regarded team of specialists providing general dental care, including endodontic treatment, cosmetic procedures, implants, as well as orthodontic treatment.

Petra Dental Care Centre

Euro Hotel Apartment Al Dhafrah **02 641 1899**
Map **2 M7**
Extremely good dental clinic offering a wide range of treatments and services, including general orthodontic work.

Royal London Dental Clinic

Al Bhadi Bldg Al Ain **03 755 7155**
www.drmonika.com
Map **4 C2**
Dental examinations, preventive treatments, restorative dentistry, gum disease treatment, root canal treatment, children's dentistry and cosmetic dentistry are all on offer from the experienced and qualified team.

Swedish Dental Clinic

Nr American Community School Al Bateen
02 681 1122
Map **1 C5**
Expert care and treatment in a well-equipped city centre general dental clinic.

Opticians & Ophthalmologists

You are never far from an optician in Abu Dhabi, with a store in most shopping malls. Prescription frames, sunglasses and contact lenses are readily available, with many larger opticians also offering eye examinations. Some have their own facilities to make your glasses on site, and you should only wait around 30 minutes for them, unless you have specific requirements. In addition, most opticians also offer contact lens fitting, stocking everything from standard lenses to disposable and coloured lenses.

The dry, dusty environment of Abu Dhabi can cause problems for eyes, even if you haven't experienced problems with your eyes before. Natural tear or refresher eye drops can increase eye comfort and these are available from most opticians and pharmacies. Spending lengthy periods in air-conditioned environments can also cause problems for contact lense wearers. Opticians can advise on the most suitable lenses and additional eye drops if required. Sunglasses are an essential accessory in Abu Dhabi, to protect your eyes from the strong sun, and prescription lenses are widely available.

For eye problems requiring specialist treatment, several hospitals and clinics, including the Sheikh Khalifa Medical City (p.166), Maghrabi Eye & Ear Centre (p.174) and the Madinat Zayed Hospital (p.165), have well-equipped ophthalmology departments catering for patients of all ages. A branch of the world-renowned Moorfields Eye Hospital (www.moorfields.ae) has also opened in Dubai, providing optometric, ophthalmic and orthoptic (relating to eye movement) care from simple eye tests to complex surgical procedures. Both Moorfields and Maghrabi Eye & Ear Centre have specialist paediatric ophthalmology units.

If you have concerns about your eyesight or the eyesight of your child, you can make a direct appointment with a specialist, or speak to your local doctor who will be able to offer a quick check-up and referral to a suitable specialist. If you want to ditch the glasses, there are several hospitals and clinics offering various laser eye surgery procedures, including LASIK eye surgery. Prices start from around Dhs.4,000 per eye, rising to around Dhs.7,500. All good laser surgery packages should include a complete year's follow-up care. Even if you have never had problems with your eyes, you will need to have an eye test done in order to get a UAE driving licence. This will take place, free of charge, at the licensing centre and only takes a minute or two to complete.

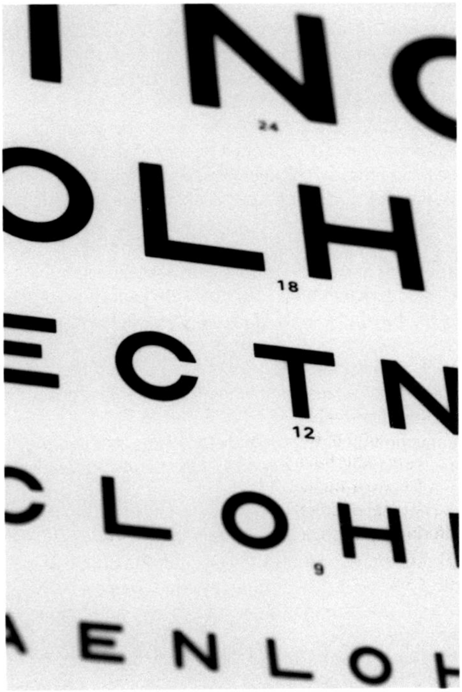

Ophthalmologists & Vision Correction Clinics

Magrabi Eye & Ear Center

Al Nakheel Tower, Bani Yas St Markaziya East
02 634 5000
www.magrabihospitals.com
Map **2 N3**

This centre offers refractive surgery, as well as having departments specialising in cataracts, vitreo-retina, glaucoma, cornea and external eye disease, paediatric ophthalmology, ocular oncology, neuro-ophthalmology and ophthalmic investigation. It can also advise on and prescribe low-vision aids and contact lenses.

Opticians

Abeer Optical Centre Sheikh Hamdan Bin Mohammed St, Markaziya East, 02 634 0014
Elite Optic Sheikh Zayed The First St, Al Khalidiyah, 02 666 6019, *www.eliteoptic.com*
Kattan Opticians Al Mullah Bldg, Sheikh Hamdan Bin Mohammed St, Markaziya East, 02 678 0818
Magrabi Optical Al Jimi Mall, Al Ain, 03 763 0680, *www.magrabioptical.com*
Moorfields Eye Hospital Dubai > *p.175* Dubai Healthcare City, Dubai, 04 429 7888, *www.moorfields.ae*
Vision Express Al Wahda Mall, Al Dhafrah, 02 443 7015
Yateem Optician Various locations, 02 627 7022, *www.yateemgroup.com*

Alternative Therapies

The UAE Ministry of Health grants licences to and administrates qualified practitioners of alternative medicine through its dedicated department for Traditional, Complementary & Alternative Medicine. Natural medicine can be very specialised, so when consulting with someone make sure that you ask questions and explain your needs and expectations to ensure practitioners can help with your situation. Prices vary but are generally comparable to western medicine, and most insurance companies will not cover the costs. As always, word-of-mouth is the best way of establishing who might offer the most appropriate treatment.

In addition to the clinics listed below, some of the main hospitals have departments offering alternative medical treatments:

National Hospital (p.165) has a holistic health clinic offering alternative and complementary therapies for disease prevention and cure, utilising drugless therapies such as hydrotherapy, mud therapy, dietetics, fasting therapy, acupressure, acupuncture and yoga therapy.

Al Noor Hospital (p.161) has a Chinese medicine clinic, and Tawam Hospital (p.168) offers acupuncture.

Ahalia Hospital (p.161) has a homeopathy department which can devise alternative therapies or complementary treatments to a wide range of conditions. Homeopathic doctors arrive at their diagnosis by considering not only your illness or condition but your body and your lifestyle; remedies are created using plant and mineral elements.

In addition, although not medical disciplines in their own right, both yoga and Pilates are effective forms of complementary therapy recommended for a wide range of conditions. Both are available at a number of studios and health clubs across Abu Dhabi, and there are classes with a focus either on the fitness aspect or on the classic, meditative form of yoga. See Yoga, p.301.

Well-being treatments, such as aromatherapy and colour therapy, are offered by various spas and salons. See Health Spas & Massage (p.181) for details and listings of addresses in Abu Dhbai.

Al Falah Natural Treatment Centre

Ahmed Al Fahim Bldg, Sheikh Khalifa Bin Zayed St Markaziya East **02 622 2709**
www.alfalahhospitals.com
Map **2 M3**

For over a decade, Al Falah has been treating Abu Dhabi residents based on the principles of Ayurveda – a system of medicine that dates back to 3,000BC. Al Falah has ayurvedic departments dealing in general medicine, surgery, ENT, gynaecology, toxicology, psychology, rejuvenation and sexology. There is also has a wellness spa, dealing in thermotherapy, acupressure, Thai massage, body cleansing and slimming. Another branch is located in Al Ain , call 03 766 5315 for details.

Gulf Chinese Medical Centre

Abdullah Hamdin Bldg, Al Nasr St Markaziya West
02 634 3538
Map **2 L3**

One of the most accomplished alternative medicine centres in town, this clinic uses traditional Chinese treatments, such as acupuncture, acupressure, reflexology and therapeutic massage to address conditions like headaches, insomnia, arthritis, asthma, gastrointestinal problems, diabetes, hypertension and prostatitis. The facility also has a herbal centre – ideal for treating allergies, heart disease, fatigue, liver and urinary dysfunctions, and obesity.

Homeopathic Medical Specialised Clinic

Nr Lifeline Hospital, Sheikh Zayed The Second St Madinat Zayed **02 621 0400**
Map **2 N4**

A clinic dedicated to homeopathy that offers curative and preventive treatments based on the healing properties of plants, animals and minerals.

Mizan Naturopathy Centre

Dubai Islamic Bank Bldg Madinat Zayed **02 633 7838**
Map **2 L3**
This centre offers a range of alternative therapies including flotation therapy for the treatment of stress, muscle pain, sleep disorders and low immunity, ear coning treatments, yoga therapy and yoga classes, plus therapeutic massage, including sports and medical massage.

Sports Injuries

Many Abu Dhabi residents lead an active lifestyle, working hard and playing harder. But accidents and injuries do happen, so whether you got roughed up playing rugby, pulled something in the gym or put your back out moving a wardrobe, you'll be pleased to hear that the city has some excellent facilities with specialists from all around the world to help you on the road to recovery. Physiotherapy is perhaps the most well-known form of sports injury rehabilitation but it can also help with neurological disorders, musculoskeletal pain and cardiopulmonary disorders, and is an effective means of preventing further injury. Chiropractic and osteopathic treatments are non-invasive and aim to improve the functioning of the nervous system, or blood supply to the body, through manipulation of the skeleton. Chiropractic therapy focuses on realigning the joints, especially those of the spinal column, while osteopathy combines skeletal manipulation with muscular massage.

Orthopaedics concerns the repair of damaged bones and joints, whether sustained through injury, disease or genetics. Pilates is said to be the safest form of neuromuscular reconditioning and back strengthening available and is becoming increasingly popular. Classes are offered by a number of gyms as part of their group exercise schedules. Soma Studio (p.301) at Al Bateen, is a dedicated pilates studio offering reformer and mat classes (www.soma.ae).

Many of the main hospitals in Abu Dhabi (p.160) have a rehabilitation or physical medicine department offering a variety of therapies, and some general practice clinics (p.158) have resident specialists. Al Mafraq Hospital (p.161) has a physical medicine department with all the facilities and expertise for all manner of physiotherapy and rehabilitation. Al Noor Hospital (p.161) boasts a state-of-the-art physiotherapy and rehabilitation department, specialising in sports injuries, spinal injuries and ligament injuries. The latest techniques are employed, including short wave and microwave diathermy, ultrasonic massage, magnetotherapy, paraffin therapy, hydrotherapy and suspension therapy. In addition to chiropody, chiropractic expertise and acupuncture, the Gulf Diagnostic Center Hospital (p.164) has dedicated physiotherapy, orthopaedic and sports medicine departments.

In Al Ain, the NMC Specialty Hospital (p.165) offers a back and neck pain clinic, as well as neuro rehabilitation, occupational therapy and speech therapy clinics, plus routine physical therapy. Also available are electro-acupuncture treatment, Thai massage and yoga classes. Oasis Hospital (p.166) has a highly recommended physical therapist who uses a combination of manual therapy, massage, ultrasound, electric current, and heated or cooled compresses to treat all manner of sporting or muscular injuries, pains and conditions.

Abu Dhabi Knee & Sports Medicine Centre

Al Saif Tower, Sheikh Zayed The Second St
Tourist Club Area **02 631 7774**
www.sportsmedicine.ae
Map **2 N4**
The first specialised orthopaedic centre in the MENA region, this facility deals solely in knee, shoulder and musculoskeletal sports injuries. It can deal with everything from surgical grafts and rebuilding joints, to the full range of physiotherapy and rehabilitation programmes.

Canadian Medical & Chiropractic Center

Sheikh Rashid Bin Saeed Al Maktoum Rd
Al Karamah **02 446 9006**
Map **2 L9**
This centre offers chiropractic adjustment, physiotherapy, sports rehabilitation, naturopathy, iridology, reflexology, orthotics customisation, as well as Swedish, Chinese, shiatsu and aromatherapy massage.

Chiropractic Specialty Clinic

Fotouh Al Khair Centre Markaziya East **02 634 5162**
www.chiropracticuae.com
Map **2 L4**
This clinic provides chiropractic care for all ages, including postural training, strength and conditioning programmes, rehabilitation, and massage therapy.

KKT International Spine Centre UAE

Villa 5, West 39 St Al Bateen **02 681 5550**
www.kktuae.com
Map **2 E5**
A specialist in non-invasive spinal treatments for conditions including spinal misalignment, injury and degeneration and general back pain.

Nutritionists & Slimming

With such a wide variety of dining options in Abu Dhabi, and with much emphasis on lounging and relaxing without sufficient physical exercise, it's easy to let your diet suffer and pile on the pounds. Thankfully, a number of slimming clubs and nutritionists are on hand to help. There are dietary and nutrition experts in many of the region's hospitals; both Al Falah Hospital (p.174) and Ibn Sina Medical Centre (p.159) have expert departments dealing in clinical nutrition and medical weight loss programmes, while Imperial College London Diabetes Centre (p.168) has a nutrition team who can help you manage the condition through diet. Eating advice for digestive disorders such as reflux, IBS and coeliacs, plus for allergies and the menopause is becoming more common – contact the main hospitals (p.160) or your local clinic for recommendations. NMC Specialty Hospital (p.165) specialises in individual health care plans. The hospital also launched Bite Rite Cafe (p.367) which opened just opposite the Al Wahda Mall. You can either eat a meal in the restaurant or choose its tailor-made healthy eating delivery service. Low-fat, low-calorie and low-cholesterol meals are devised by dieticians, freshly prepared and delivered direct to your door. It is located between Defence Road and Muroor Road. While there is not an official Weight Watchers franchise in the UAE, plenty of people follow the online version (www.weightwatchers.com) and, if you find you're struggling to stick to a new regime, you'll discover plenty of support in the online forums (see Useful Websites, p.25). Personal trainers are available at most gyms and fitness centres (p.178) to help you balance exercise regimes with sensible foods.

Cosmetic Treatment & Surgery

The UAE is becoming established as a luxury healthcare destination. This is in part due to a concerted marketing effort by the government in attracting the best renowned names in the medical industry to centres like Sheikh Khalifa Medical City (p.166), Dubai Healthcare City (p.166) and Abu Dhabi Healthcare City which is to be constructed on Reem Island over the next few years.

Cosmetic surgery is at the heart of this growth and the city now boasts several establishments that specialise in reducing, reshaping, removing and enlarging various parts of your anatomy. As well as exclusively cosmetic practices, many of the private hospitals and independent clinics offer cosmetic services, including aesthetic and reconstructive surgery (see Main Hospitals, p.160, General Practice Clinics, p.158 and Specialist Clinics, p.168).

As is the case across all medical facilities, standards are generally high, but it is worth checking out a few different clinics before you go under the knife. If you want a bit of sprucing and don't fancy slicing, a lot of the cosmetic clinics will also offer Botox and other non-surgical alternatives. Cosmetic and plastic surgery are still young industries in Abu Dhabi and, if you are unable to find exactly what you are looking for, head straight for Dubai where a multitude of cosmetic facilities await.

Cosmetic Treatment Clinics

CosmeSurge
Delma St Al Karamah **02 446 6648**
www.cosmesurge.com
Map **2 K9**
A team of experienced sub-specialist cosmetic surgeons offer surgical and non-surgical cosmetic procedures, non-invasive beauty therapy and cosmetic dentistry. A branch has recently opened in Khalifa City A (02 557 2220).

Kaya Skin Clinic
Al Karama St Al Karamah **02 445 9923**
www.kayaclinic.com
Map **2 K8**
This specialist skin clinic offers a range of aesthetic treatments including laser hair removal, Botox, anti-ageing therapies and chemical peels.

Obagi Dermatoloy & Cosmetic Centre
Hazaa Bin Zayed The First St Al Karamah
02 445 7100
www.obagi-uae.com
Map **2 K8**
Skincare experts provide surgical and non-surgical skin and cosmetic treatments, including fillers, Botox, laser, weight control, cosmetic enhancements and reductions, and aesthetic medical spa treatments.

Counselling & Therapy

Starting a new life in a different country can be a stressful process and, whether you are new to the city or not, sometimes it can help just to talk through whatever issues and anxieties you are facing. Mental health services are not as developed as in some other countries; private counsellors and therapists are uncommon. One option is to first see a general practitioner or family doctor who will be able to offer advice, and is well-placed to recommend or refer you to a suitable service; however, the limited scope of mental health services here means that medication is often the preferred treatment over other forms of psychological treatment, therapy or counselling.

There are, however, a growing number of psychiatric and neurology specialist facilities which have sprung up in Abu Dhabi in the past few years. These offer services ranging from counselling and family and couple therapy, to paediatric psychiatry, addiction support, treatment of mental health disorders and learning difficulties support. For many of these clinics, you do not need a referral, so if you are struggling with psychological issues and prefer to try alternative treatments before resorting to medication, it's worth getting in touch with them directly.

At the forefront, is the American Center for Psychiatry and Neurology (02 666 4866, ww.americancenteruae.

com). Located near Al Khalidiyah Mall, it is a dedicated mental health facility offering psychiatric evaluation, assessment and treatment for adults and children. It offers therapy on an individual basis for adjustment disorders, post-traumatic stress disorder, eating disorders, panic disorders, anger management and alcohol abuse, plus couple and marital counselling, child, adolescent and family counselling, and school and academic assessment and treatment. In addition, it offers a corporate employee assistance programme, plus seminars, workshops and in-house consultation, and it comes highly recommended.

Gulf Diagnostic Center Hospital (p.164) has a specialist mental health department offering psychiatric and psychological care and treatment, including the treatment of eating disorders. For a softer touch to mental well-being, Sharanis Wellness Spa (p.184) offers positive thinking meditation classes. For those coping with major psychiatric problems, the Behavioral Science Pavillion (p.164), at Sheikh Khalifa Medical City, is dedicated to the assessment, management and treatment of those with psychiatric disorders, and the NMC Specialty Hospital (p.165) has a dedicated psychiatric department and offers emergency evaluation and treatment, including crisis intervention and resolution. It offers a wide range of outpatient and inpatient units for adults, adolescents and children and, with a team of international experts, can offer treatment for schizophrenia, mood disorders, depression, anxiety, phobia, panic and adjustment problems, eating disorders, compulsive disorders, emotional problems, psychosexual dysfunctions and developmental disorders. It also offers student counselling and motivational courses.

As with all medical issues, check your insurance policy to see what you are covered for, and be aware that most insurers will not cover anxiety or stress-related illnesses.

FITNESS

Gyms & Fitness Clubs

Abu Dhabi is quickly becoming a hub for major sporting events in the UAE. The Abu Dhabi Tourist Authority has been tasked with turning the world's sporting eyes on the emirate and with the first Abu Dhabi International Triathlon, the Club World Cup, Formula 1 Grand Prix, UFC and European Tour golf events all making an appearance, they are well on their way to succeeding in their goal. See Spectator Sports, p.223, for more information. As a result of greater awareness of sports in the emirate, more emphasis is being placed on government-run healthy living initiatives and school sports, with new activities being introduced into both government and international schools.

Finding accommodation with its own gym facilities is difficult in Abu Dhabi. Many of the new housing complexes and tower buildings have been designed to include fitness facilities, or access to them, but the majority of tower buildings or villas on the island are too old for this.

There are, however, many options if you want to sign up for gym membership. Most of the larger hotels offer beach or health club membership. Hiltonia Beach & Sports Club (p.184) membership gives you access to the property's excellent gym facilities and full use of their beach and swimming pools. The recently opened Fairmont Bab Al Bahr (p.201) has also opened its doors to gym-goers, with separate men's and women's gyms and access to their outdoor terrace pools.

If you would rather avoid hotel guests, but would still like access to a beach, The Club (p.179) offers a family and non-family beach, swimming pool, tennis courts and a well-equipped gym; however, membership can be steep and waiting lists long.

There are also several independent gyms and fitness centres. Most charge monthly or yearly membership fees although they usually also have daily rates or visitor passes for Dhs.100 to Dhs.250. If you're deciding which gym is right for you, bigger establishments will often offer a free day of access to get your business. Try several – signing up for a full year is a hefty, if worthwhile, investment.

Group exercise classes are another great way to get in shape. The high energy levels, group motivation and fun attitude of group classes offer the perfect antidote to bunnies weary of the gym. Most fitness clubs, health clubs and hotel gyms offer some form of group class, and some are open to non-members, so it's worth calling around to find out what's on offer and trying out a few different classes until you find one that you really enjoy.

Hiltonia Gym

Whether you're a kicker, winger, fielder, striker or a hooker, there are numerous sports clubs in Abu Dhabi offering opportunities to get involved with your favourite sport at both friendly and competitive levels. To find like-minded team-mates, check out the Activity Finder on p.272.

Quick Fit

If you can't stand the thought of going to the gym, try Hypoxi therapy. The training system is said to maximise cellulite and fat burn by combining exercise with vacuum suction. The method is non-evasive and painless and can be directed at those problem areas. Visible results can be noticed after a couple of sessions and the treatment is gaining in popularity. Try it at Abu Dhabi Country Club (below), The Officer's Club (p.292) or Serenity Spa (p.184). Find out more at www.hypoxi.net.

If you need serious motivation, try one of the boot camp courses on offer from Original Fitness Co (p.179). It runs challenging, yet rewarding boot camp style group and individual training classes for all fitness levels and ages, focusing on everything from running and kick boxing to yoga and mixed martial arts. Women's only courses are also available. The Abu Dhabi Country Club also has personal trainers who offer tailored gym programmes, plus squash, tennis and swimming coaching is available should you wish to brush up on your strokes (Activities, p.272).

Abu Dhabi Country Club

Nr Al Karamah & Saeed Bin Thanoon Sts Al Mushrif **02 657 7777**
www.adhfc.com
Map **2 J13**

Extensive facilities include two gyms (one women-only), equipped with the latest fitness technology, as well as nine tennis courts, two squash courts and a basketball court. There's a swimming pool and two Jacuzzis, several outdoor all-weather football pitches; personal trainers and coaches are on hand for group and private lessons. Classes are free to members and Dhs.50 for non-members. Membership is Dhs.10,000 per year for men and Dhs.5,000 for women.

Al Forsan International Sports Resort

Nr Abu Dhabi Golf Club & Resort Madinat Khalifa A (Khalifa City A) **02 556 8555**
www.alforsan.com
Map **1 P8**

The recently opened, huge fitness complex offers classes from BodyPump, BodyBalance and BodyJam to RPM spinning. The classes are free to members of Al Forsan and cost Dhs.50 for non-members.

The Club > *p.297*

Al Meena **02 673 1111**
www.the-club.com
Map **2 V3**

Since opening its doors way back in 1962, The Club has become a bit of an institution in Abu Dhabi. Open to private members only, it has some of the best facilities in the area, including a private beach, various swimming pools, tennis, squash, badminton and a well-equipped gym. It is also home to Abu Dhabi Sailing Club (p.293) and Abu Dhabi Sub Aqua Club (p.279). While classes are reserved for members only, if you're lucky enough to wait out the waiting list, The Club offers body pump, spinning and stepping sessions, in addition to yoga instruction. Annual adult membership starts at Dhs.3,100 although it is subject to a Dhs.3,600 joining fee, plus extras depending on which sub-sections you join and which facilities you want to use.

Haddins Gym

Zayed Sport City Al Madina Al Riyadiya **050 800 6492**
www.haddins.com
Map **1 J8**

Haddin's Fitness at the newly renovated Zayed Sports City offers a broad range of group fitness classes, gym, tennis lessons and personal training, as well as their popular boxing programme. Tiered access memberships and package deals offer good value.

Original Fitness Company

C6 Tower, Baynunah St Al Bateen **02 406 9404**
www.originalfitnessco.com
Map **2 D6**

This company's claim to fame is its fitness boot camps. These are four-week military-style training programmes that are guaranteed to jumpstart you on the road to fitness by combining cardiovascular, strength and mental conditioning. The company offers individual, group and corporate training sessions and courses, from full-on boot camp style and personal training sessions, to group fitness camps and corporate bonding.

Slimming Made Easy

If your busy lifestyle makes staying in shape difficult, you could try Concept 10 10. Utilising specially designed machines at an intensity matched to your body for optimum results, Concept 10 10 claims that just 20 minutes of exercise per week with a trained Concept 10 10 instructor can get you in great shape. There is a gym on Delma Street but only one person uses the gym at any time, so booking is essential. Blocks of 10 sessions cost Dhs.1,950. Call 02 643 3353 or see www.concept1010.ae.

WELL-BEING

Whether your definition of well-being is pampering at a luxury health spa, limbering up with an invigorating massage, getting a new look for your hair or nails, or being kicked into shape by your own fitness guru, Abu Dhabi has a whole host of facilities on offer that will have you feeling relaxed and rejuvenated in body and mind in no time.

Personal Grooming

Beauty is big business in Abu Dhabi. Salons are everywhere and with certain services such as manicures, pedicures and waxing costing less than in many other international cities, you may find that a trip to the beauticians becomes a more regular diary fixture than at home. Fridays are usually the busiest day, so make sure you book ahead; on other days, many places accept walk-ins or bookings at short notice. In hotels, you'll find both male and female stylists working alongside each other, but in establishments located outside hotels, only female stylists are permitted to work in ladies' salons. These salons are very private and men are not permitted inside – even the windows are covered.

There are also numerous salons aimed primarily at Arabic ladies, which specialise in henna designs, so look out for a decorated hand poster in salon windows. The traditional practice of painting henna on the hands and feet, especially for weddings or special occasions, is still very popular with UAE Nationals. For tourists, a design on the hand, ankle or shoulder can make a great memento – it will cost about Dhs.40 and the intricate brown patterns fade after two to three weeks.

There are plenty of options for male grooming as well, with barbershops and salons to suit all budgets, and a growing number of specialist men's spas. So whether you're after a short back and sides, a traditional shave, a chest wax or a facial, there's something for all.

Many beauty salons, nail bars and hairdressers offer a combination of services, but as the quality, prices and service vary greatly, trial and error and word of mouth are the best ways to find a dependable salon. The listings below are a good starting place if you're new to the city. For a full listing of hairdressers, beauty salons and nail bars, visit www.liveworkexplore.com.

Beauty Salons & Nail Bars

Beauty salons and nail bars pop up thick and fast in Abu Dhabi, so whether your nails are in need of a polish or your skin is desperate for revitalising, you'll only need to make a quick dash down the road to your nearest shopping mall or hotel.

Many beauty salons in Abu Dhabi will offer a combination of services, from manicures and pedicures, to facials, body scrubs, Moroccan steam baths, massage, waxing, haircuts and styling. The quality of treatments and services can differ greatly so word of mouth recommendations and trial and error are probably the best ways to find a salon that is right for you. Kaya Skin Clinic (p.177) is a popular choice, with clinics based in Abu Dhabi and Dubai. They provide wonderfully rejuvenating treatments for skin dried out by the hot Abu Dhabi sun; their 'everyday radiance' treatment will have your skin feeling soft and perky again in no time. They recommend three sessions, which will set you back Dhs.1,950. If you're after something that is a little lighter on your pocket, try a 90 minute herbal facial at the Zari Spa & Beauty Centre (p.185). It'll zap life back into tried, sun-dried skin for just Dhs.175.

With the year-round sunshine holding endless possibilities for strappy shoes, flip-flops, sandals and summery wedges, there's no excuse for having less-than-perfect pinkies. It's worth trying out a few different nail bars to find one you really like as chances are you'll be making regular appearances there. Mosaic Nails (p.181) comes highly recommended for a top quality manicure and pedicure; they'll make your fingers and toes lovely and colourful for Dhs.95. In addition to sparkling and polished nails, Mosaic Nails offers hot and cold waxing, threading and tweezing, as well as Oriental and Moroccan bath treatments, massages and facials. Bridal and Shahrazad packages are also available. Nails (p.181) in Abu Dhabi Mall , and the Al Muhairy Centre and the Shangri La Souk is a firm favourite with the ladies of Abu Dhabi and you'll always find branches busy. A manicure costs Dhs.50, while a pedicure will be Dhs.60; add an extra Dhs.10 if you want a French polish.

If you fancy trying the traditional henna designs, Beautiful Henna Centre (p.181) offers a huge selection of Indian and Arabic patterns to choose from. If you'd rather relax in the comfort of your own armchair while one of their experts decorates your hand, ankle or shoulder, they also offer a home service.

Beauty Salons & Nail bars

Beautiful Henna Centre Sheikh Rashid Bin Saeed Al Maktoum Rd, Al Dhafrah, 02 634 3963, *www.noqooshaljameela.com*
The Beauty Spot Salon Marina Royal Health Club, 02 681 8817
Glow Beauty Salon One To One Hotel - The Village, Al Dhafrah, 02 495 2150, *www.uglow.ae*
La Reine Beauty Center Al Mansoury Plaza, Sheikh Hamdan Bin Mohammed St, Markaziya East, 02 677 7090
Harmony At The Club The Club, Al Meena 02 673 1111
Madonna Beauty Spa Porsche Showroom Bldg, Al Salam St, Tourist Club Area, 02 674 0666
Man/Age Luxury Men's Spa Marina Mall, Breakwater, 02 681 8837, *www.managespa.com*
Mosaic Nails & Spa Nr Delma & Al Karamah Sts, Al Karamah, 02 445 9660, *www.mosaicnailsandspa.com*
Nail Lounge Marina Mall, Breakwater, 02 681 6333
Nails Various Locations 02 644 4188
Shampoo Beauty Salon Marina Mall, Breakwater, 02 681 5898
Shamsa Beauty Salon Nr BHS Bldg, Sheikh Hamdan Bin Mohammed St, Madinat Zayed, 02 631 7063
Tips & Toes Villa 465-1, Al Khaleej Al Arabi St, Al Bateen, 02 445 8834, *www.tipsntoeshaven.com*
Zari Spa & Beauty Centre NMC Specialty Hospital Abu Dhabi, Madinat Zayed, 02 617 9150, *www.zarizardozi.com*

Hairdressers

You'll find ladies and gents hairdressers dotted throughout Abu Dhabi, and almost all shopping malls and hotels have salons. There are many small salons in the Tourist Club Area and Madinat Zayed areas of the city. In general, hairdressing in Abu Dhabi still has a long way to go until it reaches the standard you would find in most international cities, but there are a number of well-respected international salons. Finding a hairdresser you like and trust can be tricky business, but recommendations from friends and colleagues are a good place to start.

If you are looking for a simple trim and tidy-up, there are plenty of options for men and women in the city centre where you'll find a hairdresser or barber on just about every corner. Some of the smaller places are very reasonably priced and you could pay as little as Dhs.30 for a simple cut. The larger, branded salons are more expensive, with haircuts starting from around Dhs.100. For a style and a full head of highlights, prices are Dhs.300 and upwards, and you can expect to pay more for a higher quality cut and colours. Changes (02 634 1147) is a favourite amongst many of Abu Dhabi's expat ladies, as is Hairworks (02 681 6678) upstairs in Spinney's in Al Khalidiyah. Both have experienced hairdressers who offer highlights, colour and styling at reasonable prices. The newly opened Glamour Salon in Al Markaziyah has provided salvation to the blondes of Abu Dhabi with British and Australian stylists providing modern and professional cuts and colours (02 626 3002).

Barbers and gents salons offer decent, simple haircuts, traditional style shaves and, in some cases, men's facials. Men are likely to pay around Dhs.15 for a basic cut, though at upmarket salons, prices are around Dhs.60 or more. At the very high end, male spas such as The Lounge (p.184) and Man/Age (p.184) offer a range of pampering treatments for the modern male in addition to stylish haircuts.

Unbeweavable

You can find a few salons that do afro hair, braiding, relaxing and extensions in and around the city centre and Tourist Club Area, such as Dalla Beauty Saloon. However, you may find that expertise differs greatly and, for that reason, many ladies head for Elyazia Beauty Center (www.elyaziabeautycenter.com) in Dubai's International City, which has gained something of a reputation for its afro hair care, weaves, extensions and colouring.

Children are catered for too, and there are a number of specialist children's hairdressers in Abu Dhabi offering fun-shaped chairs to sit in or videos to watch while they have their hair done. Kids often receive a sweet, a balloon or a hair clip too.

Aziz Men's Salon Marina Mall, Breakwater, 02 681 8899
The Beauty Spot Salon Marina Royal Health Club, 02 681 8817
Family Beauty Salon Habib Exchange Bldg, Sheikh Hamdan Bin Mohammed St, Madinat Zayed, 02 626 0939
Fringe Benefits At The Club The Club, Al Meena, 02 673 1111
Glamour Salon El Nilein Bank Bldg, East Rd, Markaziya East, 02 626 3002
Hilton Abu Dhabi Hair Salon Hilton Abu Dhabi, Al Khubeirah, 02 681 2754
Kids Land Salon Marina Mall, Breakwater, 02 681 6316
Violet Flower Beauty Centre Baskin Robbins Bldg, Nr Al Muhairy Centre, Markaziya West, 02 634 4707

Health Spas & Massage

Soothing the body, mind and soul with a relaxing massage, cleansing facial or invigorating body scrub could be a weekly treat, a gift for someone special, or a way to de-stress after a trying time at work; whatever you're looking for, Abu Dhabi has a wide choice of luxury spas, day spas, beauty salons and massage parlours that will leave you or that special someone feeling pampered and rejuvenated.

Numerous massage and relaxation treatments are available, but prices and standards vary enormously, so it's worth doing your research into what's on offer. Options vary from five-star luxury hotel spas, to small and friendly independent establishments, which usually offer fewer options but better value for money.

At the top end of the spectrum, the Shangri-La's luxurious spa, Chi, has a wonderful range of Asian massage treatments, for which you can expect to pay around Dhs.700 for a 90 minute treatment and access to the spa's facilities; on the other hand, smaller day spas, such as Sharanis Wellness Spa, offers 60 minute signature treatments for around Dhs.270.

If you're looking for something a little different, Abu Dhabi has numerous spas offering authentic massage and relaxation treatments from around the world; Eden Spa at Le Meridien specialises in the ancient Indian practice of Ayurveda massage, Footprint Spa focuses on reflexology and the traditional Arabian hammam (p.184) is offered by many of Abu Dhabi's spas.

For sporting injuries, aches and pains, Mizan Naturopathy Centre (p.176) gives specialist sports and medical massages, as well as flotation therapy for destressing muscle pain and boosting immunity.

Abu Dhabi Country Club

Nr Al Karamah & Saeed Bin Thanoon Sts Al Mushrif **02 657 7777**
www.adhfc.com
Map **2 J13**

The on-site beauty salon at this club offers a variety of services including neck, back and shoulder massages, deep tissue and hot stone massages and reflexology. There are two basic treatments and, for a full pampering session, you can also get you hair and nails done here.

Anantara Spa

Emirates Palace Al Ras Al Akhdar **02 690 9000**
www.spa.anantara.com
Map **2 B2**

Expect the epitome of luxury at the Emirates Palace Anantara spa. This beautiful Moroccan-influenced spa only has seven treatment rooms, but each is spacious and elegantly kitted out with everything you need for some indulgent me-time. With two steam rooms, two Jacuzzis and a unique ice cave, plus a Moroccan hammam, the facilities are excellent. Treatment highlights include a caviar facial, Elemis treatments and the royal hammam ritual. The other branches at Qasr Al Sarab (p.242) and at the Desert Islands resort (p.242) offer a similar service for guests looking for a bit of luxurious pampering in these remote spots.

Body & Soul Health Club & Spa

Al Raha Beach Hotel Al Raha **02 508 0486**
www.danathotels.com
Map **1 R7**

There's a range of massages, facials, body polishes and wraps to choose from and the prices are very reasonable in comparison to many other hotel spas; complimentary use of the pool, sauna, steam room and Jacuzzi adds to the value. The small but cosy treatment rooms come complete with twinkling candles, sweet aromas and relaxing music. Check the website for regular seasonal promotions.

Bodylines

Yas Island Rotana Yas Island West **02 656 4000**
www.rotana.com
Map **1 T5**

You receive a warm welcome at the Bodylines fitness centre and, whilst the menu is limited to full body, hot stone or area-specific massage, the facility is spa-like in appearance with its cool slate walls, aromatherapy scented air and serene, spacious layout. Enjoy the option to relax in the steam, sauna and Jacuzzi facilities before your fully qualified therapist offers you

Anantara Spa

the massage pressure of your choice and the option to choose from a selection of fragrant oils. Particularly nice touches include hot towels on your feet before and after your treatment and the chance to relax on one of the day beds prolonging your feeling of Zen. There is also a gym on-site which boasts great views over the Gulf and can be enjoyed by club members.

Bodylines Health & Fitness Centre

Park Rotana Abu Dhabi Al Matar **02 657 3333**
www.rotana.com
Map **1 K7**

Like other Bodylines centres, the treatment menu is limited to full body or area-specific massages as well as heavenly hot stone treatments. Cool slate walls, aromatic air and the serene layout make for a wholly relaxing experience – top it by enjoying the steam room, sauna and Jacuzzi facilities before your treatment, then finish off by chilling out on one of the sumptuous day beds.

CHI, The Spa

Shangri-La Hotel, Qaryat Al Beri Bain Al Jessrain
02 509 8900
www.shangri-la.com
Map **1 L8**

The Shangri-La's CHI spa is a sanctum of Zen and relaxation. Arrive early to make the most of the spa pool, steam room, sauna and Jacuzzi and ready yourself for your treatment. Then choose from the extensive range of luxurious scrubs, massages, facials, signature treatment journeys and regionally inspired relaxation rituals, and sink into a state of bliss.

Corpofino Spa & Slimming Center

Villa 3/2, Airport Rd, Nr Al Wahda Mall
Shk Hamdan St, nr Al Salam St **02 445 2800**
www.corpofino.me
Map **2 L8**

Corpofino means 'fine body', and for over a decade, this spa, located in a villa near Al Wahda Mall, has been offering clients not only relaxing and rejuvenating traditional beauty treatments, but also tailor-made slimming programmes – including state-of-the-art equipment to tackle stubborn fat and cellulite. Nutritional advice is also available and once the hard work has been done, clients of this ladies only centre can reward themselves to a selection of beauty therapies from facials to Minx nails.

Cristal Spa

Cristal Hotel Abu Dhabi Madinat Zayed **02 652 0000**
www.cristalhotelsandresorts.com
Map **2 M4**

The Cristal Spa is nothing overly fancy but that's where its main advantages lie. There are three treatment rooms and a lounge area where guests can relax with

ESPA At The Yas Hotel

water or tea. There's a temperature controlled pool, a sauna and Jacuzzi and clean, modern changing rooms, but it's the no-frills quality of the treatment that will have you returning again and again. You could even fit the superb Express Facial into your lunch break.

Eden Spa & Health Club

Le Meridien Abu Dhabi Tourist Club Area
02 644 6666
www.lemeridienabudhabi.com
Map **2 S4**

The spa reception area may not be the most opulent in town, but the extensive treatment menu is very impressive – with an array of massages, facials, body wraps and body scrubs to choose from. Also on offer is balneotherapy, a hydro massage bath. The therapists know their stuff and the service is personable and to-the-point. Ayurveda therapies are also available.

ESPA At The Yas Hotel

The Yas Hotel Yas Island West **02 656 0862**
www.espaonline.com
Map **1 T5**

The luxurious ESPA at Yas Hotel offers a two-levelled sanctuary of spacious treatment rooms, relaxation zones and a Turkish hammam with chilled floors to counterbalance the warmth of the room. Dark timbers, stonework, muted lighting and designer lounges set the scene and, after a brief lifestyle consultation, you get to choose the most suitable treatment. Afterwards, you get to chill out in the impressive lounge; MetroNap rejuvenating pods are on offer in the gentlemen's area, while ladies get to relax in the soothing, fibre-optic-lit mood room. All-natural ESPA retail products are available to buy for home use.

Footprint Spa

Al Wahda Mall Al Dhafrah **02 443 7375**
www.footprint-spa.com
Map **2 M7**
This independent day spa specialises in hand and foot reflexology, and offers a range of relaxing, revitalising and pampering scrubs, soaks, massages and reflexology treatments for your fingers, toes and head. The spa takes an entirely holistic approach towards treatments and therapists discuss various benefits to meet your mind and body requirements prior to starting the treatment.

Hiltonia Health Club & Spa

Hilton Abu Dhabi Al Khubeirah **02 692 4205**
www.hilton.com
Map **2 C3**
The Hiltonia Spa is a blissful haven of tranquillity set in beautiful surroundings. Cool marble floors and ethnic decor make a soothing setting and the spacious treatment rooms come complete with private showers. As well as the popular aromatherapy and reflexology treatments, the spa also offers signature Indian head massages and an intriguing range of hydro treatments, some of which soothe the muscles and other detox. Alternatively, you can opt for one of the special packages, which combine body treatments with facials and nail care, and include the use of the sauna, eucalyptus steam room and Jacuzzi.

The Lounge

Khaleej Al Arabi St Al Bateen **02 667 7377**
www.thelounge.ae
Map **2 E6**
A men's-only spa where there is nothing whatsoever girly about the pampering on offer – the spa is decorated in reassuringly masculine earthy tones and gents can opt for a traditional shave, haircut, hair and scalp treatments, massage or steam, Moroccan and Turkish baths. The Lounge also offers IPL treatment (intense pulsed light treatment) which removes unwanted body hair in a similar way to laser hair removal. Facials, nail care, tanning and temporary tattoos are also available, and the impeccable service is fit for a king. The Lounge is conveniently located with plenty of streetside parking, but if you're too busy or shy to visit the spa, hairdressers and therapists are happy to come to your home or office.

Man/Age Luxury Men's Spa

Marina Mall Breakwater **02 681 8837**
www.managespa.com
Map **2 D1**
Pampering at the spa need not be just for the girls: this luxurious, one-stop men's spa offers male grooming including haircuts and shaving, manicures, massages and facials.

Oriental Spa & Fitness

Sultan Bin Zayed St Al Bateen **02 665 5707**
www.orientalspauae.com
Map **2 F6**
This small spa in a converted villa has a homemade feel to it but offers a good range of treatments, like massage, beauty, hair care and nail treatments. Make-up courses are also available, as are a small swimming pool, a fitness room, aerobics classes and a range of slimming and body-conditioning machines.

The Touch Of Arabia

For an Arabian pampering experience, opt for an Oriental Hammam. This treatment is traditional in the Middle East region and shares similarities with Turkish baths. The name refers to the bath (the room) in which the treatment takes place – typically an elaborate affair in Abu Dhabi's five-star spas. A hammam involves a variety of different experiences, including being bathed, steamed, washed with black soap, scrubbed with a loofah and massaged on a hot marble table; some treatments also involve mud masks and henna. While this may sound a little invasive, and more than a tad vigorous, it's a wonderfully invigorating experience which leaves your skin feeling as soft as cream. Absolute must-dos while in Abu Dhabi are the Moroccan Hammam at the Anantara Spa at Emirates Palace and the Moroccan bath at The Oryx Hotel (02 681 0001).

Serenity Day Spa By Paris Gallery

Khalidiya Centre Al Khalidiyah **02 667 8880**
www.parisgallery.com
Map **2 H4**
A surprisingly grand and extensive spa located on the top floor of Paris Gallery department store, Serenity Spa takes care of all your well-being needs with a menu of spa treatments, Clarins and Declor beauty treatments, a sauna, Moroccan bath, plus a full hairdressing and makeup salon, nail stations, and a fitness centre.

Sharanis Wellness Spa

Street 35 Madinat Khalifa A (Khalifa City A)
02 556 2601
www.sharanisspa.com
Map **1 R8**
Recently awarded 1st Runner Up Best Independent Day Spa at the Middle East Spa Awards, Sharanis Wellness Spa offers a huge range of treatments, from massage and Ayurveda to hair, nail and beauty care. Located in a spacious converted villa, the salon also holds *vinyasa flow* and *kundalini* yoga classes, plus Pilates and positive-thinking meditation classes. It's truly a one-stop shop and the therapists are well-

trained in their particular treatments. The location in Khalifa City A makes the spa a popular choice for ladies living off-island.

The SPA At Radisson Blu, Yas Island

Radisson Blu Hotel, Yas Island West **02 656 2000**
www.radissonblu.com
Map **1 S5**

A high percentage of Abu Dhabi's spas reach exceptional levels, so factors like organisation, comfort and customer service take on extra importance. The SPA has them all down to an art. Arrive early and enjoy the Jacuzzi, steam room or sauna then give your body over to the capable hands of expert therapists who make you feel like a million dollars. The aromatherapy massages and Anne Semonin facials are all a cut above, but if you've a couple of hours to spare, try the signature Radisson Blu Formulation which is about as luxuriously pampering as spa treatments get and leaves you feeling like a whole new person.

Zari Spa & Beauty Centre

NMC Specialty Hospital Abu Dhabi Madinat Zayed
02 617 9150
www.zarizardozi.com
Map **2 M4**

A longstanding favourite among Abu Dhabi ladies, Zari has been in the business of pampering for over two decades. Initially a hair salon, the spa now offers a broad range of reasonably priced beauty treatments including facials, massages, threading, eyelash extensions, pedicures and hydrotherapies. Shahnaz, an Indian range of beauty products for the skin, face, body and hair is used in all treatments. While the treatment rooms with their trio of semi-private cubicles might not be everyone's cup of tea, the spa offers excellent value and a three to six-month membership package is available to pick and choose from several treatments.

Zayna Spa

Grand Millennium Al Wahda Al Nahyan **02 495 3822**
www.millenniumhotels.com
Map **2 M7**

For head-to-toe pampering, this heavenly spa offers the ultimate in relaxation journeys. Gentle music, peppermint aroma and warm south-east Asian hospitality set the scene and each of the 10 treatment rooms is equipped with bath and changing facilities. The treatments range from luxurious caviar facials to a delightful hot stone massage.: With packages available from 30 minutes up to five hours, Zayna Spa is a perfect haven for an after-work treatment or full blown indulgence day. Treatments are available for both men and women.

Zen The Spa At Rotana

Beach Rotana Abu Dhabi Tourist Club Area
02 697 9000
www.rotana.com
Map **2 S5**

Spacious and comfortable, descending into Zen is like disappearing down a rabbit hole of relaxation. If it can be scrubbed, wrapped, hydrated, treated or massaged, then it's on the menu, and signature treatments, such as pregnancy, rejuvenation and immune boosting massages are excellent value. Each room has character, and the tranquillity suites with private changing rooms, showers and colossal baths are luxury defined. Pampering options include signature men's treatments, a *rasul* mud ritual using four different types of mud, a range of teen treatments for 12-17 year olds and couple's massage lessons.

Hilton Abu Dhabi Spa

Discover Abu Dhabi

DISCOVER ABU DHABI

Although it has taken a while for Abu Dhabi to emerge from the shadow of neighbouring Dubai, the city has well and truly put itself on the global map over the past few years as one of the top places in the region to visit. Its desire to attract some of the globe's biggest sporting events has, as planned, captured the world's attention. Its ever-changing skyline, audacious re-imagining of desert islands, vast hotels, inspired buildings and permanently sunny weather have combined with its position as an increasingly important airline hub to transform it into an international destination and the region's sporting capital.

All this is good news for expats lucky enough to have relocated to this headline-grabbing emirate – but there's more to Abu Dhabi than just the high-living holiday highlights.

Scratch the surface and you'll discover plenty of cultural delights, multicultural attractions, traditional gems and even simple, sedate everyday leisure activities. As an adopted Abu Dhabi local, there are plenty of ways to fill your leisure time. Start by exploring the city and the divide between the old and new parts of town. Head to Al Bateen and its boatyards or Heritage Village for a flavour of what Abu Dhabi used to be like before the economic boom turned it into a modern, international metropolis.

Souks, forts, local restaurants and beautiful mangrove-packed waterways provide a contrast to the mind-boggling modern developments that are replacing older buildings on the island and popping up off the island and in newly created areas. Reem Island, Yas Island, Between the Bridges, Al Raha, Capital Gate, Saadiyat, Central Market – new Abu Dhabi is a mix of spectacular buildings, high-living hotels, shopping delights and more besides.

The city's art and culture scene is starting to bubble up into something interesting too, with galleries attracting major local and international artists and several high profile festivals drawing crowds to the emirate. There's a full calendar of international events to keep sports fans happy (p.26). During the cooler months, there are some excellent outdoor options for get-togethers with family and friends; Abu Dhabi's parks (p.211) are superbly maintained, while the beaches draw crowds of sunbathers and swimmers at the weekends (p.212). There's family fun to be had too at the various amusement centres scattered around town (p.214).

You're not likely to tire of enjoying the urban attractions anytime soon but, if you do, Abu Dhabi has one of the world's biggest adventure playgrounds just beyond its city limits and it's waiting to be explored. Head off road (p.220) to make the most of the awe-inspiring desert sands and wadi beds, hike in the mountain peaks (p.219), go camping (p.218) or take to the sea for some excellent diving (p.279), snorkelling (p.222) and sailing (p.293). And that's just Abu Dhabi – there are six other emirates to get to know too (see Out Of The City, p.233).

PLACES OF INTEREST

Al Bateen

The Al Bateen area (not to be confused with Al Bateen Airport) is on the western side of the island, stretching along the coast between the InterContinental hotel (p.202) and 19th Street. It is one of the capital's most affluent areas and has a pleasant, sought-after residential neighbourhood feel. Even its well-known marina has a waiting list; mooring space is in high demand and fees have trebled in the last few years. The district feels a world away from the city centre; the sprawling suburban streets have an air of tranquillity, and there are plenty of green, open spaces.

The Bateen dhow yard is well worth a visit, with its evocative smells of freshly cut African and Indian teak. Craftsmen use traditional skills to build the dhows and racing hulls that can be seen in competitions off the Corniche. If it's not too busy, the craftsmen will happily share the intricacies of their art. The yard is open every day except Friday. The best time to visit is around 17:00. The Bateen jetty is a popular launching spot for boats, and the area around the jetty has a number of marine supply stores; if you need anything for your boat, this is the place to start. The Emirates Heritage Club's sailing department is housed here too. After strolling around and admiring the yachts you can visit one of the marina's restaurants and cafes which have scenic views across the Arabian Gulf. There are a number of diving clubs based in the marina, such as the Arabian Divers and Sportfishing Charters (p.280). However, be warned that this area is currently all change as the whole marina is being redeveloped to create the new Al Bateen Wharf (p.32). Although being developed in phases, it does mean that what's open one week may not be there the next.

The InterContinental Hotel is one of Abu Dhabi's landmark hotels, with the renowned Fishmarket (p.372) seafood restaurant overlooking the beach and the always-popular Chamas Churrascaria and Bar (p.368). You can reach the Breakwater area (p.193) in less than five minutes and the city's flagship hotel, Emirates Palace (p.201), is just at the bottom of the picturesque Baynunah Street. There isn't much in the way of shopping in the area, apart from the odd local store and Al Bateen Mall (02 666 1222), which sounds grander than it is, with some basic grocery shops and a post office.

Al Bateen has several public gardens and parks, popular for picnics and ball sports when the weather

Al Bateen

is cooler. There's a special green and pink running/cycle track along parts of 32nd Street. Wedged in between the mangroves surrounding the palace, Al Bateen Beach is usually one of Abu Dhabi's most tranquil public beaches. However, there is currently no public access due to the construction around the new sewage treatment station and the massive new bridge out to Hodariyat Island, with no word on when works will be complete and the beach reopened.

Al Karamah, Al Mushrif & Al Rowdah

Defined by 11th Street to the north, 30th Street to the east and 2nd Street to the west, the south of the area consists of wide leafy boulevards surrounding the Abu Dhabi City Golf Club and the Abu Dhabi Country Club, some small parks, and the Al Mushrif and Al Bateen Palaces.

Predominantly a residential area, it is a pleasant, family neighbourhood close to a number of international schools, open parks and green playing fields. The Women's Handicraft Centre (p.208) on Al Karamah Street is well worth visiting – a government-sponsored initiative where traditional handicrafts such as weavings, hand-made souvenirs and local artefacts are made, displayed and sold (at fixed prices). It is always best to ask before photographing the veiled women in their workshops. There's also a lovely cafe on the premises where you can sample all manner of traditional fare.

The Abu Dhabi City Golf Club (p.286) is located in the Mushrif area, in the heart of Abu Dhabi. Evening race meetings take place during the winter months, including the million dirham President's Cup race. Entrance is free and it makes for a fun night out. The international racecourse has a spectacular show-jumping area and riding school adjacent to the track. A nine-hole, par 70 floodlit course is set in the middle of the racetrack, offering golfers a novel series of challenges on some of its holes. Next door is the busy Abu Dhabi Country Club (p.179), where you can sign up to attend individual fitness classes if you don't want to pay the full membership fees.

Al Khalidiyah

Al Khalidiyah is the area between 26th and 32nd Streets, stretching up to the Corniche from 11th Street. It is one of the most upmarket areas in the city and its leafy green suburban streets lead to high-rise towers and built-up local shopping areas. There are wide-open spaces filled with beautiful public parks, bustling, busy streets with traditional shops, and eye-catching modern buildings.

The Corniche marks the boundary of Al Khalidiyah, and the Corniche Beach Park (p.211). The expanded walking area around here makes it a popular destination for local residents.

Al Hosn Palace

The best access to the Corniche from this area is at the end of 30th Street, but watch out for the traffic when entering. Close to the Corniche are Qasr Al Hosn (p.208), the oldest building in the city, and Abu Dhabi Cultural Foundation but, unfortunately, both are currently under development to create a heritage and culture centre for Abu Dhabi that will draw tourists from across the region.

Mention Khalidiyah to most local residents and they immediately think of the Khalidiyah Mall (p.337) on 26th Street, in front of one of the area's newer residential compounds. The attractive building, with its traditional Arabic design, houses 160 shops, a number of food outlets, a children's play area, and a well-stocked hypermarket.

More traditional food can be found at the shawarma stands and this area has a good supply of such joints: try Seashell Cafeteria behind Khalidiyah Tower, Zawak Al Sham near Fit Workz, Al Ramla Coast near Baskin Robbins, or Jabel Al Noor behind ADIB bank. The Folklore Gallery (p.210) on Khalidiya Street is a great place for browsing, with displays of local pottery and art, and it's also a good place for having any framing done: there's a wide range of frames and the craftsmanship is good.

The area between 7th Street and 9th Street is full of cafes and local shops, offering everything from tailoring services to laundry, and chocolate to stationery. It's a great place to get lost and explore on foot at the weekend.

This area has two large public parks in Khalidiyah Garden (p.212) and the Khalidiya Children's Garden (p.212), which is actually in Al Khubeirah, and is for ladies and children only. Both are bustling with families during the cooler weather; they are great for evening and weekend picnics, and for keeping the children entertained.

Al Maqtaa & Al Matar

These areas form the main gateway to Abu Dhabi island, lying at the southern edge of the island, just before the mainland. One of the capital's most used and well-known flyovers linking the mainland to the city, Al Maqtaa Bridge, cuts through this district.

The new Sheikh Zayed Bridge, finally open after several years of construction, has eased much of the congestion. The 842 metre long rollercoaster-style structure was designed by world famous Iraqi-born architect Zaha Hadid, and is another stunning addition to Abu Dhabi's increasingly rich architectural offering.

The most distinct landmark here is the heavily renovated Al Maqtaa Fort (p.207), one of the few remaining examples of its kind in Abu Dhabi. The 200 year old fort was originally built in the shallow channel of water at the entrance to the city as a checkpoint for those entering Abu Dhabi Island.

On the island, hidden away on a small road just before the Mussafah Bridge, is the Armed Forces Officers' Club (p.292). What makes this an interesting find is not only that it houses the best swimming pool in Abu Dhabi (one of only two 50 metre pools in the emirate), but that the rest of the sports and leisure facilities are all excellent, and include one of the best gyms around. It also has two Olympic-standard shooting ranges, three squash courts and a bowling centre. For families, Sheikh Khalifa Park (p.212), just off 2nd Street, has gardens, fountains, party halls and a dedicated area for women and children; it is busy at weekends, although quiet midweek. On occasion, the park has played host to attractions, such as circuses and a community market, although simply heading there for an evening picnic is pleasant enough.

Also providing perfect picnicking in the cooler months or evenings is the long stretch of coast beside 30th Street which is very popular, despite a lack of parking. There are a few dedicated areas for picnicking but most people seem to just pull over, unload the family, and fire up the barbecue right there.

Zayed Sports City is open seven days a week and has an ice rink (p.288), bowling alley, tennis courts, gym as well as bumper cars, video games and a cafe. Sheikh Zayed Sports City is home to the UAE's largest stadium. The landmark structure was recently

Airport Road

Airport Road is like the backbone of the island, running its entire length. Its official name is Sheikh Rashid Bin Saeed Al Maktoum Street but, like most of Abu Dhabi's main roads, residents rarely use that, opting for the far simpler Airport Road or Old Airport Road.

It starts at the Al Maqtaa Bridge and leads through the centre of the island, ending at the Corniche. It is one of the most well-used, well-known roads in the capital and the majority of Abu Dhabi's districts are accessible from it. Local, independent stores are scattered all along Airport Road between the Corniche and 27th Street and the road is also popular for its used car lots, although these will be moved off island to the new Motor World (www.motorworld.ae) development (p.60).

The 16 kilometre road passes many of the city's landmarks: the spectacular Sheikh Zayed Grand Mosque (p.208), Al Bateen Airport, Sheikh Zayed Sports City, the Diplomatic Area and the Churches Area. As you reach 11th Street, you pass Sheikh Khalifa Medical City, followed by the iconic Etisalat building, Cannon Square and Qasr Al Hosn, before the road meets the Corniche.

Al Maqtaa bridge and fort

refurbished and is now the home ground of Abu Dhabi Harlequins Rugby Club; in addition, it plays host to major international events, as does the nearby ADNEC, the National Exhibition Centre. ADNEC is now home to the captivating Capital Gate or 'The Leaning Tower of Abu Dhabi' which defies gravity with its record-breaking 18 degree lean. Just as surprising is the ADNEC grandstand which looks onto the Coast Road. It seems an odd place for it, with a prime view of passing traffic, but it does serve a practical purpose – it is used for military parades and for the International Defence Exhibition (IDEX), which is held every year.

Al Markaziyah, Madinat Zayed & Tourist Club Area

This area, bounded by the Corniche, 2nd Street and 9th Street, is an area of superlatives. Here, you'll find the oldest areas, plus the amazing recent rise of Reem Island, with at least a dozen huge towers having gone up since 2008. It has the narrowest streets, the busiest traffic, the most roadworks, the most ambitious highway construction projects, the most hospitals, the biggest mall, some of the best restaurants, and the most interesting and artistic development projects on the island. It is the centre of downtown and offers the visitor and resident alike the true taste of cosmopolitan Abu Dhabi.

Al Markaziyah is regarded as the city centre and the main business district and when you walk through the streets you will feel the unmistakable ambience of the city's heritage and history. This district is a real fusion of residential and commercial, with well-known hotels and apartments, high-rise business towers, embassies and the Al Noor Hospital, surrounded by local and international shops. Two of the busiest roads in the capital, Hamdan Street (5th Street) and Electra Street (officially called Sh Zayed The Second St or 7th Street but rarely referred to as anything but Electra Street), run through the district. It's a haven for shoppers, as the local, traditional shops share the streets with big name international stores and smaller malls.

To escape the mass of buildings, you can head to Capital Gardens (p.211), which is a refurbished public park on Khalifa bin Zayed Street. You'll find a large pond with fountains, a children's play area, a small amusement arcade and an enclosed cafeteria. The area also has its share of the city's five-star hotels with the Crowne Plaza (p.200), Sands Hotel (p.203), Millennium (p.203), and Le Royal Meridien (p 202) all within walking distance.

The Tourist Club Area got its name from the now long-gone Abu Dhabi Tourist Club and is today an area in transition, as road projects, underpasses, bridges and expressways combine with the construction work on The Quay development. Older buildings are making way for newer high-rise towers; the old marina area is also due to be razed and replaced by a collection of marinas, hotels and residential apartments. In this corner of the city, tradition meets modernity, with luxury five-star hotels neighbouring small local shops, cafes and bakeries.

When the construction work is finished in the next couple of years, it will make cross-town traffic much smoother, but, until then, you just have to accept that even taxi drivers will complain about going into this area. Nevertheless, the Tourist Club Area is buzzing with activity and is one of the most vibrant parts of Abu Dhabi. It's the perfect place to visit if you want to experience busy city life and the capital's social scene. It is located at the eastern end of the Corniche, with a cosmopolitan mix of residents and visitors. The Abu Dhabi Mall (p.334) with its 220 outlets and the Beach Rotana Abu Dhabi (p.68) with a great members only beach club and some of the best restaurants in town are the two main attractions in this part of Abu Dhabi.

Madinat Zayed is centred on the shopping centre of the same name, which is the place to go for colourful fabrics, Indian and Arabian gifts, and of course jewellery – something the next door Gold Souk (p.342) also excels in. The back streets between here and the NMC Speciality Hospital (p.165) are full of interesting shops selling the things that you can't find in the malls: musical instruments such as oudhs, bizarre electrical appliances and plastic buckets, and you'll even find the odd Ethiopian restaurant.

Al Meena

Al Meena is Abu Dhabi's main port area and an excellent place for visitors and residents to stroll around and explore.

Located on the north-eastern tip of the island, the area is dominated by low-rise apartments and quite old single-family houses, although many of the oldest buildings are being pulled down to make way for sleek modern blocks. Once you leave the residential area behind, you'll arrive at the Port Zayed area, which is best known for its souks.

This working port is home to the fish, fruit and vegetable market, the carpet souk, and the Iranian souk (p.333). The Iranian souk, in particular,

In The Club

The Meena area is where you'll find The Club (p.179), a real Abu Dhabi institution that has been going for nearly 50 years. This leisure facility is one of the most successful expat clubs in the capital, but there's a waiting list for those who want to join and guests must be signed in by a member. It has excellent facilities, including watersports, a library, a pool, a beach and an assortment of racquet and other sports. It often puts on plays and concerts not found anywhere else.

is a treasure trove to discover, selling all sorts of knickknacks. Iranians come over on dhows every three weeks or so – sometimes you'll be lucky and catch a new consignment of intricately detailed pots and plates; at other times there will be no one around. The souks offer an entirely different shopping experience to the malls, and you can utilise your bartering skills to good effect.

The dhow harbour, off Port Road, is a contrast of past and present with several hundred dhows resting in their berths. It is a fascinating place to explore early in the morning when the fishermen return from sea with their local delicacies. Try out the nearby restaurants, which offer an authentic selection of local cooking – mainly grilled meats and seafood. The harbour is also worth a visit at sunset when the dhows return. A number of dinner cruises also set sail from here.

The Other Side

Although there's a lot to see and do in the Al Meena area, it is still a working port with parts in need of modernisation and other parts under construction. The sparse industrial areas can be a little depressing, and shopping areas are occasionally a little desolate, with the pet shop area particularly soul-destroying.

Between The Bridges

Just off the island, on the city's outskirts and spanning the area between Mussafah Bridge and Al Maqtaa Bridge, this area is noted for large independent villas and compounds, the nearby Abu Dhabi Golf Club (p.286) and the cluster of new hotels. Its Arabic name is Bain Al Jessrain but, to just about everybody now, it's known as 'Between the Bridges'.

This new area is defined by the Shangri-La (p.203), Traders Hotel (p.204) and Fairmont Bab Al Bahr (p.201), which provide the main entertainment focus in the area. Sharing the same stretch of creek and beachfront, the hotels have some of the UAE's very best restaurants, plus a wide range of facilities including spas, gymnasiums and more swimming pools than you can shake a lilo at.

The hotels are part of the larger Qaryat Al Beri (p.342) development, a Disney-esque recreation of a traditional souk in a modern setting, offering a variety of shops and restaurants under one roof and connected by a waterway on which Arabic gondolas, or abras, slowly meander through the unique architecture, under arches and past restaurant terraces.

For more traditional architecture, look across the road from Qaryat Al Beri and you'll see one of the most ornate Persian-influenced mosques in the city. This small turquoise blue gem is not open for tours but you can admire the craftsmanship from outside.

Breakwater & Al Ras As Akhdar

Breakwater is an area of reclaimed land which is entirely man-made and connected by a causeway to the western end of the Corniche. Development is almost complete now, with a community of luxury villas spread across a separate promontory. The beachfront walkways are an extension of the recent Corniche development and offer some of the best spots to admire and photograph the city's superb skyline. Along the waterfront there are a number of Arabic restaurants and cafes, and the Heritage Village (p.207) which features aspects of Abu Dhabi's past, with displays of the ancient Bedouin lifestyle and an interesting collection of traditional folklore treasures.

The Abu Dhabi International Marine Sports Club (02 681 5566, www.adimsc.ae) was initially set up to

Breakwater at sunset

provide a base for the city's power boat racing, but it now offers some of the best watersports facilities in the capital. The Abu Dhabi Theatre building is also worth a look: its shape led to speculation that it was either a mosque or an observatory – regardless, it has now fallen into disuse. Next to it stands an enormous flagpole which was, for a time at least, the tallest unsupported flagpole in the world at 123.1m (until it got pipped by Jordan, then Turkmenistan).

Al Ras Al Akhdar is the area on the north-western tip of Abu Dhabi dominated by the beautiful, and massive, Emirates Palace hotel (p.201). It is a quiet, picturesque part of the city that was, until recently, surrounded by popular, long, sandy beaches. However, the entire area is now being redeveloped.

The Emirates Palace (p.201) hotel is still the city's most iconic landmark and should be at the top of every visitor's list of 'must sees' in Abu Dhabi. It is a stunning property set in more than 85 hectares of landscaped gardens, surrounded by a pristine stretch of white-sand beach and a new yacht marina. Palatial in every sense, luxury and opulence oozes from every inch of the hotel, from the huge gold domed roof in the reception area to the massive hand-woven carpets displayed on the walls. An overnight stay in one of the stunning rooms grants you access to the tranquil outdoors areas, but you can visit the public areas indoors without a reservation; the afternoon tea is one of the draws here. The hotel is also home to some exceptional restaurants, a couple of excellent galleries and a 1,500 seat auditorium that hosts a variety of shows throughout the year, including films during the Abu Dhabi Film Festival (p.29) and concerts during the Abu Dhabi Classics series (p.29).

The Corniche & Al Khubeirah

The Corniche, seen as the face of the city, runs east to west across the top of the island. The area has undergone a massive, multi-million dirham redevelopment in recent years, and now provides plenty of opportunities to get out and enjoy the open air. Home to some of the city's most impressive buildings, Corniche Road is lined with the high-rise towers that make up Abu Dhabi's spectacular skyline.

Both sides of the road have been developed to complement the paved waterfront and the inland side has been beautifully landscaped with parks, picnic grounds, small gardens, fountains, covered-seating areas lining the pavements, and cafes. All areas are easily accessible, with parking and safe (and surprisingly attractive) pedestrian underpasses.

At the western end, towards the Emirates Palace, a multimillion dirham project to modernise and expand the swimming beaches is now completed and there's a range of cafes and restaurants along the undulating shoreline. A casual stroll along the Corniche is a favourite part of many residents' evening routines and experience of the capital. The waterfront section is fully paved, making it ideal for rollerblading, jogging and walking, while the special cycle path draws both enthusiastic amateurs and more serious cyclists.

Marina Al Bateen Resort

Catering predominantly for high-end clientele, this popular resort and club, located just south of Al Khubeirah, features a range of leisure facilities. There's a fully-equipped members' gym, an attractive swimming pool area as well as a lounge bar and an Italian restaurant (p.384). The resort also has berths for 160 boats in the marina, while watersports and boat trips can be arranged (www.marinaalbateen.com).

The grassed area next to the Hilton Hotel is perfect for picnics; it is particularly popular during winter weekends when families gather and spend the day playing on the grass or swimming in the water. To explore these areas from a different perspective, visitors can cruise along by the Corniche on a traditional wooden dhow or cabin cruiser, enjoying the changing vistas of the skyline, parks and fountains. Cruises generally last for an hour, and can be booked through a tour operator (see Boat Tours, p.227).

Towering Achievements

Marina Mall is one of the most popular malls in Abu Dhabi, with hundreds of outlets housing a variety of western high street brand-names. In the centre of the shopping centre is the 100 metre high tower, at the top of which you can enjoy a cappuccino with incredible views at Colombiano Coffee House (02 681 5533) or get 360 degree views of the city teamed with a la carte cuisine at the revolving restaurant, Tiara (02 681 9090).

Between the apartment buildings inland from the Corniche, there are several luxury hotels. The Hilton Abu Dhabi is frequented by visitors and residents alike, and is renowned for its top class eateries such as BiCE (p.366), and the beachfront restaurant Vasco's (p.389). The Sheraton Abu Dhabi is on the recently refurbished eastern part of the Corniche, with the renowned, romantic seafood restaurant Il Paradiso (p.373) overlooking the beach.

The commercial buildings are occupied by many of the city's big investment banks, oil companies, and governmental departments. The skyline is ever-changing and the next couple of years will see the continued construction of a number of architectural masterpieces, including hotels, office towers and residential developments.

Yas Marina

Downtown park

Mosque near The Corniche

Heritage Park

Say Yas To Island Life

Probably the biggest addition to Abu Dhabi's attractions to date, and easily the equal of Dubai's Palm, Yas Island is home to the F1 circuit, Ferrari World and a host of hotels.

From groundbreaking in early 2007, Yas Island, an island east of the Abu Dhabi city centre, was built up with hotels, infrastructure and the brand new Yas Marina Circuit just in time to host Abu Dhabi's first Formula 1 Grand Prix in 2009. The 5.6 kilometre track stands out for its unique design which actually runs right through the island's flagship, The Yas Hotel, giving about 250 very lucky VIPs envious views of the proceedings from the bridge on race weekends. What's more, the marina is incorporated into the circuit, so that the yachting crowd can not only make grand entrances but can view the race from their boats.

Other F1 fans with more modest means can still enjoy thrilling racing moments – the grandstand was designed to offer the best views of any F1 venue. In the inaugural year, 50,000 people jammed into the Yas Marina Circuit – including celebrities, dignitaries and hardcore fans – to witness as the UAE hosted its first Formula 1 race, and the 2010 season finale took place in an equally spectacular manner.

Indeed, racing is only part of the draw of Abu Dhabi's F1 weekend: the end of each racing day in the first year brought performances from Jamiroquai, Beyoncé, Aerosmith and Kings of Leon to the outdoor arena, and in 2010, Prince, Linkin Park and Kanye West took to the stage. In 2011, the circuit will host the season's penultimate race, on 13 November.

While most famous as the home of the annual Formula 1 Etihad Airways Grand Prix, Yas Marina Circuit is a year-round venue where petrolheads can put their driving skills to the test, or take high-speed driving lessons. The possibilities include karting, drag racing, as well as a host of other options from supercar driving to passenger experiences.

To coincide with the 2010 race, Ferrari World (p.290) opened on Yas Island. The world's largest indoor theme park has enough attractions to keep motorsports enthusiasts of all ages entertained. Kids can learn to drive in a miniature Ferrari, while grown-up fans get to take a glimpse into the F1 paddock or experience race driving in a simulator. For thrillseekers, there's the world's fastest rollercoaster and the G-Force tower.

The Yas Island Show Weekends has been a popular series of concerts and events, with the 2011 lineup having included names such as Shakira and Snoop Dogg. For details on upcoming concert events, check Flash Entertainment (www.thinkflash.ae).

In the years to come, several more hotels will join the seven already open on the island, a waterpark is scheduled to open in 2012 to add to the leisure facilities, while the Yas Mall is currently under construction for scheduled opening in 2013. Currently, the main shopping draw on the island is the Middle East's largest Ikea, which opened its doors in early 2011. Other Yas attractions that are already open include a host of popular bars, restaurants and clubs; some of the top-draws include Cipriani (p.368), Kazu (p.376) and the Skylite Lounge (p.397).

The Yas Links golf course opened in March 2010, and the spectacular seaside setting has attracted plenty of attention, not to mention top golfers, to the island since then. However, Yas Island won't only be a visitor attraction. Master developer, Aldar (p.74), is working on several residential communities, including the first ever signature Ferrari villas. They're unlikely to be cheap but you can bet they'll look good.

The New Corniche

The Corniche should not be confused with the New Corniche (or Eastern Corniche), which runs along the eastern side of the island and is also known as the Eastern Ring Road (or, in fact, Al Salam Street or 8th Street). A popular place for barbecues, picnics and a spot of fishing, the area is now undergoing a huge facelift, with resort hotels, cafes and restaurants on the way, creating another outdoor area for Abu Dhabi's residents to enjoy.

The Islands

Exploring Abu Dhabi needn't mean being confined to the streets of the capital. You can also take to the seas and view more than 200 islands that are scattered in the waters around the main island. Many of these hidden treasures are just a short boat ride away; they vary in size and the majority are flat, sandy and uninhabited.

The waters around the islands are rich in marine life and you may be lucky enough to spot the local population of humpbacked dolphins or the endangered dugongs on your trip. Between March and July, head farther out and there is the possibility of catching a glimpse of the migrating whale species found in the region, including the blue whale, Bryde's whale and Risso's dolphin. Several of the larger islands are currently closed to the public, as they are in the hands of developers in the middle of creating a variety of tourism destinations.

Getting There

There are no organised tours to the islands but Net Tours (p.231) can tailor a trip for you. You can choose which islands you would like to sail by or visit and enjoy a personalised island-hopping programme. Prices start from Dhs.1,800 to hire a speedboat for two hours, which accommodates up to seven people, or Dhs.2,400 to hire a larger boat for two hours which will take up to 19 people. The cost includes land transfers.

Arabian Divers & Sports Fishing Charters (p.228) has nearly two decades of experience sailing around the islands and can organise private charters. Prices start from Dhs.900 for a two hour trip in a small speedboat that carries up to six passengers. It also has large touring boats which can accommodate up to 19 people, plus a 23 metre luxury yacht.

You can hire a fully staffed boat for a couple of hours and sail around the Arabian Gulf, observing the natural beauty of these unspoiled islands. There are still plenty of islands where you can stop off and enjoy the fantastic opportunity to explore, barbecue or simply relax in absolute peace.

Saadiyat Island

Saadiyat Island, to the east of the city, used to be a popular spot for weekend breaks and daytrips. It is now the site of a massive development project that is transforming the island into a major tourism and commercial hub. Saadiyat, translated as the 'island of happiness', will be home to around 145,000 residents and a host of leisure and cultural activities. Internationally renowned architects have been hired to design a Guggenheim Museum, a Louvre gallery and the Zayed National Museum. The whole project should be completed in 2018 but several elements, including the Manarat Al Saadiyat (p.210) visitor centre and exhibition space, and the Saadiyat Beach Golf Club (p.287) have already opened., with another beach club, the Monte-Carlo, opening in September 2011. The first hotels on Saadiyat will also open in late 2011 (see New Hotels, p.198).

The large, man-made Lulu Island can be seen directly opposite the Corniche, and is protected from the sea by a breakwater. Once a day trip retreat open to the public, Lulu Island is currently off limits due to planned redevelopment work, with no date for reopening available.

Situated 12 kilometres north-east of Abu Dhabi is Al Sammaliah Island, where plans are underway to develop the heritage and environmental aspects of island life for educational purposes, and a habitat restoration programme is in progress. The island covers 35 square kilometres and is home to one of the world's largest artificial mangrove plantations, covering some eight square kilometres.

You can moor your boat at Bahraini Island and spend the day on its unspoiled beaches or visit the wildlife sanctuary. It is a 40 minute trip, but a worthwhile journey as you may be able to spot dolphins swimming in the waters, and you pass by many of the other islands in Abu Dhabi's archipelago. You will need to take supplies with you as there are no facilities on the island.

Futaisi Island is five kilometres – or a 10 minute boat ride – to the south of Abu Dhabi. The island's history dates back hundreds of years; its inhabitants used to supply sweet water and stone for building forts and rulers' houses to the main Abu Dhabi island. It covers an area of around 50 square kilometres and part of this land is currently being turned into an eco-tourism destination. The rest of the island will remain quiet and undisturbed, creating a very effective wildlife sanctuary. Gazelles run and jump across the flats and spiny-tailed lizards roam the sands. The island is also an important transit point for migrating birds, and flamingos are commonly seen on the shores. Sightings of the endangered green sea turtle, as well as dolphins, are evidence of the rich marine life in the waters. There is a regular boat service that takes you to the island in the morning and brings you back to Abu Dhabi at the end of the day; alternatively, rent one of the beachfront chalets at the Futaisi Country Club (see www.futaisi.com for details of boat and accommodation).

Horseshoe Island is a small, flat and sandy isle, 25 minutes away from Abu Dhabi's east coast. It is home to a number of desert foxes and offshore is Surf Reef – a great spot for windsurfing. The island has been inaccessible to the public of late, so check ahead.

ABU DHABI HOTELS

One thing you'll discover quickly is that much of the social scene revolves around the city's many hotels. Whereas in, say, Europe, where generally a city hotel's main purpose is to provide accommodation and host the odd corporate function, in Abu Dhabi, hotels also act as places for residents to go for a drink, for dinner, to a nightclub, for a workout and to relax at the weekend.

There are dozens of the world's leading hotel brands to be found here, many of them housed in some of the city's most interesting buildings. Your first encounter with them may be when you come to Abu Dhabi on a reconnaissance mission before you make the decision to move permanently. You might also find yourself staying in one when you first move out, often hosted by your new company, while you find your feet and look for some accommodation of your own.

Once you're settled in, you'll soon become familiar with many of the places listed in this section. Whether you're going out for Friday brunch, after-work drinks or a romantic dinner, the UAE's licensing laws – alcohol can only be served in hotels or sports clubs – mean that it's likely to take place in a hotel.

Putting your visitors up in a hotel (should lack of space dictate and budget allow) is also something you may need to do; Abu Dhabi's popularity as a tourist destination means that most hotels are excellently geared up for holidaymakers, with several located on the beach or near to some of the main attractions.

There is a vast array of hotels, ranging from one of the most superlative and opulent in the world, the Emirates Palace (p.201), with a rack rate in the region of Dhs.6,000 for a night in a standard suite, right down to the cheapest digs in areas such as those in Al Salam Street costing under Dhs.250 a night. While the hotels at the higher end of the market offer superb surroundings and facilities, those at the cheaper end vary – and you certainly get what you pay for.

For people arriving in Abu Dhabi on a holiday package, hotels are normally five or four star, but if you are looking for cheaper accommodation at the lower end of the market, make sure you check out the hotel and have a look at one of the rooms before checking in. Remember that, as with anywhere else in the world, you can usually get a discount on the rack rate or published price if you negotiate.

Many hotels also offer seasonal discounts to GCC residents, particularly in the hot summer months when prices can be 50% lower than at peak times, providing a great opportunity for a bargain break. .

The Abu Dhabi Tourism Authority (ADTA) oversees a hotel classification system that gives an internationally recognised star rating to hotels and hotel apartments so that visitors can judge more easily the standard of accommodation they will receive. See www.adta.ae for more details.

For restaurants and bars that operate in Abu Dhabi's hotels, refer to the index at the back of the book. Just look up the hotel name and all of its outlets that are featured in the book will be listed underneath.

New Hotels

Anyone visiting Abu Dhabi for the first time would be forgiven for thinking that the city was immune to the recent financial crisis, especially with all the hotels that have recently sprung up. In 2009, 10 new hotels opened in the capital, of which seven were located on Yas Island to coincide with Abu Dhabi's first ever Formula 1 race and the launch of extensive leisure facilities from golf courses to indoor theme parks. Three more hotels opened their doors in 2010 and around two dozen new establishments scattered across the city and emirate are slated to open by the end of 2011. Some of these are likely to be delayed, but confirmed openings include the first hotels on Saadiyat Island: Park Hyatt Abu Dhabi will welcome its first guests in October 2011 and St. Regis Saadiyat Island Resort looks set to follow suit in November. Yet more hotels are getting ready to launch operations across the turquoise waters on Abu Dhabi's main island. Rocco Forte, operator of London's famed Brown's Hotel, will lure business travellers with its brand new venue, set in the heart of the city's commercial hub, from late 2011. Other big names looking to set up by the end of 2011 include Hyatt Capital Gate and Dubai-based Jumeirah, whose first ever hotel in the capital, Jumeirah at Etihad Towers, is scheduled to formally open by November 2011 in Al Khubeirah, opposite Emirates Palace. Also on Abu Dhabi island, Anantara has been confirmed as manager of the brand new Eastern Mangroves resort, off the New Corniche. Further out, the same operator is expanding its offering on the Desert Islands where the Al Sahel Lodge and Al Yamm Lodge will add a new level of accommodation in private villas, some of which are located within the island's nature reserve itself. Golfers, meanwhile, will have a new option close to the city once the Westin Golf Resort & Spa opens its doors in November 2011.

Emirates Palace In Numbers

Emirates Palace cost approximately $3 billion to build. It took 20,000 construction workers three years. The hotel sits on 100 hectares of land and, wing to wing, covers a kilometre. The hotel has 128 kitchens and pantries which use up 5kg of pure edible gold and 200 tonnes of fresh oranges each year. The building features 114 domes and 1002 chandeliers. No wonder it was the first hotel in the world to feature a vending machine selling gold bars.

Other Options

Quaint is not a word that readily comes to mind when describing Abu Dhabi. The area is not exactly known for cute little B&Bs or guesthouses nestling in the woods or on a secluded patch of beach. And hostels? Forget about it. However, Dubai, Sharjah and Fujairah all have youth hostels if you're in the market for a budget weekend. There's even a UAE Youth Hostel Association (www.uaeyh.com for more information).

What Abu Dhabi is known for is grand, luxurious, palatial hotels. Probably the closest thing to a guesthouse would be the hotel apartments. In addition to catering to residential clientele, many of these places rent rooms by the night, complete with a kitchen if you're into fixing your own meals. Obviously, these are good for extended stays, giving the traveller a bit more autonomy and flexibility in day-to-day affairs.

The Abu Dhabi Tourism Authority has a hotel and apartment search engine at www.visitabudhabi.com. Approach the list with caution, however, as many places listed as having gardens, gyms and pools have nothing of the sort. The closest thing to a pool at some of the places is a puddle in the pavement in front of the entrance.

Get Away

If you'd like to escape the city for a day or two, there are a number of excellent desert, beach and mountain resorts within the UAE that are worth checking out. See Out Of The City, p.234 for full details.

Abu Dhabi Airport Hotel

Abu Dhabi International Airport 02 575 7377
www.abudhabiairporthotel.ae
Map **1 V7**

This convenient stopover is a godsend for weary travellers who have long transit times at the airport. Alternatively, you could check in the night before and just walk to the boarding gates having had a good night's sleep in this comfortable hotel.

Al Ain Palace Hotel

Corniche Road East Markaziya East **02 679 4777**
www.alainpalacehotel.com
Map **2 P3**

The Al Ain Palace (fondly known as Ally Pally) is one of Abu Dhabi's more established hotels. It offers international restaurants and a well-known British-style pub which serves great food. Situated close to the Corniche with 110 deluxe rooms and suites, plus self-contained studios and chalet-style rooms, it's a good base from which to discover Abu Dhabi.

Al Diar Capital Hotel

Al Meena St Tourist Club Area **02 678 7700**
www.aldiarhotels.com
Map **2 R3**

The Capital Hotel is well-positioned in the centre of Abu Dhabi, close to both the business district and some of the city's major attractions. It has 200 rooms, 80 of which are suites and studios, and guests have access to the modern gym, swimming pool and beauty salon. The property also boasts six bars and restaurants making it a popular hangout for residents as well as visitors.

Al Diar Dana Hotel

Shk Zayed Second St Tourist Club Area **02 645 6000**
www.aldiarhotels.com
Map **2 R4**

Located in the Tourist Club Area, near Abu Dhabi Mall, this hotel has 112 spacious rooms, each with its own kitchenette for self-sufficiency, coupled with the perks of a hotel. On the dining front, those perks include a choice between a European pub, a pizzeria, a coffee shop and 49er's The Gold Rush (p.360), a Wild West themed rooftop restaurant and bar.

Al Diar Regency Hotel

Al Meena St Al Meena **02 676 5000**
www.aldiarhotels.com
Map **2 Q3**

A stone's throw from the business district, guests here have the option of rooms and suites with sea or city view balconies and all are equipped with kitchenettes. There is a business centre, a conference hall and a health club, while the in-house restaurant and popular pubs make for ideal retreats from busy city life.

Al Jazira Club Hotel

Street 17, Al Jazira Sports & Cultural Grounds
Al Madina Al Riyadiya **02 443 3966**
Map **2 M12**

The 75 room Sport City Hotel is a modern and luxurious affair located right next to the Sports City stadium. The fitness and spa facilities are, as you'd imagine, exceptional, with an Olympic size swimming pool and two indoor playing fields.

Al Raha Beach Hotel > p.344

Nr Al Raha Mall Al Raha **02 508 0555**
www.danathotels.com
Map **1 R7**

In a city known for its big, brash, luxurious hotels, Al Raha was Abu Dhabi's first boutique resort and, although it is located just 20 minutes from the airport and is next door to a large shopping mall, it is rapidly becoming known as a retreat to escape to. The rooms enjoy sea views and there is a selection of excellent dining outlets. Leisure facilities at the resort include a health club, spa, two pools, squash courts, watersports and a children's playground.

Aloft Abu Dhabi

Abu Dhabi National Exhibition Centre (ADNEC)
Al Safarat **02 654 5000**
www.aloftabudhabi.com
Map **1 H8**

Part of the Starwood group, Aloft Abu Dhabi is a true designer offering located at the Abu Dhabi National Exhibition Centre (ADNEC). Aloft is a modern, trendy 408 bedroom hotel with full business and events facilities, a state-of-the-art gym and rooftop splash pool, and a range of bars and restaurants, from Dine, the all-day buffet option, to the cool rooftop lounge bar Relax@12 (p.396) which is a popular hangout among local expats. Check the website for regular special offers.

Beach Rotana Abu Dhabi

Liwa St, Nr Abu Dhabi Mall Tourist Club Area
02 697 9000
www.rotana.com
Map **2 S5**

An Abu Dhabi landmark, the hotel boasts a conference centre and luxury suites with 414 sea-facing rooms. It offers some of the most popular dining options in Abu Dhabi (such as Rodeo Grill, p.384) as well as direct access to the Abu Dhabi Mall. The Rotana's many leisure facilities include a private beach, a covered children's play area, tennis and squash courts, and swimming pools. In addition, the large Zen Spa is another major draw to both tourists and local residents alike.

Cassells Ghantoot Hotel & Resort

Nr Racing & Polo Club Ghantoot **02 506 8888**
www.cassellsghantoothotel.com
Map **3 D3**

Around 45 minutes north of the city along Sheikh Zayed Road, very close to the Racing and Polo Club on the Abu Dhabi-Dubai border, Cassells is a slightly old-fashioned but pleasant beachfront resort hotel with an Arabic restaurant and coffee shop, and recreational facilities including a pool, sauna, Jacuzzi and access to watersports and horse riding.

Centro Yas Island

Golf Plaza Yas Island West **02 656 4444**
www.rotana.com
Map **1 T5**

One of the crop of seven Yas Island hotels that opened in time for the 2009 F1 GP, Centro is a modern and luxurious business hotel with 259 bedrooms, conferencing facilities, plus a fitness centre with gym, pool and steam rooms. F&B offerings are simple but stylish, with a buffet style restaurant, a deli for takeaways or room service, and a modern but informal lounge bar.

Cristal Hotel Abu Dhabi

Off Electra St Madinat Zayed **02 652 0000**
www.cristalhotelsandresorts.com
Map **2 M4**

This 192 room and suite hotel is right in the heart of the action, next to the downtown banking district. It has state-of-the-art conferencing facilities, a couple of decent F&B offerings in the shape of a cafe and an all day restaurant, and the Cristal Club Lounge is a popular venue for informal business meetings. The 19th floor spa and fitness club are both excellent.

Crowne Plaza Abu Dhabi

Shk Hamdan Bin Mohamed St Markaziya East
02 621 0000
www.ichotelsgroup.com
Map **2 N4**

Situated in the heart of the city and only a few minutes' walk from the shopping district and beach, the Crowne Plaza is another well-established landmark hotel, ideal for both business and leisure travellers. The hotel has a lobby cafe and four restaurants – including popular Asian and Italian offerings – two bars, a health and fitness centre, and the rooftop has stunning views

Crowne Plaza

of the city. The hotel is a good venue for business with 13 meeting rooms, three executive floors and an excellent business centre.

Crowne Plaza Yas Island

Yas Island Yas Island West **02 656 3000**
www.ichotelsgroup.com
Map **1 S5**

Sitting right next to Yas Links Abu Dhabi golf course, this 428 room hotel has a fully-equipped health and fitness centre that includes squash courts and a 25 metre swimming pool. Four excellent restaurants and two bars are also on hand to tempt guests and visitors. It boasts excellent conferencing facilities and, for sports and leisure fans, is just a five minute walk from both the Yas Marina Circuit and Ferrari World.

Emirates Palace

Corniche Road West Al Ras Al Akhdar **02 690 9000**
www.emiratespalace.com
Map **2 B2**

Arguably Abu Dhabi's most famous and instantly recognisable landmark, the $3bn Emirates Palace – reported to be the world's most costly hotel – boasts 392 opulent rooms and suites, all decked out with the latest technology and sumptuous decor. Operated by the exclusive Kempinski group, there are several outstanding food outlets offering seven-star service and some of the most indulgent dishes the city has to offer. The afternoon high tea is a must. Guests can enjoy the 1.3km stretch of private beach, two amazing pools and the exclusive Anantara spa, not to mention several galleries, exhibits and boutiques.

Fairmont Bab Al Bahr

Nr Al Maqta & Mussafa Bridges Bain Al Jessrain **02 654 3333**
www.fairmont.com
Map **1 L8**

Located next to the creek in the Souk Qaryat Al Beri area, the 369 room hotel is every bit as luxurious as you'd expect from a Fairmont. It has two pools and great views over the creek to Abu Dhabi island. The hotel's bars and restaurants have proven popular among locals, with Frankie's (named after owner and champion jockey Frankie Dettori, p.372), Marco Pierre White's Steakhouse and Grill (p.378) and The Chocolate Gallery (p.368) arguably the pick of the bunch.

Golden Tulip Al Jazira Hotel & Resort

Dubai – Abu Dhabi Rd, Nr Racing & Polo Club Ghantoot **02 562 9100**
www.goldentulipaljazira.com
Map **3 D3**

Located on a large, quiet canal that encircles the hotel in Ghantoot – a quiet resort around 45 minutes north of Abu Dhabi island – the 80 room hotel is a stone's throw from the Ghantoot Racing and Polo Club, and offers a large pool area to chill out in, direct marina access, varied watersports facilities and four cafes and bars. Please note that Plastik, the resort's St Tropez style beach club, is now closed.

Grand Continental Flamingo Hotel

Hamdan St Markaziya East **02 690 4000**
www.gcfhotel.net
Map **2 P3**

This intimate, boutique style hotel is centrally located in the business and commercial district. It has 155 rooms, all of which offer good views of the city. There are three restaurants, including the popular Peppino Italian restaurant (p.381). The hotel has a host of handy business facilities and a well-equipped gym.

Grand Millennium Al Wahda

Al Wahda Complex, Hazaa Bin Zayed St Al Nahyan **02 443 9999**
www.millenniumhotels.com
Map **2 M7**

In a great location next to Al Wahda Mall and almost slap-bang in the middle of downtown Abu Dhabi, The Grand Millennium Al Wahda is a giant testament to high-end hospitality. Its 844 rooms, suites and apartments are bright, modern and even more spacious than you'll find in most luxury hotels; the second floor spa and fitness areas are among the city's very best; while the rooftop pool, sunbathing area, juice bar and relaxation beds are the cherry on the cake. Its F&B outlets – Toshi and Porto Bello in particular – are excellent.

Hilton Abu Dhabi

Corniche Rd West Al Khubeirah **02 681 1900**
www.hilton.com
Map **2 C3**

Conveniently located between Abu Dhabi's financial district and Marina Mall, the Hilton is one of the capital's landmark hotels and has 350 beautifully decorated rooms and suites. The Hiltonia Beach Club is one of the city's most popular, with a private beach, swimming pools and a luxurious gym and spa. The restaurants and bars are also among Abu Dhabi's top entertainment options, particularly Hemingways (p.394), renowned Italian restaurant BiCE (p.366), and the funky Jazz Bar (p.394).

Holiday Inn Abu Dhabi

31st Street, Btn East Rd & Shk Rashid Bin Al Maktoum Rd Al Rehhan **02 657 4888**
www.holidayinn.com
Map **1 H7**

Located near to both Al Bateen Airport and ADNEC, the recently opened 203 room hotel has an excellent, fully staffed business centre and a roof level fitness centre with gym, pool, sauna and steam room. The fitness centre even offers a smattering of reasonably priced spa treatments, such as Swedish, Thai and aromatherapy massages to help take the edge off a busy working day. Food and drink options are limited but of good standard, with a restaurant, a cafe and a lounge bar.

InterContinental Abu Dhabi > p.369

Bainunah St Al Bateen **02 666 6888**
www.ichotelsgroup.com
Map **2 C4**

This landmark hotel was completely renovated in 2006 and now provides 390 modern rooms and suites in a prime location overlooking the Arabian Gulf and a lovely marina. There is a choice of superb eateries, including the always popular Fishmarket (p.372) and Belgian Beer Cafe (p.391), state-of-the-art business facilities, and, for relaxation, there is a 24 hour gym, outdoor pool, squash court, tennis courts and a beautiful private beach next to the marina.

Khalidiya Palace Rayhaan By Rotana

Corniche Road West Al Ras Al Akhdar **02 657 0000**
www.rotana.com
Map **2 A3**

Although just a stone's throw from the city centre, this new hotel's location on Corniche Road West gives the illusion of being away from the hustle and bustle of the city: some of the rooms offer balconies and tranquil views of the hotel's private beach and there are six sea view conference rooms to boot. There's also a fitness club, inclusive of spa, as well as three restaurants.

Kingsgate Hotel

Nr Abu Dhabi Mall Tourist Club Area **02 499 5000**
www.millenniumhotels.com
Map **2 R5**

The 108 room Kingsgate Hotel is located near to the Abu Dhabi Mall (p.334) in the busy Tourist Club Area. Smaller and quieter than some of the area's bigger hotels, it is an understated but classy affair with nicely appointed but simple conference and banqueting facilities, sports and leisure offerings and one tasteful restaurant-cafe concept.

Le Meridien Abu Dhabi

Liwa St, Nr Old Abu Dhabi Co-op Society
Tourist Club Area **02 644 6666**
www.lemeridienabudhabi.com
Map **2 S4**

A recent facelift has rejuvenated this landmark hotel's 234 guest rooms and suites. There are plenty of leisure facilities, including a private beach, kids' and adults' swimming pools and a health club and spa. The European-style courtyard houses many of the hotel's food and beverage outlets, including a popular traditional pub, The Captain's Arms (p.391), and upmarket French, Thai and Italian restaurants.

Le Royal Meridien Abu Dhabi > p.229

Sheikh Khalifa St Markaziya East **02 674 2020**
www.leroyalmeridienabudhabi.com
Map **2 P3**

This hotel – one of the city's best known and most visited – has 265 beautiful rooms and suites, most with spectacular views of the Corniche and Arabian Gulf. There are 13 restaurants and bars, all of which are excellent – particularly Al Fanar (p.361), the revolving rooftop restaurant, and the Shuja Yacht (p.387), upon which you can take a romantic dinner cruise. Leisure facilities include both indoor and outdoor swimming pools, and a fitness centre.

Mafraq Hotel

Nr Mafraq Hospital, Al Mafraq Airport Area
02 659 6666
www.mafraq-hotel.com
Map **2 U13**

Originally opened in 1996, this hotel has been going through renovations; call in advance to enquire about availability. Conveniently located just 10 minutes from Abu Dhabi International Airport, the hotel features 121 rooms and four suites with an excellent choice of leisure facilities that include a swimming pool and a recreation club. The Mafraq's revamp will also see an adjoining 129 room wing and chalet block added. Other facilities will include larger swimming pools, a ballroom and a new conference centre.

New Options

2011 will see the opening of a number of new hotels in Abu Dhabi. On Saadiyat Island (p.35), Park Hyatt Abu Dhabi and St. Regis Saadiyat Island Resort will open their doors. Meanwhile, Jumeirah, Ritz-Carlton and Rocco Forte are among the scheduled openings on the main island. Further out, Anantara is expanding on the Desert Islands (p.240). See New Hotels, p.198.

Mercure Centre Hotel

Shk Hamdan Bin Mohd St, Nr Liwa Centre
Markaziya East **02 633 3555**
www.mercure.com
Map **2 M4**

Located in a central spot near Liwa Centre in Markaziya East, this hotel has 215 rooms and suites, comprehensive meetings facilities and enough to sate the appetite of most fanatical fitness freaks, in the form of a gym, swimming pool, sauna and Jacuzzi. There's also an array of F&B outlets, including a poolside sports bar, a piano lounge, a cafe, a Chinese restaurant and a popular French restaurant.

Millennium Hotel Abu Dhabi

Sheikh Khalifa Bin Zayed St Markaziya East
02 614 6000
www.millenniumhotels.com
Map **2 P3**

The modern Millennium Hotel, located near the Corniche, offers great city panoramas. It has 325 elegantly decorated rooms and three restaurants serving Moroccan, Italian and International cuisine. The hotel is best known for its champagne and cigar bar, Cristal (p.392). The business and leisure facilities are comprehensive with boardrooms, a business centre, a fitness club and a swimming pool.

One To One Hotel – The Village

Al Salam St, Nr Dar Al Shifa Hospital Al Dhafrah
02 495 2000
www.onetoonehotels.com
Map **2 Q8**

The One to One Hotel differs from many establishments in that it resembles a small, European boutique hotel. The One to One group was launched in 2007 and seeks to redefine the region's notion of hospitality, so expect a more personal experience than you're likely to get from the big chains. The hotel is a little way from downtown, but is close to the airport and exhibition centre. It is becoming increasingly popular with the city's younger residents who are drawn to its stylish but relaxed cafes, bars and restaurants.

Oryx Hotel

7th Street Al Khalidiyah **02 681 0001**
www.oryxhotel.ae
Map **2 F4**

There are 96 luxurious rooms and 32 suites at this boutique-style hotel in Al Khalidiyah, just five minutes walk from the Corniche. It has a spacious and well-equipped gym, a soothing spa and a rooftop pool, as well as a range of services aimed specifically at the business traveller. The hotel has two restaurants, while a drink in the top floor Blue Bar is a must, if only to take in the panoramic views of Abu Dhabi's skyline.

Park Inn By Radisson Abu Dhabi, Yas Island Hotel

Golf Plaza Yas Island West **02 656 2222**
www.parkinn.com
Map **1 T5**

A modern, affordable offering on Yas Island, the Park Inn has a particular eye for business travellers and those visiting Yas Marina circuit or Ferrari World. There are 204 rooms, two modern meeting rooms, a pool bar and two very good restaurants with the Mexican, Amerigos (p.361), gaining a reputation as a fun venue for groups. Swankier restaurant, bar and spa offerings are available just next door at Yas Island's other hotels.

Park Rotana Abu Dhabi

Nr Sheikh Khalifa Park Al Matar **02 657 3333**
www.rotana.com
Map **1 K7**

Located in the new government-backed business area near Khalifa Park, the bridges off the island, the Grand Mosque and ADNEC, its 308 rooms are lavishly laid out, while there are all the usual leisure and business facilities you'd expect from a five-star establishment. Its food and drink outlets, Teatro restaurant (p.388) and Cooper's gastro pub (p.392) in particular, have gained popularity among those living just off the island, thanks to the hotel's convenient location.

Radisson Blu Hotel, Abu Dhabi Yas Island

Golf Plaza Yas Island West **02 656 2000**
www.radissonblu.com
Map **1 S5**

With views over both the marina and the Yas Links Abu Dhabi golf course, the new Radisson Blu is located on the western side of Yas Island. It is a large, comfortable and well-equipped hotel with excellent meeting, pool, fitness and spa facilities. However, it is the hotel's F&B that is getting most attention; Filini (p.372) is already considered one of the city's best Italians, while Assymetri (p.362) draws the Friday brunch crowds in.

Sands Hotel

Sheikh Zayed Second St Madinat Zayed **02 615 6666**
www.danathotels.com
Map **2 N4**

Centrally located, the Sands Hotel is a popular option, especially with business travellers. Offering quick access to the commercial and financial districts, it has excellent conferencing amenities, including secretarial services and meeting and banqueting capacity for up to 1,000 people. It also has some excellent food and drink outlets, including the lively Harvester's English Pub. There is a rooftop pool, a sundeck and a good gym.

Shangri-La Hotel, Qaryat Al Beri

Qaryat Al Beri Complex Bain Al Jessrain **02 509 8888**
www.shangri-la.com
Map **1 L8**

This luxury resort hotel overlooks the creek that separates Abu Dhabi island from the mainland. The 214 spacious rooms and suites all have private terraces with stunning sea views. Its two gyms, kilometre of private beach and five swimming pools make it one of the most popular and luxurious holiday retreat in the capital. The spa and outlets – particularly Bord Eau (p.367) and Pearls and Caviar (p.396) – are extremely popular with the city's well-to-do residents looking for an atmospheric night out by the water's edge. The Shangri-La also has direct access to Souk Qaryat Al Beri (p.342), an Arabian style souk with shops, cafes and restaurants connected by waterways. The souk has emerged as one of Abu Dhabi's favourite dining destinations so you will not be short of options here even after you've covered all of the hotel's own dining outlets.

Sheraton Abu Dhabi Hotel & Resort

Corniche Rd Markaziya East **02 677 3333**
www.sheratonabudhabihotel.com
Map **2 Q2**

The recently refurbished 272 room Sheraton Abu Dhabi is situated on the revamped area of the Corniche. The hotel is a longstanding favourite dining venue for many Abu Dhabi expats. There are 12 restaurants and bars, including the romantic seafood restaurant, Il Paradiso (p.373), to choose from. In addition, there's a popular English pub, which is good for watching sports. As for leisure activities, the facilities are varied: there are climate controlled outdoor pools, squash and tennis courts, a fitness centre and a private beach offering watersports and volleyball.

Sheraton Khalidiya Hotel Abu Dhabi

Sheikh Zayed The First St Markaziya West
02 666 6220
www.sheratonkhalidiyaabudhabi.com
Map **2 J4**

This downtown hotel is in the upmarket Al Khalidiyah area, close to Abu Dhabi's business and commercial districts in the heart of the city. A 2007 refurbishment added a state-of-the-art business centre with extremely well-equipped meeting rooms to lure business travellers. The hotel has 285 guest rooms and its other facilities include a rooftop gym, a sundeck and a pool. There are also two solid restaurant offerings, while The 3rd Avenue bar is proving to be a welcome addition to the expat social scene in this part of town.

Traders Hotel, Qaryat Al Beri

Qaryat Al Beri Complex, Btn the Bridges
Bain Al Jessrain **02 510 8888**
www.shangri-la.com
Map **1 L8**

Part of the large and picturesque Souk Qaryat Al Beri (p.342) complex that peers over the creek between the mainland and Abu Dhabi island, Traders offers 301 luxurious rooms and suites, a private beach and very well appointed gym and relaxed pool area. The hotel has just the one restaurant, a lobby lounge and a pool bar, but it also has direct access into Souk Qaryat Al Beri, where a maze of cafes, shops and restaurants await to be explored. Guests also have access to the neighbouring Shangri-La hotel's facilities, including one of the city's most highly regarded spas and a myriad of other options.

Tulip Inn Al Rahba

Shk Zayed Rd, Rahba City
02 563 8557
www.tulipinnalrahba.com
Map **3 D2**

Half an hour from the city centre along the Abu Dhabi-Dubai highway, this 52 room hotel offers good value with regular offers on its website. It has a tennis court, a basketball court, swimming pools for adults and children and a Jacuzzi, with work to add a fitness club with spa underway. It has two bars, a shisha bar and a cafe, with one main restaurant specialising in Arabic cuisine.

The Yas Hotel > *p.363*

Nr Yas Marina Yas Island West **02 656 0000**
www.theyashotel.com
Map **1 T5**

Abu Dhabi's latest icon, the stunning The Yas Hotel is an architectural wonder that straddles the F1 race track – the bridge over the track perhaps offering the best views of all come race day. Its futuristic shell is illuminated at night, while the interiors are no less modern or spectacular. The hotel has 499 rooms, excellent fitness and spa facilities, and is also popular for meetings and conferences. Its F&B offerings are all developing reputations as some of the very best the city has to offer, with Amici (p.361) and Kazu (p.376) real stand outs. The top floor Skylite Lounge (p.397) is one of Abu Dhabi's coolest night time haunts.

Yas Island Rotana

Golf Plaza Yas Island West **02 656 4000**
www.rotana.com
Map **1 T4**

A superb hotel on the up-and-coming Yas Island, The Yas Island Rotana has 308 rooms and suites which ooze modern luxury, while there are also more sports, fitness and spa facilities than you can shake a tennis racquet at. Another of the city's popular meetings and conferences venues, its F&B outlets are also starting to make a splash, particularly Blue Grill (p.367) and Rangoli (p.381).

ART & CULTURE

Heritage & Cultural Sites

Abu Dhabi has a handful of interesting places to visit, offering glimpses into a time not so long ago when the city was nothing more than a small fishing, pearling and trading port. Many of the pre-oil heritage sites have been or are currently being carefully restored, with close attention being paid to traditional design and the use of original building materials.

The Yas Hotel

InterContinental Abu Dhabi

Khalidiya Palace Rayhaan By Rotana

Shangri-La, Qaryat Al Beri

Where For Art Thou?

With big and bold new developments, Abu Dhabi is aiming to become the cultural capital of the Middle East – but what of its current art scene?

Since the capital is gearing up to become the cultural centre of the UAE, one might think the art scene would be buzzing. Well, not quite yet. But (and it's a big but) the best is yet to come. In typical UAE style, when they do it, they tend to go all out, and that's the attitude for the upcoming Guggenheim and Louvre Abu Dhabi museums, both slated to open in the next few years. The models for these buildings look like something from outer space, as if the architects (Frank Gehry and Jean Nouvel, respectively) were given free reign and a blank cheque. Indeed, the buildings will be things to behold, and the art housed inside promises to take viewers to new levels. In the meantime, there are options. Foremost of these is the Abu Dhabi Art Fair, held in November. The exhibition, held in the Emirates Palace Ballroom, has previously showcased work from 50 galleries in 19 countries to thousands of attendees during the four-day event. When names like de Kooning, Richter and Basquiat are tossed around, the art world listens; Jeff Koons even made an appearance at the 2010 fair. The next edition is again scheduled for November and, as is often the case with these events in this neck of the woods, expect each year to show notable growth and improvement (www.abudhabiartfair).

Other events at the Emirates Palace have included a Picasso exhibition, previews of both the Louvre and Guggenheim, and a sprawling display of Islamic art. Check the Arts Abu Dhabi website (www.artsabudhabi.ae) for upcoming gallery shows and other events.

Of the bigger venues, the new Manarat Al Saadiyat (p.210) is an exciting addition. A multi-purpose venue, it houses lecture theatres, an auditorium and acts as a visitors' centre to the Saadiyat project. It also contains three galleries and, although it is still early days for Manarat Al Saadiyat, the first exhibitions have shown its potential, with some fascinating exhibitions examining the notion of Middle East unity organised by guest curators from around the region, one of the definite highlights to date.

Although there are still only a handful of independent galleries in Abu Dhabi, the capital does have a burgeoning gallery scene. One of the premier spaces in Abu Dhabi is the Ghaf Art Gallery (p.210). The oldest contemporary art gallery in the capital, Ghaf concentrates on showcasing contemporary local and regional artists, as well as solo and mixed exhibits featuring international names.

Qibab Art Gallery (p.210) specialises predominantly in Iraqi art but as a gallery it is also dedicated to showing both local and foreign contemporary artists, often including handicrafts and traditional bazaars along with the art to give the viewer a real cultural experience. Acento Gallery (p.210), strangely enough, specialises in Mexican and Spanish art but in recent years it has shown artists from New York as well as locally-based artists from places like New Zealand, Uganda and Pakistan. Newcomer, Salwa Zeidan Gallery (p.210) shows international and Middle Eastern contemporary masters, as well as emerging artists from varied backgrounds. The gallery also shows a wide range of mediums, from painting, photography and sculpture to installation and performance art.

Finally, the Abu Dhabi Festival, billed as the UAE's premier classical arts event, takes place during March and April each year. Though concentrating on music, the festival showcases works by a couple of artists each year and often commissions new works. In 2010, the festival included the exhibit Middle Eastern Modern Masters, with works by Parviz Tanavoli and Adam Henein shown in the Emirates Palace. In addition to showing the artists' works, the festival featured lectures by the artists as well as panels about art in the UAE.

What The Future Holds

Although the incredible structures themselves will take a lot of the plaudits, both the Guggenheim and Louvre Abu Dhabi will be genuinely exciting spaces of international note. Guggenheim has already named its curators and says the gallery will exhibit a collection focused on international post-war art. The Louvre meanwhile – the first ever outside the original Paris location – will feature global works with particular focus on those creating a dialogue between east and west. Other than that, Louvre chiefs have said that the museum's location in a Muslim country will have no effect on the pieces that will go on show.

Abu Dhabi Authority For Culture & Heritage (ADACH)

Airport Rd, Nr Zayed Sports City Al Madina Al Riyadiya **02 657 6171**
www.adach.ae
Map **1 J8**

Previously housed in a remarkable building next to Qasr Al Hosn (p.208) that had become the heartbeat of the city's thriving community arts scene, ADACH (the foundation in charge of Abu Dhabi emirate's culture and heritage offerings) is now based in a temporary location near Zayed Sports City and ADNEC. Meanwhile, the entire city centre block that contains the foundation and heritage site Qasr Al Hosn (p.208), is undergoing major renovations with the aim of creating the UAE's foremost cultural visitor attraction. The foundation continues to oversee the emirate's culture and heritage and organises exhibitions, screenings, performances and lectures all over the city. See the website for a full calendar.

Al Maqtaa Fort

Nr Maqtaa Bridge Al Maqtaa
Map **1 L8**

This heavily renovated fort is one of the few remaining examples of its kind in Abu Dhabi city. Your first glimpse of the monument will likely be as you approach the Al Maqtaa Bridge towards Abu Dhabi island. The 200 year old fort, standing on the edge of the island, was built to fend off bandits and provides a wonderful contrast to the modern bridge right next to it. Be careful when taking photographs here as it is a sensitive military zone and there are often police patrols.

Bateen Dhow Shipyard

Nr InterContinental Abu Dhabi Al Bateen
Map **2 B6**

Connected to the island via a short causeway over Khor Al Bateen, the Bateen Shipyard is a cluttered, busy and charmingly atmospheric area where proud boat builders continue to craft vessels in the way they have done for decades. Visit early in the morning or late in the afternoon and you'll be rewarded by friendly workers who are happy to explain their craft and be photographed.

Emirates National Auto Museum

South of Abu Dhabi, Hamim Rd, Off E11
www.enam.ae
Map **3 D3**

Located 45 kilometres south of Abu Dhabi, this impressive pyramid houses an assortment of cars from one dedicated collector: Sheikh Hamad bin Hamdan Al Nahyan, aka the 'Rainbow Sheikh'. After officially opening to the public in 2005, the museum has recently undergone development and is now home to almost 200 cars, including a vast collection of off-road vehicles, classic American cars, the Sheikh's rainbow collection of Mercedes and the largest truck in the world. Some exhibits were showcased in the BBC television programme Top Gear. Even if you're not particularly interested in cars, this is a fascinating collection and a great place to stop on the way to or from Liwa. Opening times are currently 09:00 to 18:00 seven days a week, but this can change. Entry, formerly free, is now Dhs.50 per adult with kids still free.

Heritage Village

Nr Marina Mall Breakwater **02 681 4455**
www.torath.ae
Map **2 F2**

The picturesque Heritage Village is situated on the Breakwater near Marina Mall, facing Abu Dhabi's waterfront. Run by the Emirates Heritage Club, it offers an interesting glimpse into the country's past. Traditional aspects of the Bedouin way of life, including a camp fire with coffee pots, a goats' hair tent, a well and a falaj irrigation system, are attractively displayed in the open museum. There are workshops where craftsmen demonstrate traditional skills, such as metal work and pottery, while women sit weaving and spinning. The craftsmen are happy to share their skills and may occasionally give you the chance to try them out. The little spice shop is a treat – you can get a range of dried herbs, handmade soap and plenty of chatter. It's a great place to buy saffron; the world's most expensive spice is available in the shop at far less than you would pay in major supermarkets. After visiting the village, sample some typical Arabic cuisine at the waterside restaurants with great views of the Corniche. Close by is a pleasant kids' play area. Entry is free.

Heritage Village

Petroleum Exhibition

Corniche Rd East, Nr Commercial Bank Markaziya East **02 444 6900**
www.adnec.ae
Map **2 L2**

The recently revamped Petroleum Exhibition covers Abu Dhabi's phenomenal development from a desert oasis to a thriving cosmopolitan city. Spread across three rooms, there are scale models, photographs and maps charting the earliest oil exploration in the desert and the Gulf, to the first oil export from Das Island in 1962. Interactive displays, like giant drill bits and documentary films (in English, French and German), give a fascinating insight into one of the world's largest oil and gas producers. Entrance is free.

Ramadan Timings

During Ramadan, timings for many companies in Abu Dhabi change significantly. Museums and heritage sites usually open slightly later in the morning, and close earlier in the afternoon. Check before you go.

Qasr Al Hosn

Al Nasr St Al Manhal **02 621 5300**
www.adach.ae
Map **2 K4**

Qasr Al Hosn (also known as the Old Fort or the White Fort) is the oldest building in Abu Dhabi, dating back to 1793. It was the official residence of the rulers of Abu Dhabi when they moved from the Liwa Oasis to the island. Unfortunately, Qasr Al Hosn, along with the neighbouring Cultural Foundation, is closed for major renovations: the area is being redeveloped by ADACH (p.207) and there are plans to reopen the fort as a museum and public monument.

Sheikh Zayed Grand Mosque

Shk Rashid Bin Saeed Al Maktoum St Al Maqtaa **02 441 6444**
www.szgmc.ae
Map **1 K8**

The stunning Sheikh Zayed Grand Mosque opened in 2007, and has captivated worshippers and visitors since. This architectural work of art is one the largest mosques in the world, with a capacity for an astonishing 40,000 worshippers. The mosque's first event was the funeral of its namesake, Sheikh Zayed, who is buried at the site. It features 80 domes, over 1,000 columns, 24 carat gold-plated chandeliers and the world's largest hand-woven Persian carpet. Unlike other mosques in Abu Dhabi, Sheikh Zayed Mosque is open for non-Muslims to tour. One hour tours start at 10:00, 11:00 and 17:00 daily, but not on Fridays. For more information or to book a tour, call the number above or visit the website. This is one not to be missed.

Women's Handicraft Centre

Women's Association Complex, Al Karamah St Al Mushrif **02 562 1918**
Map **2 K11**

This creative and arty initiative is government sponsored and run by the Abu Dhabi Women's Association as a showcase for local art and crafts. The museum within may be a little on the small side but it does offer the chance to examine the handiwork of local artists and learn something about the work on display. There is also a shop onsite where you can buy some of the items which are produced, making for an original and interesting keepsake. The round buildings near the museum are workshops where female artists display distinctive Arabian oils, handmade souvenirs, incense, local dress, silver thread work and weaving. It is suggested you remove your shoes before entering each hut and note that photography is not encouraged. This is an excellent place to experience the traditional art of henna. For just Dhs.10 you can get a small henna design painted on your hand, which will last about two weeks.

Art Galleries

While there's nothing of international acclaim in Abu Dhabi yet, there are a number of galleries that have interesting exhibitions of art and traditional Arabic artefacts, and more are springing up. Most operate as a shop and a gallery, but some also provide studios for artists and are involved in the promotion of art within the UAE.

Culture Reigns In Al Ain

As the UAE's birthplace – the oasis where the Emirates' tribes originally settled before heading to the coast – Al Ain is the country's most culturally rich city and area. Located 140km inland from Abu Dhabi, it is home to many heritage attractions such as the National Museum (p.235), the Palace Museum (p.235), Al Jahili Fort and Park (p.236). See Out Of The City, p.234 for more information about Al Ain.

Abu Dhabi Authority For Culture & Heritage (ADACH)

Airport Rd, Nr Zayed Sports City Al Madina Al Riyadiya **02 657 6171**
www.adach.ae
Map **1 J8**

ADACH hosts art exhibitions throughout the year. As a government organisation, it is charged with preserving and promoting local artistic expression, and does so successfully and enthusiastically. In addition to the regular art displays, the foundation also hosts performing arts shows, poetry readings, lectures and film screenings. The foundation is

Sheikh Zayed Grand Mosque

currently based in a temporary location while the area around its original Khalidiyah Street home is being developed into a major heritage site; regardless, it continues to organise all manner of cultural activities throughout the city.

Acento Gallery

Street 13, Warehouse 6, Al Meena Port Area
Al Meena **02 673 6900**
www.acentogallery.com
Map **2 U1**

A modern, warehouse-loft style gallery in the old port area of the city, Acento is the city's largest art space and represents a roster of international artists, covering everything from paintings and etchings to sculptures. The gallery displays functional and decorative art, as well as more subjective pieces and exhibitions showcasing talent from all over the world which changes regularly.

The Barakat Gallery

Emirates Palace Al Ras Al Akhdar **02 690 8950**
www.barakatgallery.com
Map **2 B2**

Located in Emirates Palace Hotel, this recently opened and dynamic addition to Abu Dhabi's developing art scene has branches in London and Los Angeles. Barakat specialises in ancient art and has on display a multitude of antiquities from China, Egypt, the Near East, Africa, Greece and Rome. Items vary widely and include statues, jewellery, coins, necklaces and pottery.

Folklore Gallery

Sheikh Zayed First St Al Khalidiyah **02 666 0361**
www.folkloregallery.net
Map **2 G4**

A simple but welcoming art and exhibition space, this gallery focuses on local artistic and craft offerings, with traditional Bedouin ceramics and jewellery available at reasonable prices. Art comes in the form of prints and paintings that have been inspired by the country's landscape.

Gallery One

The Souk At Qaryat Al Beri Bain Al Jessrain
02 558 1822
www.g-1.com
Map **1 L8**

Gallery One at Souk Qaryat Al Beri has become a significant player on the Abu Dhabi art scene. It regularly hosts exhibitions of international note, the most prominent to date being Art of Islam and Picasso Abu Dhabi in 2008. Exhibitions also bring together diverse works from across the Middle East and UAE. Gallery One usually runs a series of lectures alongside each exhibition, and entry to all shows and events is free.

Ghaf Art Gallery

Al Khaleej Al Arabi St, Nr Khalidiyah Gardens
Al Khalidiyah **02 665 5332**
ghafgallery.blogspot.com
Map **2 G5**

The funky Ghaf Art Gallery opened its doors to art lovers in 2006, intent on presenting local artists to Abu Dhabi residents. It hasn't disappointed, with Ghaf becoming a notable player in the city's arts scene. Exhibitions are both mixed and individual, showcasing local and also sometimes international artists, with new artists regularly exhibiting their work. The gallery is open from 09:00 to 13:00 and 17:00 to 21:00, but is closed on Fridays.

Manarat Al Saadiyat

Sadiyat Island **02 406 1400**
www.saadiyat.ae
Map **1 G1**

Although the most eagerly anticipated elements of Saadiyat Island – the Guggenheim, Louvre and the Zayed National Museum – may still be a few years away from completion, the first of the island's new artistic offerings has already opened its doors. Manarat Al Saadiyat is a 15,000 square metre visitor centre that is home to the Arts Abu Dhabi Gallery, the Contemporary Art Gallery and the Universal Art Gallery, a restaurant as well as several auditoriums and other interesting display spaces. With an impressive programme of exhibitions that is set to pick up pace as the year goes on, this new and exciting addition to Abu Dhabi's art scene is already exhibiting some fascinating works and collections.

Qibab Art Gallery

Corniche Rd East Al Manhal **02 665 2350**
www.qibabgallery.com
Map **2 G5**

With a focus on Middle Eastern contemporary art, Qibab Art Gallery specialises in promoting the work of Iraqi artists in particular and showcasing future trends to Abu Dhabi's art enthusiasts and collectors. Exhibitions change regularly, so there's often something new to check out.

Salwa Zeidan Gallery

Al Khaleej Al Arabi St 30, Villa 256 Al Khalidiyah
02 666 9656
www.salwazeidangallery.com
Map **2 G5**

A lovely, bright and large space that showcases not just painting, sculpture and photography, but also works of installation and performance pieces. Works are fresh and thought-provoking, and many provide an interesting comment on the current state of Islam. The gallery hosts many exhibitions and is also the driving force behind an annual sculpture symposium.

PARKS, BEACHES & ATTRACTIONS

Parks

Abu Dhabi has a number of excellent parks, most of which have lush green lawns and a variety of trees and shrubs, creating the perfect escapes from the concrete and construction jungle of the city. During the winter months, the more popular parks can get very busy at weekends. Most have a kiosk or a cafe selling snacks and drinks, and some even have barbecue pits – just remember to bring your own wood or charcoal.

Regulations among the parks vary, with some banning bikes and rollerblades, or limiting ball games to specific areas. Pets are not permitted and you should not collect plant cuttings either. Some parks have a ladies' day when entry is restricted to women, girls and young boys, and certain smaller ones actually ban anyone other than ladies through the week, while allowing families only at the weekends. Entrance to the smaller parks is generally free, while the larger ones charge up to Dhs.5 per person. Opening hours of most parks change during Ramadan.

Al Nahyan Garden

Shk Zayed First St Al Khalidiyah
Map **2 H4**

One of a number of small children's parks found throughout the city, this well-maintained and compact park located near the Sheraton Khalidiya (p.204) ensures your little ones can't get up to too much trouble. Simple play equipment helps the kids let off steam. Entrance is just Dhs.1 but single men without their children or family will not be allowed entry.

Capital Gardens

Nr NBAD Markaziya East
Map **2 N3**

This refurbished park is a welcome patch of green in the middle of the city centre. Each little cove of the garden has a small selection of climbing frames, swings and slides. A large pond in the middle erupts periodically with bursts from the stunning fountains, taking visitors by surprise. Vending machines and an enclosed cafeteria provide refreshment – and there is a popular takeaway pizza place right across the road. There is also a small mosque and a municipal plant shop.

The Corniche

Off Corniche Rd, Central Abu Dhabi Al Khubeirah
Map **2 J3**

Extensive land reclamation and park development along the Corniche has created an expansive series of lush green spaces for everyone to enjoy. Corniche Road now boasts an impressive six kilometres of parks that include children's play areas, a separate cycle and

DUBAI'S ART DELIGHTS

While Abu Dhabi's art scene is growing, an hour down the road in Dubai, it's positively flourishing, especially in the Al Quoz industrial area, where galleries, artists' spaces and cultural communities have popped up consistently over the past few years. Art Sawa (www.artsawa.com), The Third Line (www.thethirdline.com), Total Arts Gallery (www.courtyard-uae.com), Gallery Isabelle Van den Eynde (www.ivde.net) and Meem Gallery (www.meemartgallery.com) are some of the best; if you're looking for an artsy community, then head for The Jam Jar (www.thejamjardubai.com) or Shelter (www.shelter.ae). At the other end of the spectrum, Dubai International Finance Centre (DIFC) has top notch galleries, such as Artspace (www.artspace-dubai.com), The Farjam Collection (www.farjamcollection.com), The Empty Quarter (www.theemptyquarter.com) and Cuadro (www.cuadroart.com), which house quality pieces from masters such as Picasso and Matisse.

Art Dubai (www.artdubai.ae) is an annual get-together of industry people from across the Middle East and Asia. Held in March at Madinat Jumeirah, one of the main events is the Global Art Forum, which attracts artists, curators, museum groups and international media. Several exhibitions and events also run alongside the forum, drawing thousands of visitors. During Art Dubai, the ArtBus (04 341 7303, www.artinthecity.com) ferries culture vultures between Dubai's best venues. For major arts festivals or exhibitions, the ArtBus links Dubai-based art lovers with the country's capital to get a taste of what Abu Dhabi has to offer.

Ayyam Gallery, Al Quoz

pedestrian path, cafes and restaurants, and Corniche Beach, a life-guarded beach park. There is the Family Park near King Khalid bin Abdul Aziz Street (26th Street), noted for its creative climbing structures; the Urban Park near Sheikh Rashid bin Saeed Al Maktoum Street, with its beautiful garden; the Lake Park near Muroor Street, known for its 'lake'; and the Formal Park by Baniyas Street, noted for its architecture and maze. There is plenty of parking on the city side of Corniche Road, and pedestrian underpasses at all the major intersections connect to the waterfront side.

Khalidiya Children's Garden

Nr THE One Al Khubeirah
Map **2 F4**

This is one of the more popular parks in the city with the area's residents flooding here during the cooler months. Costs of the various rides and play equipment vary, but the standard entry fee remains at Dhs.1.

Khalidiyah Garden

Al Khaleej Al Arabi St Al Khalidiyah
Map **2 G4**

Taking up a whole block, this large city park is popular with families. It has a variety of safe play areas for toddlers and older children. Its lovely grassy areas are great for picnics, with a number of large trees providing excellent shade. A branch of the Abu Dhabi Cooperative Society operates on the south side of the park, allowing for the shopping to be done once the children have let off steam.

Mosque Gardens

Shk Hamdan Bin Mohd St Markaziya East
Map **2 R4**

Also known as Electra Park, this is yet another serene retreat in the heart of the city. Like most other parks, it offers swings and slides for children to play on. It's rarely busy and therefore ideal for families. The park is located on Electra Street, between 4th and 5th Streets.

Mushrif Central Park

Al Karamah & Mohammed bin Khalifa Sts, Nr Choueifat School Al Mushrif
Map **2 K11**

This large park near Airport Road has been going through renovations aimed at turning it into a varied people's park. The whole park is unlikely to open to the public before late 2011 at the earliest. However, a jogging track is already open and the future plans include a museum and a petting zoo.

Old Airport Garden

Nr Sheikh Zayed Sport Centre Al Madina Al Riyadiya
Map **1 J8**

This is a quiet park and an ideal place if you want to relax after taking the kids ice skating at the adjacent rink. One side of the park has swings and small tidy gardens, while the other side is more ornamental, with plenty of trees offering shade. Maintenance takes place in the mornings, so be prepared to move quickly if the sprinkler system is switched on. If the hunger pangs strike, there's a KFC right on the edge of the gardens. And for any unfortunate injuries, Al Noor Hospital's (p.161) newest facility has opened near the park's southern boundary.

Park on The Corniche

Sheikh Khalifa Park

Nr Al Bateen Airport Al Matar **800 22220**
www.adm.gov.ae/khalifa_park
Map **1 K7**

Located in Al Matar, off the Eastern Ring Road, Khalifa Park is one of the city's largest parks and is now a major landmark. The inspiration for the designs of the gardens has been drawn from Arabic and Islamic architecture, as well as from some of the great gardens around the world, including Chatsworth House in England and the Al Hambra Palace in Spain. The gardens are set in a landscape of canals, fountains, lakes and waterfalls, and mini train tours of the park are available. With play equipment for children, picnic facilities and an outdoor auditorium, it's a popular spot in the cooler evenings and at weekends. During cooler months, a community market sees stalls set up in the park every evening. A host of activity programmes for kids are regularly run at the park as well.

Beaches

A visit to one of Abu Dhabi's beaches is a perfect way to spend the day – warm turquoise waters, white sandy beaches and stretches of lush greenery will transport you a hundred miles from the stresses of city life. Swimwear is not the norm on the public beaches so prepare for a few stares if you decide to strip off.

An upside to the public beaches in Abu Dhabi is that, unlike in other places in the UAE, vehicles can't get onto the beaches, so you won't find 4WD enthusiasts churning up the sand. Not all beach-goers are good at disposing of their litter so make sure to wear sandals or water socks to prevent unwanted injuries.

Coast Roads

In addition to the normal parks, both the roads that flank Abu Dhabi's island – the Eastern Ring Road on one side and Coast Road on the other – are fringed with lovely green, leafy spaces that hug the shoreline and look out over neighbouring mangroves. Although finding somewhere to park is not always easy, it is worth the effort, as shaded areas, benches and barbecues await. However, both these roads are prone to roadworks and general upheaval, with areas of both being developed to create new corniches for the city, complete with restaurants, bars and even resort hotels.

There are surprisingly few public beaches to choose from, and numbers have been further depleted by closures due to construction and redevelopment works. Most options located close to the city centre have been affected by the ongoing development in Abu Dhabi. The remaining options are very popular for barbecues and picnics, as well as perfect settings for a casual stroll. Like the parks, the beaches are busiest during the cooler months and at weekends.

Located on the north-western tip of Al Ras Al Akhdar, for years Abu Dhabi Public Beach was the city's most popular public beach. Prior to the construction of Emirates Palace, the beach used to extend across to the Marina Mall causeway. Now smaller, it is pretty basic, with no facilities, and is currently closed due to the building of a new presidential palace opposite. The beach is Al Bateen Beach, popular with locals and used for fishing and swimming is also currently closed due to nearby construction of a bridge. Once it's re-opened, head west on 19th Street (Saeed bin Tahnoon St) and turn left onto 16th Street when it ends. After 200 metres, you'll see the beach in front of Sheikh Sultan bin Sayed Playground. For other options to tip your toes in the warm waters of the Gulf, see Hotels, p.198.

Waterparks

Although a huge, game-changing water park is set to grace Yas Island in the next few years, for the moment, Abu Dhabi's slide enthusiasts will have to make do with the small indoors waterpark in Mushrif Mall (p.342) – or head north to Dubai, Umm Al Quwain and Ras Al Khaimah to get wet and wild. Thankfully, Wild Wadi, Aquaventure and the brand new Ice Land Water Park are all well worth the journey from Abu Dhabi if water fun is what you're after.

Aquaventure

Atlantis The Palm Dubai **04 426 0000**
www.atlantisthepalm.com

Aquaventure is the ultimate destination for wet and wild thrill seekers. To get the adrenaline pumping, head straight to the Leap of Faith, a 27 metre near-vertical drop that shoots you through a series of tunnels surrounded by shark-infested waters. Alternatively, The Rapids will take you on a tumultuous 2.3 kilometre river journey around the whole park, complete with waterfalls and wave surges. For the little ones, there is Splashers, a giant water playground, while those looking for more tranquil pursuits can lounge on the park's beach where chairs are provided. Open daily from 10:00 until sunset. Entrance for those over 1.2m is Dhs.200, and Dhs.165 for those under that height. Children younger than 2 years old and Atlantis hotel guests get in for free. Special promotional rates for residents are frequently offered during Summer. On selected Thursdays throughout the warmer months, Aquaventure holds its Cool Summer Nights parties, when the park stays open until midnight, with music and entertainment also on offer.

Dreamland Aqua Park

North of UAQ, RAK Rd Umm Al Quwain **06 768 1888**
www.dreamlanduae.com

Over 25 water rides spread across 250,000 square metres of green, landscaped grounds. Adrenaline junkies will not be disappointed with rides such as the Black Hole, the Kamikaze, and the four 'twisting dragons'. For a more leisurely experience, there's the lazy river, a wave pool, and a high-salinity pool for floating about. The Aqua Play area has 19 games and attractions for the whole family and, if you prefer not to get wet, you can burn rubber on the 400 metre go-kart track. There's a variety of cafes and restaurants, as well as a licensed pool bar and shisha majlis. Overnight accommodation is also available, either in a tent (provided for you) or a 'cabana' hut. Admission costs Dhs.100 for adults and Dhs.70 for children under 12, while children under 3 go free. The park is open all year round (check the website for timings). Fridays, Saturdays and holidays are reserved for families only.

Swim Safely

Although the waters off the coast generally look calm and unchallenging, very strong rip tides can carry the most confident swimmer away from the shore very quickly and drownings have occurred in the past. Take extra care when swimming off the public beaches where there are no lifeguards.

Ice Land Water Park
Al Jazeera Ras Al Khaimah 07 206 7888
www.icelandwaterpark.com
Located in Ras Al Khaimah, this brand-new, gigantic waterpark opened in mid-2011.The park has a capacity to welcome10,000 guests per day and the attractions include Penguin Falls (the world's tallest man-made waterfall), Penguin Bay (a rain dance pool), Arctic Slides and Tundra Baths. In addition, you'll find aqua games fields and a coral bay reef for snorkelling. General admission costs Dhs.150 for adults and Dhs.100 for kids, while annual and quarterly membership plans start from Dhs.750 per adult.

SplashLand
WonderLand Theme & Water Park Dubai
04 324 1222
www.wonderlanduae.com
The waterpark within the WonderLand amusement park offers fun for kids or adults, with nine rides including slides and twisters, a lazy river, an adults' pool and a children's activity pool with slides, bridges and water cannons. Alternatively, you can just relax by the pool and sunbathe.

Wild Wadi Water Park
Al Sufouh Rd Dubai 04 348 4444
www.wildwadi.com
Spread over 12 acres beside Jumeirah Beach Hotel (p.249), the park has 23 aquatic rides and attractions to suit all ages and bravery levels. One of the first you'll encounter is Wipeout, a permanently rolling wave giving you the chance to show off your body-boarding skills. Admission is Dhs.200 for adults and Dhs.165 for children under 1.1m in height. There is also a 'sundowner' rate (for the last three hours of opening), when adults pay Dhs.165 and children pay Dhs.135.

Wildlife

Abu Dhabi Falcon Hospital > p.vii, 138, 215
Nr Abu Dhabi International Airport Al Shamkha
02 575 5155
www.falconhospital.com
Map 3 D3
Abu Dhabi Falcon Hospital opened in 1999. Affiliated with the Environment Agency – Abu Dhabi (www.ead.ae/en), the team of specialists here provide diagnosis, treatment and disease prevention for falcons, other bird species and even poultry. Renowned for its work in the field, ADFH provides training opportunities to veterinary practitioners, students and technicians from around the world. Responding to keen interest from the general public, the hospital also offers guided two hour tours on weekdays (these must be booked in advance). Contact the hospital on the number above or see the website for more information. Also on this site is the Animal Shelter (www.abudhabianimalshelter.com).

Abu Dhabi Wildlife Centre
Al Ain Rd, Nr Al Wathba 050 614 4024
www.abudhabiwildlifecentre.com
Map 3 D3
Abu Dhabi Wildlife Centre was created with a vision of caring for sick and orphaned animals – specifically cheetahs. It is now a a fully fledged rehabilitation and breeding centre for endangered species and rare animals. Entrance costs Dhs.45 for adults, while kids under the age of 12 get in for Dhs.35; the prices are inclusive of an informative and entertaining 60 minute long tour of the facilities. The centre is open for educational visits too – call to arrange in advance.

Kids Park
Al Bahya, 35km from Abu Dhabi 02 563 3100
www.kidsparkuae.com
Map 3 D2
The recently opened Kids Park is the emirate's first petting zoo. Located 35 kilometres outside the city on the road to Dubai, the Kids Park offers children the chance to get up close to their favourite animals, combining learning with touch. The five acre farm houses peacocks, ostriches, ibex, camels, horses, raccoons, ferrets, and exotic fish and birds. The park is open every day; see the website for more details.

Amusement Centres

Action Zone
Mina Centre Al Meena 02 673 4577
www.actionzoneuae.com
Map 1 D2
Action Zone is big, bright and noisy – a kid's paradise. There are themed carousels, amusement rides, a bungee trampoline, video games and a climbing

maze. Food is served and birthday parties hosted. To play, you purchase a swipe card (Dhs.3) and load it with credit. Games are Dhs.3 to Dhs.15. Open weekdays from 10:00 to 23:00.

Fun City

Marina Mall Breakwater **02 681 5527**
www.funcity.ae
Map **2 D1**

Themed as a tropical forest, the park has a dramatic entrance built into a rock with the sound of thunder crashing all around. An array of computer and video games, carousels and other funfair facilities await inside. This is certainly not a 'learning through play' centre, but a high-tech, bright lights amusement outlet – and a very good option for keeping your kids busy while you shop. To get started, you need to purchase a play credit card (Dhs.3) which is then loaded with as much credit as you like. Games and rides cost Dhs.10 to Dhs.12.

Fun Island

Al Jernain Center Al Manhal **02 665 9009**
Map **2 K4**

Aimed at the under 5s, this play centre has a large area of safe, soft play apparatus, such as tube slides, ball ponds, hanging ropes and cruiser rollers. There is also a Lego room and computer games for older children. Birthday party packages are available. The entrance fee is Dhs.15 per child.

Fun World

Al Muhairy Bldg, Hamdan Bin Mohamed St
Al Manhal **02 632 2255**
Map **2 K4**

Fun World has a range of computer games that are intended to encourage kids to draw, paint and solve puzzles; they can also thread beads and try their hand at sand art. There's a soft play area for the little ones (Dhs.15), a coffee shop and a children's hairdresser all on the same floor. You need to purchase a Fun World credit card (Dhs.3) that you load with credit so your child can access the games (Dhs.3.50 to Dhs.8 each).

FunZone

Al Mariah Mall Al Markaziyah **02 677 1741**
www.almariah.com
Map **2 P3**

This indoor family entertainment centre has popular arcade games from bumper cars to video games and virtual reality simulators.

Kidoos

Abu Dhabi Mall Tourist Club Area **02 645 9070**
Map **2 S5**

Kidoos is a good and busy play club for younger children. There is plenty for youngsters to do with a large, soft play area, a sand pit, an art centre, numerous computers and even a small climbing wall. Refreshments are also available. Operating hours are 10:00 to 22:00 daily except Thursday (10:00 to 23:00) and Friday (14:00 to 23:00). Admission costs Dhs.35 on weekdays, and Dhs.45 from Thursday to Saturday.

Wild Times

Although the animal offerings in Abu Dhabi itself may be a little limited, there are several high quality offerings beyond the city limits that are well worth a visit for wildlife lovers. Al Ain Wildlife Park and Resort (p.236) is undoubtedly the best, with tie-ins with the world-renowned San Diego Zoo. However, Sharjah has the Arabian Wildlife Centre and Children's Farm (p.251) and there's also Dubai's Ras Al Khor wildlife sanctuary (04 606 6822) which is a stopping-off point for thousands of migrating birds each year, including more than 1,500 flamingos.

Head out to the islands off Abu Dhabi's coastline to see more of Mother Nature's best work. Arabia's biggest nature reserve, the Arabian Wildlife Park, is out on Sir Bani Yas (Out Of The City, p.234), while there are several other sanctuaries that can only be accessed by boat (p.223).

Play & Learn

Marina Mall Breakwater **02 681 5990**
Map **2 D1**

Located near to the cinema at Marina Mall, Play & Learn offers computer and PlayStation games for older children, along with a soft play area, a sand pit, an art centre and kitchen facilities for the younger family members, who will enjoy the crafts and dressing-up, while parents tend to take heart from the fact that there's an emphasis on learning and development through play. Entrance is Dhs.35 on weekdays and Dhs.45 from Thursday to Saturday. There is also a branch at Al Raha Mall (02 681 5994).

Sparky's

Khalidiyah Mall Al Khalidiyah **02 635 4317**
Map **2 H5**

A large, shiny and brand new family fun centre that takes up a large section of Khalidiyah Mall's top level, Sparky's has a kids' roller coaster, bumper cars, a 4D cinema, a bowling alley, a football striker zone and a soft play area, as well as arcade games. Another Sparky's (02 559 1744) operates from Mazyad Mall.

Wanasa Land

Al Wahda Mall Al Dhafrah **02 443 7654**
www.wanasaland.com
Map **2 M7**

For younger children, this new centre has a large, soft play area and animal themed carousels and

Under Starter's Orders...

The Ferrari World has thrillseekers, fans of Italian performance cars and motorsports addicts all purring in delight.

The UAE has made catching up an art form. Where once there were sleepy fishing villages, vast sandy expanses and shipyards full of dhows, we now see majestic towers, sprawling communities and cutting-edge marinas

Resorts, restaurants and attractions have all risen from the desert sands but the one thing that was strangely lacking until late 2010 – a top quality theme park. Amazing waterparks, yes, but due to the long delays affecting the mammoth Dubailand project, fans of white-knuckle rides, roaring rollercoasters and high speed rushes had to look elsewhere for their kicks. Not so any more. Open since October 2010, Ferrari World is slated as 'the world's biggest indoor theme park' and we certainly wouldn't challenge the claim. Part theme park, part simulator and part museum/learning centre for the legendary Italian brand, Ferrari World has won the hearts of UAE petrolheads and visitors alike.

Out-and-out theme park fans should be impressed by the Formula Rossa – billed as the world's fastest rollercoaster, it reaches speeds of up to 240km/h. It's so fast riders have to wear safety goggles. The G-forces an F1 driver experiences are imitated by a 62m high ride that drops vertically through the park's roof, while a flume style water ride leads visitors through a series of twists, turns, rises and falls based on the workings of a Ferrari 599 engine.

State-of-the-art simulators used to train Ferrari drivers give a realistic experience of being in the break-neck hustle and bustle of a real Grand Prix, while young wannabe Schumachers and Alonsos can attend a driver school.

If fast paced thrills and spills aren't your thing, there are also plenty of more demure and educational attractions – especially for those with an interest in cars and Italy. Bell'Italia is an aerial tour of a miniature Italy, where all manner of traditional Italian foods and flavours are on offer. And anyone who has ever wanted, well, just about anything adorned with the famous 'prancing horse' logo won't go home disappointed after a visit to the flagship store.

Ferrari World Abu Dhabi is open Tuesday to Sunday from 12:00 until 22:00 and general admission tickets cost Dhs.225. For further details and current news and event, log onto www.ferrariworldabudhabi.com.

amusement rides. The older children have a choice of 45 high-tech computerised games, an electronic shooting range and five hair-raising funfair rides. The food court is next door and has nine restaurants and fastfood outlets. There is no entrance fee; rides start from Dhs.5 or you can buy a swipe card for your child and put a set amount of money on it.

OUT & ABOUT

The UAE has much more to offer than its headline-grabbing, metropolis-based attractions. Beyond the city limits, in all directions, is a varied and fascinating landscape that has great potential for exploring and leisure-time activities. Getting out into the deserts and wadis by 4WD is a must-do while you're an Abu Dhabi resident and, once you're out there, there are some super hiking and camping spots to take advantage of too. The sea that surrounds the country is also a great adventure playground, and the warm Gulf waters provide a wonderful opportunity to try snorkelling, diving and sailing.

Off-Roading

With the vast areas of virtually untouched wilderness in the UAE, wadi and dune bashing are very popular pastimes. Every other vehicle on the road in Abu Dhabi seems to be 4WD, but unlike in many countries, in the UAE there's ample opportunity to truly put them to the test in an off-road environment. Dune bashing, or desert driving, is one of the toughest challenges for both car and driver, but once you have mastered it, it's also the most fun. Driving in the wadis is a bit more straightforward. Wadis are (usually) dry gullies, carved through the rock by rushing floodwaters, following the course of seasonal rivers.

Some of the UAE's regional highlights include:

Al Ain: The oasis town (p.234) is worthy of a visit in its own right, while nearby are the imposing Jebel Hafeet and Hanging Gardens, a great trekking spot.

Liwa: A trip to Liwa (p.241) is one you'll never forget – it's one of the few remaining chances to experience unspoiled dunes. The drive from Abu Dhabi is long, more suitable for a two or three day camping trip, but the journey is worth it. Prepare for the most adventurous off-road driving the UAE has to offer, and some of its most incredible scenery.

Northern Emirates: For a full day out or weekend away, with some of the best driving in the Emirates, combine the mountains around Wadi Bih, near Ras Al Khaimah (p.254), with one of the interesting wadi routes on the east coast.

East Coast: From Abu Dhabi, the east coast (p.256) can be reached in about three hours. The mountains and beaches are fantastic spots for camping, barbecues and weekend breaks, as well as various other activities. There are some great wadi and mountain routes here, and the area is also renowned for its diving and snorkelling opportunities, particularly around Snoopy Island.

Hatta: The Hatta (p.244) region is home to the popular Big Red sand dune, a huge draw and a must-do challenge for off-roaders and quad bikers, as well as the Hatta Pools, a great swimming spot in the Hajar Mountains. For further information and tips on driving off-road, check out both the *UAE Off-Road Explorer* and *Oman Off-Road Explorer*. These books feature a multitude of detailed routes and give advice on how to stay safe, where to camp and things to do along the way.

If you want a wilderness adventure but don't know where to start, contact any of the major tour companies (see Tour Operators, p.230). All offer a range of desert and mountain safaris.

If you're really keen to learn, OffRoad-Zone (04 339 2449, www.offroad-zone.com), located in Jebel Ali on the way to Dubai, runs a driving centre at the Jebel Ali Shooting Club where you can practise tackling various obstacles that you might find while off-roading, including deep water, loose rocks and steep descents.

Camping

Constant sunshine and an awe-inspiring array of locations make camping a much-loved activity in Abu Dhabi and the UAE. In general, warm temperatures and next to no rain mean you can camp with much less equipment and preparation than in other countries, and many first-timers or families with children find that camping becomes their favourite weekend break. For most, the best time to go is between October and April, as in the summer it can get unbearably hot sleeping outside. Choose between the peace and tranquility of the desert, or camp among the wadis and mountains next to trickling streams in picturesque oases. Many good campsites are easily accessible from tarmac roads so a 4WD is not always required. You can camp just about anywhere, but there are some stand-out spots that are super places to pitch up.

Jebel Yibir is the UAE's highest peak and, as such, camping out on the mountain (there's a road up to the summit) is a good option for the warmer months as the temperatures up there are much cooler than down below. The Wadi Sidr off-road route leads to a plateau that offers some good places to camp, with great views, while both Fossil Rock (p.257) and the drive from Madam to Madah provide terrific, accessible dune driving and camping spots. On the outskirts of Al

DRIVE WITH CARE

To protect the environment from damage, you should try to stick to existing tracks rather than create new tracks across virgin countryside. While it may be hard to deviate from the track when wadi bashing, dunes are ever-changing, so obvious paths are less common. Although the sandy dunes may look devoid of life, there is a surprising variety of flora and fauna that exists.

The main safety precaution to take when wadi bashing is to keep your eyes open for rare, but not impossible, thunderstorms – the wadis can fill up quickly and you will need to make your way to higher ground pretty quickly to avoid flash floods.

Ain, close to the border with Oman, camping near the mountains can be just as spectacular. The ground is rockier, and some of the driving can be questionable, with rocks the size of footballs scattered throughout the gravel tracks. Upon reaching a camping spot, however, the adventurous camper is blessed with solitude, amazing rock formations, wadis, and a sky bursting with stars. There are even waterfalls and pools to be found in this area of the country.

The ultimate camping experience is to be had in the sea of dunes at Liwa, where you can go to sleep beneath a perfect starry sky and then wake up completely surrounded by one of the world's most mesmerising dunescapes (see Out Of The City, p.234). For more information on off-road adventuring and places to camp, refer to the *UAE Off-Road Explorer*.

Hiking

Despite Abu Dhabi's flat terrain, spectacular hiking locations can be found just a few hours outside the city limits. In the very north of the UAE, the Ru'us Al Jibal Mountains contain the highest peaks in the area, standing proud at over 2,000 metres, while the impressive Hajar Mountains stretch from Musandam in the north all the way down to the Empty Quarter desert in the south. Inland, Al Ain provides some excellent hiking routes, with plenty of mountains, including the imposing Jebel Hafeet, teamed with seven lush oases. Routes range from short, easy walks leading to spectacular viewpoints, to all-day treks over difficult terrain, and can include major mountaineering. Some hikes follow centuries-old Bedouin and Shihuh mountain paths, a few of which are still being used. One of the easiest places to reach is the foothills of the Hajar Mountains on the Hatta Road, near the Oman border. After passing through the desert, the flat, stark, rugged outcrops transform the landscape. Explore any turning you like, or take the road to Mahdah, along which you'll find several options. Other great areas for hiking and exploring include the mountains in and around Musandam, and the mountains near the east coast. The mountains in the UAE don't generally disappoint, and the further off the beaten track you get, the more likely you are to find interesting villages where residents live in much the same way as they did centuries ago.

For somewhere a bit further afield see *Oman Trekking*, a guide book from Explorer Publishing with pull-out maps covering major signed routes in Oman. As with any trip into the UAE 'outback', take sensible precautions. Tell someone where you are going and when you should be back, and don't forget to take a map, compass, GPS equipment and robust hiking boots. Don't underestimate the strength of the sun – take sunscreen and, most importantly, lots of water. For most people, the cooler and less humid winter months are the best season for serious mountain hiking. Be particularly careful in wadis (dry riverbeds) during the wet season as flash floods can immerse a wadi in seconds. Also note that there are no mountain rescue services in the UAE, so anyone venturing out should be reasonably experienced or accompanied by someone who knows the area. See Activities, p.271, for companies that offer organised hikes.

CARRY WHEN CAMPING

Although the UAE has low rainfall, care should be taken in and near wadis as flash floods can and do occur. Remember, it may be raining in the mountains, kilometres away from where you are, but the effects are no less risky.
You should consider taking the following equipment:

- Tent
- Lightweight sleeping bag (or light blankets and sheets)
- Thin mattress (or air bed)
- Torches and spare batteries
- Cool box for food
- Water (always take too much)
- Camping stove, or BBQ and charcoal if preferred
- Firewood and matches
- Insect repellent and antihistamine cream
- First aid kit (including any personal medication)
- Sun protection (hats, sunglasses, sunscreen)
- Jumper/warm clothing for cooler evenings
- Spade
- Toilet rolls
- Rubbish bags (ensure you leave nothing behind)
- Navigation equipment (maps, compass, Global Positioning System)
- Mobile phone (fully charged)

Beginners' Guide To Desert Driving

Off-road driving is exciting and adventurous, but it shouldn't be undertaken lightly; it requires skill, the correct equipment and a little planning before venturing out for the first time.

The key to driving on sand is maintaining controlled momentum and always looking ahead so you can plan for obstacles before you reach them. Most of the tracks on routes such as Fossil Rock (see the feature in Out Of The City, p. 234) shouldn't present any problems, but they will get you used to how your car handles on sand and the different style needed to driving on hard surfaces. Before you start driving, deflate your tyres to 15-18psi. This increases the surface area of the tyre in contact with the sand, providing added traction for the soft conditions and saving your engine from being overworked. Make sure you are in 4WD (high range), and use the lower gears at higher than normal revs. You will find you use first and second a lot, but on more open and flatter tracks, you will get into third and even fourth, and at times it will feel very similar to driving on the road. When the track becomes undulating or you head into the

Don't worry too much about getting stuck – it happens to everyone. Clearing a little sand from around the wheels and getting a few people pushing will get most cars out of minor problems.

dunes, slow down, keep a steady pace and stay alert for obstacles. You should try to use the accelerator more than anything else, barely touching the brakes or clutch. If you do brake, do so lightly and smoothly to avoid sinking into the sand.

At first, even small dunes can seem quite extreme, so take things carefully. Plan your ascents to take the smoothest route and try to reduce your speed so that you coast over the top of a rise or a dune at close to walking pace so you will be in control for the descent. Go easy on the gas – it is far better to fail to make a climb because you were going too slowly than to end up jumping over the top of a dune.

When you get over the top, brake gently and, if you decide to stop, do so just on the downward slope. This will allow you to start going again easily. You will often not know what the slope is like until you are right on it; point your car straight down the dune and let your engine do most of the controlling of your speed. Drivers of automatic cars can do the same using the accelerator; pressing down hard will change down gears, but you may need to use the gear stick to ensure the car doesn't change back up before you want it to, robbing you of the momentum and power you need to climb dunes. Descending, you will need to change into first or second so the car doesn't race away from you.

Don't worry too much about getting stuck, it happens to everyone. If you do, don't keep revving the engine – chances are it will just dig you in further. Get out of your car to assess the situation, and try to work out how it happened so you can learn for next time. Usually, clearing a little sand from around the wheels and getting a few people pushing will get most cars out of minor problems. If you are in deeper, you may need to dig the car free, lower the tyre pressures more or get someone to tow you out.

Essential Equipment

There are some basic technical requirements for anyone driving in the desert. A well-maintained and fully serviced vehicle, a spare tyre in good condition, a jack, a tool kit including everything to change a tyre, a sturdy plank or block of wood in case you need to change wheels in sand, a tow rope and shackles, a pressure gauge, and a shovel are all essential. And, as with any other time you venture out into the desert, you should always have at least one other car with you – even on the simplest routes you might get stuck deep enough to need towing out. Remember to make sure you have plenty of fuel in the tank too.

Other things that can help get you out of sticky situations include sand mats or trays (or your floor mats if you are not too attached to them), a compressor to re-inflate tyres, heavy duty gloves, jump leads, a fully charged mobile phone, and a GPS, which can help take the guesswork out of navigation. Also make sure everyone in your car has plenty of water, sun cream and a hat, and shoes rather than sandals, as the sand can still get very hot.

Diving

The UAE offers diving that's really very special; the lower Arabian Gulf and the Gulf of Oman will satisfy all tastes and levels of experience for divers and snorkellers alike. You can choose from over 30 wrecks in relatively shallow water, tropical coral reefs and dramatic coastlines that are all virtually undived. Better still, they're bathed in comparatively warm water all year round.

Water temperatures range from a cooler 20°C in January to a warmer 35°C in July and August. Although the land temperatures can be in the high 40s in the summer months, it is rarely too hot when out at sea for dipping into the water.

While the visibility is not quite as spectacular as in the best dive sites in the tropics, it's rarely a problem.

The UAE's coastal waters are home to a variety of marine species, coral life and quite a few shipwrecks, so you won't run out of stuff to see. You'll see some exotic fish, like clownfish and seahorses, and possibly even spotted eagle rays, moray eels, small sharks, barracuda, sea snakes and stingrays. Most of the wrecks are on the west coast, while the beautiful flora and fauna of coral reefs can be seen on the east coast.

There are many dive sites on the west coast that are easily accessible from Abu Dhabi. Cement Barge, Mariam Express and the MV Dara wrecks are some of the more popular dive sites. Off the east coast, a well-known dive site is Martini Rock, a small, underwater mountain covered with colourful soft coral, with a depth range of three to 19 metres. North of Khor Fakkan is the Car Cemetery, a reef that has thrived around a number of cars placed 16 metres below water. Visibility off both coasts varies by the time of the year; generally, it ranges from five to 20 metres.

Another option for diving enthusiasts is to take a trip to Musandam (p.262). This area, which is part of the Sultanate of Oman, is often described as the 'Norway of the Middle East' due to the many inlets and the way the sheer cliffs plunge directly into the sea. It offers some spectacular dive sites. Sheer wall dives with strong currents and clear waters are more suitable for advanced divers, while the huge bays, with their calm waters and shallow reefs, are ideal for the less experienced. Visibility here is between 10 and 35 metres. If you plan to travel to Khasab, the capital of the Musandam peninsula, you may not be able to take your own air tanks across the border and will have to rent from one of the dive centres there. You may also require an Omani visa. Alternatively, from Dibba on the UAE east coast, you can hire a fast dive boat to take you anywhere from five to 75 kilometres up the coast. The cost ranges between Dhs.150 and Dhs.500, for what is usually a two-dive trip.

There are plenty of dive companies in the UAE that can help you should you want to try diving for the first time, or improve on your existing diving skills (see Activities, p.271). Padi training is available from beginner level through to instructor qualifications. Most companies offer both tuition and straightforward dive outings, with equipment.

Snorkelling

Snorkelling is a great hobby and, with conditions in the UAE creating relatively calm waters for most of the year, this is the perfect place to get into it. Whatever your age or fitness levels, snorkelling will get you into the sea and the minute you get your first glimpse of bright reef life, you'll be hooked.

Snorkelling offers a different experience to diving, with many interesting creatures such as turtles, rays and even sharks all frequently seen near the surface. It's a great way for the family to enjoy an activity together and all you need is some basic equipment and you're ready to go.

You can pretty much snorkel anywhere off a boat – all you need is a mask and fins, and you'll

ADRENALINE SPORTS

Adrenaline junkies don't need to head out to sea or jet across to distant shores to get a taste of extreme adventure; there may not be any actual jumping out of a plane or stomach-in-chest feelings, but Spacewalk, located in the Abu Dhabi Country Club (p.179), is an indoor skydiving centre that uses a vertical wind tunnel to keep thrill-seekers flying for minutes at a time.

If driving extremely fast sounds more exhilarating, Yas Marina Circuit (p.290) holds periodic track days that allow drivers to try out the performance and handling of their own cars on the Grand Prix circuit before the Formula 1 racers take to the track again in November. Or, for a hefty fee, professional drivers take passengers along for the full F1 experience. Check out the website www.yasmarinacircuit.com or call 02 446 0384 for details.

For those who need to feel the rush more often, there's always the Dubai Autodrome (www.dubaiautodrome.com), where racers can rent different types of cars or just wheel around in go-carts, in addition to the regular track days.

Finally, if you're hankering after cooler climes and are missing your fix of powder and mountains, head to Ski Dubai (p.296) – the indoor piste in the heart of the city, complete with its very own 'black run'. Lessons for beginners are available, while experienced downhillers can go on Freestyle Night to get some serious air on the jumps, kickers and rails.

likely see something swimming around – but there are certain areas where you're guaranteed to enjoy greater marine action. The east coast is a plum area for snorkelling and has the most diverse marine life. Most dive centres take snorkellers out on their boats (along with divers, and the trip lasts for about two hours in total). Some centres can make arrangements to take you to Shark Island (also called Khor Fakkan Island) where you can spend the day. They'll come and collect you at the time you agree on. If that's what you'd like to do, it's best to arrange this with your dive centre in advance. Depending on your swimming ability and the water conditions, you can go to Sandy Beach Hotel (p.259) and spend the day on the beach and swim out to Snoopy Island, just a short distance from shore. In winter time, the water recedes a long way and the distance you have to swim is even less – but the water temperature will be considerably cooler too.

Water Choice

As well as boating, diving and snorkelling, there are plenty of other water-based activities to fill your leisure time with. Windsurfing, jet skiing and waterskiing are all available from various beachfront hotels and sports clubs (p.178), while canoeists and kayakers can take advantage of the mangroves and lagoons on both sides of Abu Dhabi island for some first-class exploring (see p.197). Kitesurfing (p.301) is a growing pastime worldwide, and there are a couple of good spots in town, with more out on the islands, down in Al Gharbia or up in Dubai, while surfing (p.300) is possible in the UAE, although the waves are a far cry from Hawaiian tubes. Stand up paddle boarding (p.300) is a relaxing way to view the coast of Abu Dhabi from a new vantage point and get fit at the same time. You can get inspiration watching the very best in action at the Al Gharbia Watersports Festival (p.28).

The west coast is not so great, with the best places for seeing fish being the waters by harbour walls, but take care: on the outside of harbour walls the waves tend to bash against the rocks and you may get caught off guard by a rogue wave (created by boats in the construction areas). You can snorkel on the inside of the harbour walls, but the water there is rather still and tends to silt up. The fish also prefer the outside walls.

Musandam offers good snorkelling too, but the waters there can have strong currents so it's a good idea to go with a tour company and have a guide to point out the best sites. The best fish life is to be found between the surface and 10 metres below, so try to snorkel along the side of rocks and islands. There are a number of tour companies that offer dhow trips for dolphin watching and snorkelling, and the boats usually moor in areas that are safe to snorkel in (see Boat Tours p.227).

Boating

With calm waters and year-round sunshine, the UAE offers ideal conditions for those wishing to sample life on the ocean waves. A number of companies provide boat charters, offering everything from sundowner cruises of a couple of hours and overnight trips with snorkelling stopovers, to scuba diving excursions to remote destinations such as Musandam.

Large sailing yachts, speedboats and other motorboats can be hired for private charter and corporate events; other companies offer outings on dhows and also cater to weddings and birthday parties. Fishing trips and watersports packages are also available. If you're on the east coast and fancy a traditional boating experience, large independent groups can charter a dhow from the fishermen at Dibba. If you haggle you can usually knock the price down substantially. Respected UAE charter companies operating out of Abu Dhabi include Belevari Marine (www.belevari.com), ART Marine (www.artmarine.net), Croatian Emirates (www.pyc.hr), Ocean Active (www.oceanactive.com) and Arabian Divers & Sportfishing Charters (www.fishabudhabi.com). See Activities, p.271, for more details and, if you're a boating enthusiast, pick up Explorer's *UAE Yachting & Boating* book.

SPECTATOR SPORTS

For eight months of the year, Abu Dhabi residents can enjoy a calendar packed with sporting events, many of which are world class and feature leading names from tennis to Formula 1 and sailing. The UAE's sunny winter climate, its location within easy reach of Europe and Asia, its development of some excellent sporting facilities, and its ability to stump up monstrous sums as prize money mean the country is growing ever more attractive as a venue for international sporting associations to include on their schedules. All of this is great news for sport fans. From big headline events, such as the Grand Prix and FIFA Club World Cup, to regular tennis and golf tournaments, and even local horse and camel racing meets, there's an awful lot going on.

Boat Racing

With both the Abu Dhabi Grand Prix in November and then the Dubai Grand Prix in December, the UAE is the only country with two stops in the Class 1 World Power Boating Championship (www.class-1.com). These boats are something to behold, reaching speeds of 250km/h and sometimes barely even touching the water. In addition to Class 1 events, there is the F1 Abu Dhabi Grand Prix, the Wooden Power Boats Championship, the UAE Jet Ski Championships (see www.adimsc.ae for all those events), sailing competitions and dhow races throughout the year at the Abu Dhabi International Marine Sports Club.

Dubai International Marine Club (www.dimc.ae) is just as busy, if not more so, with many events planned in partnership with the ADIMSC. For something completely different, however, every year there's the Dubai Dragon Boat Festival (www.dubaidragonboat.com) in April, with teams from all over competing in the races.

Sailing is a sport that is really on the up in Abu Dhabi and the world's biggest sailing event, the Volvo Ocean Race (www.volvooceanrace.com), will make a stop in town during January 2012. The event will see racing teams, including the new Team Abu Dhabi, sail over 39,000 nautical miles of the world's most treacherous seas via ports around the world. Abu Dhabi will be the first Middle East port ever to host the racers, and there's a lot of buzz surrounding the event, which is expected to bring huge crowds to the capital and the brand new marina at Emirates Palace.

Camel Racing

Camel racing? Seriously? This popular local sport is actually very serious business with racing camels changing hands for as much as Dhs.10 million each, while as much as Dhs.25 million in prizes is won each year. A camel owner with a star racer can do very well for himself, and it shows at the races as the owners drive alongside the track, keeping up with the animals. The Al Watba Camel Race Track is 45km from Abu Dhabi, on the road to Al Ain. There are two tracks; the main one is grandstanded and the secondary track is out towards the Endurance Racing Center. If you run out of direction signs, just follow the herds of camels going to the tracks to train. Morning races take place throughout the winter on Thursday and Friday from as early as 06:30 to 08:30. Periodically, major races are held on public holidays like National Day. Admission to the track is free.

Cricket

Sheikh Zayed Cricket Stadium, near Khalifa City A on Airport Rd, is host to many international matches of cricket, which is a popular sport in Abu Dhabi, largely thanks to the big number of expats from several cricket countries. In addition to recent test matches held at the venue, Pakistan has made the stadium its second home because of foreign teams' refusals to play in Pakistan due to security concerns. In fact, Pakistan has played all its 'home' one day internationals and Twenty20 games in Dubai or Abu Dhabi for over a year. There's almost always something going on at the stadium, with England training there last year in preparation for their series in India and other teams regularly using it for pre-season preparation. See www.emiratescricket.com.

Endurance Racing

For those who like to watch athletes pushing their bodies to mind-altering limits, there's the Abu Dhabi International Triathlon (www.abudhabitriathlon.com) in March. Including a 3km swim in the lagoon at the Emirates Palace, a 200km bike section that travels the length of the island before zipping around The Yas Marina F1 circuit and a 20km run up and down the Corniche, spectators are sure to catch sight of plenty of iron men and women, including some of the biggest names in the sport, attracted by the early season race, exotic scenery and large prize purse.

Endurance athletes are also on show at January's Dubai Marathon (www.dubaimarathon.org) which, thanks to its flat, fast course and generous prize money, has also become one of the biggest in the calendar over the past few years, with spectators able to cheer on the likes of world record holder Haile Gebrselassie.

Racing Robots

Racing camels used to be ridden by children, but this practise has since been outlawed – and robotic jockeys have taken over. The operators follow the race in 4WDs while directing the jockeys by remote control – quite a bizarre sight.

Football

Football is as popular in the UAE as it is the world over and, in recent years, there has been plenty of action for fans of the game to watch. Abu Dhabi was awarded the honour of hosting the FIFA World Club Cup in 2009 and 2010, a tournament which sees the champions of each continent competing in a one-off knock-out competition. Matches are held at Zayed Sports City and Mohammed bin Zayed Stadium.

There's a strong domestic competition too – the UAE Football League – and attending one of these games makes for a really colourful experience.

Emirati supporters are fanatical about their teams and there are some strong local rivalries. Abu Dhabi's Al Jazira were crowned champions of the 2011 Etisalat Pro-League after winning on their home pitch against Dubai. There are plenty of stars on display too, with Fabio Cannavaro (Italy's 2006 World Cup winning captain and World Player of the Year for the same year) currently plying his trade at Dubai's Al-Ahli, while Argentinian legend Maradona is the new coach of Al Wasl. For information on international tournaments, see www.uaefa.ae.

Golf

Golf fans have plenty to keep them entertained throughout the year, with three major tournaments taking place in the UAE. First, the Abu Dhabi Golf Championship (www.abudhabigolfchampionship.com) is staged each January at the National Course at Abu Dhabi Golf Club, near Khalifa City A. The championship is the opening event on the European PGA Tour's Middle East-based Desert Swing Trio, with over $2 million in prize money given away each year.

Dubai, too, has become a major golf destination, with two world-class events held each year. The Dubai Desert Classic (www.dubaidesertclassic.com), held each February, has previously been won by the likes of Tiger Woods and Ernie Els. In addition, the Dubai World Championship (www.dubaiworldchampionship.com) is held in November or December each year; now in its third year, more than 50,000 golf fans have turned up in previous years to witness the culmination of the European Tour's Race To Dubai. The tournament takes place from 8 to 11 December 2011.

Horse Racing

Horse racing is extremely popular in the Emirates and is accessible to everyone through free admission at all the tracks. Meetings are held in the afternoons or evenings throughout the cooler months (the season runs from November to early April). Emirates Racing Authority (www.emiratesracing.com) is the internationally recognised governing body for horse racing in the UAE and oversees all aspects of the sport. With four tracks spread among Abu Dhabi, Dubai and Sharjah, there are plenty of places to catch the action.

Abu Dhabi Equestrian Club (www.adec-web.com) in Al Mushrif offers races on Sunday evenings beginning at 18:00 during the racing season, with show jumping and endurance events also taking place. Sharjah's Equestrian and Racing club holds a handful of events each year, but Dubai's tracks, Jebel Ali and the brand new supertrack Meydan, host most races. The culmination and the highlight of the racing season is the Dubai World Cup (www.dubaiworldcup.com), the world's richest horse race, held every year in March in Dubai.

Gambling is not allowed in the UAE, but everyone can take part in various free competitions to select the winning horses, with the ultimate aim of taking home prizes or cash.

It may be a fair drive from the city, up next to the Dubai border, but Ghantoot Racing & Polo Club (www.grpc.ae) is definitely worth a visit, as the only club in Abu Dhabi that is dedicated to the equine sport that is growing rapidly in popularity throughout the region. The club has a modern infrastructure for sports and events, and the polo calendar is full of regular chukka tournaments and high profile international games. For a bit of a chuckle, look out for games of camel polo.

A golfer's paradise

Motorsports

The Yas Marina Circuit (p.290) has been a boon to motorsports fans in the capital. Ever since the facility opened for the Grand Prix in 2009, announcements of new events just keep pouring in. In addition to the Grand Prix, easily the UAE's headline motor racing event, the circuit has held endurance races, drag racing, a GT1 battle of the brands and a leg of the Australian V8 Supercars. Check the website www.yasmarinacircuit.com for information on upcoming events.

Dubai Autodrome also hosts events of various categories all year round. The website www.dubaiautodrome.com lists a full calendar of events.

For fans of more rugged terrain, the Abu Dhabi Desert Challenge (www.abudhabidesertchallenge.com), which has stages right across the whole emirate, is the opening round of both the FIA and the FIM Cross Country Rally World Cups.

Desert Slickers

As well as the Abu Dhabi Desert Challenge (p.27), there are numerous other desert rally events that take place throughout the year right across the emirate and deep into the Liwa desert, like the dune drag races that see motors storm up the almost sheer face of Moreeb Dune. See http://emsfuae.org for the latest events.

Rugby

Although amateur club matches take place in Abu Dhabi, Al Ain and Dubai throughout the year (see Abu Dhabi Harlequins, p.292), the big rugby event takes place every December in Dubai, when fans and party-goers from the UAE and far beyond head to The Sevens Stadium on the Al Ain road for the Emirates Airline Dubai Rugby Sevens (www.dubairugby7s.com).

This 'light' version of the sport is fast paced and competitive, with young, up-and-coming international stars taking centre stage in the knock-out format. As much about the atmosphere as the sport, as evidenced by the hugely popular 'Rugby Rock' concert held on the final night of the event, The Sevens is without doubt one of the region's biggest parties and sporting spectacles.

However, rugby fans based in Abu Dhabi are now increasingly treated to one-off matches, such as the first round of the Asian 5 Nations Rugby tournament in April 2011.

Tennis

The UAE's tennis fans are blessed with a couple of stellar tournaments that help get the year off to a good start. First is the Abu Dhabi Mubadala World Tennis Championships (p.29), usually kicking off around the New Year's celebrations at the International Tennis Complex at Zayed Sports City. For the past few years, the three-day tournament has attracted six of the top players in the world, including Roger Federer and Raphael Nadal, to the capital.

February sees the Dubai Duty Free Tennis Championships (p.27), which is held at the Aviation Club. It is a great opportunity to catch some of the top male and female players on the tour, such as 2011 winners Novak Djokovic and Caroline Wozniacki.

TOURS & SIGHTSEEING

What better way to experience Abu Dhabi than customised land, sea or sky tours? As exhilarating for those who are in the city for just a short time as they are for longtime residents, desert safaris or dhow cruises allow you to take in the beauty of the area while also getting a feel for the traditional culture. Abu Dhabi's spectacular geographic location makes for an ideal touring site and indeed, with the city's tourist numbers growing rapidly every year and millions of dirhams being pumped into promotional marketing for the emirate, the different types of tours and thrills will only continue to multiply in the years to come. Already, most tour companies offer desert safaris and dhow cruises, but some offer helicopter tours (see listings on the left), as well as diving and snorkelling trips. Many tour companies will work with adventurers who want to customise their own experience.

The most classic option, however, is the desert safari. Expert drivers blast 4WD vehicles up, down and around massive dunes while passing old Bedouin villages and pointing out beautiful natural attractions. Mountain safaris lead passengers through the narrow wadis and steep passes of the Hajar Mountains. This tour makes for an exhilarating experience not to be missed. Most driving safaris include pick-up from your place of residence and lunch. Some end the day of wild driving at a replica Bedouin camp where passengers can watch a belly dancer, eat Arabic delicacies and smoke shisha. Many operators even run overnight safaris that combine desert and mountain safaris.

When booking, it is often advisable to reserve spaces three or four days in advance.

Bus Tours

For a tourist wanting a quick peek at the main attractions of the city, a bus tour is the way to go and the Big Bus Company (www.bigbustours.com, 800 244 287) has a fleet of London-style double decker buses that provide a hop-on hop-off service, with commentary for attractions across Abu Dhabi and Dubai. In Abu Dhabi, Marina Mall is the main starting point, but riders can get on or off at any of the eleven stops that include Sheikh Zayed Mosque, Abu Dhabi Mall, the Meena souks, the Corniche, the Public Beach and Heritage Village.

Desert & Mountain Tours

Desert safaris are by far the most popular variety of tours available, perhaps because a good safari offers many activities in one day. Starting with an exciting ride up and down some of the desert's biggest dunes, you can try sand skiing before watching the sun set over the dunes. After driving a short distance further to a permanent Bedouin-style camp, you are treated to a sumptuous barbecue, followed by shisha, belly dancing, camel rides and henna painting. You can vary the length of your safari, choosing to stay overnight or combine it with a trip into the mountains, if desired. However, a safari to the mountains is highly recommended, if only to see how the landscape changes from orange sand dunes to craggy mountains within the space of a few kilometres.

The approximate cost for a desert safari is Dhs.150-Dhs.350 (overnight up to Dhs.500). Many companies offer these types of tours (see Main Tour Operators, p.230); below is a selection of typical itineraries you can choose from.

Dune Dinners

Enjoy some thrilling off-road desert driving before settling down to watch the sun set behind the dunes. Starting around 16:00, tours typically pass camel farms and fascinating scenery that provide great photo opportunities. At an Arabian campsite, enjoy a delicious dinner and the calm of a starlit desert night, returning around 22:00.

Full-Day Safari

This day-long tour usually heads out into the vast expanses of desert dunes, passing the occasional traditional Bedouin villages or camel farm in the desert on the way. Between taking on sand dunes of varying colours and heights, a cold buffet lunch may be provided in the wide open expanses before the drive home.

Sick Of Safari

Even the milder, shorter safaris involve some fairly vigorous off-road driving and, if you tend to experience motion sickness in cars, the chances are that you'll not enjoy the ride, especially as, in the middle of the desert, you can't really just get out. Equally, pregnant women, and anyone with back or neck problems should probably avoid 4WD safaris.

Hatta Pools Safari

Hatta is a quiet, old-fashioned town nestled in the foothills of the Hajar Mountains, famed for its fresh water rock pools that you can swim in. The full-day trip usually includes a stop at the Hatta Fort Hotel, where you can enjoy the pool, landscaped gardens, archery, and nine-hole golf course. Lunch is served either in the hotel, or alfresco in the mountains.

Mountain Safari

Normally, a full-day tour takes you to the east coast, heading inland at Dibba and entering the spectacular Hajar Mountains. You will travel through rugged canyons onto steep winding tracks, past terraced mountainsides and ancient stone houses that offer a glimpse of life as it used to be. The journey homewards can often take in Masafi Market on the way.

Overnight Safari

This 24 hour tour starts at about 15:00 with a drive through the dunes to a Bedouin-style campsite. Dine under the stars, sleep in the fresh air and wake to the smell of freshly brewed coffee, before heading for the mountains. The drive takes you through spectacular rugged scenery, past dunes and along wadis, before stopping for a buffet lunch and returning to Abu Dhabi.

Don't Forget Your Camera

The UAE is absolutely stacked with picturesque sights, so keep your camera handy and don't forget to use it to capture your memories and keep them forever. See p.314 of Shopping for information on where to purchase or repair camera equipment.

Boat Tours

There's nothing like a breezy evening under the stars just off the Corniche while taking in Abu Dhabi's arresting skyline. Dinner cruises range from hearty affairs to more romantic versions, and most companies offer private charter services. Alternatively, book a daytime tour to soak up the sun while gliding through the sparkling, turquoise waters of the Gulf, admiring Abu Dhabi's stunning coastline with its countless islands and beautiful mangroves. In addition to organised sightseeing tours, there are also catamaran rentals and the inflatable speedy crafts of The Yellow Boats (p.228).

Al Dhafra

Nr Meena Fish Market Al Meena **02 673 2266**
www.aldhafra.net
Map **2 S1**

As well as dinner cruises, Al Dhafra has several traditional Arabic dhows available for charter. Most clients take their own equipment as there is only a

Exploring the desert

limited amount on board. Food can be supplied at additional cost. Charters cost from Dhs.600 per hour for a dhow that can take 20 people. For more details on Al Dhafra, see the review on p.361 in Going Out.

Arabian Divers & Sportfishing Charters > p.283
Al Bateen Marina Al Bateen **050 614 6931**
www.fishabudhabi.com
Map **2 C6**
As well as sportfishing, scuba and snorkelling, this firm offers sightseeing trips and chartered tours that you can tailor, from island hopping to cruises and dolphin watching.

Blue Dolphin Company
Airport Rd Al Khubeirah **050 492 6887**
Map **2 C5**
Private dinner cruises, island trips on a traditional dhow, a full day island-hopping with BBQ lunch and watersports, Arabic night tours and more. Also runs desert safaris, snorkelling and fishing trips.

Noukhada Adventure Company
Al Meena St Al Meena **050 721 8928**
www.noukhada.ae
Map **2 S2**
Offers fantastic sailing and kayaking adventures along the coastline and through the mangroves. Options start with two-hour kayak tours and go through to full moon tours, two day expeditions around Abu Dhabi island and sailing trips to wildlife rich Belghailam Island.

Sea Tourism
Nr Marina Mall Breakwater **02 681 3064**
www.seatourism.net
Map **2 D1**
Offers cruises, island camping trips and pick up/drop off services for anyone keen to explore the islands. Can also arrange fishing trips, scuba and parasailing.

Shuja Yacht > p.229
Le Royal Meridien Abu Dhabi Markaziya East **02 674 2020**
www.lemeridien.com/royalabudhabi
Map **2 P3**
These exquisite dinner cruises head along the Corniche for superb views of the Abu Dhabi skyline while enjoying a romantic meal. For more details, see the review on p.387 in Going Out.

The Yellow Boats
Marina Mall Breakwater **800 8044**
www.theyellowboats.com
Map **2 D1**
These high speed RIBs offer tours of Abu Dhabi waters and the nearby islands and are not for the faint of heart. The 30 minute rides where the skipper shows off the boat's abilities cost Dhs.150. The boats can also be chartered by the hour or hired for corporate events.

Dhow & Out
Large, independent groups can charter a dhow from fishermen at Dibba on the east coast to travel up the coast to Musandam (p.262). Be prepared to haggle – around Dhs.2,500 per day for a 20-25 person dhow, or Dhs.100 per hour for a smaller one is standard. Take your own food and water, as there's nothing onboard except ice lockers. Conditions are basic, but you'll have the freedom to plan your own route to see the Musandam's fjord-like scenery. Turtles and dolphins can often be seen from the boat. If you leave from Dibba (or Daba), Omani visas are not required even though you'll be in Omani waters. It's also possible to arrange stops along the coast and take camping equipment, although you can sleep on board.

Aerial Tours
With views as varying as towering skyscrapers and shifting sand dunes, rocky peaks and turquoise waters, Abu Dhabi reveals plenty of its wonders from the air. Swoop over the cityscape in a helicopter or take in the serenity of the desert from a graceful hot air balloon. Either option will make memories to last a lifetime.

Falcon Aviation Services
Nr Marina Mall Breakwater **02 444 0007**
www.falconaviation.ae
Map **2 D1**
Take off from Marina Mall in a luxurious six-seater Eurocopter EC130 for a bird's eye view over Abu Dhabi, Saadiyat and Yas. A 20 minute tour costs Dhs.625.

Hala Abu Dhabi
Muroor St, Etihad Bld, Nr Madinat Zayed Shopping Centre & Gold Ctr Madinat Zayed **02 617 7811**
www.halaabudhabi.ae
Map **2 M5**
Helicopter tours in an EC130 or a Bell 206 sweep the Corniche before heading out over Saadiyat and Yas to the amazing F1 track, taking in Al Raha Beach, Sheikh Zayed Mosque and Emirates Palace on the way back. Prices vary depending on the tour.

Seawings
Jebel Ali Golf Resort & Spa Dubai **04 883 2999**
www.seawings.ae
Offers aerial tours all over the UAE, including Abu Dhabi, in its fleet of seaplanes. Tours last 35-45 minutes, depending on take-off point, and up to nine people can

fly at a time. Head over The Yas Marina Circuit or check out the Bu Tinah nature reserve. Contact for prices.

Main Tour Operators

Almost all tour operators offer the main types of excursions: city tours, desert safaris and mountain safaris. Some, however, offer more unique activities, such as fishing or diving trips, expeditions to see the Empty Quarter in Liwa (p.241), helicopter tours and desert driving courses. The main tour companies and those that offer something a little bit different are listed in this section, along with some of their highlights – contact them directly for their full programmes.

Absolute Adventure

Al Diyafah Centre Dubai **050 625 9165**
www.adventure.ae

Organises a host of activities, including mountain biking, trekking, climbing, kayaking, watersports, 4WD safaris and motorised hang glider flights. Also offers training for outdoor pursuits instructors, and can organise treks, safaris and travel to far flung places like Nepal and Mongolia. The activity centre, located directly on Dibba's beach, can accommodate 14 people for group stays with a barbecue on the beach.

Tour Tips

If you are booking a tour, make sure you call around to get the best price. Abu Dhabi is dedicated to discounts, particularly at this point in time, and you can often get a better rate as a full-time resident. Just remember, it is all about putting on the charm – not being a cheeky customer. Also, keep an eye on local newspapers and magazines throughout the year for some great sightseeing discounts.

Abu Dhabi Travel Bureau

Corniche Rd, Nr Chamber of Commerce
Markaziya West **02 622 1100**
www.abudhabitravelbureau.com
Map **2 L2**

One of the UAE's biggest travel and tour operators with 40 years of experience in the UAE and 14 offices throughout Abu Dhabi alone, with another in Al Ain. Organises all manner of travel, including desert safaris, cruises, cultural trips and educational visits.

Advanced Travel & Tourism

Hamdan Bin Mohammed St, Nr Qatar Airways
Markaziya East **02 634 7900**
www.advancedtravels.net
Map **2 N3**

General agent offering tour packages and family trips throughout the UAE, and the greater region.

Al Badeyah Eyes Tourism

Nr Al Safeer Center, Mohd Bin Zayed City Mussafah **02 559 6155**
www.abet-uae.com
Map **1 R7**

Based close to Al Raha Beach, this tour company offers desert safaris, dhow cruises and city tours.

Al Badie Travel Agency

Al Badie Tower, Al Nasr St Markaziya West **02 632 2775**
www.albadietravel.com
Map **2 K3**

Large, general travel agency that can organise everything from golf trips and F1 stays to off-roading in the Empty Quarter, culinary tours and Bedouin style desert safaris, with sand skiing and falconry thrown in for good measure.

Arabian Adventures

Emirates Travel Shop, Corniche Rd Al Khalidiyah **02 691 1711**
www.arabian-adventures.com
Map **2 P2**

One of the big tour operators in the country, Arabian Adventures offers a range of tours and itineraries including desert safaris, city tours, sand skiing, dhow cruises, camel riding, and wadi and dune bashing.

Cyclone Tours & Travels

Omeir Holidays Bld, Khalifa St Markaziya East **02 627 6275**
www.cyclonetours.com
Map **2 N3**

Offers everything from urban city tours of Abu Dhabi and Al Ain to overnight desert safaris in remote locations. Desert driving courses, fishing trips and dinner cruises on traditional dhow boats are also available to arrange on request.

Desert Adventures

Al Raha Beach Hotel Al Raha **02 556 6155**
www.desertadventures.com
Map **1 R7**

A Dubai-based company with an Abu Dhabi office that organises tours throughout the Emirates and the wider Gulf region. City and culinary tours, safari adventures and cruises in traditional dhows are the company's specialities.

Desert Rangers

Nr American Hospital, Street 18 Dubai **04 357 2200**
www.desertrangers.com

Desert Rangers offers one of the most comprehensive ranges of tours and safaris, including a number of special interest trips such as dune buggy safaris, rock climbing, deep sea fishing. Different activities take place across the Emirates; see the website for details.

Emirates Adventures
Al Salam St, Nr NBAD No Area Listed **02 644 5117**
www.emiratesadventurestours.com
Map **2 R3**
Offers city tours of Abu Dhabi, Dubai and Al Ain, as well as desert safaris, dune buggy tours and wadi treks.

Emirates Travel Express
Main St, Nr Clock Tower Signal Al Ain **03 765 0777**
www.eteholidays.ae
Map **4 E2**
With 30 years of experience in the United Arab Emirates, Emirates Travel Express offers the usual range of city tours, safaris and dhow cruises, but also caters for those with a taste for adventure further afield, offering cruises and safaris in India, the Masai Mara and more.

Hala Abu Dhabi
Muroor St, Etihad Bld, Nr Madinat Zayed Shopping Centre & Gold Ctr Madinat Zayed **02 617 7811**
www.halaabudhabi.ae
Map **2 M5**
A part of the Etihad group, Hala organises a wide range of tours and sightseeing activities, from desert safaris and dhow dinner cruises to helicopter tours and Hatta treks, city highlights tours and helicopter trips.

Kurban Tours
Al Nasr St, Nr Arab Bank Markaziya West **02 555 0566**
www.kurbantours.com
Map **2 K3**
Tour company specialising in the UAE, Lebanon and Oman, with trips including golf experiences, cultural sightseeing, Bedouin desert safaris, east coast tours, deep sea fishing and Hatta adventures.

Net Tours Abu Dhabi
Sheraton Abu Dhabi Hotel & Resort Markaziya East **02 679 4656**
www.netgroupauh.com
Map **2 Q2**
Covers all the main tour types with both half day and overnight desert safaris, Liwa desert adventures, tours of all the UAE's main cities, helicopter tours, dhow cruises and adventure sports breaks, including cycling, hiking, dune buggying, sand skiing and camel riding. Also has a branch in Al Ain (03 768 7400).

Omeir Travel Agency
Airlines Tower, Sheikh Khalifa St 02 612 3456
www.omeir.com
Map **2 N3**
One of the UAE's largest general travel agencies with 50 years' experience in the region, Omeir Travel Agency offers all the usual tours – desert, city and cruises – as well as some extremely good offers on local accommodation, should you wish to flesh out your tour with an overnight stay away from home one weekend. The company has a second branch in Al Ain (03 765 5517).

Orient Tours
Nr Sheraton Kalidiyah Markaziya West **02 667 5609**
www.orienttours.ae
Map **2 J4**
Provides city tours, safaris, 4WD adventures and cruises. Also caters for corporate events and private parties on request.

Safar Travel & Tourism
Liwa St Markaziya East **02 418 0888**
www.safar.ae
Map **2 N3**
Safar Travel & Tourism has a dedicated adventure arm looking after tours and sightseeing. Island tours, desert safaris in a 4WD or driving quads, cultural city tours, wadi trekking, wildlife adventures, outdoor shows, dhow dinner cruises, fishing and watersports trips are all on the menu.

Fascinating Falconry
Falconry is a national sport in the UAE and the two hour guided tour available at the Abu Dhabi Falcon Hospital provides a unique opportunity to learn about these impressive creatures. The guided tour, which needs to be booked online (www.falconhospital.com), is conducted twice daily from Sunday to Thursday. Also on site is the Animal Shelter (www.abudhabianimalshelter.com)

Salem Travel Agency
Muroor Rd (4th St), Nr Abu Dhabi Commercial Bank Al Nahyan **02 621 8000**
www.salemtravelagency.comMap **2 98**
Operates Arabian Odyssey – dedicated to tours throughout the country. Pick from falconry tours, city tours, cruises, treks, desert safaris and hot air ballooning. Also has Al Ain branch (03 766 2915).

Sunshine Tours
Various Locations **02 444 9914**
www.adnh.com
Offers a wide range of tours from heritage site visits to scenic helicopter rides and dhow cruises on Abu Dhabi's turquoise waters. Desert safaris and overnight trips can also be booked, while excursions to the most popular destinations in other emirates can be arranged on request.

your neighborhood Mall
Beauty
Dining
Shopping
Enjoy
مَـزْيَـدْ مـول
MAZYAD MALL
your neighborhood Mall
Mohamed Bin Zayed City, Mussafah, Abu Dhabi
T: +971 2 5532200, F: +971 2 5532211
www.mazyadmall.com
Managed by - Line Investments & Property LLC

Out Of The City

OUT OF ABU DHABI

Abu Dhabi may have everything from mangroves and marinas to boutiques and beaches, but there are a number of interesting and varied areas outside the city and country that deserve a place in your weekend plans. There are six other emirates in the UAE and five other countries in the GCC, all of which warrant exploration.

All six of the other emirates in the UAE – Dubai, Sharjah, Ras Al Khaimah, Umm Al Quwain, Fujairah and Ajman – are within a few hours' drive of the centre of the capital. From the sleepy streets of Umm Al Quwain and the rugged mountains of Ras Al Khaimah to the cultural grandiose of Sharjah, each emirate has something different to offer, and each can be explored, at least in part, over a weekend. The country's vast deserts and harsh-looking mountains are equally accessible with a copy of the *UAE Off-Road Explorer* and can be reached easily and quickly if you need to escape civilisation for a while.

With Abu Dhabi and Dubai both being international travel hubs, it's easy to find quick, cheap flights to the neighbouring GCC countries of Oman, Saudi Arabia, Qatar, Bahrain and Kuwait, none of which are more than an hour and a half flight away. Oman is considered by many to be one of the most beautiful and culturally interesting countries in the region, and it can easily be reached and explored by car – Muscat is only a five hour drive from Abu Dhabi.

Like the UAE, the countries in the GCC are growing at a phenomenal rate and are trying to attract more tourism. Many hotels in the GCC, including in the UAE, regularly hold promotions or offer discounted rooms, especially in the summer months. It's a good idea to sign up for the mailing lists of regional travel agencies, such as Salem Travel (www.salemtravelagency.com) and Dnata (www.dnata.ae), to find out about any weekend getaway packages they offer.

ABU DHABI – REST OF THE EMIRATE

Al Ain

Al Ain is the capital of the eastern region and Abu Dhabi emirate's second city. Its greenery and the fact that it is the birthplace and childhood home of Sheikh Zayed bin Sultan Al Nahyan, the former (and much-loved) ruler of the UAE, gives it special status in the hearts and minds of the people.

In the days before the discovery of oil, the journey from Abu Dhabi to Al Ain took five days by camel. Today, it only takes an hour and a half by car and most tour companies offer excursions to this fascinating Garden City that straddles the border with the Sultanate of Oman; the UAE side is known as Al Ain and the Oman side as Buraimi.

The fortresses around the city, 18 in all, illustrate Al Ain's importance as part of the ancient trade route from Oman to the Arabian Gulf, and there is evidence of the area having been inhabited for at least the last 7,000 years. Indeed, the city's archaeological legacy is of such significance that Al Ain is now a Unesco World Heritage Site.

Throughout his life, Sheikh Zayed pursued his vision of creating an oasis of greenery in the desert by initiating a series of 'greening' projects. As a result, Al Ain's seven natural oases are now surrounded by tree-lined streets and beautiful urban parks. The main Al Ain Oasis is home to palm plantations, many of which are working farms. The palms provide welcome shade and a haven from the noise and bustle of the city. Most of the farms still use the ancient falaj system of irrigation, which taps into underground water. If you do go exploring in the palm plantations, it is best to stick to the paved areas that weave between the walled-in farms. On the outskirts of the city, you will also find a Camel & Livestock Souk (p.235) which is worth a visit.

Jebel Hafeet

Jebel Hafeet is unmissable – in more ways than one. Rising abruptly from the surrounding countryside, it dominates the area, and the views from the top are stunning. On a clear day you can see the surrounding desert plains, oases, wadis, and the Hajar Mountain range in the distance. At 1,240 metres, the mountain provides a dramatic backdrop to the city, which itself is 300 metres above sea level. The winding road to the top is regularly referred to by international motoring magazines as one of the world's best driving roads. It is in excellent condition with a number of strategically placed viewpoints, all with plenty of parking spaces (and portable toilets). It snakes its way to the top through a series of twists, turns and hairpins. The more energetic could try cycling – a gruelling hour or so up, then 10 minutes down. The five-star Mercure Grand Hotel (p.238) is set in a commanding position, at 915 metres, with splendid views of the surrounding area.

The hot springs at the base of Jebel Hafeet are reputed to have healing properties – although the water temperature may be just too hot in the summer – and the facilities at the striking Green Mubazzarah Park (03 783 9555) include chalet accommodation and a boating lake. There's also the Al Ain Al Fayda Resthouse (03 783 8333) which has a really lovely setting and provides a brilliant green contrast to the starkness of Jebel Hafeet towering above.

Buraimi

Visitors from the UAE don't need a visa to enter the Oman side of the Buraimi Oasis, as long as you are an official resident in the UAE. In 2008, the Al Mudeef border was closed to non-GCC traffic, but the Al Hili

Al Ain Camel & Livestock Souk

checkpoint is still open, either for a trip through to Buraimi and back (with only passport and residence visa checks), or you can get stamped out of the UAE here if you are planning on entering Oman.

The entry point to Oman is about 50 kilometres from the centre of Al Ain, along the road to Sohar. The only real problem you should have in getting from Al Ain to Buraimi is finding it: there are almost no signs to Buraimi in Al Ain. As a general guide, once you are on Khalifa bin Zayed Street, keep going until you get to the large roundabout, then turn left (heading north) and go past the university (on your left). As you look to the right, everything you see is Oman. The border crossing is ahead on your right.

If you are not travelling with your own car, transport in and around Buraimi will need to be by one of the local orange and white taxis. You'll also see UAE taxis, but once they've crossed the border their meters all magically stop working, so know where you are going and agree a price beforehand. Drivers usually accept payment in both Omani riyals and UAE dirhams, and a trip within the township of Buraimi will generally cost no more than Dhs.3 or 300 baisa (RO 0.3). If you are driving yourself and decide to enter this part of the oasis, make sure your car insurance covers Oman as this is not always the case.

The Buraimi Souk is worth a visit for the local atmosphere and colour – along with more mundane household goods, there are a few souvenir shops selling pottery, silver jewellery and woven crafts. Behind the souk is Al Hili Fort, a good starting point from which to explore the oasis. Al Khandaq Fort, located in Hamasa town in Welayat Buraimi, is believed to be about 400 years old. Like many of Oman's forts, it has been extensively restored, and it is great to wander around and admire the views from the battlements.

Al Ain Attractions

Al Ain Ladies Park

Zayed Al Awwal St Al Ain
Map **4 D2**

Commonly known as Basra Park, this quiet garden is for women and children only (boys under the age of 10). There are plenty of benches under the shady trees. Play areas with swings, slides and climbing frames are sure to keep the kids busy.

Al Ain National Museum

Nr Sultan Fort, Zayed Bin Sultan St Al Ain **03 764 1595**
www.adach.ae
Map **4 E2**

Divided into three main sections – archaeology, ethnography and gifts – the presentations include photographs, Bedouin jewellery, musical instruments, weapons and a traditional majlis.

Al Ain Camel & Livestock Souk

Nr Bawadi Mall Al Ain
www.adach.ae
Map **4 E3**

Conditions in the souk have improved dramatically with spacious pens for the animals and ample parking for visitors. A visit to the market is a fantastic way to mingle with locals and witness camel and goat trading like it's taken place for centuries. The locals arrive in pick-ups laden with animals and settle in to do some hard bargaining. Arrive early, preferably before 09:00, to soak up the true essence and atmosphere.

Al Ain Oasis

Nr Al Ain Museum Al Ain
www.adach.ae
Map **4 E2**

This impressive oasis in the heart of the city is filled with palm plantations, many of which are still working farms. The cool, shady walkways transport you from the heat and noise of the city to an otherworldly, tranquil haven. You are welcome to wander through the plantations, but it's best to stick to the paved areas. The farms have plenty of working examples of falaj, the traditional irrigation system which has been used for centuries to tap into underground wells. There are eight different entrances, some of which have arched gates, and there is no entry fee.

Al Ain Palace Museum

Al Ain St Al Ain **03 751 7755**
www.adach.ae
Map **4 D2**

The museum was originally a palace belonging to Sheikh Zayed bin Sultan Al Nahyan, dating back to 1937. Now, it tells the story of its previous owner and his remarkable achievements turning the desert state into a wealthy, popular and thriving country. The museum is a lovely, quiet place to stroll and explore.

Al Ain Public Garden

Zayed Bin Sultan St Al Ain
Map **4 D2**
As the main park in the city of Al Ain, the Public Garden is a tranquil spot amid the hustle and bustle. Walkways wind their ways under shady trees, fountains are attractively lit up at night and areas for younger children offer a variety of fun and safe play equipment. For older kids, there's a small amusement arcade tucked away near the back entrance.

Al Ain University Natural History Museum

University of Al Ain Al Ain **03 713 4224**
Map **4 D2**
Aimed at those interested in the flora and fauna of the UAE, this museum is a small but informative centre run by the university. It includes a herbarium and collections of various species of animals and birds. An assortment of rocks, minerals and fossils is on display.

Al Ain Wildlife Park & Resort

Nhayyan The First St Al Ain **800 2977**
www.awpr.ae
Map **4 D3**
Stretching over 900 hectares, this is one of the largest and best zoos in the Gulf region. With ample greenery, a casual stroll through the paths that criss-cross the park makes for a wonderful family day out. As well as seeing large mammals, reptiles, and big cats, you can get up close to some rare and common local species such as the Arabian Oryx and sand gazelle, or pay a visit to the fantastic birdhouse. Since its founding, the zoo has been a centre for endangered species' conservation and visitors can look forward to spotting true rarities. Nearly 30% of the 180 species are endangered and the park is even home to a stunning pair of white tigers and white lions. Family nights with activities from sports games to cartoon screenings take place on Wednesdays. A park train regularly departs from the central concourse, providing a whirlwind tour of the zoo. The park is open daily from 09:00 to 20:00 in winter and from 16:00 to 22:00 during summer. Entrance is Dhs.15 for adults, Dhs.5 for children and it's free for those under 2 years.

Al Jahili Fort

Nr Central Public Gardens Al Ain **03 784 3996**
www.adach.ae
Map **4 D2**
Celebrated as the birthplace of the late Sheikh Zayed bin Sultan Al Nahyan, the picturesque fort was erected in 1891 to defend Al Ain's precious palm groves. It is set in beautifully landscaped gardens and visitors are encouraged to explore the exterior.

Hili Archaeological Park

Hili Al Ain
www.adach.ae
Map **4 E1**
Located 10 kilometres outside Al Ain on the Dubai-Al Ain highway, the gardens are home to a Bronze Age settlement (2,500 – 2,000BC), which was excavated and restored in 1995. Many of the artefacts found during the excavation are now on display in the Al Ain National Museum (p.235).

Hili Fort

Nr Date Farm & Hili Oasis Al Ain
Map **4 E1**
Across the border in Buraimi, the Hili Fort is located at the edge of a date palm plantation near the Buraimi Souk. The area features several delightful mud-walled paths that lead out from the back into the oasis.

Hili Fun City > *p.186*

Off Emirates St Al Ain **03 784 5542**
www.hilifuncity.ae
Map **4 E1**
The recently renovated 22 hectare park may not compete with the world's greatest theme parks in terms of the rides on offer, but the spacious, leafy grounds make Hili Fun City a perfect destination for family outings. There are plenty of arcade games and refreshment stands, or you could bring your own picnic. Located on the eastern side of the park is a mammoth 60 by 30 metre ice rink. The park is open 16:00 to 22:00 (Monday to Thursday), 12:00 to 22:00 (Friday and Saturday), with Wednesdays reserved for ladies and children only. The park is closed on Sundays and for Ramadan (when annual maintenance takes place). Special opening hours apply for the June-August period. Entrance costs Dhs.45 (Mondays and Tuesdays, Dhs.40); free for kids up to 89cm tall. The Dhs.25 admission fee to the ice rink includes the rental of skates for one hour.

Camel Safaris

Al Ain Golden Sands Camel Safaris offers a selection of tours that include a camel ride over the dunes of Bida Bint Saud. The rides usually last one to two and a half hours and include transfers from Al Ain. Call 050 447 7268 for the details.

Muraijib Fort

Al Jimi St Al Ain
Map **4 D2**
Built in 1816, the Muraijib Fort is the oldest fort in Al Ain. It is located on Al Jimi Street and the restored remains of the fort are situated within beautifully landscaped gardens, which are reserved for women and children only.

Al Ain Oasis

Al Jahili Fort

Al Ain Wildlife Park & Resort

Al Ain Palace Museum

Silmi Garden

Mohammed Bin Khalifa St Al Ain
Map 4 D2

Silmi Garden is a popular spot with locals. Like all other parks in Al Ain, it is well cared for with plenty of trees, shrubs, flowers, fountains and a play area with swings and slides. Unfortunately, you have to park on the street and all the signs are in Arabic. You needn't worry if your Arabic isn't great; the park is quite easy to locate, especially at night as the walls are lit with multi-coloured lights.

Al Ain Hotels

Al Ain Rotana

Sheikh Zayed Rd Al Ain 03 754 5111
www.rotana.com
Map 4 D2

Located in the centre of the city, the hotel's rooms, suites and chalets are extremely spacious and modern. The other facilities include a beautiful garden pool and good fitness facilities. In addition, the hotel is also a nightlife hub with six dining venues, including the ever-popular Trader Vic's and a highly recommended Lebanese restaurant.

Al Massa Hotel

Nr Hamdan Bin Mohd & Al Baladiah Sts Al Ain 03 763 9003
www.almasahotels.com
Map 4 D2

This city centre establishment has 50 rooms and 12 suites, along with a cafe and Lebanese-style restaurant. It is a little dated but clean and welcoming if you're simply looking for a place to stay in the centre of town.

Ayla Hotel

Khalifa Bin Zayed Al Anwal St Al Ain 03 746 0918
www.aylahotels.com
Map 4 D2

A new hotel near the town centre, the rooms are practical and tasteful, while there's a modern gym, indoor pool, sauna, Jacuzzi and basic spa offerings. Dining options are simple but adequate, but Ayla is aimed mainly at an Arabic market (and a business one at that) and outlets are not licensed. Western tourists shouldn't be put off – the hotel has a local flavour that creates a welcoming, relaxed atmosphere.

City Seasons Hotel Al Ain

Nr Ruler's Diwan, Sheikh Khalifa Bin Zayed St, Al Ain 03 755 0220
www.cityseasonsgroup.com
Map 4 D2

This hotel has 77 lovely rooms and suites with excellent facilities. Executive suites have a separate living room and kitchen facilities. The hotel has a fitness centre, swimming pool and sun deck.

Danat Al Ain Resort

Khalid Bin Sultan & Al Salam St Al Ain 03 704 6000
www.danathotels.com
Map 4 E2

One of the most enjoyable inland resorts in the UAE, this hotel has landscaped gardens, swimming pools, luxurious guestrooms, deluxe villas and a Royal Villa with a private Jacuzzi. It also has great facilities for families and a delightful spa.

Hilton Al Ain

Khalid Bin Sultan St Al Ain 03 768 6666
www.hilton.com
Map 4 E2

Located near the heart of Al Ain, this ageing hotel is a key landmark and sits in lush, landscaped gardens that contain a nine hole golf course, tennis and squash courts, a health club and a nice pool area. It is particularly convenient for visiting the wildlife park and Jebel Hafeet. The Hiltonia Sports Bar and Paco's Bar are both popular haunts.

Mercure Grand Jebel Hafeet Al Ain

Al Ain 03 783 8888
www.mercure.com
Map 4 D4

Situated in a spectacular location near the top of Jebel Hafeet, the Mercure offers incredible views of Al Ain from all of its simply decorated rooms and terraced restaurants. There are also three swimming pools, and a water slide. There is a pub, buffet restaurant and poolside cafe serving excellent evening barbecues.

Al Gharbia

Located way west of Abu Dhabi, and further than most people usually venture on or off-road, Al Gharbia (or the Western Region) actually makes up over two-thirds of the UAE. Along its hundreds of kilometres of coastline can be found some stunning beaches, as well as a number of islands, which are increasingly being developed and promoted for visitors. But the main reason to make the drive is Liwa – a destination that will blow you away with massive expanses of awesome desert and the biggest dunes this side of the Sahara.

Prepare for the most adventurous off-road driving the UAE has to offer, and some of its most incredible scenery. For an overview of what you can find in the area, read on; for detailed routes and information, get a copy of *UAE Off-Road Explorer.*

The Pearl Coast

If you head west along the coast from Abu Dhabi, the first port of call is Mirfa. A long-established fishing port and pearling centre, Mirfa has a rather quiet feel these days, but this is all set to change following the inauguration of the Mirfa Corniche

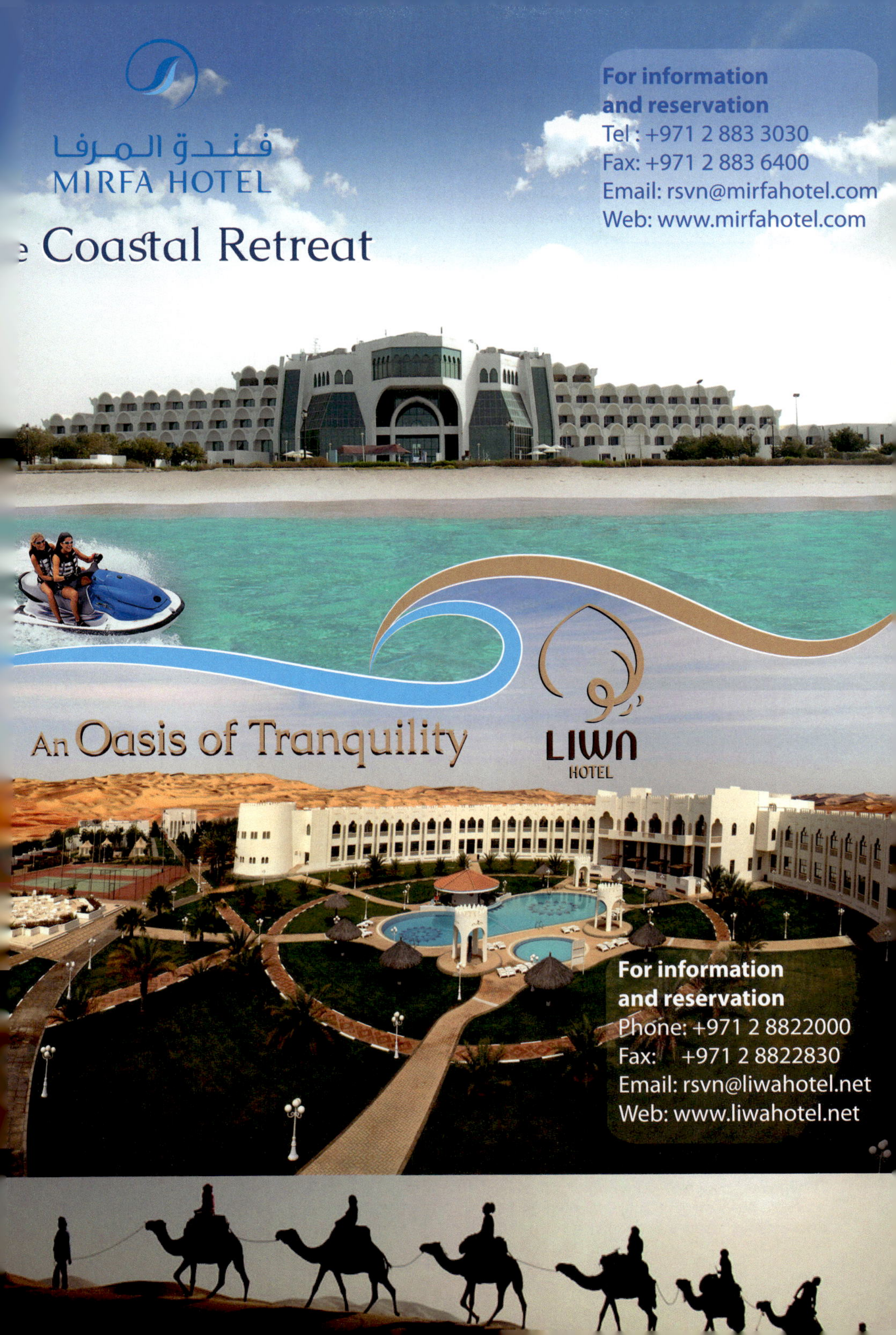

فندق المرفا
MIRFA HOTEL
e Coastal Retreat
For information
and reservation
Tel : +971 2 883 3030
Fax: +971 2 883 6400
Email: rsvn@mirfahotel.com
Web: www.mirfahotel.com
An Oasis of Tranquility
LIWA
HOTEL
For information
and reservation
Phone: +971 2 8822000
Fax: +971 2 8822830
Email: rsvn@liwahotel.net
Web: www.liwahotel.net

development in March 2011. The project is part of Abu Dhabi's 2030 development plan for the whole region. While the works are under way, new life has recently already been blown into the area by the opening of the refurbished Mirfa Hotel. Developed by Al Marfa Pearl, the resort now consists of 114 rooms and wide-ranging leisure facilities designed to attract a growing number of visitors to this part of the emirate. For now, the biggest annual draw remains the Al Gharbia Watersports Festival (p.28), held on the beach opposite the hotel. Each year the event wakes up Mirfa with a weekend of crowds, fireworks and competitive kitesurfing, wakeboarding and kayaking.

Delma Ferry

A new car ferry travels between Jebel Dhanna and Delma Island at 10:00, 13:00 and 16:00, making the return trip at the same times.

A hundred kilometres further along is Jebel Dhanna, another stopping point for history's pearl divers. With a great beach and the clear, shallow sea, the two hotels are among the region's best kept secrets. The Dhafra Beach Hotel (p.242) has been there for 30 years now, home to long-term residents that work in the area, and to the late Sheikh Zayed's ornate presidential suite, which is now available to visitors and popular with honeymooners at a cost of around Dhs.3,000 a night. Just along the beach, the Danat Jebel Dhanna Resort (p.242) is a real find. A good-value, five-star resort with a country club feel, it has great facilities and its bars and restaurants are particularly impressive. Both hotels are popular with international expats based in industrial outposts in the region, but at just a two-hour drive from the capital, they make for great weekend getaways for Abu Dhabi residents too.

Nearby, Ruwais is a purpose-built town, inhabited entirely by ADNOC employees from all over the world. It has a small stretch of shops, a pool and a recreation club, but holds little interest for visitors.

The last stop before you hit the Saudi Arabia border is Sila, a true frontier town. With sleepy streets and wide empty vistas, there is little happening in Sila today, but there is great potential for change as the proposed GCC railway network will stop here. Until then, visitors should head down from the town to the quiet harbour, where at the Abu Dhabi Fishermen's Cooperative Society (02 673 0888) you can buy some fresh catch. Alternatively, call in at the tackle shop (02 872 1385) to see if you can arrange a fishing trip of your own. For a beach barbecue, pick up extra provisions at Al Rahi Home Grocery next to the Fishermen's Cooperative. Drive north, with the quarry-scarred embankment on your left, along the beach track, and find a spot away from the beach houses. This is one of the few spots along the coast where you can camp; two headlands further west, you'll find an even more pristine spot. It is there that you will find the powder white sand, calm turquoise sea and bobbing pink flamingos.

Desert Islands

As part of the plan to develop Al Gharbia for tourism, this huge, eight island project is one of the most exciting developments in the whole emirate. The islands include the larger Sir Bani Yas and Delma islands, and the six Discovery Islands, which will provide eco-tourism accommodation on small islands modelled after those in the Maldives.

Sir Bani Yas Island was once Sheikh Zayed's personal retreat and is now becoming a noted wildlife reserve, green energy champion and internationally renowned holiday resort. The Desert Islands Resort & Spa (p.242) has received accolades for its sensitive and stylish luxury. Located off the coast from Jebel Dhanna, it has succeeded in bringing tourists to the area to enjoy region-specific activities from safaris to snorkelling, and kayaking to mountain biking.

Far beyond Sir Bani Yas lies Delma Island. A two-hour ferry ride from Jebel Dhanna, this was the most important island in the Gulf for all but the most recent history. With rare and precious fresh water reserves, it was a favourite stopping point for traders, fishermen and pearlers, and has been inhabited for over 7,000 years. Important archaeology, fascinating history and fertile plantations are expected to appeal to future visitors too.

Arabian Wildlife Park

The Arabian Wildlife Park (www.desertislands.com) houses thousands of animals; the species include the endangered Arabian oryx, sand gazelle and mountain gazelle, as well as cheetahs, hyenas, Barbary sheep, Arabian rock hyrax, Arabian hares, northern ostriches and Ethiopian hedgehogs. Research and conservation play leading roles in the park's development, which has been an unprecedented success. Since the early 1960s, when the Arabian oryx was declared extinct in the wild, more than 500 born on Sir Bani Yas have been released back into the wild. Human interference has been removed from the park, but tourism and education are key to the park's success, and visitors are encouraged to take part in game drives, nature trails, mountain biking or even opt for an exclusive outdoor dining experience. Only those staying at The Desert Islands Resort & Spa by Anantara (p.242) can enter the park and, even then, you have to do so with an official guide provided by the resort.

The volcanic landscape literally sparkles and big ospreys watch over fields of ostrich, but even with two new car ferries plying the route from the mainland, Delma's attractions are still very much under construction and the barren island is scarred with quarrying, construction and watchtowers. It feels like a deserted service station, which in marine terms it is. Currently the only accommodation available is at the Delma Motel (02 878 1222); another option is to camp – either up in the hilly moonscape interior or on a quiet stretch of beach.

Liwa

For most visitors to Al Gharbia, all roads lead to Liwa. On the way, they pass through tumbleweed towns like Ghayathi (good for stocking up on authentic Bedouin souvenirs) and the regional capital Madinat Zayed.

The land here is ancient; at Bu Ghar, eight million year old fossils have been found. There are oases dotted throughout the region, and occasional farmsteads. Modern Bedouin, with entire bungalows on the back of big-wheeled trucks, criss-cross the interior all the way to Liwa.

Liwa Oasis is one of the largest oases on the Arabian Peninsula. This fertile crescent stretches over 150km and is home to the Bani Yas tribe, ancestors of the ruling family of Abu Dhabi. Dotted with date plantations, small towns and ancient forts, it's a quiet area, visited for traditional falconry, camel racing and trading, and because Liwa is the gateway to the great desert.

The Rub Al Khali is the biggest sand desert on the planet and is one of the world's great attractions with its unsurpassed majesty and scale. Covering parts of Oman, Yemen, the southern UAE and almost all of southern Saudi Arabia, the Rub Al Khali was historically regarded as the edge of civilisation by people living in the region. There is an extraordinary beauty to this landscape, despite it being so harsh and inhospitable. Even today man has been able to make little mark on it. Desert driving in this area is more of an expedition than just a spot of dune bashing, so go prepared for the adventure of a lifetime.

Something Fishy

Perhaps the most unusual place to visit in the Liwa area is the fish farm near Khanur, where the water arrives from underground sources. There are pools and breeding tanks filled with tilapia, bulti, catfish and even some carp. To get there, and to learn about other off-the-beaten-track adventures in the region, pick up the *UAE Off-Road Explorer*.

The opportunities for camping in the region are endless, and sleeping under the stars is a great way to experience the peace and tranquillity of the desert. If you don't feel like roughing it, a clutch of stunning hotels have recently been added, ensuring that you need not go without your home comforts. Qasr Al Sarab (p.242) is the easily the most scenic and atmospheric choice: managed by Anantara, the luxurious resort sits in the midst of stunning red sand dunes and features Arabic-themed, spacious rooms and villas. Other alternatives include the Liwa Hotel (p.242), a comfortable resort with great leisure facilities; the Tilal Liwa Hotel (p.243), between Madinat Zayed and Liwa, and styled like a traditional fort; or the Liwa Resthouse (p.242) in Mezaira'a, although the main reason for stopping here is to stock up on fuel and provisions before heading into the brilliant wilderness.

The Empty Quarter

Al Gharbia Hotels

Danat Jebel Dhanna Resort

Jebel Dhanna Ruwais **02 801 2222**
www.danathotels.com
Map **3 B3**

Sitting on 800 metres of private, picturesque beach, this hotel offers 109 luxurious rooms and suites including six waterfront villas. It has a health club and a spa that includes beach massage huts and a pool area with swim-up bar. The five dining venues include an Italian restaurant, all-day buffet restaurant, cafe and shisha bar.

Desert Islands Resort & Spa By Anantara

Sir Bani Yas Island Jebel Dhanna **02 801 5400**
www.desertislands.anantara.com
Map **3 B3**

Probably one of the most unique resorts anywhere in the world, the Desert Islands Resort is accessible only by boat or the hotel's private aircraft (from Abu Dhabi International Airport). Once you arrive, luxurious leisure awaits – from stylish rooms and private beach villas to the wonderful beachside restaurant Samak, and the soothing treatments at the adjacent Anantara Spa. Outside the hotel is the Arabian Wildlife Park (p.240), with nature and wildlife drives, kayaking, snorkelling, trekking, hiking, archery and guided game walks. New, boutique style villas are scheduled to open by the end of 2011 (p.198), some of them located directly inside the wildlife park.

Arabian Nights Under The Stars

An essential part of any Liwa adventure, camping in the desert is a truly unforgettable experience. The expanses of sand rolling into the distance at early dawn and the snaking silvery dunes in the moonlight are quite magical. This area provides some of the best desert views in the UAE. You can camp just about anywhere, so take any of the roads and tracks into the desert off the main road through the oasis. Find somewhere near to where you'd like to be for the next day's driving, but just make sure that you drive far enough from roads, habitation and activity to find a peaceful spot. Try to get settled in your campsite long before the sun goes down, both for safety reasons and to prevent getting stuck in the dark (and of course, to allow you to enjoy the sunset). One particularly good area is on the road to Moreeb Hill passing the Liwa Resthouse. This minor, paved road heads into the desert for 11.5km, leading you into some of the best dunes, and crossing plenty of sabkha flats – any one of which allows you to get off-road and into some sheltered areas, far from disturbances, in quite a short time.

Dhafra Beach Hotel

Jebel Dhanna Ruwais **02 801 2000**
www.danathotels.com
Map **3 B3**

A very pleasant and reasonably priced hotel with a variety of rooms and suites to choose from, as well as a handful of dining options, a fitness centre with a sauna, and two swimming pools.

Liwa Hotel > *p.239*

Nr Mezzaira Village, Mezaira Liwa **02 882 2000**
www.liwahotel.net
Map **3 C4**

With a raised location giving spectacular views of the Rub Al Khali, the green oasis and a palace on the hilltop opposite, Liwa Hotel is a good option if you're not keen on camping. The hotel has spacious rooms and green, landscaped grounds with an attractive pool. The quality of the facilities and the service in the hotel are good, and there's a choice of dining options and evening venues.

Liwa Resthouse

Mezaira Liwa **02 882 2075**
Map **3 C4**

One of a number of resthouses in Abu Dhabi, Liwa Resthouse is a little past its prime and has been eclipsed by the nearby Liwa Hotel. Its (mainly Arab) clientele includes visiting business travellers, government officials and families on holiday. Although the accommodation and facilities are pretty basic compared to local hotels, it is clean and functional, and for the cheapest alternative to camping, it's worth a look.

Mirfa Hotel > *p.239*

Dubai – Sila Highway, 160 Kms From Abu Dhabi Mirfa **02 883 3030**
www.mirfahotel.com
Map **3 C3**

Located in the quiet town of Mirfa, 160 kilometres from Abu Dhabi, this hotel is perfect for a weekend break or as a stopover if you're driving to Saudi Arabia. The hotel has just been renovated and now features 114 comfortable rooms and suites, and lush gardens that include a fantastic range of regional flora and attract plenty of local fauna. Leisure facilities consist of two pools, floodlit tennis courts, a volleyball court, a fitness centre and a kids' playground.

Qasr Al Sarab Desert Resort By Anantara

1 Qasr Al Sarab Rd Liwa **02 886 2088**
www.qasralsarab.anantara.com
Map **3 D4**

The Qasr Al Sarab resort offers five-star, Arabian-style, luxury accommodation on the edge of the vast Rub Al Khali desert near Hamim. The hotel has 150 rooms, plus one, two and three-bedroom villas and a tented village. As well as a sensational pool area with a swim-up bar, it offers desert excursions, and there's an observatory from where guests can gaze into the desert night skies. Unsurprisingly for an Anantara resort, the spa, which features hammam baths amid peaceful courtyards, fountains and aromatic plants and flowers, is every bit as stunning as the endless dunes beyond.

Tilal Liwa Hotel

Nr Madinat Zayed, Rub Al Khali Liwa **02 894 6111**
www.danathotels.com
Map **3 C3**
One of the newest hotels in Al Gharbia, this four-star desert hideaway stretches around a charming pool area and offers a range of rooms and suites which blend old and new design elements, and look out over the endless sands. There are a few options for eating and drinking, and the gym, sauna and steam rooms keep guests busy, although desert safaris in the dunes should be at the top of all visitors activity itineraries.

UAE – THE OTHER EMIRATES

Dubai

Cliches tend to trip off the tongue when describing Abu Dhabi's little brother – the city of gold, sleepy fishing village transformed into modern metropolis, the Vegas of the Middle East, and so on. The truth is that, while the emirate boasts an incredible number of attractions claiming to be the tallest, biggest or longest, it's not all bright lights – the atmospheric old town around the Creek, and the restored Bastakiya area are musts for any visitor wanting to scratch Dubai's cultural surface, and the beautiful Jumeira Mosque (p.245) is one of the few mosques in the region open to non-Muslims, offering a rare chance to learn about the impact of Islam on the local people.

Dubai is also a great place for families and, from amusement parks and aquariums to child-friendly hotels and restaurants, you'll find plenty of ways to keep the kids busy while in town.

Beyond the city, the desert opens up further possibilities and many visitors choose to combine a city break with a couple of nights camping with a tour group, or relaxing at a luxury desert resort such as Al Maha (p.246) or Bab Al Shams (p.246). That said, if it's bright lights you're after, Dubai outshines the rest of the region. The emirate has been successful in its quest for economic diversification, and its focus on tourism revenues has resulted in a fantastic array of superlative-laden attractions for tourists and residents alike. From skiing on real snow at Ski Dubai (p.245) and plunging through shark-infested waters at Aquaventure (p.213), to shopping till you drop at Dubai Mall (p.244) and surveying the entire city from the world's tallest building, Burj Khalifa (see below), a weekend trip to Dubai promises an action-packed break.

Its selection of five-star hotels, restaurants, bars and clubs will ensure a well fed and watered stay, and luxury spas and clean beaches provide ample opportunities to relax.

For more help on planning a trip to Dubai, grab a copy of the *liveworkexplore* magazine or log on to www.liveworkexplore.com where you can find listings of up-coming events and further information about Dubai hotels and attractions, and where you can order a copy of *Dubai Mini Visitors' Guide* – the essential guide for your weekend break.

Dubai Attractions

Adventure HQ

Time Square Dubai **04 346 6824**
www.adventurehq.ae
Map **3 E2** Metro **Noor Islamic Bank**
In addition to stocking up on active wear and outdoors goods, adrenalin addicts will find indoors thrills from the Cable Climb to the Chill Chamber.

At The Top

Burj Khalifa Dubai **800 2884 3867**
www.burjkhalifa.ae
Map **3 E2** Metro **Burj Khalifa/Dubai Mall**
In less than 60 seconds, a high-speed lift whisks visitors up to the 124th floor of the world's tallest tower. From the Burj Khalifa observation deck, you can survey a 360 degree view of the city. Advance bookings are Dhs.100 for adults and Dhs.75 for children; tickets bought on the day cost Dhs.400.

Downtown Dubai

HATS OFF TO HATTA

Out of the city, but not strictly out of Dubai, is the mountain town of Hatta. It lies within Dubai emirate, about an hour's drive south-east of the city, but makes for a great addition to any out-of-town trip to Dubai.

The Hatta Fort Hotel (04 809 9333, www.jebelali-international.com) is a perfectly secluded mountain retreat in tranquil gardens. The hotel is fully equipped with numerous facilities and activities, including two swimming pools, a children's pool, a bar and restaurant, the Senses Beauty Salon, a driving range and chipping green, floodlit tennis courts and archery. The 50 spacious chalet-style rooms and suites all come with patios overlooking the impressive Hajars.

There are several good off-road options for those who want to do some 4WD exploring, including the nearby Hatta Pools, which you can swim in. They're fairly accessible from the town along an unpaved road, and there signs to guide you there. Pick up a copy of *UAE Off-Road Explorer* for other great routes in the area. Back in town is the Hatta Heritage Village. It is constructed around an old settlement and was restored in the style of a traditional mountain village. Explore the tranquil oasis, the narrow alleyways and discover traditional life in the mud and barasti houses.

Hatta's history goes back over 3,000 years and the area includes a 200 year-old mosque and the fortress built by Sheikh Maktoum bin Hasher Al Maktoum in 1896, which is now used as a weaponry museum. Entry is free.

Dubai Aquarium & Underwater Zoo

The Dubai Mall Dubai **04 448 5200**
www.thedubaiaquarium.com
Map **3 E2** Metro **Burj Khalifa/Dubai Mall**

Located in the middle of Dubai Mall, this aquarium displays over 33,000 tropical fish to passing shoppers free of charge. For a closer view of the main tank's inhabitants, which include fearsome looking but generally friendly sand tiger sharks, you can pay to walk through the 270° viewing tunnel. Also well worth a look is the Underwater Zoo, which includes residents such as penguins, piranhas and an octopus. If you're feeling really adventurous, you can even go for a scuba dive in the tank (call ahead to book).

The Dubai Mall

Nr Interchange 1, Financial Centre Rd Dubai
800 38224 6255
www.thedubaimall.com
Map **3 E2** Metro **Burj Khalifa/Dubai Mall**

One of the world's largest shopping malls, The Dubai Mall is a shopper's paradise housing some 1,200 stores, including the famous New York department store, Bloomingdales. Even if you're not in town to shop, you should make a trip to the mall anyway to view the many attractions within. There is an Olympic sized ice rink, an indoor waterfall, a 22 screen cinema, Sega World indoor theme park, KidZania edutainment centre, the Dubai Aquarium & Underwater Zoo and some great alfresco dining venues with views of the spectacular musical displays of the Dubai Fountain.

Dubai Museum

Al Fahidi Fort Dubai **04 353 1862**
www.dubaitourism.ae
Map **3 E2** Metro **Al Fahidi**

Located in Al Fahidi Fort, this museum is creative, well thought-out and interesting for all the family. The fort was originally built in 1787 as the residence of the ruler of Dubai and for sea defence, and then renovated in 1970 to house the museum. All aspects of Dubai's past are represented. You can walk through a souk from the 1950s, stroll through an oasis, see into a traditional house, get up close to local wildlife, learn about the archaeological finds or go 'underwater' to discover the pearl diving and fishing industries. There are some entertaining mannequins to pose with too. Entry costs Dhs.3 for adults and Dhs.1 for children under 6 years old. Open daily 08:30 to 20:30 (14:30 to 20:30 on Fridays).

Heritage & Diving Village

Nr Sheikh Saeed House Dubai **04 393 7151**
www.dubaitourism.ae
Map **3 E2** Metro **Al Ghubaiba**

Located near the mouth of Dubai Creek, the Heritage & Diving Village focuses on Dubai's maritime past, pearl diving traditions and architecture. Visitors can observe traditional potters and weavers practising their craft the way it has been done for centuries. Local women serve traditionally cooked snacks – one of the rare opportunities you'll have to sample genuine Emirati cuisine. It is particularly lively during the Dubai Shopping Festival and Eid celebrations, with performances including traditional sword dancing. Open daily 09:00 to 21:00 (Fridays 15:00-22:00). The village is very close to Sheikh Saeed Al Maktoum's House, the home of the much-loved former ruler of Dubai, which is a good example of a traditional home and houses a number of interesting photographic exhibits.

Jumeira Mosque

Jumeira Rd Dubai **04 353 6666**
www.cultures.ae
Map **3 E2** Metro **Al Jafiliya**

This is the most beautiful mosque in the city and perhaps the best known, as its image features on the Dhs.500 banknote. The Sheikh Mohammed Centre for Cultural Understanding (www.cultures.ae) organises mosque tours for non-Muslims on Saturday, Sunday, Tuesday and Thursday mornings at 10:00. Visitors are guided around the mosque and told all about the building, and then the hosts give a talk on Islam and prayer rituals. The tour offers a fascinating insight into the culture and beliefs of the local population, and is thoroughly recommended. You must dress conservatively – no shorts and no sleeveless tops. Women must also cover their hair with a head scarf or shawl, and all visitors will be asked to remove their shoes. Cameras are allowed, pre-booking is essential and there is a registration fee of Dhs.10 per person..

KidZania

The Dubai Mall Dubai **04 448 5222**
www.kidzania.ae
Map **3 E2** Metro **Burj Khalifa/Dubai Mall**

This new addition to Dubai Mall offers kids the chance to become adults for the day. Billed as a 'real-life city' for children, youngsters can dress up and act out more than 75 different roles, from policeman to pilot and doctor to designer. The KidZania city even has its own currency, which children can earn and spend. It's intended to be both fun and educational. Dhs.95 – 125 entry.

The Lost Chambers

Atlantis The Palm Dubai **04 426 0000**
www.atlantisthepalm.com
Map **3 E2** Metro **Nakheel**

The ruins of the mysterious lost city provide the theme for the aquarium at Atlantis. The maze of underwater halls and tunnels provide ample opportunity to get up close to the aquarium's 65,000 inhabitants, ranging

Jumeira Mosque

from sharks and eels to rays and piranhas, as well as multitudes of exotic fish. The entrance fee is Dhs.100 for adults and Dhs.70 for 7 to 11 year olds.

SEGA Republic

The Dubai Mall Dubai **04 448 8484**
www.segarepublic.com
Map **3 E2** Metro **Burj Khalifa/Dubai Mall**

This indoor theme park located in Dubai Mall offers a range of thrills and spills, courtesy of the nine main attractions and the 150 arcade games. A Power Pass (Dhs.140) gets you all-day access to the big attractions, which include stomach-flipping rides like the Sonic Hopper, the SpinGear and the Halfpipe Canyon. Unlike many other shopping mall amusement centres, SEGA Republic is for all ages, and features some truly unique thrills.

Ski Dubai

Mall Of The Emirates Dubai **04 409 4000**
www.skidxb.com
Map **3 E2** Metro **Mall of the Emirates**

Ski Dubai is the Middle East's first indoor ski resort, with more than 22,500 square metres of real snow. The temperature hovers around -3 celcius, even when it's closer to +50 outside, to make for a cooling excursion from city life. Competent skiers and boarders can choose between five runs and a freestyle area, skiing and snowboarding lessons are available for beginners, and there is a huge snowpark for the little ones. Slope pass and lesson prices include the hire charge for jackets, trousers, boots, socks, helmets and either skis and poles or a snowboard, but it's worth bringing your own gloves as these are charged extra on top of everything else. Freestyle nights are held every other week on Mondays from 20:00 to 23:00.

Just Deserts

With thousands of square kilometres of desert and a little sprinkling of luxury, the sands of the UAE make the perfect place for a short break from city life.

Bab Al Shams

If there are two things that the UAE does better than most other international tourist destinations, it is five-star luxury and the desert experience. Holidaymakers fly across the globe to indulge in the unique blend of opulence and landscape, but UAE residents have all this on their doorstep. From the mountains of RAK to the endless sea of sand two hours from Abu Dhabi, there are several excellent locations for a memorable desert getaway. Here are the highlights:

Al Maha, A Luxury Collection Desert Resort & Spa

Dubai-Al Ain Rd **04 832 9900**
www.al-maha.com

The Al Maha Desert Resort & Spa is the definitive place to get away from it all. Accessible only by a 4WD driven by your own field guide, the resort is congruously set on the slopes of a rising dune in the form of a Bedouin camp and blends into the desert as if it has been there as long as the sands. Rooms resemble a traditional Bedouin tent but are the epitome of luxury. Surrounded by colourful gardens and accessed by golf buggy, every one of the 42 suites has a private wooden-decked terrace and infinity plunge pool.

Inside, circular suites are full of gloriously decadent touches, including two chaise-longues, regal drapes, an array of fascinating artefacts and a vast, luxurious bathroom bigger than most hotel rooms. Panoramic windows look out over the desertscape and doors open onto the patio area, which comes complete with a pair of powerful binoculars to spot the wild Arabian oryx (maha) that wander the resort.

Activities include a sunrise falconry display, horse riding, dune safaris, nature walks, archery, a sunset camel ride and champagne toast on the dunes, and there's the Timeless Spa for a full range of pampering. Eat in Al Diwaan restaurant with its great wine list or on your private terrace.

Should you fancy a spot of night swimming, there are pool lights to help you see where you are going, and the water temperature is adjustable.

Bab Al Shams Desert Resort & Spa

Nr Dubai Endurance Village **04 809 6100**
www.themeydan.com

Like a desert mirage come to life, Bab Al Shams is a Bedouin fantasy escape away from the hectic streets of the cities. Bamboo torches guide you to the low-rise building which blends into the imposing dunes that surround it. Your welcome, marked with the traditional ritual of dates and kahwa, is one of the many personal touches that infuse Bab Al Shams with Arabian hospitality and warmth.

The rooms, although luxurious, have been designed to evoke a feeling of Bedouin living; walls seem to be made of clay, furnishings are crafted from dark wood, and curtains are made of hessian. The bathroom is similarly designed and features clay pots, rustic tones and a large bath that looks like it could have been carved straight from the earth.

Camel rides on the dunes are available or, if you prefer relaxation, you can chill out in one of the holistic swimming pools. The infinity pool's horizon drops off into the sand dunes. Swim up to the in-pool bar for a cocktail or an icy cold beer and enjoy the splendour of the sunset over the dunes – you really do feel as though you are in an isolated world of tranquillity. You can take the pampering up a notch by heading to the Satori Spa, which offers a range of signature treatments.

As the evening sets in, head to the Al Sarab Rooftop Lounge for shisha and a selection of drinks. For dinner, you could choose to eat in the hotel's Al Forsan restaurant which serves an international buffet for breakfast, lunch and dinner, but the highlight is Al Hadheerah, which offers not just a dinner but a full-on Arabian experience, including a huge buffet, horse and camel displays, belly dancing and traditional music.

Banyan Tree Al Wadi

Ras Al Khaimah **07 206 7777**
www.banyantree.com

Hidden in the undulating desert of Ras Al Khaimah emirate, from the access road, the impressive resort appears out of the sand like a mirage. Guests have a choice of either the traditional mudbrick inspired Al Rimal villas with mighty wooden doors and high ceilings, or the spacious nomad-style tented villas (over 250 sq m). All villas have their own pool, and luxury is around every corner.

The resort is set in 100 hectares, 60 of which are a nature reserve where Arabian gazelles, camels and oryx roam. There's even a watering hole for the wildlife strategically located under the balcony of one of the restaurants. Activities include archery, cycling and horse and camel rides, and there is a kids' club and falconry centre too. The spa is immense, with treatment pavilions (the word 'room' isn't enough) offering the ultimate in sublime pampering and state-of-the-art hydrotherapy treatments. The restaurants are equally opulent and there are great views from the roof-top bar. For a memorable romantic getaway with a touch of exotic desert scenery, Banyan Tree Al Wadi fits the (large) bill.

Liwa Hotel > *p.239*

Nr Mezzaira Village, Mezaira'a **02 882 2000**

The Liwa Hotel was originally conceived as a sheikh's palace, but prior to occupation was converted into a hotel. While it may not quite match royal standards, a stay here makes for an enjoyable weekend break with a difference, thanks to the stunning setting: the hotel offers beautiful, peaceful views of the desertscape. Rooms all have large terraces, so you can relax and enjoy the scenery, with five suites and three villas available. The decor is fairly basic, but it fits in with the calm, minimalist surroundings, only interrupted every now and then by the occasional revving of a 4WD or quad bike on its way back from a jaunt on the dunes. The restaurant serves buffet breakfast and dinner. Leisure-wise you'll find a large swimming pool and surprisingly lush grounds, perfect for relaxing. There is also a sauna, Jacuzzi and steam room, tennis and volleyball courts and a separate kids' pool and play area. But the real star of the show is the stunning surroundings.

Qasr Al Sarab Desert Resort By Anantara

1 Qasr Al Sarab Rd Nr Hameen **02 886 2088**
www.qasralsarab.anantara.com

Set on the edge of the Empty Quarter, at the birthplace of the Al Nahyan family, this palatial hotel's graceful windtowers and traditional Emirati architecture rise out of the impressive dunes in hues that blend the new with the age-old desert. Luxurious, five star touches make it a true retreat from Abu Dhabi life.

Each spacious room is lavishly adorned, with decor in earthy tones contrasting with cutting edge lighting, sound and entertainment facilities. Extravagant bathrooms with rain showers and circular bathtubs, and expansive terraces and balconies, all with views across the Empty Quarter, provide endless opportunities for rest and relaxation. The luxurious Anantara spa and excellent restaurants provide the finishing touches for a truly relaxing escape from city life.

For those looking to dig a little deeper into Liwa's heritage, more than 2,500 cultural artefacts are on display throughout the resort, culminating in a stunning library stocked with literature about the region. Guests can enjoy a host of cultural and experiential activities from archery practice and dawn desert hikes to hamman spa treatments, sampling Emirati cuisine in a traditional Bedouin tent, and star gazing to a backdrop of oud music.

For a full range of regional getaway options, from desert to city to coast, get hold of a copy of *Weekend Breaks Oman & UAE* by Explorer.

Qasr Al Sarab Desert Resort by Anantara

Souk Al Bahar
The Old Town Island Dubai **04 362 7011**
www.soukalbahar.ae
Map **3 E2** Metro **Burj Khalifa/Dubai Mall**
With atmospheric passageways, Souk Al Bahar is designed to resemble a traditional souk. It houses a host of designer boutiues and shops selling Arabian wares such as carpets, paintings, jewellery, clothes and perfumes, but its main attractions are the restaurants and bars, many of which have terraces with views of the Dubai Fountain and Burj Khalifa.

Souk Madinat Jumeirah
Al Sufouh Rd Dubai **04 366 8888**
www.jumeirah.com
Map **3 E2** Metro **Mall of the Emirates**
This modern shopping mall is a recreation of a traditional souk with confusingly winding passageways, authentic architecture and interconnecting waterways traversed by motorised abras (traditional boats). It houses a collection of boutique shops, galleries, cafes and bars and the al fresco dining venues are always buzzing during the evenings of the cooler months.

Take A Tour
Why not view the city from the upper floor of a doubledecker bus, learning some fascinating facts about Dubai along the way? The Big Bus Company (www.bigbus.co.uk) allows you to hop on and off as you like at various attractions, while the amphibious Wonder Bus even takes to water (www.wonderbustours.net).

Stargate
Zabeel Park Dubai **04 325 9988**
www.stargatedubai.com
Map **3 E2** Metro **Al Jafiliya**
Kids will love Stargate; this massive complex, located in Zabeel Park, is free to enter, with access to the five giant play domes paid for by a rechargeable card. Each area contains a different adventure; there's a multistorey soft-play area, two go-kart tracks, an ice rink, an indoor rollercoaster and a 3D fun zone. The walkways connecting the play domes house plenty of food venues and retail outlets, and there are enough arcade games dotted throughout to keep everyone happy.

Dubai Hotels

The Address Downtown Dubai
Emaar Blvd Dubai **04 436 8888**
www.theaddress.com
Map **3 E2** Metro **Burj Khalifa/Dubai Mall**
Even at over 300 metres in height, The Address is dwarfed by its neighbour, the Burj Khalifa – but breathtaking views, beautiful interiors and eight dining outlets (including Neos, the panoramic bar on the 63rd floor) make this one of the most popular spots in town. There are also two more The Address hotels, located at Dubai Mall and Dubai Marina.

Atlantis The Palm
Crescent Rd Dubai **04 4260 000**
www.atlantisthepalm.com
Map **3 E2** Metro **Nakheel**
With a staggering 1,539 rooms and suites, all with views of the sea or the Palm Jumeirah, Atlantis is certainly one of Dubai's grandest hotels. It has no less than four restaurants featuring the cuisine of Michelin-starred chefs, including a branch of Nobu. It is also home to Aquaventure, the biggest water park in the Middle East, and the Lost Chambers aquarium.

Bonnington Jumeirah Lakes Towers
Nr Almas Tower Dubai **04 356 0000**
www.bonningtontower.com
Map **3 E2** Metro **Jumeirah Lakes Towers**
This British five-star institution made its Dubai debut in Jumeirah Lakes Towers. Containing both hotel suites and serviced apartments, as well as six restaurants and bars, and a leisure deck with infinity pool, it has great connections to Dubai Marina, as well as the rest of the city via the nearby Metro stop.

Burj Al Arab
Nr Wild Wadi, Jumeirah Rd Dubai **04 301 7777**
www.jumeirah.com
Map **3 E2** Metro **Mall of the Emirates**
Standing on its own man-made island, this dramatic Dubai icon's unique architecture is recognised around the world. Suites have two floors and are serviced by a team of butlers. To get into the hotel as a non-guest, you will need a restaurant reservation.

Desert Palm Dubai
Al Awir Rd Dubai **04 323 8888**
www.desertpalm.ae
Map **3 E2**
Located outside the bustle of the city, Desert Palm is so tranquil you'll never want to leave. Overlooking polo fields, guests can chose from suites, or private villas with a pool. The extensive spa menu features massage and holistic therapies including reiki. Signature restaurant Rare is a must for meat lovers, while Epicure is a lovely gourmet deli and a great breakfast venue.

Dubai Festival City
Al Rebat St Dubai **04 213 6213**
www.dubaifestivalcity.com
Map **3 E2** Metro **Emirates**
DFC has two hotels to choose from. The InterContinental (04 701 1111) has extensive spa

facilities and great views from all its rooms and suites; next door is the Crowne Plaza (04 701 2222) with the ever-popular Belgian Beer Café.

Hilton Dubai Creek

Nr Economic Dept, Baniyas Rd Dubai **04 227 1111**
www.hilton.com
Map **3 E2** Metro **Al Rigga**
With very flash yet understated elegance, this ultra-minimalist hotel features interiors of wood, glass and chrome. Centrally located and overlooking the Creek, with splendid views of the Arabian dhow trading posts, the hotel has two renowned restaurants in Glasshouse and Gordon Ramsay's Verre.

Jumeirah Beach Hotel

Nr Wild Wadi, Jumeirah Rd Dubai **04 348 0000**
www.jumeirah.com
Map **3 E2** Metro **Mall of the Emirates**
Shaped like an ocean wave, with a fun and colourful interior, the hotel has 618 rooms, all with a sea view. It is also home to some excellent food and beverage outlets, including Uptown for happy hour cocktails and a great view of the Burj Al Arab. Kids and families will love Wild Wadi Water Park, which is located here.

Kempinski Hotel Mall Of The Emirates

Mall Of The Emirates Dubai **04 341 0000**
www.kempinski-dubai.com
Map **3 E2** Metro **Mall of the Emirates**
Located in Mall Of The Emirates, this chic hotel's 400 deluxe rooms enjoy direct access to the shopping extravaganza of the iconic mall and Ski Dubai, the indoor ski slope. Check into one of the 15 exclusive ski chalet rooms, remove your boots, put your feet up to the (fake) fire and tuck into an apres-ski afternoon tea while watching the world slide by.

Madinat Jumeirah

Nr Burj Al Arab, Jumeirah Rd Dubai **04 366 8888**
www.jumeirah.com
Map **3 E2** Metro **Mall of the Emirates**
This extravagant resort has two hotels, Al Qasr and Mina A'Salam, with no fewer than 940 luxurious rooms and suites, and the exclusive Dar Al Masyaf summer houses, all linked by man-made waterways navigated by wooden abra boats which whisk guests around the resort. Nestled between the two hotels is the Souk Madinat, with over 75 shops and 45 bars, restaurants and cafes to choose from.

One&Only Royal Mirage

Jumeira Rd Dubai **04 399 9999**
www.oneandonlyresorts.com
Map **3 E2** Metro **Nakheel**
This stunningly beautiful resort is home to three different properties: The Palace, Arabian Court and Residence & Spa. The hotel features unparalleled service and dining (opt for the Beach, Bar & Grill for a romantic evening out; try delectable Moroccan cuisine in the opulent Tagine; or enjoy cocktails with a view in the Rooftop and Sports Lounge), and a luxury spa treatment here is the ultimate indulgence.

The Palace – The Old Town

Emaar Blvd, The Old Town Island Dubai **04 428 7888**
www.theaddress.com
Map **3 E2** Metro **Burj Khalifa/Dubai Mall**
Palatial indeed, The Palace faces the mighty Burj Khalifa and the spectacular Dubai Fountain. Styled with traditional Arabic architecture, this opulent hotel boasts 242 luxurious rooms and suites, a beautiful spa and some excellent restaurants, including Argentinean steakhouse Asado, and majlis-style shisha tents arranged around the stunning pool.

Aquaventure at Atlantis

Park Hyatt Dubai

Nr Dubai Creek Golf & Yacht Club Dubai **04 602 1234**
www.dubai.park.hyatt.com
Map **3 E2** Metro **GGICO**

Enjoying a prime waterfront location within the grounds of Dubai Creek Golf & Yacht Club, the Park Hyatt is Mediterranean in style with low-rise buildings, natural colours and stylish decor. The hotel has 225 rooms and suites, all with beautiful views, as well as some great dining outlets and one of the city's best spas, which features a luxury couples' massage option. Excellent restaurants include The Thai Kitchen and Traiteur.

Raffles Dubai

Wafi Dubai **04 324 8888**
www.raffles.com
Map **3 E2** Metro **Healthcare City**

With 248 stunning suites, the renowned Raffles Amrita Spa and a unique Botanical Sky Garden, this is one of Dubai's most noteworthy city hotels. Nine food and beverage outlets offer a mix of international and far eastern cuisine.

The Ritz-Carlton, Dubai

Nr Le Royal Meridien Dubai **04 399 4000**
www.ritzcarlton.com
Map **3 E2** Metro **Dubai Marina**

Even though it is the only low-rise building amid the sea of Marina towers behind it, all 138 rooms have beautiful views of the Gulf – the Ritz-Carlton was, after all, here years before the rest of the marina was built. Afternoon tea in the Lobby Lounge is a must, and there are several other excellent restaurants and a very good spa onsite. Ritz-Carlton has also added another property to its offerings, with a new 341 room hotel in the DIFC area.

The Westin Dubai Mina Seyahi Beach Resort & Marina

Al Sufouh Rd Dubai **04 399 4141**
www.westinminaseyahi.com
Map **3 E2** Metro **Nakheel**

Set on 1,200 metres of private beach, The Westin has 294 spacious rooms and suites with all the luxury amenities you would expect of a five-star hotel, including the aptly named Heavenly Spa. There are plenty of dining venues, including perennially popular Italian Bussola, Senyar for cocktails and tapas, and wine and cheese bar Oeno.

Sharjah

Despite being eclipsed by its close neighbour Dubai in terms of international spotlight, Sharjah has substantially more culture and heritage to offer visitors. So much so that it was named the cultural capital of the Arab world in 1998 by Unesco, thanks to its eclectic mix of museums, heritage preservation and traditional souks.

Sharjah is built around Khalid Lagoon, also known as the Creek, and the surrounding Buheirah Corniche is a popular spot for an evening stroll. From various points on the lagoon, small dhows can be hired to see the city lights from the water. Joining Khalid Lagoon to Al Khan Lagoon, Al Qasba (p.251) is home to a variety of cultural events, exhibitions, theatre and music – all held on the canal-side walkways or at dedicated venues.

The city's main cultural centres, The Heritage Area (p.252) and The Arts Area, are two of the most impressive collections of museums and heritage sites in the country. The ruling Al Qassimi family are renowned collectors of historical artefacts and art, and in an emirate known for its conservatism, many of the works held within the Arts Area are surprising in

Sharjah Corniche (image courtesy SCTDA)

their modernity. Sharjah's cultural worth is indeed so great that visitors should avoid trying to absorb it all in one trip.

Shoppers will have a blast as well, searching for gifts through Sharjah's souks. Souk Al Arsah has recently been renovated and is the oldest souk in the emirate, while the Central Souk is known for its well-respected carpet shops. There's also high-street shopping at Sharjah Mega Mall (www.sharjahmegamall.com, 06 574 2574) for days when culture and curiosities aren't on the agenda.

Sharjah Attractions

Al Hisn Kalba

Nr Bait Sheikh Saeed Bin Hamed Al Qasimi, East Coast Kalba
www.sdci.gov.ae
Map **3 E1**

Located in the East Coast town of Kalba, this complex consists of the restored residence of Sheikh Sayed Al Qassimi and Al Hisn Fort, which houses the town's museum and contains a limited display of weapons. It won't take long to get round but luckily there's also a collection of rides for children. Entrance is Dhs.3 for individuals and Dhs.6 for families.

Al Mahatta Museum

Nr Dept of Immigration Sharjah **06 573 3079**
www.sharjahmuseums.ae
Map **3 E1**

Home to the first airfield in the Gulf, opened in 1932, Sharjah played an important role as a primary stop-off point for the first commercial flights from Britain to India, and the museum looks at the impact this had on the traditional way of life in Sharjah and this part of the world overall. Four of the original propeller planes have been fully restored and are on display. Located behind Al Estiqlal Street, entry is Dhs.5 for adults and Dhs.10 for families.

Al Qasba

Nr Al Khan Lagoon Sharjah **06 556 0777**
www.qaq.ae
Map **3 E1**

With an ever-changing events calendar that includes Arabic poetry readings, film viewings and musical events, the emphasis at Al Qasba is clearly on culture, but there's more on offer. The complex's shops, event spaces and restaurants are laid out between Sharjah's two lagoons and are packed on cooler evenings with window shoppers, diners and families. Motorised abras provide tours up and down the canal, but the biggest and most visible draw is the Eye of the Emirates – a 60 metre high observation wheel with air-conditioned pods offering amazing views over Sharjah and across to Dubai.

Sharjah Aquarium

Nr Sharjah Martime Museum Sharjah **06 528 5288**
www.sharjahaquarium.ae
Map **3 E1**

Although eclipsed by the two aquariums that opened in Dubai in 2008, Sharjah Aquarium is the city's newest attraction and draws big crowds, especially at the weekends. Situated next door to Sharjah Maritime Museum at the mouth of Al Khan Lagoon, its location allows visitors to view the Gulf's natural underwater life. There are over 250 species in the aquarium, as well as many interactive displays to educate visitors. Opening hours are 08:00 to 20:00 Monday to Thursday, 16:00 to 21:00 on Fridays and 08:00 to 21:00 on Saturdays and closed Sundays. Admission is Dhs.20 for adults, Dhs.10 for children and Dhs.50 for families.

Sharjah Archaeology Museum

Sheikh Rashid Bin Saqr Al Qasimi Rd Sharjah **06 566 5466**
www.archaeologymuseum.ae
Map **3 E1**

This hi-tech museum offers an interesting display of antiquities from the region. Using well-designed displays and documentary film, the museum traces man's first steps and progress across the Arabian Peninsula through the ages, and one area features the latest discoveries from excavation sites in the UAE. The museum is closed on Sunday, and for part of the afternoon on other days, so it is best to call before you visit to check times.

Sharjah Art Museum

Sharjah Arts Area Sharjah **06 568 8222**
www.sharjahmuseums.ae
Map **3 E1**

The Arts Area centrepiece, the Art Museum was originally built to house the personal collection of over 300 paintings and maps belonging to the ruler, HH Dr Sheikh Sultan bin Mohammed Al Qassimi. Permanent displays include the work of 18th century artists, with oil paintings and watercolours depicting life in the Arab world, while other exhibits change frequently. There's an art reference library, bookshop and coffee shop, and the museum hosts various cultural activities. The museum is closed on Friday mornings, while Wednesday afternoons are for ladies only.

Sharjah Desert Park

Interchange 9, Al Dhaid Rd Sharjah **06 531 1501**
www.epaa-shj.gov.ae
Map **3 E1**

Located 25 kilometres outside the city, Sharjah Desert Park comprises the Natural History Museum, the Arabian Wildlife Centre, the Childrens' Farm and the recently opened Sharjah Botanical Museum. The Natural History and Botanical Museums feature interactive displays on the relationships between man and the natural world in the UAE and beyond, while at the Arabian Wildlife Centre you get the chance to see many reptiles, birds, mammals and creepy crawlies, including the rare Arabian leopard. The facilities are excellent and the animals are treated well. There is also a Children's Farm with animals that can be fed and petted. Picnic areas are available, plus cafes and shops. Closed on Tuesdays, entry costs Dhs.5 for children, Dhs.15 for adults and includes access to everything.

Sharjah Discovery Centre

Nr Interchange 4, Al Dhaid Rd Sharjah **06 558 6577**
www.sharjahmuseums.ae
Map **3 E1**

The Discovery Centre is a great family day out and children of all ages, including toddlers, can explore the many themed areas and experiment and interact with the exhibits. The underlying aim is to teach youngsters about the biological, physical and technological worlds in a practical, and interesting, way. There is good pushchair access, an in-house cafe serving a light menu and ample parking. Entrance is Dhs.5 for children and Dhs.10 for adults. The centre is open from 08:00 to 14:00 Sunday to Thursday, and 16:00 to 20:00 Friday and Saturday. Be aware it can get busy at weekends.

Sharjah Heritage Area

Nr Sharjah Arts Area, Al Merraija Sharjah **06 569 3999**
www.sharjahtourism.ae
Map **3 E1**

The beautifully restored heritage area includes a number of old buildings including Al Hisn Fort (Sharjah Fort), Sharjah Islamic Museum, Sharjah Heritage Museum (Bait Al Naboodah), the Maritime Museum, the Majlis of Ibrahim Mohammed Al Midfa and the Old Souk (Souk Al Arsah). Traditional local architecture and life from the past 150 years is described, depicted and displayed throughout the extensive area. Toilets can be found at each venue and there's an Arabic coffee shop in the shady courtyard of Souk Al Arsah.

Sharjah Maritime Museum

Nr Sharjah Aquarium Sharjah **06 522 2002**
www.sharjahmuseums.ae
Map **3 E1**

With the goal of documenting the development of seafaring in the Middle East, the museum's displays feature fishing, trading, pearl diving and boat construction methods native to the UAE. Each room in the museum informs visitors about a different aspect of the marine industry. The museum also houses several real examples of traditional seafaring boats.

Sharjah Museum Of Islamic Civilization

Nr Sharjah Creek, Corniche St Sharjah **06 565 5455**
www.islamicmuseum.ae
Map **3 E1**

With vaulted rooms, and impressive galleries and halls, the architecture of this new museum alone makes a visit worthwhile, but with over 5,000 Islamic artefacts, and reams of information, this is one of the best places to learn about Islam and Islamic culture. The museum is organised according to five themes: the Islamic religion, Islamic art, artefacts, craftsmen and weaponry, each in its own gallery; the Temporary Exhibition Gallery hosts a programme of visiting exhibitions. Entry for adults is Dhs.5; children are free.

Sharjah Science Museum

Nr Sharjah TV station Sharjah **06 566 8777**
www.sharjahmuseums.ae
Map **3 E1**

The interactive museum's exhibits and demonstrations cover subjects such as aerodynamics, cryogenics, electricity and colour. There's also a planetarium and children's area where the under 5s and their parents can learn together. The Learning Centre offers more in-depth programmes on many of the subjects covered in the museum. Entry costs Dhs.5 for children aged 3 to 17 years; and Dhs.10 for adults.

Sharjah Hotels

Coral Beach Resort

Al Muntazah St Sharjah **06 522 9999**
www.coral-international.com
Map **3 E1**

Sitting on a perfect white beach,this resort boasts a convenient location and wide-ranging sports facilities.

Lou' Lou'a Beach Resort

Al Meena St Sharjah **06 528 5000**
www.loulouabeach.com
Map **3 E1**

Beach resort situated on the Sharjah coast. Offers watersports and spa facilities.

Radisson Blu Resort Sharjah

Corniche Rd Sharjah **06 565 7777**
www.radissonblu.com
Map **3 E1**

Located on the Sharjah Corniche, close to the city's main cultural attractions, the hotel has its own beach.

Sharjah Rotana

Al Arouba St Sharjah **06 563 7777**
www.rotana.com
Map **3 E1**

Located in the centre of the city, the Rotana caters mostly to business travellers.

Ajman

The smallest of the emirates, Ajman is around 10 kilometres further up the coast from Sharjah city centre, and the two cities almost merge with each other along the coast. There is a nice stretch of beach and a pleasant corniche to walk along. The Ajman Kempinksi Hotel & Resort is a grand offering for those who want a luxurious stay, while there are some other cheaper options along the beach. Ajman Museum (p.253) houses a variety of interesting displays in a restored fort that is worth visiting as much for the building itself as for the exhibits. The tiny emirate is known for being one of the largest boat building centres in the region, and while it is mainly modern boats that emerge from the yards these days, you may still catch a glimpse of a traditionally built wooden dhow sailing out to sea. The emirate's main souk is a reminder of a slower pace of life, while Ajman City Centre (06 743 2888) holds plenty of shops and a cinema.

Ajman Attractions

Ajman Museum

Nr Etisalat, Museum R/A Ajman **06 742 3824**
www.am.gov.ae
Map **3 E1**

Ajman Museum's interesting and well arranged displays have descriptions in both English and Arabic. The museum has a variety of exhibits, including a collection of Ajman-issued passports and dioramas of ancient life, but it's the building itself that will most impress visitors. Housed in a fortress dating back to around 1775, the museum is a fascinating example of traditional architecture, with imposing watchtowers and traditional windtowers. Entry is Dhs.5 for adults. Morning opening times are 09:00 to 13:00 then 16:00 to 19:00 in the evening. Closed on Fridays.

Ajman Hotels

Ajman Beach Hotel

Nr Kempinski Hotel Ajman Ajman **06 742 3333**
www.ajmanbeachhotel.com
Map **3 E1**

A decent budget hotel with rooms facing the sea and the creek, the location is excellent for visiting Ajman's best sites and you can almost fall out of bed on to the white, sandy beach.

Kempinski Hotel Ajman

Sheikh Humaid Bin Rashid Al Nuaimi St Ajman **06 714 5555**
www.kempinski.com
Map **3 E1**

Visitors to Ajman can relax on half a kilometre of the Kempinski's private beach or around its superb pool facilities. The hotel has 185 seaview rooms and a diverse range of international restaurants, cafes and bars, as well as a grand ballroom. The Laguna Spa offers a comprehensive spa menu, including an outdoor Balinese massage.

Umm Al Quwain

Nestled on the coast between Ajman and Ras Al Khaimah, not much has changed in Umm Al Quwain of late. The main industries are still fishing and date cultivation. The emirate has six forts, and a few old watchtowers surround the town.

With plenty of mangroves and birdlife, Umm Al Quwain's lagoon is a popular weekend spot for outdoors enthusiasts. In addition to bird watching, it's possible to come here for boat trips, windsurfing and other watersports. North of the lagoon is known for being a regional activity hub. The Emirates Motorplex (www.motorplex.ae) hosts all types of motorsport events, including the Emirates Motocross Championship which takes place here on a specially built track. One of the emirate's most popular attractions is Dreamland Aqua Park (p.253). Another favourite is the adjacent Barracuda Beach Resort (see below) which is particularly popular thanks to its well-stocked duty-free liquor store. The emirate has not escaped the attention of the developers completely and a project currently underway will see over 9,000 homes and a marina emerge on the shore of the Khor Al Beidah wildlife area. What impact this will have on the abundant plant and animal life remains to be seen.

Umm Al Quwain Attractions

Dreamland Aqua Park

North of UAQ, RAK Rd Umm Al Quwain **06 768 1888**
www.dreamlanduae.com
Map **3 E1**

With over 25 water rides, including four 'twisting dragons', Dreamland Aqua Park is massive. If extreme slides aren't your thing, there's the lazy river, a wave pool, an aqua play area, and a high-salinity floating pool. Overnight accommodation in provided tents or huts is also available. Admission is Dhs.135 for adults and Dhs.85 for children under 1.2m, while children under 2 go free. The park is open all-year-round; Fridays, Saturdays and holidays are for families only.

Umm Al Quwain Hotels

Barracuda Beach Resort

Nr Dreamland Aqua Park, Khor Al Baida Umm Al Quwain **06 768 1555**
www.barracuda.ae
Map **3 E1**

Known throughout the UAE for its popular tax-free booze emporium, Barracuda is also a pleasant resort for quick weekend getaways. Aside from the main hotel, the resort offers several lagoon-side one-bedroom chalets that can each accommodate up to five people. The chalets come with kitchenettes and barbecues – perfect for private overnight parties. There's also a large pool and Jacuzzi.

Flamingo Beach Resort

Nr Horsehead R/A Umm Al Quwain **06 765 0000**
www.flamingoresort.ae
Map **3 E1**

Cheap and cheerful, this resort is surrounded by a shallow lagoon interspersed with many green islands that attract a variety of birdlife, including migrating flamingos. Evening crab hunting adventures around the mangrove islands are available for non-guests.

Imar Spa

Nr Palma Beach Hotel Umm Al Quwain **06 766 4440**
www.imarspa.com
Map **3 E1**

This five-star ladies-only spa haven is in the heart of Umm Al Quwain, in a peaceful, seaside setting. The hotel has a small private beach and terrace, a fabulous temperature-controlled pool and a saltwater aqua therapy pool. There are only two twin rooms and three singles so booking in advance is advised.

Ras Al Khaimah

With the majestic Hajar Mountains rising just behind the city, the Arabian Gulf stretching out from the shore and the desert starting just to the south near the farms and ghaf forests of Digdagga, Ras Al Khaimah (RAK) has possibly the best scenery of any emirate in the UAE. The northern-most emirate in the country, a creek divides the main city into the old town and the newer Al Nakheel district. The past couple of years have witnessed RAK's transformation into a prominent weekend destination, and several new resorts have opened for the overworked residents of Abu Dhabi and Dubai. If you're visiting for the day you should make time to visit the souk in the old town and the National Museum of Ras Al Khaimah, which is housed in an old fort. Manar Mall (www.manarmall.com) is a large shopping and leisure facility, housing a cinema complex, family entertainment centre, a watersports area and dining options overlooking the creek and mangroves. Other shopping destinations include Al Hamra Mall (www.alhamramall.com) and Safeer Mall (www.mysafeer.com), while Ice Land Water Park (p.214) provides cooling water fun. Outdoors activities from mountaineering to kayaking can be arranged by Al Shaheen (www.alshaheenme.com). Al Hamra Marina (07 243 4540, www.alhamramarina.com) offers boat excursions, waterskiing and fishing trips, as well as jetski rentals. Golfers can choose between the Tower Links Golf Course (www.towerlinks.com) and Al Hamra Golf Club (www.alhamragolf.com). The former, a popular weekend haunt, is laid out among the mangroves around the creek and features a clubhouse, restaurant and gym. The latter has a gym, three dining options and a seaside sundeck.

The town is also a good starting point for exploring the surrounding mountains, visiting the ancient sites of Ghalilah and Shimal, the hot springs at Khatt and the camel racetrack at Digdagga. Ras Al Khaimah boasts several archaeological sites, some dating back to 3000BC. Take the Al Ram road out of the Al Nakheel district towards the Hajar Mountains to discover some of the area's history, including the Dhayah Fort, Shimal Archaeological Site and Sheba's Palace. The bare ruins of the Dhayah Fort can be spotted from the road, but you might need a 4WD to access them. Further inland is the Shimal archaeological site and Sheba's Palace. Both are a little obscure, but worth the difficulty of finding them. Shimal includes a tomb from the Umm An Nar period, roughly 5,000 years ago. Further down the same road is another tomb, which dates back to the Wadi Suq period (2000BC).

Many of the artefacts from these locations can be found at the National Museum at Ras Al Khaimah (see below). There are also several chances to get into the mountains up the coast, as well as south of RAK in places like Jebel Yibir – the tallest mountain in the country, where a new track takes you nearly to the top for spectacular views.

Ras Al Khaimah Attractions

National Museum Of Ras Al Khaimah

Nr Police HQ Ras Al Khaimah **07 233 3411**
www.raktourism.ae
Map **3 F1**

Housed in an impressive fort that was once the home of the present ruler of Ras Al Khaimah, this museum focuses on local natural history and archaeological displays, including a variety of paraphernalia from pre-oil, Bedouin life. Look out for fossils set in the rock strata of the walls of the fort – these date back 190 million years. The building has battlements, a working windtower and ornate, carved wooden doors. Entrance is only Dhs.2 for adults and Dhs.1 for children, and directions can be found on the museum website. Open every day except Tuesday and during public holidays: September to May from 10:00-17:00; June to August from 08:00-12:00 and 16:00-19:00.

Stellar Cellar

The Al Hamra Cellar, owned by MMI (www.mmidubai.com), is a tax-free liquor store that is well worth the trip. You won't find dodgy booze past its sell-by date; instead, you can browse a wide range of fine wines, spirits and beers at competitive prices. Call 07 244 7403 for more info.

Ras Al Khaimah Hotels

Al Hamra Fort Hotel & Beach Resort

Off the E11 Ras Al Khaimah **07 244 6666**
www.alhamrafort.com
Map **3 E1**

With traditional Arabic architecture set among acres of lush gardens and along a strip of sandy beach, this hotel offers a peaceful getaway. A range of watersports and activities, including two floodlit golf courses and an onsite dive centre, will keep you entertained, and the eight themed eateries offer a wide variety of international cuisines and atmosphere.

Banyan Tree Al Wadi

Al Mazraa Ras Al Khaimah **07 206 7777**
www.banyantree.com
Map **3 F1**

Banyan Tree Al Wadi combines superior luxury with exclusive spa facilities, desert activities and a wildlife conservation area. Set within Wadi Khadeja, the villas are designed for optimum relaxation.

The Cove Rotana Resort

Nr Directorate of Police Ras Al Khaimah **07 206 6000**
www.rotana.com
Map **3 F1**

Built into the hills overlooking the Arabian Gulf, The Cove's sprawling layout of 204 rooms, 72 private villas and winding pathways is reminiscent of an old Mediterranean hill town. The resort revolves around an immaculate lagoon, protected from the sea by 600 metres of pristine beach. A Bodylines spa and several impressive restaurants round out the package.

Golden Tulip Khatt Springs Resort & Spa

Nr Hajjar Mountains, Khatt Ras Al Khaimah
07 244 8777
www.goldentulipkhattsprings.com
Map **3 F1**

Simple and subdued, Golden Tulip Khatt Springs Resort & Spa relies on mountain views, uninterrupted tranquillity and incredible spa packages to attract weekend visitors. Next to the hotel, you can take a dip in the public Khatt Hot Springs – piping hot water which, it is claimed, has curative powers. Men and women have separate pools and a variety of massages is also available. It's a good idea to visit the hot springs in the morning and avoid Fridays as it can get very busy with families.

Hilton Ras Al Khaimah Resort & Spa

Al Maareedh St Ras Al Khaimah **07 228 8844**
www.hilton.com
Map **3 F1**

Tucked away on an exclusive bay, out of sight of the city, the resort's many guest rooms and villas are perfect for a beach break. The pool bar, spa and laid-back dining options make this one of the most relaxing destinations in the region. Guests of the older Hilton Ras Al Khaimah (07 288 8888, www.hilton.com), located in the city, can use the facilities.

Fujairah

A trip to the east coast is a must for any west coast resident. Made up of the emirate of Fujairah and several enclaves belonging to Sharjah, the villages along the east coast sit between the rugged Hajar Mountains and the gorgeous Gulf of Oman. The three-hour drive from Abu Dhabi passes through some of the UAE's most scenic mountain passes. Fujairah city has seen little development compared to west coast cities, but the real draw here is the landscape. Mountains and wadis stretch west of the coast, offering some of the country's best and most accessible camping spots. The beaches, reefs and villages attract visitors throughout the year.

Bidiyah

The site of the oldest mosque in the UAE, Bidiyah is one of the oldest settlements on the east coast and is believed to have been inhabited since 3000BC. The mosque is made from gypsum, stone and mud bricks finished off with plaster, and its original design of four domes supported by a central pillar was considered unique, but the shape was changed to stepped domes during the recent renovation. The building is believed to date back to the middle of the 15th century. The mosque is still used for prayer, so non-Muslim visitors can't enter. Built next to a low hillside with several restored watchtowers on the ridge behind, the area is now lit up at night with coloured light.

East Coast Made Easy

To reach the UAE's east coast from Abu Dhabi takes about three hours by road. The most popular route is to pick up the E611 outside of Dubai, turning onto the E88 that runs from Sharjah to Masafi, and then turn left to Dibba or right to Fujairah. A quieter alternative is the S116, which heads south-east out of Sharjah, past Fossil Rock and through the Hajar Mountains, hitting the coast at Kalba. It's faster than the E88, it's smooth, it's got tunnels, great scenery, and is so quiet you'll wonder why no-one else seems to know about it yet.

Dibba

Located at the northern-most point of the east coast, on the border with Musandam (p.262), Dibba is made up of three fishing villages. Unusually, each part comes under a different jurisdiction: Dibba al Hisn is

Exploring Fossil Rock

A brief guide to the perfect route for first-timers.

Fossil Rock is the UAE's easiest desert route to access, and to drive, with some superb and varied scenery along the way. Starting at Al Awir, off the E44 Hatta Road about 20 minutes outside the city of Dubai, it is the perfect drive for absolute beginners and novices to cut their teeth on in the desert and gain some valuable lessons. It provides a slightly more rugged landscape than the oceans of dunes that accompany all off-road adventures nearer to Abu Dhabi. As with anywhere, it's definitely better to accompany an experienced driver the first couple of times you head out.

The route is pretty straightforward to navigate – the driving starts along a sandy track then graduates to rolling through some easy medium-sized dunes later on. Making its way to the starting point in the fertile oasis town of Al Awir, the road weaves through a surprising amount of greenery, trees and farms, and many palaces and stately homes. Keep a look out for the estate that's home to herds of gazelle and deer, race horses that can often be spotted training, and the long wall of the summer palace belonging to the Al Maktoum family.

Existing tracks normally define the best path to take, especially on this route. They offer the easiest route, with only gentle inclines and descents, and limit damage to flora and fauna. However, when you start to get the hang of it, there are some places where you can climb up to the top of the dunes following alongside the track to weave your way along the ridges. The first half of the route finishes in sight of a main road, where it turns and follows the sandy river bed of Wadi Fayah along the bottom of the dunes. This fast and fun track weaves through bushes, trees, dunes and some rocky outcrops to a short gravely climb out onto the road.

After crossing the road, sticking with the main undulating sandy track heading up into the dunes will take you quite smoothly and easily towards Fossil Rock, clearly visible ahead. If you are feeling confident with your new skills, there is plenty of adventurous terrain just off the main track to test your driving among the dunes and bowls on either side, including in the area around the rock known as Camel Rock.

The striking Fossil Rock is always there as a landmark to avoid getting lost, and whenever you have had enough, just pick up the track again and head towards the rock. When you reach the hard track under the pylons with Fossil Rock directly in front of you, the quickest and easiest exit route is to turn right and head back past the village of Maleihah and the main road. It is possible to head straight on for even more challenging driving and the climb up to Fossil Rock (or Jebel Maleihah as it is officially called) itself, but this is more one for expert drivers. If you do make it up to the top, whether on foot or behind the wheel, it is a fun place for a scramble, and for the views and a poke around to see if you can spot a fossil or two.

After leaving the desert, don't forget to re-inflate your tyres as soon as possible, as driving on tarmac with soft tyres can cause blowouts. To get to the nearest petrol station, when you meet the tarmac road turn left and it is roughly two kilometres along the road on the right. If you carry on a little further, you will reach the S116 – the fastest way back to civilisation.

Off-Road Expert

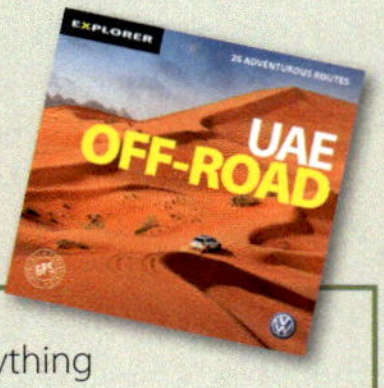

For more information on everything to do with driving off road and exploring all corners of the country, pick up a copy of the *UAE Off-Road Explorer.* Fossil Rock is one of 26 routes featured in full detail, with annotated satellite images and detailed descriptions of the route, along with attractions and activities along the way.

part of Sharjah, Dibba Muhallab is Fujairah and Dibba Bayah is Oman. The three Dibbas share an attractive bay, fishing communities, and excellent diving locations – from here you can arrange dhow trips to take you to unspoilt dive locations in the Musandam. The Hajar Mountains provide a wonderful backdrop, rising in places to over 1,800 metres. There are some good public beaches too, where your only company will be the crabs and seagulls, and where seashell collectors may find a few treasures.

Fujairah

The town of Fujairah is a mix of old and new. The surrounding hillsides are dotted with ancient forts and watchtowers, which add an air of mystery and charm. Most of these also appear to be undergoing restoration work, too. Fujairah is also a busy trading centre, with its modern container port and a thriving free zone attracting major companies from around the world. Off the coast, the seas and coral reefs make a great spot for fishing, diving and watersports. It is also a good place for birdwatching during the spring and autumn migrations as it is on the route from Africa to Central Asia. Since Fujairah is close to the mountains and many areas of natural beauty, it makes an excellent base from where to explore the countryside and discover wadis, forts, waterfalls and even natural hot springs.

Kalba

Just to the south of Fujairah you'll find Kalba, which is renowned for its mangrove forest and golden beaches. It's a pretty fishing village that still manages to retain much of its historical charm. There is a road through the mountains linking Kalba to Hatta which makes for an interesting alternative when returning.

Khor Kalba

Set in a beautiful tidal estuary (khor is Arabic for creek), Khor Kalba is a fascinating mangrove forest and home to a variety of plant, marine and birdlife not found anywhere else in the UAE. The mangroves flourish in this area thanks to a mix of seawater and freshwater from the mountains. The delicate wetlands are receding due to the excessive use of water from inland wells, but there is still plenty to see. For birdwatchers, the area is especially good during the spring and autumn migrations when the routes of migratory birds mean rare species can be spotted. The bird species frequently seen include the resident reef heron and the area is also home to a rare subspecies of white collared kingfisher, which breeds nowhere else in the world (except nearby in Oman). A canoe tour by Desert Rangers (p.230) is ideal for reaching the heart of the reserve. Furthermore, there's also the possibility of seeing one of the region's endangered turtles.

Fujairah Attractions

Dibba Castle

Dibba
Map **3 F1**

Hidden away in the Omani part of Dibba (aka Daba), next to vast farms and plantations, Dibba Castle is an interesting place to have a poke around. Built over 180 years ago, it has been restored and, while there aren't a lot of artefacts on show, you can access all the rooms and climb up the towers, where you'll get views over the castle and its surroundings. It is signposted off the road past the UAE border check post.

Fujairah Fort

Nr Fujairah Museum Fujairah
Map **3 F2**

Part of the east coast's rich heritage, Fujairah Fort has recently undergone a major renovation programme. Although you cannot enter the fort itself, the surrounding heritage buildings are open for viewing. Carbon dating estimates the main part of the fort to be over 500 years old.

Fujairah Heritage Village

Nr Ain Al Madhab Garden Fujairah
Map **3 F2**

Situated just outside Fujairah City, this collection of fishing boats, simple dhows and tools depicts life in the UAE before oil was discovered. There are two spring-fed swimming pools for men and women and chalets can be hired by the day.

Fujairah Museum

Nr Fujairah Fort & Archaelogical Site Fujairah
09 222 9085
Map **3 F2**

This interesting museum offers permanent exhibitions on traditional ways of life including the not-so-distant nomadic Bedouin culture. There are also several artefacts on display that were found during archaeological excavations throughout the emirate. Some of the items include weapons from the bronze and iron ages, finely painted pottery, carved soapstone vessels and silver coins. The museum is closed on Saturdays. Entry fee is Dhs.5.

Fujairah Tennis & Country Club

Nr Rd 89 Fujairah **09 224 4880**
www.ftcc-sim.ae
Map **3 F2**

The recently renovated sporting and leisure complex makes a great destination for a weekend away. In addition to six flood-lit hard courts and a centre court, the general sports and fitness facilities are fantastic, and overnight stays are possible at the adjacent boutique hotel which features 14 cosy rooms.

Fujairah Hotels

Fujairah is home to several great beach hotels, many of which offer scuba diving. In addition to the below, overnight stays are possible at the Fujairah Tennis & Country Club (p.258)

Fujairah Rotana Resort & Spa – Al Aqah Beach

Al Aqah Beach Fujairah **09 244 9888**
www.rotana.com
Map **3 F1**

Each of the 250 guest rooms and suites has its own balcony and view over the sea. The hotel offers some of the best dining options on the east coast, as well as an indulgent spa, a private beach and a huge pool.

Golden Tulip Resort Dibba

Nr Daba Beach Dibba **+968 268 36654**
www.goldentulipdibba.com
Map **3 F1**

Simple, clean and with a great beach, this is a good option for an affordable getaway. From the nearby Dibba Port you can take a dhow cruise and the hotel is also in a great location for snorkelling in the pristine waters of the Gulf.

Hilton Fujairah Resort

Al Ghourfa Rd Fujairah **09 222 2411**
www.hilton.com
Map **3 F2**

The Hilton Fujairah Resort, set at the north end of Fujairah's corniche, just a stone's throw from the foothills of the grand Hajar Mountains, is a relaxing resort with all facilities needed for a wonderful weekend away. If you get tired of lounging by the temperature-controlled swimming pool, or of activities such as tennis, snooker, basketball or even of all the watersports on the private beach, you could always explore the rugged splendour of the surrounding mountains. The hotel is great for families, and there is a safe play area for children.

Le Meridien Al Aqah Beach Resort

Le Meridien Al Aqah Beach Resort

Dibba – Khor Fakkan Rd Fujairah **09 244 9000**
www.lemeridien-alaqah.com
Map **3 F1**

All of the rooms at Le Meridien Al Aqah have views over the Indian Ocean, and the grounds are covered by lush foliage. It is particularly geared up for families, with a kids' pool and outdoor and indoor play areas. There's an extensive spa, a dive centre, and entertainment options include a cinema, bars and restaurants serving a range of Thai, Indian and European cuisine.

Radisson Blu Resort Fujairah

Dibba Fujairah **09 244 9700**
www.radissonblu.com
Map **3 F1**

Its pastel exterior might be an acquired taste, but the modern, business-like interior and wonderful restaurants that lie within are a treat to the senses. The whole place is reminiscent of a spa, with clean lines and wholesome colours. There's also a wonderful Japanese spa and plenty of private beach.

Sandy Beach Hotel & Resort

Dibba – Khorfakkan Rd Fujairah **09 244 5555**
www.sandybm.com
Map **3 F1**

Snoopy Island is one of the best diving spots in the country and is right off the coast from the Sandy Beach Hotel, making it a firm favourite with UAE residents. Day trippers can purchase a day-pass to the hotel to access the temperature-controlled pool, watersports and beach bar services. There is also a Five-Star Padi Dive Centre within the hotel that rents diving and snorkelling gear for exploring the reefs around Snoopy Island.

Bull Butting

On Friday afternoons during winter, crowds gather between the Hilton Hotel and the Khor Kalba area to watch 'bull butting'. This ancient Portuguese sport consists of two huge bulls going head to head for several rounds, until after a few nudges and a bit of hoof bashing, a winner is determined. It's not as cruel or barbaric as other forms of bullfighting, but animal lovers may still want to avoid it.

LONG WEEKEND TRIPS

Make the most of a long weekend by heading off to one of many great travel destinations within easy reach of the UAE.

Abu Dhabi's central location makes it an ideal base for exploring the region beyond the GCC countries. If you can't find a cheap flight from Abu Dhabi International Airport, don't hesitate to look for better deals departing from either Dubai, Sharjah or even Al Ain. The country now has two low-cost carriers, Air Arabia at Sharjah Airport and flydubai at Dubai Airport. Both offer some incredible deals. If you'd rather fly in style, both Etihad and Emirates fly to enough locations to keep you planning for years to come.

Cyprus

It's hard to believe that this idyllic Mediterranean island is such a short flight from Abu Dhabi. Three main towns, Larnaca, Limassol and Paphos, each offer unique accommodation and leisure options, and capital city Nicosia is great for shopping and nightlife. Whether you choose to rent a self-catering apartment or stay in a luxurious hotel on full board, a holiday in Cyprus is a huge change from the Gulf. You can drive up mountains for crisp, cool air and some awesome views, and explore quiet local villages off the beaten track.

Flights:

Air Liban – Abu Dhabi to Larnaca, Dhs.4,400
Emirates – Dubai to Larnaca, Dhs.4,200
Etihad – Abu Dhabi to Larnaca, Dhs.2,600

Egypt

Egypt is an ideal trip for history fans. It's one of the oldest civilisations in the world and home to famous historical sites such as the Pyramids and Sphinx. It also has some amazing scenery: there is the moon-like White Desert and the isolated Siwa Oasis in the west, the Red Sea and the vast Sinai Peninsula in the east, and, of course, the Nile, which flows south to north through the country, past the incredible ruins between Aswan and Luxor. Cairo's chaotic streets are a constant adventure and the city has an active nightlife.

Flights

Etihad – Abu Dhabi to Cairo, Dhs.1,700
flydubai – Dubai to Alexandria, Dhs.1,700
Air Arabia – Sharjah to Luxor, Dhs.1,200

Kerala

India

India is a land of many guises, from the beautiful beaches of Goa and the vibrant city of Mumbai to the imposing mountains of Kashmir and lush coastline of Kerala. It's best to avoid the summer monsoon, but if you do get caught in the rain, you can take advantage of good off-season deals. Some areas such as Ladakh in northern India and the desert state of Rajasthan receive very little, if any, rain all year.

Flights

Air India Express – Al Ain to Kozhikode, Dhs.2,100
Jet Airways – Abu Dhabi to Delhi, Dhs.1,300
Air Arabia – Sharjah to Kochi, Dhs.1,700
Sharjah to Jaipur, Dhs.1,300
Sharjah to Hyderabad, Dhs.1,500
Jet Airways – Dubai to Delhi, Dhs.1,600

Jordan

Jordan is packed with religious and historical sites, incredible architecture, and friendly, welcoming people. The capital, Amman, offers enough dining and cultural attractions to fill up a few days, but to truly experience the country, you'll need to get out of the city. Head south to feast your eyes on Petra, the ancient city built into solid rock canyons. On your way, don't miss the opportunity to float atop the waters of the Dead Sea. History and religious experts will be fascinated by the many holy sites that dot the country, and movie buffs shouldn't miss a trip to Wadi Rum, where Lawrence of Arabia was filmed.

Flights

Etihad – Abu Dhabi to Amman, Dhs.1,300
Air Arabia – Sharjah to Amman, Dhs.1,100
flydubai – Dubai to Amman, Dhs.1,500

Lebanon

Lebanon's blossoming development as a vibrant tourist destination has suffered some knockbacks with conflicts both internally and externally. But never a nation to take things lying down, it is doing everything possible to rebuild itself. Beirut's nightlife is considered by many to be the best in the Middle East, and its culinary excellence is well-known. Outside of Beirut is just as interesting; the massive Roman temples in Baalbek are not to be missed, and the many villages scattered throughout the country hold the key to Lebanon's incredible hospitality. Come the winter, you can enjoy a spot of skiing at Mzaar-Kfardebian (www.skimzaar.com).

Flights

Etihad – Abu Dhabi to Beirut, Dhs.1,400
Air Arabia – Sharjah to Beirut, Dhs.1,400
flydubai – Dubai to Beirut, Dhs.2,100

Sri Lanka

The beauty of Sri Lanka, apart from the short flight time from the UAE, is that you can either have a fantastic holiday on a small budget or indulge in luxury of a lifetime. Colombo has several attractions, but most holidaymakers choose to spend their time in the lush mountains or at the untouched beaches.

Flights

Sri Lankan Airlines – Abu Dhabi to Colombo, Dhs.1,100
Air Arabia – Sharjah to Colombo, Dhs.1,000

Stunning Petra

Emirates – Dubai to Colombo, Dhs.2,100
Qatar Airways – Dubai to Colombo, Dhs.3,700

Syria

With Damascus, the oldest continuously inhabited city in the world, Aleppo, the food capital of the world, and untouched countryside, Syria is a traveller's dream. However, in mid-2011 there was a period of civil unrest which resulted in many countries issuing warnings against all travel here – at the time of writing it is unclear whether the situation will resolve itself quickly, so check with your embassy before booking your trip. Once it is safe once more, the old part of Damascus is a joy to explore on foot thanks to the many souks and unique architecture. The ancient city of Palmyra (known as Tadmor in Syria) is only a four-hour bus ride from Damascus and a must for anyone interested in the country's incredible past. Syria is a great choice for budget-minded travellers, as flights to and from the UAE are cheap and you could spend an entire week eating only the delicious street food.

Flights

Etihad – Abu Dhabi to Damascus, Dhs.1,500
Air Arabia – Sharjah to Damascus, Dhs.900
flydubai – Dubai to Damascus, Dhs.1,300

Turkey

Perfectly placed between contrasting cultures of east and west, Turkey is a popular holiday destination with beautiful landscapes, great weather, sun, sea and mountains. Istanbul is an amazing city – full of history, great food and vibrant nightlife. Alternatively, take a road trip to the capital, Ankara, for a taste of Turkish student life and a glimpse of the country's most modern city. If you need a break from big-city life, head south to the equally impressive Bursa, where you'll find the iconic Ulu Cami mosque and huge, communal thermal baths.

Flights

Etihad – Abu Dhabi to Istanbul, Dhs.2,300
Turkish Airlines – Abu Dhabi to Istanbul, Dhs.1,600
Air Arabia – Sharjah to Istanbul, Dhs.1,300
Emirates – Dubai to Istanbul, Dhs.2,500

DIRECTORY:

Air Arabia – www.airarabia.com
Air India Express – www.airindiaexpress.in
Emirates – www.emirates.com
Etihad – www.etihadairways.com
flydubai – www.flydubai.com
Jet Airways – www.jetairways.com
Sri Lankan Airlines – www.srilankan.aero
Turkish Airlines – www.turkishairlines.com

GCC

Over the past decade, the countries that make up the Gulf Cooperation Council (Bahrain, Kuwait, Oman, Qatar, Saudi Arabia and the UAE) have been building their tourism industries in an effort to diversify their oil-based economies. Several international brands have opened hotels in the region and the respective governments have made a real effort to promote their heritage and culture. To learn more about the region's history, see the UAE chapter on p.1.

Oman

The most accessible country in the GCC for residents of Abu Dhabi, Oman is a peaceful and breathtaking place, with history, culture and spectacular scenery. The capital, Muscat, has enough attractions to keep you busy for a good long weekend, including beautiful beaches, some great restaurants and cafes, the mesmerising old souk at Mutrah, and the Sultan Qaboos Mosque. Out of the capital you will find many historic old towns and forts, and some of the most stunning mountain and wadi scenery in the region. Salalah (p.262) in the south has the added bonus of being cool and wet in the summer.

A flight from Abu Dhabi to Muscat takes 60 minutes, but when you factor in check-in times and clearing customs it's not much quicker than driving. There are daily flights from Abu Dhabi, Dubai and Sharjah with Etihad, Emirates, Oman Air and Air Arabia (p.53). Regular flights direct to Salalah are also available.

There is also a daily bus service between Abu Dhabi and both Muscat and Salalah, taking 7 and 17 hours respectively, and costing from Dhs.50 for the Abu Dhabi to Muscat trip (www.ontcoman.com).

For further information on Oman check out the *Oman Mini Visitors' Guide, Oman Off-Road Explorer* and *the Oman Trekking Explorer* – see www.liveworkexplore.com/shop.

Musandam

The UAE's northern neighbour, Musandam is an isolated enclave belonging to Oman. The region is dominated by the same Hajar Mountains that run through the eastern UAE. As the peninsula juts into the Strait of Hormuz, it breaks up into a myriad of jagged, picturesque fjords. Spending a day exploring the fjords on a wooden dhow is a must for any Abu Dhabi resident. Most of the trips originate from the region's capital, Khasab, and day trips from Khasab Travel & Tours (04 266 9950) cost around Dhs.200 per person and include lunch, soft drinks and an informative guide. Alternately, you can access the famous Wadi Bih off-road route from Dibba and spend a weekend camping atop some of the region's most magnificent mountains. See the *UAE Off-Road Explorer* for information about the route.

Nizwa

After driving deep into the Hajar Mountains, you'll find Nizwa, the largest city in Oman's interior. This oasis city offers fascinating sights and heritage, including the 17th century Nizwa Fort and the Jabrin Fort, notable for its secret passageways.

Visas

Visas for Oman are required whether entering by air or road, and different regulations apply depending on your nationality and how long you want to stay. Nationalities are split into two groups – check out the Royal Oman Police website, www.rop.gov.om, for full lists (click on 'Directorates', then 'DG of Passports'). People in group one can get a visit visa at the border for a nominal fee. Residents from group two, however, will need to get a visa from the Oman consulate or embassy in advance, which may take a few days to process so check before you head out for the border to avoid being stuck. Oman does have a common visa facility with the UAE, meaning people on an Abu Dhabi visit visa will not need a separate visa to visit Oman.

Salalah

Home to several museums and souks, Salalah is best known for its lush landscape. The scenery is especially attractive during the summer months, when the area catches the Indian monsoon. Salalah is also a major frankincense producer and you can visit the farms along the Yemen border to witness how it is extracted. A 16 hour drive from Abu Dhabi, plan on spending a few days here to make the most of it.

Oman Hotels

The Chedi Muscat

Boushar Beachfront Muscat **+968 24 524 400**
www.ghmhotels.com

This beautiful boutique hotel on the shore is famed for its clean lines, luxury and an impressive sense of calm. The stunning spa and outstanding restaurant don't hurt either. With an infinity pool, private beach and library, this is a destination for a break from bustle and perhaps isn't an ideal choice for families.

Crowne Plaza Hotel Muscat

Qurum St, Qurum Heights Muscat **+968 24 660 660**
www.ichotelsgroup.com

This established hotel boasts cliff top views over Al Qurum and the beach below. Many of the 200 guest rooms benefit from the striking vistas and several of the restaurants also boast outdoor terraces. There's a large swimming pool, gym, spa and dolphin watching trips available, making this hotel a great choice for those looking for relaxation and for visitors who want an action packed break.

InterContinental Muscat

Al Kharijiyah St Muscat **+968 24 680 000**
www.ichotelsgroup.com

This is an older hotel that has recently undergone a major facelift. The InterContinental continues to be popular for its outdoor facilities, international restaurants and regular entertainment in the form of dinner theatres and visiting bands. Alfresco restaurant, Tomato, is a must-try. Trader Vic's, with its legendary cocktails, is perennially popular. All of the rooms have views of Qurum Beach, landscaped gardens or the mountains.

Hoota Cave

This cave has a large chamber with some amazing rock formations, an underground lake and a fascinating ecosystem. Facilities include a train that transports you into the cave, knowledgeable guides, a restaurant and a natural history museum. Photography is not allowed. Visitors must book at least 24 hours in advance, as there are only a limited number of people allowed in at any time. (+968 24 490 060, www.alhootacave.com).

Oman Dive Center

Nr Qantab, Bandar Jussa Muscat **+968 24 824 240**
www.omandivecenter.com

Just south of Muscat, a stay here is an amazing experience, enjoyable whether you're a diver or not. You can book a barasti hut (they are actually made of stone, with barasti covering) for an average of RO.66 for two people (depending on season). The room price includes breakfast and dinner in the centre's licensed restaurant. For keen divers, the centre offers dive training and excursions, as well as boat tours in the surrounding area.

Shangri-La's Barr Al Jissah Resort & Spa

Off Al Jissah St Muscat **+968 24 776 666**
www.shangri-la.com

With three hotels catering for families, business travellers and luxury-seekers, the Shangri-La is one of the most gorgeous resorts in the region. The hotels have several swimming pools and enough play areas to keep children occupied for days. The exclusive, six-star Al Husn is incredibly luxurious and perfect for a weekend of out-of-town pampering.

Six Senses Zighy Bay

Zighy Bay, Musandam Muscat **+968 26 735 555**
www.sixsenses.com

Located in a secluded cove in Musandam, the resort has been designed in true rustic style and is made up of individual pool villas. Like all Six Senses resorts, the focus here is on relaxation. The spa treatments available are of the highest quality and expertly prepared dinners can be enjoyed from the comfort of your own villa, or from the mountainside restaurant with breathtaking views of the bay.

Bahrain

Just a 40 minute flight from Abu Dhabi, Bahrain has been a popular destination since the 1970s thanks to a mix of architecture, miles of souks, excellent shopping and some truly outstanding bars and restaurants. However, in early 2011, there was a period of civil unrest, which resulted in some countries issuing travel warnings on the island nation. At the time of writing, it remains unclear whether the situation will resolve itself quickly, so check with your embassy.

The Chedi Muscat

Bahrain Attractions

Bahrain Fort
Nr Karbabad Village Karbabad
www.bahraintourism.com
This impressive 16th century Portuguese fort is built on the remains of several previous settlements, going back to the Dilmun era around 2800BC. There are several large, informative notices dotted around the area, and some information booklets are available in English. Entry is free and the fort is open from 08:00 to 20:00 every day including Friday. The village at the entrance to the fort is worth a visit on its own. Nearly every square inch of the place, from walls to satellite dishes, is covered in brightly coloured murals.

Race To Bahrain
Long before Abu Dhabi hosted its first GP, Bahrain was welcoming the F1 circus to its own desert racetrack. After a break in 2011 (due to civil unrest, see p.263), the race will return in 2012. In the meantime, there are are other regular races, running through the winter months, or you can take to the track yourself in a single-seater Caterham Xtreme. The karting zone is a real rush, as is testing a monster 4WD across a range of obstacles at the Hummer Academy – one of just two anywhere in the world. See www.bahraingp.com for details of all of these activities.

Bahrain National Museum
Nr Sheikh Hamad Causeway & Al Fatih Highway, East Corniche Manama **+973 1729 8777**
www.bahraintourism.com
Situated on the corniche, this museum documents Bahraini life before the introduction of oil. Children will love the Hall of Graves and the museum often hosts impressive international exhibits.

Beit Al Qur'an
Nr Diplomat Hotel Manama **+973 1729 0101**
www.bahraintourism.com
The building may not look like much from afar, but a closer inspection reveals walls covered in beautiful Arabic calligraphy. The museum displays examples of historical calligraphy and Islamic manuscripts. Entrance is free, but donations are welcome.

The Burial Mounds
Manama
www.bahraintourism.com
One of the most remarkable sights in Bahrain is the vast area of burial mounds at Saar, near A'ali Village, at Hamad Town and at Sakhir. The mounds were built during the Dilmun, Tylos and Helenistic periods and are anything from 2,000 to 4,000 years old. The largest burial mounds, which are known as the Royal Tombs, are found in and around A'ali Village.

La Fontaine Centre Of Contemporary Art
92 Hoora Ave Manama **+973 1723 0123**
www.lafontaineartcentre.net
This place is a true architectural gem. The wind towers, cool corridors, a Pilates studio that has to be seen to be believed, world-class restaurant, extensive spa, regular film screenings and art exhibitions make La Fontaine a unique jewel in Bahrain's crown. The enormous fountain in the courtyard is worth a visit.

Bahrain Hotels

Al Areen Palace & Spa
Nr Al Areen Wildlife Park Juffair **+973 1784 5000**
www.lhw.com
Located close to the F1 International Circuit, this all-villa resort offers an extensive spa, outstanding restaurants and good conference facilities.

Al Bander Hotel & Resort
Maámeer Riffa **+973 1770 1201**
www.albander.com
Located at the southern end of Sitra, this resort has a wide range of facilities including swimming pools and watersports at their private beach. Rooms are either cabana style or in chalets, and there are activities for kids and a variety of food and dining options.

The Diplomat Radisson Blu Hotel, Residence & Spa
Nr King Faisal Highway & Shk Hamad Causeway Manama **+973 1753 1666**
www.radissonblu.com
Overlooking the Gulf, on the edge of the Diplomatic area and close to the National Museum, this is a five-star property with a spa, a large lagoon pool and a range of dining and drinking venues.

The Gulf Hotel Bahrain
Bani Otbah Ave Manama **+973 1771 3000**
www.gulfhotelbahrain.com
Just five minutes from the city centre, the popular Gulf Hotel has 352 rooms including eight suites. Its facilities include an outdoor swimming pool, a gymnasium, a beauty salon, shops and babysitting services. It has several popular restaurants and bars

Novotel Al Dana Resort
121 Sheikh Hamad Causeway, Al Muharraq Manama **+973 1729 8008**
www.novotel.com
The only city beach resort in Bahrain, the Novotel is a great choice for families with both an indoor and

outdoor play area, a large pool and a small private beach; there are also watersports facilities

The Ritz-Carlton Bahrain Hotel & Spa

Bahrain International Exhibition Center, Manama Bay Manama **+973 1758 0000**
www.ritzcarlton.com

The hotel has one of the best beaches in Bahrain, in a man-made lagoon surrounded by lush gardens. The 600 metre private beach sweeps round the lagoon with its own island and private marina. Along with the nine quality dining venues and comprehensive business facilities, hotel residents have access to all of the club facilities, including the racquet sport courts, the luxurious Spa and watersport activities.

Kuwait

Kuwait may be one of the world's smallest countries but its 500 kilometre coastline has endless golden beaches that remain refreshingly tranquil. From the Grand Mosque to the Kuwait Towers there are many architectural splendours to explore, while Al Qurain House, which still shows the scars of war with its immortal bullet holes, gives you a fascinating insight into the troubled times of the Iraqi invasion. There is also Green Island, an artificial island linked by a short bridge which is home to restaurants, a children's play area and a great alternative view of Kuwait's shoreline. For accommodation options, try the Four Points by Sheraton (www.starwoodhotels.com), Courtyard by Marriott (www.marriott.com) or Radisson Blu (www.radissonblu.com).

Qatar

Qatar once had a sleepy reputation, but things are changing fast. The amount of development and investment in the country means it is becoming increasingly popular with visitors. With an attractive corniche, world-class museums and cultural centres, and plenty of hotels with leisure and entertainment, the capital Doha makes a perfect weekend retreat for UAE residents. Away from the city, the inland sea (Khor Al Udaid) in the south makes a great day trip, usually as part of an organised tour. For further information and full details of the below activities and attractions, grab a copy of Explorer's *Qatar Mini Visitors' Guide,* whichs also includes a free pull-out map. See www.explorerpublishing.com/shop.

Qatar Attractions

Cultural Village of Katara

Nr Exhibition Centre, Lusail St Doha **+974 4411 3027**
www.katara.org.qa

This is a unique development, bringing together all the artistic elements in Qatar including music, dance, theatre, photography, painting and sculpture. The site, which looks like a large village, allows artists to meet and collaborate on different projects. It is also open to the public with two concert halls designed for opera, ballet and large theatrical productions, an outdoor amphitheatre which holds 5,000 people, as well as galleries, workshops, cafes, 16 restaurants and souks.

Museum Of Islamic Art

The Corniche Doha **+974 4422 4444**
www.mia.org.qa

Architect IM Pei has created an elegant home for this impressive collection. The building is beautifully subtle, with details drawn from a wide range of Islamic influences. The collection is showcased as a journey through time, countries and cultures, and the oldest pieces date from the ninth century.

Souk Waqif

Al Jasra St Doha

The city's oldest market, Souk Waqif, was renovated in 2004 using traditional building methods and materials. The resulting complex is now one of the most beautiful and authentic modern souks in the Gulf. The most refreshing aspect of the souk area is its dual purpose – tourists can easily stroll the narrow alleys in search of souvenirs while locals can purchase everything from fishing nets to pots and pans. Aside from the many shops and restaurants, there is the Waqif Art Center, which houses several small galleries and craft shops.

Qatar Hotels

Four Seasons Hotel

Corniche St Doha **+974 4494 8888**
www.fourseasons.com

One of the finest hotels in the city, the Four Seasons has an exclusive beach and marina, first-class service and excellent restaurants, including the classy Italian eatery Il Teatro.

La Cigale Hotel

60 Suhaim Bin Hamad St Doha **+974 4428 8888**
www.lacigalehotel.com

La Cigale has a reputation for first-class hospitality and is an exclusive nightlife destination.

Mövenpick Hotel Doha > *p.269*

Corniche Rd Doha **+974 4429 1111**
www.moevenpick-hotels.com

This modern hotel boasts breathtaking views of the corniche, where guests can enjoy a morning jog or afternoon stroll. Popular with business travellers, this boutique-style hotel also attracts tourists with its excellent restaurants and leisure facilities which include a swimming pool, whirlpool and steam bath.

MUSCAT

Sandwiched between spectacular rocky mountains and beautiful beaches, Muscat is one of the Middle East's most striking cities.

Muscat is one of the most attractive and charismatic cities in the Middle East, and once you've visited you'll understand why many count it as their favourite regional city. It is visually striking and hugely varied, set out between the Gulf of Oman and the Hajar mountains. While generally characterised by white, low-rise buildings, Muscat has many separate areas nestling between the low craggy mountains and the ocean. This is because the city is actually formed by three smaller towns that have grown together over history to form what is now known as Muscat. Indeed, there is no one area that defines Muscat on its own – each part has its own distinctive character and charm.

Great care has been taken to ensure that, while it is definitely a modern city, there is a cohesive and traditional Arabic element which has been retained. Visit the old town of Muscat or the Mutrah Souk for an idea of what life has been like for decades for the people that still live in the area. Muscat is clean and features a lot more greenery than you may be used to in Abu Dhabi. With beautiful beaches, bustling souks, a collection of great restaurants and cafes, and some fascinating museums, you'll need at least a few days to fully discover this friendly city. The main areas worth exploring are around the old town and the fishing port of Mutrah, although taking long walks along the beach in Qurum or exploring the natural lagoons in Qantab are also worthwhile activities.

The Old Town Of Muscat

The old town of Muscat is situated on the coast at the eastern end of the greater Muscat area between Mutrah and Sidab. It is quiet and atmospheric, based around a sheltered port that was historically important for trade. The area is home to some very interesting museums. Muscat Gate Museum is located in one of the fortified gates of the old city walls, and illustrates the history of Muscat and Oman from ancient times right up to the present day. The view from the roof over the old town is worth the visit alone. Bait Al Zubair is in a beautifully restored house and features major displays of men's traditional jewellery, including the khanjar, women's jewellery and attire, household items, and swords and firearms. The Omani French Museum celebrates the close ties between these two countries, and is on the site of the first French Embassy. Other highlights include the striking Alam Palace, home of Sultan Qaboos, and Jalali Fort and Mirani Fort overlooking the harbour.

Mutrah

Mutrah rests between the sea and a protective circle of hills, and has grown around its port, which today is far more vibrant than the port of Muscat's old town. Mutrah Corniche is lined with pristine gardens, parks, waterfalls and statues. Further east you'll find Riyam Park, where a huge incense burner sits on a rocky outcrop, while nearby is an ancient watchtower overlooking Mutrah – the view from the top is lovely and well worth the steep climb. One of Muscat's most famous shopping experiences lies in this area: the Mutrah Souk. It is always buzzing with activity and is renowned as one of the best souks in the region.

Other Areas

Although primarily a residential area, Qurum has some great shopping, good quality restaurants and cafes, the

Mutrah Corniche

city's largest park (Qurum National Park) and arguably the best beach in Muscat. It is also home to some of the top hotels, all of which have superb leisure facilities. The villages of Al Bustan and Sidab provide an interesting diversion from the main Muscat areas. Head south along Al Bustan Street out of Ruwi on the spectacular mountain road to get to the village of Al Bustan and the Al Bustan Palace Hotel, one of the most famous hotels in the region.

Further down the coast, the mountains increase in height and the landscape gets more rugged. However, this undulating rocky coastline hides a number of beautiful secluded coves. These bays, mostly reachable by roads winding over the mountains, are home to the beaches of Qantab and Jassah, the Oman Dive Center (www.omandivecenter.com) – one of the top dive centres in the world – and the new Shangri-La Barr Al Jissah Resort. Many of the bays in this area have stretches of sandy beach sheltered by the rocky cliffs, and crystal clear waters that are perfect for snorkelling, diving and fishing.

Outside Muscat

Not much further out of Muscat than the Shangri-La Barr Al Jissah Resort, Yiti Beach, while once a popular daytrip from Muscat, is now sadly becoming off limits due to the construction of a huge development called Salam Yiti. As Sifah beach, a little further down the coast, is very popular. The well-travelled path past the last of the houses in As Sifah leads to a beach which slopes gently towards the ocean at low tide. If you're keen to snorkel, head towards the northern edge of the beach. If you enjoy hiking, you can explore the headlands on foot (and maybe even find a secluded beach or two further along).

There are some excellent off-road routes you can take from Muscat within a day, or on an overnight camping trip. For more information on off-roading in Oman, get a copy of the *Oman Off-Road Explorer*.

Ramada Plaza Doha

Salwa Rd Doha **+974 4428 1428**
www.ramadaplazadoha.com
With a new wing and plenty of restaurants, bars and lounges, the Ramada is a staple of Doha's nightlife.

The Ritz-Carlton, Doha

West Bay Lagoon Doha **+974 4484 8000**
www.ritzcarlton.com
The opulent Ritz-Carlton is a perfect stop-off if you're sailing in the region, with its 235 berth marina and clubhouse. You can expect 5 star touches as standard at this resort. All of the 374 rooms and suites have breathtaking views over the sea or marina. The beach club has a great selection of watersports and there's a lavish spa. You'll be spoilt for choice with nine international and local restaurants, and can finish the night with either a cigar at Habanos or a cocktail at the Admiral Club.

Sharq Village & Spa

Ras Abu Abboud St Doha **+974 4425 6666**
www.sharqvillage.com
Reminiscent of a traditional Qatari town, Sharq Village & Spa is another example of Qatar's insistence on spectacular architecture. The Six Senses Spa was constructed using traditional building techniques and the resort's restaurants are some of the finest in Doha.

W Doha Hotel & Residences

West Bay Doha **+974 4453 5000**
www.whoteldoha.com
Adding a touch of fun to Doha's rather conservative luxury hotel scene, the W Hotel chain is known for its funky design and an fabulous level and quality of individualised service. Every inch of the hotel is an exercise in architectural minimalism, and its central location makes exploring Doha easy.

Saudi Arabia

The biggest GCC country, the Kingdom of Saudi Arabia boasts some incredible scenery, fascinating heritage and archaeological sites, and diving locations by the Red Sea that are arguably among the best in the world. Sadly, due to the difficulty in obtaining tourist visas, most expats and visitors to this part of the world are unlikely to ever experience this intriguing country. Limited transit visas are available through agents, allowing visitors a three day stay in Saudi Arabia en route to another country, such as the UAE or Bahrain. Recent press reports suggest that the Kingdom may begin to issue more tourist visas to boost the country's budding tourism industry (religious tourism in particular), and to give better access to business travellers now that Saudi Arabia is part of the World Trade Organization. Until then, visit www.sauditourism.com.sa to see what you're missing.

Doha highrises

Activities & Hobbies

ACTIVITIES & HOBBIES

With so many different cultures converging in Abu Dhabi, it should come as little surprise that there is such a diverse range of activities to fill your free time with. Everything from simulated jumping out of an airplane to singing is covered in this section, and for every traditional pursuit such as tennis or football, there is the opportunity to try something a little different, such as kitesurfing, martial arts or even a spot of salsa. For the more adventurous at heart, the UAE's diverse topography lends itself perfectly to a wide range of outdoor pursuits, including rock climbing, mountain biking, dune bashing, wadi driving and skydiving. Thanks to the endless kilometres of coastline, watersports are particularly popular as well, with scuba diving, snorkelling, sailing, surfing, jetskiing and water skiing all firm expat favourites.

Of course, not all activities require a mammoth dose of adrenaline or even the great outdoors, and there is an increasing number of groups that meet with indoor comforts for everything from art classes to amateur dramatics. Whatever your hobby or interest, the chances are that there are already plenty of like-minded people in Abu Dhabi that would love to enjoy it with you. If you don't find what you're looking for, why not set up a club yourself? Social networking sites like Facebook, MeetUp and Social Circles UAE are a great way to reach people with similar interest to you. For more information on fitness and well-being see p.180.

American Football

For those who miss their glory days of high school quarterbacking or college wide-receiving, or would just like to give this fun and sociable sport a try, there's 'Monday Night Lights' – Duplays' Abu Dhabi flag football league. Games are played every Monday night between April and June with cross-city games against Dubai's best ball players coming soon too. Cost of joining is Dhs.400 for individuals and Dhs.3,600 for teams. For more information visit www.duplays.com.

Archery

Following the opening of Al Forsan, there's now a local option for Robin Hood style fun with bows and arrows; more facilities are located a short drive away in Dubai.

Al Forsan International Sports Resort

Nr Abu Dhabi Golf Club & Resort Madinat Khalifa A (Khalifa City A) **02 556 8555**
www.alforsan.com
Map **1 P8**

The newly opened Al Forsan has ten archery lanes offering distances of up to 60 metres. Lessons are on offer from Dhs.100 – more for private instruction.

Dubai Archers

Sharjah Wanderers Golf Club Sharjah **050 558 0951**
www.dubaiarchers.com

Meets at Sharjah Wanderers Golf Club on Fridays. Beginners' classes run from 09:00 to 12:30 and cost Dhs.50 for non-members.

Activity Finder

Hatta Fort Hotel

Dubai – Hatta Rd Hatta **04 809 9333**
www.jebelali-international.com
The 25 metre range has eight targets and hosts an annual archery competition. Dubai Archers (above) also holds its annual tournament here. Dhs.60 for 30 minutes target practice, with equipment included.

Sharjah Golf & Shooting Club

Emirates Rd, Nr Tasjeel Auto Village Sharjah
06 548 7777
www.golfandshootingshj.com
The shooting club's indoor range offers target practice at Dhs.60 for 20 arrows. You can also try your hand at pistol and rifle shooting.

Art Classes

Abu Dhabi Music & Arts Foundation

Kanoo Group Bldg, Najda St Markaziya East
02 677 8432
www.admaf.org
Map **2 P4**
As well as organising and running the annual Abu Dhabi Festival, ADMAF holds year-round educational activities dealing with everything from film and music to poetry. Some of these are open to the public, with others limited to certain professional and academic communities. Often, visiting artists, musicians or writers will lead workshops or give lectures.

National Theatre

Shk Rashid bin Saeed Al Maktoum St, Nr Al Jazira Club Al Nahyan **02 657 6355**
www.adach.ae
Map **2 L12**
Since the Cultural Foundation closed in 2009, the art classes that were regularly taking place there have moved to the National Theatre. Classes include painting, sculpture, ceramics and silk painting. They run from Sunday to Thursday, and prices start from Dhs.300 for monthly courses. See the ADACH website for a complete timetable.

Aussie Rules

It started with the Dubai Dingoes and then came the Dubai Heat. Now, the Abu Dhabi Falcons have entered the arena. It seems that Aussie Rules is gaining a foothold here in the Emirates, and with the influx of Australian expats it's about time.

The Falcons compete in the Middle East AFL competition that runs from October to March each year with teams based in Dubai, Muscat, Bahrain, Qatar and Abu Dhabi. All are welcome, regardless of skill level or experience. For more information contact Steve Watson on 056 109 2346 or visit www.abudhabifalcons.com.

Badminton

You wouldn't really think of badminton as a sport with a huge Middle East following, but it seems to be gaining popularity in a big way in Abu Dhabi with a competitive league and a number of die-hard fans of the sport. Members of The Club (p.179) can enjoy weekly matches in the indoor court with occasional leagues introduced, while Duplays (www.duplays.com) runs a recreational co-ed ten-week season for those who want to meet new people and work up a playful sweat in the process. Games are played on Wednesdays at Al Raha School and cost Dhs.350, or Dhs.700 for a two-person team. Alternatively, if you already have the gear and a partner, many sports clubs and hotels have courts that can be hired on an hourly basis.

Basketball

Hoops is certainly alive and well in the capital. In addition to the leagues listed below, there are a number of public ball courts around town. Also, many of Abu Dhabi's hotels have a basketball court (usually outdoor) free for members to use. Duplays runs the Hoosiers League, giving players the chance to run and gun in a competitive set-up for an eight-week season which includes playoffs. Games are usually played on Wednesday nights, and cost Dhs.500 and Dhs.3,200 for a team. New leagues are periodically added, so check the website for more details.

Birdwatching

The increasing lushness of the area attracts ever more birds, many of which are not easily found in Europe or the Middle East. Over 80 species breed locally, while over 400 have been recorded on their migration between Africa and Central Asia. Species spotted include the socotra cormorant, chestnut-bellied sandgrouse, crab plover, and Saunders' little tern. Good areas for birdwatching include the eastern lagoon on the New Corniche, the port area, Mushrif Palace Gardens and around the Abu Dhabi Equestrian Club. Extensive records of sightings and descriptions are kept by Tommy Pedersen who maintains a detailed and constantly updated website (www.uaebirding.com), and all twitchers are encouraged to participate. Other excellent places for birding around the Emirates include the mangrove swamps in Umm Al Quwain and at Khor Kalba (p.258) – the only place in the world where you can spot the white-collared kingfisher. During the migrating periods (September/October and March/April), enormous flocks of wading birds can be found. The flamingos that feed here are always a spectacular sight. Access is restricted to permit holders, but birds can be watched from the car if you park along the Ras Al Khor creek and use binoculars. Desert Rangers arrange canoe tours through Kalba's mangroves (04 357 2200).

Bowling

A number of the shopping centres around town have excellent ten-pin bowling facilities which are ideal for an inexpensive family outing. Bowling City has seven locations in the UAE, including three in Abu Dhabi and one in Al Ain. Abu Dhabi Country Club in Al Mushrif (p.179) has a four lane facility which is often booked for birthday parties. The cost for one game is Dhs.20 and to hire the lane for one hour will cost Dhs.100 (www.adhfc.com). The biggest bowling alley in Abu Dhabi is Khalifa International Bowling Centre, which regularly hosts competitive bowling as well as bowling for the general public.

Bowling City

Abu Dhabi Mall Tourist Club Area **02 676 0444**
www.bowling-city.com
Map **2 S5**

With billiard lounges, karaoke booths, internet cafes and gaming zones, there is so much more to Bowling City than just bowling. If you do feel like hitting the lanes, it costs Dhs.12 per game or Dhs.15 including shoes; socks are an additional Dhs.3. There are seven locations across the country to choose from including Abu Dhabi Mall (02 676 0444), Khalidiyah Mall (Sparky's Family Fun Centre, 02 635 4317) and Al Mariah Mall (02 676 9001) in Abu Dhabi, with another at Al Ain Mall (03 751 0006). Parties, corporate events or competitions between groups of friends can all be arranged.

Khalifa International Bowling Centre

Nr Zayed Sports Complex Al Madina Al Riyadiya
02 403 4648
www.capitala.ae
Map **1 J8**

This state-of-the-art bowling centre, located just off Airport Road, boasts 40 lanes and is apparently one of the most modern bowling alleys in the world. Prices start from Dhs.10 per game with shoe hire an additional Dhs.2. Billiards is also on offer, with an hour's play starting at Dhs.20.

Canoeing & Kayaking

Not only are canoeing and kayaking great ways to get out and enjoy the weather when it's not so hot, but both also offer a moment of peace and quiet in a city that can drive one to near craziness with all the horns and jackhammers. Of course, the azure waters of Abu Dhabi are temptation enough, but with mangrove forests all around the area and a good chance of catching sight of wild flamingos and dolphins, getting out on the water is one of the best ways to get free of the city without actually leaving the city limits. Not only that, but the relatively calm waters can make it easy for beginners to learn, especially in kayaks with their low centre of gravity.

Abu Dhabi Ocean Warriors

Abu Dhabi Marina Sports Club Breakwater
050 837 2436
www.adowsurfski.wordpress.com
Map **2 E1**

Abu Dhabi Ocean Warriors (ADOW) is a surfski club that operates out of Abu Dhabi Marine Sports Club near Marina Mall. Surfskis are long kayaks used for ocean racing, and the club caters to paddlers of all abilities, from racing speedsters to those enjoying a leisurely paddle. ADOW meets every Friday morning for a time trial; contact Roland at the above number for more details.

Desert Rangers

Nr American Hospital, Street 18 Dubai **04 357 2200**
www.desertrangers.com
Metro **Oud Metha**

Desert Rangers offers guided trips through the mangroves of the unique nature reserve at Khor Kalba on the east coast, in two-seater Canadian canoes. Initial instruction is followed by hands on practice to develop skills and confidence. All trips depart from Dubai and cost Dhs.300 per person.

Noukhada Adventure Company

Al Meena St Al Meena **050 721 8928**
www.noukhada.ae
Map **2 S2**

Noukhada was started over two years ago to promote eco tourism in the area. They offer kayak tours of the mangroves and even offer sunrise/sunset tours for those who want to get out on the water before or after work. However, if you're a keen kayaker, Noukhada also offers an annual membership for Dhs.3,000, which gets you free use of kayaks and equipment, a free monthly guided tour and discounts for friends.

Caving

The cave network in the Hajar Mountains is extensive and much of it is yet to be explored. Some of the best caves are located near Al Ain, the Jebel Hafeet area and just past Buraimi near the Oman border. Many of the underground passages and caves have spectacular displays of curtains, stalagmites and stalactites, as well as gypsum flowers. In Oman, the range includes what is believed to be the second largest cave system in the world, as well as the Majlis Al Jinn Cave – the second largest chamber in the world. To arrange caving trips in Oman, contact a local tour operator such as Gulf Leisure (+968 9901 3424, www.gulfleisure.com) or Muscat Diving & Adventure Center (+968 2454 3002, www.holiday-in-oman.com). Within the region, caving ranges from fairly safe to extremely dangerous and, as no mountain rescue services exist, anyone venturing out into mountains should always be well-equipped and accompanied by an experienced leader. Mountain

حلبة مرسى ياس
YAS MARINA CIRCUIT
FEEL LIKE A CHAMPION
Drive:
• Yas Driver Experiences
• Yas Track Day
• Karting
• Chevrolet Drag Experience
• Yas Drift Nights
Ride:
• F1 2-Seater
• Yas 3-Seater Dragster
• Hot Laps
Learn:
• Driver Tuition
• ATCUAE Licensing
• Yas Venue Tours
• Drag Racing Academy
800 YAS (927)
www.yasmarinacircuit.ae

High (050 659 5536, www.mountainhighme.com) offers guided tours in and around the caves of Al Ain plus canyoning and other adventures from Dhs.500 per person per day.

Chess

The chess scene revolves around Abu Dhabi Chess & Culture Club, which runs a host of tournaments.

Abu Dhabi Chess & Culture Club

Sheikh Rashid Bin Saeed Al Maktoum Rd, Nr Islamic Bank Madinat Zayed **02 633 1110**
www.abudhabichess.com
Map **2 N5**

Abu Dhabi Chess & Culture Club was opened in 1979, and regularly participates in a wealth of local and international chess tournaments, including an annual tournament run by the Abu Dhabi Authority For Culture & Heritage (ADACH). The club has sponsored numerous competitions and enrols members of all ages. All are welcome.

Climbing

For those who feel at home on a vertical plane, excellent climbing can be found in various locations around the UAE, including Ras Al Khaimah, Dibba, Hatta and the Al Ain/Buraimi region; more than 600 routes have been recorded since the 1970s. These vary from short outcrop routes to difficult mountain routes of alpine proportions. Most range from (British) Very Severe, up to extreme grades (E5). However, there are some easier routes for new climbers, especially in Wadi Bih and Wadi Khab Al Shamis.

To meet like-minded people, head to Wadi Bih where you're sure to find climbers nearly every weekend, or go to the climbing walls below, where most of the UAE climbing fraternity hangs around (ahem). One excellent resource is Toby Foord-Kelcey's website www.redarmadapublishing.com.

Also, www.uaeclimbing.com features an active forum and a wealth of information for anyone interested in climbing in the UAE. If you're not ready to go it alone, Al Shaheen Adventure Training (07 244 5171), based in Ras Al Khaimah, offers outdoor lessons for both beginners and more experienced climbers looking to advance their skills and confidence.

Climbing Dubai

Dubai World Trade Centre Dubai **04 306 5061**
www.climbingdubai.com
Metro **World Trade Centre**

Climbing Dubai has daily climbing programmes, outdoor climbing tours and international climbing expeditions. The group seeks to attract new climbers and promotes walk-ins at the evening sessions which cost Dhs.60 and include all necessary equipment.

The Club > *p.297*

Al Meena **02 673 1111**
www.the-club.com
Map **2 V3**

The Club has a five metre outdoor climbing wall which overlooks the main swimming pool. Open to members only, adults and children from the age of 4 can try out their climbing skills. Full safety gear is provided.

Desert Rangers

Nr American Hospital, Street 18 Dubai **04 357 2200**
www.desertrangers.com
Metro **Oud Metha**

Desert Rangers offers rock climbing trips to well-established locations, suitable for the absolute beginner or experienced climbers. Trips include instruction, all necessary safety equipment and lunch. All excursions depart from Dubai and a day of scaling the peaks will cost Dhs.400 per person.

Pharaohs' Club

Wafi Dubai **04 324 0000**
www.wafi.com
Metro **Healthcare City**

The indoor climbing wall at Pharaohs' Club lets climbing enthusiasts improve their skills, and offers a range of courses for kids and adults of all abilities, as well as public sessions for experienced climbers.

Climbing in the UAE

Lessons for non-members cost Dhs.62 per hour, need to be booked in advance and are limited to six people per instructor. The wall consists of varied climbing routes, and crash mats are present for bouldering.

Cookery Classes

For a city that is such a mixing pot of cultures, backgrounds, sights and sounds, Abu Dhabi is found a little lacking when it comes to teaching the tastes. The city's hotels do, on occasion, hold cooking nights or short cookery courses and Royal Orchid on Salaam St (02 677 9911) periodically hosts classes for Thai and Indian cooking. By and large, however, the responsibility falls to PartiPerfect (050 126 4819, partiperfect@gmail.com) which offers regular cookery classes in the city: every month (during non-summer months) Chef Lana plans the class schedule and menus range in style from Middle Eastern to Turkish; during holidays, they also bravely run cookery classes for kids.

Cricket

With such a mixture of nationalities and cultures in Abu Dhabi, cricket is a passion shared across many communities. Many organisations have their own cricket teams for inter-company competitions and the sport is becoming more popular in schools. Car parks, rough land and grassy parks all sprout stumps at weekends and evenings, when a mix of ages come out to play. International matches are regularly hosted in the UAE at grounds in Abu Dhabi, Dubai and Sharjah.

Abu Dhabi Cricket Council

Al Salam St Tourist Club Area **02 645 9790**
www.uaecricket.com
Map **2 Q4**

The council was established to promote and run cricket affairs in the emirate. There are currently 65 local clubs registered, with over a thousand players of many nationalities. If you want to play cricket, the council will put you in contact with a suitable club. The council also runs a cricket academy and organises local and international matches at the purpose-built cricket stadium near Khalifa City.

Al Ain Cricket Association

Al Khateem St Al Ain **03 712 1167**
www.uaecricket.com
Map **3 E3**

The association is the oldest cricketing body in the UAE and has been running cricket affairs in Al Ain since April 1989. There are currently 20 teams (seniors and juniors) with over 350 resident players of many nationalities. It has a new location with four new grounds, including a floodlit pitch for play at night. Coaching is available five evenings a week. For more information see website.

Cycling

Abu Dhabi is not the most bike-friendly of places but if you're willing to brave some crazy drivers, there are plenty of areas where you can ride, including the Corniche (p.194), where there are cycle paths, and it is even possible to hire bikes. The only expat road cycling club in the UAE is Dubai Roadsters, based in Dubai (04 339 4453, www.dubairroadsters.ae), but Abu Dhabi has a triathlon club (www.abudhabitriclub.org) through which it is possible to meet regular cyclists. The website www.cyclechallenge.ae is an excellent resource for two-wheelers, while Cycle Safe UAE regularly organises evenings of riding at Yas Island Circuit and Dubai Autodrome. See Cycle Safe UAE's Facebook page for details.

Dance Classes

Sociable, great fun and excellent exercise for all ages and levels of ability, dance has a universal appeal that breaks down barriers and inhibitions (sometimes). In addition to the following organisations, some health clubs, bars and restaurants hold weekly sessions in ballroom, flamenco, jazz dance, salsa, samba, and so on. The Club (p.179) offers ballet, hip hop and tap dance classes to children of all ages; the adult lessons include dance fusion and ballet. The Clubhouse at Zayed Sports City hosts regular nights dedicated to salsa lessons and Latin music.

Alternatively, this is definitely the right part of the world to learn belly dancing with all its charms. Surprisingly, there aren't a huge number of studios that advertise it, but health clubs and social clubs will sometimes offer classes, and there are quite a few private teachers. Clara Ball (050 417 6226) teaches lessons at the Beach Rotana and One to One hotels and gives private lessons by appointment. Lessons are also offered at the International Music Institute (02 6211299). Also, don't forget that the true belly dancing capitals of the world, like Cairo and Istanbul, are a short flight away (see Out Of The City, p.233).

Abu Dhabi Salsa

Various Locations
www.abudhabisalsa.com

This organisation's mission is to share the love and passion of Latin dancing and salsa with other people, while promoting the Abu Dhabi salsa scene. Apart from holding classes for different dance styles, it also organises events. Visit the website for more information on the instructors and rates.

Dance Abu Dhabi

Various Locations **050 410 1535**
www.danceabudhabi.com

Offering Latin and ballroom dance lessons for everyone from children and beginners to those who already think they can hold their own on the dance floor. With classes taking place at both the Hiltonia Beach and Health Club and the Intercontinental Health Club, there are plenty of opportunities to foxtrot, waltz or cha-cha.

Expressions Of Dance & Drama

23rd Street, Muroor Rd Al Nahyan **02 448 2778**
Map **2 M10**

The trainers at Expressions Of Dance & Drama offer children and adults a fun way to exercise or dance their way to fitness. Classes in ballet, tap, jazz, hip hop and even Argentine tango are on offer for the seriously inspired.

International Music Institute

Khalidiyah St, Nr Grand Stores Al Khalidiyah
02 621 1299
www.imi-jmc.net
Map **2 F4**

With classes in ballet, as well as modern dance and even belly dancing, the International Music Institute offers much more than just music. Visit the website for class times and information.

Irish Dancing

Various Locations **050 314 1922**
www.irishsocietyabudhabi.com

Irish dancing lessons for children are available through the hugely active Irish Society Abu Dhabi (p.42). Beginners, intermediate and advanced dancers are taught separately and anyone is welcome to join. For more details, contact Deirdre Mallon.

Salsa With Brando

International Music Institute Al Khalidiyah
050 268 4520
www.salsawithbrando.com
Map **2 F4**

The founder of the annual Abu Dhabi International Salsa Festival, Orson Brando is passionate about spreading the love of salsa in Abu Dhabi. Not only does he offer classes at the International Music Institute, for both beginners and the more experienced, but he's also a bit of a salsa scholar with plenty of information about the history of salsa in the region. The energetic classes start at Dhs.250 for eight lessons.

Scottish Dancing

The Club Al Meena **055 948 4658**
www.adscots.com
Map **2 V3**

Don your kilt and sporran and join in with this fun class for some traditional highland dancing. People of all levels are welcome – it doesn't matter if you've never danced before. Contact Francine Quastel for more information.

Turning Pointe Dance Studios

Shop 12 & 14, V23 Bldg, Intnl City Dubai
800 32623
www.turningpointe.ae

This Dubai-based, RAD-accredited dance school offers lessons at Pearl Primary School in Abu Dhabi and, from September 2010, at Al Yasmeena School as well. Ballet training, from baby ballet to Grade 1 examinations, is offered, with girls and boys aged 3-10 accepted. Entries are accepted throughout the year, with an admissions and information day held at the beginning of each term; examinations are held in April.

Diving

The warm seas and clear, calm waters of the Arabian Gulf on the UAE west coast and the Gulf of Oman on the east are perfect for exploring the region's varied underwater life. Popular places for snorkelling on the east coast include Snoopy Island, just off the beach of the Sandy Beach Hotel & Resort (p.259). There are also good spots further north, such as the beach north of Dibba village, where the coast is rocky and there's coral close to the shore. For somewhere closer to home, the seas around Abu Dhabi's numerous islands have a fair amount of marine life. Most hotels or dive centres rent equipment (snorkel, mask and fins); costs vary greatly, so shop around.

If you prefer to go deeper, there are a good number of interesting dive sites, especially wrecks, some of which are within easy reach of Abu Dhabi. There are plenty of dive companies who will get you there and help you improve your diving skills. Courses are offered under the usual international training organisations. If you've already got the know-how and the gear, and want to find out more about diving and snorkelling sites in the UAE, see p.222.

7 Seas Divers

Nr Khor Fakkan Souk, East Coast Khor Fakkan
09 238 7400
www.7seasdivers.com

This PADI dive centre offers day and night diving trips to sites around Khor Fakkan, Musandam and Lima Rock. Training is provided from beginner to instructor level, in a variety of languages.

Abu Dhabi Sub Aqua Club

The Club Al Meena **02 673 1111**
www.the-club.com
Map **2 V3**

This club is affiliated to the British Sub Aqua Club (BSAC); safety standards are high, and training courses are regularly held for all levels, including beginners. Dive trips are held at weekends, and include locations around Abu Dhabi, Musandam, Fujairah and five other sites in the region.

Al Mahara Diving Center
Dalma Mall Mussafah **050 720 2833**
www.divemahara.com
Map **1 N13**
This centre organises PADI training, ranging from beginner to open water and specialist diving. If you're looking for a career change, the centre also offers instructor training with experienced teachers. special training includes children's programmes, underwater photography and videography. The centre also organises trips to the east coast, Musandam and even overseas; snorkelling sessions near the Breakwater offer a chance to see a number of local species.

Arabian Divers & Sportfishing Charters
Al Bateen Marina Al Bateen **050 614 6931**
www.fishabudhabi.com
Map **2 C6**
With over 10 years' experience in diving and boat charters, this company has a complete range of on-site facilities in the Al Bateen Marina, including a shop, a classroom, a training dive pool and boats for charters. PADI courses from beginner to advanced are available, as well as dives to sites around the UAE coast. The company prioritises individual attention and small diving groups, making sure that safety comes first. In addition to diving and sportfishing, this company also offers snorkelling charters, with experienced captains who know the best local spots.

Emirates Diving Association
Heritage & Diving Village Dubai
04 393 9390
www.emiratesdiving.com
Metro **Al Ghubaiba**
This non-profit group aims to conserve, protect and restore the UAE's marine resources by promoting the importance of the environment. It looks after the well-being of UAE corals as part of its coral monitoring project, and organises annual Clean-Up Arabia campaigns. A quarterly newsletter, Divers for the Environment, details current activities and the website has lots of useful info. Divers are encouraged to join, with membership costing Dhs.100 per year.

Freediving UAE
Various Locations
www.freedivinguae.com
This group of diving enthusiasts promotes and practises the art of freediving – diving without the aid of breathing apparatus. Freediving AIDA accredited courses are also offered to give beginner, intermediate and advanced freedivers the physical skill, mental preparation and theory training required to freedive safely and successfully. Training sessions are held every week on Sundays and Tuesdays, with trips to dive sites in Khor Fakkan organised periodically.

Sandy Beach Diving Centre
Sandy Beach Hotel & Resort Fujairah **09 244 5555**
www.sandybm.com
Located in a chalet beach resort, the centre, which sells and rents dive and snorkelling equipment, is open year-round. Nearby Snoopy Island, alive with hard coral and marine life, is an excellent spot for snorkelling and diving. Beach access for the day is Dhs.75. Snorkelling equipment is available for hire at Dhs.60 a day.

Scuba 2000
Al Bidiya Beach Fujairah **09 238 8477**
www.scuba-2000.com
Located on the east coast between Dibba and Fujairah, this centre offers boat trips to the east coast's best diving and snorkelling sites, in addition to diving courses, night dives, snorkelling trips and equipment rental. You can also snorkel directly from the beach, and accommodation is available. A two-dive boat trip with full equipment costs Dhs.330, while a night dive with full equipment costs Dhs.400. A Discover Scuba Diving course is on offer for Dhs.500 and the PADI Open Water Diving course is available at Dhs.2,350. Diving packages, with two free dives, are also offered for certified divers. Snorkelling trips start at Dhs.170, inclusive of boat ride, fins, mask, snorkel and boots, plus refreshments.

Dragon Boat Racing
The ancient sport of dragon boat racing involves long boats, each with twenty members paddling furiously from the start of the race, like a team paddle boat sprint, over relatively short distances. The name comes from the fact that boats are often adorned with striking dragon heads and tails. Abu Dhabi's pristine turquoise waters and year-round warm weather make for a perfect setting for outings of all sorts, and neighbouring Dubai is home to more dragon boating activities for dedicated enthusiasts.

The UAE Dragon Boat Association (www.dubaidragonboat.com) lists all of the country's dragon boating crews who meet, along with international competitors, for the annual Dubai International Dragon Boating Festival.

Abu Dhabi MAR
Shangri-La Hotel, Qaryat Al Beri Bain Al Jessrain
050 926 2764
Map **1 L8**
This group meets on Monday and Wednesday evenings at the Shangri-La Hotel, Qaryat Al Beri. The group is open to absolutely everyone, and there's a nice balance of competitive spirit with general social camaraderie between the members. For further information and exact timings, call Warren on the above number for details.

Capital Dragons

Abu Dhabi Marine Sailing Club Breakwater
02 696 7831
Map **2 E1**

This group is open to paddlers of all ages, and training sessions run on Monday and Wednesday evenings at the Marina Yacht Club close to Marina Mall, often paddling to nearby Lulu Island for a social picnic or swim. Call the above number for more information.

Drama Groups

The performing arts are growing in popularity both in terms of performances staged in the capital and opportunities for residents to get involved themselves. While major cultural developments are being geared up by the government, there's already a bunch of opportunities to give your creative side a go and release your inner performer. The Abu Dhabi branch of the New York Film Academy (www.abudhabifilmschool.com) opened in 2008 and offers intensive four and six week film acting courses, as well as one and two year acting diplomas. Drama Workshops Dubai (www.dramaworkshopsdubai.com) sometimes organises workshops in Abu Dhabi; check the website for updates. For those who dream of treading the boards themselves, there are a number of dance schools in Abu Dhabi (p.278).

Abu Dhabi Dramatic Society

The Club Al Meena **02 673 1111**
www.abudhabidrama.com
Map **2 V2**

As with almost all activities at The Club, the Abu Dhabi Dramatic Society is open to members only. However, the productions are open to the public as long as they're guests of a member. The society puts on four productions a year and offers children's programmes and workshops.

Environmental Groups

As it currently stands, there's little chance that Abu Dhabi would be mistaken for a bastion of greendom, but the government is committed to ambitious environmental goals to gradually turn the city into a model for sustainable development. Masdar City is at the forefront of the emirate's aim to become a global leader in environmental development. On the grassroots level, there are other developments. For example, Abu Dhabi's Centre of Waste Management recently undertook a massive marketing campaign to encourage adoption of the three 'Rs' – reduce, reuse, recycle; and private companies like Spinneys have also implemented recycling efforts. Elsewhere, a government-led programme to phase out plastic bags over the next few years is in place. In the meantime, here are the local standbys when it comes to the environment.

Al Ain Wildlife Park & Resort

Nhayyan The First St Al Ain **800 2977**
www.awpr.ae
Map **4 D3**

Al Ain Wildlife Park houses a wide range of animals on its spacious, leafy grounds and one of the park's principal goals is to educate visitors in matters relating to environment, conservation and sustainability. In addition, the park is active through several local schools and communities.

Emirates Environmental Group

Villa 117A, Nr Dubai Zoo, JMR 68 Dubai
04 344 8622
www.eeg-uae.org
Metro **Financial Centre**

This voluntary organisation is devoted to protecting the environment through education, action programmes and community involvement across the Emirates. Activities include evening lectures and special events such as recycling collections and clean-up campaigns. Annual membership costs Dhs.200 for adults and Dhs.50 for students.

Emirates Natural History Group

Various Locations **02 604 3313**
www.enhg.org

The ENHG has groups in both Abu Dhabi and Al Ain, with regular field trips, and lectures on various subjects, ranging from astronomy to zoology. The Abu Dhabi group now meets in the main auditorium at Abu Dhabi Men's College of the Higher Colleges of Technology, at 19:30 on the first and third Tuesdays of each month, with the exception of July and August, when there are no meetings, and during Ramadan when meetings begin no earlier than 20:00.

The Al Ain chapter meets on the second and fourth Tuesday of each month (July, August and December excepted) at 19:30 at the Danat Al Ain Resort. Membership costs Dhs.100 per calendar year.

Emirates Wildlife Society

Abu Dhabi Chamber Of Commerce & Industry
Markaziya West **02 634 7117**
www.uae.panda.org
Map **2 L2**

The Emirates Wildlife Society (EWS) works alongside the World Wildlife Fund (WWF) in the UAE. Together they operate a volunteer programme open to anyone who can spare a few hours a month to assist with valuable conservation work in the Emirates. Volunteer activities include admin, fundraising, assisting with wildlife surveys, clean-up operations and educational presentations, as well as awareness campaigns. To find out more about how to get involved and how to volunteer with the society, log onto www.uae.panda.org to complete the online application form.

Feline Friends
Various Locations **050 582 2916**
www.felinefriendsuae.com
This non-profit organisation of volunteers aims to care for sick and injured street cats and kittens, as well as controlling the cat population by sterilisation. It rescues abandoned cats and fosters them until permanent homes can be found.

K9 Friends
Dubai **050 274 1949**
www.k9friends.com
K9 Friends has a re-homing service for stray and abandoned dogs; the group promotes responsible dog ownership and encourages a neutering programme to help control the population of stray dogs. Volunteers and foster homes are always needed.

Strays Of Abu Dhabi (SAD)
Various Locations **050130 7392**
www.straysofabudhabi.com
Strays of Abu Dhabi (SAD) is committed to re-homing stray and abandoned animals in Abu Dhabi. It deals primarily with dogs, but will occasionally assist other animals in need of help too. The non-profit group is always on the lookout for reliable volunteers to walk the dogs; provide weekend foster families; or act as phone volunteers and fundraisers.

Fishing
A boat isn't necessarily required to enjoy a great afternoon or evening of fishing. There are plenty of places along the Corniche where fishermen tend to congregate, but be aware that you must first obtain a licence. You can apply and pay online for an annual (Dhs.120) or weekly (Dhs.30) fishing licence (www.abudhabi.ae). For a chance of hooking bigger bites, or to let someone else handle the licence admin, it's best to get out on the water and hire a fishing guide. From September to April is the peak fishing season, although it's still possible to catch queenfish and sailfish in the summer months. Other commonly caught fish include dorado, jacks, kingfish, shari and tuna. If you're after a really big catch and have some cash to spare, deep-sea fishing and trawling are offered by specialist operators.

Arabian Divers & Sportfishing Charters > *p.283*
Al Bateen Marina Al Bateen **050 614 6931**
www.fishabudhabi.com
Map **2 C6**
This experienced boat charter company offers dolphin watching trips, scuba diving and snorkelling, boat charters and big game sport fishing. An IGFA (International Game Fishing Association) certified captain is on hand to help you reel in your catch.

Beach Rotana Abu Dhabi
Nr Abu Dhabi Mall, Liwa St Tourist Club Area
02 697 9000
www.rotana.com
Map **2 S5**
The hotel's boat is available for hire for fishing or cruising the pristine waters of the Arabian Gulf. The driver will suggest different fishing spots depending on the season, but with hundreds of small islands just off the coast, good fishing and scenery are guaranteed. For details, contact the hotel or call Mr Anamul on 050 315 9181.

Hiltonia Health Club & Spa
Hilton Abu Dhabi Al Khubeirah **02 692 4205**
www.hilton.com
Map **2 C3**
An experienced guide from the Hiltonia Beach Club can organise fishing trips, an island cruise or a combination of both which includes a barbecue for the catch. Though the best fishing is during the cooler months, under expert guidance there are big fish to be caught even in the height of summer.

Noukhada Adventure Company
Al Meena St Al Meena **050 721 8928**
www.noukhada.ae
Map **2 S2**
For something a little different, Noukhada brings you closer to the action with kayak fishing. Because the company focuses on eco-tourism, catch and release is promoted, but that only means bigger fish in the stories you tell your friends. Fly fishing options are also offered.

The Oceanic Hotel & Resort
Beach Rd Khor Fakkan **09 238 5111**
www.oceanichotel.com
Fishing trips from the hotel head to a favourite local spot where catches are guaranteed. For hotel guests, the catch of the day can then be cooked according to your taste by the hotel chef. Non-guests can take their catch home with them. Trips leave from 14:00 onwards. The hotel also organises whale and dolphin watching trips, as well as the chance to swim with sharks.

Sheraton Resort Health Club
Sheraton Abu Dhabi Hotel & Resort Markaziya East
02 677 3333
www.sheraton.com/abudhabi
Map **2 Q2**
Expeditions are run from the resort for deep sea fishing, with large catches of barracuda, hammour, kingfish and shari (seasonal) virtually guaranteed. Everything is provided, including refreshments, equipment and experienced guides to ensure every trip is a success.

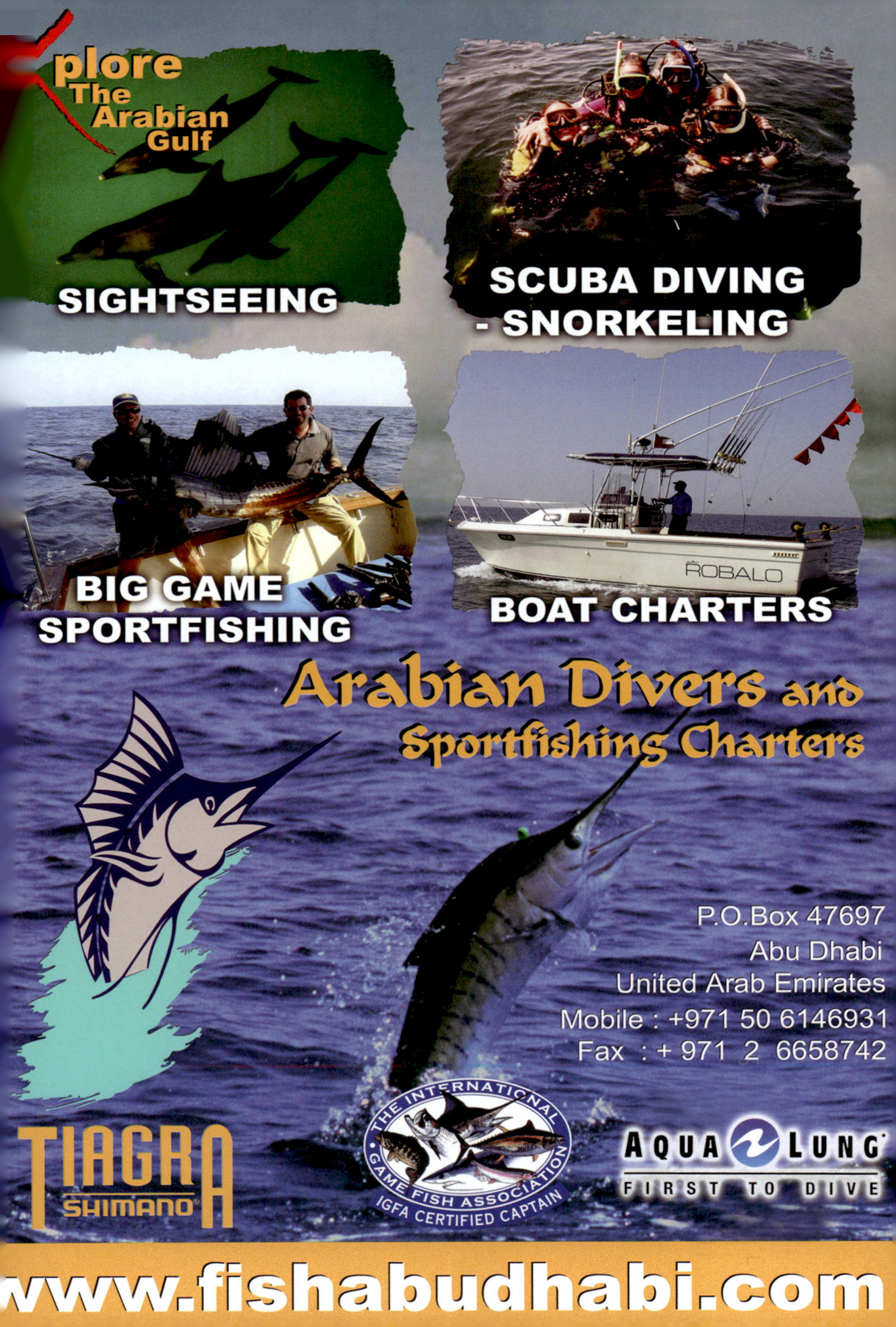
Xplore The Arabian Gulf
SIGHTSEEING
SCUBA DIVING
- SNORKELING
BIG GAME
SPORTFISHING
ROBALO
BOAT CHARTERS
Arabian Divers and
Sportfishing Charters
P.O.Box 47697
Abu Dhabi
United Arab Emirates
Mobile : +971 50 6146931
Fax : + 971 2 6658742
TIAGRA
SHIMANO
THE INTERNATIONAL GAME FISH ASSOCIATION
IGFA CERTIFIED CAPTAIN
AQUA LUNG
FIRST TO DIVE
www.fishabudhabi.com

Flying

At present, there are no private flying clubs up and running in the Abu Dhabi or Al Ain areas. However, Dubai-based Micro Aviation Club (see below) occasionally offers lessons in Abu Dhabi too. Otherwise, those keen to learn can travel north to Dubai or Umm Al Quwain, or even east to Fujairah. Those with a private pilot's licence can contact the Dubai Flying Association; while at Fujairah Aviation Academy' the brave can pick up the high habit and obtain their pilot's licence. If you are after a private flight, but would prefer someone else to handle the controls, you can arrange a charter through Abu Dhabi Aviation (02 575 8000).

Emirates Flying School

Dubai International Airport Dubai
04 299 5155
www.emiratesaviationservices.com
The only approved flight training institution in Dubai offers private and commercial licences, and will convert international licences to UAE. A Private Pilot Licence course costs upwards of Dhs.51,920.

Fujairah Aviation Academy

Fujairah International Airport Fujairah
09 222 4747
www.fujaa.ae
Facilities include single and twin-engine aircraft, an instrument flight simulator and a repair workshop. Training is offered for private and commercial licences, instrument rating and multi-engine rating. Pleasure flights and sightseeing tours are also available, and those with a pilot's licence can enquire about aircraft for hire by calling the above number.

Jazirah Aviation

Dubai – Ras Al Khaimah Highway, Jazirat Al Hamra Ras Al Khaimah **07 244 6416**
www.jac-uae.net
The club is dedicated solely to microlight/ultralight flying, although it does also offer training and pleasure flights. A Microlight Pilot's Licence course involves around 25 hours flying time at a cost of Dhs.500 per hour.

Micro Aviation Club

Nr Bab Al Shams, 20km from Emirates Rd Umm Al Quwain **055 212 0155**
www.microaviation.org
The Dubai-based Micro Aviation Club offers full training courses in microlight flying, paragliding and paramotoring. Its office is located at Dubai Men's College, in Dubai Academic City. Courses start from Dhs.3,500, with an addtional annual registration fee of Dhs.250.; Lessons are sometimes held in Abu Dhabi as well as in Dubai.

Football

Football (or soccer for any American expats) is, as in most of the rest of the world, the most popular sport in the United Arab Emirates and it enjoys a large number of spectators as well as plentiful players. During the evenings and at weekends, parks, beaches and any open areas seem to attract a game, generally with a mix of nationalities taking part. However, you could also leave the street football behind and join The Club's (p.179) Monday Soccer group, which runs on Monday evenings and is open to men and women (members only). Alternatively, you could try one of the clubs listed below. The football field at Abu Dhabi Country Club (p.179) serves as the primary practice facility for football programmes. If you'd rather watch than play, the UAE's national league has regular fixtures at the Al Jazira and Al Wahda stadiums in town (see Spectator Sports, p.223). For Gaelic football, see Gaelic Games on p.286; for American football, see p.272; for Australian Rules, see p.273.

Abu Dhabi Strollers

Al Ghazal Golf Club Airport Area
Map **1 V8**
This club holds kickabouts every Sunday in Abu Dhabi from 19:30-21:00, and has a team in the seven-a-side and eleven-a-side Abu Dhabi leagues. There's also an annual trip to Phuket in Thailand for the sevens tournament every November. Email Roland at the above address for more information.

Duplays Fifth Element League

The Dome@Rawdat,Shk Rashid Bin Saeed Al Maktoum Rd Al Madina Al Riyadiya **055 224 0186**
www.duplays.com
Map **1 J8**
For five-a-side action, the Abu Dhabi branch of sporting community Duplays organises competitive leagues every couple of months. Games are played weekly at the newly built Dome @ Rawdhat, and it costs Dhs.400 to sign up per individual, or Dhs.3,000 per team of eight.

Manchester United Soccer Schools

The Dome@Rawdhat, Shk Rashid Bin Saeed Al Maktoum Rd Al Madina Al Riyadiya **02 449 8480**
www.manutdsoccerschools.ae
Map **1 J8**
Manchester United Soccer Schools offers a range of football courses for kids, as well as youth football camps to children and young adults aged between 6 and 18 years. The courses run several times a year. at the Dome @ Rawdhat, and various age groups are on offer to book. All players are given the opportunity to take part in a series of skills challenges, with selected participants being given the chance to attend the World Skills Final event in the UK.

Abu Dhabi Golf Club

Walking along The Corniche

Zayed Sports City

Sea fishing

Gaelic Games

Abu Dhabi Na Fianna

www.abudhabinafianna.com

The sister association of Abu Dhabi Irish Society (p.42), Na Fianna offers a sporting programme of Gaelic games, including Gaelic football and hurling. In addition to regular training and competitions, the group runs a busy social calendar which includes golf days, themed social events and fundraisers.

Gardening

Abu Dhabi Flower & Garden Group

www.adfgg.com

This non-profit volunteer organisation aims to create environmental awareness and promote gardening at home and in the Gulf by planting seeds, flowering plants and trees. Meetings are held once a month, and there are various workshops and field trips, as well as exhibits by floral artists.

Golf

The UAE is quite rightly known as the best golf destination in the Gulf, with excellent year-round facilities and many important tournaments being held here. Courses are either fully grassed or brown (sand) courses, or a mixture of the two. Abu Dhabi is home to a variety of local tournaments held on an annual or monthly basis, such as the regular Abu Dhabi Duty Free Medal, while on the international scene, the Abu Dhabi Golf HSBC Championship (p.26) has become an annual stop on the European PGA Tour. A great event to watch, it attracts some of the sport's top names; and in Dubai, the Emirates Golf Club hosts the well-established Dubai Desert Classic (p.27) and the Jumeirah Golf Estates hosts the Dubai World Championship (p.29) in November, the culmination of the European Tour's Race to Dubai.

Abu Dhabi City Golf Club

Saeed Bin Tahnoon St Al Mushrif **02 445 9600**

www.adcitygolf.ae

Map **2 H13**

This unusual course is set within a horseracing track and its par 70 course boasts one of the longest par five holes in the Gulf, at 630 yards. Competitions are held each Friday and the Junior Golf Academy offers an eight-week teaching programme for 8 to 14 year olds. Although there are only nine holes, there are alternative tees for the back nine. All facilities are free to members. Green fees for visitors vary depending on the time of day and year; an off-peak nine holes during the summer starts at Dhs.165 including cart hire. A range of balls are available starting at Dhs.25. The luxurious clubhouse also features an excellent restaurant, pool and Jacuzzi for use by members.

Abu Dhabi Golf Club

Umm Al Nar St Madinat Khalifa A (Khalifa City A)

02 558 8990

www.adgolfclub.com

Map **1 N8**

Located just 30 minutes from the centre of Abu Dhabi, the club's excellent facilities include 27 holes, including a par 72 world-class 18 hole course, a driving range, putting and pitching greens and a golf academy that holds lessons for juniors as well. There is a wide range of membership categories designed to suit every type of golfer. Managed by Troon Golf, the club is the host of the Abu Dhabi Golf HSBC Championship (p.26), a stop on the European PGA Tour. The falcon-shaped clubhouse also features bars, restaurants, pro-shop, gym, pool and spa.

Al Ain Golf Club

Nr Danat Al Ain Resort Al Ain **03 768 6808**

Map **4 E2**

The Al Ain Golf Club, near the Danat Al Ain Resort, boasts an 18 hole sand course, a clubhouse and a floodlit driving range. Handicaps gained here are valid internationally. Visitors are welcome, but should phone ahead.

Al Ghazal Golf Club

Nr Abu Dhabi Intl Airport Airport Area

02 575 8040

www.alghazalgolf.ae

Map **1 V8**

This golf course has 'browns' instead of 'greens' with a purpose-built 18 hole sand golf course, driving range, academy and licensed clubhouse is situated two minutes from the capital's airport, and is home to the World Sand Golf Championship. Anyone can play here, including transit passengers with a few hours to kill – airlines can arrange free 96 hour passenger transit visas for travellers who want to play golf or use the facilities. Lessons are available, and green fees range from Dhs.70 for nine holes for members (weekdays), to Dhs.165 for eighteen holes for non-members at weekends. A branch of the Abu Dhabi Duty Free Shop is situated on the premises (see www.addf.ae).

Emirates Golf Federation

Dubai Creek Golf & Yacht Club Dubai

04 295 2277

www.ugagolf.com

Metro **Deira City Centre**

This non-profit organisation governs amateur golf in the UAE. It is overseen by the General Authority of Youth & Sports, and actively supports junior players and the development of the national team. The affiliate membership rate is Dhs.200 per quarter, and the UGA Handicap Scheme costs Dhs.795 per year.

Hilton Al Ain Golf Club

Hilton Al Ain Al Ain **03 768 6666**
www.al-ain.hilton.com
Map **4 E2**

This par three course has an average distance of about 80 yards between each hole and, although short in length, it can play tough. The course has nearly 30 bunkers and very small quick greens. It is open to non-members, and lessons are available. There is an entrance fee of Dhs.76 for non-members and green fees are also Dhs.23; club hire starts from Dhs.35 for a half set and Dhs.8 per golf ball.

Rotana Junior Golf League

Abu Dhabi City Golf Club Al Mushrif
02 445 9600
www.adcitygolf.ae
Map **2 H13**

When it comes to learning golf, the younger you start the better. This junior golf league operates from September to May, with tournaments held every month and lessons given weekly. The cost of instruction is Dhs.600 for eight lessons, plus a registration fee of Dhs.150.

Saadiyat Beach Golf Club

Saadiyat Island 02 557 8000
www.sbgolfclub.ae
Map **1 H1**

Abu Dhabi's latest golf course, and the only one designed specifically for pay and play daily members, Saadiyat Beach is a par 72, 18 hole links-style Championship course designed by golfing legend Gary Player. The spectacular location features three lakes and 60 bunkers. UAE residents can play at a discounted rate of Dhs.250 during the week and Dhs.350 at weekends, with visitor prices at Dhs.300 and Dhs.450 respectively. The Golf Institute by Troon Golf can help you perfect your swing with an introduction to the course, world-class coaching for all levels, and a junior development programme.

Yas Links Abu Dhabi

Nr Yas Marina Circuit, Yas Island Yas Island West
02 810 7777
www.yaslinks.com
Map **1 T4**

Open since 2010 and designed by Kyle Phillips, Yas Links is undeniably one of the region's top golf destinations. It boasts an 18 hole course in a stunningly scenic setting as part of the Yas Island development, with gorgeous seashore views. Yas Links is also home to a nine hole academy course, clubhouse, golf academy and floodlit practice facilities. Individual membership costs Dhs.14,000 per year with an initial Dhs.5,000 joining fee, while rack rates start at Dhs.599 for non-members.

Hashing

Billed as 'drinking clubs with a running problem', Hash House Harriers is a worldwide network of social running clubs where the emphasis is on taking part, and socialising afterwards, rather than on serious running. Members run or walk around a course laid out by a couple of 'hares'. It's a fun way to get fit and meet new people.

Abu Dhabi Island Hash House Harriers

Various Locations **050 669 2667**
www.auh4.wordpress.com

If you think you need the drinking capacity of an elephant and the running ability of Sebastian Coe to join a hash, think again. Sprint, run, walk or hobble – it's up to you. The hash meets on Monday nights at various locations around the city. Membership costs Dhs.150 and includes a welcome pack and T-shirt. Under 16s join free with parents. Runs cost Dhs.50 for adults and Dhs.10 for under 16s. Call Derek Griffin for more information.

Abu Dhabi Mainland Hash House Harriers

Various Locations

The Mainland Hash was started as an alternative to the Island Hash. It usually meets off-island on Monday evenings year-round. Food and beverages are provided in return for a small contribution. For more information email John Arkley at jrl-a@hotmail.com.

Al Ain Hash House Harriers

Various Locations Al Ain **050 623 0411**

Started in 1984, this hash has run over a thousand times with no break, despite rain, lightning and the occasional near hurricane. The runs vary in difficulty and start at various locations around Al Ain on Mondays, at 17:30 in the winter and 18:00 in the summer. It's a family affair that welcomes people of all ages and holds special events. Contact Georges on 050 623 0411 or Jude on 050 618 7244 for further details and information.

Horse Riding

Horses are of great significance in this part of the world, both in historical and modern terms, and the UAE has a wealth of equine talent. Recreational riding is extremely well supported, and most stables offer quality horses, whether for hacking in the desert or rides along the beach. Courses are on offer from the beginner level all the way to advanced. Horse racing and endurance riding are also extremely popular and races are held throughout the year. In March each year, Dubai hosts the world's richest horse race, the $10 million Dubai World Cup (p.28), which is one of the major events on the UAE's social calendar and takes place at the impressive Meydan racetrack.

Al Forsan International Sports Resort

Nr Abu Dhabi Golf Club & Resort Madinat Khalifa A (Khalifa City A) **02 556 8555**
www.alforsan.com
Map **1 P8**
The newly-opened complex offers fantastic premises and lessons for all levels; indoor and outdoor training areas; show jumping facilities; and a polo field. Lessons start from Dhs.180 and discounted package deals are available.

Abu Dhabi Equestrian Club

Al Saada St Al Mushrif **02 445 5500**
www.adec-web.com
Map **2 H13**
As well as races and show jumping events during the cooler winter months, the club offers comprehensive instruction at different levels of expertise, starting with riding for beginners right through to show jumping. Private lessons start from Dhs.200 for members and Dhs.350 for non-members. The facilities include modern stables, a polo field and an equine swimming pool.

Ice Hockey

Abu Dhabi Falcons Ice Hockey

Zayed Sports City Al Safarat **050 268 0446**
www.falconsabudhabi.com
Map **1 J8**
This club is dedicated to the development of youth ice hockey in a fun, safe environment. Practice sessions are held at Sheikh Zayed Sports City and the teams participate in local tournaments against Al Ain, Dubai, Dhahran, Doha and Muscat. The club also holds an annual camp with professional Canadian coaches. Boys and girls aged between 5 and 18 are welcome.

Abu Dhabi Scorpions Ice Hockey

Abu Dhabi Ice Rink Al Madina Al Riyadiya
050 621 6464
Map **1 J8**
You don't have to play like Wayne Gretsky to join this team – all players over 18 are welcome. The Scorpions participated in the inaugural Emirates Hockey League, along with the Abu Dhabi Storms (an Emirati team), two teams from Al Ain and a team from Dubai. The league is impressively organised, and highly competitive. For more information about either the Scorpions or the Storms, contact chairman Ali Kaddas (alikaddas1976@gmail.com).

Ice Skating

Abu Dhabi now has two ice rinks to call its own. The Abu Dhabi Ice Rink is the oldest and largest, and it's where most of the capital's ice sporting events take place. The newest edition, the SnowWorld rink at Marina Mall (02 681 8300), is a smaller rink, but it should prove to be popular with children, and with shoppers who are looking for exercise that's a little more interesting and challenging than mall walking. Similarly, Al Ain has a small rink in Al Ain Mall (03 766 0333) to supplement the more serious, full-size rink at Hili Fun City.

Abu Dhabi Ice Rink

Zayed Sports City Al Safarat **02 444 8458**
Map **1 J8**
This Olympic size rink has great facilities with a separate children's area, a French cafe and arcade entertainment. Lessons for all levels of ability are available. There is a Dhs.5 entrance fee and a Dhs.15 skating fee but children under 3 get in for free. It's advisable to call ahead as the rink is sometimes closed for ice hockey practice.

Hili Fun City > *p.186*

Off Emirates St Al Ain **03 784 5542**
www.hilifuncity.ae
Map **4 E1**
Located on the eastern side of the park, this mammoth 60 by 30 metre rink has seating for 3,000 spectators. Besides public skating sessions, there are ice hockey tournaments and ice skating competitions held throughout the year.

Ice skating

Martial Arts

Abu Dhabi Aikido Club

Various Locations **050 412 2395**

Aikido literally means harmony and love with the spirit of the universe, and the training is designed to give you the ability to defend yourself while gaining control of your assailant without inflicting injury. Classes take place at the Abu Dhabi Hilton and Asian Karate Center (behind the Russian Embassy). Call Freddie on the number above for more information.

Abu Dhabi Combat Club

Abu Dhabi Equestrian Club Al Mushrif **02 443 0355**
www.adcombat.com
Map **2 H13**

Headed by HE Sheikh Hazza Bin Zayed Al Nahyan, this club focuses on Brazilian jiu-jitsu but cross trains in boxing, kickboxing, judo, wrestling and various other arts beneficial to no rules fighting. Membership costs Dhs.200 for one month and Dhs.800 for six months for children, and Dhs.200 for one month and Dhs.1,500 for one year for adults. Classes take place every day except Friday and Saturday, from 17:00 to 18:00 for children and 19:00 to 20:00 for adults.

Fighting Fit

Karate, kung fu, kickboxing and self defence classes taught by Sensai Shan, a bronze medal winner in the Karate World Championships, are available for adults and junior members of The Club (p.179). Call 02 673 1111 for enquiries.

Baroudy's Sports Club

ADCB Building, Corniche St Markaziya East
02 626 8122
Map **2 Q2**

Baroudy's teaches taekwondo, which embraces the traditional beliefs of honour, integrity, loyalty and compassion. Taekwondo teaches self defence and also improves physical fitness and mental discipline. The club runs a children's summer camp. For details, contact Tony Baroudy on the number above.

Cobra Muay Thai Abu Dhabi

Zayed Sports City Al Safarat **055 616 0996**
Map **1 J8**

Cobra Muay Thai has something to offer everybody, welcoming all skill levels from beginners to advanced students. Chief instructor Mat Dryden divides his time between hosting classes at Zayed Sports City but is looking for a dedicated facility. Classes include Muay Thai and traditional boxing training as well as a Fitness for Fighters class that promises to push even the most in-shape participants to their limits. For details, call Mat at the above number.

Emirates Sports Centre

Nr Al Salama Hospital Tourist Club Area
050 820 5734
www.shaolinemirates.com
Map **2 R3**

Sessions in karate and kung fu are conducted by Master Jai. With over 15 years of martial arts experience and a trunkload of awards, expect only the best level of instruction.

The Oriental Karate & Kobudo Club

Tourist Club Area **02 677 1611**
www.orientalkarate.com
Map **2 R4**

This active Abu Dhabi club offers classes for all skill levels. Lessons are held at various locations; call the number above or get in touch with one of the following centres: Madinat Zayed (02 634 5080), Airport Road (02 445 7375), Khalifa Street (02 622 4182) and Al Khalidiyah (02 621 8773). Classes cost Dhs.250 a month (two sessions per week), excluding a Dhs.100 admission fee and Dhs.100 for the uniform.

Sheraton Resort Health Club

Sheraton Abu Dhabi Hotel & Resort Markaziya East
02 677 3333
www.sheraton.com/abudhabi
Map **2 Q2**

Sheraton Resort Health Club offers classes in martial arts ranging from judo and kickboxing to karate at the club facility. The instructor is a highly experienced martial arts black belt who focuses on defence and safety. Lessons are available for different levels of skill, as well as for children. Individual sessions costs Dhs.40 for non-member adults and Dhs.30 for children.

Tai Chi Club

The Club Al Meena **02 673 1111**
www.the-club.com
Map **2 V3**

The Tai Chi Club has a trained professional leading regular, weekly sessions of the ancient Chinese martial art; you must be a member of The Club (p.179) or be accompanied by a member to take part.

Martial Arts **Dan Cady,** participant at Cobra Muay Thai

I've been training martial arts for several years now, but Muay Thai is a new discipline for me. I train because it makes me recognise my own limitations physically and mentally and work to surpass them. Martial Arts add balance and discipline to my life and really help me alleviate the stresses of work and everyday life.

Mini Golf

To combine a spot of mini golf with a trip out of town, day visitors can play at the Hatta Fort Hotel (04 809 9333) for Dhs.30 per hour, from 09:00 till 18:00, while at the Mercure Grand Jebel Hafeet (03 783 8888), mini golf is charged at Dhs.24 per hour from 09:00 till 23:00. Guests can play at both hotels for free. The Mercure Grand's course is set against a backdrop of the magnificent mountains. Balls and clubs can be hired from the hotel.

Motorsports

Abu Dhabi MX Club

Various Locations **050 818 4668**

Abu Dhabi MX Club is a social group that meets on certain weekends and some week nights (from about 16:00 to 19:00) to ride in the desert. It has several practice tracks that it uses and riders of all standards are welcome.

Al Forsan International Sports Resort

Nr Abu Dhabi Golf Club & Resort Madinat Khalifa A (Khalifa City A) **02 556 8555**

www.alforsan.com

Map **1 P8**

Abu Dhabi finally has a karting facility: the ultra-modern Motor Sports Centre boasts a 1.2km track with a Supermoto section built to FIM regulations and three models of karts, the fastest reaching speeds of 110km/h. There is also a child-safe track as well as a 2km off-road circuit.

Emirates Motor Sports Federation

Villa 1, Casablanca Rd, Nr Aviation Club Dubai **04 282 7111**

www.emsf.ae

Metro **GGICO**

Emirates Motor Sports Federation organises events throughout the year, such as the 4WD 1000 Dunes Rally, the Champions Rally for saloon cars, road safety campaigns and classic car exhibitions. Membership including competition licence is Dhs.500 per year; non-members can race for a fee. Check out the website for a full calendar of events and keep an eye on daily newspapers. A number of international rallies either start or end in Abu Dhabi, or pass through during their stages.

Ferrari World Abu Dhabi

Yas Island Yas Island West **02 496 8001**

www.ferrariworldabudhabi.com

Map **1 T4**

The world's largest indoor theme park has enough attractions to keep motorsports enthusiasts of all ages entertained. Kids can learn to drive in a miniature Ferrari, while grown-up fans get to take a glimpse into the F1 paddock or experience race driving in a simulator. For thrillseekers, there's the world's fastest rollercoaster and the G-Force tower.

Yas Marina Circuit > *p.275*

Yas Island Yas Island West **02 446 0384**

www.yasmarinacircuit.com

Map **1 T5**

While most famous as the home of the annual Formula 1 Etihad Airways Grand Prix, Yas Marina Circuit is a year-round venue where petrolheads can put their driving skills to the test, or take high-speed driving lessons. The possibilities include karting and drag racing, as well as a host of other options from supercar driving to passenger experiences.

Mountain Biking

Away from the cities, the UAE has a lot to offer outdoor enthusiasts, especially mountain bikers. On a mountain bike it's possible to see the most remote and untouched places that are not even accessible in 4WDs. For hardcore, experienced mountain bikers there is a good range of terrain, from the super-technical rocky trails in areas like Shuwayah and Shawka, to mountain routes like Wadi Bih, which climb to over a thousand metres and can be descended in minutes.

The riding is mainly rocky, technical and challenging. Even if you are an experienced biker, always be sensible and go prepared – it's important to remember that the sun can be very strong, you will need far more water than you think, and it's easy to get lost. You'll find wide, knobbly tyres work much better on the loose, sharp rocks. For further information on mountain biking in the UAE, including details of possible routes, refer to the *UAE Off-Road Explorer.*

Hot-Cog Mountain Bike Club

Various Locations Dubai **056 170 8087**

www.hot-cog.com

Hot Cog MTB is an active group of Dubai-based enthusiasts who ride every weekend, all over the country, all year round. They also camp, hike and barbecue, and new riders are always welcome. Visit the website for more information.

Noukhada Adventure Company

Al Meena St Al Meena **050 721 8928**

www.noukhada.ae

Map **2 S2**

Since there are no mountains in the area, Noukhada will take you on trails out in the desert. Expect to run into camels and people riding horses, and to view the setting sun and stars coming out over the plains. Noukhada supplies a helmet, gloves and a bike for Dhs.50 per person per hour. Individuals with their own gear can join for free on Tuesday nights at Yas Island.

Music Lessons

There are a few companies that offer music lessons in Abu Dhabi. As well as the companies included below, Royal Music & Arts (02 622 5442) also offers lessons for a range of common instruments.

Beethoven Institute Of Music

Al Nasr St, Nr Clock Tower & Fish Market
Al Khalidiyah **02 632 7588**
Map **2 K3**

Started in 1984, this was one of the first music institutes in the UAE. On offer are lessons on the drums, guitar, piano and organ. Children can start as young as 6 years old, and summer courses are also held. For more information contact the number listed or Ms Shahnaz on 050 782 7947.

International Music Institute

Khalidiyah St, Nr Grand Stores Al Khalidiyah
02 621 1299
www.imi-jmc.net
Map **2 F4**

Founded in 1994 in order to nurture musical education in the capital, IMI offers lessons taught by professionally trained instructors of piano, string, wind and percussion instruments. The institute offers both individual lessons and group classes based upon the skill levels of its students.

The Young Musician Music Institute

Nr Zayed Shopping Centre Madinat Zayed
02 556 2080
www.theyoungmusician.com
Map **2 M5**

With a highly trained faculty, this institute teaches a variety of instruments and genres including classical, rock, jazz, blues, pop, flamenco and even heavy metal. The organisation offers custom-made and advanced courses which are recognised by the Trinity College of Music, Royal School of Music, Trinity Rock School of Music and London College of Music.

Netball

Abu Dhabi Netball League

www.adnetball.com

Netball is the largest organised weekly women's sporting event in Abu Dhabi. This league has been in existence for 10 years and the teams also participate in the Inter-Gulf Netball Championships. The players range from beginners to experts and even men – and it now has 150 girls playing every week. New players are always welcome. A yearly membership fee of Dhs.375 is payable by each player to cover administration costs.

Off-Road Driving

With vast areas of rarely visited wilderness to explore, dune and wadi bashing are popular pastimes in the UAE. When heading off-road, it's always advisable to travel with at least two vehicles. If anything goes wrong, you'll be glad of an extra pair of hands, or a tow. If you're desert driving for the first time, go with an experienced person – driving on sand requires very different skills to other surfaces. Tour companies offer a range of desert and mountain safaris (see Tour Operators p.230). 4WDs can be hired from most car hire companies (for Car Rental Agencies see p.60). One point about the word 'bashing' – while it is a popular term for this form of entertainment, it can be misleading. Most, if not all, of your journey should be on existing tracks to protect the environment from further damage. For more information of where to head, get a copy of the *UAE Off-Road Explorer*.

Off-road adventures

Abu Dhabi 4x4 Club

www.AD4x4.com

This off-road club welcomes off-roaders based in Abu Dhabi. The club also tries to include family members in its range of activities and events. Members can meet other enthusiasts and share off-road driving tips and experiences. The club's website is also very informative.

Paintballing & Laser Games

Al Forsan International Sports Resort

Nr Abu Dhabi Golf Club & Resort Madinat Khalifa A (Khalifa City A) **02 556 8555**

www.alforsan.com

Map **1 P8**

Paintballing fans get to choose from three separate, themed indoor spaces: The Wild West, Alien Encounter and Pacific Island Zone. It also contains an international standard tournament field, as well as laser tag modifications for children.

Armed Forces Officers Club & Hotel

Nr Grand Mosque Al Maqtaa Officers Club **02 441 5900**

www.afoc.mil.ae

Map **1 K9**

The Officers' Club boasts two paintball fields complete with cinder block shelters, wrecked cars and other detritus of urban warfare. The cost is Dhs.150 for an hour, with a minimum of seven players to reserve exclusive use of the field. Advance bookings are essential.

The Emirates National Paintball League

www.enpl.ae

Dying to hurl a few paintballs at unsuspecting victims? Get it in contact with ENPL through the website above and get started. The group is run by experienced paintball players who want to share their passion for the game with other enthusiasts. The club also holds four tournaments every year.

Polo

Ghantoot Racing & Polo Club

Ghantoot **02 562 9050**

www.grpc.ae

Map **3 D3**

Popularity for this sport has increased dramatically over the last few years. Ghantoot Racing & Polo Club boasts modern infrastructure for sports and events, and the centre's calendar features regular chukka tournaments and high profile international games. The club sprawls over 300 hectares close to the Abu Dhabi–Dubai highway. The quality of horses and play is high, and spectators are always welcome. There is also a restaurant and a library on the premises.

Pottery

Abu Dhabi Pottery

16th Street, Nr Khalidiya Garden Al Khalidiyah **02 666 7079**

www.abudhabipottery.com

Map **2 G4**

Creative-minded adults and children aged 5 and up can try hand building and wheel pottery under the guidance of friendly staff. A chance to explore your creative side costs Dhs.150 per session for adults and Dhs.85 for children.

Rugby

Rugby is played by men, ladies and children throughout the UAE, with the larger teams taking part in Gulf league and cup competitions. The highlight of the year, for players and fans, is the annual Emirates Airlines Dubai Rugby Sevens Tournament (p.29), held at the new ground, The Sevens.

Abu Dhabi Harlequins Rugby Club

Al Ghazal Golf Club Airport Area **050 614 5199**

www.abudhabiquins.com

Map **1 V8**

Formerly the Abu Dhabi Rugby Football Club, the Abu Dhabi Harlequins is an active club boasting over 400 members, including men, women and children. All are welcome to join in. For further information contact chairman Richard Harris at the above number, or club captain David Stolzenberg at 050 592 0717.

Al Ain Amblers Rugby Club

Al Ain Equestrian, Shooting & Golf Club Al Ain **03 702 6431**

www.palmsportsresort.com

Map **4 C3**

Formed way back in 1981, the club embraces rugby players of all different standards. There are future plans to include a youth set-up and a mini section for children aged 10 to 16. For more information contact the club chairman.

Ecole Française de Rugby

Sports Stadium, Delma St Al Nahyan

www.efrabudhabi.com

Map **2 P9**

If your child is a fan of this adrenaline-pumping sport, and they are between the ages of 6 and 19, then look no further. This club has several groups welcoming beginners and players of all nationalities. Visit the website for information on training sessions, coaches and the season schedule.

Running

For more than half the year, the weather is ideal for running, although even in the height of summer, you'll find dedicated runners pounding the streets across the country. In the hottest months, the evenings and early mornings are the best times to run. Clubs and informal groups meet regularly, for casual and competitive runs and for training towards running events organised throughout the year. Regular, short distance races are held, as well as a variety of biathlons, triathlons and hashes. A favourite competition is the epic Wadi Bih Run. Teams of five run the 70km from Ras Al Khaimah to Dibba over mountains topping out at more than a thousand metres. Backed by a support vehicle, runners take turns on the different stages. The Dubai Marathon (p.26) is held in January each year.

Abu Dhabi Striders

www.abudhabistriders.com

Formed in 1983 by runners in search of fellow enthusiasts, members come from all walks of life with varying standards of fitness. There are organised runs every Wednesday and interval training on Sundays. Each year the club holds 10km, half marathon, full marathon and cross-country races, and participates in races across the UAE, while organising various social events. Contact them on admin@abudhabistriders.com.

Al Ain Road Runners

Nr Danat Al Ain Resort Al Ain **050 472 1566**

Map **4 E2**

Al Ain Road Runners are generally runners and hashers who want to do a 'bit more'. Each training session encompasses two routes: a 5km jogging route, and a longer one for the more serious runners. The group meets outside the Danat Al Ain Resort on Sundays and Thursdays, and all are welcome. Contact Phil (philip.almond@hct.ac.ae) for more details.

Running along the Corniche

Sailing Courses

While the summer months can be scorching, the winter is perfect for setting sail. From hotels that charter boats for excursions to an offshore island, to friends who moor their catamarans and speedboats at the marina – opportunities to get out on the water are plentiful. Membership at one of the sailing clubs will often mean you can use its leisure facilities, join in with activities, hire sailing and water sports equipment and moor or store your boat. Several clubs offer lessons if you are new to sailing.

Abu Dhabi Sailing Club

The Club Al Meena **02 673 1111**

www.abudhabisailing.com

Map **2 V3**

Abu Dhabi Sailing Club is a sub-section of The Club (p.179). It has a fleet of Kestrels, Lasers and Optimists, and meets regularly both on the water and socially. Social races are held every week and they participate in a number of national regattas every year in Dubai and Abu Dhabi. Membership is open only to members of The Club but beginner sailing courses are offered for adults and children from the age of 6. Annual membership of the sailing club is Dhs.1,600. For more information contact them on the number above or see the website.

Noukhada Adventure Company

Al Meena St Al Meena **050 721 8928**

www.noukhada.ae

Map **2 S2**

For those who want to learn how to sail, Noukhada is a perfect starting point. Its Hobie catamarans are light and easy to manoeuvre and the staff have been sailing for years. For expats who are already accomplished sailors without access to a boat, Noukhada's sailing club (Dhs.5,000 per year) offers the use of its boats for a set number of hours and a discounted rate once those hours have been exceeded. And there's not the headache of storage or upkeep.

Sandboarding & Skiing

The big dunes at Liwa are a wonderful place to try this exciting and unusual sport. It's easy to learn and it doesn't hurt (too much) when you fall. The boards are usually standard snowboards but as the sand is quite hard on them, they often can't be used for anything else afterwards. Some sports stores sell 'sand boards', which are a cheaper and more basic type of snowboard. As an alternative for children, a plastic sledge is enough to provide a lot of fun. All the major tour companies (p.230) offer sandboarding or skiing experiences with basic instruction on how to stay up, surf and fall properly and safely. This experience is often available either as part of another tour or as a dedicated sand boarding tour.

Shooting

The shooting ranges and facilities available in Abu Dhabi have increased significantly following the opening of Al Forsan. Alternatively, more options are available just a short drive away in neighbouring Dubai and Ras Al Khaimah.

Al Forsan International Sports Resort

Nr Abu Dhabi Golf Club & Resort Madinat Khalifa A (Khalifa City A) **02 556 8555**
www.alforsan.com
Map **1 P8**

The newly-opened shooting ranges at Al Forsan provide what Abu Dhabians were previously lacking: dedicated indoor and outdoor ranges, including the first clay shooting course in the Gulf region. With simulated game flush shooting, Olympic trap and skeet fields, rifle ranges and a laser shooting simulator, the options are plentiful. Lane rentals start from Dhs.100 and training is available.

Caracal Shooting Club

Armed Forces Officers Club & Hotel Officers Club **02 585 4441**
www.caracal.ae
Map **1 K9**

Caracal has a 25 metre shooting range and a simulator room, so if your day at work has been particularly bad you can relieve a little stress the Wild West way. Entry to the club cost Dhs.130 – you will then have to pay for your bullets.

Jebel Ali International Shooting Club & Centre Of Excellence

Nr Jebel Ali Golf Resort & Spa Dubai
04 883 6555
www.jebelali-international.com

This club has five floodlit clay shooting ranges that consist of skeet, trap and sporting. Professional instructors give comprehensive lessons and experienced shooters are welcome to try their hand at clay shooting or archery. Indoor and outdoor ranges, as well as a specialised pistol range, are available. Non-members are welcome. Refreshments are available and corporate or group activities can be arranged. Prices available on request.

Ras Al Khaimah Shooting Club

Nr RAK Airport Ras Al Khaimah **07 236 3622**

This club welcomes interested parties that want to learn how to shoot, whether it's shotguns or long rifles. The club boasts a 50m indoor and 200m outdoor rifle range, and has a canteen selling snacks and soft drinks. If you ring them you may want to have an Arabic speaker standing by. Otherwise, just drop by the next time you're in RAK.

Singing

Abu Dhabi Choral Group

Al Muna School Al Markaziyah **050 442 0029**
abudhabichoralgroup.com
Map **2 N4**

The largest and longest-running choral group in the capital, ADCG has been active for over three decades. The choir is open to anyone, and annual membership dues are Dhs.100 with rehearsals normally held on Tuesday evenings at Al Muna school in Khalidiyah. The four part harmony choir stages two major performances a year, selecting pieces from popular musicals for a spring production and festive tunes for a series of December concerts.

Blue Fever

Various Locations **050 442 0029**

Passionately belting out love songs and big band hits (in a four to eight part harmony), these jazz and a cappella singers have performed at a range of locations including the Emirates Palace. Contact coordinator and founder Laura Roberts on the number above for more details. Space is limited, so there are friendly auditions.

Men's Barbershop

Various Locations **050 442 0029**

This brand new group sings songs from doo-wop style to traditional barbershop blends in a cappella concerts. This is the first group of its kind in Abu Dhabi. A 'friendly' audition is required and there must be a commitment to attend practices regularly. Call or email for more information.

Voices Of Harmony

Abu Dhabi Authority For Culture & Heritage (ADACH) Al Madina Al Riyadiya **050 442 0029**
Map **1 J7**

This is an all women's barbershop group in Abu Dhabi that sings a cappella style. The group performs at hotel events, fund raisers and dinner parties, as well as at National Day parties for the United States Embassy, ADACH (Abu Dhabi Authority for Culture & Heritage), the Emirates Palace Hotel and the Crowne Plaza. A casual audition is required, as well as a commitment to attend practices regularly.

Skateboarding & Rollerblading

Good fun and great exercise, rollerblading is a sport for all the family. The best places to skate have few people and enough slopes and turns to make it interesting and to improve your balance and skill. The Corniche (p.194) and Breakwater have long paved areas, best when they're not too crowded – the view is a bonus. Although it gets busy in the evenings, the New Corniche (p.197) is another good spot, with views

A racing dhow

across the mangroves. Prepare for the inevitable falls by wearing the necessary safety gear: a helmet and elbow, knee and wrist pads. See p.328 for sportswear stockists. For more serious skaters, there is a skate park opposite the Hilton Baynunah. Skate Arabia (www.skatearabia.com) is an online skating community which posts blogs, information about events being held in the region and photos of enthusiasts. It also occasionally organises competitions and events in Abu Dhabi.

Skiing & Snowboarding

The ski slope at SnowWorld in Marina Mall (p.338) is still under construction and is already years past its opening date so, in the meantime, those wanting to hit the slopes will have to either buy a plane ticket or head to Dubai for their snow fix.

Dubai Ski Club

Ski Dubai Dubai
www.dubaiskiclub.com
Metro **Mall of the Emirates**

The club has over 1,400 members and meets at 18:00 on the last Saturday of every month, next to Ski Dubai's ticket counter, for social skiing or snowboarding, race training and races, followed by apres ski. Membership benefits include a reduced fee for the slope pass and use of the 'advance booking' lane when purchasing tickets, plus special offers on equipment, clothing, accessories and holidays. Membership is Dhs.300.

Ski Dubai

Mall Of The Emirates Dubai **04 409 4000**
www.skidxb.com
Metro **Mall of the Emirates**

The Middle East's first indoor ski resort, Ski Dubai has more than 22,500 square metres of real snow. Competent skiers and boarders can choose between five runs and a freestyle area, skiing and snowboarding lessons are available for beginners, and there is a huge snowpark for the little ones. Slope pass and lesson prices include the hire charge for jackets, trousers, boots, socks, helmets and either skis and poles or a snowboard, but make sure you bring gloves as these are charged for additionally on top of everything else. Freestyle nights are held every other week on Mondays from 20:00 to 23:00.

Skydiving

iFLY Dubai

Mirdif City Centre Dubai **04 231 6292**
www.iflyme.com
Metro **Rashidiya**

With Umm Al Quwain's Aeroclub unfortunately no longer offering skydiving, at least you can get a taste of the adrenalin-soaked sport when in the north at the new iFly in Dubai. Using super strong fans, the experience is realistic and challenging. First flight packages (instruction, gear and two flights) cost Dhs.195.

Spacewalk Indoor Skydiving

Abu Dhabi Country Club Al Mushrif **02 446 3653**
www.spacewalk.ae
Map **2 J13**

Located at the Abu Dhabi Country Club, this is the perfect way to safely experience the thrill of free falling and skydiving without the dare-devil act of jumping out of an airplane. It is safe, fun for the whole family and an exhilarating experience for beginners (ages 3 and up) and those with experience. An Intro Flight ticket costs Dhs.180, with a First Class ticket costing Dhs.290. Your introductory flight includes your training session, use of all flight gear, two one-minute flights (two two-minute flights for First Class), and one-on-one personal assistance from your instructor. You will also learn the basic free fall position. A family package (up to five flyers) costs Dhs.720.

Snooker

Snooker here is a largely informal affair. A number of golf clubs have snooker and billiards facilities available for practising and for friendly competitions, but other than at The Club, there are no formal leagues.

The Club > *p.297*

Al Meena **02 673 1111**
www.the-club.com
Map **2 V3**

The Snooker Section at The Club (p.179) has a snooker room with three full size tables available for members only. Weekly league matches and regular tournaments are played. In addition to The Club membership fees, an additional Dhs.125 annual subscription is required for The Snooker Section. For more information call The Club or see www.abudhabisnooker.com.

Shooters

Danat Al Ain Resort Al Ain **03 768 6686**
www.danathotels.com
Map **4 E2**

Home to four pool tables and a snooker table, available for use by anyone wanting to brush up their skills. Prices are Dhs.30 per table per hour; free if you order drinks. The club aims to be closely associated with other pool and snooker clubs around the country. Refreshments and snacks are available.

Squash

Courts are available for hire through hotel sports and health clubs and private clubs. The squash league at The Club provides the best opportunities for competitive playing and meeting new players,

although Duplays (www.duplays.com) has recently launched its own league at the Officers' Club. Duplays' online noticeboard is also a good place to get in touch with other players looking for a game.

Abu Dhabi Golf Club

Umm Al Nar St Madinat Khalifa A (Khalifa City A)
02 558 8990
www.adgolfclub.com
Map **1 N8**

Squash courts are available here for members' use. Guests of members are charged Dhs.150 for 45 minutes.

The Club > *p.297*

Al Meena **02 673 1111**
www.the-club.com
Map **2 V3**

The Club has an active squash section with social evenings, internal box leagues and, for the more competitive player, representation in the Abu Dhabi Squash League. There is also a junior squash section with regularly organised games, practise sessions and tournaments. You must be a member of The Club (p.179) to play in competitions. Call for more details and timings, or see www.abudhabisquash.com.

Hiltonia Health Club & Spa

Hilton Abu Dhabi Al Khubeirah **02 692 4205**
www.hilton.com
Map **2 C3**

Squash coaching is available at the Hiltonia Health Club & Spa. Prices for a single lesson start at Dhs.115 for members and Dhs.125 for non-members. A discounted package is available if you book a set of 10 lessons: Dhs.1,035 for members and Dhs.1,150 for non-members.

Le Meridien Abu Dhabi

Liwa St, Nr Old Abu Dhabi Co-op Society
Tourist Club Area **02 644 6666**
www.lemeridienabudhabi.com
Map **2 S4**

Le Meridien's squash courts are available to outside guests at Dhs.70 per person per hour during the week and Dhs.90 at weekends. Health club members and hotel guests can use the courts for free. Health club membership starts at Dhs.8,500 per year.

Sheraton Abu Dhabi Hotel & Resort

Corniche Rd Markaziya East **02 677 3333**
www.sheratonabudhabihotel.com
Map **2 Q2**

Squash court hire is Dhs.50 per hour to non-members and non-guests. Individual membership to the healthclub starts at Dhs.7,700 and includes use of the squash courts.

Swimming

Abu Dhabi's location on the Arabian Gulf means easy access to water that's relatively clean and at a pleasant temperature for most of the year. During the hottest months of the summer, the water near the beach is often warmer than a bath. Swimming off the beaches is possible at public beaches (p.212), beach parks (p.213) and private beaches belonging to hotels (p.198). On public beaches, you're advised to be modest in your choice of swimwear and, while bikinis and other swimwear are perfectly acceptable at most hotel pools, beaches and beach parks, be sure to cover up as soon as you leave the beach or pool area.

Don't underestimate the strength of the tides and currents when swimming in the sea. Even off the safest-looking beaches rip tides have been known to carry people out to sea. Also, it's advisable to keep an eye out for jellyfish.

There are no public swimming pools but most hotels have swimming pools that are open for use by the public for a day entrance fee; the Abu Dhabi Marina and Yacht Club also has a pool open to day guests. Entrance charges vary, but range from Dhs.50 to Dhs.100 on weekdays and Dhs.100 to Dhs.200 at weekends and sometimes include beach access if the hotel has a private beach. Swimming lessons are available. Pools are usually cooled for the summer months. Hiltonia Health Club & Spa offers swimming lessons for kids and adults. Prices start from Dhs.120 (members) or Dhs.150 (non-members) for a private lesson, while group lessons are on offer from Dhs. Dhs.270 for a set of four sessions.

Table Tennis

Most beach, health and sports clubs offer at least one table tennis table. Contact the hotels (p.198), and gyms and fitness centres (p.178) for more details.

Tennis

Tennis players are well catered for, with courts available for public use in Abu Dhabi hotels (p.198), or for members only in private clubs. Nearly all courts are floodlit to allow play in the evenings – the coolest time of the day, and about the only time you'll want to play outside in the summer. Prices for hiring courts vary between Dhs.25 and Dhs.50 on weekdays, but you may be charged as much as Dhs.100 at the weekends. Group and individual coaching is widely available.

For those interested in professional tennis, the Mubadala World Tennis Championship (p.29) has become an annual fixture which kickstarts the sporting year. Abu Dhabi's first international tennis championship was held in January 2009 and top players, including Roger Federer and Rafael Nadal, have taken part each year ever since. The event features family attractions as well as a series of tennis-based activities and tournaments during the run-up to the event, including the Community Cup. A month later, Dubai's annual competition, the million dollar Dubai Duty Free Tennis Open, is held at Dubai Tennis Stadium. For further information, see www.dubaitennischampionships.com

Abu Dhabi International Tennis Complex

Zayed Sport City Al Madina Al Riyadiya
www.capitala.ae
Map **1 J8**

Part of Zayed Sports City, the Abu Dhabi International Tennis Complex is home to Abu Dhabi's Mubadala World Tennis Championship each January. The state-of-the-art, Association of Tennis Professionals (ATP) standard tennis facility has six training courts and a centre court with a spectator capacity of 5,000. Family membership is available from Dhs.2,500 and individuals from Dhs.1,200, while court hire starts from Dhs.40 per hour. In addition to the court facilities, members have access to a gym, sauna and steam room for the post-play wind-down.

The Club > *p.297*

Al Meena **02 673 1111**
www.the-club.com
Map **2 V3**

With four floodlit tennis courts and a professional coach available for members at The Club, you're sure to have your backhand perfected in no time. Tennis social evenings and tournaments regularly take place. For those after a more competitive edge, there are annual club championships and teams from The Club are put forward to compete in the Abu Dhabi Tennis League. For more details, call The Club or see www.abudhabitennis.com.

Hiltonia Health Club & Spa

Hilton Abu Dhabi Al Khubeirah **02 692 4205**
www.hilton.com

Tennis coaching is available from Dhs.180 (members) and Dhs.200 (non-members). Ten lessons for two people costs Dhs.1,000 per person (members) and Dhs.1,100 (non-members). Group lessons are also available and all groups will be divided by ability and age into Maxi, Midi and Mini tennis groups.

Triathlon

Abu Dhabi Tri Club

Various Locations
www.abudhabitriclub.org

The Abu Dhabi Triathlon Club is a friendly and active group of swimming, running and cycling enthusiasts who train all year round. In addition to regular training sessions, the members organise and attend competitions and events across the region. There is no formal membership; just show up to the next session.

Emirates Triathlete

Golden Tulip Al Jazira Hotel & Resort Ghantoot
www.emiratestriathlete.com
Map **3 E2**

Picking up from the now defunct Dubai Tri Club, Emirates Triathlete is a hub for the UAE's multisporters and organises monthly sprint distance triathlon races at Golden Tulip Al Jazira (p.201) in Ghantoot throughout the year (with the exception of the most sizzling summer months), which are aimed at absolute beginners as well as the more serious athletes.

Walking

The Corniche

The Corniche is a special place. Nearly seven kilometres long, it is a place where everyone can get away from the city without actually leaving it. The turquoise waters soothe and calm the most harassed city dweller and, in the evening, there's usually a breeze blowing in, bringing welcome respite in hot weather. It's easily the most popular gathering place in the city and is great not only for stretching your legs but also for people-watching. On the city side of the street, there are parks, gardens and play areas, which make for a pleasant walk as well. In the evenings, the parks are busy with families who congregate while the kids let off steam.

Sheikh Khalifa Park

At the opposite end of the island is the huge Sheikh Khalifa Park. The expansive area makes the park a favourite among walkers and, with a miniature train that circles the perimeter, it gets the kids excited as well. There is plenty of other play equipment for the young at heart, with a pool for women and children only. The many trees, pergolas and gazebos offer shade from the hot sun, and the fountains add to the park's pleasant feel. If you want a break from walking, duck into the Heritage and Maritime Museums.

Khalidya Park

Another favourite for families with children, this park boasts lots of grass and space, so is perfect for walks. There's a charge of Dhs.1 in the evenings and on Fridays, but it's worth it for all the play equipment geared to younger children, such as swings, slides, climbing frames, monkey bars and the climbing wall, and areas for football and bike riding.

Al Mushrif Central Park

The recently opened jogging circuit in the park, located off Khaleej Al Arabi St, features a 2.4 kilometre rubberised track, the only one of its kind in the capital. Future expansion of the track will add stations for water coolers, vending machines, and benches. The park as a whole is currently undergoing development;

upon completion, it will have a sculpture garden, petting zoo and a performing arts centre. which wind their way through and around the green spaces, are promised for walkers, joggers and cyclists.

Tourist Club Area

No one in their right mind would recommend this as a place for a quiet stroll, but for sheer street activity it can't be beaten. The sights, sounds and smells lurking on every corner promise something new with every visit to the area. And with hole-in-the-wall restaurants dotted around, there are plenty of places to refuel when you become tired from dodging cars, construction and the endless stream of pedestrians.

Watersports

During cooler months, beaches come alive as people enjoy water-based activities. Most beach hotels offer watersports and there are a handful of special interest groups if you want to take one up on a regular basis. Activities at hotel beach clubs are often discounted to members and guests; day guests will likely have to pay a fee to access the beach, although some hotels offer a special weekend brunch + beach package. Call hotels directly for details, as week and weekend charges vary. For info on canoeing and kayaking, see p.274; for snorkelling and diving, see p.279; for sailing, see p.293; for boating, see p.223.

Abu Dhabi Stand Up Paddling Club

Various Locations **050 905 9743**
www.abudhabisup.com

Stand up paddling, or SUP, is exactly what it sounds like: participants stand on an oversized surfboard and use a paddle to propel the board. Hour-long group lessons are available through the club for Dhs.125 per person, and boards may be rented at the Sheraton and Fairmont hotels. The group is active, with paddle fit lessons on a weekly basis and occasional group paddles through the mangroves. Check the website for details.

Al Forsan International Sports Resort

Nr Abu Dhabi Golf Club & Resort Madinat Khalifa A (Khalifa City A) **02 556 8555**
www.alforsan.com
Map **1 P8**

If you're tired of rinsing the salt out of your hair, Al Forsan is the place to go. Two purpose-built freshwater lakes, one for beginners and the other for experts, offer the only cable system in the Middle East. Wakeboarders, kneeboarders, and waterskiiers are pulled along at speeds of 29-38km/h, the controlled environment allowing for quick progress. When you've fallen one too many times, nurse your wounded pride at the adjacent Beach Bar.

Watersports off Abu Dhabi

Jetski Restrictions

Private jetski owners must now licence their jetskis but you can jetski almost anywhere. It is prohibited around the public beaches, and in the middle of 2010, the Abu Dhabi Coast Guard began to crack down on jetskiers driving recklessly or getting too close to beaches and other boats. There are patrols near Corniche Beach Park that chase away violators getting too close to shore. A good location for launching is Al Bateen Beach (p.212), and jetskiing here is popular. Despite restrictions, there's a lot of water out there to cover, and many hotels, such as the Hilton Abu Dhabi (p.201) rent jetskis for private use.

Beach Rotana Abu Dhabi

Nr Abu Dhabi Mall, Liwa St Tourist Club Area
02 697 9000
www.rotana.com
Map **2 S5**

Offers a good range of watersports, including windsurfing, waterskiing, wakeboarding, banana boat rides and laser dinghies. There's a beach access charge but, if you visit on a weekday for watersports without beach access, the fee is waived. Windsurfing is Dhs.60 per hour, waterskiing costs Dhs.60 for two sessions of 10 minutes each, and a wakeboarding taster costs Dhs.55 for two circuits of around 10 minutes each.

Hiltonia Health Club & Spa

Hilton Abu Dhabi Al Khubeirah **02 692 4205**
www.hilton.com
Map **2 C3**

For non-club members, a day pass will set you back Dhs.150 on a weekday, and Dhs.185 at weekends and holidays. A range of watersports is then available to you; try wakeboarding at Dhs.75 for 20 minutes.

Kite4Fun

Various Locations **050 813 3134**
www.kite4fun.net

Learn kitesurfing with IKO certified instructor Marc Hofrichter, or up to five people can head out on the Kite4Fun Sea Ray for wakeboarding or waterskiing. Prices range from Dhs.300 to Dhs.1,000. Kitesurfing lessons take place at different spots, according to ability levels (beginner or advanced).

Sheraton Abu Dhabi Hotel & Resort

Corniche Rd Markaziya East **02 677 3333**
www.sheratonabudhabihotel.com
Map **2 Q2**

Has a range of beach activities and watersports. High-adrenaline wakeboarding is available for Dhs.70 for 10 minutes; waterskiing is charged at the same rate.

UAE Kitesurfing

Various Locations **050 562 6383**
www.ad-kitesurfing.net

Kitesurfing is a fast-growing sport which has a good UAE following. It's not windsurfing, it's not surfing, it's not wakeboarding, and it's not kite flying, but a fusion of all four. With instructors in both Abu Dhabi and Dubai, UAE Kitesurfing is a group of IKO certified gurus who will get you up and kiteing in no time. Call Jakub at the above number for details.

Wine Tasting

African & Eastern (02 631 2300) and Gray Mackenzie & Partners (02 676 5954) both arrange occasional tastings on an ad hoc basis at various branches around town. To take part in either, you do, however, need to have a liquor licence. Contact them directly to find out when the next sessions take place. MMI (04 424 5000) also has a Wine Society in Dubai – Grapewine members receive monthly newsletters, discounts and invites to tastings and dinners.

Yoga

Yoga is a low-impact (but challenging) form of holistic exercise that has been practised in the East for centuries. It involves holding sequences of poses, or 'asanas' that, combined with breathing exercises, gently but powerfully help your body to become stronger and more flexible, as well as improving mental wellbeing. In addition to the studios below, many health and fitness clubs (p.178) offer yoga as part of their weekly schedule, as do some of Abu Dhabi's alternative therapy centres (p.174) and sports injury specialists (p.176).

It's Yoga Time

If you decide to follow the example of millions of practitioners across the world and sign up for yoga classes, don't forget the first golden rule: punctuality. Rushing in late after a class has started won't win you any points with classmates who are trying to concentrate.

Yoga Tree & Soma Pilates Studios

Villa 405/1, Al Khaleej Al Arabi St & Hazaa Bin Zayed The First Sts Al Bateen **02 667 6579**
www.yogatree.ae
Map **2 G6**

A favourite with local yoga and pilates enthusiasts. Offers group, individual and partner training sessions, pre-natal and natal partner yoga, *Hatha, Kripalu Flow, Ashtanga* and *Vinyasa* practices, children's yoga and belly dancing. Group drop-in classes cost Dhs.60 an hour with a 10 class package priced at Dhs.540. Private classes are available for Dhs.250 per hour. See the website to download the latest schedule.

Shopping in your communit
Supermarket
Restaurants & Cafes
Cinema
Salons & services
Fashion Boutiques
... and more
راحة مول
Al Raha Mal
Shopping in your communit
Al Raha Beach, Dubai - Abu Dhabi Highway, Abu Dhab
Tel: 02 5562229. www.al-rahamall.con
www.ADLINEad.com

Shopping

SHOPPING

Shopping plays a big role in everyday life in this part of the world. The malls are gathering places, especially during the hotter summer months when they offer an oasis of cool in the sweltering city – somewhere to walk, shop, eat and be entertained.

One thing that makes shopping here so appealing is the variety – you can offload Dhs.30,000 on a state-of-the-art watch, or pick up one for Dhs.10 in a supermarket or souk (p.332). You can spend thousands on a designer outfit from one of the top names in fashion, or buy a length of fabric and have a tailor (p.306) make you up your very own creation for next to nothing. You can buy a treasured Arabian antique from days gone by, or a super-modern home entertainment system (p.320).

The variety of goods on sale in the city means there is very little that is not available. For most items there is enough choice to fit any budget, from the fake designer goods in Markaziya East (between Sheikh Khalifa Bin Zayed Street and Sheikh Zayed Second Street), to the shops in the malls that sell the real thing.

You will be amazed at how cosmopolitan the goodies are that are loaded in your shopping trolley. However, like many countries, the cost of living is increasing and while some of what is available is still cheaper than elsewhere, groceries seem to be more expensive every week. You may find that imported items and brands, particularly from the international high-street stores, carry an extra few dirhams to compensate for the cost of importing the goods. If you are an expert bargainer (p.305), you can get better deals at the souks (p.332). And for those items with non-negotiable prices, the trick is to wait for the sales – they happen a few times a year and prices are slashed quite significantly.

Cars are, on the whole, a good buy and petrol, though prices are rising, is still cheap enough to make large 4WDs practical for the school run. Electronics can be cheaper but it depends what you are used to; this region is also a major re-exporter of gold.

One of the few retail sectors where Abu Dhabi is still lacking is second-hand shops (see Second-Hand Items on p.327), although there are a few linked to various charities. With the population still being largely transitory, there is no shortage of second-hand goods, many of which are advertised on the notice boards in supermarkets, in the classified section of newspapers, and on websites (such as www.expatwoman.com).

Shopping hours take some getting used to and a bit of forward planning, especially over Ramadan when almost all shops are closed from noon until about 19:00. However, you can often do your grocery shopping till midnight, and a few of the major supermarkets are even open 24 hours. The malls are particularly busy at the weekends, especially on Friday evenings.

Online Shopping

The online shopping scene in Abu Dhabi is still developing; unlike in some other countries, you won't find a huge catalogue of online fashion stores and you usually can't do your grocery shopping online. There are, however, a few exceptions as more local retailers get on the online bandwagon.

The past few years have seen the birth of online shopping sites such as www.souq.com and www.uaemall.com, which sell items from a number of companies. There's a wide range of products available to buy, but navigation can prove a bit time consuming. In addition, a growing number of independent retailers are setting up an online presence with quick and affordable nationwide delivery. For example, Jacky's Electronics (www.jackys.com) has a fairly comprehensive site with good online deals; Magrudy's website (www.magrudy.com) allows for both buying and reserving books and www.kentessa.com offers gifts for delivery.

There are also sites based in the region that will arrange for gifts to be delivered both here and internationally, for example, www.papagiftexpress.com, which deals with India, Sri Lanka and the UAE.

Quick Reference

Hellwafashion (hellwafashion.com) is an online resource providing information on the clothes on offer in nearby Dubai's independent stores and designer boutiques, and online shopping is also available at designer wear specialist Boutique 1 (www.boutique1.com). For books detailing the best off-road routes in the UAE or Oman or a guide to weekend breaks in the region, visit the online store at www.liveworkexplore.com.

The web is an increasingly good bet to hunt down second-hand items; try sites such as www.dubizzle.com and www.expatwoman.com.

The range of products you can find on international online shopping sites adds to the retail therapy available in Abu Dhabi's many malls and souks. If you shop around, you may be able to find discounted prices, which make online shopping more appealing, particularly for items you can't find locally. More and more international online retailers now deliver to the UAE, so it may make sense to shop around if you are after a special purchase. However, not all companies will ship to the UAE and if they do, the shipping charges can be prohibitive and it may take time for the goods to clear customs.

International credit cards are accepted by most vendors and you should have no problems paying with your UAE card provided international delivery is available. The use of PayPal can often cause problems, but vendors on sites like eBay may be flexible if you explain the situation. Many sites will accept other forms of payment. Sites like Amazon should provide little difficulty, although its branded packaging may be opened at customs. Companies without representation in the region will sometimes agree to sell directly to individual customers, so it is worth sending them an email.

Aramex (see also Shipping p.306) provide a 'Shop & Ship' service which sets up a mailbox in both the UK and US, great for dealing with sites which do not offer international shipping. Borderlinx (www.borderlinx.com) provides a similar service for stores that will only ship to the USA. Aramex also offers a Web Surfer card, a prepaid MasterCard for use online – this can be set up through the mailboxes and is a solution to PayPal problems.

Refunds, Exchanges & Consumer Rights

The policies on refunds and exchanges vary from shop to shop. There is more chance of success with faulty goods rather than if you have simply changed your mind, and it is more common to be offered an exchange or credit note rather than a refund. Even with tags attached, many stores will not even consider an exchange unless you have the receipt. For some items, such as those in sealed packages, shops insist that the packaging should be intact so that the item can be resold. This is ok if the item was unwanted – however, it has been known for claims for faulty goods to be rejected as the packaging has been damaged; but how could you know if it was faulty if you hadn't opened it?

If you are having no success with customer services, ask to speak to the manager, as the person on the shop floor is often not authorised to deviate from standard policy whereas managers may be more flexible.

The Consumer Protection Department of the UAE Ministry of Economy has been established to safeguard the interests of shoppers. The department tracks and regulates retail prices and has rejected planned price increases for staple goods. Consumers wishing to complain about a retailer can complete a form on the website www.adeconomy.ae, send an email to consumer@adeconomy.ae, or call the freephone hotline on 600 522 225. The hotline is manned by non-English speakers so it may be best to stick to other methods. The Abu Dhabi Food Control Authority (02 495 4000, www.adfca.ae) primarily deals with unfit food. The Dubai Government's consumer rights website (www.consumerrights.ae) provides tips and further information on consumer rights.

How To Pay

There are facilities for exchanging or withdrawing money pretty much everywhere there is a chance to spend it. If you need to withdraw cash, ATMs are available all over the country, in banks, malls and some petrol stations. They accept most cards – check your bank card for logos of international organisations like CIRRUS or PLUS, and look out for cash machines bearing the same logos. Credit cards are widely accepted in malls and bigger shops but cash still rules in the souks and local convenience stores. Most international credit cards are accepted, including American Express, Visa, MasterCard and sometimes Diners Club. Discounting the high rates of interest you will have to pay, local banks reward their credit card users with a number of promotions, competitions and discounts. If you want to pay in foreign currency, you'll find that dollars, sterling and GCC currencies are accepted in really big stores like Carrefour and IKEA, but in other shops they may only accept dollars, if anything. For the astute shopper though, the best bargains are secured by using local currency; there are numerous money exchange bureaus in all major shopping areas. Having dirhams in your pocket will make shopping quicker and easier, and can potentially translate into some great discounts for you.

Bargaining

Bargaining is still common practise in the souks and shopping areas of the UAE; you'll need to give it a go to get the best prices. Before you take the plunge, try to get an idea of prices from a few shops, as there can often be a significant difference in prices. Once you've decided how much you are willing to spend, offer an initial bid that is roughly around half that price. Stay laidback and vaguely uninterested. When your initial offer is rejected (and it will be), keep going until you reach an agreement or until you have reached your limit. If the price isn't right, say so and walk out – the vendor will often follow and suggest a compromise price. The more you buy, the better the discount. When the price is agreed, it is considered bad form to back out of the sale.

Bargaining isn't commonly accepted in malls and independent shops. However, use your discretion, as some shops such as jewellery stores, smaller electronics stores and eyewear optical centres do operate a set discount system and the price shown may be 'before discount'. Ask whether there is a discount on the marked price and you may bag a bargain.

Buyer Beware

Traps for the unwary shopper do exist in Abu Dhabi. Some of the international stores sell items that are far more expensive than in their country of origin (you can often even still see the original price tags). Prices can be as much as 30% higher, so beware.

Sending Gifts Home

Sending gifts to your friends and family back home shouldn't be too taxing as there are several online stores that offer international delivery services. For cards and flowers, www.moonpig.com is a great online store where you can customise your own cards by uploading photos and have them sent to a variety of locations. Interflora (www.interflora.co.uk) also delivers a selection of gifts internationally and can often accommodate same day or next day delivery.

Shoes & Clothing Sizes

Figuring out your size isn't rocket science, just a bit of a pain. Firstly, check the label – international sizes are often printed on them. Secondly, check the store – they will often have a conversion chart on display. Otherwise, a UK size is always two higher than a US size (so a UK 10 is a US 6). To convert European sizes into US sizes, subtract 32 (so a European 38 is actually a US 6). To convert European sizes into UK sizes, a 38 is roughly a 10. As for shoes, a woman's UK 6 is a European 39 or US 8.5 and a men's UK 10 is a European 44 or a US 10.5. If in doubt, ask for help.

Sizing

Clothing sizes in Abu Dhabi's stores usually range from a UK 8 to 16. Petite ranges are available in many stores including Debenhams (p.329) and Marks & Spencer (p.329). For plus-size clothing you can head to H&M, New Look, Wallis, Bhs, Liz Claiborne, Debenhams (p.329), Marks & Spencer and Splash (look out for Evans in Debenhams and Scarlett's in Splash). For more exclusive lines for the fuller figure, head to Dubai for Oui (04 324 2167) or Charisma (04 324 0200) in The Beach Centre in Jumeira.

Men looking for larger sizes should head to Big & Tall (02 681 6703) in Marina Mall which caters for waist sizes from 40 plus and shirts up to 6XL.

Repairs & Cobbling

Abu Dhabi's multitude of tailors will repair or alter garments for a reasonable price, but there are fewer companies who mend shoes. Minutes (02 681 6380) in Marina Mall also offer shoe repairs as well as their key cutting service. You can also try Clogs Shoe Repair (02 626 2750) on Hamdan Street or Jeeves (02 666 3755) in Abela Supermarket (p.330).

Shipping

Due to the number of international and local shipping and courier agencies, it is possible to transport just about anything. Both air freight and sea freight are available; air freight is faster and you can track the items, but it's more expensive and not really suitable for large or heavy objects. Sea freight takes several weeks to arrive but it is cheaper and you can rent containers for larger items. It is worth getting a few quotes and finding out what will happen when the goods arrive; some offer no services at the destination while others, usually the bigger ones, will clear customs and deliver right to the door. Empost (600 565 555), the Emirates Postal Service, offers both local and international courier and air freight services – its prices are competitive and packages can be tracked.

Several courier companies can arrange for items to be delivered to Abu Dhabi, and Aramex (02 555 1911) offers a great service called 'Shop & Ship', for those wishing to buy online. If a site doesn't offer international delivery or their postage rates are high, for a one-off payment of $35, Aramex will set up a mailbox for you in both the UK and the US. The company will then arrange deliveries up to three times a week and packages can be tracked; the rates are calculated by the total weight of your packages.

Tailoring & Bespoke Services

There are numerous tailors in Abu Dhabi and most operate from small shops tucked away down side streets. The cost of fabric and workmanship is comparatively cheap, and having a shirt, suit, summer dress or even wedding dress custom made can be a surprisingly affordable option. Tailors can copy a pattern, a garment, or even a photograph, and any good service will include at least one fitting before the garment is finished. Standards of workmanship vary, so ask around to get recommendations of good tailors. In addition, different tailors specialise in different styles of garment, such as saris, abayas, western-style clothes, suits and wedding dresses, so while most tailors will tell you that they can stitch anything you need, you're more likely to be happy with the results if you go to one that can demonstrate their experience in that style.

Agree on the price of the item before the tailor starts work. When the garment is finished, you will be able to try it on and have minor adjustments made if necessary.

Personal recommendations are the best way to find a trusted tailor, but Sposa Haute Couture (02 622 1768) or Joury Tailors (02 631 7323) are good places to start. See Textiles & Haberdashery on p.328 for places to buy fabric.

WHAT & WHERE TO BUY

With so much choice there should be little problem finding what you need. From antiques to the latest technology, and from tools to toys, the aim of this section is to let you know what is available in Abu Dhabi and the best places to buy it.

Alcohol

It is legal for anyone over the age of 21 to buy alcohol in Abu Dhabi's licensed restaurants and bars, and some clubs, for consumption on the premises. If you wish to drink at home you will need a liquor licence (see p.44 for more information). While it is relatively easy to get your licence, there are certain limits – Muslims, for example, are not permitted to apply, and the amount of alcohol you are allowed to buy is dependent on your monthly salary.

Four companies operate liquor stores in Abu Dhabi. All have several branches in the city, the most handy being the ones near supermarkets. Visit the websites on the right for details of locations. Generally speaking, the selection is decent but certain brands are offered exclusively in certain stores, so it is worth looking around if you are after something specific, or something a little different. Unlike in Abu Dhabi's neighbouring emirate Dubai, where a 30% tax is added at the till, no tax is added in Abu Dhabi – the price you see on the shelf is exactly what you end up forking out at the till. There is also a good selection of alcohol (and several other products including perfume, confectionary and cosmetics) available at the airport Duty Free.

There are a number of 'hole in the wall' stores in the northern Emirates that sell duty-free alcohol to members of the public, even if you don't have a licence. Prices are reasonable and there is no tax. There is a large store within the Barracuda Beach Resort (06 768 1555, www.barracuda.ae), next to Dreamland Aqua Park in Umm Al Quwain (p.253), and also Al Hamra Cellar in Ras Al Khaimah (www.mmidubai.com) is another. You don't need to worry about being busted buying booze illegally, but you should be careful when driving home, because it is the transporting of alcohol that could get you into trouble, especially if you are stopped within the borders of Sharjah emirate, which is completely dry. There have been reports of random police checks on vehicles driving from Ajman into Sharjah. Also, if you have an accident and you're found to have a boot full of liquor, your day could take a sudden turn for the worse.

African & Eastern (A&E) > ***p.309*** Sheikh Zayed First Street, Al Khalidiyah, 02 667 6808, *www.africaneastern.net*
Gray Mackenzie Partners Nr Mitsubishi Showroom, Baniyas St, Al Baladia, 02 671 4400, *www.admmi.com*
High Spirits Nr Carrefour, Off Mussafah Rd, Al Madina Al Riyadiya, 02 444 9821, *www.highspirits-adnh.com*
Spinneys Liquor Nr Khalidiyah Public Gardens, Al Khubeirah, 02 681 2356, *www.spinneysonline.com*

Art

Abu Dhabi is not well known historically for its galleries and exhibitions, but the capital's art scene is on the verge of new realms of cultural diversity with branches of the Louvre and Guggenheim due to open by 2013, and the industry is enjoying steady growth in preparation. Most of the galleries in Abu Dhabi display traditional and contemporary art by Arabic and international artists, and many of the works are for sale.

At the higher end of the spectrum is Gallery One (p.210), at Emirates Palace, which hosts art fairs throughout the year showcasing modern and contemporary art from all over the world. Emirates Palace is also home to The Barakat Gallery (p.210) which has branches in London and Los Angeles, and specialises in ancient art. On display are antiquities from China, Egypt, the Near East, Africa and ancient Greece and Rome. Every item on display in the cabinets is also for sale.

The Emirates Palace is something of an arts hub and, in November, it's the venue for Abu Dhabi Art (p.29) – an innovative new platform for modern and contemporary art from the four corners of the globe. It's also a great opportunity to snap up a bargain or something truly original. Acento Gallery (p.210) specialises in Mexican and Spanish art, but also displays works by artists from other parts of the world. Salwa Zeidan Gallery (p.210) showcases a varied range of art by international and Middle Eastern contemporary artists; in addition to paintings, photography and sculpture art, the gallery occasionally houses installations and performance art.

For more traditional, and affordable, art, craft and gift items from the Arab World, check out the Folklore Gallery (p.210) in Khalidiya which sells prints and paintings inspired by the UAE landscape, as well as traditional Bedouin jewellery, ceramics and a picture framing service. Falcon Gallery (02 634 4375) in Fotouh Al Khair shopping centre sells kitsch oil paintings and prints, alongside its stock of elaborate home furnishings. If it's framing that you're after, you can also head for Posters in the Tourist Club Area (02 672 4724) or Al Wahda Mall (02 443 7089).

Art & Craft Supplies

A number of shops sell a good range of art and craft supplies and you should find there is enough choice, whether you need paints and crayons for children or top quality oils. Particularly good places to find materials are All Prints in Khalidiya (02 633 6999) and United Bookstore in Mina Zayed (02 673 3999), both of which stock an extensive range of stationery, arts and craft supplies for all ages, in addition to related specialist and educational books.

The Tourist Club branch of Posters (02 672 4724) also offers a limited range of painting and watercolour supplies, as well as a picture framing service. Magrudy's (p.314) in Al Wahda Mall sells stationery items, as well as knitting needles and wool, and a few haberdashery items. For more specialist artist materials, check out Green Branch on Sheikh Zayed the Second Street (02 621 4507), Folklore Gallery (p.210) and Artists Material Suppliers in the Mohamed Al Makhawi Establishment (02 644 3141).

Baby Items

The basic baby items are all available in Abu Dhabi and, while you may not find the range you would back home, you should find nursery essentials, like bottles, buggies, car seats, changing bags, cots, prams, rocking chairs and travel cots. Supermarkets stock formula, nappies and wipes and many also sell bottles and feeding equipment. If you can't find an item, check with the store because some are kept behind the counter. A good range of jars of baby food are available but prices are slightly higher than you'd pay at home. Pharmacies sell baby essentials and some have breast pumps.

For bigger baby items, such as pushchairs and car seats, try Mamas & Papas, Mothercare or Toys R Us (p.322). The quality of the items is good and most conform to international safety standards. Various brands of car seats are available and should fit most cars; all shops will offer to help fit car seats but the staff aren't always knowledgeable about what is most suitable. You can also rent car seats, buggies, strollers and other equipment from Dubai-based Rentacrib (www.rentacrib.ae) – if you hire a car seat its staff will fit it for you free of charge. Call 050 253 2535 to find out delivery options for Abu Dhabi.

The range of slings on sale is pretty limited and backpacks to put your baby in are hard to find, so you may want to order these items from overseas or look online at Bubs Boutique (www.bubsboutique.com) or BabySouk.com (www.babysouk.com).

When it comes to clothing, there are several stores to choose from. Abu Dhabi Mall (p.334) has the widest range of well-known stores, offering brands such as Mothercare, Adams and Bossini. Online store DubaiBabies (www.dubaibabies.com) also stocks a fabulous range of products for babies and parents, and delivers to Abu Dhabi for a nominal fee. IKEA (p.318) has nursery furniture such as cots, changing tables and bathtubs. It also makes cot sheets and blankets and some baby-safe toys. Worth waiting for are Babyshop's sales which occur several times a year. For more information on having a baby, see p.131.

Babyshop

Marina Mall Breakwater **02 681 8894**
www.babyshopstores.com
Map **2 D1**

Babyshop sells low-cost baby clothing and essentials; pick up feeding items, clothing, toys and even baby monitors here. It also stocks feeding pillows, safety rails and sterilisers. Its affordable newborn items come in value packs, perfect for the temporary items you can't live without, but know you won't keep. Other locations are on Sheikh Zayed Bin Saeed Al Maktoum Road (02 634 7012), Tourist Club Area (02 644 7739) and in Madinat Zayed (02 884 0438).

Dubai Babies

Dubai **050 600 3199**
www.dubaibabies.com
Map **3 E2**

You can shop at your leisure at this online boutique selling blankets, feeding essentials, slings and skincare products, among other items. The store also offers a good selection of gifts that are perfect for baby showers, such as cupcakes, gift baskets, balloons and books for new parents.

Just Kidding

Gold & Diamond Park Dubai **04 341 3922**
www.justkidding-uae.com
Map **3 E2** Metro **First Gulf Bank**

Not for the budget conscious, but still worth a browse, Just Kidding sells a good range of baby items, furniture and clothes from Europe, including Bugaboo buggies, Little Company bags and Stokke high chairs. You'll find interesting toys for playtime and a catalogue of items that includes maternity wear, gift sets and slings. The store is located in Al Quoz in Dubai, but you can also shop online and have your items delivered. The store also offers an online gift registry service for baby showers.

Top 10 Things That Are Cheaper In Abu Dhabi

Eating Out

Enjoying a three-course dinner and a few rounds of drinks in a fine-dining restaurant will probably cost more-or-less the same as in other cities, but cheap, street-side dining is one of Abu Dhabi's great bargains. Whether you snack on a Dhs.3 chicken shawarma in the Tourist Club Area, or feast on a Thali lunch (refillable pots of yummy vegetarian curry) from one of Hamdan Street's many great curry houses, it's hard to find such delicious, authentic food at a cheaper price.

Home Help

Having a cleaner come in a few times a week to hoover and dust would be an unaffordable luxury for most people living in the UK, but here in Abu Dhabi it is as normal as eating breakfast in the morning. For as little as Dhs.20 per hour, you can get a maid service in to do all the stuff you're too busy – or too lazy – to do. Frazzled parents can also rejoice at the bargain babysitters' rates available in Abu Dhabi. Call Abu Dhabi Maids for more info (p.99).

Personal Grooming

Having pretty hands and feet comes cheap in Abu Dhabi, where there is seemingly a nail salon on every street corner, and you'll pay as little as Dhs.70 for a manicure and pedicure. Even the boys aren't left out: gents can enjoy a shampoo, a hot oil treatment, a haircut, a shave and a head massage all for around Dhs.40 at your typical city centre men's salon.

Cigarettes

That Dhs.9 pack of Marlboro Lights would set you back the equivalent of over Dhs.30 in the UK, around Dhs.15 in the USA, and Dhs.25 in Australia. It's good news for visiting relatives, who always want to take back a few sneaky cartons, and bad news for smokers, who have little financial incentive to quit here; but at least you don't have to charge your friends every time they pinch a smoke off you.

Taxis

In many of our home countries, a night on the tiles would involve an elaborate plan to recruit a designated driver, or a lengthy wait in a queue for a taxi. Here in Abu Dhabi, walking out of a restaurant or club to find a line of cabs ready and waiting to take you home, at a very reasonable price, never gets old. And just when you thought it couldn't get any better, a whole new fleet of taxis have been put on the roads, to make sure you never have to wait too long.

Soft Drinks

Seemingly, since the beginning of time, a can of Coke or Pepsi cost just one little dirham in a cornershop, a petrol station or a supermarket. The price per can was even cheaper when you bought your favourite fizzy drink by the case. Recently, inflation caught up with the soft drinks industry and a can now costs Dhs.1.50. It's still a bargain by international standards but, unfortunately, the price doesn't always survive the transition to restaurant menus, where that same drink can set you back a shocking Dhs.15 or more. That's quite a mark-up.

Petrol

Although the price of petrol has been increased in the UAE of late, filling up the tank here is cheaper than in many other countries, and often significantly so. For a litre of petrol you'll pay around Dhs.1.70 at an Abu Dhabi pump. As a rule of thumb, to fill a tank it costs roughly one fourth of what you'd pay in parts of Europe; a third of that in Australia or India, and about half of the price in America.

Cinema Tickets

You'll pay between Dhs.30 and Dhs.40 for a cinema ticket in Abu Dhabi (Dhs.40 is becoming standard if you opt for a 3D performance). A ticket will set you back around Dhs.50 in London, Dhs.45 in New York, Dhs.45 in Dublin and Dhs.67 in Tokyo. The downside is that here in Abu Dhabi there are no concessions if you are a child, a student or a pensioner, and the ticket price is the same, no matter what time of day it is (whereas in other cities, morning and matinee shows are cheaper).

Tailoring

Having a tailor whip up a made-to-measure piece of clothing is prohibitively expensive in cities such as London, where a simple shift dress could cost you as much as Dhs.1,000 and you'll need at least Dhs.5,000 for a bespoke suit. In Abu Dhabi, however, there are tailors who can whip up a long dress for around Dhs.100, a blouse for Dhs.50, and a suit starting from as little as Dhs.1,600.

Trips To Oman

It's fast becoming one of the most popular Middle Eastern destinations for tourists from Europe, and it's not hard to understand why. Oman is a breathtaking country combining scenery, culture and luxury hotels. And it's just a one-hour flight or a five-hour drive to Muscat from Abu Dhabi. For more information see Out Of The City, p.233.

Mamas & Papas

Marina Mall Breakwater **02 681 6689**
www.mamasandpapas.com
Map **2 D1**

This store has become a household name for providing well-designed, stylish products for babies and mums-to-be. A good variety of items are on offer including toys, car seats, pushchairs, cribs, nursery items and decorations, maternity clothes and feeding items. Although this is one of the more costly options, it remains a popular spot for gifts and newborn essentials. Another branch is located in Al Wahda Mall (02 443 7273).

Mothercare

Abu Dhabi Mall Tourist Club Area **02 645 4894**
www.mothercare.com
Map **2 S5**

Mothercare is a long-established store which remains a reliable place to shop for baby essentials. It has a particularly good selection of clothes and many of its larger stores stock cots, prams and car seats. You can order mattresses in specific sizes, and items you've seen online or in a UK catalogue can also be ordered, but the delivery time is a minimum of four weeks and often longer. There are other branches on Hamdan Street (02 621 9700), in Al Muroor (02 449 8115), at Marina Mall (02 681 1781) and at Al Wahda Mall (02 443 7252).

Bicycles

There aren't a lot of bike shops in Abu Dhabi for serious cyclists, but things have got a lot better in the last few years. Studio R (02 681 7676) in Marina Mall has a concession for the excellent Specialized bikes, clothing and accessories, while Tamreen Sports (02 622 2525) stocks Cannondale, GT, Mongoose and Schwinn. For the BMX biker, a branch of Rage opened in Al Wahda Mall (02 443 7617) in 2010. Alternatively, head out to Dubai where Wolfi's Bike Shop (04 339 4453) stocks the likes of Kona, Giant, Santa Cruz, Scott, Felt, Merida and Storck; there's also a Trek shop (04 323 7966) in the Gold & Diamond Park. The internet based Probike (www.probike.ae) is the official UAE importer of Planet X and Ridley brands, with prices often little more expensive than they are in the UK or USA.

For the casual cyclist, various sports shops (p.328) sell more basic models at reasonable prices, while fans of something a little different can check out the eccentric vintage bike selection at Middle East Bicycle Trading (050 541 5170) on Post Office Road in Madinat Zayed. Children's bicycles are widely available in bike and sports shops, and shops like Babyshop (p.308) and Toys R Us (p.322) have a range for tiny Lance Armstrong wannabes, as do some supermarkets, such as Carrefour (p.330). Both adults' and children's helmets are available at the main retailers. Supermarket noticeboards and online classifieds, such as www.dubizzle.com, are good places to look for second-hand bikes.

Books

You'll find both international bookstores and good local bookstores in Abu Dhabi which stock a decent selection of international books and magazines. Virgin Megastore (02 644 7882) carries an interesting selection of books related to music and popular culture. Magrudys, Jashanmal Bookstore and United Bookstore have a wide selection of English language books, covering everything from popular fiction and self-help to classics, autobiographies, guide books and photography books. United Bookstore also happens to have one of the best arts and crafts selections in town; it stocks stationery and office supplies, computers and accessories, school supplies, magazines, party goods, gifts and a very good selection of greetings cards. You will also find a small selection of books in larger supermarkets like Carrefour (p.330), Abela Supermarket (p.330) and Abu Dhabi Co-operative Society (p.330).

If you cannot find a publication, the larger stores often have customer service sections where you can search for titles, place an order or enquire whether it is available in another branch. Most shops are happy to order the title for you if you are not in a last minute

Explorer products

rush. Otherwise, popular online store Amazon delivers to the UAE – it's usually better to order from the UK site (www.amazon.co.uk) than the US site (www.amazon.com), so that you can take advantage of cheaper delivery rates. Unless you choose the super-expensive express delivery, it will take around two weeks to receive your order and your package may be inspected by UAE customs.

For second hand books, try St Andrews Thrift Centre (02 446 4193) or look out for carboot and yard sales advertised on supermarket noticeboards and in online classifieds. Alternatively, House of Prose stocks a wide selection of used books at its new store in the Dubai Garden Centre (04 344 9021).

Become An Explorer

If you've found this book useful, pick up some of Explorer's other popular titles. Find out more about the region with the *Mini Visitors' Guides* to cities such as Dubai, Muscat and Doha. Get adventurous with off-road guides to the UAE and Oman, *UAE Yachting & Boating*, or *UAE Underwater*. Or get a souvenir of your time in the UAE with a photography book like *Impressions of Abu Dhabi*.

Book Corner Marina Mall, Breakwater, 02 681 7662, *www.bookcorner.ae*
Booksplus Khalidiyah Mall, Al Khalidiyah, 02 635 4944, *www.appareluae.com*
Isam Bookshop & Stationery Sheikh Zayed First Street, Markaziya East, 02 634 3557
Jashanmal Bookstore > *p.313* Abu Dhabi Mall, 02 644 3869, *www.jashanmalgroup.com*
Magrudy's Al Wahda Mall, Al Dhafrah, 02 443 7172, *www.magrudy.com*
United Bookstore Mina Centre, Al Meena, 02 673 3999, *www.jarirbookstore.com*

Camera Equipment

Both amateur and serious photographers will be able to find most of what they need on the shelves in Abu Dhabi. Prices from agents are usually fixed but quite reasonable, although it is still a good idea to shop around before you buy, as many famous brands can be found in smaller shops where the price is negotiable. Asking for added extras, such as free memory cards, camera cases or print vouchers, can add extra value to your purchase. However, watch out for parallel (or grey) imports – these products are not counterfeit but they have been imported from another country where they are cheaper, so that dealers can increase profits or undercut the competition. The problem arises if the item is faulty, because you won't have a valid warranty. Similarly, if you are buying the camera to take to another country, ensure that the warranty is international: don't just take the retailer's word for it, ask to open the box and read the warranty to make sure. Make sure the warranty is stamped and dated upon purchase. Opinion is divided as to whether it's cheaper to buy cameras in the UAE than elsewhere. Due to low import costs, cameras here are less expensive than in the UK for instance, but that doesn't mean that the UAE is the cheapest place in the world – Hong Kong and Singapore are both cheaper, if you know what you are looking for. It's always worth waiting for the sales to begin before splashing out on big ticket items such as SLR cameras. Don't be afraid to ask the staff — some camera and electronics store sales staff will happily tell you when the next sale is coming up, and a few weeks' wait can save you big bucks on the same item.

For specialist equipment and a good range of film cameras, the main outlets are Grand Stores, Salam and National Store. Grand Stores sells Fuji, Nikon, Canon and Mamiya; Salam Studio carries Bronica, Leica, Minolta and Pentax, and National Store stocks Canon, Lexar, Petra, Karcher, Moser, and Westinghouse products. They all sell a selection of filters, tripods and studio equipment. The alternative to buying locally is to use an online retailer. B&H Photo (www.bandhphoto.com) and Adorama (www.adorama.com), in New York, are extremely popular.

For compact, point-and-shoot cameras, basic model SLRs, video cameras and home printers, you should find a decent selection of competitively priced items at electrical stores like Plug-Ins (p.321), Jumbo Electronics (p.321), and at hypermarkets like Carrefour (p.330).

For second-hand photography equipment, www.gulfphotoplus.com has an active equipment noticeboard (as well as being a great source of information and a good networking site for locally based photography enthusiasts, with information on everything from photography tips to training courses and shooting trips in the vicinity).

Should your equipment need to be repaired, Grand Stores offers a repair service. Film and disposable cameras are readily available in supermarkets, local shops and hotel foyer shops, and there are plenty of outlets such as United Colour Film (02 677 1967, www.ucfq.com), in the Tourist Club Area, that can develop films for you.

Grand Stores

Abu Dhabi Mall Tourist Club Area **02 645 1115**
www.grandstores.com
Map **2 S5**

This is the main retailer for Nikon cameras in Abu Dhabi. The store also stocks Fuji, Canon and Mamiya too and you can also have you camera cleaned and repaired in its stores. Also at Marina Mall (02 681 7817) and in Al Khalidiyah (02 631 2100).

National Store

Omeir Travel Agency Bldg, Sheikh Khalifa Bin Zayed St Markaziya East **02 622 2437**
www.jk.ae
Map **2 N3**

This store is a distributor of Canon, Lexar, Petra, Karcher, Moser, and Westinghouse products and you'll find a good selection of cameras, printers and camera accessories in store.

Salam

Abu Dhabi Mall Tourist Club Area **02 645 6999**
www.salams.com
Map **2 S5**

Salam stocks a complete range of professional-grade camera and studio equipment, including a good selection of filters and tripods. It carries Bronica, Leica, Minolita and Pentax. Also in Al Ain Mall (03 751 5000).

Car Accessories

Cars and their accessories are big business in Abu Dhabi, so you won't struggle to find the accessories you need. ACE (p.323) and Carrefour (p.330) have large departments selling everything from steering wheel covers to fridges which run off the car battery. Near the intersection of Al Salam and Al Falah streets you'll find a number of small workshops where you can buy accessories such as alloys, window tints and custom seat covers and you can get them all fitted there too. It's worth taking a drive to Yellow Hat (04 341 8592) in Times Square in Dubai for a fantastic range of products from spare parts and in-car technology, to imported, custom-made alloys and under car lighting. GPS systems are available from major stores such as Plug-Ins (p.321), Sharaf DG (p.321) and Jumbo Electronics (p.321), plus other big retailers such as Carrefour (p.330) and ACE (p.323). Car stereos are widely available, and are sold by most electronics shops, with some of the car dealerships stocking alternative models for their cars. To have them fitted, head either to a dealer, service centre or to the workshops around Al Salam and Al Falah – it should cost around Dhs.500 if you are providing all the parts.

Many car owners try to beat the heat by having their car windows tinted. The legal limit is 30% tint; if you get your windows tinted any darker you could be fined, and your car won't pass its annual inspection. The options range from the Dhs.75 plastic film from the workshops around Al Salam and Al Falah, up to Dhs.5,000 at V-Kool (02 443 5333), which is also covered by a warranty, and its clear film is more heat resistant than the tinted one.

If you are just looking for some memorabilia, or if you simply love fast cars, head out to Ferrari World (p.217).

Carpets

Carpets are one of the region's signature items. The ones on sale here tend to be imported from Iran, Turkey, Pakistan and Central Asia. Carpets vary in price depending on a number of factors such as its origin, the material used, the number of knots, and whether or not it is handmade. The most expensive carpets are usually those hand-made with silk, in Iran.

Inspect carpets by turning them over – if the pattern is clear on the back and the knots are all neat, the carpet is of higher quality than those that are indistinct. Do some research, so you have a basic idea of what you are looking for before you go, just in case you happen to meet an unscrupulous carpet dealer who could take advantage of your naivety. Fortunately, crooked carpet conmen are rare, and most will happily explain the differences between the rugs and share their extensive knowledge. If you ask the dealer, you can often garner some interesting

Traditional carpets

information about the carpets and where they were made – for example some carpets have family names sewn into the designs.

The Carpet Souk at the Port end of Meena Road is the most obvious place to start; Meena Souk (also known as Afghan Souk) is similarly well stocked. However, if you prefer a more genteel way of purchasing your carpet, a number of the malls have well-stocked carpet shops. For instance, Gulf Antiques & Carpets (02 645 9956) and Handmade Carpet House & Antiques (02 644 3444), both located in the Tourist Club's Khalifa Centre, are a good place to start your carpet hunt. They're less crowded and pushy than the myriad vendors at the Carpet Souk. Most places will not deliver, so it is best to purchase them one at a time.

Ask to see a variety of carpets so that you can get a feel for the differences between hand-made or machine-made, silk, wool or blend carpets. Of course, asking may not be necessary, since vendors will undoubtedly start unrolling carpets before you at a furious pace.

Carpets range in price from a few hundred dirhams to tens of thousands. It is always worth bargaining; make sure the seller knows you are not a tourist, and remain polite at all times to maximise the success of your haggling.

If you happen to venture further out, the road to Hatta (p.244) is lined with stalls selling carpets and the Friday Market in Fujairah is also a good place to pick them up. The Blue Souk in Sharjah has a great range too.

Mall of the Emirates and The Dubai Mall have a good selection of shops selling traditional carpets; just bear in mind that prices may be steeper here.

For something practical rather than decorative, IKEA (p.318) is always a safe bet, or try Carrefour (p.330) and THE One (02 644 8100).

Computers

You should have few problems submerging yourself in the latest technology here – whether it's hardware or software, numerous outlets sell up-to-the-minute merchandise. The major electronics stores, including Jumbo (p.321), Sharaf DG (p.321) and Plug-Ins (p.321) all sell computer hardware and software, and EMax (02 674 4937) on Hamdan Street is particularly good for gamers. You will even find a small selection of computers at Carrefour (02 681 7100). The market is dominated by PCs, but Macs are available from iSTYLE (www.istyle.ae) in Abu Dhabi Mall (02 644 4934) and Marina Mall (02 681 9161). The UAE government, together with the Business Software Alliance is clamping down heavily on the sale of pirated software. As a result, most computer shops are reputable and offer the usual international guarantees.

If you are really serious about computers and the latest technology, it's worth driving to Dubai to check out GITEX (www.gitex.com). Each year, usually during October, the Dubai World Trade Centre houses this exhibition and a broad range of computer companies participate. There's also a GITEX Shopper held at the Airport Expo in Dubai, so when you've cruised the stands and decided which latest gizmo you can't live without, you can pop along and buy it, with a good discount.

Fashion

From Bhs to Benetton, and Mango to Marchesa, Abu Dhabi has clothes shopping covered. Upmarket designer stores are usually found in shopping malls and hotels. If your budget doesn't stretch to thousand-dollar threads, department stores like Next (02 443 7033), Marks & Spencer (p.329) and Woolworths (p.330) will probably be your hunting ground. In addition, the new branches of H&M (02 671 8799) and Desigual (02 671 9975) in Abu Dhabi Mall certainly caused ripples among the budget-minded fashionistas of late. And if you're on a really tight budget, you can sometimes find some excellent bargains in the souks (p.332). Hypermarkets such as Carrefour (p.330) are another option, or you could try your luck at affordable boutiques like Splash (02 644 5565) and Forever 21 (02 681 8118).

There is a good range of international high street brands including Topshop (02 681 8242), Banana Republic (Al Wahda Mall, 02 443 7006) and Gap (Marina Mall, 02 681 1255).

For something that stands out of the crowd, boutiques (p.331) like S*uce (p.331), Ounass (p.331) and Grafika (02 443 7111, www.grafikauae.com) step away from the mainstream selections and offer trendy togs from up-and-coming designers.

High street fashion

If you love designers but not the price tags, browse the selection online at www.mapochette.com. The online store stocks designer bags from Miu Miu, Versace and Prada, and offers a rental service which will deliver one of its designer bags straight to your door.

Of course, most of the shops loved by women also have excellent men's sections, such as Debenhams (p.329), Marks & Spencer (p.329), Next (02 443 7033), or Zara in Marina Mall (02 681 8080).

When it comes to shoes, the choice is enormous. Designer labels like Jimmy Choo (sold at Ounass, p.331) and Gucci (Marina Mall, 02 681 6844) mingle with middle-of-the-range creations from the likes of Aldo (02 644 4058), while cheap-as-chips flip-flops and sandals are sold in the big hypermarkets. For stylish shoes on a budget try Shoe Mart (02 644 9543) which carries fashionable and practical shoes.

Most malls have a good selection of quality clothing outlets and there is an increasing trend towards international brands that sell the same items the world over, changing their stock every four to six weeks. Handily, most of these shops also show the retail price in each country on the tag, so it can be quite satisfying to know that you are paying no more than your friends back home (although some stores do charge slightly inflated prices compared to your home country). Mass summer sales generally take place around August or September, and there are more in January when stores get rid of the old and bring in the new. During the January sales in particular, the offers here can be amazing. The Eid sales, around the end of Ramadan, are like the January sales back home – busy and intense, but well worth it if you're an avid bargain hunter unafraid of equally fervent fellow shoppers.

Fashion – Shoes

AK Anne Klein Abu Dhabi Mall, Tourist Club Area, 02 644 4710, *www.anneklein.com*
Aldo Abu Dhabi Mall, Tourist Club Area, 02 644 4058, *www.aldoshoes.com*
Bata Marina Mall, Breakwater, 02 681 6834, *www.bata.com*
Cesare Paciotti Marina Mall, Breakwater, 02 681 3900, *www.tfgroup.ae*
Charles & Keith Abu Dhabi Mall, Tourist Club Area, 02 645 6240, *www.charleskeith.com*
Clarks Marina Mall, Breakwater, 02 681 5717, *www.clarks.com*
Dumond Al Wahda Mall, Al Dhafrah, 02 443 7497, *www.dumond.com.br*
Dune Abu Dhabi Mall, Tourist Club Area, 02 645 0315, *www.dune.co.uk*
Ecco Marina Mall, Breakwater, 02 681 7120, *www.ecco.com*
Hush Puppies Al Wahda Mall, Al Dhafrah, 02 443 7447, *www.hushpuppies.com*
K Corner Khalidiyah Mall, Al Khalidiyah, 02 635 4418, *www.kcornershoes.com*
Nine West Abu Dhabi Mall, Tourist Club Area, 02 645 6880, *www.ninewest.com*
Paris Hilton Marina Mall, Breakwater, 02 681 4993
Shoe Mart Abu Dhabi Cooperative Society Bldg, Al Baladia, 02 644 9543, *www.shoemartgulf.com*
Spring Abu Dhabi Mall, Tourist Club Area, 02 645 1297, *www.myspringshoes.com*
Tod's Marina Mall, Breakwater, 02 681 6562, *www.tods.com*

Furniture

This is one of Abu Dhabi's most buoyant retail sectors, perhaps because of the wide variety of villas and apartments all in need of furnishing. Most tastes are catered for, from ethnic pieces to the latest designer concepts and specialist children's furniture stores.

Some of the more popular furniture shops sell just about everything you need to furnish your entire home under one roof (the only thing they don't sell is electrical appliances). Fans of IKEA (p.318) will love the brand new store on Yas Island. At 33,000 square metres, it's the largest in the Emirates. IKEA is famous around the world for its basic (but attractive) designs, low prices and huge range – the only downside is that you have to assemble it all yourself. However, they do offer a home delivery and assembly service at a nominal rate (and it's free if you spend over Dhs.2,500).

Other large furniture shops specialise in different styles: 2XL Furniture & Home Décor (02 673 3008, www.2xlme.com) is middle-of-the-range as far as prices go, whereas Home Centre (p.318) and Homes r Us (02 631 2020) both stock some lovely furniture at bargain prices. Zara Home's (02 681 5560, www.zarahome.com) fresh, European designs are available in Marina Mall, or try the stylish range of contemporary furniture at Natuzzi in Abu Dhabi Mall (02 644 4048, www.natuzzi.com).

You can also pick up a good selection of outdoor furniture at ACE on Mina Zayed road (02 673 1665, www.aceuae.com).

If you fancy the trip, there is a great selection of stores in Dubai; The Walk, Jumeirah Beach Residence has a few independent homeware stores, and Mall of The Emirates (04 409 9000, www.malloftheemirates.com) and The Dubai Mall (800 382 246 255, www.thedubaimall.com) are worth checking out too.

Second-hand bargain hunters can either pay a visit to Nefertiti's warehouse on the Corniche at Khaleej al Arabi St or peruse the offerings online (www.useditemsuae.com, 050 641 9861). Then of course, there are plenty of deals to be found in the classified section of newspapers or on supermarket noticeboards. For something completely different, head to the warehouse stores in Sharjah. The hot, dusty warehouses are not the choicest of options, but prices are excellent and after a good polish the furniture looks fabulous. This is a particularly good place to pick up wooden furniture – Pinky Furniture & Novelties in Industrial Area 10 (06 534 1714, www.pinkyfurnitureuae.com) is a great option; Bayti in Marina Mall (02 681 8107) also stocks a good selection.

Genuine antiques are available but very rare (and therefore very expensive); many antique pieces come from Oman and Yemen. You'll also find plenty of shops selling accessories to add the finishing touches to your home. Souvenir shops (p.327) often sell a good range of regional items including fabric wall-hangings and ornaments. Next (02 443 7033) has a small home accessories section and Debenhams (p.329) is good for homeware, bedding and kitchenware.

For something unique, MacKenzie Art (04 341 9803, www.mackenzieart.com, can assist you with some amazing finishing touches to your home, including murals and trompe l'oeils.

Home Centre

Liwa Centre Markaziya East **02 639 1918**
www.homecentre.net
Map **2 M4**

Step into this store and you won't know which way to turn – it is crammed with bath towels, kitchenware and accessories. You'll also find a conservative selection of wooden tables, sofas and bedroom furniture. Its other branches are located in Centrepoint (02 681 4050) and Dalma Mall (02 550 2415).

IKEA

Nr Ferrari World Abu Dhabi Yas Island **02 493 5888**
www.ikeauae.com
Map **1 T4**

IKEA's enormous showroom sells a great range of good value furniture. Its selection is suitable for most budgets, and it stocks everything from Dhs.1 tealight holders to Dhs.20,000 kitchens. The store also has a selection of reasonably priced kids' furniture (its range of bunkbeds is consistently popular).

Lucky's

Street No. 2 Sharjah **06 534 1937**
Map **3 E1**

Although this store is in Sharjah, it remains popular with expats looking for well-priced wooden furniture. The range of products is vast, but one of the staff will happily explain the origin and design of the pieces and they can also varnish, paint or make alterations.

Marina Exotic Home Interiors

Abu Dhabi Mall Tourist Club Area **02 645 5488**
www.marinagulf.com
Map **2 S5**

The items sold here should add an exotic touch to your home – you can pick up key pieces that reflect the region. The selection includes large wardrobes, tables, ornate chests and various other types of wooden furniture and garden furniture.

THE One

Abu Dhabi Mall Tourist Club Area **02 644 8100**
www.theoneplanet.com
Map **2 S5**

A favourite among the expat crowd, this store's only downfall is the fact that those divine cushions you bought will most likely pop up in your acquaintances' homes from time to time. But, there is a reason why it's so popular: its funky, modern style (that is highly decorative, but not gaudy) and good selection of home accessories can add a much-needed flourish to impersonal apartments. Another branch is located in Khalidiya (02 681 6500).

ChenOne Marina Mall, Breakwater, 02 681 8110, *www.chenonehome.com*
ID Design Al Wahda Mall, Al Dhafrah, 02 443 7557, *www.iddesignuae.com*
Interiors Shk Hamdan Bin Mohammed St, Markaziya East, 02 6797 040, *www.interiorsfurniture.com*
Pan Emirates Shk Rashid Bin Al Maktoum Rd, Madinat Zayed, 02 621 1030, *www.panemirates.com*
Pier Import Nr Sheraton Khalidiya, Al Nasr St, Markaziya West, 02 665 8395, *www.pierimport-me.com*

Gold & Diamonds

Whatever your taste in jewellery you'll find an abundant supply here. Gold is available in 18, 21, 22 or 24 carats and is sold according to the international daily gold rate. This means that for an identical piece, whether you buy it in the mall or the Gold Souk, there will be very little difference in the price of the actual gold. Where the price varies is in the workmanship that has gone into a particular piece.

For adventurous jewellery shoppers, there is plenty to choose from, such as silver jewellery from Oman, cultured pearls from Japan, and ethnic creations from India crafted in rich yellow gold. The Gold Souk (p.342) in Madinat Zayed on 4th Street has many jewellers including some of the largest jewellery shops in the Gulf. The outlets in these areas cater for all tastes, so have a browse around to see a full variety of Arabic, Indian and European styles.

Costume jewellery can be found in most department stores; several fashion stores also stock a small range of jewellery. Branches of Accessorize (02 681 3431) and Claire's Accessories (02 645 4861) are great for inexpensive items and hair accessories for children and they can be found in many of the malls.

When it comes to watches, there is also plenty of choice. You'll get plastic cheapies for no more than a few dirhams, or diamond-encrusted designer time pieces coming in at over a hundred thousand dirhams,

Shopper's delight

and everything in between. Check out the souks – not only will you find all the brands you know, plus some you don't, but you'll have fun haggling with the colourful shop owners – The Hamdan Centre (p.340) is a good place to start.

Al Futtaim Jewellery Abu Dhabi Mall, Tourist Club Area, 02 645 2004, *www.watches.ae*
Al Jazira Jewellery Shk Hamdan Bin Mohammed St, Markaziya East, 02 634 4141
Al Manara Jewellery Marina Mall, Breakwater, 02 681 0888
Al Mandoos Jewellery Marina Mall, Breakwater, 02 681 6555
Carcassone Gold & Diamond Hamdan Centre, Markaziya East, 02 634 7676
Damas Khalidiyah Mall, Al Khalidiyah, 02 635 4420, *www.mydamas.com*
Le Portique Jewellery Sheikh Khalifa Bin Zayed St, Markaziya East, 02 626 9133
Tiffany & Co. Abu Dhabi Mall, Tourist Club Area, 02 644 1182, *www.tiffany.com*

Home Appliances

Whether you are setting up home in Abu Dhabi, or you are moving house, you'll have to spend some time looking for white goods. While you may be used to essential items like a cooker, washing machine or fridge, coming as part and parcel of a lease, in Abu Dhabi, unfurnished really means unfurnished and you'll have to fork out for the most standard items like curtain rails for your windows.

Unsurprisingly, there are several places for you to buy goods and several large international brands are sold here like LG, Samsung and Siemens. Marina Mall (p.338) and Abu Dhabi Mall (p.334) have a large selection of shops.

Many of the larger hypermarkets like Carrefour (p.330) and Lulu (p.331) stock a superb range of goods from well-known brands (and some lesser known ones that also do the job) and they usually offer a delivery and installation service. Sharaf DG (p.321), Jacky's Express (p.321), Jumbo Electronics (p.321), Better Life (02 443 7567), Costless Electronics (02 673 4150), Eros Electricals (02 645 4624), Geco (02 443 6866) and Universal Electricals (02 633 6252) all stock a selection of home appliances. Al Ghandi Electronics (www.alghandielectronics.com) stocks Kitchen Aid products in addition to more mainstream brands such as Philips and Whirlpool.

You can buy coolers and water dispensers in the larger supermarkets or you can buy them directly from the companies that deliver bottled water (see p.94).

Competition is high, so prices are reasonable and most dealers will offer warranties – some will offer a warranty extension for an extra year or two. Check that the warranty is valid internationally if you wish to take items back to your home country. Also check that the item will work in all areas of the world and whether you will have to pay any import duty if you return back home. Also check who will service the items if there are problems. For second-hand items, check the adverts placed on supermarket noticeboards and online classifieds like www.dubizzle.com.

Home Audio & Visual

When it comes to home entertainment, the stores in Abu Dhabi don't scrimp on size, quality or range. There are several stores dedicated to electronics in each of the larger malls and you'll find large sections in the supermarkets which stock top-of-the-range high-definition televisions, plasma screens, DVD players, games consoles and stereos. Whether or not the items sold here are cheaper than those sold in

Abu Dhabi Mall

other countries depends on where you compare it too, but it does pay to wait for the sales as there can be a noticeable difference in prices.

Many stores display operational products so you can check the quality, and staff are happy to explain the differences between models and brands. Bang & Olufsen (Abu Dhabi Mall, 02 644 0587) and Bose (Marina Mall, 800 7584467) offer a pricey but stylish range of goods for the home, but you'll find a good range of products in all of the electronic stores. Many stores also offer delivery and installation services, which take the hassle out of mounting a plasma screen or setting up your surround sound system.

Mobile Phones

Mobiles are big business and you won't need to go too far to find one. Most of the larger supermarkets have areas dedicated to the bigger brands, while smaller shops around the Madinat Zayed and Al Markaziyah areas may offer some bargains on older models. Handsets can also be bought directly from du (p.96) or Etisalat (p.96); it is often cheaper to buy a phone from them as part of a package.

Jacky's Express

Bawadi Mall Al Ain **03 784 0747**
www.jackys.com
Map **4 E3**

A wide range of electronics is stocked here including well-known brands – particularly Sony products. The store offers home delivery and installation for some of its products as well as warranties and protection plans.

Jumbo Electronics

Shk Hamdan Bin Mohammed St Markaziya East **02 632 7001**
www.jumbocorp.com
Map **2 P4**

The selection on offer at this store is vast; head here for its popular brands, good deals and helpful staff. This is also a good place to go to if you are looking for Sony LCD televisions and home theatre systems. Several branches of this store are located in Abu Dhabi in the Tourist Club Area (02 679 0298) and Al Wahda Mall (02 443 7143) among others.

Plug-Ins

Marina Mall Breakwater **800 758 4467**
www.pluginselectronix.com
Map **2 D1**

Representing over 300 brands, a full range of electronics is offered at this store. From audio to appliances and from entertainment to office gadgets, you're likely to find what you're looking for here. Some of the brands include Panasonic, Bose, Sony and LG.

Home Audio & Visual

If you are looking for ways to amp up your parties, or you want to set up a home cinema or sound system in your home, AVE (050 676 2864) offer all the advice and assistance you'll need. An independent audiovisual consultant will provide installation services for home audio equipment, projector systems and multi-room audio installation.

Sharaf DG

Times Square Dubai **04 341 8060**
www.sharafdg.com
Map **3 E2**

This is many residents' first port of call because of its range of gadgets and good service. Its stores carry everything from plasma televisions and laptop computers to mobile phones and irons. Previously, the only Abu Dhabi store was in the airport, but there's now a new branch at Abu Dhabi Mall (02 650 3570) too.

Hardware & DIY

While it is usually easier to get someone in to tackle all those niggling domestic jobs, many still prefer to do it themselves. DIY enthusiasts will find the tools they need to get the job done at ACE (p.323). Customised paints, glazes, special paint effect materials, electronic tools and hardware materials can also be found here. A basic range of items can be bought at IKEA (p.318). Carrefour (p.330), in Marina Mall, also has a DIY section where you can pick up the basics.

Health Food & Special Dietary Requirements

The health food trend is growing in Abu Dhabi and there are now quite a few specialist stores. Nutrition Zone (www.nutritionzoneltd.com), which specialises in vitamins and other health supplements, has branches in both Abu Dhabi Mall and Marina Mall. Longstanding Dubai institution, the Organic Store (p.331), opened its first Abu Dhabi branch in Masdar City in 2011, bringing a wide selection of organic food and eco-friendly home care products to the doorstep of capital dwellers.

Eat Smart Market (p.330) also offers a range of organic products, while jones the grocer (p.331), the Australian purveyor of gourmet and artisan foods, also carries a range of organic produce at its three Abu Dhabi locations.

Larger supermarkets sell an increasing (but still limited) range of organic and allergy-friendly products and they all carry products for diabetics; Spinneys (p.331), for example, carries a limited selection of organic products. Abu Dhabi Co-operative stores (p.330) have aisles dedicated to organic foods, including muesli, honey, biscuits and teas, while

Carrefour's (p.330) range is increasing and, in addition to the basic items that most supermarkets carry, it has a selection of its own brand of organic products; readymade meals are an alternative option for those with special dietary requirements and those counting calories. BiteRite Cafe and Restaurant (p.367) specialises in healthy balanced foods, which are particularly good if you want to lose weight, or if you have a restricted diet due to conditions such as diabetes or high cholesterol levels. For added convenience, you can also try its four week or 14 day meal plans, which are delivered free to home and office (www.biterite.ae). BiteRite approved products are also available at Zari Zardozi restaurant (p.390) in Al Raha Mall and Foodlands Restaurant (p.372), and you can find its range of guilt-free, meal-on-the-go options in ADNOC garages. The D Club (www.thedclub.com, 02 644 6461) specialises in balanced, nutritious organic meals, painstakingly planned down to the last calorie. There are packages available for monthly meal deliveries, and options for specific health needs, as well as a catering service for events. Keep an eye out for a D Club restaurant opening in the future.

Kids' Items

There is a high concentration of shops selling toys and clothes for children and you'll find a good selection of well-known stores and smaller outlets. Most electronics stores stock a wide range of games for the various platforms. Carrefour (p.330) also has a good selection, and the hypermarket's toy department is a good address to stock up on inexpensive birthday presents and stocking fillers. Remember that not all toys conform to international safety standards and therefore should only be used under supervision. When it comes to clothing, many of the department stores (p.329) have children's departments or you could splash out on high-end designer gear at Cacharel (02 681 6633).

For babies and younger children, Babyshop (02 681 8894), Mamas and Papas (02 681 6689), Mothercare (02 645 4894), Woolworths (p.330) and Next (02 443 7033) carry the essentials and have some great outfits at reasonable prices. Okaidi (02 681 7740) and Pumpkin Patch (02 635 4527) sell bright, colourful and practical clothes. Monsoon (02 635 4523) has a great range of party clothes, particularly for girls. The majority of children's clothes shops also stock shoes and there are some specialist stores. Shoe Mart (p.317) and Debenhams (p.329) have children's sections. Adams (02 644 0608) and The Athlete's Foot (04 368 5246) also carry a good range. For party costumes check out the Early Learning Centre (p.322) or Toys R Us (p.322), year round. Supermarkets and hypermarkets (p.330) stock some items in the run up to festive events like Halloween and Christmas.

Early Learning Centre

Abu Dhabi Mall Tourist Club Area **02 645 4766**
www.elc.com
Map **2 S5**

Early Learning Centre stocks a good range of educational products and toys that stimulate play and imagination. There are several outlets in Abu Dhabi stocking a good selection of children's books and some wooden toys.

Toys R Us

Nr Royal Furniture, Mina Zayed Rd Al Meena
02 673 2332
www.toysrus.com
Map **1 D2**

This well-known emporium offers a good selection of products, whether you are looking for small toys to amuse kids or larger gifts like bikes, electronic games and play sets.

Maternity Items

While maternity fashion is still limited in Abu Dhabi, if you shop around you will find an interesting range to cater to different price brackets. Many of the main retailers have jumped on the maternity fashion bandwagon and now offer fashionable outfits, so that mums-to-be can look as stylish as everyone else. Zara (02 681 8080) stocks a limited range of stylish maternity wear. Similarly, the new H&M (02 671 8799) in Abu Dhabi Mall has a small but trendy selection available at affordable prices. Woolworths at Marina Mall (p.338) also stocks some maternity clothes. Specialist stockists include Mamas & Papas (p.312), Mothercare (p.312), Premaman (02 645 8600) in Abu Dhabi Mall, and Formes in Marina Mall. Next (02 443 7033) and the eclectic Najo Secret (02 673 6622) in Mina Centre also stock some maternity wear. Online shopping is an alternative if you can't find what you're after in store. Just Kidding (www.justkidding-me.com), which carries Noppies (www.noppies.com) maternity wear from the Netherlands, and Isabella Oliver (www.isabellaoliver.com) both deliver to Abu Dhabi, and while they are comparatively expensive, they offer a huge variety of extremely stylish choice. Another option could be to join Abu Dhabi Mums (www.abudhabimums.ae), where you can hire maternity wear. For other maternity items, such as cool packs, creams and bras, you'll have to shop around in Mothercare (p.312), Babyshop (p.308), and Marks & Spencer (p.329), as available ranges vary and may be limited. Babyshop, Mothercare and Najo Secret all stock a range of breast pumps, or you could try one of the larger pharmacies (p.160) if you want a really heavy duty one. Other essential accessories for pregnancy are available here – one example is a 'Bump Belt', which redirects your car seatbelt under your bump, and can be found in Mothercare. For more information on having a baby see p.131, and for shopping for items for your new arrival, see Baby Items, p.308.

Music & DVDs

Although the selection isn't as large or as up to date as in North America, Asia or Europe, you will find a number of audio and video stores selling the latest releases from all over the world. Unless you have particularly eclectic taste, you should find a satisfying collection of music in the city's supermarkets and record stores. The advantage of Abu Dhabi's multicultural society is that you can open yourself up to new genres – Arabic dance music, for example, is very popular. Everything has to go through the censor, so any music or DVDs deemed offensive will not be sold here, unless it can be edited to make it more acceptable.

Hollywood blockbusters and mainstream titles can be picked up in many supermarkets. Music and DVDs are generally more expensive than they are in other countries. Virgin Megastore (02 644 7882) at Abu Dhabi Mall has the widest range of new music, as well as classics. It also stocks a great selection of films and TV series box sets on DVD, at competitive prices.

Videos are in the PAL format and there are numerous video rental stores around the city – check one out in your area. Rental prices range from Dhs.4 to Dhs.10 per video and around Dhs.10 (as well as a hefty deposit sometimes) either per DVD, or just for membership when you join. Al Mansoor Audio & Video (02 678 3456) stocks a range of DVDs and videos to rent and buy, in addition to audio CDs. Recordable CDs, DVDs, audio and videotapes are sold at major grocery stores.

Carrefour (p.330) and Spinneys (p.331) have good value bargain bins and, although they are usually filled with Hollywood titles, there are occasional gems and the odd BBC children's title. Bollywood films are extremely popular and available in most shops.

Retailers will order titles that are on the approved list for the UAE. Online shopping is an alternative if you can't find an item and you'll find more variety on sites like Amazon (www.amazon.com and www.amazon.co.uk). Amazon's postal charges are often fairly high and its branded packages are occasionally inspected at the post office (see Online Shopping p.304).

Musical Instruments

Whether you are already an accomplished musician or you have recently decided to explore your hidden talents, you may find the selection of musical instrument stores in Abu Dhabi a little disappointing. Thomsun Electronics (02 672 4703, www.thomsunpuremusic.com) on Hamdan Street has a decent range of acoustic and electric guitars as well as some keyboard models. Sonia Electronics sells some musical instruments as well as leasing sound equipment. The company has an office in Abu Dhabi, but its main showroom is located in Dubai (04 227 2395, www.soniaelectronic.com) – you can view its selection of electronics on its website. Some basic items are sold in Carrefour (p.330) and AKM Music Centre (02 621 9929) which has a decent range of musical instruments including pianos and sheet music. If you can't find what you're looking for, it may be worth a trip to Sadek Music (04 368 6570, www.sadek-music.com) and Zak Electronics (04 336 8857, www.zakelectronics.com) in Dubai where you'll find a greater choice. Sadek Music offers a repair service and music lessons and you can also rent a selection of its instruments.

Outdoor Goods

Exploring the great outdoors is a popular pastime in the UAE, especially when the weather cools. While there are no specialist camping shops, the basic gear is readily available in Carrefour (p.330) and ACE (p.323). Items are suitable for weekend campers, but would not withstand extremes, so if you are intending to do anything more strenuous you should consider ordering kit online.

Caveman Make Fire (04 347 6167, www.cavemanmakefire.com) produces a range of barbecues and heaters which you can have delivered free of charge. GPS equipment can be found in most electronics stores. For outdoor sports enthusiasts there are a number of options (see Sports Goods, p.328).

Serious climbers and hikers should consider getting their boots and equipment from overseas, but a small and decent selection of packs and boots are available at Jack Wolfskin (02 443 7802) in Al Wahda Mall.

Alternately, you can order a good range of items from REI (www.rei.com) and Mountain Equipment Co-op (www.mec.ca).

While hydration packs (backpacks that you can fill with water, complete with a long tube and mouthpiece) are becoming more widely available in sports shops, anything larger than a day pack should be bought overseas.

Similarly, hiking accessories for people with small children, such as backpack carriers, are not widely available here and your best bet would be to buy these goods overseas or order them online.

ACE

Mina Zayed Rd Al Meena **02 673 1665**
www.aceuae.com
Map **1 D2**

ACE is the place to go to for hardware, outdoors equipment and camping gear. You can buy all the basic equipment you need for your jaunt in the desert at this store, including tents, sleeping bags and cool boxes. The store also stocks a good range of hardware and accessories.

Places To Shop For Kids

Whether you need to get a gift, re-stock a wardrobe or fulfil a curriculum requirement, shopping for your (or your friends') kids can be an expensive and exhausting task. But with a little bit of planning and a lot of imagination you can have the best-dressed, educated and well-occupied child in Abu Dhabi.

Kids' Fashion

The good news is that Abu Dhabi has a wide variety of international brands (see Kids' Items, p.322) and many adult fashion stores have kids' ranges. Marks & Spencer (p.329) has a great range of on-trend kids' clothes and shoes, while Bhs (02 621 1242) and Next (02 443 7033) have good quality ranges. Check out Women'secret (02 681 8070) for unique items for children, and Beyond the Beach (02 443 7201) for some super cool surf gear. For novelty t-shirts and babygrows with 'My Dad's Cooler Than Yours' across the front, check out concession stalls found in the bigger malls. Katakeet (02 650 3604) stocks brands like Baby Dior, Tartine et Chocolat and Burberry.

Kids' Sportsgear

For swimming suits with built in floats check out Mothercare (p.308), Early Learning Centre (p.322) and most sports shops (p.328). Sun and Sand Sports (02 681 8330) has a great range of sporting items for kids, including roller blades, trampolines (also try Toys R Us, p.322), bikes (see also p.312), miniature pool tables, tennis racquets and golf clubs. For specialist sportswear, like martial arts outfits and ballet outfits you will probably have to buy from one of the academies (see Activities for Kids, p.133), although Marks & Spencer (p.329) and Claire Kids (02 681 5990) sometimes carry ballet outfits.

Musical Instruments

There are a few specialist shops (see p.323) but you can also find basic drum kits and keyboards in Toys R Us, and Virgin Megastore (02 644 7882) have an excellent range of keyboards, as well as digital music games. You might be able to pick up a second-hand guitar or piano from www.dubizzle.com or put a notice on www.expatwoman.com. If you're looking for sheet music (often teachers will request parents to buy the required sheet music) Magrudy's has a large range, including exam papers, and can generally order specific books for you.

Bedroom Design

If you want to decorate your kid's room but don't want to paint it you can get family photos printed on canvas, recreate a night time scene (with stars and a moon) or garden setting (with flowers and a ladybird) in wall lighting from IKEA (p.318). Alternatively go for wall stickers – Just Kidding in Dubai stocks wall stickers for children, from funky and friendly animal stickers for nurseries to flowers and rockets for young children's rooms. Order online at www.justkidding-me.com or pop to Dubai to browse the store (800 5878).

Abu Dhabi is home to all manner of kids' items – from novelty t-shirts to toys galore. So, head out for a shopping trip and get ready to spoil the little ones!

Bags & Stationery

While a lot of schools have book bags as part of their uniform, many kids also take their own school bag in order to fit in their gym kit and packed lunch. Pull along wheeled bags are popular and can be found in Toys R Us in all manner of characters. If you're looking for pencil cases and the like, then Magrudy's, Toys R Us and Early Learning Centre stock good ranges, as do almost all of the city's biggest hypermarkets. While you're there, you can stock up on most types of stationery – if they don't have something, Magrudys, Book Corner (p.314) or Booksplus (p.314) almost certainly will.

Affordable Gifts

Once your kids get to school age you will find that they will be invited to a birthday party nearly every month. So buying birthday gifts can get expensive – if they have a sweet tooth, try Sugar Daddy's (04 330 8700) or Cupoof Cupcakes (050 660 6964) for the very best cupcakes in town. Rico Gifts (02 681 7622) in Marina Mall has all sorts of fun items like glow sticks, temporary tattoos, wacky T-shirts and wigs, while The Party Centre in Raha Mall is ideal for novelty balloons and costumes (02 556 5563).

Party Accessories

Most major supermarkets and stationery stores sell the basic party paraphernalia, and if you go to the more specialised shops, you'll find an even wider range. From cards, balloons, candles, table settings and room decorations to gift wrapping, fancy dress outfits, bouncy castles and entertainers, the choice for both children's and adults' parties is comprehensive. If you're entertaining at home, but don't want the hassle of cooking, there are a number of companies who will be happy to relieve you of the burden (see Parties At Home, p.352).

Carrefour (p.330) and Toys R Us (p.322) stock party essentials such as themed plates, cups and hats. The selection isn't great though, so if your child is attached to a particular character, you may find that online options are more fruitful. UK-based Characters4Kids (www.characters4kids.co.uk) and its sister site Heroes For Kids (www.heroesforkids.co.uk) have an endless range of products for kids' birthday parties. US store Oriental Trading Company (+1 800 875 8480, www.orientaltrading.com) accepts international orders by phone. With any online retailer, be sure to order in plenty of time to allow for delivery hold-ups.

Japanese discount store Daiso (02 631 1514), in Madinat Zayed Shopping Centre, is good for stocking up on knick-knacks for children's party bags. If you're after a fancy dress costume, many of the small tailors in Abu Dhabi are able to copy designs from pictures. Expressions Dancewear & Costumes (www.expressions-dancewear.com) has a fancy dress hire department. You can order your costume online and have it delivered, or collect it from the shop. For everything else, try The Party Centre in Al Raha Mall (02 556 5563, www.mypartycentre.com).

Alcohol retailer Gray Mackenzie, on Khalifa Street (02 612 3545, www.admmi.com) offers a free party service. A deposit of Dhs.500 will allow you use of 24 pint beer glasses, 24 wine glasses, two ice buckets, two waiter trays, two bar towels and 24 coasters. Items should be returned within five days of payment of the deposit – a minimum breakage charge of Dhs.6 per glass will be deducted from the deposit and the balance refunded.

Birthday cakes are available at branches of Lenôtre (02 621 9888, www.lenotre.fr) as well as in the bakery section of all major supermarkets. You can have custom made cakes created by Tickls Celebration Cakes (055 516 0825, www.ticklscakes.webs.com). Ice cream cakes are available from Baskin Robbins (www.baskinrobbins.com).

If you'd rather someone did all the work, leaving you to enjoy the event along with your guests, Events R Us (02 645 6605, www.events-r-us.net) can provide everything from the catering and balloons, to entertainment. Although they are based in Dubai, the Balloon Lady (04 344 1062, www.balloonladyuae.com), Cheeky Monkey Parties (056 691 3552, www.cheekymonkeyparties.com) and Flying Elephant (800 72789, www.flyingelephantuae.com) can provide bouncy castles, fancy-dress costumes, party favours and games. And if you need a marquee (of any size), you should contact Harlequin Marquees and Event Services (04 347 0110, www.harlequinmarquees.com).

Perfumes & Cosmetics

Perfumes and cosmetics are big business here, from the local scents like frankincense and oudh, to the latest designer offerings. These perfumes and scents tend to be strong and spicy – you can often locate the stores by the smell of the incense they burn in their doorways. The department stores (p.329) and local chains such as Areej (www.altayer.com) and Paris Gallery (www.parisgallery.com) are located in most of the larger malls and they stock the most comprehensive ranges of international brand perfumes and cosmetics. The Body Shop, Boots, Red Earth, M.A.C and Make Up Forever are also located in many of the city's malls. M.A.C has a great selection and its staff will also offer tips on application. Larger supermarkets and pharmacies stock skincare products and some make-up. Anti-allergenic ranges are available at some of the larger pharmacies. Most needs are covered but if yours aren't, specialist retailers often have online shopping facilities.

Arabic perfumes

Fragrant outlets of Arabian Oud (www.arabianoud.com) are found in most malls, but they tend to cater to the Arab population and don't always have English-speaking shop assistants on duty.

Prices for perfumes and cosmetics are similar to those in some other countries, although certain nationalities might find perfume is cheaper here than in their home country. There are no sales taxes, so there is rarely a difference between Duty Free and shopping mall prices.

Amouage

Marina Mall Breakwater **02 681 6662**
www.amouage.com
Map **2 D1**

Made in Oman, Amouage, 'the world's most expensive perfume,' is a high-end brand that can also be found in Paris Gallery. The brand is the epitome of luxury with a range of perfumes that smell fantastic and are totally unique.

L'Occitane

Marina Mall Breakwater **02 681 6691**
www.loccitane-me.com
Map **2 D1**

Head here for natural skin care products and fragrances; all of its products are certified 100% organic and are made using ingredients like almond, orange, lavender, green tea and shea butter.

Second-Hand Items

The fairly transitory nature of much of the population results in an active second-hand market. If you are looking to buy or sell second-hand goods, the supermarket noticeboards and the classifieds sections in newspapers are a good place to start. There are also several community websites with classifieds sections – try www.dubizzle.com, www.abudhabiwoman.com, www.expatwoman.com, www.souq.com and www.websouq.com. In most cases you will have to arrange for the items you buy to be transported – head down to the carpark next to the Central Post Office in Madinat Zayed, and negotiate with the drivers there for the use of a small truck. The price should include a driver and a few men to help you carry larger items. The St Andrew's Thrift Shop (02 446 4193) sells a range of second-hand items. If you are selling second-hand goods, a number of the local second-hand shops will come to your home and give you a quote (usually way below the purchase price, so be prepared to haggle).

Souvenirs

From typical holiday trinkets to tasteful ornaments and keepsakes, there is a wide range of souvenirs to be found in Abu Dhabi. Many of the items are regional rather than local, and several are mass produced in India, Pakistan and Oman. The generic holiday mementos such as t-shirts, mugs, keyrings and, of course, stuffed camels, can be found in the retail outlets in the international airport as well as at Posters (02 672 4724) in the Tourist Club Area and most of the larger hotel gift shops.

The range of ornamental gifts available is endless, with perennial favourites being the Arabic coffee pot and cups (a symbol of Arabic hospitality), metallic decorative plates (traditionally used for serving coffee, and the larger ones for food), framed khanjars (traditional Arabian daggers), wooden trinket boxes and larger handcrafted wooden wedding chests and furniture. For these kind of traditional or regional items, the souks (p.332), particularly the Iranian Souk (p.333), and individual gift shops are the best places to look. Prices and quality vary enormously, and the souks generally offer the best prices – as long as you haggle.

Within the Tourist Club Area are an array of souk-style shops in the Khalifa Centre (p.340), opposite Abu Dhabi Mall, which sell Persian rugs and other carpets from the Middle East, in addition to trinkets and cultural souvenirs; try Gulf Antiques & Carpets Exhibition (02 645 9956), Golden Antique Exhibition (02 645 5591), or Handmade Carpet House & Antiques (02 644 0344). More expensive souk-style shops can be found in The Souk At Qaryat Al Beri (p.342), including Gallery One (www.g-1.com) which sells a selection of stylish photographs and canvas prints and is particularly good if you want images of the region. You'll also find some of these items at the Heritage Village (p.207) in the workshops where craftsmen ply their trades and produce souvenir replicas, as well as more contemporary keepsakes such as keyrings, t-shirts and bags. Reshie Handicrafts (www.reshie.com, 02 681 2747) in Marina Mall, Khalidiyah Mall and Madinat Zayed Shopping Centre sells a variety of embroidered, decorative fabrics including pashminas, wall hangings, rugs and garments, which make beautiful souvenirs but, being imported from Kashmir, aren't indicative of the Middle East.

For ladies, pashminas are in abundant supply and make lightweight, handy gifts for family and friends. The Women's Handicraft Center (p.208) showcases and sells local handicrafts and is ideal for picking up authentic jewellery or pashminas. In some of the souvenir shops, you'll find simple, but extremely heavy, silver wedding jewellery. If the style is not to your liking, these coveted pieces of historical art make excellent displays when mounted in a glass box frame.

Alternatively, if gold is more to your taste, the UAE's legacy as a gold trading post means a vast selection of jewellery and excellent prices for shoppers. The Gold Centre at Madinat Zayed Shopping Centre (p.342) offers the capital's largest collection of gold vendors and jewellers under one roof. The cost of workmanship is also very competitive, so if you have something specific in mind, but don't find the exact piece, you can create your own designs. For more on buying gold, see Gold & Diamonds, p.318.

Once valued more highly than gold, the dried resin from the frankincense tree of southern Oman has been traded for centuries and, nowadays, is often sold in a small wooden chest and with a charcoal burner to give off its evocative scent. You will either love or hate the smell of incense and the heavy local perfumes, but they are great as authentic Middle East gifts, and all available from the souks in Al Meena (p.192). Oud is a popular and expensive oil used in many of the perfumes, while myrrh and other sweet smelling mixtures are also sold. Ask for some to be burned, so you can smell it before deciding on your purchase. Arabian Oud has kiosks and shops in most malls (www.arabianoud.com). Amouage is an exclusive Omani brand of frankincense based-perfumes, which includes some of the world's most valuable perfumes, made from rare ingredients. Its products can be found in branches of Paris Gallery (02 681 6662) and in Abu Dhabi Duty Free at the airport.

Shisha or hubbly bubbly pipes are fun souvenirs which, along with flavoured tobacco, make a great gift. The more authentic versions can be picked up in the souks or in the Arabic stores on the top level of Marina Mall but, if your friends and family are unlikely to know any better, good but cheaper shisha pipes and tobacco, in flavours such as apple, strawberry and grape, are sold in Carrefour (p.330).

Where edible souvenirs are concerned, look out for delicious Lebanese sweets (usually made from pastry, honey, ground nuts and dates) or local dates. You can find dates, both preserved and (in season) fresh, plus date-based products like date paste and date-flavoured honey, in all supermarkets (p.330). Most are imported from Iran or Saudi Arabia. Iranian caviar is widely available and good value for money, as it is sold without import duty or any added tax.

For a more easily transportable souvenir, pick up a good coffee table book such as *Images of Abu Dhabi and the United Arab Emirates* by Explorer Publishing. This artistic photographic book, available in all good bookshops, offers a refreshing and insightful visual perspective on this part of the world. Explorer's range of photographic calendars also make great gifts and mementos. In addition, most of Abu Dhabi's tourist attractions also offer their own souvenir shops where you can purchase items to remember your visit.

Sports Goods

Abu Dhabi is a great place for a variety of sports, from common activities such as tennis, sailing, golf or football, to more unusual pursuits like sand skiing. General sports shops stock a good variety of items including racquets or sports clothing. You can also find specialist sports shops around the city. For the fishing fanatic, there is a string of bait and tackle shops along Tourist Club St near Hamdan St, while BMX enthusiasts will find a range of bikes at Rage in Al Wahda Mall (02 443 7617). Indeed, unless yours is an unusual sport or you require a more specialised piece of equipment, you should have little difficulty finding what you require. Studio R (02 681 7676) in Marina Mall sells a selection of active wear lifestyle brands such as Quiksilver, Rockport and Union Bay, and sports brands (Adidas, New Balance, Reebok and Speedo). The store also has sales throughout the year where stock is heavily discounted.

Many of the major brand names have multiple outlets in Abu Dhabi, including Adidas (02 681 4046), Nike (02 635 4707) and Timberland (02 681 2611). Larger shops dedicated to sportswear such as Sun & Sand Sports (02 681 8330), City Sports (02 681 4922) in Marina Mall and Megasports (02 645 6166) stock a variety of brands. You can also pick up a few basic items at Carrefour (p.330).

Textiles & Haberdashery

To buy fabric, head to Madinat Zayed Shopping Centre & Gold Centre, or the streets behind Marks & Spencer in Markaziyah, both of which have a high concentration of textile stores. You'll find all kinds of fabric from the most delicate broderie anglaise to practical cottons. Compare prices between stores and don't forget to haggle. Look out for sales – the prices are too low to resist. Cairo is a fabric emporium located near Al Noor Hospital on Khalifa Street. It has three floors of textiles from elegant silks to plain cotton. Also look out for Green Branch (02 621 4507) on Electra Street, Kashmir Traders (02 621 0347) on Al Nasr St or Rivoli Textiles (02 679 2996) on Hamdan Street. Al Omara Textiles has branches in Madinat Zayed (02 634 5292) and Madinat Zayed Shopping Centre & Gold Centre (02 632 1930), and Paris Textiles has branches on Khalifa Street (02 622 5030), in Al Khalidiyah (02 632 6156) and Al Ain (03 766 7723). If you don't fancy pounding the streets, Al Esayi Textile (02 645 0313), in Abu Dhabi Mall, stocks a range of printed and plain cottons and silks, and IKEA (p.318) has a good range of bright, colourful cottons, plus curtain fabrics.

For embroidery details such as pearls, thread and ribbons, try Malik & Shaheed behind Madinat Zayed Shopping Centre. If it's quality European upholstery fabrics you're after, Areeca Furniture & Curtains in the Tourist Club Area (02 679 0010) and Sedar just opposite have an impressive range, but you'll need to order in advance as they don't keep stock.

Wedding Items

Abu Dhabi is a great place to have your wedding, with sunshine pretty much guaranteed for your big day and a whole host of world-class five-star hotel venues to choose from to make sure you have an unforgettable day. Almost all the large hotels offer wedding planning services if you book your wedding and/or reception with them, and can guide you through every little detail to ensure it all comes together perfectly on the day.

Bridal gowns are, however, hard to come by in the capital with most options reflecting the flamboyant Arabic style. The best-known bridal shop in Abu Dhabi is Rahmanian (02 676 7079) at the Tourist Club Area end of Hamdan Street. Dubai has a broader range of dresses on offer and has several excellent bridal shops to choose from. Beach Road is home to several bridal stores, including The Bridal Room (04 344 6076) and Frost (04 345 5690, www.frostdubai.com). Pronovias (04 339 8770, www.pronovias.com) has a store in The Dubai Mall. For high-end designer gowns head to Saks Fifth Avenue's (04 351 5551, www.saksfifthavenue.com) bridal department in the BurJuman Centre which stocks the latest off-the-peg designer wedding gowns by Vera Wang and Reem Acra. The store keeps some gowns in stock, but others can be ordered (allow around four months for delivery). The bride will need to attend a number of fittings, but alterations are done in-house and are to couture standards.

There are several specialist bridal designers with workshops in Dubai, but Arushi (04 344 2277, www.arushi-fashion.com) is renowned as one of the best. You can select the fabric yourself or it can be selected during the first meeting with the designer. Gowns take around one month to make, but as Arushi is so popular, there is often a waiting list. Some of the tailors in Abu Dhabi are also able to work from pictures to create your ideal dress, but proceed with caution as, while most tailors will tell you they can sew anything you want, standards vary hugely, so it's best to ask to see samples of similar work before commissioning an expensive garment like a wedding dress.

Mothers of the bride and groom, and guests, are well catered for at Coast, Debenhams and Monsoon among many others, all of which sell a good selection of dresses suitable for bridesmaids as well.

A Little Bit of Sol (http://solinvitations.blogspot.com) and Chic Design (www.chicdesign.org) both make bespoke wedding stationery. For any items that you can't find here, www.confetti.co.uk accepts international orders. Debenhams (p.329) and THE One (p.318) both offer wedding list services and there are also a couple of local online gift list services (www.uniquegiftservices.com and www.whiteme.net).

As well as offering wedding planning services, several of Abu Dhabi's main hotels can be commissioned to make the wedding cake; alternatively, Lenôtre (02 621 9888, www.lenotre.fr), Le Pont Café in Khalidiya (02 666 4022, www.lepontcafe.com) and Tickls Celebration Cakes (www.ticklscakes.webs.com) create beautiful wedding cakes. Most of the capital's florists can turn their hands to wedding bouquets and arrangements; discuss your requirements with them to find out what will be available. For more information on tying the knot in Abu Dhabi, see Getting Married on p.130.

PLACES TO SHOP

Department Stores

Department stores anchor some of Abu Dhabi's biggest malls and in addition to British stalwarts like Marks & Spencer and Debenhams, South Africa's trusted Woolworths and regional powerhouse Jashanmal provide the essentials for the whole family.

Debenhams

Khalidiyah Mall Al Khalidiyah **02 635 4994**
www.debenhams.com
Map **2 H5**

A mainstay of the British high street, Debenhams is a go-to for perfumes, cosmetics and clothing for men, women and children. There are also several concessions including Evans, for plus-size clothing, Motivi, Warehouse, Oasis and Dorothy Perkins. There's also a good selection of homeware, including cookware by Jamie Oliver. Debenhams' reputation for selling good quality items at reasonable prices is continued by its Designers at Debenhams ranges by John Rocha, Jasper Conran and Pearce Fionda.

Jashanmal > *p.313*

Abu Dhabi Mall Tourist Club Area **02 645 6454**
www.jashanmalgroup.com
Map **2 S5**

This department store may have escaped your notice but it offers an interesting selection of items. Its homeware section is particularly good for linen and crockery. It also sells a small range of clothing and underwear, perfume and books, and its luggage section is particularly good. It's also located in Marina Mall (02 681 5419) and Khalidiyah Mall (02 635 4545).

Marks & Spencer

Fotouh Al Khair Centre Markaziya East **02 621 3646**
www.marksandspencerme.com
Map **2 L4**

One of the best known brands from the UK, M&S, as it is known, sells men's, women's and children's clothes and shoes, along with a small, but ever popular, selection of food. The clothing lines are not the most exciting from the fashion point of view, but M&S is famous for their underwear and have a reputation for quality. The UAE stores carry selected ranges which include Per Una – high street chic – as well as more classic lines.

Woolworths

Marina Mall Breakwater **02 681 0881**
www.woolworths.co.za
Map **2 D1**
This is home away from home for South Africans – Woolworths in South Africa is similar to Marks & Spencer in the UK. It is renowned as the place to go for high-quality clothes, shoes and home textiles (towels and bedding). They also do a great range of accessories and underwear. In the UAE, Woolworths may be slightly less impressive than the original stores, but the items are still high quality and the range offers something a little different to standard (UK) goods.

Supermarkets & Hypermarkets

Abela Supermarket

Khalidiya Centre Al Khalidiyah **02 667 4675**
Map **2 H4**
Abela is a 'super-store', with a range of shops offering stationery, video rental, books and magazines, dry-cleaning services and jewellery (and much more). In terms of food, Abela has a good selection with a pork section and a good fresh fish counter. Also located at the Shangri-la Hotel (02 558 1468) and Khalifa Street (02 556 7061).

Abu Dhabi Co-operative Society

Abu Dhabi Mall Tourist Club Area **02 645 9777**
www.adcoops.com
Map **2 S5**
With branches all over the city, Abu Dhabi Co-operative Society is a popular store selling international products. It has a good selection of fresh food and vegetables and it sells its own brand of goods. Other locations include the Mina Centre (02 673 4848), Hamdan Street (02 676 6766) and Madinat Zayed Shopping Centre & Gold Centre (02 632 4500).

Al Maya Supermarket

Nr Hitachi Showroom Tourist Club Area **02 644 4012**
www.almayagroup.com
Map **2 R6**
With enough items to help you keep your pantry well-stocked, Al Maya Supermarkets sell moderately priced goods. Its stores offer a good selection of regional and international items, and often have a small bakery and fresh meat and fish sections. Other branches are located in Al Dhafrah (02 8840 410) and Al Ain City Centre (03 768 8777).

Carrefour

Rashid Bin Al Maktoum Rd Al Madina **800 73232**
www.carrefouruae.com
Map **1 J8**
Branches of this French hypermarket chain can be found throughout the city. As well as a full range of foods, each large store carries fairly comprehensive ranges of electronics, household goods, luggage, mobile phones, and white goods. Camping gear, sporting and car accessories are also on sale, in addition to clothes and shoes for men, women and children, garden furniture, hardware, music and DVDs, and stationery. The store offers a good range of French products (it's the best place to get crusty, freshly baked French sticks) and it even has a small health food section. Carrefour is renowned for its competitive pricing and special offers. Other branches are located in Dalma Mall (02 652 5999), Marina Mall (02 681 7100), Al Jimi Mall (03 762 0044) and Bawadi Mall (03 703 5101).

> **Shop & Drop**
>
> Carrefour is the latest store in the UAE to launch itself into the digital world. You can buy a range of electrical, household and non-perishable personal items from its online shop, www.ic4uae.com, and have them delivered directly to your door.

Choithram

Nr Sheraton Khalidiya Hotel Al Khalidiyah
02 666 0610
www.choithram.com
Map **2 J4**
Choithram has several outlets in the UAE. It is renowned for stocking British, American and Asian products that can't be found elsewhere, but they are also known for being expensive. Its stores have excellent frozen sections and a great range of baby products – particularly food and formula. Other branches can be found on Corniche Road (02 681 6930), Al Mada Complex (03 765 6798), Khalifa Street (03 765 6300) and Mega Mart in Al Ain (03 755 570).

Eat Smart Organic Market & Cafe

Fotouh Al Khair Centre Markaziya East **02 634 6624**
Map **2 L4**
Conveniently located in the city, Eat Smart has a range of organic products, as well as a cafe offering tasty, healthy meals. The products are sourced from around the world and include a range of natural delicacies such as Manuka honey from New Zealand.

Emirates General Market

Sheikh Zayed The First St Markaziya East
02 631 6262
www.luluhypermarket.com
Map **2 N3**
Owned by the same group as the Lulu chain of supermarkets, Emirates General Market is a destination for the cheap and cheerful rather than designer chic. Known locally as EmGen, you'll find clothes, sportswear, watches, electronics, music and

more at this lively and affordable mall. The store is also located in Ruwais (02 876 2272), Muroor Road (02 448 0490), Shawamekh (02 584 0850) and Hamdan Street (02 674 7500).

jones the grocer

Al Mamoura Bldg B, Muroor Rd Al Nahyan **02 443 8762**
www.jonesthegrocer.com
Map **2 N10**

A gourmet food store that offers a selection of deli items and fresh produce. It stocks international produce (that is largely free from additives and preservatives) and is a particularly good place to fill up your picnic basket. It also has a bakery and cafe and offers a catering service. Also located in Al Raha Gardens (02 557 4882) and Khalidiyah (02 639 5883), in the Pearl Plaza Tower.

K.M. Trading

Nr Emirates Driving School Mussafah **02 551 2030**
www.kmt-group.com
Map **1 M10**

Large new hypermarket serving the Mussafah area with a huge range of goods: from fresh fruit and vegetables, bread and hot takeaway food, to fashion, footwear, toys, luggage, electronics, household and more. K.M. Trading also has five more locations throughout Abu Dhabi island and two in Al Ain.

Lulu Hypermarket

Khalidiyah Mall Al Khalidiyah **02 635 4100**
www.luluhypermarket.com
Map **2 H5**

The store is great for those on a budget; its hot food counters, salad bars and fish monger are particularly good value. There's not much that isn't sold at this store – from luggage and electronics to food and clothing and home appliances. The Lulu Center on Salam Street (02 678 0707) is more like a mini mall selling practically everything under the sun – from electronics, sportswear and toys to stationery, clothing, cosmetics and travel accessories. Other branches can be found at Al Wahda Mall (02 443 7500), Al Sanaiya (03 722 0055) and Al Kuwaitat (03 764 0555).

Organic Foods & Cafe

Masdar City
www.organicfoodsandcafe.com
Map **1 U7**

Long an institution in Dubai, Organic Foods and Cafe now has a branch in Abu Dhabi. The store is an organic supermarket, as well as a cafe, and has a good range of products from fruits and vegetables to skincare and cleaning products. Catering and delivery services are also available.

Spinneys

Nr Adnoc, Corniche St Al Khubeirah **02 681 2897**
Map **2 E4**

Spinneys keeps the Brits happy with its Waitrose range among other British products, but the store also stocks a great range of South African, Australian and American products. The bakery is always brimming with freshly baked treats and it is definitely one of the best places to go for fresh fish and pork. It also has its very own car park so parking is never a problem. See the website for a full list of its outlets.

Boutiques & Independent Shops

The independent shopping scene is not as prolific as it is in other countries. However, there are a few stores, mainly selling fashion, that offer capsule collections of regional and international designers.

Grafika

Al Wahda Mall Al Dhafrah **02 443 7111**
www.grafikauae.com
Map **2 M7**

Grafika is all about stunning Emirati elegance. It offers one-of-a-kind gowns, blouses and dresses from vibrant designers and, although the emphasis is very much on Arabic and Indian inspired shapes and colours, women of all cultures will enjoy checking out the designs, especially those wanting something a little special or different. Prices range from the 'well, I guess I could...' to the 'how much?' category. If you shop here however, you can be more confident that you'll not turn up to a party in the same outfit as someone else.

Ounass

Marina Mall Breakwater **02 681 8667**
www.altayer.com
Map **2 D1**

Ounass (which means 'people' in Arabic) appeals to the ultra-sophisticated party people of the UAE, stocking lines from Marchesa and Alberta Ferretti. As well as fashionable creations and designer treats, the walls are lined with artwork from regional artists, so you can buy beautiful creations for your home as well as your wardrobe.

S*uce

Marina Mall Breakwater **02 681 8650**
www.shopatsauce.com
Map **2 D1**

Unapologetically girlie, S*uce is a haven for those who like things chic with a feminine touch. All of its stores follow the same theme and funky accessories, quirky fashion and individual pieces are the hallmark of this boutique. Head here for unique items and international designers.

Markets & Souks

Souk is the Arabic word for market or a place where any goods are bought or exchanged. Historically, dhows from the Far East, China, Ceylon (Sri Lanka) and India would offload their cargo, and the goods would then be haggled over in the souks adjacent to the docks. Souks have traditionally been the social and commercial centres of life in the Arabic world, providing a place to meet friends and socialise outside the family. In lots of ways, the souk is the Arabic equivalent of a Western style mall, and, increasingly so, modern souks and malls tend to feature elements of both here.

Over the years, the items on sale have diversified dramatically from spices, silks and perfumes, to include electronic goods and the latest kitsch consumer trends. Traditionally, the souks developed organically and were a maze of shady alleyways, with small shops opening on to the paths. Nowadays most of these have been redesigned and replaced by large, air-conditioned developments. Although Abu Dhabi's souks aren't as fascinating as others in the Arab world, such as Fes in Morocco or Mutrah in Oman, they are worth a visit for their bustling atmosphere, eclectic variety of goods, and the traditional way of doing business. Some of the souks have porters who will carry your goods and follow you around, for a few dirhams (agree on a price though, before they start).

Al Ain Souk

Zayed Bin Sultan St Al Ain
Map **4 E2**

Also known as the Central or Old Souk, the Al Ain Souk is a great place to explore, savour the local atmosphere, and to practise your bargaining skills. Selling an interesting mix of household goods – including pots and pans, and plastic buckets of every size and colour – and fruit and vegetables, the souk itself is a fittingly diverse affair, but the prices are good and it is different from many of the other modern, rather sterile, air-conditioned markets that are appearing elsewhere.

Carpet Souk

Al Meena Rd Al Meena
Map **2 T2**

Also known as the Afghan Souk, Yemeni mattresses and machine-made carpets dominate here, but bargains can be found if you know what you are looking for. Some of the vendors will make Arabic 'majlis' cushions to order for a very reasonable price. Don't forget to haggle.

Fish, Fruit & Vegetable Souk

Nr Iranian Souk Al Meena
Map **2 U1**

Fish doesn't get much fresher than this. The day's catch is loaded onto the quayside and sold wholesale for the first two hours of trading (usually 04:30 to 06:30). They move onto smaller quantities after 06:30 and you have to be there early to get the best fish. While the atmosphere is electric, it is not a place for the faint-hearted, as the smell can be pretty strong. Don't wear your best clothes – you'll be closer to the action than you'd think.

Across the road from the Fish Market, a visit to Al Meena Fruit and Vegetable Market is a more relaxed affair. Cruise around until you spot a shop stocking most of the items you need – their wares are normally arranged outside the shops. The price and quality of the stock is often better than in the supermarkets and you can buy by the kilo or the box, but do arrive early

Regional ceramics

Fruit & Vegetable Souk

as the best produce exchanges hand in the first hours of trading. There is another fish and vegetable souk in town between Al Istiqlal Street and Al Nasr Street.

Iranian Souk

Nr Fish, Fruit & Vegetable Souk Al Meena
Map **2 U2**

It may not be air-conditioned, but fresh batches of Iranian goods arrive at this authentic souk every three days by dhow or barge. Everything is on sale, from household goods and terracotta urns, to decorative metal, cane and glass items. It's also a great place for plants – both indoor and outdoor. As it is part of the working port, photography is prohibited.

Muwajei Souk

Nr Jebel R/O, Shk Khalifa Bin Zayed St Al Ain
Map **4 D2**

This modern souk is a long strip of handy shops, including big guns like Choithram, Shoe Mart and The Body Shop. There is also a bakery, a baby shop, a butcher's and a toy shop –and even more outlets can be found across the road.

Souk Al Bawadi

Bawadi Mall Al Ain
Map **4 E3**

Along with Souk Al Qaws, this makes up part of the Bawadi Mall complex. While Souk Al Qaws is more a tourist construct for modern services, Souk Al Bawadi does focus on more traditional and heritage type items. It's well worth visiting if you're in Al Ain and searching for souvenirs.

Souk Al Zaafarana

Nr Emirates International Hospital Al Ain
Map **4 D2**

A few years ago, Al Ain's traditional souk was handed a new home in the shape of Souk Al Zaafarana. Although it took a while for the old vendors to warm to the idea, there are now plenty of stores in the souk selling lots of traditional items, including a vast variety of dates and spices, although souvenirs and knick-knacks are also plentiful.

Shopping Malls

Shopping malls are not just places to shop; a definite mall culture exists here and people come to the malls to meet, eat, play and mingle. Many malls provide entertainment and people of all ages can easily spend hours in them. Recent changes to the law have resulted in a smoking ban in all of Abu Dhabi's malls (and some of the bars attached to them) which has been welcomed across the city.

With so much choice out there, most malls try to offer something unique to draw the crowds. In terms of architecture, Souk Qaryat Al Beri and the Souk

Souk shopping

At Central Market feature remarkable, modern re-imagining of a traditional Middle Eastern marketplace. Indeed, the line between a mall and a souk is becoming increasingly blurred as developers roll out modern 'souks' which are effectively malls.

Khalidiyah Mall boasts stunning Islamic architecture and is home to over 160 shops, a cinema and the ever-popular Sparky's Family Fun Centre (p.337). The Marina Mall has a couple of top attractions, including an indoor ice skating rink. Abu Dhabi Mall offers all the biggest brands right in the city centre, while Mushrif Mall has generated a buzz with its its ambitious architecture and an array of shops and entertainment options – including Abu Dhabi's first indoor waterpark.

Summer in Abu Dhabi (www.summerinabudhabi.ae) is a festival that runs through the summer months in malls throughout the capital, as well as at Abu Dhabi National Exhibition Centre. In addition to prize giveaways and special offers in almost all stores, there are several other events and attractions aimed at the younger members of the family. There is another sale period in January and February, when big discounts are offered throughout stores. In addition, the annual Dubai Shopping Festival, which runs for a month around this time of the year and features gradually increasing discounts, is an important attraction (p.27). Although they're often remarkably quiet and pleasant to stroll through during the day, almost all of Abu Dhabi's malls get extremely busy during special events such as Summer in Abu Dhabi. Regular weekends and evenings, particularly weekend evenings, also attract hoards of shoppers to the malls; if you're not a fan of big crowds, it's probably best to avoid hitting the mall at these times. Most of the malls have plenty of parking and well-served taxi ranks, although both are often stretched to their limits at the weekends when everyone turns up to shop and stroll.

Abu Dhabi Mall

Nr Beach Rotana Hotel Tourist Club Area **02 645 4858**
www.abudhabi-mall.com
Map **2 S5**

One of the main destinations for shopaholics, Abu Dhabi Mall has more than 200 retail outlets spread over four floors, and attracts 25,000 visitors each day. It has a broad range of shops and is particularly good if you're looking for jewellery or gifts. The stores that really bring in the shoppers are the large Abu Dhabi Co-op (p.346), Paris Gallery (02 645 2000) and Virgin Megastore (02 644 7882) which, as well as music, games and DVDs, also sells tickets to local events. There are some gems in terms of smaller boutiques, such as The White Company (02 645 7002). Visiting Abu Dhabi Mall is about more than just shopping, and there are restaurants on every floor, a nine-screen cineplex, a food court and a children's play area. The 3,000 covered parking spaces and the taxi rank mean you won't struggle to get home. The mall is good at looking after the needs of its shoppers; baby trolleys are available for hire, and you can pick them up next to Mugg & Bean (a good place to stop for a pre-shop breakfast) on level one. The mall also provides shop-mobility assistance and rents electric wheelchairs at the customer service desk on level one. There is also a mother and child room and a mothers' feeding area. The mall hosts exciting promotional exhibitions throughout the year, including the popular Christmas Market, which takes over the walkways of the mall and, if you like to combine your window shopping with your workout, the mall is open every day from 07:00 to 10:00 for members of its walking club. Pick up a registration form at the customer service desk.

Abu Dhabi Mall Stores

Books & Stationery
Book Gallery (Jashanmal)
Carlton Cards
Gulf Greetings
Paper Moon

Department Stores
Al Sharief
Bhs
Grand Stores
Salam

Electronics & Computers
Axiom Telecom
Bang & Olufsen
Braun
iStyle
Nokia
Virgin Megastore

Fashion
Aeropostale
Bench
Bershka
Bossini
Bugatti
Cartise
Enrico Marinelli
Evans
Gant
Giordano
Guy Laroche
Hang Ten
Jack & Jones
Jeans West
La Senza
Levi's
Liz Claiborne
Mango
Massimo Dutti
Nautica
Nayomi
Next
Pepe Jeans
Phat Farm & Baby Phat
Pierre Cardin
Pull & Bear
Salsa
Share
Springfield
Stradivarius
Tommy Hilfiger
Triumph
Uterque
Vero Moda
Women'secret
Xanaka
Zara

Furniture & Home Appliances
2XL
Marina Furniture
Museum for Linens & Embroidery
Natuzzi
Sara (Villeroy & Boch)
THE One
The White Company

Kids' Items
Adams
Early Learning Centre
Geekay Games
Krash Toys & Gadgets
La Senza Girl
Mothercare
Pablosky
Premaman

Perfume & Cosmetics
Al Jazira Perfumes
M.A.C
Paris Gallery
Red Earth
The Body Shop
Yas

Services & Utilities
Al Ansari Exchange
Etihad
Al Manara Pharmacy
Al Masood Travel & Services
Dry Cleaning
Fast Rent-A-Car
NBAD
UAE Exchange

Sports & Outdoor Goods
Adidas
Fila
Mega Sport
Puma

Supermarkets, Hypermarkets & Confectionery
Abu Dhabi Co-Operative
Salehia Dates
Bateel
La Casa Del Habano
Patchi

Al Ain Mall

Al Qwaitat St Al Ain **03 766 0333**
www.alainmall.net
Map **4 E2**

When it opened in 2001, Al Ain Mall changed the face of not just shopping in the 'garden city' but of its leisure time and attractions too. Although it has since been eclipsed in size, it's still the city's most popular mall and meeting place. There are more than 100,000 square metres of retail and entertainment space, spread over three floors, in this bright and modern mall, with the 175 stores selling everything from greeting cards to gold jewellery. Large anchor stores include Grand Stores, Home Centre, Splash, Peacocks, Paris Gallery and a MegaMart Hypermarket, but there's plenty of choice and more than enough to satisfy even the most hardcore shopper. There are a number of stores focused on high-end goods and fashions, while The Bride's House is a must-visit for those preparing for their wedding. Electra, Jumbo and i2 should have all the electronics you'll need.

If you're all shopped out, head for the family entertainment area with its 12 lane bowling alley and multi-screen cinema – there's even an indoor ice-skating rink, bumper cars and an action games zone. There are coffee shops throughout, for quick shopping pitstops, and you'll find most of the big fastfood chains present. Covered parking for 1,000 cars is located on the ground floor.

Al Ain Mall Stores

Department Stores
Al Mandoos
LifeStyle
Salam
Sana

Electronics & Computers
Axiom Telecom
Cellucom
Grand Stores
i2
Jumbo Electronics

Fashion
Balestra Fashion Design
Blue Ocean
Can Can
Cloud Nine
Enzo Studio
Evans
Giordano
Hang Ten
Heaven
High Fashion
Kayra
La Senza
Mexx
Nayomi
Next
Parma Moda
Paul Jordan
Peacocks
Pierre Cardin
Sahra
Splash
Ted Lapidus
The Bride's House
Tina Fashion
Velvet

Eyewear & Opticians
Al Ain Optical
Badie Optical
Grand Sunglasses
NYS
Optifashion
Yateem Optician

Footwear
K-Corner
Milano
Nicoli
Peacocks
Shoe Mart
Spring

Furniture & Home Appliances
Unique Furniture
Design Furniture
Grand Stores
Intercoil Therapedic
LifeStyle

Kids' Items
Babyshop
Bambini
Early Learning Centre
Hobby Centre
Microbio
MotherCare

Perfume & Cosmetics
Arabian Oud
Grand Stores
Karji Perfumes
M.A.C
Make Up For Ever
Mikyagi
Nabeel Perfume
Nectar
Paris Gallery
Sterling Perfume
Tawash
Yas

Services & Utilities
Al Ansari Exchange
Al Manara Pharmacy
Al Masaood Travel & Services
Al Tawash Rent A Car
Mall Automatic Laundry
Mall Car Wash
VIP Rent A Car

Sports & Outdoor Goods
Adidas
Nike

Supermarkets, Hypermarkets & Confectionery
Megamart

Al Wahda Mall > p.343

Nr Al Wahda Sports Club, Hazaa Bin Zayed The First St Al Dhafrah **02 443 7000**
www.alwahda-mall.com
Map **2 M7**

Located right in the heart of the city, Al Wahda is one of Abu Dhabi's newer malls and has become a firm must-visit shopping destination. Its spacious sun-roofed design is fresh and inviting and, although the layout is open and spacious, it also has a myriad of side passages leading shoppers to hidden delights. In one store you can taste-test various Italian and Spanish olive oils and vinegars, or you can eat at a restaurant dedicated to chocoholics. The mall features a wide range of western brand stores including Gap, Banana Republic, Next and Mamas & Papas, while there's a sizeable branch of Magrudy's that doesn't just cater to the needs of reading fans, but also stocks toys and supplies for a whole host of crafts and hobbies. One of the mall's biggest draws is Lulu Hypermarket which has a huge choice of quality products and is particularly popular for its deli counter and pre-prepared meals and salads.

As for entertainment, Wanasa Land is the mall's family entertainment centre which has 10 pin bowling, arcades and pool tables. While the mall is home to the usual host of cafes and fast food joints, there is a sprinkling of higher end restaurants providing slightly more substantial fare too. The hypermarket is open daily from 08:00 to 24:00, while the rest of the mall is open between 10:00 and 22:00.

Al Wahda Mall Stores

Books & Stationery
Gulf Greetings (Hallmark)
Magrudy's
Red Rock

Electronics & Computers
Axiom Telecom
E-City
Jumbo Electronics
Techzone

Eyewear & Opticians
Optifashion
Pearle Opticians
Sunglass Hut
X-Stream Sunglasses
Yateem Optician

Fashion
Armani Exchange
Banana Republic
Cache Cache
Gap
Giordano
Grafika
Intimo Tre
La Senza
Le Chateau
Mango
Marco Firri
Nayomi
Next
Oysho
Pierre Cardin
Pimkie
Riva
Springfield
Ted Lapidus
Tommy Hilfiger
Xanaka

Footwear
Aldo
Bata
Dumond
Hush Puppies
Milano
Moreschi
Tala Shoes

Furniture & Home Appliances
@Home
Better Life
Dwell
Id Design
Stokes
Wall Arts Decor

Jewellery & Accessories
Al Futtaim Jewellery
Aldo Accessories
Claire's
Damas Les Exclusive
Pure Gold
Rivoli
Swatch
The Watch House

Kids' Items
Accessorize Tape A Loeil
Adams Kids
Early Learning Centre
Mamas & Papas
Mothercare
Pumpkin Patch

Perfume & Cosmetics
Areej
Inglot
Mikyajy
Missha
Solace Organics
Swiss Arabian
Tammy Vipera Cosmetics
The Body Shop

Services & Utilities
Abu Dhabi Islamic Bank
Al Ansari Exchange
Al Fardan Exchange
Boots Pharmacy
Etihad Airways
Saber Watch Repairing

Sports & Outdoor Goods
Adidas
Animal
Columbia
Ecko Unltd
Jack Wolfskin
Nike
Oakley, Ripcurl & Beyond The Beach
Orlando Sports
Rocawear

Supermarkets, Hypermarkets & Confectionery
Quatro Dates & Nuts
Sweet Factory

Khalidiyah Mall > p.341

King Khalid Bin Abdulaziz Saeed St Al Khalidiyah
02 635 4000
www.khalidiyahmall.com
Map **2 H5**

Not to be confused with the older, smaller Khalidiyah Centre just up the road, Khalidiyah Mall opened in 2008 and has become one of Abu Dhabi's most popular shopping venues. Located on Al Nahyan Street in the city centre, it is designed in a distinctive Islamic architectural style and is nicely spaced out over three floors.

Home to over 160 stores, the highlights are a large branch of Lulu Hypermarket, which is spread over the first and second floors, and department stores such as Debenhams, Bhs and Paris Gallery. There are plenty of choices for fashionistas with high street labels like Monsoon and Springfield teamed with a couple of higher-end and more traditional outlets. Sports enthusiasts can turn to the excellent, bargain-filled Sports Direct, and other stores sell everything from electronics to accessories and books.

The food and drink outlets go a little further than the bog standard food court offerings, with Bricco Café, Cantina Laredo and Chilis offering more substantial and higher quality fare. Khalidiyah Mall is particularly popular thanks to its entertainment attractions: the large Sparky's Family Fun Centre (p.216) includes rides and a bowling alley, while the CineRoyal cinema shows all the latest Hollywood flicks.

Khalidiyah Mall Stores

Books & Stationery
Booksplus
Bookworm
Gulf Greetings
Photo Magic

Department Stores
Jashanmal
Lulu Deparment Store
Tchibo

Electronics & Computers
Jumbo Electronics
Nokia
Techzone

Eyewear & Opticians
Optifashion
Rivoli Eye Zone
Yateem Optician

Fashion
Alcott
Aldo
Azzaro
Bendon
BHS
Bossini
Brantano
Calonge
Debenhams
Fouad Sarkis
Giordano
K Corner
La Senza
Laura Ashley
Marco Firri
Mario Zognelle
Monsoon
Nayomi
Nine West
Piquadro
Signe
Springfield
Tammy
Via Spiga

Furniture & Home Appliances
Options Furniture

Jewellery & Accessories
Accessorize
Al Zain
Aldo Accessories
Claire's
Damas 22K
Damas Les Exclusive
Hour Choice
Lozan House
Oriental Stores
Paris Gallery
Rivoli
Visconti

Kids' Items
Adams
Bhs Kids
Early Learning Centre
Khabbaz Kids
Pumpkin Patch
Tape A Loeil

Perfume & Cosmetics
Ajmal Perfumes
Faces
Loccitane
Mikyajy
Paris Gallery
The Body Shop
Yas Perfumes

Services & Utilities
ADCB
Al Ansari Exchange
Etihad Holidays
Lulu Khalidiyah Pharmacy
UAE Exchange

Sports & Outdoor Goods
Nike
Sports Direct
Sun & Sands Sports
Timberland

Supermarkets, Hypermarkets & Confectionery
Bateel
Edible Arrangements
Lulu Hypermarket

Marina Mall

Corniche St Breakwater **02 681 2310**
www.marinamall.ae
Map **2 D1**

Situated in Breakwater, but still within easy reach of the city's main residential areas, this mall offers a breath of fresh (sea) air to its customers, especially those looking for a mix of familiar western brands with a few individual boutiques and a sprinkling of local goods. Popular outlets include global favourites, such as Carrefour, IKEA, Plug-Ins, Sun & Sand Sports and Woolworths. Restaurants, fastfood outlets and coffee shops aplenty offer fuel for weary shoppers, while committed bargain hunters should pencil in a couple of visits during the big sale period that lasts from mid January to the end of February.

If you get bored of shopping, the nine-screen Cinestar complex, Fun City (02 681 5527), and the musical fountains near the main entrance will keep you entertained. There's also one of the city's biggest bowling centres and a small ice rink, while those with a taste for heights and views can have a coffee or a bite to eat in the mall's viewing tower.

On the same plot but with a separate entrance is the large Centrepoint department store, where you'll find everything from shoes, fashion and baby items to a home and garden store.

Marina Mall Stores

Books & Stationery
Book Corner
Gulf Greetings

Department Stores
Jashanmal
Woolworths

Electronics & Computers
Cool Gadgets
I Style
Plug-Ins
Vertu

Fashion
Armani Exchange
Baby Phat
BC Bulgari
Bench
BillaBong
Burberry
Calvin Klein
Chanel
Converse
Diesel
Dior
Ed Hardy
Ermenegildo Zegna
Esprit
Fendi
Gap
Guess
Hugo Boss
Jennyfer
Kookai
La Senza
Lacoste
Levi's
Mango
Monsoon
Nayomi
Next
Oasis
Phat Farm
Pierre Cardin
Quiksilver
Sauce
Springfield
Steve Madden
Stradivarious
Ted Lapidus
Timberland
Top Shop
Valentino
Women'secret
Zara

Furniture & Home
Appliances
Home Sweet Home
Homes Art
IKEA
Silica
Zara Home

Kids' Items
Adams Kids
Bambini
Early Learning Centre
Mamas & Papas
Mothercare
Pumpkin Patch
Sanrio
Tape A L'oeil

Perfume & Cosmetics
Arabian Oud
Areej
Faces
L`Occitane
M.A.C
Natural Looks
Paris Gallery
Swiss Arabian Perfumes
The Body Shop

Services & Utilities
Al Ansari Exchange
Al Manara Pharmacy
Bin Sina Pharmacy
Etihad Airways
Etisalat
Minutes
Moments
Orbit Showtime
Tamweel
UAE Exchange

Sports & Outdoor Goods
Adidas
Studio R
City Sport/Sports Link
Ocean & Woods
Sun & Sand Sports
Timberland

Supermarkets, Hypermarkets & Confectionery
Al Dhafra Dates
Candy Land
Carrefour
Patchi
Sweet Factory

Abu Dhabi Co-operative Society

Nr Dana Hotel Tourist Club Area **02 644 0808**
www.abudhabicoop.com
Map **2 R4**

This older shopping centre still buzzes, especially during weekends and evenings. It was once home to the Abu Dhabi Co-op (now in Abu Dhabi Mall), hence the name, but its main draws are now Splash, Shoe Mart, Lifestyle and The Baby Shop.

Al Falah Plaza

Al Falah St Al Dhafrah **02 642 5800**
Map **2 N6**

Situated near Habib Bank, this mall is a cheap and cheerful place to stock up on household essentials. Apart from the Lulu Hypermarket on the ground floor, you'll also find a music shop, a pharmacy, a fastfood restaurant, a cafe, and much more. Timings for the supermarket are from 09:00 to 23:30, while stores are open from 09:00 to 14:00 and 16:30 to 23:00 on weekdays, and 09:00 to 23:30 on Fridays.

Al Foah Mall

Al Ain – Dubai Rd, Al Foah Al Ain
03 766 3560
Map **4 E1**

Al Ain's latest mall opened its doors in December 2010 to bring shopping facilities, including a Lulu Hypermarket, closer to residents in this part of town.

Al Mariah Mall

Hamdan St Al Markaziyah **02 677 1741**
www.almariah.com
Map **2 P3**

Located in downtown Abu Dhabi, this mall hosts a range of regional and international shops with a focus on brands that won't break the bank. The shops include Milano and Splash, while eating options range from Chilli's to MacDonald's.

Al Muhairy Centre

Shk Zayed The First St Al Manhal **02 632 2228**
Map **2 L4**

This shopping centre occupies the commercial floors of one of new Abu Dhabi's most recognisable mixed-use developments. It is yet to fully find its place in the hearts and minds of Abu Dhabi residents – mainly as there's nothing here you can't find elsewhere – although the mall does have a nice collection of stores, with a focus on high-end shopping. You'll find a couple of designer labels, as well as some of the city's top-end tailors and dressmakers here, with a smattering of coffee shops, cafes, a doctor's surgery and a couple of beauty salons. Perhaps its greatest offering is for kids: in addition to children's accessories and a medical shoe store, there are two play areas for the younger family members.

Al Raha Mall > *p.302*

Off Abu Dhabi-Dubai Rd Al Raha **02 556 2229**
www.al-rahamall.com
Map **1 R7**

A welcome addition to this rapidly developing area, Al Raha Mall provides all the daily necessities and some entertainment options to those living in the new, off-island, residential communities nearby. Al Raha Mall is more for local convenience than a tourist attraction in its own right. This said, the mall succeeds in offering locals more than the bare essentials. The Lulu Express supermarket is not huge, but it is well-stocked and has fresh, appetising produce. The mall also has a pharmacy, an optician and several of the biggest banks are represented. Grooming and beauty care services are also available, including hair saloons, a Kaya Skincare Clinic and Nails Magic. There are a few fashion outlets; Betterlife provides homeware and appliances; Avenue Home Furniture other house fixtures; while Orlando's Sport is a decent sports shop with a wide enough stock to suit most needs. There are a number of restaurants and cafes in the foodcourt, and a small cinema plays the latest releases. For parents with younger children, Play & Learn (p.216) is a supervised children's centre. Parking is plentiful, and the mall is open from 10:00 to 22:00 during the week, and from 10:00 to 23:00 at weekends.

Bawadi Mall

Zayed Bin Sultan St Al Ain **03 784 0000**
www.bawadimall.com
Map **4 E3**

The modern, bright and spacious building houses almost 400 stores covering every possible purchasing need, from the giant Carrefour hypermarket and department stores such as Centrepoint and Marks & Spencer, to high street fashion chains (including Zara, Oasis, La Senza and Etam) and shops selling more specialist goods (including sports gear, sunglasses, jewellery, luggage and DIY items). Bawadi Mall is packed with banks, services and eateries (there's a particularly good foodcourt), but it also has a unique offering: there is a separate heritage village and two other souk sections, which resemble traditional Arabic marketplaces, with over 100 stores. There's also a Grand Bawadi Cinema, which has a VIP screen, and a 10,000 square metre family entertainment centre with an arcade, bowling alley and ice rink.

Dalma Mall

Nr Mohammed Bin Zayed City Mussafah **02 550 6111**
Map **1 N13**
www.dalmamall.ae

This huge, brand new mall in Mussafah caters to residents of Mohammed Bin Zayed City. Dalma Mall is becoming a favourite for off-island dwellers: Abu Dhabi's largest mall is anchored by Carrefour and Home Centre, and the gigantic structure is also home to several international retail chains' largest branches in town. Kids entertainment oasis FunCity keeps the little ones occupied while the 14-screen CineStar movie theatre is Abu Dhabi's largest.

Dalma Mall

Dana Plaza

Nr Khalidiya Garden, Khalidiya St Al Khalidiyah
02 665 1333
Map **2 H4**

Packed with outlets selling everything from cosmetics and stationery, to household goods, linen and fashions for the whole family; most of the stores cater largely to local tastes. The ground floor houses a branch of the Abu Dhabi Co-op (open 24 hours a day) and bargain hunters should head for the third floor to find a selection of purse-friendly outlets.

Fotouh Al Khair Centre

Shk Rashid Bin Saeed Al Maktoum St Markaziya East
02 681 1130
www.fotouhalkhair.com
Map **2 L4**

Several of the world's favourite brands are jammed into this spacious mall – Marks & Spencer, Adams, Monsoon, Nine West, and many more. Other shops include Al Rani Bridal Wear, Bendon Lingerie, Dune, Nail Fashion, Pumpkin Patch, Watch House, and Falcon Gallery – great for Christmas decorations, candles and other fancy goods.

Hamdan Centre

Shk Hamdan Bin Mohd St Markaziya East
02 632 8555
Map **2 N4**

Something of an institution on the local shopping scene, and located right in the heart of the city, this vibrant centre is a good place to buy clothing, leather, shoes, bags, perfumes, sports equipment and touristy knick-knacks, all at reasonable prices. Look carefully, and you'll also find a few designer outlets. The centre also houses a pharmacy.

Khalifa Centre

Nr Abu Dhabi Co-operative Society
Tourist Club Area
Map **2 R4**

Located behind the Abu Dhabi Co-op building and opposite Abu Dhabi Mall (look for Al Mandoos), this mall is teeming with craft and souvenir shops, as well as shops selling Persian and Baluchi carpets. It's a great place to take visitors looking for mementos, or to browse in air-conditioned comfort, as opposed to the souks. Be aware that you may find a few questionable or controversial items, such as African ivory. If you have strong feelings about this, check before you buy.

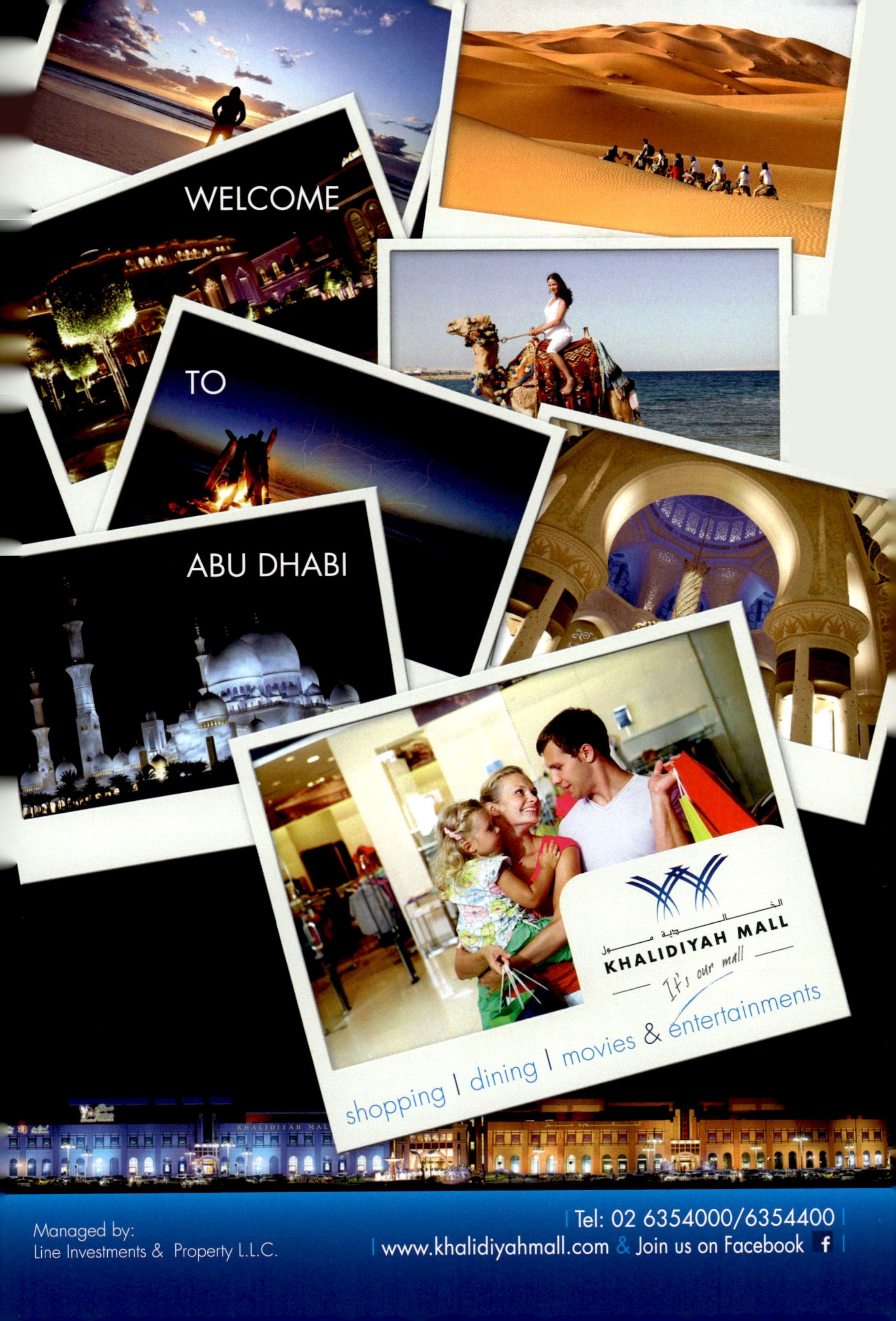
WELCOME
TO
ABU DHABI
KHALIDIYAH MALL
It's our mall
shopping | dining | movies & entertainments
Managed by:
Line Investments & Property L.L.C.
Tel: 02 6354000/6354400
www.khalidiyahmall.com & Join us on Facebook

Liwa Centre

Shk Hamdan Bin Mohd St Markaziya East
Map **2 M4**

This is where to head on Hamdan Street for designer jewellery, clothes, makeup, perfume and more. Be sure to visit the vibrant food court on the second level or relax in the coffee shop, which is open until midnight.

Madinat Zayed Shopping Centre & Gold Centre > *p.66*

Nr Post Office, East Road Madinat Zayed
02 633 3311
Map **2 M5**

Shopaholics will love this mall – it has over 400 outlets selling just about everything from home accessories to clothing. The Madinat Zayed Gold Centre, adjacent to the main mall, glitters with the finest gold, diamond and pearl jewellery. The supervised toddlers' area and the games arcade will keep the kids entertained.

Mazyad Mall > *p.232*

79th Street Mohammed Bin Zayed City **02 553 2200**
www.mazyadmall.com
Map **1 P10**

This light, airy mall is not what you'd call a shopping hotspot, but there's a well stocked Lulu Express supermarket, as well as fashion outlets, cafes and a small foodcourt. Great for general mall outings, and with sporting goods, jewellery stores and electronics all covered, Mazyad Mall leans more towards family outings than fashionista shopping sprees.

Mina Centre

Nr Toys R Us Al Meena **02 673 4848**
Map **1 D2**

This small and quiet commercial centre in the port area of the city is mainly visited for three reasons: the excellent branch of the Abu Dhabi Co-op, the Costless Electronics that it houses, and the great art and craft section in the United Bookstore. The Co-op has arguably the city's largest assortment of fruit, vegetables, fresh bread, meat and fish, while the Costless has the capital's biggest collection of electronic goods under one roof. United Bookstore has a vast array of art and craft supplies, and a good range of educational books. There's the usual collection of coffee shops, fastfood joints and a kids' play centre, plus a carpet store and an interiors store.

MultiBrand

Nr Shk Hamdan Bin Mohd St & Baniyas St
Markaziya East **02 621 9700**
www.alshaya.com
Map **2 P4**

This large, open plan store houses well known shops such as Mothercare, Claire's, Next and Oasis. If your taste in fashion is more USA than UK, you'll find the Liz Claiborne outlet a welcome addition. Alternatively, indulge your shoe fetish at Milano.

Mushrif Mall > *p.v*

Sheikh Rashid Bin Saeed Al Maktoum Rd Al Mushrif
02 690 4444
www.mushrifmall.com
Map **1 G7**

The newest of the capital's mall options has generated a buzz among Mushrif residents with its ambitious architecture and an array of shops and entertainment options. Anchored by Lulu Hypermarket, there's also the Indoor Market, which is the largest of its kind in Abu Dhabi and a destination in itself. What's more, many of the branded retail outlets are the first of their kind in Abu Dhabi, and some stores indeed in the whole country. Finally, there's an enormous dining court and a small indoor water park – another first for the UAE.

Rotana Mall

Al Khaleej Al Arabi St Al Khalidiyah **02 681 4433**
Map **2 G4**

Located between Khaleej Al Arabi Street and Sheikh Zayed The First Street, this mall is best known for a couple of shops selling antiques, carpets, handicrafts, Arabic pottery and wall hangings.

The Souk Central Market

Shk Hamdan Bin Mohd St
Map 2 M3

The Souk at Central Market opened in 2011 after extensive redevelopment and the beautifully themed setting has already attracted faithful regulars, particularly at its many cafes and restaurants. With a growing number of shops and boutiques now opening their doors, the development looks set to transform the shopping scene in this part of town.

The Souk At Qaryat Al Beri

Qaryat Al Beri Complex Bain Al Jessrain **02 558 1670**
www.soukqaryatalberi.com
Map **1 L8**

A contemporary adaptation of a typical souk, Qaryat Al Beri forms part of a larger creekside complex with the Shangri-la and Traders hotels. This area is a rabbit's warren of outlets, bound together by romantic water canals on which abras transport visitors. The outlets are predominantly aimed at tourists and, as such, are a little over priced, although residents looking for certain niche items, such as antiques, heritage items, souvenirs or even gifts of flowers, dates and chocolates will find what they're looking for here. The real reason for Souk Qaryat Al Beri's increasing popularity, however, is its extensive and diverse collection of cafes, bars and restaurants. Almost all offer alfresco dining with views over the creek.

EXPLORE
الوحدة مول
AL WAHDA MALL
HAVE IT ALL & MORE
PUBLISHED BY: AL WAHDA MALL | ANNUAL ISSUE
SHOPPING
Tel: 02 4437000
www.alwahda-mall.com
Al Wahda Mall Extension Nearing Completion
Fashion Piazza
Jewellery Boulevard
Tech City
Food Station
Home Improvement Square
Entertainment World
Health, Beauty & Wellness Zone
Kids County
AL WAHDA MALL
ANNUAL EVENTS & OFFERS
CUSTOMER SATISFACTION
TESTIMONY
AWARDS & APPRECIATIONS
PUBLIC SERVICE COMMITMENTS
AL WAHDA MALL

Going Out

GOING OUT

Abu Dhabi's gastronomic landscape is fairly impressive, and continues to grow at an ever-increasing rate. At one end of the spectrum, celebrity chefs, picturesque cocktail lounges and well-appointed clubs compete for your hard-earned dirhams. At the other end, bargain eateries, drink-deal bars and bang-for-your-buck brunches are there to help at the end of the month. Abu Dhabi's social scene revolves around club nights, raucous brunches and laid-back shisha cafes, so expect to go out more than you ever did back home.

Thursday and Friday nights are the big ones, with reservations required in restaurants. During the week you'll find drinks deals across the city and all manner of dining promotions, so the town is still buzzing. Since alcohol can only be served in hotels and sports clubs, chances are you won't have a 'local' at the end of your street; instead, you might have a roster of four or five favourites within a 10 minute taxi drive. Most of the city's popular restaurants are located in hotels for the same reason – but don't let the absence of a wine list deter you from exploring the many outstanding independent restaurants that Abu Dhabi has to offer. You can always eat first and drink later.

The live entertainment scene lags behind other cities, but with ADNEC focusing increasingly on live events, Emirates Palace and Yas Island opening their doors to concerts, and some of the city's festivals incorporating a healthy dose of music, more and more big names are being lured over to perform and the scene is improving all the time (see Concerts & Live Music, p.351).

Ramadan Rules

During Ramadan, opening and closing times of restaurants change considerably. Because eating and drinking in public is forbidden during daylight hours, many places only open after sunset and then keep going well into the early hours. Restaurants in some hotels remain open, but will be screened off from public view. Alcohol will also only be sold after sunset. Live entertainment is not allowed, so while some nightclubs remain open, all dancefloors are closed.

Opening Hours

In general, cafes and restaurants close between 23:00 and 01:00, with bars and nightclubs split between those that close 'early' at 01:00 and those that go on until 03:00. The legal drinking age is 21, and it's best to avoid getting staggeringly drunk as it may land you behind bars. Most importantly, don't even think about getting behind the wheel of a car after drinking – Abu Dhabi maintains a strict zero tolerance stance on drunk driving. Respect the laws and you'll have nothing to worry about – apart from your dwindling finances.

Dressing Up

Generally speaking, shorts and T-shirts are a no-no for Abu Dhabi's bars and restaurants, and even some pubs will frown at your beach-bum attire, especially at the weekend. While trainers aren't strictly outlawed it will depend on the whole ensemble, and many places don't let you in wearing flip-flops – even if they're nice ones. Abu Dhabi's dress code is on the smarter side – more beautiful than bohemian – so shine your shoes when you're stepping out.

EATING OUT

The majority of Abu Dhabi's most popular restaurants are located within hotels and leisure clubs, and their popularity is partly down to the fact that these are virtually the only outlets where you can drink alcohol with your meal. Almost all other restaurants are unlicensed. If you're the type who requires a glass of vino to make a meal complete, it's best to phone ahead to check whether the establishment serves alcohol. There's quite a hefty mark-up on drinks, with a decent bottle of wine often costing as much as your meal.

Bottled water also seems to rocket in price in the five-star venues, and if you ask for water you'll often be given an imported brand, costing up to Dhs.40 a bottle. You should specify 'local' water when ordering, but even then you can expect to pay Dhs.10 or Dhs.20 for a bottle of still water that costs less than Dhs.2 in the supermarket.

However, the city has some superb independent restaurants and cafes that shouldn't be ignored just because they don't serve booze. Most of these serve up Arabic or Asian cuisines and, along with a more traditional dining experience, you'll often be faced with a bill that, for two people, comes to less than that bottle of imported water.

Hygiene

Food and drink outlets are subject to regular checks by the Abu Dhabi Food Control Authority (www.adfca.ae), and unclean outlets are warned to either scrub up or shut down. ADFCA also regulates food stores and wholesalers. You can be fairly confident that restaurants within hotels and most independent restaurants meet basic health and hygiene requirements. The city isn't immune to the odd food poisoning incident, however, so if a place looks like it might have some hygiene issues, it's best to avoid it.

If you feel a restaurant you have visited could use an inspection, you can call ADFCA (800 555).

Food Allergies

If you suffer from food allergies, take extra care when eating out in Abu Dhabi's restaurants. Many restaurants in the larger chain hotels now adhere to western practices in catering to and warning those with allergies about the contents of dishes, and menus are generally well-labelled for nuts and shellfish. In smaller and independent eateries, however, a lack of clearly-marked menus and a serving culture that is trained to tell customers what they think they want to hear can combine to form a dangerous situation. Don't hesitate to inform servers about the seriousness of your allergies if you don't think they are catching the drift of your questioning.

Taxes & Service Charges

Look out for the small print at the bottom of your menu and you may spot the dreaded 'prices are subject to 10% service charge and 6% tourism fee'. In some hotel restaurants and bars, these extras are already included, but they appear as extras on bills in a large number of outlets, particularly independent eateries. The 10% service charge is perhaps incorrectly named as often it isn't passed on to the staff, and you have no option of withholding it if you receive poor service. If you want to reward the waiting staff directly then the standard rule of a 10 – 12.5% tip will be appreciated, but give them cash if you can, or your tip may go straight in the till.

Street Food

Throughout the city, you will find counter windows selling 'shawarma' (rolled pita bread filled with lamb or chicken as well as chips and a yogurt sauce). Costing about Dhs.5 each, this is not only an inexpensive option but also well worth trying as an excellent alternative fast food to the usual hamburger. These places usually sell other dishes too, such as 'foul' (a paste made from fava beans) and 'falafel' (or ta'amiya), small savoury balls of deep fried chickpeas. And if it's value for money you're after, for just Dhs.15, you can buy a whole grilled chicken, salad and hummus. While most counter window restaurants offer virtually the same thing, slight differences make some stand out from the rest. People are often adamant that their particular favourite serves, for example, the best falafel in town. Every restaurant has its own way of doing things and you might find that the best place is, surprisingly, the smallest, most low key restaurant you happened upon by chance.

Arabic coffee

Vegetarian Food

Vegetarians should be pleasantly surprised by the variety available to them in Abu Dhabi's restaurants. For starters, Abu Dhabi is home to a large population from the subcontinent who are vegetarian by religion, and numerous Indian restaurants offer a range of cooking styles and tasty vegetarian dishes, especially in the small restaurants centred around the Tourist Club and Al Markaziyah areas. Try Royal Vegetarian (p.384), Evergreen Vegetarian Restaurant (p.372) or super budget Ruchi (02 679 5679). In other restaurants (even in steakhouses), you'll often find at least one or two vegetarian options. Arabic cuisine, although heavy on meat-based mains, offers a great range of mezze that are mostly vegetarian.

Abu Dhabi's cafes also represent decent sources for vegetarian food. Of particular note is BiteRite (p.367). The D Club, (www.thedclub.com) offers an organic food delivery service in the capital, and has plans to open a restaurant in the near future.

A word of warning: if you are a strict veggie, confirm that your meal is completely meat free. Some smaller restaurants cook their 'vegetarian' selection with animal fat or on the same grill as the meat dishes. Also, in some places you may need to check the ingredients of the vegetarian items before ordering.

Cultural Meals

Al Markaziyah is the best place in the city to eat while soaking up some of the local atmosphere. This traditional city centre may be non-stop hustle and bustle, but strolling through the streets and dining at one of the many small, independent restaurants and cafes is an enjoyable experience. Both the Heritage Village (p.207) and Women's Handicraft Center (p.208) have small eateries where you can try traditional Emirati flavours, while an Emirati buffet is there to be dived into at Al Arish (02 673 2266) – a real local, cultural gem in the Al Meena port area. To enjoy Abu Dhabi – and the Corniche in particular – in the way that Abu Dhabians themselves enjoy it, head for Mirage Marine Café (p.379) or Café Layali Zaman (02 626 4555), which both serve up local cuisine and shisha in waterfront locations. Top-end Emirati cuisine is on offer at Mezlai (p.379), located in the sumptuous Emirates Palace (p.201).

Independent Restaurants

While hotel restaurants tend to draw in the crowds, especially at the weekend, Abu Dhabi's independent choices are not to be missed. Areas like Al Markaziyah, Tourist Club Area and Al Khalidiyah are home to restaurants serving everything from authentic Arabic kebabs (Lebanese Flower, p.378) and tempting teppanyaki (Samurai, p.384) to Indonesian dishes (Bandung, p.366) and fiery Pakistani curry (Karachi City, 02 677 6055). Whether you pop in for a hearty lunch or have a teetotal evening you shouldn't ignore the culinary, and affordable, delights of these independent restaurants.

NIGHTLIFE

Bars, Pubs & Clubs

You can't expect authenticity from Abu Dhabi's pubs, but then when they're mostly in hotels, in the desert, in the Middle East, that won't come as a surprise. What you can look forward to is some inviting, friendly spots with a decent selection of draught and bottled beers and reliably good grub. Many of these mostly English and Irish places are popular when there's a big game on. And they're all comfortable, raucous and smoky enough to feel like the real thing.

Door Policy

Certain bars and nightclubs have a 'selective' entry policy, and sometimes the 'members only' sign on the entrance needs a bit of explaining. Membership is usually introduced to control the clientele frequenting the establishment, but is often only enforced during busy periods. At quieter times, non-members may have no problems getting in, even if not accompanied by a member. Some places seem to use the rule to disallow entry if they don't like the look of you or your group.

Local Liquids

Fresh juices are widely available, either from small restaurants or juice shops. They are delicious, healthy and cheap, and made on the spot from fresh fruits such as orange, mango, banana, kiwi, strawberry, avocado, cantaloupe melon, watermelon, grapefruit and pineapple. If you can't decide, go for the mixed fruit cocktail or the refreshing lemon mint. Yoghurt is also a popular drink, often served with nuts, and the local milk is called 'laban' (a heavy, salty buttermilk that doesn't go well in tea or coffee). Arabic mint tea is available but probably not drunk as widely here as it is in other parts of the Arab world. However, Arabic coffee (thick, heavy and strong) is extremely popular and will have you buzzing on a caffeine high for days.

Large groups (especially all males), single men and, sometimes, certain nationalities may be turned away without explanation. You can avoid the inconvenience, and the embarrassment, by breaking the group up or by going in a mixed-gender group. If you do find yourself being discriminated against it's not worth arguing with the doorman – it won't work. Most companies do everything to avoid bad publicity, so try taking the issue up with the local media instead. Pre-booking a table is a good option for ensuring that you gain entrance into a popular club. But keep in mind that table reservations usually come with a required minimum spend.

Dress Code

While many bars have a reasonably relaxed attitude towards dress code, some places will not allow you in if you are wearing shorts and sandals, while others require a collared shirt and have a 'no jeans or trainers' policy. You'll find that dress codes get stricter at the weekend too, when relaxed sports bars you've watched matches in wearing shorts and flip-flops during the week will turn you away for the same attire. In general, nightclubs are stricter, so dress to impress.

Certain bars and nightclubs have a 'selective' entry policy, and sometimes the 'members only' sign on the entrance needs a bit of explaining. Membership is

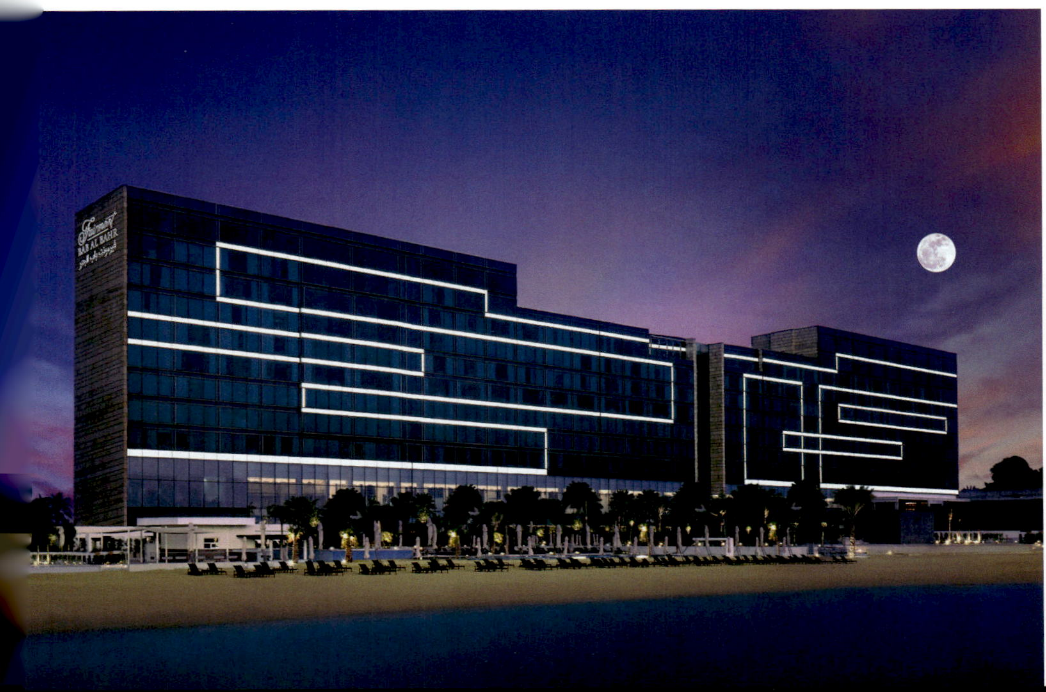

usually introduced to control the clientele frequenting the establishment, but is often only enforced during busy periods. At quieter times, non-members may have no problems getting in, even if not accompanied by a member. Some places seem to use the rule to disallow entry if they don't like the look of you or the look of your group overall.

Large groups (especially all males), single men and, sometimes, certain nationalities may be turned away without explanation. You can avoid the inconvenience, and the embarrassment, by breaking the group up or by going in a mixed-gender group. If you do find yourself being discriminated against it's not worth arguing with the doorman – it won't work. Most companies do everything to avoid bad publicity, so try taking the issue up with the local media instead.

Pre-booking a table is a good option for ensuring that you gain entrance into a popular club. But keep in mind that table reservations usually come with a required minimum spend.

Under Age

The law in Abu Dhabi states that drinkers must be 21 or over. If you're lucky enough to look like you were born after the 1980s, make sure you carry some form of ID that shows your age – a passport or driving licence is best. Even if you think you're flattering your slightly wrinkled self, it's better to be safe than sorry. Otherwise you'll be on lemonade all night, or, worse still, left outside alone.

Driving Under The Influence

Drinking and driving is illegal in Abu Dhabi. There is zero tolerance; if you are caught with even a hint of alcohol in your system you will be sent to prison. Be responsible and always take a taxi – they're cheap, reliable and plentiful. For more information on drink driving and the law, see p.127.

Cinemas

There are a number of cinemas around Abu Dhabi – the majority of them situated in shopping malls. Grand Cinemas operates a pair of cinemas, while Vox Cinemas runs the Marina Mall cinema. Abu Dhabi's movie offerings are largely mainstream Hollywood and Bollywood films with multiple screenings; see www.liveworkexplore.com for listings. There are also a couple of smaller independent cinemas in Abu Dhabi, which focus mainly on Hindi films. Unfortunately, there are no IMAX screens in Abu Dhabi, so those wanting the full 3D experience will have to head for Ibn Battuta Mall in Dubai where the Grand Megaplex has an IMAX screen, or to Screen 22 at Dubai Mall's Reel Cinema which offers an IMAX-like experience.

There are local cinema idiosyncrasies – freezing air conditioning, people chatting to each other or talking on their mobile phones, and the heavy hand of the censor can all affect your experience. Also, the sound quality can be a little off and Arabic (and often French) subtitles cover the bottom of the screen.

An annual cinematic highlight is the Abu Dhabi Film Festival (p.29). The event runs for a week in October, taking place mainly at the Emirates Palace and showcasing an impressive mix of mainstream, world and local cinema, from short films and documentaries to full-length features.

Alternative Screenings

Several of Abu Dhabi's big hotels hold occasional movie nights featuring giant or even poolside screens but, unfortunately, none of these as yet make regular appearances on the cultural calendar. The Alliance Française's Cine Club (www.af-aboudabi.net) has regular screenings of French language films while some of the more progressive art spaces occasionally arrange film nights. ADACH (the cultural foundation, see p.207) teams up with consulates and embassies to put on film nights from time to time, although these have become less frequent since the foundation moved from its Al Hosn home. Check www.adach.ae for details of upcoming screenings and events. New York University Abu Dhabi (www.nyuad.nyu.edu), in collaboration with the Abu Dhabi Film Festival, runs a series of Cinema Chats during the academic year. The series generally features movies by Arab filmmakers, who take questions from the audience following the film. Check the website for scheduled viewings.

Cine Royal Khalidiyah Mall, Al Khalidiyah, 02 681 9444, *www.cineroyal.ae*
Grand Abu Dhabi Mall Abu Dhabi Mall, Tourist Club Area, 02 645 8988, *www.grandcinemas.com*
Grand Cineplex Cinema Al Ain Mall, Al Ain, 03 751 1228, *www.grandcinemas.com*
Grand Rotana Al Ain Rotana, Al Ain, 03 754 4447, *www.grandcinemas.com*
Vox Cinemas Marina Mall, Breakwater, 02 681 8484, *www.voxcinemas.com*

Comedy Nights

The regular comedy scene in Abu Dhabi is, unfortunately, quite limited. However, there are regular visits from The Laughter Factory as well as the occasional comical theatre production or one-off event. Comedy shows tend to be aimed at the British population, so other nationalities may not always get the joke. Events are often promoted only a short time before they actually take place, so keep your ears to the ground for what's coming up.

Based on a concept that has been tremendously successful in the UK, America and Hong Kong, The Laughter Factory (02 621 0000, www.thelaughterfactory.com) provides acts by both established and up and coming comedians. The artists, imported straight from the UK comedy circuit, are carefully selected to entertain the mainly expat audiences in this region. The winning formula of three distinct comedy styles performed in one evening caters to a wide range of comic tastes. Shows are usually held monthly at the Crowne Plaza Yas Island (p.201). If you can't make the Abu Dhabi date, see the website for the busier Dubai schedule.

Concerts & Live Music

In Abu Dhabi, there is no regular calendar of events for music lovers, although recent years have seen a decided increase in happenings in the music scene. At different times of the year (mainly in winter), international sporting events, concerts and festivals feature international artists, bands and classical musicians (see Abu Dhabi Calendar, p.26). Ticket prices may be higher than you would expect to pay elsewhere.

Emirates Palace has established itself as a venue for large scale concerts in the capital and, in the couple of years since opening, a number of international artists have played in the palace gardens including Andrea Boccelli, Bon Jovi, The Killers and Coldplay; Emirates Palace's concert hall has also played host to a number of renowned international orchestras. More recently, however, the biggest concerts have taken place on Yas Island in Flash Forum, a large concert pavilion adjacent to Ferrari World. Linkin Park, Kanye West, and Prince played the 2010 Formula One Weekend, while Stevie Wonder, Eric Clapton and Shakira have also recently performed.

Stretch In Style

If you're feeling a bit flash (or are on a stag or hen party), you can rent a stretch Lincoln, SUV or even Hummer limo from Dubai-based company Connection Chauffeur (www.uae-limousine.com) so that you can arrive at your destination in style. Al Ghazal (www.adnh.com) also has a fleet of Mercedes, Audi and Chevrolet limos ready to dispatch.

Club events, such as Ministry of Sound nights, have also taken place in Abu Dhabi, and the Abu Dhabi Music & Arts Foundation (www.admaf.org) has hosted several cultural events. The Abu Dhabi Classics programme, which runs throughout the winter months, is well attended (www.abudhabiclassics.com). Moreover, Dubai's popular Jazz Festival (p.28) in November and the Latino Festival in March (organised by Chillout Productions – 04 391 1196) are two annual events that are not to be missed.

Also worth noting is that WOMAD (p.28), Peter Gabriel's 'World of Music and Dance' festival,

WOMAD

appears to have become an annual fixture, while the wakeboarding festival Wakestock Abu Dhabi (p.28), which in 2010 saw De La Soul and MaximioPark perform, seems likely to follow suit.

Promoters usually have no long term programmes and details are only available about a month in advance, so for details of events, visit Explorer's website at www.liveworkexplore.com, check the daily press or monthly magazines, and listen out for announcements and advertisements on Emirates 1 and 2 FM as well as the northern radio stations Channel 4 FM and Dubai 92 FM. If you're experiencing live music deficiency and suffer from severe withdrawal symptoms, hop over to neighbouring Dubai to see what's going on there.

Ticket Tips

Tickets for concerts and events go on sale at the venues and often through other outlets, such as Virgin Megastore, Centrepoint and Starbucks too. Tickets for the majority can be purchased online at www.boxofficeme.com, www.thinkflash.ae or www.itptickets.com.

Parties At Home

There are several companies in Abu Dhabi that can do all the cooking, decorating and cleaning up for you, leaving you with more time to concentrate on your witty after-dinner anecdotes. All of the companies listed offer a complete service from event organisation to the hiring of performers and equipment rental. For a novel outdoor party idea, you can get your own shawarma stand set up in the garden, complete with shawarma maker. Several Arabic restaurants provide this service, which works out as a very reasonable and easy way to sustain hordes of party guests. Also, many popular Indian restaurants offer catering services at great prices. You can order off the menu and specify the number of guests (although the general rule is reduce it by a few unless you want to be eating curry for a week). In addition to specialist companies, many restaurants, hotels, and clubs, including the Beach Rotana (p.200), Hilton Abu Dhabi (p.201) and The Club (p.179), have catering departments, so pick your favourite and ask if they can help out. Depending on what you require, caterers can provide just the food or everything from crockery, napkins, tables, chairs, waiters and doormen to a clearing up service for afterwards.

The D Club

Tourist Club Area **02 644 6461**
www.thedclub.com
Map **2 N4**

The first organic catering company in the UAE can arrange healthy food for your get-togethers at home.

Events R' Us

Sultan Al Qubeisy Bldg Tourist Club Area **02 645 6605**
www.events-r-us.net
Map **2 R4**

This events company can take care of all your party requirements from delivering quality catering for an intimate dinner to providing party food, themed decor and serving staff for big bashes.

Flying Elephant

Sheikh Zayed Rd Dubai **04 347 9170**
www.flyingelephantuae.com
Map **3 E2** Metro **Noor Islamic Bank**

This Dubai-based events company offers everything from entertainment and themed decorations to catering and waiting staff for all kinds of events, from weddings and kids' birthdays to office parties and corporate team-building events.

Parti Perfect

Khaleej Al Arabi St Al Manhal **050 126 4819**
Map **2 G5**

This company offers food themed parties where you or, better still, your kids get to create your own party food as part of the celebration. Standard party catering is also available.

Theatre

The theatre scene in Abu Dhabi remains rather limited, with fans relying chiefly on touring companies and the occasional amateur dramatics performance. However, there are some developments.

Amateur theatre, in the form of Abu Dhabi Dramatic Society (p.281), always welcomes new members, and there are occasional drama workshops to get involved with, most of which hold a performance at the end of the workshop (see Drama Groups, p.281).

As for bigger shows, the usual suspects – ADNEC (www.adnec.ae) and Emirates Palace (p.201) – are usually the venues. However, the National Theatre (p.273) does see some performances. Much like musical concerts, shows tend to come in fits and starts rather than on any consistent basis. The exception is the Abu Dhabi Festival (p.28), during which there should be plenty to keep theatre fans happy.

The recently opened Manarat Al Saadiyat (p.273) has a large auditorium which may well attract performances – especially as the venue is a precursor to Saadiyat's Performing Arts Centre, due for completion in 2013, and will then surely make theatre a staple part of the Abu Dhabi events calendar. In the meantime, you could head to Dubai, where the First Group Theatre at Madinat Jumeirah (www.madinattheatre.com), the Palladium (www.palladium-dmc.com), and the Centrepoint Theatre at DUCTAC (www.ductac.org) have regular shows.

Savour The Souk Flavour

Got the munchies? Head to Souk Qaryat Al Beri, arguably Abu Dhabi's top foodie destination that's packed with a multitude of restaurants and cafes.

Although it's located away from the traditional city centre and the tourist magnet that is the Corniche, the southeast end of the island and just across the bridge on the mainland are arguably Abu Dhabi's most up-and-coming areas. And in the middle of it all is Souk Qaryat Al Beri.

There are some lovely, unique stores and boutiques in this traditional style marketplace, but this is one souk where shopping doesn't take centre stage. Here, you'll find everything from simple bites to some seriously high-end fine dining restaurants, but the main draw is the relaxed atmosphere, alfresco eating and drinking. The maze of walkways is interlinked by canals on which small abras motor, delivering visitors from one end to the other of the complex.

There are piles of dining options in Souk Qaryat Al Beri, serving up just about every popular cuisine available. If you can't decide what you're in the mood for, just go for a wander and you'll soon stumble upon something that takes your fancy. For lunch, there's little to rival the healthy skewers, salads, pita sandwiches and smoothies from Le Paradis du Fruit (02 558 1212), although coffee and carrot cake from Starbucks is always a decent back-up option.

Come dinnertime, steak and burger lovers will likely head straight for The Meat Co (p.378), although they shouldn't be too quick to decide as the African themed Mombasa Grille (02 558 1868) is also an excellent option. The Lebanese restaurant Abdel Wahab (p.360) offers more than just meat, but its kebabs are really something special.

Luxurious European option, Eight Restaurant & Bar (p.370), is fairly new on the scene but has already won rave reviews and, staying in Europe, Certo (p.368) is widely considered to be one of the best Italian joints in town.

As you look east on your global Souk Qaryat Al Beri gastronomy tour, you arrive at the award-winning Indian fare of Ushna (p.389), the unfussy but delicious servings from The Noodle House (p.380) and, finally, the super chic Sho Cho restaurant where cool Japanese cuisine is served up daily. Red Carpet Restaurant (02 558 7660) may not strictly be a Japanese restaurant, but its sushi is delicious.

Although it may be best to enjoy dining at Souk Qaryat Al Beri's restaurants at night, when they spill out on to the creekside and offer up amazing views across the water to an illuminated Sheikh Zayed Mosque and Abu Dhabi island, bear in mind that many of the flashier restaurants also have some jaw-droppingly good lunch deals.

Finally, if you feel like continuing your evening, head to the excellent Left Bank (p.395) which serves up all manner of beers, wines and cocktails, while also having a pretty decent bar food menu. And, if all that's not enough, all the goodies in the Shangri-La, Traders and the Fairmont, including Hoi An (p.373), Pearls and Caviar (p.396) and Frankie's (p.372) and Chameleon (02 654 3238) are a short stroll away.

Souk Qaryat Al Beri

RESTAURANTS BY CUISINE

Italian

Japanese

Mediterranean

Mexican

Moroccan

Nepalese

Polynesian

Portuguese

Seafood

Steakhouses

Tex Mex

Thai

Al Matar

Park Rotana Abu Dhabi

Al Meena

Nr Meena Fish Market

The Club

Al Mushrif

Abu Dhabi Country Club

Al Nahyan

East Rd, Nr Red Crescent Bldg

Grand Millennium Al Wahda

Al Raha

Al Raha Beach Hotel

Al Raha Mall

Al Ras Al Akhdar

Emirates Palace

Khalidiya Palace Rayhaan By Rotana

Al Safarat

Aloft Abu Dhabi

Bain Al Jessrain

Fairmont Bab Al Bahr

Shangri-La Hotel, Qaryat Al Beri Hotel

The Souk At Qaryat Al Beri

Venues By Location

Tourist Club Area

Abu Dhabi Marina & Yacht Club
Bam Bu!, Chinese p.362
Colosseum, Nightclubs p.392
Portofino, Italian p.381
The Alamo, Tex Mex p.361

Al Diar Capital Hotel
Ciro's Pomodoro, Italian p.370
Rock Bottom Cafe, American Bars p.396
The Palm, International p.380

Al Diar Dana Hotel
49er's The Gold Rush, American p.360

Al Nuaimi Tower, Al Meena St
Samurai Restaurant, Japanese p.384

Beach Rotana Abu Dhabi
Bay View, International p.366
Benihana, Japanese p.366
Brauhaus, German p.391
Essence, Buffet p.372
Finz, Seafood p.372
Indigo, Indian p.374
Prego's, Italian p.381
Rodeo Grill, Steakhouses p.384
Trader Vic's, Polynesian p.389

Le Meridien Abu Dhabi
Al Birkeh, Arabic/Lebanese p.360
Captain's Arms, Bars p.391
G Club, Nightclubs p.394
La Brasserie, Buffet p.376
Le Bistrot, French p.377
NRG Sports Cafe, International p.395
Opus Bar, Bars p.396
Pappagallo, Italian p.380
Talay, Seafood p.388
Wakataua Terrace, Beach/Waterfront Bars p.397

Nr Al Madina Supermarket, Nadi Shahid St
Bandung, Indonesian p.366

Nr Kia Showroom
Le Shaderwan, Arabic/Lebanese p.377

Nr Lebanese Flower Restaurant, Al Salam St,
Al Aqsa Sweets, Arabic/Lebanese p.360

Obaid Al Romaisi Bldg, Nr Emirates Islamic Bank
Al Qasr Restaurant & Grill, Arabic/Lebanese p.361

Yas Island

Yas Yacht Club
Allure By Capriani, Nightclubs p.390
Cipriani, Italian p.368
Stars 'n' Bars, American p.397
Yotto, Japanese p.389

Yas Island West

Centro Yas Island
c.taste, International p.367

Crowne Plaza Yas Island
Barouk, Arabic/Lebanese p.366
Jing Asia, Asian Subcontinent p.374
Stills Bar & Brasserie, Bars, Pubs & Clubs p.397

Park Inn By Radisson Abu Dhabi, Yas Island Hotel
Amerigos, Mexican p.361

Radisson Blu Hotel, Abu Dhabi Yas Island
Assymetri, International p.362
Filini, Italian p.372

The Yas Hotel
Amici, Italian p.361
Angar, Indian p.362
Atayeb, Arabic/Lebanese p.362
Kazu, Japanese p.376
Noodle Box, Contemporary Asian p.380
Origins, International p.380
Rush, Bars, Pubs & Clubs p.396
Skylite Lounge, Bars, Pubs & Clubs p.397

Yas Island Rotana
Blue Grill, Steakhouses p.367
Rangoli, Indian p.381
Y Bar, Bars, Pubs & Clubs p.397

Yas Links Abu Dhabi
Hickory's Sports Bar, Sports Bars p.394

RESTAURANTS & CAFES

The Yellow Star

This yellow star highlights places that merit extra praise. It might be the atmosphere, the food, the cocktails, the music or the crowd, but any review that you see with the star attached is sure to be somewhere that's a bit special.

Restaurants & Cafes

18Oz — Steakhouse

This elegant restaurant is an ever-popular part of Abu Dhabi's dining scene. 18Oz specialises in mouth-watering steaks and chops, serving choice cuts of Angus beef drenched in a selection of no fewer than eight sauces. Non-carnivorous diners are catered to as well, however; seafood appetisers and lamb, chicken and vegetarian main dishes can also be found on the menu. The modern decor and attentive service feels just right, and even the desserts are delicious – if you have any space left after the meaty feast. They're open for lunch (12:30 to 15:30) and dinner.

One To One Hotel – The Village Al Dhafrah
02 495 2000
www.onetoonehotels.com
Map **2 Q8**

49er's The Gold Rush — American

Centrally situated, this popular venue is usually packed, so get there early to enjoy an entire evening of entertainment American-style. The rich timber finishes reflect the ranch style atmosphere, and the food is delicious, with steaks that melt in your mouth. Service is excellent, and with live music and quite reasonable prices, you can't go too wrong – this is a great venue. Check out the various theme nights for added spice.

Al Diar Dana Hotel Tourist Club Area **02 645 6000**
www.aldiarhotels.com
Map **2 R4**

Abdel Wahab — Arabic/Lebanese

The Abu Dhabi branch of this legendary Beirut establishment does, by and large, live up to the hype, with authentic but refined Lebanese cuisine in nice, if not stunning, surroundings. The Levantine-inspired menu won't shock anyone with novelty – think flatbread, hummus, mezzes and lamb dishes – but it's all prepared as well as you'll find anywhere else, and with reasonable prices to boot.

The Souk At Qaryat Al Beri Bain Al Jessrain
02 558 1616
Map **1 L8**

Al Aqsa Sweets — Arabic/Lebanese

Al Aqsa does only one thing and it does it extremely well: kanafeh. Made of very fine shredded pastry dough on top of a soft cheese, drizzled with sugary syrup and crushed pistachios, and served hot, the sweet is beloved throughout the Arab world. This tiny shop, near Gad Restaurant, sells two kinds of kanafeh by weight; there are small tables to sit at but you'd be just as well to take it wrapped to go.

Nr Lebanese Flower Restaurant, Al Salam St Tourist Club Area **02 644 2159**
Map **2 Q5**

Al Atlal — Arabic/Lebanese

Al Atlal is within easy reach of just about everywhere, and popular with locals. Authentic Lebanese served in a cosy atmosphere, complemented by loud, lively music and belly dancing. A set menu includes an expansive mezze and grilled mixed kebabs, plus many more dishes to satisfy ravenous diners. Overall, service meets requirements and it is a reasonably priced, offering food and lively entertainment for a hungry soul.

Sands Hotel Madinat Zayed **02 615 6666**
www.aldiarhotels.com
Map **2 N4**

Al Birkeh — Arabic/Lebanese

Widely touted as one of the best pan-Arabic restaurants in town, this established venue serves traditional Middle Eastern fare in an atmospheric setting, complete with live music and a belly dancer to set the mood. Start your culinary journey with a selection of hot and cold mezze before moving on to a main course of grilled meat or fish (and lots of it, too). The portions are generous and, for the adventurous or gastronomically brave, the menu also

18Oz

includes some rather exotic Lebanese dishes such as raw liver, washed down with the strong aniseed drink, arak, that perfectly cleans the plate.
Le Meridien Abu Dhabi Tourist Club Area **02 644 6666**
www.lemeridienabudhabi.com
Map **2 S4**

Al Dhafra — Dinner Cruise
This traditional dhow offers daily dinner cruises in a tranquil setting as the atmospheric vessel floats along the picturesque Corniche. The upper deck boasts a majlis while the lower deck is air-conditioned and can seat approximately 50 people. A sumptuous menu includes lavish international fare which can be tailored to individual preferences. As you dine, the ethnic charm of the dhow, and the serenity of the calm Arabian waters, ensures an unforgettable evening. The dhow can also be hired for private functions.
Nr Meena Fish Market Al Meena **02 673 2266**
www.aldhafra.net
Map **2 S1**

Independent Reviews
All of the outlets in this book have been independently reviewed by writers based in Abu Dhabi. Their aim is to give clear, realistic and unbiased views of each venue. If you feel you have been unwittingly led astray, or your much-loved local or hidden gastronomic gem has not been included, let us know by emailing info@explorerpublishing.com. Alternatively, if you think you know better and have sufficiently discerning taste buds, log on to www.liveworkexplore.com and submit your own reviews.

Al Fanar — International
The revolving Al Fanar restaurant on the very top of the Le Royal Meridien hotel in Abu Dhabi is the perfect venue for a first date: the constantly changing vista of the capital's skyline offers welcome opportunities to fill any awkward conversation lulls while the extensive menu provides a good selection of inventive dishes including seafood, meat and vegetarian options. Al Fanar takes 1 hour and 45 minutes to do a full rotation – during which the polite waiters cater to your every whim, enhancing the feeling of other-worldliness. If you are all romanced out, Al Fanar also hosts lively Friday brunches and has set course business lunches.
Le Royal Meridien Abu Dhabi Markaziya East
02 674 2020
www.leroyalmeridienabudhabi.com
Map **2 P3**

Al Qasr Restaurant & Grill — Arabic/Lebanese
Tender appetisers of stuffed vine leaves and well balanced moutabel pave the way for main courses of hammour and mixed grill. Lunch offers an astounding selection of 99 dishes, including Middle Eastern rice, curries and other specialities, with service staff that are capable and eager to please.
Obaid Al Romaisi Bldg, Nr Emirates Islamic Bank
Tourist Club Area **02 644 9933**
Map **2 R5**

The Alamo — Tex Mex
The Alamo, with its cantina-style atmosphere and Mexican-inspired memorabilia, is renowned for its frozen margaritas, succulent spare ribs, sizzling fajitas and Friday brunch. Friendly and polite service staff complete the ingredients for a perfect 'casual night out' venue.
Abu Dhabi Marina & Yacht Club Tourist Club Area
02 644 0300
Map **2 S4**

Amalfi — Italian
The chef is Italian and so are many of the guests – the fact that Amalfi is favoured by Italian expats speaks volumes of the restaurant's commitment to produce all-Italian classics using top-notch ingredients. From antipasti to pesce, insalate and carni, you'll find all the usual suspects on the menu; the home-made pasta dishes are a particular standout. The grandiose setting, an extensive wine list and live music top the experience.
Le Royal Meridien Abu Dhabi Markaziya East
02 674 2020
www.leroyalmeridienabudhabi.com
Map **2 P3**

Amerigos — Mexican
Suitable for casual or formal occasions, this spacious Mexican restaurant has modern colourful decor with a large TV at one end, dedicated mainly to sports. If you prefer, you can enjoy the views from the poolside restaurant area. Choose from traditional fajitas and quesadillas with fresh guacamole, or try tender meats and fish dishes, all prepared to a high standard and served by friendly staff. Alternatively, just sip a long cocktail at the large bar. A bustling restaurant that almost always results in a lively, social evening.
Park Inn By Radisson Abu Dhabi, Yas Island Hotel
Yas Island West **02 656 2222**
www.parkinn-abudhabi.com
Map **1 T5**

Amici — Italian
Amici is an Italian restaurant with an almost futuristic vibe thanks to a large outside dining terrace, calming water feature, moulded white structures and furniture

and green glass hanging sculptures. Fresh bread and a trio of flavoured olive oils start your meal, delivered by staff who are attentive and helpful. While the menu is small (you choose from an antipasti buffet for your appetiser), there is quite obviously an Italian chef passionate about food in the kitchen, as every morsel is authentic and delicious.
The Yas Hotel Yas Island West **02 656 0600**
www.theyashotel.com
Map **1 T5**

Angar — Indian

Follow your nose through The Yas Hotel, and you'll be lead straight to Angar, the hotel's delightful Indian eatery. Authentic tastes of India mix with contemporary luxury, served in one of the most exciting recent additions to Abu Dhabi's five-star dining scene. The beautiful terrace has views of the brightly coloured hotel dome and a small water feature; inside, you can watch chefs prepare your curries from scratch to whet your appetite. Each course is carefully constructed, balancing flavours and textures. The extensive menu features authentic dishes in numbers that prove that variety really is the spice of life.
The Yas Hotel Yas Island West **02 656 0600**
www.theyashotel.com
Map **1 T5**

Arabic Cafe — Arabic/Lebanese

The waft of fruity shisha and dulcet notes of Arabic music welcome you to this relaxed little cafe set in the heart of the Hiltonia Beach Club overlooking the shimmery, turquoise waters of the Arabian Gulf. The concise menu offers Arabic staples from mezze to Shawarma and grilled chicken with sumac alongside international bar food classics from burgers to croque monsieurs. Similarly, the desserts menu features regional treats like Om Ali and halawat al geban as well as ice cream and eclairs.
Hilton Abu Dhabi Al Khubeirah **02 681 4344**
www1.hilton.com
Map **2 C3**

Asian Garden — Asian

Don't let the rather plain look of this restaurant fool you – what's on offer is a culinary tour of East Asia at bargain prices. From Thai curries to Filipino noodles and Chinese fried rice, the food is faultless and the prices cheaper than what you'd pay at a mall food court. Watch out if you order something spicy, though: perhaps true to authentic Southeast Asian cooking styles, the chef can have a heavy hand with the chili peppers.
Nr El Dorado Cinema, Sheikh Zayed Second St Markaziya East **02 676 3350**
Map **2 Q4**

Assymetri — International

Perfect for families with children, this restaurant has its own clown, an assortment of toys and a swimming pool right on the doorstep. The international cuisine, by its very nature, caters for all and the live cooking stations make for dynamic entertainment as fresh dishes are concocted before your very eyes. The restaurant itself is large, with an abundance of natural light and views over the Arabian Gulf, allowing you to admire the beauty of Abu Dhabi's islands.
Radisson Blu Hotel, Abu Dhabi Yas Island Yas Island West **02 656 2000**
www.radissonblu.com
Map **1 S5**

Atayeb — Arabic/Lebanese

At Atayeb, located in the Yas Hotel, you can savour traditional Emirati cuisine while looking out over a Formula One racetrack – an experience that perfectly captures the mix of old and new in Abu Dhabi. Its name translates as 'many delicious things' and the menu is indeed full of dishes ranging from Moroccan tagines to pan-fried Gulf hammour. Indoors, the soft, orange-hued lighting and candle-lit tables create a modern Middle Eastern feel and, come Thursday evening, a belly dancer performs as you linger over a bottle from the extensive wine list. Outdoors, the large terrace offers spectacular views of the racetrack and harbour.
The Yas Hotel Yas Island West **02 656 0600**
www.theyashotel.com
Map **1 T5**

Azur — Mediterranean

At a first glance, the rather clinical modern decor could be off-putting, which is a pity since 'Azur' hides a cornucopia of wholesome high-end dishes predominantly made with organic ingredients. The menu features hearty meat dishes, seafood and super fresh vegetables; there's even organic wine on menu. Thefood arrives piping hot and service is surprisingly knowledgeable and friendly, albeit a little slow.
Al Raha Beach Hotel Al Raha **02 508 0555**
www.danathotels.com
Map **1 R7**

Bam Bu! — Chinese

Whether out for a romantic dinner or a celebration with all your friends, you can't go wrong with Bam Bu! – a little slice of the Orient with an enchanting view of the yachts in the marina. The brunch option is a good choice for the uninitiated – just sit back and relax while a constant stream of freshly prepared delicacies are brought to your table. Speciality dishes such as lobster or peking duck are charged for accordingly.
Abu Dhabi Marina & Yacht Club Tourist Club Area **02 645 6373**
Map **2 S4**

Where To Go For What

Abu Dhabi is a pick 'n' mix of eateries, drinking spots and entertainment options vying to please a highly diverse audience. Whether you want a daytime binge of five-star cuisine, a raucous night out dancing to live music, an evening of brain teasers or an early morning rendition of 'I Will Survive', you will find it all within Abu Dhabi's restaurants, cafes, pubs, bars and nightclubs.

Alfresco

Between late October and early May, the weather in Abu Dhabi is perfect for alfresco dining. Popular spots for dinner with a waterfront view are The Fishmarket (p.372) and The Yacht Club (p.397) at the InterContinental Abu Dhabi, while Finz (p.372) at the Beach Rotana is on a pontoon-like wooden structure that stretches out over the water and BBQ Al Qasr (p.366) at Emirates Palace is right there on the sand. Boccaccio (p.367) and Riviera (p.384) both have lovely outdoor areas. Several venues, including Pearls and Caviar (p.396), Left Bank (p.395) and Ushna (p.389), at Souk Qaryat Al Beri are great alfresco watering holes that also serve up tasty treats under the stars. The recently opened Central Market development is home to several increasingly popular options too; try Tarboush (p.388) for shisha and fruit mocktails unders the stars.

Celebrity Chefs

Does food prepared by famous hands really taste better? Check out Marco Pierre White's eponymous grill restaurant (p.378) or Frankie's (p.372), both found at the Fairmont Bab Al Bahr, to see for yourself. At Emirates Palace, the delectable Emirati dishes on offer at Mezlai (p.379) are created by the country's first Emirati chef, Chef Ali Salem Musbeh Al Badawi. Alternatively, hop over to Dubai to check out what's cooking by chefs including Gordon Ramsay, Pierre Gagnaire, Gary Rhodes, Nobu Matsuhisa, Santi Santamari and Michel Rostang.

Fish & Chips

You may not find a British-style 'chippy' in Abu Dhabi, but if you're really hankering for some good old fish and chips there are a few choices at your disposal. To keep the takeaway feel, head for Al Wahda Mall where there's a London Fish & Chips (02 443 7701) in the foodcourt, although these are a far cry from the real deal. For something more authentic, Ally Pally Corner (p.390) and Rock Bottom Café (p.396) get the big British pub portions and low prices spot on while, if you take your fish and chips seriously, try Hemingway's (p.394) or Stills (p.397), for some of the best fish and chips in the city.

Dancing

There are a few clubs to boogie the night away in, as well as a handful of places for impromptu dance routines. Should you fancy wiggling to something slightly more alternative while out on the town, then you're likely to be disappointed. Rock Bottom Café (p.396) is about the only place in town where rock or indie are played, although the cover band at The Tavern (p.397) on Thursday nights is worth checking out. Cinnabar's (p.392) dance floors are often full, especially for Saturday's salsa night. By and large,

Skylite at The Yas Hotel

dancing in the capital is a fairly glitzy affair, with Etoiles (p.394), Pearls and Caviar (p.396) and Sho Cho (p.396) popular options.

Late & Lively

In addition to the dedicated clubs listed in this chapter, Abu Dhabi's nightlife also includes several bars and restaurants which transform late evening into lively joints with hopping dancefloors. These include Beachcomber (p.390), Colosseum (p.392), Aloft's Relax@12 (p.396) and Skylite (p.397) at The Yas Hotel.

Karaoke Bars

There are a few places in Abu Dhabi where you can show off your vocal abilities, or even just belt out a comedy version of Ice Ice Baby. Wasabi (02 678 1000) in the Al Diar Mina Hotel is a popular haunt, with its authentic Japanese style private booths, while the karaoke cabins at Bowling City (p.274) even allow you to record your vocal gymnastics on to CD for future playback. Tambayan (02 679 4777) at Al Ain Palace Hotel is a popular choice, as is the karaoke room at PJ O'Reilly's (p.396).

Ladies' Nights

Lucky ladies in this fair city can go out almost any night of the week and enjoy free drinks. Of course, this isn't a charitable venture for Abu Dhabi's bar scene; where ladies are drinking, the men and their wallets inevitably follow. Wednesday is the biggest ladies' night with many bars and pubs offering at least two free drinks, and some of the most popular venues include PJ O'Reilly's (p.396), Cooper's (p.392), Zenith (p.397), Left Bank (p.395), 49er's (p.360) and Etoiles (p394).

Quiz Nights

If you want to test your brain power and knowledge of useless trivia then head to one of Abu Dhabi's many quiz nights. Try Hemingway's (p.394) on a Sunday, Heroes (p.394) on a Monday or Ally Pally Corner (p.390) every Tuesday. If you're lucky enough to be a member of The Club (p.179), then the bar there runs a popular quiz on Wednesdays which always attracts a decent crowd.

And The Rest...

Abu Dhabi also has a few fun alternatives for when you need a break from the bar and restaurant scene. Aloft's Mai Café (p.395) takes the party to the pool with its Full Moon Splash parties, which include a shisha lounge. There are several large dhows, such as Al Dhafra (p.227) and Shuja Yacht (p.228), that offer dinner cruises for the best Corniche view in town, while numerous charter companies (p.227) will provide boats for hire – you can then bring your own food and drinks on board. For something really different, why not head for one of the quiet islands off the coast and set up camp with a barbecue?

Bandung — Indonesian

Another Tourist Club gem, this Indonesian restaurant might not be a delight for the eyes but its food is a feast for the taste buds. The meat and fried fish dishes are all tasty and the food always arrives piled high.
Nr Al Madina Supermarket, Nadi Shahid St Tourist Club Area **02 645 2008**
Map **2 R5**

Barouk — Arabic/Lebanese

This Lebanese joint offers an authentic taste of the Middle East – with a Turkish twist. With a wide selection of hot and cold mezze, sharing is advisable in order to sample a range of the delights. Main course options are predominately a choice of juicy lamb or chicken kebabs. To sweeten things up, try the exquisite Turkish delight to accompany the restaurant's own belly dancer who makes an appearance between 21:00 and 22:00, transforming the atmosphere from quiet and refined to lively and vibrant.
Crowne Plaza Yas Island Yas Island West **02 656 3000**
www.crowneplaza.com
Map **1 S5**

Bay View — International

If alfresco dining beneath beach brollies, sipping cocktails and watching sunsets sounds appealing, then head to Bay View in the Beach Rotana's rather plush sports complex (you need to be a club member or pay the 'day guest' entry fee to eat here). An abundance of freshly prepared salads, mains and desserts awaits, and there's also a fine choice of drinks. The food, although pricey, is tasty, healthy and well presented, but the service could use a bit of fine tuning.
Beach Rotana Abu Dhabi Tourist Club Area
02 697 9011
www.rotana.com
Map **2 S5**

BBQ Al Qasr — Arabic/Lebanese

With high-quality chargrilled food, served on purpose-built pagoda platforms right on Emirates Palace's very own private stretch of beach, this is barbecuing VIP style. The setting is perfect for a romantic evening out; musicians play chilled out tunes until late into the night as you sample the Arabic-inspired barbecue menu. Although there are non-meat options – such as tasty grilled seafood dishes – ultimately this is carnivore territory. A shisha is the perfect way to end the meal.
Emirates Palace Al Ras Al Akhdar **02 690 7999**
www.emiratespalace.com
Map **2 B2**

The Beach Restaurant — Seafood

Located next to the beach and pool, this aptly named restaurant offers a reasonably priced range of internationally-inspired seafood. You'll have the choice to dine al fresco by the pool or indoors within the cozy terracotta walls and murals. The Atlantis, an iced seafood platter, is worth a special mention – not only does it come overflowing with aquatic treats of all manner, but it also features rare-to-find Ceviche. Otherwise, the menu features dishes ranging from Mexican lobster quesadillas to Mediterranean coconut crusted yellow fin tuna.
Khalidiya Palace Rayhaan By Rotana
Al Ras Al Akhdar **02 657 0000**
www.rotana.com
Map **2 A3**

Beijing Restaurant — Chinese

The large restaurant, tucked away behind Madinat Zayed mall, gets packed at the weekend and doesn't win many points for ambience, but with food this authentic, it doesn't need to. Classics like scallion pancakes, fried green beans and Kung Pao chicken are perfect for sharing and the rotating tabletops mean that everyone gets a chance to dig in.
Al Falah St, Nr Shoe Mart Madinat Zayed
02 621 0708
Map **2 M5**

Benihana — Japanese

Contemporary Asian cuisine, minimalist decor and crowd-pleasing chefs make this a 'must do' on the Abu Dhabi restaurant circuit. The menu includes soups, salads and desserts, but don't miss out on the sushi teppanyaki, prepared at live stations by entertaining chefs. Prices seem high, but for a feast of treats, it's good value, especially on the teppanyaki theme nights.
Beach Rotana Abu Dhabi Tourist Club Area
02 697 9011
www.rotana.com
Map **2 S5**

BiCE — Italian

For modern Italian cooking with a touch of romance, BiCE is a good choice. Low lighting and flickering candles create an intimate atmosphere, and the crisp white tablecloths offset by dark wood fittings provide a feeling of relaxed elegance. The hand-made pasta, and good range of seafood dishes, are all prepared with care and presented with a flourish. It's Italian but with a twist on the traditional recipes; expect to spot specialties such as spaghetti with lobster bolognaise. The service is professional and prompt, and the staff are friendly. Live piano music provides a nice touch, though the acoustics are not great and it's a little too easy to overhear the conversations at neighbouring tables.
Hilton Abu Dhabi Al Khubeirah **02 681 1900**
www1.hilton.com
Map **2 C3**

BiteRite
Cafe

A healthy eating cafe-restaurant where nutritional, well-balanced lunches and dinners are the name of the game. The menu offers a jigsaw of flavours, with sandwiches, wraps and stir-fries rubbing shoulders with curries, pizzas and pastas. The decor is reflective of the menu – clean, bright and original. BiteRite also does a range of healthy-eating programmes, and can deliver nutritionally-controlled meals direct to your home or office.

Nr Red Crescent Bldg, East Rd Al Nahyan
02 641 1660
www.biterite.ae
Map **2 N8**

Blue Grill
Steakhouse

Elegant in shades of blue with touches of dark wood, this light and airy restaurant displays an extensive wine cellar and an impressively large show kitchen. An innovative a la carte menu focuses on prime beef and seafood, and is replaced on Fridays with a truly fine dining brunch experience. With freshly squeezed juices and the option of free flowing Laurent Perrier champagne served by attentive staff, your gastronomic journey starts with an exquisite array of appetisers including oysters, foie gras and lobster. Follow with your choice of freshly prepared main, including fillet steak with truffle mash, eggs Benedict with smoked haddock and perfectly cooked duck breast, but save room to sample the enticing handmade desserts on display.

Yas Island Rotana Yas Island West **02 656 4000**
www.rotana.com
Map **1 T5**

Boccaccio
Mediterranean

Boccaccio offers some of the best Italian food in town, at surprisingly reasonable prices. Choose between dining outside on the deck overlooking the charming marina or eating in the elegant, warmly lit interior, decorated by the illuminated bar and wine rack, where the mood is added to by the talented, resident acoustic trio. The newly expanded menu contains a large number of pastas, pizzas, starters and mains, all extremely well prepared. The quality of the food makes dining here a real pleasure, and it is equally suitable for a romantic tete a tete as for a group gathering, as it's fairly buzzing when it's busy. To round off a superb meal, ask for the chef's recommendations for his truly wicked, adult desserts.

InterContinental Abu Dhabi Al Bateen **02 666 6888**
www.ichotelsgroup.com
Map **2 C4**

Bord Eau
French

Bord Eau has quickly established itself as one of the very best restaurants in the city, but good food doesn't come cheap here and, while the chef produces some undeniable gastronomic masterpieces, dinner for two will do some considerable damage to your wallet. The menu takes established luxuries – delicacies such as foie gras, scallops, lobster thermidor and Wagyu beef – and adds a subtle but distinctive twist. There is the hushed and refined air of fine dining, and people come here for business (when someone else is picking up the cheque) or for special occasions. The views of the creek through the large picture windows are interesting, and the service faultless. One of Abu Dhabi's finest.

Shangri-La Hotel, Qaryat Al Beri Bain Al Jessrain
02 509 8888
www.shangri-la.com
Map **1 L8**

c.taste
International

The Centro hotel is all about high-quality and well-presented but simple functionality and its main restaurant reflects just that. An all-day, buffet style eatery, its decor is modern, light and airy, while the kitchen serves up a vast selection of dishes from just about every type of cuisine you can think of. It may not push any culinary boundaries but c.taste is certainly good value.

Centro Yas Island Yas Island West **02 656 4444**
www.rotana.com
Map **1 S5**

Cafe Arabia
Cafe

Located in a nondescript villa out of the heart of the city, Cafe Arabia is worlds apart from the typical cafe in the Capital. Each of the three floors, as well as the rooftop terrace, is tastefully decorated with plush sofas, elegant tables, and bookcases inviting you to stay and read over coffee. The menu offers light fare based on recipes the owner has collected from family and friends, as well as some inventive hot and cold beverages. Thanks to art shows and coffee mornings, this new spot has quickly established a well-deserved following.

Nr Mushrif Park, Mohammed Bin Khalifa St
Al Mushrif **02 643 9699**
Map **2 K10**

Caravan Restaurant
Indian

If you're looking for a cheap, 'no frills' Asian meal, Caravan delivers the goods. The menu offers a tasty selection of Chinese, Indian and Thai cuisine, and the evening buffet (incredible value for money) includes soups, salads, a selection of main courses and desserts. The service is remarkably friendly and helpful given that this is a low cost venue. A home delivery service is available.

Al Hamed Centre Madinat Zayed **02 639 3370**
www.sterlingcaravan.com
Map **2 M4**

Certo
Italian

The Souk Qaryat Al Beri's reputation as Abu Dhabi's greatest food destination is growing almost daily and a good part of the credit for that must be given to Certo. The Abu Dhabi branch follows the same blueprint as its namesake in Dubai, and serves up a masterclass in how to do high-end Italian cuisine. It's a little pricey but it's also very tasty, serving up modern versions of traditional Mediterranean meat, fish, pizza and pasta dishes.
The Souk At Qaryat Al Beri Bain Al Jessrain
02 558 1161
Map **1 L8**

Chamas Churrascaria & Bar
Brazilian

Eat as much red meat as you like for a fixed price; Chamas' concept is great but the road to red-meat heaven is a long one. First navigate salad bar purgatory, before steering through steaming bowls of polenta, hash browns, black beans, vegetable rice and fried bananas; then negotiate various barbecued meats. Resist all of these wayside temptations and you'll finally arrive at steak heaven, serving sirloin, flank, rib eye and tenderloin. This noisy, frantic place with its enthusiastic band, is great for large groups and is packed every night, proving that Chamas has got the formula for Brazilian churrascaria (that's barbecue for the uninitiated) just right.
InterContinental Abu Dhabi Al Bateen **02 666 6888**
www.ichotelsgroup.com
Map **2 C4**

Chequers
Mediterranean

This modern, intimate venue is a pleasing choice if you fancy a cosy meal accompanied by good wine and a spot of live music. The service is attentive and the meals beautifully presented, but if you are a particularly picky diner, you may find the food a little bland. However, thanks to the excellent wine list, the singer and her sidekick on the baby grand piano, your evening at Chequers will be a largely enjoyable one.
Sands Hotel Madinat Zayed **02 615 6666**
www.aldiarhotels.com
Map **2 N4**

China Restaurant
Chinese

This restaurant has been dishing up yummy Chinese cuisine for 24 years and it is still going strong. The food and service are both of consistently high standards, with the peking duck and kung pao prawns worthy of a special mention. The authentic decor and lighting enhance the warm, welcoming ambience – all in all this is a highly recommended venue.
Mercure Centre Hotel Markaziya East **02 633 3555**
www.mercure.com
Map **2 M4**

Cho Gao
Asian

The menu reads like an eclectic collection from a food travelogue – an ingredient from China, a recipe from Thailand, a technique from Vietnam; salad, soup, dim sum. Recommended are the steak, duck and seafood options, but you'll also find some of the most creative vegetarian options in town. The ambience is calm and the decor authentic, while the service is attentive without being intrusive. It's the perfect place for a low-key but special night out with friends or loved ones. The bar, with its two-for-one happy hour, is great for a quick drink and a snack after work.
Crowne Plaza Markaziya East **02 621 0000**
www.crowneplaza.com
Map **2 N4**

The Chocolate Gallery
Cafe

This restaurant-cafe-heaven just about screams luxurious indulgence, and is a chocoholic's paradise. Choose between chocolate delights from crepes to muffins, and chocolate martinis to a mouth watering, not to be missed, chocolate fondue with all the trimmings. Special sculptured chocolate models and cakes can be ordered in advance and can be seen on display around the cafe; you can watch the talented chocolatiers work their Willy Wonka magic through glass windows too. Don't fret if you don't have a sweet tooth – an array of savoury paninis, crepes and salads are also available.
Fairmont Bab Al Bahr Bain Al Jessrain **02 654 3238**
www.fairmont.com
Map **1 L8**

Cipriani
Italian

This nautically-themed joint's sleek cream and navy interiors make it feel like a superyacht – complete with

Cho Gao

an attentive crew and top-notch chef. The menu offers signature Italian fare from light bites to soups, pasta and risotto, as well as tasty grilled mains. Culinary treats aside, the adjacent bar is an atmospheric hangout; with its eclectic collection of coffee table books to flick through, it's an easy place to while away the hours over a drink.
Yas Yacht Club Yas Island **02 565 0050**
www.cipriani.com
Map **1 T5**

Ciro's Pomodoro — Italian

If you just can't resist a charming Italian, then this unique, trendy venue is perfect for you. The menu covers all the classics like pastas, salads, pizzas and grilled dishes, and the numerous pictures of celebrities visiting Ciro's around the world will keep you entertained while you wait for your meal to arrive. The food is delectable, the service friendly and attentive, and a live band is there most days to serenade you through your meal.
Al Diar Capital Hotel Tourist Club Area **02 678 7700**
www.aldiarhotels.com
Map **2 R3**

Yas Marina Yacht Club

One of Abu Dhabi's most popular dining destinations is also one of the city's swankiest – which is saying something in this five-star city. You can sample exquisite sushi at Yotto, taste Italian treats at fine-dining Cipriani (see the previous page), enjoy bar food and big screen sports at Stars 'n' Bars (p.397) or sashay the night away to DJ tunes at Allure by Cipriani (p.368).

CuiScene — International

CuiScene offers diverse all-day dining with an almost embarrassingly large assortment of international fare represented. Buffet style, with five live cooking stations, there's definitely something for everybody here. The Arabic and Indian dishes excel, the sushi is extremely good and the dessert station is big enough to get lost in. The chefs are ready with recommendations and advice, as are the immaculate waiting staff. It's worth booking a table ahead of time, as CuiScene can get busy with both Emirati and western diners. The restaurant serves buffet breakfast, lunch and dinner, with an a la carte menu and a Friday brunch. The decor of the restaurant, meanwhile, is the last word in cool and contemporary: hot pink, black and silver grace the interiors to complete the experience. There is also a popular outdoor eating area.
Fairmont Bab Al Bahr Bain Al Jessrain **02 654 3238**
www.fairmont.com/babalbahr
Map **1 L8**

Curry House — Nepalese

Take your tastebuds on a culinary journey to Nepal at this unpretentious restaurant. The traditional Nepalese fare includes vegetable dishes, soups and curries, as well as a variety of momos (Nepalese dumplings) accompanied by a spicy sauce. The naan bread, served fresh and hot, is particularly memorable. Indian and Chinese specialities are also available. This venue is a bit more upmarket than your local thali joint, and is recommended for a tasty, inexpensive meal.
Nr Janata Bank, Shk Zayed First St Markaziya East
02 632 8860
Map **2 N4**

Dine — International

As simple as the name suggests, Dine is an all-day buffet restaurant that offers few airs and graces with a bright, breezy atmosphere and unfussy retro-style fittings. Appetisers are limited to the salad bar, while the mains feature more international dishes, such as red Thai chicken curry, lamb and steamed fish, with steaks and pasta options prepared at live cooking stations. The wine menu leans predominantly towards new world offerings, with a few prestigious champagnes.
Aloft Abu Dhabi Al Safarat **02 654 5000**
www.aloftabudhabi.com
Map **1 H8**

Eight Restaurant & Bar — International

Another big name establishment with a track record elsewhere – this time in Lebanon – that has transferred its success to Abu Dhabi. Style and class are two words that spring immediately to mind as you enter, and the food has all the idiosyncratic delights of the decor. From spinach-fringed gnocchi and grilled fish, to beef fillet and ribs, each dish feels like a luxurious treat, as do the wines and cocktails.
The Souk At Qaryat Al Beri Bain Al Jessrain
02 558 1988
Map **1 L8**

El Sombrero — Mexican

Peachy terracotta walls, signature sombreros and live Mexican music set the scene at this lively restaurant, which comes recommended, whether you're out for a relaxed dinner for two or a raucous night with your amigos. The impeccably dressed maitre d plays an active role in servicing the tables as guests wade through the menu which offers Mexican staples. The Fiesta Platter is perfect for sharing and the house specialty, homemade guacamole, is prepared fresh at the table. Mains are a feast of Mexican-style meat and fish dishes, burritos, tacos and enchiladas.
Sheraton Abu Dhabi Hotel & Resort Markaziya East
02 677 3333
www.starwoodhotels.com
Map **2 Q2**

Filini

Jing Asia

The Garden Restaurant

El Sombrero

Frankie's Italian Restaurant & Bar

Escape — International
Swimmers and beach-goers alike can find welcome refuge from the sun in this casual poolside restaurant with its full canvas canopies and multiple electric fans; the setting is ideal for a casual family dinner or a few lazy sundowners. The hearty sandwiches and healthy, original salads make Escape a great place to recharge after a hard day relaxing on the beach. Kids are welcome and there's a special menu for hungry little tummies.
Hilton Abu Dhabi Al Khubeirah **02 681 1900**
www1.hilton.com
Map **2 C3**

Essence — Buffet
Hotel buffet can fall victim to trying to cater to everybody, but Essence manages to do a decent job of the tricky task. The food is of solid quality, the setting classy and even though it's a family-friendly restaurant, there's an unusual aura of serenity. The international buffet has something for just about anyone and some of it you get to witness being prepared at the live cooking stations.
Beach Rotana Abu Dhabi Tourist Club Area
02 697 9011
www.rotana.com
Map **2 S5**

Evergreen Vegetarian Restaurant — Vegetarian
This is a traditional vegetarian Indian restaurant where the emphasis is very much on fresh, healthy ingredients. The restaurant is clean but reassuringly basic in the way that only the very best independent restaurants get away with and, true to form, the food is authenticity itself. To delight local residents, the restaurant also does takeaways.
Nr Al Safa Supermarket, Sheikh Zayed Second St
Madinat Zayed **02 676 7361**
Map **2 M4**

Figaro's Pizza — Italian
More a family or fast food style Italian restaurant than a venue for a romantic evening, Figaro's serves up pizza and pasta which are both fairly tasty and decent value. It's a good place to stop and carb-up before taking on a second round of shopping.
Marina Mall Breakwater **02 681 3300**
www.figaros.com
Map **2 D1**

Filini — Italian
This is a spacious, modern restaurant where warm beiges, creams and dark woods calm the senses; if the weather allows, the terrace is equally as peaceful a dining space. Filini is unashamedly Italian, and classic, simple and seasonal fare is served up from a menu that holds no surprises. Pizza, fish, meat or pasta are the main choices, but they're done very well, and the wine list, like the service and presentation, is excellent. The bar is also very good for a quiet chat over a deep claret tinto.
Radisson Blu Hotel, Abu Dhabi Yas Island Yas Island West **02 656 2000**
www.radissonblu.com
Map **1 S5**

Finz — Seafood
Sitting apart from the other Beach Rotana restaurants, Finz feels like something of a seafood pilgrimage. Finz is serious about seafood and, with several pages detailing different preparations and offerings, the place doesn't disappoint. From lobster to sea bass to huge prawns, Finz keeps you salivating. It's not cheap, but it's almost worth it for the half shell oysters alone. Attentive service and a gorgeous terrace setting (currently suffering from construction noise) can turn a Monday night into an evening fit for a holiday.
Beach Rotana Abu Dhabi Tourist Club Area
02 697 9011
www.rotana.com
Map **2 S5**

The Fishmarket — Seafood
With the tropical island decor and the always smiley service, the Fishmarket feels a very long way from Abu Dhabi, and the food furthers that illusion. From the extensive array of fresh seafood and the cartload of fresh vegetables, noodles and rice, customers choose the style of cooking (grilled, sautéed or fried), the kind of sauce (green curry, red curry or oyster sauce), and the accompaniments. Not a place for committed meat lovers, this place concentrates on seafood and raises the bar to another level by doing so.
InterContinental Abu Dhabi Al Bateen **02 666 6888**
www.ichotelsgroup.com
Map **2 C4**

Foodlands Restaurant — Indian
Foodlands is a good place to go for a reasonably priced family meal. There are two separate areas, depending on whether you are dining or just fancy a quick snack, and both offer tasty Indian, Chinese, Arabic and continental cuisine, all served with a smile. Parking can be a problem, so prevent road rage on busy nights by taking a taxi. Foodlands is also open for breakfast.
Al Hamily Bldg, Shk Rashid Bin Al Maktoum Rd
Al Manhal **02 633 0099**
www.foodlands.com
Map **2 K5**

Frankie's Italian Restaurant & Bar — Italian
Frankie Dettori's collaboration with Marco Pierre White offers world-class dining in a chic, romantic

setting. Attention to detail is key, from the eclectic decor, mouthwatering menu and outstanding service, right down to the lighting. Diners can feast on the freshest Italian fare, ranging from home-made pastas and wood-fired pizzas to gourmet treats like grilled Canadian lobster and beef tenderloin. Dessert is a must, with home-made gelatos and tiramisu, while the sommelier can guide you through the extensive wine list. Open for dinner only, the restaurant often has midweek early bird two-for-one offers on main courses and cocktails.
Fairmont Bab Al Bahr Bain Al Jessrain **02 654 3238**
www.frankiesitalianbarandgrill.com
Map **1 L8**

The Garden Restaurant — International

This lovely eatery offers an assortment of themed brunches through the week. Stylish decor, an easy atmosphere and homely charm make it a thriving favourite. The Mojito Bubbly Brunch (Dhs.160) on Fridays offers unlimited mojitos, bubbly and live music. A divine buffet, live cooking stations and an exceptional wine list accompany every meal. So whether you're into Mexican, Far Eastern, seafood, Italian, or all of these (international night), book a table and enjoy, but remember to dress on the smart side.
Crowne Plaza Markaziya East **02 621 0000**
www.crowneplaza.com
Map **2 N4**

Hakkasan — Far Eastern

From the moment it opened its doors in June 2010, this infamous establishment with its signature 'Hakkasan' decor and world class cuisine, has been a popular choice for anyone who loves Chinese food.

Hakkasan

The restaurant's layout offers each party of diners a secluded area where they can enjoy privacy, but still observe their surroundings and the stunning interiors. The menu offers a mouthwatering choice of Cantonese specialities and innovative creations. For those who may fear a dent to your wallet due to Hakkasan's location in Emirates Palace, fear not; whilst it is possible to spend a fortune on the a la carte menu, there are very reasonable options too – particularly the highly recommended Dim Sum brunch.
Emirates Palace Al Ras Al Akhdar **02 690 7999**
w3.hakkasan.com
Map **2 B2**

Haveli — Indian

Unfussy restaurant delivering hearty Indian fare, warm service and rock bottom prices. It does a range of chicken and lamb kebabs prepared in a tandoor oven, as well as tasty curries, ranging from mild to fiery. Traditional north Indian thalis offer the chance to sample a number of curries and desserts in small portions.
Nr New Etisalat Bld Al Dhafrah **02 632 1448**
Map **2 M6**

Hawksbill Restaurant — International

It may be a golf course restaurant but Hawksbill offers much more than your average clubhouse. Named after Saadiyat's local turtle species, it welcomes non-member diners in search of a modern setting, great views, a range of reasonably priced drinks and a varied menu. It serves up everything from designer burgers to Thai dishes, but the common theme is huge portion sizes. The large terrace is great for a long weekend lunch.
Saadiyat Beach Golf Club 02 557 8000
www.sbgolfclub.ae
Map **1 H1**

Hoi An — Vietnamese

An upmarket taste of Vietnam overlooking the shores of Al Maqta Channel. The comprehensive menu comprises traditional Vietnamese favourites and delicious originals, such as kobe steak in a rich foie gras sauce. The staff are friendly and accommodating, tailoring dishes to suit the palates of chilli lovers and loathers alike. Subtly decorated in a far eastern style indoors, the outdoor tables offer a more secluded dining experience.
Shangri-La Hotel, Qaryat Al Beri Bain Al Jessrain **02 509 8888**
www.shangri-la.com
Map **1 L8**

Il Paradiso — Seafood

The Sheraton's signature restaurant and a leading player in the city's competitive seafood scene.

Making the most of the hotel's position at the end of the Corniche overlooking the beach, it offers one of the capital's most scenic outdoor dining experiences. The setting is intimate with live entertainment that sets the tone. Seafood lovers will not be disappointed by the range of fish and shellfish, all imaginatively presented. This is one of Abu Dhabi's pricier restaurants – watch out for the 'cooking charge' – but the food is good and the service is friendly and efficient.
Sheraton Abu Dhabi Hotel & Resort Markaziya East
02 677 3333
www.starwoodhotels.com
Map **2 Q2**

Central Market

Located on the site of the city's old souk, the newest destination for shopping and dining in Abu Dhabi is exquisite, with intricate wood architecture and a rooftop terrace perfect for enjoying a (non-alcoholic) drink with friends. Although the Market is still in its infancy, there are already many shops and restaurants open. Stop by Kababs & Kurries (p.376) for upscale Indian, feel Parisian at the Crepe Café, sample some of the Southern hemisphere's finest ice cream at New Zealand Natural, or get a taste of the Middle East at Tarbouche (p.388). The Central Market often holds cultural events and book fairs on weekends, so stay tuned as Abu Dhabi's newest souk finds its niche.

Il Porto — Italian

Il Porto is located in the Mirage Marine complex. The restaurant's stylish interior is eclipsed by its outdoor terrace with views over blue waters. On offer is an intriguing mix of contemporary Italian fare and sushi (which feels a bit odd, but just about works). Food is simple, service is fine, and dishes are mouth-watering, but this good restaurant is elevated by its location. Within the complex, a Lebanese restaurant, shisha garden and cafe also serve up treats, and Mirage Marine is fast becoming an essential, though unlicensed, hangout.
Mirage Marine Complex, Nr Marina Mall Breakwater
02 635 9957
Map **2 D2**

India Palace — Indian

This unassuming restaurant features an extensive menu and is busy at lunchtimes and evenings with a mix of diners. The flavoursome, authentic dishes are generously portioned and offer good value for money. As certain dishes are pretty fiery, those with delicate palates can request milder versions. Quick, courteous waiters will patiently guide you through the menu if you are not an expert on north Indian cuisine.
Al Salam St, Nr ADNOC Markaziya East **02 644 8777**
www.sfcgroup.com
Map **2 Q5**

Indigo — Indian

Offering a lighter take on Indian cuisine, with distinct Thai and Malaysian twists to some of the dishes, Indigo is popular with Indian families as well as expats. Although one of the more expensive Indian restaurants in the capital, Indigo serves high quality fare in stylish surroundings with a good atmosphere. Wooden screens separate the restaurant into private areas making it suitable for groups of all sizes as well as intimate couples. Opt for terrace dining to make the most of the view of the beach and harbour, with the lights of the ever-growing Reem Island twinkling in the distance.
Beach Rotana Abu Dhabi Tourist Club Area
02 697 9011
www.rotana.com
Map **2 S5**

Jing Asia — Asian

Contemporary and colourful on the inside, with a rejuvenating sea view from the outside, the ambience at Jing Asia is impressive either way. Attentive, friendly staff prepare fresh ingredients in the open kitchen which hosts traditional Asian cuisine, from sushi to stir fries; Friday brunch casts the net wider, even boasting a traditional roast with Yorkshire puddings. Ideal for large groups or parties, there are a variety of themed nights throughout the week.
Crowne Plaza Yas Island Yas Island West **02 656 3000**
www.crowneplaza.com
Map **1 S5**

jones the grocer — International

The Australian-based chain is a firm favourite among Abu Dhabi expats with a taste for high quality food, organic produce and rustic style. The cafe, nestled within a larger food emporium that includes a fromagerie and bakery, offers natural gourmet food sourced from around the world. It has a decidedly rustic feel, with simple decor and food often served on cutting boards. Sit outside on wooden benches to soak up some sun as you enjoy a mouth-watering brunch or light lunch, and you'll soon understand the hype; the breakfast here comes particularly highly recommended. Other branches are located in Khalidiyah (02 639 5883) and Al Raha Gardens (02 557 4882).
Al Mamoura Bldg B, Muroor Rd Al Nahyan
02 443 8762
www.jonesthegrocer.com
Map **2 N10**

YOU ARE WELCOME!

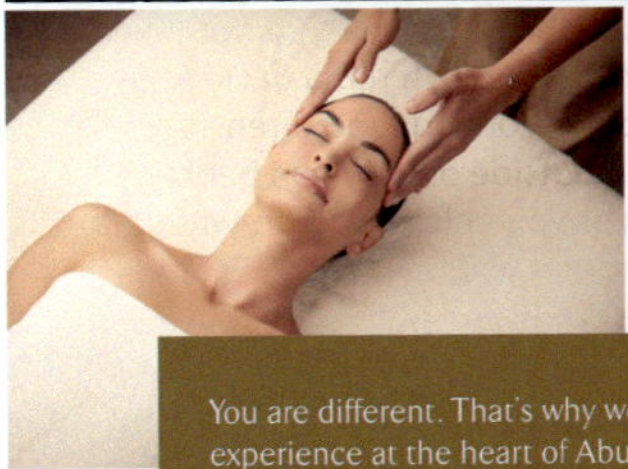

Kababs & Kurries — Indian

Located in the brand-new Central Market, this upscale restaurant offers, as the name suggests, both Indian and Arabic food. The selection of kababs, ranging from chicken tikka to a more adventurous shikampuri lamb, should please any meat lover while the curry selection showcases the best of the subcontinent.

The Souk Central Market Markaziya East
02 628 2522
Map **2 M4**

Kazu — Japanese

There are some very good restaurants in Abu Dhabi but Kazu makes the difficult leap to stand out. The interior is nothing spectacular – it's simple, modern and nicely lit; however the terrace, overlooking Yas Marina and the race circuit, makes for a unique backdrop to a social restaurant where sharing is the best way to sample as much of the menu as possible. Head chef Yu Cao trained under Nobu Matsuhisa but, in Kazu, it's possible that the apprentice has eclipsed his master's Dubai offering. The exceptional lightness and clarity of flavours almost defies belief; wash them down with a Japanese beer or some sake. Presentation is excellent, as is service.

The Yas Hotel Yas Island West **02 656 0600**
www.theyashotel.com
Map **1 T4**

Kwality — Indian

If you like authentic Indian food at a very reasonable price, then Kwality is one of the best options in town. From north Indian tandoori dishes to Goan curries, Kwality offers the diner a wonderful culinary tour through India. Watch the chefs in the open kitchen prepare succulent kebabs and hot, fluffy naans, while you whet your appetite with peppery poppadoms and spicy chutneys. The food, service and welcoming atmosphere make this one of the 'must do' Indian restaurants in the capital.

Al Salam St, Nr National Bank of Fujairah Markaziya East **02 672 7337**
Map **2 Q3**

L'Auberge — Arabic/Lebanese

Although L'Auberge may have slipped down somewhat on the list of top Arabic restaurants in the city, its prime location in the heart of the business district ensures a bustling lunchtime trade. The menu covers a wide range of Lebanese specialities and European fare, and the Friday brunch is very popular. The venue is modern and spacious, albeit fairly plain, but the waiters are all friendly and very helpful. Prices veer a little towards the high side.

Shk Khalifa Bin Zayed St Markaziya East **02 627 3070**
Map **2 N3**

L'Opera Brasserie — International

At first glimpse, this restaurant may appears small, but once you're seated, it doesn't feel crowded and the small size makes for an intimate ambiance. Alfresco dining next to the hotel pool is an option in cooler weather. The Friday brunch offers a good quality buffet with a wide selection of well presented international dishes. It also caters for children, with a separate mini-buffet and TV, allowing parents the freedom to eat in peace. It has a calm, relaxed atmosphere with prompt, responsive staff. During the rest of the week, the restaurant offers an a la carte menu, and caters for breakfast, lunch and light dinners.

Le Royal Meridien Abu Dhabi Markaziya East
02 674 2020
www.leroyalmeridienabudhabi.com
Map **2 P3**

La Brasserie — Buffet

This established eatery, overlooking Le Meridien's lively Culinary Village, serves a good selection of French regional cuisine, whether you opt for the varied buffet or choose from the extensive a la carte menu. Themed evenings add variety: the seafood buffet on Monday night is particularly popular due to the wide range of treats on offer – crab, lobster and crayfish sit alongside sushi and all manner of fish dishes from near and far. Another favourite is the Friday brunch. Thursday nights are Meat Nights, featuring a carnivorous buffet for pocket change. When the weather is cooler, the terrace is a wonderful place for an evening of laidback alfresco dining.

Le Meridien Abu Dhabi Tourist Club Area
02 644 6666
www.lemeridienabudhabi.com
Map **2 S4**

La Mamma — Italian

This spacious, well-appointed restaurant has a homely atmosphere, which makes you immediately feel welcome. With the exception of the antipasti buffet which has a number of exotic dishes, the food is fairly standard but is well prepared and of good quality. Presentation is unfussy and leaves the food to speak for itself. The restaurant caters to a wide range of appetites, from quick and filling pizza to delicious and generous helpings of pasta and seafood. The staff are unobtrusive but attentive and quick to offer extras such as perfumed towels and freshly grated parmesan cheese. An excellent choice of restaurant for an intimate romantic evening, a fun family feast or a respectable business meal.

Sheraton Abu Dhabi Hotel & Resort Markaziya East
02 677 3333
www.starwoodhotels.com
Map **2 Q2**

La Piazza — Italian

Refreshingly free from cliched 'traditional' decor, La Piazza offers quiet respite. The menu, on the other hand, stays true to its Italian theme with a good selection of authentic starters, main dishes and desserts that are all enjoyable, good value and well presented. A popular buffet is also available.
Sands Hotel Madinat Zayed **02 615 6666**
www.danathotels.com
Map **2 N4**

La Terrazza — Mediterranean

The decor of this bustling, open-plan restaurant is stylish and modern, and the dazzling buffet display doubles up as decoration. There are a number of stations, each with a culinary theme, and it is easy to miss one out in your enthusiasm to pile your plate with delectable titbits. For all the quantity of food, the quality is not compromised. Resist the temptation to fill up before reaching the exquisitely presented dessert table. Busy, without being crowded, Wednesdays and Thursdays are theme nights, and on all other nights the buffet serves international cuisine.
Hilton Abu Dhabi Al Khubeirah **02 681 1900**
www1.hilton.com
Map **2 C3**

La Veranda — International

This intimate, formal dining establishment has four different reasonably priced dinner menus, plus a brunch buffet, and the excellent quality of food makes up for the somewhat limited choice. There is a tempting selection of international dishes and, if you fancy lobster, steak or prawns, each food type has its own menu, detailing the varying sauces, cooking methods and accompaniments. Reserve a table by the windows for a view of Al Khalidiya Street.
Sheraton Khalidiya Hotel Abu Dhabi Markaziya West **02 666 6220**
www.sheratonkhalidiyaabudhabi.com
Map **2 J4**

Le Beaujolais — French

With its red checked tablecloths and French speaking, glass clinking clientele, Le Beaujolais transports you to a charming little bistro in Paris. The menu offers a choice of traditionally prepared seafood and meat dishes, rounded off perfectly by a dessert selection which includes favourites such as creme brulee and cheese plates. A daily set menu is also available. This is one of the few places in Abu Dhabi where you can treat yourself to a cheese or meat fondue. The service, headed by a friendly maitre d', is welcoming and attentive, but never obtrusive.
Mercure Centre Hotel Markaziya East **02 633 3555**
www.mercure.com
Map **2 M4**

Le Vendôme Brasserie

Le Bistrot — French

Fans of natural ingredients, fine wines and elegant French cuisine will enjoy a superb culinary experience at Le Bistrot in Le Meridien's central garden. In the cooler months, the terrace offers a great opportunity to watch the world go by, while feasting on some top quality fare. The menu is not long, and vegetarians are not particularly well catered for, but fans of classically French simple fish and meat dishes will be more than happy. Cheap it's not, but here you get what you pay for. The only downside is the loud music played at Le Meridien's Village at the weekends.
Le Meridien Abu Dhabi Tourist Club Area **02 644 6666**
www.lemeridienabudhabi.com
Map **2 S4**

Le Shaderwan — Arabic/Lebanese

Le Shaderwan is one of the few Arabic restaurants that are neither high-end hotel nor chaotic cafe. The atmosphere is almost cave-like and the menu, which features informative images of the dishes, has all the traditional Arabic staples covered. Prices are reasonable, portions generous, and the food served promptly. The restaurant is also a popular indoor shisha spot for those seeking tranquillity amid the hustle and bustle of Tourist Club.
Nr Kia Showroom Tourist Club Area **02 645 5400**
Map **2 Q4**

Le Vendôme Brasserie — International

If you are a fan of luxurious opulence and sampling cuisines from all around the world in one sitting, then Le Vendôme is your kind of place. This all-day restaurant offers a wonderful buffet and if weather permits you can sit outside on the beautiful terrace. Alternatively, you can enjoy the stunning decor

inside the restaurant, where tables are laid out under gothic-inspired archways. In a happy departure from the norm at buffet restaurants, the tables at Le Vendôme are set well apart from each other, so you won't be knocking elbows with the strangers at the next table.
Emirates Palace Al Ras Al Akhdar **02 690 7999**
www.emiratespalace.com
Map **2 B2**

Lebanese Flower — Arabic/Lebanese
The pavement location of this popular joint results in a few parking difficulties, with cars lining up outside to collect takeaway orders. Once inside the brightly lit, comfortable interior, you'll find a range of high quality grilled meats and fish accompanied by fresh Arabic bread from the nearby bakery. A selection of Middle Eastern curries and meat dishes are available at lunchtime. The service is super efficient.
Nr Electra & 26th Sts Al Khalidiyah **02 665 8700**
Map **2 F4**

Marakesh — Moroccan
Despite the elaborate decor, Marakesh has a fairly casual ambience which suits business and leisure diners alike. Exotic and delectable Moroccan food (with more than a hint of Lebanese influence) is served in generous portions and delivered to your table by a bevy of highly efficient waiters. A live band adds atmosphere and, later in the evening, an eye-poppingly beautiful belly dancer makes a dramatic appearance. The air conditioning is rather frosty, so go prepared. Marakesh is open seven days a week for dinner only.
Millennium Hotel Abu Dhabi Markaziya East **02 614 6000**
www.milleniumhotels.com
Map **2 P3**

Marco Pierre White Steakhouse & Grill

Marco Pierre White Steakhouse & Grill — Steakhouse
If a beautifully appointed restaurant with exact yet friendly service delivering classic, hearty British comfort food, elevated to superbly delicious standards, sounds like your idea of heaven, then get yourself to Marco's Abu Dhabi restaurant. He may be a celeb chef but one bite into the foie gras or pepper sauce topped fillet and you'll know this is anything but style over substance. It's a dinner only restaurant but you'll want to spend the whole night wallowing in the wine-fuelled experience.
Fairmont Bab Al Bahr Bain Al Jessrain **02 654 3238**
www.fairmont.com
Map **1 L8**

Marroush — Arabic/Lebanese
The multitude of cars lined up outside this Lebanese street cafe is the first thing to catch your attention – and given the somewhat grimy decor, it is not surprising that the bevy of drive-by customers choose to take their food away. However, the standard Lebanese dishes on the menu are delicious and freshly grilled, and there is the usual range of decadent fruit cocktails piled high with syrup, nuts and cream. Marroush is recommended as a cost effective venue for light meals and takeaways.
Nr Abu Dhabi Chamber of Commerce & Industry Markaziya West **02 621 4434**
Map **2 L2**

Mawal — Arabic/Lebanese
An Arabian belly dancer and singer top the bill at Mawal, but the excellent food, colourful service and lively atmosphere are enough draw in themselves. In addition to an exhaustive range of hot and cold Lebanese mezze, there's is a selection of superb kebabs grilled to perfection. If you plan to stay for the show, reservations are essential as the place really comes alive later on. The show starts at 22:30 Saturday to Wednesday and at 23:00 at weekends, and there is a minimum spend on food of Dhs. 275 (weekdays) or Dhs. 325 (weekends) per person for the show.
Hilton Abu Dhabi Al Khubeirah **02 681 1900**
www1.hilton.com
Map **2 C3**

The Meat Co — Steakhouses
The Meat Co is a deceptively large restaurant, covering two floors plus a big outdoor deck. It's open plan to the extreme with an open kitchen, and even an open pantry and store cupboard. The energy of the kitchen spills out to the restaurant giving the place a frenetic atmosphere, which is augmented by the loud music, making it popular with large groups. When not rushed, the service has a casualness that isn't reflected in the steep prices. The meat, the best reason for

coming here, is good with Wagyu sirloin, Australian and South African Grade A, and US Black Angus beef on offer.
The Souk At Qaryat Al Beri Bain Al Jessrain **02 558 1713**
www.themeatco.com
Map **1 L8**

Mezlai
Emirati

Appropriate for a restaurant which prides itself on being the UAE's first Emirati restaurant, Mezlai's Arabic-themed decor features majlis corners and memorabilia from the country's early days while stained glass lanterns cast an atmospheric spell. The food relies on traditional staples – rice, meat and fish – with a sprinkling of regional influences from across the Middle East. True to the UAE's culinary traditions, there's a definite emphasis on seafood and you'll get to sample specialities like Weld-Al Walad – a shark soup – and grilled Gulf hammour, while carnivores are treated to camel meat and Lamb Medfoun. The restaurant's Emirati chef (see p.364) is also touted as a regional first.
Emirates Palace Al Ras Al Akhdar **02 690 7999**
www.emiratespalace.com
Map **2 B2**

Mezzaluna
Italian

From the moment the complimentary breads and olives are placed in front of you, until the time you devour the last crumb of your wicked (but wonderful) dessert, your experience at Mezzaluna will be heavenly. The Italian head chef uses divine inspiration to create a host of beautifully presented dishes that include fresh pasta concoctions, seafood creations and meat dishes, many of which are surprisingly easy on the pocket. If you can't fit in one of its delicious desserts then don't miss out on an after-dinner coffee, served with a selection of Italian biscotti and rich dipping sauces. Whether seated out on the covered terrace or indoors, the stunning decor set beneath church-like arches creates an opulent atmosphere that you'll want to return to time and again – this is a rare opportunity to experience food and service of regal standards, without having to pay a king's ransom.
Emirates Palace Al Ras Al Akhdar **02 690 7999**
www.emiratespalace.com
Map **2 B2**

Mirabel
International

Located in the Marks & Spencer building, Mirabel stands out from the standard shopping mall cafes; the menu encompasses delicious breakfast, lunch and dinner options made of fresh ingredients by the European-led kitchen crew – and if you can't leave the office for lunch, the online automated ordering system will see a warm delicious meal delivered without the usual hassle of location explanation.
Fotouh Al Khair Centre Markaziya East **02 631 5111**
www.mirabel.ae
Map **2 L4**

Mezlai

Mirage Marine Cafe
Arabic/Lebanese

A favourite among locals, this large Lebanese restaurant-cafe features a main restaurant, a covered shisha bar and an outdoor garden. Very popular for shisha and coffees, the mezze and mixed grills are also all well above par.
Mirage Marine Complex Breakwater **02 635 9957**
Map **2 D2**

Nihal Restaurant
Indian

This well-established restaurant offers great curries at very reasonable prices, and the menu is extensive enough to tickle just about anyone's fancy. The fragrant spices of the subcontinent are expertly blended into tasty traditional dishes, served up with the usual relishes, yoghurts and chutneys. If Indian food is not your favourite, there are also various Chinese dishes on offer. Nihal does a bustling takeaway trade, and has a well reputed outside catering service. This is cheap chow at its best.
Sheikh Zayed Second St, Nr Sands Hotel Madinat Zayed **02 631 8088**
Map **2 N4**

Noodle Box — Asian

The Noodle Box boasts a chic but calm romantic setting with an outdoor terrace overlooking Yas Marina and the F1 track. The menu is simple, but expertly designed. From signature dim sum and prawn cakes with fresh chillies and lime leaves, to wok specialties that include Singaporean black pepper crab and a tantalising Thai green chicken curry, each dish holds a myriad of flavours to tempt even the most discerning of taste buds. The well selected wine list and, particularly, the house speciality beer, Tsingtao, complement the cuisine perfectly and the service is impeccable.

The Yas Hotel Yas Island West **02 656 0600**
www.theyashotel.com
Map **1 T5**

The Noodle House — Chinese

Views of the Souk Qaryat Al Beri, coupled with delicately prepared oriental dishes, mean that The Noodle House is a popular choice at any time of the day. With a wide selection for vegetarians, spice lovers and healthy eaters, everyone leaves satisfied. The zen ambience and oriental music make this modern slice of Asia ideal for any type of social gathering, although it's best suited to lunch with friends and family, or dinner before a night out. The service is fast but this doesn't hinder the excellent quality of the food. Another branch in Al Wahda mall is also popular for those seeking a quick, quality meal between shops.

The Souk At Qaryat Al Beri Bain Al Jessrain
02 558 1699
www.thenoodlehouse.com
Map **1 L8**

Oceans Seafood Lounge — Seafood

African masks and heavy wicker furniture decorate this excellent restaurant. Offering a range of Indian, Thai and Malay dishes, the menu is dominated by seafood, though it does have a good selection of meat dishes, and there are a few salads. Low lighting and widely spaced tables offer a feeling of intimacy, although the tables are a little large for two people. There are special promotions and occasional live music. The venue also offers terrace dining in the cooler weather, as well as a private function room.

Le Royal Meridien Abu Dhabi Markaziya East
02 674 2020
www.leroyalmeridienabudhabi.com
Map **2 P3**

THE One Cafe — Cafe

Located inside the eponymous furniture store in Khalidiya, The One Café is a great place to relax in the middle of a shopping adventure. Not surprisingly, given the location, the cafe is strikingly decorated, and the menu, though not extensive, offers both traditional and more inventive cuisine, as well as delicious desserts.

Sheikh Zayed First St Al Khalidiyah **02 681 6500**
www.theoneme.com
Map **2 G4**

Origins — International

The setting has the feel of a futuristic movie set, but the most striking feature of Origins is the amazing view of the Yas Marina Circuit (and some pretty swanky boats). The international buffet is well spread out and presented, with loads of time honoured favourites from around the world. The salad and dessert bars stand out, offering an excellent selection of fresh, quality produce, and tempting sweet treats. Come the weekend, brunch deals are offered.

The Yas Hotel Yas Island West **02 656 0600**
www.theyashotel.com
Map **1 T5**

The Palm — International

Ideal for families, The Palm offers a reasonably priced buffet packed with fresh, tasty salads, hot meals and desserts, with various theme nights during the week. The simple decor is clean and inviting, and large glass windows allow an abundance of light into the cheerful dining area.

Al Diar Capital Hotel Tourist Club Area **02 678 7700**
www.aldiarhotels.com
Map **2 R3**

Pappagallo — Italian

Pappagallo is like a little slice of Tuscany right in the heart of Le Meridien's Culinary Village. The menu offers all the usual Italian favourites, such as pastas and pizzas, as well as a wonderful antipasti buffet. Whether you dine alfresco or indoors, the food is decent and the informal setting of the restaurant allows for a relaxed experience; if undecided as to where to go for a simple night out, then Pappagallo is definitely a safe bet.

Le Meridien Abu Dhabi Tourist Club Area
02 644 6666
www.lemeridienabudhabi.com
Map **2 S4**

Gourmet Abu Dhabi

Abu Dhabi gastrophiles should look forward to the month of February as that's when Gourmet Abu Dhabi hits the kitchens of the capital. Organised by Abu Dhabi Tourism Authority, Gourmet Abu Dhabi is a 10 day culinary tour-de-force that sees Michelin-starred and celebrity chefs from all over the world showcase their skills, and discuss their art, at several of Abu Dhabi's biggest hotels. See www.gourmetabudhabi.ae for more info.

Peppino — Italian

Peppino has been around for a long time and, although this shows in the decor, the food is still good. While it offers a decent spread of standard Italian fare, Peppino is most famous for its pizza with interesting toppings; note that the wine list is no longer on offer, though. The service here is good, but takeaways and home delivery options are available, if you prefer.
Grand Continental Flamingo Hotel Markaziya East **02 690 4000**
www.gcfhotel.net
Map **2 P3**

Poolside — International

Set alongside the beach and overlooking the creek, Poolside serves great food with signature cocktails and juices. Healthy dishes, such as tuna tartare with avocado, cucumber and arugula and an interesting array of salads feature alongside more calorific mains. The gourmet burgers are delicious – choose from Atlantic lobster, chargrilled lamb loin, or The Full Monty: Australian Wagyu beef, black truffle, foie gras, caramelised onions and parmesan in a onion bun.
Fairmont Bab Al Bahr Bain Al Jessrain **02 654 3238**
www.fairmont.com
Map **1 L8**

Porto Bello — Italian

Porto Bello stands out among Abu Dhabi's many Italian restaurants thanks to its first-class food, discreet service and classy setting. Whether you dine indoors or on the atmospheric terrace, you'll get to sample a good but not confusingly large choice of dishes, each of which is a lesson is flavoursome simplicity.

Porto Bello

The lasagna – overpowering bechamel is shunned in favour of layers of ricotta and mozzarella cheese – is a fine example of its attributes, as are the smoked duck risotto and osso buco Milanese.
Grand Millennium Al Wahda Al Nahyan **02 443 9999**
www.millenniumhotels.com
Map **2 M7**

Portofino — Italian

Although it probably won't win any awards for food quality, the menu offers nicely prepared Italian classics like pizza, pasta and tiramisu. On the plus side, portions are generous and prices are reasonable. The main draw is the pleasant location overlooking the pool, which lends itself to relaxed outdoor dining in the winter months. Shisha pipes are available, if desired.
Abu Dhabi Marina & Yacht Club Tourist Club Area **02 644 0300**
Map **2 S4**

Prego's — Italian

Prego's boasts an enchanting setting with its large, airy interior and superb terrace overlooking the beach. The food is wonderful – in addition to a varied pizza bar, the menu has a selection of both classic and innovative pasta dishes, main courses and desserts, and an impressive wine selection. Pizzas are prepared in an authentic wood-fired oven. Prego's is family friendly, but it's good for an intimate dinner too.
Beach Rotana Abu Dhabi Tourist Club Area **02 697 9011**
www.rotana.com
Map **2 S5**

Rainbow Steak House — International

This refurbished venue is definitely worth a visit. Contrary to its name, steaks are not its forte so stick to the seafood, Chinese, Indian and continental cuisine. Lunch and dinner buffets are available daily at unbelievably low prices, with friendly, efficient service.
Rainbow Hotel Apartment Markaziya East **02 632 6333**
www.rainbowauh.com
Map **2 N3**

Rangoli — Indian

With a la carte options available and friendly staff, Rangoli offers a good value curry fix. The buffet, with a focus on North and South Indian cuisine, is fresh and attractive. Starters and mains include vegetable samosas and meat, fish and vegetable curries. Sweet lovers can choose from traditional desserts. Cushioned booths and a formal dining area enveloped in dark wood with flashes of bright colour, and a glass-fronted show kitchen, create a laid back atmosphere.
Yas Island Rotana Yas Island West **02 656 4000**
www.rotana.com
Map **1 T5**

Let's Do Brunch

Brunch may have been invented in the States, given kudos in New York, and be setting itself a place mat in the hipper centres of western Europe, but in this particular Middle Eastern city, it's a hobby, a social skill, a weekend institution. It's the calorific glue that holds the weekend together.

Far from the genteel image of croissants, scrambled eggs and good coffee over the day's newspapers, brunch in Abu Dhabi is synonymous with triumphantly eating your own body weight in food and washing it down with free-flowing champagne. And all for a set price.

Having eaten and quaffed the entire day away, brunchers are renowned for then throwing themselves into misguided rampages around the city's nightspots, and suffering spirit-crushing hangovers the following morning. New arrivals are quickly asked whether they've been to a brunch yet, typically by an expat with more Abu Dhabi-years under their (loosened) belt, and a knowing glint in their eye.

So why is this gluttonous sport so popular in Abu Dhabi? This city's predominantly expat community probably has a lot to do with it. There are plenty of work-hard, play-even-harder type young revellers looking to blow off steam and mingle, so Abu Dhabi has a sociable culture to match. The fact that you boil alive if you venture outside for more than 10 minutes during at least three months of the year also helps keep people inside and ingesting at the weekends.

Whatever the reason, brunch has become quite the art form; one which diners master by flexing their (softening) stomach muscles at the masses of competitive, creative and uniquely reasonable deals available from the city's fleet of five-star hotels. Formerly purely a Friday fun-for-all, the pursuit is now spreading through the week, almost to the point where brunch becomes a round-the-clock way of living, rather than just a way of eating.

The Yacht Club

Brunch. You might think that the word is self-explanatory: a portmanteau of 'breakfast' and 'lunch' – a meal you have between the two more widely accepted dining anchors. If so, you clearly haven't lived in Abu Dhabi for very long.

If you want to throw yourself in at the deep end, head out to The Yas Big Brunch. Held every Friday and Saturday, Dhs.200 will buy you an extensive array of dishes to choose from and you'll get to wash it all down with unlimited house beverages – before heading to the Skylite bar for an after party; for Dhs.100 extra, house beverages will be free-flowing all through the night and you even have the option to stay overnight at the Yas Hotel for a discounted Dhs.450, should the party carry on to the point of no return.

Once you've flaunted your daytime partying prowess, you might want to prove you can keep the same pace going. In that case, head for the InterContinental's Yacht Club (p.397) where the Friday late lunch runs from 14:00 to 18:00 and offers unlimited food from the menu along with more mojitos than are served during the average Havana public holiday.

Le Vendome Brasserie (p.377) offers a brunch experience with finesse. The deal at this Emirates Palace favourite epitomises Abu Dhabi's posh and pricey all-inclusive. For a princely sum, you can feed on the entire world (from Japan to Europe via India), and swig from a champagne flute all afternoon. And while at Emirates Palace, there's no better address in town for local flavour than Mezlai (p.379). A booze-fuelled fiesta it may not be, but for Dhs.280, you can tuck into Emirati delicacies from camel shawarma to grilled Gulf hammour every Friday. Prepared under the guidance of the UAE's first Emirati chef, it's a local feast, in a spectacular Emirates Palace setting to boot.

Across town, you could do worse than head out to Fairmont Bab Al Bahr's CuiScene, where Dhs.520 buys you a brunch with unlimited Moet & Chandon. Bubble lovers would be equally pleased at Left Bank (p.395), where you get to select whatever you fancy from an a la carte menu and the bubbly is free-flowing too.

Thankfully, tucking into the stuff of brunch-time legends need not mean breaking the bank. Priced at Dhs.138, c.taste's budget option is hard to beat. In addition to the offerings of an irresistible waffle station, you'll be treated to unlimited house beverages and complimentary pool access.

Somewhere in the middle of the brunch-ometer lies a trove of average-priced bargains that take the feasting mission slightly less seriously, and are therefore ideal for a laidback meal with chums or a family outing. Assymetri's Friday Family Brunch is priced at Dhs.180 and the deal runs till 15:30 every Friday.

Talking of families, both Sevilla (p.386) and Assymetri (p.362) have fun-filled Friday family brunches with both food and entertainment aimed at kids as well as parents. Both also represent fantastic value. Sevilla costs Dhs.174, while Assymetri sneaks in at Dhs.180. Both include certain house beverages, while children are half price. Just as fun is the Friday Family Brunch at Jing Asia (p.374), where you can enjoy an extensive selection of eastern and international delicasies. And so there it is. Brunching in Abu Dhabi is as big as football in the UK, sumo wrestling in Japan and basketball in the US. So raise your fork and join in.

The Restaurant — Buffet

This members-only dinner venue features an impressive entrance area, complete with a fireplace constructed of stone and wine bottles, which leads to a softly lit, Roman-style interior – the perfect setting for a romantic evening out. With theme nights every night except Saturdays and brunches on Friday and Saturday, The Restaurant offers a superb choice of tasty cuisines and culinary experiences. The prices are reasonable and there is live music on most nights.
The Club Al Meena **02 673 1111**
www.the-club.com
Map **2 V3**

Resto! — International

Warm, modern decor, the quiet hum of easy listening tunes, and friendly staff set the tone at Resto! and the international menu is equally crowd-pleasing: the buffet includes curries, sushi, grilled meats and vegetarian dishes, with the pasta bar a definite highlight – closely followed by the colourful treats from the dessert bar.
One To One Hotel – The Village Al Dhafrah **02 495 2000**
www.onetoonehotels.com
Map **2 Q8**

Riviera — Italian

Riviera is a guilty pleasure courtesy of executive chef Salvatore Cozzi, who came from Naples to bring authentic Italian cooking to the heart of Abu Dhabi. From hearty homemade pasta, pizza and irresistible breads that will satisfy your carb cravings to the terraced seating that overlooks the tranquil marina, dining at Riviera is a relaxed affair that deserves ample time to savour.
Marina Al Bateen Resort Al Bateen **02 665 0144**
www.marinaalbateen.com
Map **2 C6**

Eat In Al Ain

It may not be a global culinary capital but find yourself in Al Ain and there are a few decent options to help ward off hunger. Danat Al Ain's (p238) Luce, The Wok and Tanjore are all excellent eateries, while Casa Romana at the Hilton Al Ain (p.238) is an Italian restaurant worth checking out. The Al Ain Rotana (p.238) also has some good restaurants, with Gardenia and Trader Vic's arguably the top picks.

Rodeo Grill — Steakhouses

Part old English drawing room, part old American shooting lodge, Rodeo Grill is reminiscent of a high-end Argentinean ranch. Resplendent in green leathers and deeply hued wood, it's an unashamedly masculine restaurant geared to carnivores who enjoy full-bodied reds. That said, salads, seafood and even a few veggie options make it on to the menu, but the spotlight shines firmly on the fantastic range of steak cuts, with the grade nine marble Wagyu and the bison rib eye stealing the show. Wash it all down with a pinot noir and you're in meat-lovers' heaven. Prices are certainly not cheap, but this is a truly excellent restaurant.
Beach Rotana Abu Dhabi Tourist Club Area
02 697 9011
www.rotana.com
Map **2 S5**

Royal Orchid — Thai

The extensive menu at this small tucked away joint allows you to break convention. It alternates between light, fragrant Thai and succulent Chinese spices – the deep fried black bean chilli chicken wings are as deliciously indulgent as they sound. Like the cooking, the decor effuses elegant Thai style with more than a hint of Chinese flair. Families are welcome, but the intimate seating is best suited to couples, small groups and business occasions. Ample portions and reasonable prices make for a satisfying experience.
Hilton Abu Dhabi Al Khubeirah **02 681 3883**
www1.hilton.com
Map **2 C3**

Royal Vegetarian Restaurant — Indian

In the city centre, it can be hard to tell one Indian restaurant from another – shoddy on the outside and tasty on the inside is something of a running theme. Taste the thali at Royal Vegetarian, however, and you'll soon have its location stored firmly in your memory. Serving up everything from soups and snacks to curries, it's fast, cheap and delicious.
Shk Hamdan Bin Mohd St Markaziya East
02 678 7272
Map **2 P3**

Samurai Restaurant — Japanese

There aren't too many Japanese restaurants in Abu Dhabi, and those that there are tend to veer towards the pricier end of the spectrum. If you're a devotee of sushi, maki and yakiniku, then Samurai is a special little find. The food is top draw, while the atmosphere, like the decor, is a lot of fun.
Al Nuaimi Tower, Al Meena St Tourist Club Area
02 676 6612
Map **2 R3**

Sardinia — Mediterranean

Hidden away in an area not known for its fine dining, every course at Sardinia is both an event and a work of art, served by a white-gloved, highly professional waiting team. Only the finest ingredients are used and while some of the amuse-bouches are off-the-wall,

Riviera Italian Resturant

Enjoy the cooking of our Italian Executive Chef

- -"Homemade" pasta, pizza & breads.
- - Terraced seating overlooking the marina.
- - Fully licensed bar.

Open for lunch & dinner for reservation call 02-6650144

Dock Side Pool Bar

Comfortable outdoor seating overlooking the marina.

- -Home made baguettes & sandwiches.
- -Grilled Kababs, steaks&Shisha.
- -Fully licensed bar.

Open from 11:00 am till late For reservations call 056-6089955

Health Club & Pool

Experience the serenity of our facilities With professional personalized training.

- -35 of the latest "LifeFitness interactive fitness solutions" machines & free weights.
- -Pool with temperature control & in-water bar.
- -Limited number of members.
- -Swimming lessons.
- -Scuba diving instruction.

Gym opens 07:00am till 11:00pm daily Pool opens 07:00am till sunset daily

Call 02-6657255

Waves Lounge Bar

-Outdoor Functions, Indoor Functions, Live Music &DJ Private Parties *Call 056- 6089944*

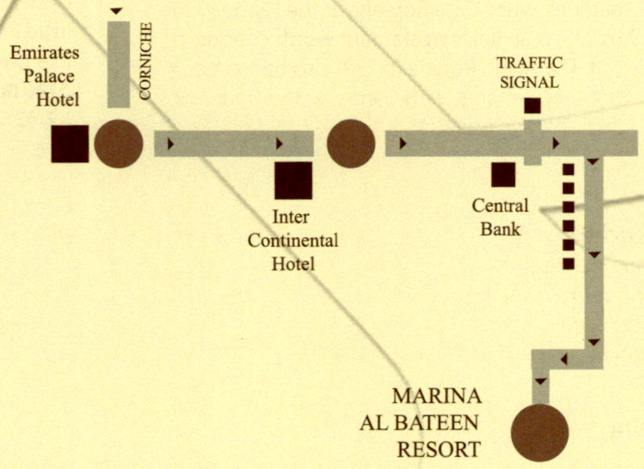

مارينا البطين

MARINA AL BATEEN RESORT

Tel: 02 6650144
Fax: 02 6665755
P.O.Box: 44044, Abu Dhabi
United Arab Emirates

هاتف: ٠٢ ٦٦٥٠١٤٤
فاكس: ٠٢٦٦٦٥٧٥٥
ص.ب: ٤٤٠٤٤، أبوظبي
الإمارات العربية المتحدة

such as foie gras with chocolate and passion fruit, most are sublime mouthfuls. Opt for the twelve course 'regular' dinner accompanied by four types of wine (Dhs.750) for a sensational culinary journey. Certainly one of the best restaurants in Abu Dhabi.
Abu Dhabi Country Club Al Mushrif **02 446 5455**
www.sardinia.adhfc.com
Map **2 J13**

Sayad — Seafood

As one of the key restaurants at the luxurious Emirates Palace, you can expect the ultimate high-end dining experience. This superb eatery offers a seasonal menu of fresh seafood, sourced from across the globe. The modern glass interior could look stark, but the blue-green lighting adds a touch of class and quiet charm. The wine list is extensive, offering the top eight wines from every wine-producing region in the world. You can select your own fish or lobster from the tanks along the wall to be prepared to your taste. If the choice of so many well-designed dishes is overwhelming, simply opt for the five-course set menu for a taste of everything from sushi to the catch of the day. A sublime dining option.
Emirates Palace Al Ras Al Akhdar **02 690 7999**
www.emiratespalace.com
Map **2 B2**

Selections — International

Few restaurants are more aptly named than Selections. Buffets and live cooking stations are the name of the game here, with the variety reflecting no less than Lebanese, Asian and Mediterranean cuisines. Breads, salads and soups make up the starters; fish, fresh pastas and curries account for the main courses; desserts are more numerous than you could possibly imagine. Ideal for a business meeting during the week, or family brunch at the weekend, the large, light restaurant looks out over the pool and the shimmering Arabian Gulf beyond.
InterContinental Abu Dhabi Al Bateen **02 666 6888**
www.ichotelsgroup.com
Map **2 C4**

Sevilla — International

Situated in the grand lobby of Al Raha Beach Hotel, Sevilla offers a daily dining buffet with a different theme depending on the night of the week. There is an extensive wine list and the buffet which is supplemented with a salad bar, a large selection of bread and a small dessert trolley, whilst not prolific at any one time, is tasty and freshly prepared. Inside you can relax to the tinkling sounds of the harpist and outside on the terrace overlooking the pool and the gardens of the hotel, enjoy your evening under the stars.
Al Raha Beach Hotel Al Raha **02 508 0555**
www.danathotels.com
Map **1 R7**

Sevilo's — Italian

In the more temperate months, make use of Sevilo's poolside terrace which offers stunning views of the city and gardens. The varied yet uncomplicated menu delivers classic Italian cuisine, which is freshly prepared and generally of a high standard. Sevilo's is a pleasant, intimate and trustworthy eatery which delivers a trio of high points: good food, pleasant setting and great service, which should provide an enjoyable evening.
Millennium Hotel Abu Dhabi Markaziya East **02 614 6000**
www.milleniumhotels.com
Map **2 P3**

Sayad

Shang Palace

Shakespeare & Co. — International

Stepping into Shakespeare & Co. is a little like stepping into the book Alice In Wonderland; the shabby chic Victorian decor, with pastel colours and mismatched chairs, is delightful and instantly inspires an urge for a cup of tea and some sweets. The menu has an eclectic mix of English, American, Italian, and Arab cuisine at moderate prices. The desserts, neatly showcased in a pastry case, are decadent and – almost – too beautiful to eat.

The Souk Central Market Markaziya East
02 639 9626
www.shakespeareandco.ae
Map **2 M4**

Shang Palace — Chinese

There are so many reasons to visit Shang Palace. The extensive menu covers Cantonese and Szechuan cuisine in addition to many non-Chinese items, and seafood features prominently. The atmosphere is great, the service faultless, the staff impeccably dressed, the food superb, and the large portions offer excellent value for money. The breathtaking views from the romantic terrace are more than enough reason to come and linger for the evening in the large, solid chairs. Highly recommended, and deservedly popular, reservations for terrace dining are advised.

Shangri-La Hotel, Qaryat Al Beri Bain Al Jessrain
02 509 8888
www.shangri-la.com
Map **1 L8**

Shuja Yacht — Dinner Cruise

All aboard for a voyage which makes you feel like the 'king of the world'. From the lowliest deckhand to the captain, every staff member goes all out to ensure you have a memorable and impressive trip. The downstairs area is dedicated to dining, while the upstairs is saved as a pre dinner retreat with a bar and open air deck to enjoy the cool evening breeze with your complimentary drink as you sail along the Abu Dhabi corniche. A vast selection of seafood is on offer, including some delicious clams, as well as some hot dishes.

Le Royal Meridien Abu Dhabi Markaziya East
02 674 2020
www.leroyalmeridienabudhabi.com
Map **2 P3**

Soba — Japanese

Soba is a tranquil, comfortable, minimalist haven, where you'll find a taste of the far east and a chance to unwind. The emphasis is on fresh, good quality: the signature sushi rolls are perfectly formed and delicious, but if raw fish isn't your thing there are plenty of cooked alternatives to tempt the taste buds. The dessert menu is limited, but a great end to the meal – the green tea icecream is particularly good. Open for lunch and dinner, Soba is perfect for groups and singles, but may not be the best place for children due to the muted ambience. The open kitchen gives a view of the quiet skill of the chefs, and if the menu inspires you, Soba offers sushi-making classes on Saturdays, morning and afternoon.

Le Royal Meridien Abu Dhabi Markaziya East
02 674 2020
www.leroyalmeridienabudhabi.com
Map **2 P3**

Sofra Bld — International

Any restaurant that can boast three chocolate fountains is worth a visit, and while an a la carte menu is available, it is Sofra's luxury buffet, surrounding its centrepiece of fountains, that is the restaurant's main attraction. A breathtaking selection of cuisine is offered which covers all four corners of the globe – from fresh sushi to shawarmas, kebabs and parrot fish. The light and airy interior is less suited to intimate occasions, while the outside terrace provides a perfect vantage point for viewing the neighbouring Sheikh Zayed Grand Mosque.

Shangri-La Hotel, Qaryat Al Beri Bain Al Jessrain
02 509 8888
www.shangri-la.com
Map **1 L8**

Spaccanapoli Ristorante — Italian

This Italian haunt is squarely Neapolitan and, although thoroughly modern, it has plenty of rustic features which nod to a menu that embraces the traditional quality of simple Italian fare, rather than the modern trend for fusion offerings. Treats such as baked aubergine with mozzarella, parmesan, tomato and

basil get the meal off to an excellent start, and all the traditional main courses are represented. Try the veal escalope, the fresh fish or, if you're hungry, the metre-long pizza. The food is excellent, the prices reasonable and, best of all, the atmosphere is traditionally Italian.
Crowne Plaza Markaziya East **02 621 0000**
www.crowneplaza.com
Map **2 N4**

Sushi Bar — Japanese

On the first floor of the Abu Dhabi Golf Club, this casual joint offers made to order sushi. Prices are reasonable; four pieces of sushi costs Dhs.35 and the chef's special, which includes an assortment of around 15 different pieces, is just Dhs.85. On Monday evenings, enjoy a leisurely all-you-can-eat sushi deal for Dhs.105 per person. The Sushi Bar also offers a takeaway option – it's advisable to call ahead so that they can have your order ready when you arrive.
Abu Dhabi Golf Club Madinat Khalifa A (Khalifa City A) **02 558 8990**
www.adgolfclub.com
Map **1 N8**

T-Garden — Afternoon Tea

Tea aficionados in the capital are treated to a wide range of brews from ginger to Darjeeling and the comfortable sofas make a good spot for relaxing with a book. Should you get peckish sipping your third cup, there's a selection of finger food – choose from a range of panini, sandwiches and Asian small eats, or satiate your sweet tooth by opting for one of the luxurious cakes on display.
One To One Hotel – The Village Al Dhafrah
02 495 2000
www.onetoonehotels.com
Map **2 Q8**

Talay — Seafood

This Thai restaurant is a wonderful place to sip cocktails as you watch the daylight fade away over a quiet beach – a great tonic for frazzled nerves at the end of a long day. Choose from the fresh display of seafood (with live lobsters), and have it prepared to your personal tastes – the Chu Chee prawns are a particular treat. Alternatively, the a la carte menu offers a good range of starters, seafood, meat, rice and noodle dishes – all flavoured to suit western palates. The typically Thai service is attentive, but not intrusive and, despite the range of wine and drinks on offer, this restaurant is more on the quiet side, making it a good choice for an intimate occasion or business dinner.
Le Meridien Abu Dhabi Tourist Club Area
02 644 6666
www.lemeridienabudhabi.com
Map **2 S4**

Trader Vic's

Tarbouche — Arabic/Lebanese

The ground floor location offers views of the new souk, but it's the roof terrace where Tarbouche excels: alive and buzzing with people drinking fruit cocktails and enjoying shishas, it's fast becoming one of the most popular lounges in the city. Comfortable sofas and chairs are arranged in groups to allow you and your friends to socialize while taking in the downtown view. Both food and drinks are available and service is efficient, though expect to pay slightly higher prices than average.
The Souk Central Market Markaziya East
02 626 0700
Map **2 M4**

Teatro — Fusion

An eclectic mix of Venetian masks, crystal beads, thick white candles and modern furniture creates a dramatic, but informal, atmosphere at Teatro, which is echoed by a huge show kitchen that hides nothing. Choose from an impressive and extensive a la carte menu, which covers a spectrum of east to west fine dining cuisine with many favourites available. For special occasions, you can book the exclusive chef's table which can seat up to eight people. Service is impeccable, with nothing too much trouble. Teatro is fast becoming a firm favourite.
Park Rotana Abu Dhabi Al Matar **02 657 3333**
www.rotana.com
Map **1 K7**

Toshi — Asian

'Fusion' is sometimes shorthand for a restaurant with an identity crisis but when it's done well – as it is here at Toshi – it gives you access to a wide-raging and delicious menu. The restaurant delivers a good range of Japanese, Chinese and Thai dishes, but it's

the teppanyaki that steals the show – try black tiger prawns, Canadian lobster or jumbo scallop: light, healthy and delicious.
Grand Millennium Al Wahda Al Nahyan **02 443 9999**
www.millenniumhotels.com
Map **2 M7**

Trader Vic's
Polynesian

Trader Vic's is a tropical retreat serving fusion cuisine from Polynesia alongside the chain's legendary cocktail menu, of course. Live Cuban and Latin music complete the picture and the lively atmosphere draws in the crowds most days of the week. The menu ranges from finger food to tasty treats from the Wood Fire Oven selection.
Beach Rotana Abu Dhabi Tourist Club Area
02 697 9114
www.tradervics.com
Map **2 S5**

Ushna
Indian

Ushna's sophisticated surroundings perfectly complement the beautifully prepared food. The service mirrors the superb setting and there's a good selection of traditional North Indian dishes to choose from, as well as a large range of premium wines and cocktails. During the cooler months, bag a table by the water overlooking the Grand Mosque.
The Souk At Qaryat Al Beri Bain Al Jessrain
02 558 1769
Map **1 L8**

Vasco's
Portuguese

Vasco's is a contemporary, fine-dining venue that serves up a fusion of European, Arabic and Asian cuisines. Food is prepared to a very high standard, imaginatively presented, and delivered to your table by friendly, knowledgeable waiters. As this is one of the more popular restaurants in the capital, reservations are essential for lunch and dinner. During the winter, the patio offers a pleasant alfresco setting.
Hilton Abu Dhabi Al Khubeirah **02 681 1900**
www1.hilton.com
Map **2 C3**

The Village Club
International

Situated in a garden with huge, shady trees, this is a great place to linger over a leisurely lunch or a relaxed supper. At the buffet, starters include soup, mezze and salads; the barbecue offers a variety of meat, fish and side dishes. Weekends are good for families; there's plenty of space for kids and two trampolines keep them occupied.
One To One Hotel – The Village Al Dhafrah
02 495 2000
www.onetoonehotels.com
Map **2 Q8**

The Vista
International

A great outdoor venue with one of the best restaurant views in Abu Dhabi. Steaks, tapas, grills and seafood dominate the menu; best of all may be the Wagyu tenderloin and Omani lobster. The reasonable prices make The Vista a regular hangout for club members and their families.
The Club Al Meena **02 673 1111**
www.the-club.com
Map **2 V3**

Waves
Far Eastern

This relaxed beachfront joint caters to fans of pan-Asian cuisine. The menu offers a fusion of Far Eastern flavours from Peking Duck to tempura and kim-chi. Open for members and their guests, the alfresco setting makes for a tranquil evening out.
The Club Al Meena **02 673 1111**
www.the-club.com
Map **2 V3**

Wokcano
Far Eastern

This friendly joint with creative flair offers a taste of Asia: the glossary at the back of the extensive Pan-Asian menu guides your decision between a range of sushi, dim sum and a host of innovative specialities as you dine in the beautifully presented setting.
One To One Hotel – The Village Al Dhafrah
02 495 2000
www.onetoonehotels.com
Map **2 Q8**

Yotto
Japanese

This bright and minimalist restaurant, located in Yas Yacht Club, features a pleasing fusion of nautical and

Yotto

Japanese design. Japanese classics from sushi to noodles and tempura grace the menu; the signature Alaskan black cod with sweet miso glaze merits a return visit – and is often sold out at the weekends. End your meal with the pastel mocha: sweet and chewy bites of pounded rice moulded around ice cream. Though dinner for two, at upwards of Dhs.700, does not come cheaply, it is difficult to find a more memorable Japanese meal in the capital.
Yas Yacht Club Yas Island **02 565 0722**
www.cipriani.com
Map **1 T5**

Zari Zardozi — Indian

The theme of Indian opulence, silk and spice is clearly reflected in Zari Zardozi with its rich red walls, copper ceiling and fragrant incense. Intimate seating arrangements add to the exotic mood and accompany the north and south Indian menu – which is extensive to say the least. The chef and staff will happily come to your table and discuss your preferences for spicy culinary treats. Other options include fusion food, a diet menu and 'tandushi' – which combines tandoori cooking with sushi.
Al Raha Mall Al Raha **02 556 5188**
www.zarizardozi.com
Map **1 R7**

Zen — Japanese

While the minimalist decor is a touch on the drab side, and the high-pitched, xylophonic zinging of the background music is clanging at times, Zen has a string of satisfied customers, including many from the Japanese expat community of Abu Dhabi. The secret of this success is simple: the food is authentic, delicious and fresh. Whether you choose the sophisticated sushi or the dishes served at the teppanyaki bar, you'll quickly forgive the shortcomings of the decor thanks to the impresse simplicity and subtlety of the flavours on offer.
Al Ain Palace Hotel Markaziya East **02 679 4777**
www.alainpalacehotel.com
Map **2 P3**

Zest — Cafe

With a light, zesty twist throughout the menu, this bistro style eatery offers an array of light, healthy snacks and fillers. Delectable soups, salads and sandwiches appeal, with the roasted corn and pumpkin soup and the chicken and mango Thai style salad recommended. Situated in the fitness centre of The Club, Zest also provides pump for the pros with a range of Myoplex infused smoothies, and low carb and high protein alternatives. For the not so health conscious, there is a selection of well earned afters to indulge in.
The Club Al Meena **02 673 1111**
www.the-club.com
Map **2 V3**

Allure By Cipriani

BARS, PUBS & CLUBS

Allure By Cipriani — Nightclub

High-end nightclubs can be synonymous with a pretentious crowd too beautiful to dance, but Allure, even while offering Dhs.68,000 bottles of champagne, strikes a fine balance and does a decent job in its attempt to create a club scene reminiscent of Ibiza. Stunning all-white decor, top DJs and monthly theme nights attract a crowd looking to genuinely have a good time while moving to pulsating beats.
Yas Yacht Club Yas Island **050 596 9543**
www.nightcluballure.com
Map **1 T5**

Ally Pally Corner — Bar

A bit of an Abu Dhabi expat institution, the goal is a British style boozer and the execution is almost perfect. Beers, wines and spirits run freely, while the food is hearty and, in most cases, served with chips. Sport is shown on the large screens, and there's a pool table and darts board to keep drinkers entertained.
Al Ain Palace Hotel Markaziya East **02 679 4777**
www.alainpalacehotel.com
Map **2 P3**

The Beachcomber — Bar

This chilled-out beach bar feels more Caribbean than UAE. Popular with after-work and weekend crowds, it serves up a tapas menu that, while not truly Spanish, ideally accompanies the cocktails and shisha that are both also must-tries. Beachcombers is closed during the warmest summer months.
Sheraton Abu Dhabi Hotel & Resort Markaziya East **02 677 3333**
www.sheraton.com
Map **2 Q2**

Belgian Beer Cafe

Pub

A lively, European-style café setting with lots of noise and hearty laughter coming from the bar. The specialty is steamed mussels – what else, this being a Belgian joint – and you'll get to sample the Belgian classic dish cooked with broths ranging from curry to white wine and tarragon. The restaurant boasts some of the best fries in the city, as well as pork cooked in a number of ways. Other alternatives include steaks, chicken and vegetarian selections, all of which makes for an escape into Belgian vibes, if only for a few hours. The extensive choice of beers made this a favourite hangout among expats.
InterContinental Abu Dhabi Al Bateen **02 666 6888**
www.ichotelsgroup.com
Map **2 C4**

Sporting Life

The glitz and glamour of the A-lister bars is all very well, but sometimes you just want a joint where you can catch the big match and enjoy a pint with your mates. Unfortunately, Abu Dhabi is a little lacking when it comes to out-and-out sports bars (try Heroes p.394, or NRG p.395) but there are plenty of other bars where the screens are big and the beers are cold. Harvester's (02 615 6666) and The Captain's Arms (p.391) are popular options, while Cooper's (p.392) is a good venue for those living at the other end or off the island.

Black Pearl

Bar

An excellent choice for a sophisticated evening out. The bar has a small but varied menu of mostly light meals. While the food is delicious, it is definitely more a bar than a restaurant and is a great choice for pre-dinner drinks or as a stop-off during an evening out. The comfortable leather couches provide intimacy, while stools grouped around the bar are ripe for those who want to mix and mingle. Black Pearl also has a small selection of cigars on offer.
Al Raha Beach Hotel Al Raha **02 508 0555**
www.danathotels.com
Map **1 R7**

Brauhaus

Pub

This cosy pub features all things German in a setting almost authentic enough to make you forget you are indeed in Abu Dhabi. The dark wood panelling and hunting gear mounted on the walls give this establishment a feel of a remote lodge and European sports is shown on the many TV screens. The menu offers hearty German fare including pretzel dumplings with a ragout of forest mushrooms; pork knuckle with sauerkraut and mashed potato; as well as five types of German sausages – with all the trimmings. The signature apple strudel with vanilla sauce and cinnamon ice cream is the perfect finish if you can fit it in.
Beach Rotana Abu Dhabi Tourist Club Area
02 697 9118
www.rotana.com
Map **2 S5**

Bravo Tapas Bar

Bar

An intimate setting with lovely decor, this is a great place for a date or catching up with a friend. While chatting away and sipping on a glass of Iberian tinto or cold Estrella beer, dive into the exceptional tapas.
Sheraton Abu Dhabi Hotel & Resort Markaziya East
02 677 3333
www.sheraton.com
Map **2 Q2**

Captain's Arms

Bar

Located in the Village Courtyard and overlooking the gardens, this tavern has a cosy interior and upbeat, outdoor terrace. It offers a traditional British pub ambience and, by and large, Abu Dhabi's expat scene soaks it up. The daily happy hour (17:00 to 19:00), nightly entertainment and food and drink specials bring in those crowds and, although you won't find many culinary surprises, food portions are generous and satisfying. The service could be better, but it is the value for money on drink specials that appeals.
Le Meridien Abu Dhabi Tourist Club Area
02 644 6666
www.lemeridienabudhabi.com
Map **2 S4**

Chill Out Lounge

Bar

The unrivalled views from the top floor location make Chill Out Lounge a perfect spot to while away

Cinnabar

the hours over drinks and shisha. The in-house band provides cool tunes to relax to while the attentive staff make sure you won't run out of anything while watching the sun go down. Whether you turn up solo to wind down, or with friends to chill out, you'll be soaking up some of the best vistas in town.
Grand Millennium Al Wahda Al Nahyan **02 443 9999**
www.millenniumhotels.com
Map **2 M7**

Cinnabar — Nightclub

With an eclectic mix of RnB and popular funk, Cinnabar offers a stylish way to round off your night. From the rich ruby drapes to the minimalist sofas and candlelit tables, it is more sophisticated than most Abu Dhabi nightspots. Guests can either strut their stuff on the dancefloor or simply sit back, relax and let one of the waitresses guide them through the cocktail menu. The champagne and fresh strawberry cocktails slip down very easily but, don't fear, the Dhs.100 price tag will keep your excesses in check and sore heads at bay. Quiet on weeknights, the club comes alive after midnight at weekends when the party set let their hair down. It is also the venue for weekly salsa nights.
Hilton Abu Dhabi Al Khubeirah **02 681 1900**
www.hilton.com
Map **2 C3**

Cloud Nine – Cigar Bar — Bar

If a refined evening of cognac, caviar and the finest cigars appeals to you, Cloud Nine is a place you'll want to call home. From the first puff on your hand-picked Cohiba, Monte Cristo or Bolivar (delivered to you on a silver platter, of course), to the last taste of Beluga that passes your lips, this luxurious venue exudes a pleasing mix of old boys' club charm and trendy sophistication. Service is pleasant and discreet, and a pianist adds further elegance to a classy (if a bit smoky) evening out. Happy hour is from 17:00 to 20:00.
Sheraton Abu Dhabi Hotel & Resort Markaziya East **02 677 3333**
www.sheraton.com
Map **2 Q2**

The Club Bar — Bar

A lively members' bar, with an extensive drinks menu and a great range of pub food at attractive prices. It shows major sporting events and there's a weekly quiz night on Wednesdays. The Club's Sports Bar is on a similar tip and is also an excellent, laidback venue.
The Club Al Meena **02 673 1111**
www.the-club.com
Map **2 V3**

Colosseum — Nightclub

Visit this Roman-style nightclub any night of the week to rub shoulders with the young and hip on the snug, yet pumping, dancefloor. Tuesday is Arabic night, while the rest of the week sees a live band and decent DJs belting out the latest RnB and pop beats, making this multi-cultural venue one of the city's favourite hotspots. Entrance is Dhs.100 (which includes three free drinks). As an added bonus, drinks are reasonably priced and ladies get in free.
Abu Dhabi Marina & Yacht Club Tourist Club Area **02 644 0300**
Map **2 S4**

Cooper's Bar & Restaurant — Pub

Coopers draws in the football fans: not only can you find a friendly pint and some superb pub grub, the pub also shows all major football matches (call ahead for details), is convenient for both on-island and off-island clientele and boasts competitive prices with 50% off selected beverages during its extended 'happy hour'. It can entertain a large number of drinkers and diners with its spacious interior and additional seating outside, making it a convenient location for informal social gatherings.
Park Rotana Abu Dhabi Al Matar **02 657 3333**
www.rotana.com
Map **1 K7**

Al Ain Watering Holes

Wetting your whistle in the oasis city of Al Ain is a generally quiet but enjoyable affair, with the Horse & Jockey (03 704 6000) offering the most authentic pub ambiance in town – come the weekend, the atmosphere can get pretty lively too. Across town is Paco's (03 768 6666), part bar part Mexican cantina and an equally popular haunt among local expats. And that's not even mentioning the ever reliable Trader Vic's (03 754 5111) where the cocktails are so strong they should come with health warnings, and the live entertainment is just as addictive.

Cristal — Bar

Experience the tranquil but trendy ambience of this bar, where elegantly understated decor is set off perfectly by an excellent range of champagne, sparkling wine and other tipples. The bar manager will help you select the perfect drink while you sit back and relax in surroundings of polished wood, leather and subdued lighting – the tinkling tunes played by the in-house classical jazz pianist are the perfect accompaniment. Head there from 17:00 to 19:00 for happy hour drink deals.
Millennium Hotel Abu Dhabi Markaziya East **02 614 6000**
www.milleniumhotels.com
Map **2 P3**

NRG Sports Café

Trader Vic's

Pearls & Caviar

Dock Side Pool Bar — Bar

After a hectic week, relaxing by the water with a drink in hand is just what the doctor ordered. Dock Side Pool Bar, at Marina Al Bateen Resort, is the ideal place to kick back with friends or get the family together for a casual meal overlooking the marina. Dine alfresco on home-made baguettes, hearty kebabs and steaks ,or just watch the sun go down with a drink from the licensed bar with a shisha pipe at your side. Open from 11:00 until late.
Marina Al Bateen Resort Al Bateen **02 665 0144**
www.marinaalbateen.com
Map **2 C6**

Etoiles — Nightclub

It's hard to decide whether this is a lounge bar, restaurant or nightclub, such is the venue's success at walking a delicate line between all three. The food is tasty European haute cuisine, while the decor is Paris, New York or Milan chic turned all the way up to 11. A backdrop of loud house music may be a little bizarre as you finish your meal, but as the evening gets later and the venue hits full on club mode, Etoiles stands out as one of the UAE's very best. It's where the A-listers party when they're in town, which pretty much says it all.
Emirates Palace Al Ras Al Akhdar **02 690 7999**
www.etoilesuae.com
Map **2 B2**

G Club — Nightclub

G Club, previously known as Gauloises, may be a nightclub that is a little past its peak, but its drink promotions and prime location seem to keep it hopping along. The dancefloor is vastly under used, thanks in part to the rather lacklustre DJ.
Le Meridien Abu Dhabi Tourist Club Area
02 644 6666
www.lemeridienabudhabi.com
Map **2 S4**

Havana Club — Bar

In keeping with the grandeur and opulence of the hotel, the Havana Club exudes sumptuousness and luxury. The delicious lingering scent of fine cigars and cigarillos entices from the moment you set foot in this old boys' bar. The club itself has a split personality, with the rowdy bar area having a younger, more outgoing spirit, while the leather armchairs in the back recess are the epitome of refinement. Relax and enjoy the imaginatively mixed and decorated exotic cocktails or sample one of the many vintage brandies and other spirits – or even test-smoke the cigars and cigarillos.
Emirates Palace Al Ras Al Akhdar **02 690 7999**
www.emiratespalace.com
Map **2 B2**

Hemingway's — Pub

Tucked away at the back of the Hilton hotel, this lively bar-restaurant offers an unpretentious all-in-one experience. The restaurant area serves the standard Mexican fare and it opens out onto a bar (which can get quite raucous at the weekends) with TV screens and live music, making Hemingway's more of a fun venue than one for an intimate rendezvous. There are regular ladies' nights and quiz nights.
Hilton Abu Dhabi Al Khubeirah **02 681 1900**
www1.hilton.com
Map **2 C3**

Heroes — Bar

Heroes is your typical sports bar early in the evening and during weekend afternoons. However, once the DJ begins at 21:00, followed by the band at 22:00, don't bother trying to watch TV – the lively, good-natured crowd will be more interested in throwing shapes on the dancefloor. The pub grub is plentiful and well-priced, with mains around Dhs.60. Arrive early if you plan to eat – seats are hard to come by once things kick off. Monday is quiz night and Tuesday is ladies' night. Parking around the hotel is nightmarish so use the underground carpark next to the Crowne Plaza or take a cab.
Crowne Plaza Markaziya East **02 621 0000**
www.crowneplaza.com
Map **2 N4**

Hickory's Sports Bar — Bar

A cosy club restaurant with sensational views over the lake and golf course, Hickory's is a sports bar, but that title doesn't really do it justice. Sure, major sporting events and news adorn the large plasma screens, but the feel is of a private members' club; the robust menu of wood-fired pizzas, huge pies and steaks is also a cut above. For something different, try the tasty tapas-style snacks on the terrace.
Yas Links Abu Dhabi Yas Island West **02 810 7777**
www.yaslinks.com
Map **1 T4**

Illusions — Bar

One of Abu Dhabi's best known nightspots, Illusions plays loud, banging dance music in a futuristic venue. The crowd tends to be fairly male dominated and it's not the place to go if you're after a cosy chat with friends. Saturday and Monday are ladies' nights.
Le Royal Meridien Abu Dhabi Markaziya East
02 674 2020
www.leroyalmeridienabudhabi.com
Map **2 P3**

The Jazz Bar & Dining — Bar

Small tables and hug-around chairs allow you to rub elbows with neighbours also enjoying the music at

this stylish but laidback nightspot. The select menu offers elite bites, including oysters and foie gras, and is priced to match, while dishes in the dining area are more conducive to larger and less exclusive appetites. The floor staff keep the unique, jazz-themed cocktails flowing and the live band entertains with cover versions; although there's no official dance floor, at weekends, wherever there's floor there's dancing.
Hilton Abu Dhabi Al Khubeirah **02 681 1900**
www1.hilton.com
Map **2 C3**

Left Bank — Bar

With views of Sheikh Zayed Grand Mosque, and chic contemporary European cuisine, Left Bank has a lot to offer. The terrace bears Arabic influences, while the interior echoes any exclusive London venue, complete with VIP section and inexhaustible cocktail menu. The combination of excellent food, friendly staff and stylish surroundings has earned Left Bank a good reputation among the expat community, so visitors are advised to book ahead.
The Souk At Qaryat Al Beri Bain Al Jessrain
02 558 1680
www.emiratesleisureretail.com
Map **1 L8**

Level Lounge — Bar

High above Hamdan Street, Level Lounge serves up mellow tunes and tasty tapas in a cosy, chilled-out rooftop setting. Wild mushroom risotto balls and braised calamari will take the edge off your appetite and, without a roof to obstruct the view, you can hunt for stars or just enjoy the twinkling city lights. Cooling off in the swimming pool next to the bar is an option on Friday afternoons, otherwise, Level Lounge is open nightly from 19:00. Check it out on Thursday and Friday nights when a DJ drops by to spin some tunes.
Crowne Plaza Markaziya East **02 621 0000**
www.crowneplaza.com
Map **2 N4**

Mai Cafe — Bar

A poolside restaurant-cum-lounge bar, ideal for spending hours draped over retro lounge chairs with drinks and shisha for company. Alternatively, move to the poolside tables and choose from the many Arabic and international dishes that adorn the menu. On Thursday evenings, get down early to make the most of the all-you-can-eat BBQ which includes unlimited house drinks.
Aloft Abu Dhabi Al Safarat **02 654 5000**
www.aloftabudhabi.com
Map **1 H8**

Mood Indigo — Pub

With its colonial furnishings and live music courtesy of the resident pianist and band, this is a sophisticated hangout. A snack menu of sandwiches, burgers and light bites is available as you prop up the very long, custom-made bar. This all-day bar stays open later than most other outlets at the hotel, closing at 02:00.
Mercure Centre Hotel Markaziya East **02 633 3555**
www.mercure.com
Map **2 M4**

NRG Sports Cafe — Pub

Armchair athletes flock to this sports cafe, with its multitude of TV screens, reasonably priced snacks and happy hour that lasts from 19:00 to 21:00. Decorated in sporting colours and paraphernalia, it combines an arena ambience with an open kitchen that pumps out fast and furious fusion food; NRG is a great spot to catch your favourite game live on TV. You can try out

Left Bank

your best moves on the dancefloor or, better still, keep your eyes glued to the score line.
Le Meridien Abu Dhabi Tourist Club Area **02 644 6666**
www.lemeridienabudhabi.com
Map **2 S4**

Opus Bar — Bar

This elegant bar is the kind of place you might take your boss for an after-work drink – with its comfy chairs and civilised noise levels, you'll be able to discreetly demand that promotion without having to shout over the music. The food is the usual pub fare (think Arabic mezze, chicken fingers, burgers and sandwiches), and it is served up in a more refined setting than your usual local.
Le Meridien Abu Dhabi Tourist Club Area **02 644 6666**
www.lemeridienabudhabi.com
Map **2 S4**

Pearls & Caviar — Bar

Inside, this popular venue is a sleek world of black, white and chrome – Downstairs, you can enjoy Mediterranean-Levantine culinary treats in a soothingly dark decor (Caviar), while the airy rooftop lounge (Pearls) serves cocktails and tapas to the backdrop of the white marble of Sheikh Zayed Mosque. As you might expect, three types of caviar are on offer: Beluga, Sevruga and Oscietra. Prices and service reflect the luxury and, while dinner for two will set you back around Dhs.1,200, this has not dimmed the restaurant's popularity. Expect a lively Lebanese and Emirati contingent on Fridays.
Shangri-La Hotel, Qaryat Al Beri Bain Al Jessrain
02 509 8888
www.pearlsandcaviar.com
Map **1 L8**

PJ O'Reilly's — Pub

One of Abu Dhabi's most popular pubs, with a friendly atmosphere. The menu is bar grub with flair – large portions prove good value for money. There's a lively bar downstairs, but you can escape to the quieter upstairs or outdoor areas. Bright and comfortable, it seldom feels crowded, despite its popularity. Large screen TVs show sport, though the sound is generally only on during live matches. Happy hour runs from 12:00 to 19:00 every day.
Le Royal Meridien Abu Dhabi Markaziya East
02 674 2020
www.leroyalmeridienabudhabi.com
Map **2 P3**

Relax@12 — Bar

The name says it all – chill out in the sleek lounge, nibble on some Asian bites and down a cocktail or two as you sink into one of the inviting sofas on the terrace overlooking Abu Dhabi's gorgeous skyline. The decor is modern with glowing bars, dim lighting and angular furniture, and both the terrace and huge-windowed bar attract a refreshingly broad mix of clientele. The view alone is worth a visit, but the extensive menu of beer, wine and cocktails, along with sushi and Japanese snacks, makes this a perfect spot for a night out.
Aloft Abu Dhabi Al Safarat **02 654 5138**
www.relaxat12.com
Map **1 H8**

Rock Bottom Cafe — Bar

This vibrant American diner has a split personality – go early in the evening to enjoy a quiet dinner, or hang around until later when the live music starts and the pace becomes frenetic. The menu features succulent steaks, sizzling seafood and innovative salads, as well as a range of lighter snacks. Quality food and value for money are distinct characteristics. The daily happy hour extends until 21:00.
Al Diar Capital Hotel Tourist Club Area **02 678 7700**
www.aldiarhotels.com
Map **2 R3**

Rush — Bar

The sort of swanky and effortlessly elegant lounge bar you'd expect from the people behind the global Buddha Bar chain. It still hasn't quite hit its stride and is not always as busy as the bar and setting merit, but Rush is still a great place for afterwork cocktails, an early stop or a chilled-out but classy night out. The cocktails are excellent, and there's some top quality finger food on the menu too.
The Yas Hotel Yas Island West **02 656 0600**
www.theyashotel.com
Map **1 T5**

SAX — Bar

Loved by the chic set for its vibrant and trendy NYC style. Staff are welcoming and remain so throughout the evening. A live jazz band and a well-stocked bar contribute to the vibey atmosphere as you unwind on comfortable sofas in the sunken lounge area, with one of the many exotic cocktails on offer. The decor is clean-cut with avant-garde lighting, which suits the sophisticated young clientele looking for a stylish venue to meet and mingle.
Le Royal Meridien Abu Dhabi Markaziya East
02 674 2020
www.leroyalmeridienabudhabi.com
Map **2 P3**

Sho Cho — Bars

One of Dubai's most achingly hip restaurants and nightspots has successfully made the leap to Abu Dhabi. The interiors are a delight, while the decking area boasts enviably incredible creekside views. The

cuisine is perhaps best described as oriental fusion, with plenty of fish and sushi dishes on the menu. This is fast becoming a weekend favourite among Abu Dhabi's elite socialites.
The Souk At Qaryat Al Beri Bain Al Jessrain
02 558 1117
www.sho-cho.com
Map **1 L8**

The Shore — Bar
The Club's members all tend to talk highly of The Shore which brings to mind the easy glamour of old St Tropez. Located on the beachside, during the day members can dip in the sea and then head straight for a light bite and cocktail at The Shore.
The Club Al Meena **02 673 1111**
www.the-club.com
Map **2 V3**

Skylite Lounge — Bar
You can't help but be blown away by the stunning views from this rooftop lounge bar, and even the most style conscious will appreciate the modern, imaginative decor. There are light bites and long wine, champagne and cocktail lists to choose from, while the dress code errs on the smart. The best time to enjoy Skylite is as the sun goes down, but it's easy enough to spend all night here too.
The Yas Hotel Yas Island West **02 656 0600**
www.theyashotel.com
Map **1 T5**

Stars 'n' Bars — American
Located on the water's edge of the Yas Marina, this hive of fun with an unmistakable all-American facade gives out its welcome message loud and clear: Stars n Bars prides itself on being far more than a restaurant – it offers 'eatertainment'. In addition to serving unashamedly American food from Tex Mex favourites to the ultimate 'Burgernator,' there's a pool table, live music, DJ and dancing – not to mention the countless screens showing sports of all kind.
Yas Yacht Club Yas Island **02 565 0101**
www.starsnbars.ae
Map **1 T5**

Stills Bar & Brasserie — Pub
This lively bar serves the cool youth as well as the gracefully aged. There's a nice list of speciality cocktails and whiskys, as well as several beers on tap and a cigar humidor. The gastro-pub menu serves light bites. There's also a DJ Pool Party night once a month, and Stills serves as a sometime-stopover for touring bands.
Crowne Plaza Yas Island Yas Island West **02 656 3000**
www.crowneplaza.com
Map **1 S5**

Tavern Pub — Pub
The Tavern may not epitomise sophisticated dining, but it does cracking roast dinners which will please those in need of some 'morning after' carb-loading. The no frills approach, comfortable dining area and the limited yet familiar menu create a relaxed, functional atmosphere with no pretension. Early birds get the armchairs.
Sheraton Abu Dhabi Hotel & Resort Markaziya East
02 677 3333
www.sheraton.com
Map **2 Q2**

Wakataua Terrace — Bar
With an idyllic setting on the water's edge, Wakataua is popular with those seeking a sundowner spot. A limited range of light snacks (chicken satay, buffalo wings and nachos) is available to help you curb the munchies.
Le Meridien Abu Dhabi Tourist Club Area
02 644 6666
www.lemeridienabudhabi.com
Map **2 S4**

The Yacht Club — Bar
If you're a vodka martinis fan then, with 52 different kinds of vodka, The Yacht Club should definitely be on your hit list. An excellent fusion menu is jam-packed with tasty Asian and western dishes. The terrace benefits from harbour vistas, while, inside, the sparkly decor is one part disco and one part ship's galley. There's a DJ on hand at the weekend.
InterContinental Abu Dhabi Al Bateen **02 666 6888**
www.ichotelsgroup.com
Map **2 C4**

Y Bar — Bar
Hit the bar area, with its long wooden tables and sport on TV or try the outside terrace with its views of the other Yas hotels. The extensive drinks menu focuses on cocktails and spirits while the food menu provides tasty basics, such as shepherd's pie, steak and chips and a few bar snacks.
Yas Island Rotana Yas Island West **02 656 4000**
www.rotana.com
Map **1 T5**

Zenith Club — Nightclub
One of the city's most popular clubs, tunes are of the house and RnB varieties and the crowd is diverse and intent on partying. Saturday is Arabic night, and ladies drink for free on Mondays, Tuesdays and Wednesdays.
Sheraton Abu Dhabi Hotel & Resort Markaziya East
02 677 3333
www.sheraton.com
Map **2 Q2**

# #

A

D

E

F

G

H

M

T

EXPLORER

Live Work Explore Guides

Mini Visitors' Guides

Mini Maps

Check out **www.liveworkexplore.com**

Photography Books

Maps

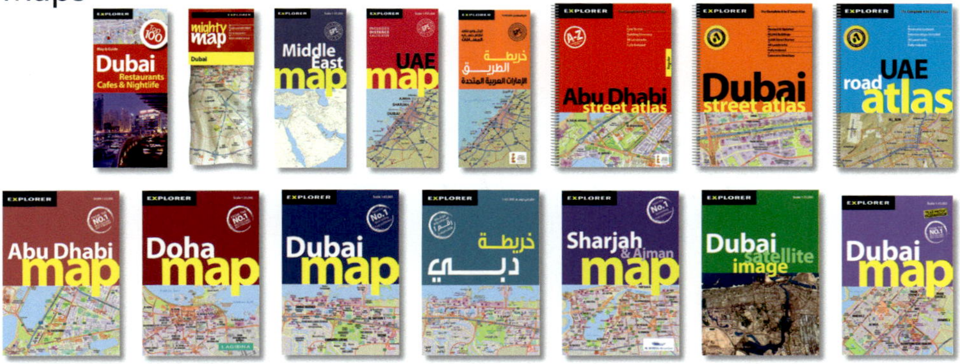

Lifestyle Guides

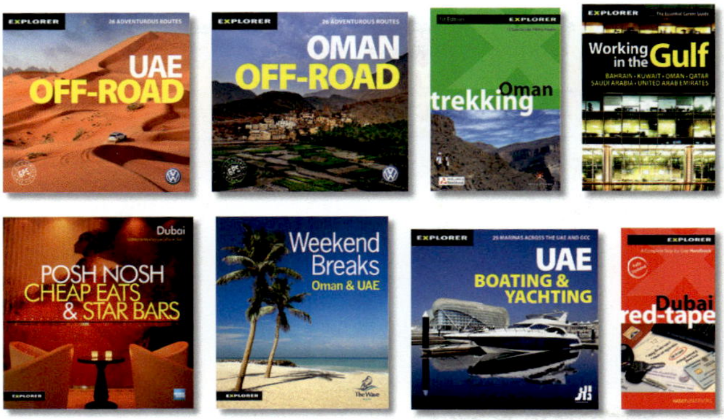

Magazine

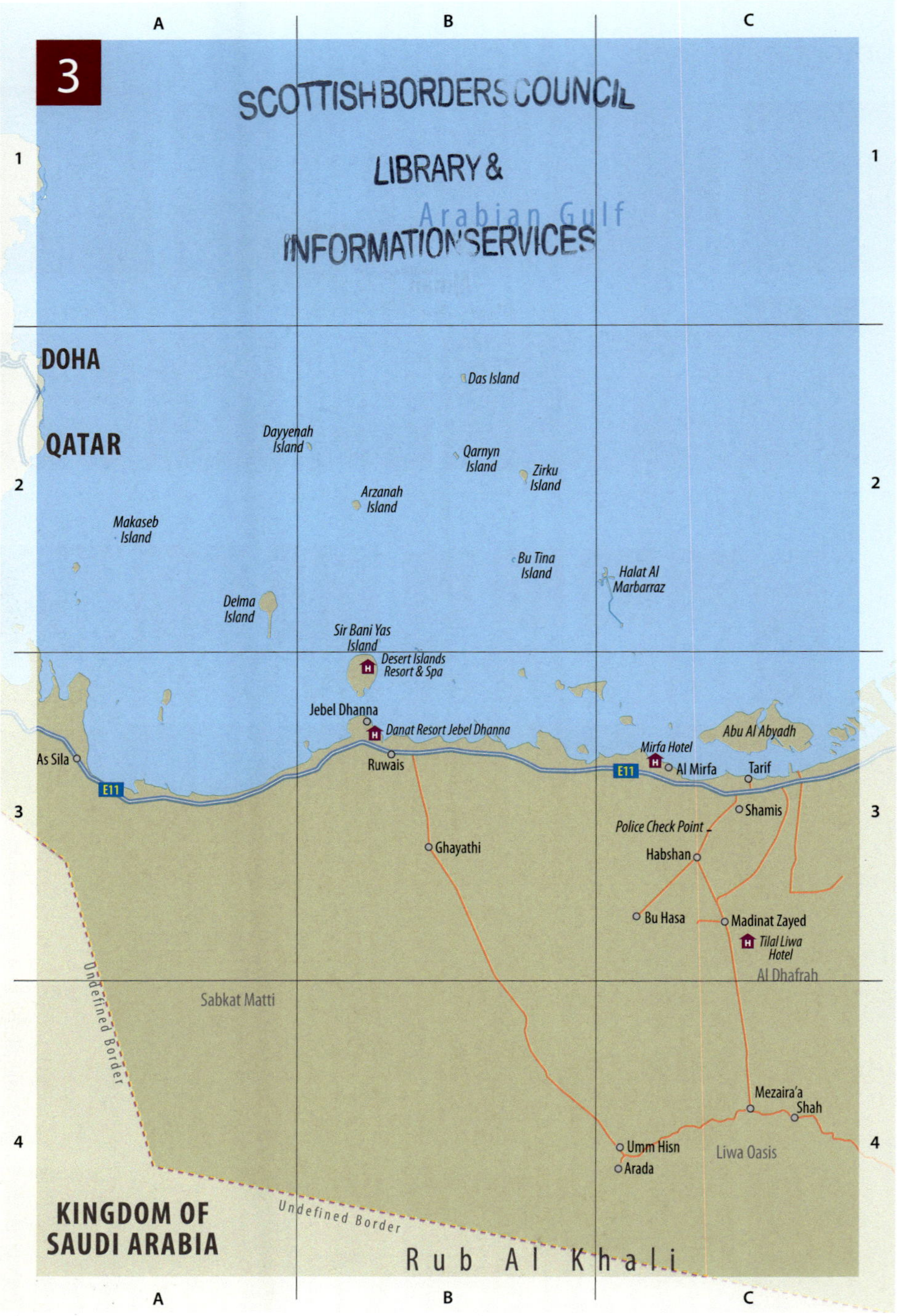
3
A
B
C
1
2
3
4
Arabian Gulf
DOHA
QATAR
Das Island
Dayyenah Island
Qarnyn Island
Zirku Island
Arzanah Island
Makaseb Island
Bu Tina Island
Halat Al Marbarraz
Delma Island
Sir Bani Yas Island
Desert Islands Resort & Spa
Jebel Dhanna
Danat Resort Jebel Dhanna
As Sila
Ruwais
E11
Mirfa Hotel
Al Mirfa
Abu Al Abyadh
Tarif
Shamis
Police Check Point
Ghayathi
Habshan
Bu Hasa
Madinat Zayed
Tilal Liwa Hotel
Al Dhafrah
Sabkat Matti
Undefined Border
Mezaira'a
Shah
Umm Hisn
Arada
Liwa Oasis
KINGDOM OF SAUDI ARABIA
Rub Al Khali

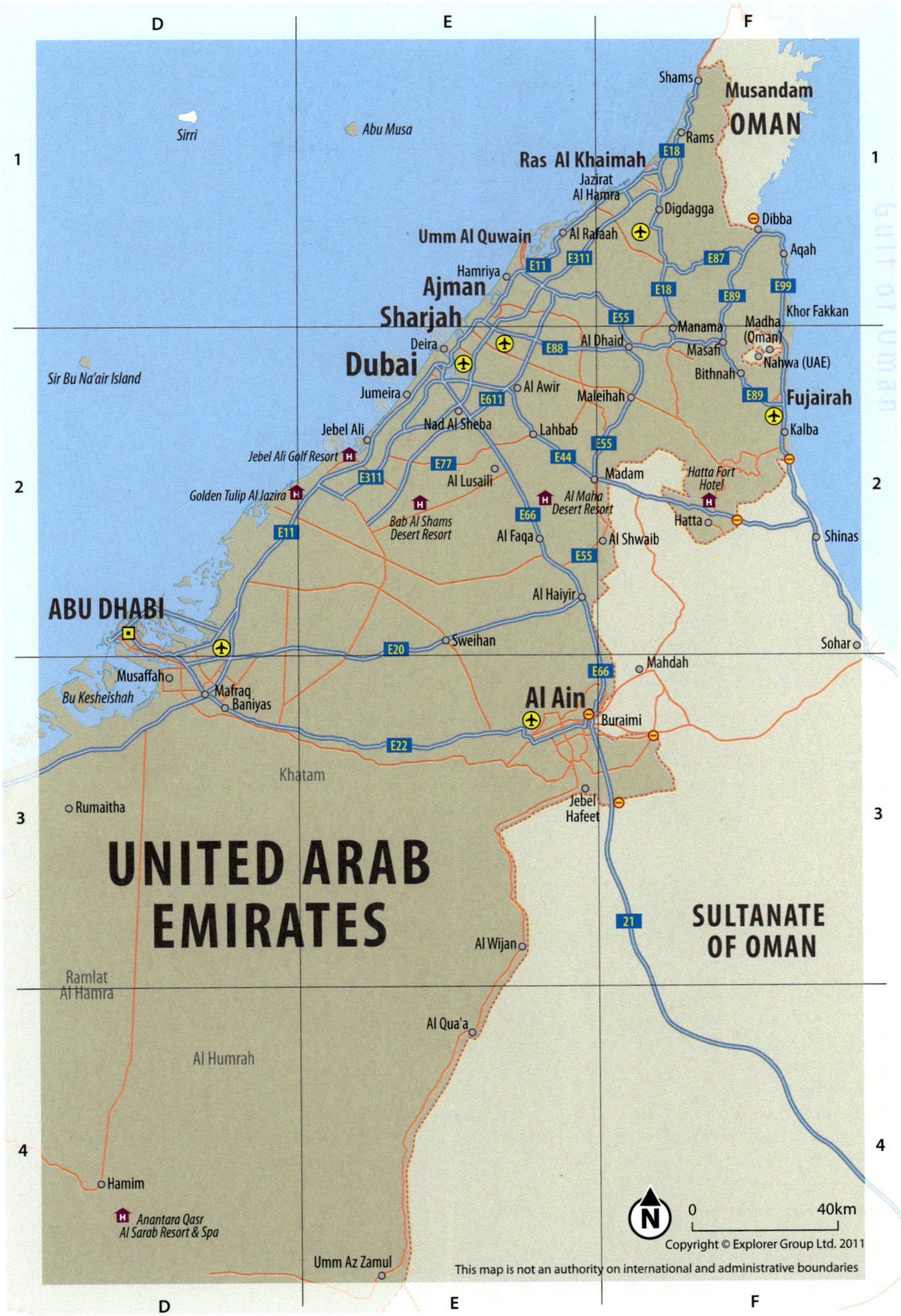

D
E
F
1
2
3
4
Musandam
OMAN
Shams
Rams
Ras Al Khaimah
Jazirat Al Hamra
Digdagga
Dibba
Aqah
Umm Al Quwain
Al Rafaah
Hamriya
Ajman
Sharjah
Dubai
Deira
Jumeira
Khor Fakkan
Manama
Madha (Oman)
Masafi
Nahwa (UAE)
Bithnah
Fujairah
Kalba
Al Dhaid
Al Awir
Maleihah
Nad Al Sheba
Lahbab
Jebel Ali
Jebel Ali Golf Resort
Golden Tulip Al Jazira
Al Lusaili
Madam
Hatta Fort Hotel
Hatta
Bab Al Shams Desert Resort
Al Maha Desert Resort
Al Faqa
Al Shwaib
Shinas
Sirri
Abu Musa
Sir Bu Na'air Island
ABU DHABI
Al Haiyir
Sweihan
Sohar
Mahdah
Musaffah
Bu Kesheishah
Mafraq
Baniyas
Al Ain
Buraimi
Khatam
Rumaitha
Jebel Hafeet
UNITED ARAB EMIRATES
SULTANATE OF OMAN
Al Wijan
Ramlat Al Hamra
Al Qua'a
Al Humrah
Hamim
Anantara Qasr Al Sarab Resort & Spa
Umm Az Zamul
E18
E311
E11
E87
E89
E99
E55
E88
E611
E44
E77
E66
E20
E22
21
Gulf of Oman
N
0
40km
Copyright © Explorer Group Ltd. 2011
This map is not an authority on international and administrative boundaries

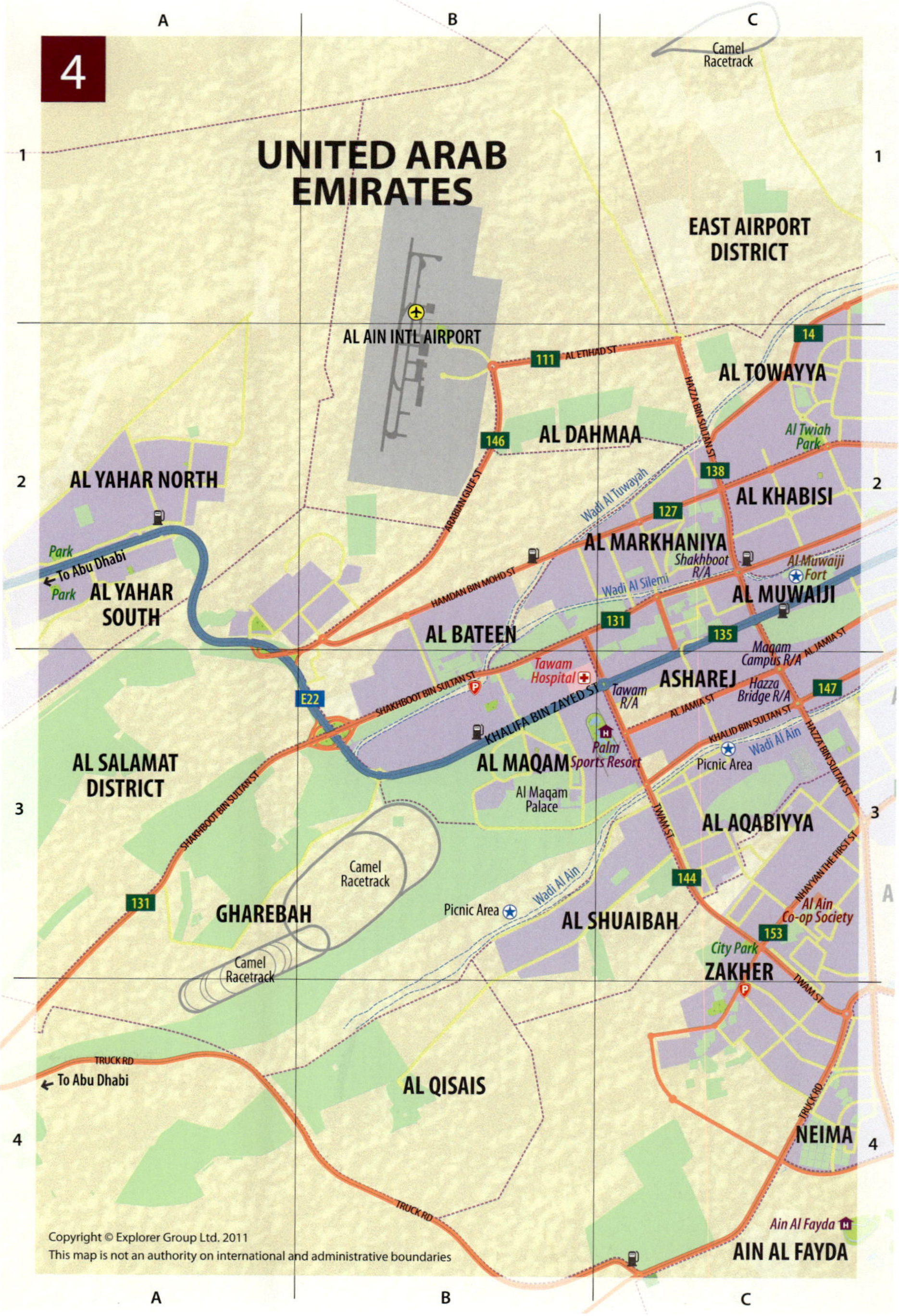
4
UNITED ARAB EMIRATES
AL AIN INTL AIRPORT
EAST AIRPORT DISTRICT
Camel Racetrack
AL TOWAYYA
AL DAHMAA
Al Twiah Park
AL KHABISI
AL YAHAR NORTH
Park
To Abu Dhabi
Park
AL YAHAR SOUTH
AL MARKHANIYA
Shakhboot R/A
Al Muwaiji Fort
AL MUWAIJI
Wadi Al Tuwayah
Wadi Al Silemi
AL BATEEN
Tawam Hospital
ASHAREJ
Maqam Campus R/A
Tawam R/A
Hazza Bridge R/A
AL MAQAM
Palm Sports Resort
Al Maqam Palace
Picnic Area
Wadi Al Ain
AL SALAMAT DISTRICT
AL AQABIYYA
Camel Racetrack
GHAREBAH
Camel Racetrack
Picnic Area
Wadi Al Ain
AL SHUAIBAH
Al Ain Co-op Society
City Park
ZAKHER
To Abu Dhabi
TRUCK RD
AL QISAIS
NEIMA
TRUCK RD
Ain Al Fayda
AIN AL FAYDA
AL ETIHAD ST
HAZZA BIN SULTAN ST
ARABIAN GULF ST
HAMDAN BIN MOHD ST
SHAKHBOOT BIN SULTAN ST
KHALIFA BIN ZAYED ST
AL JAMIA ST
KHALID BIN SULTAN ST
TWAM ST
NHAYYAN THE FIRST ST
E22
14
111
146
138
127
131
135
147
144
153
131
A
B
C
1
2
3
4
Copyright © Explorer Group Ltd. 2011
This map is not an authority on international and administrative boundaries

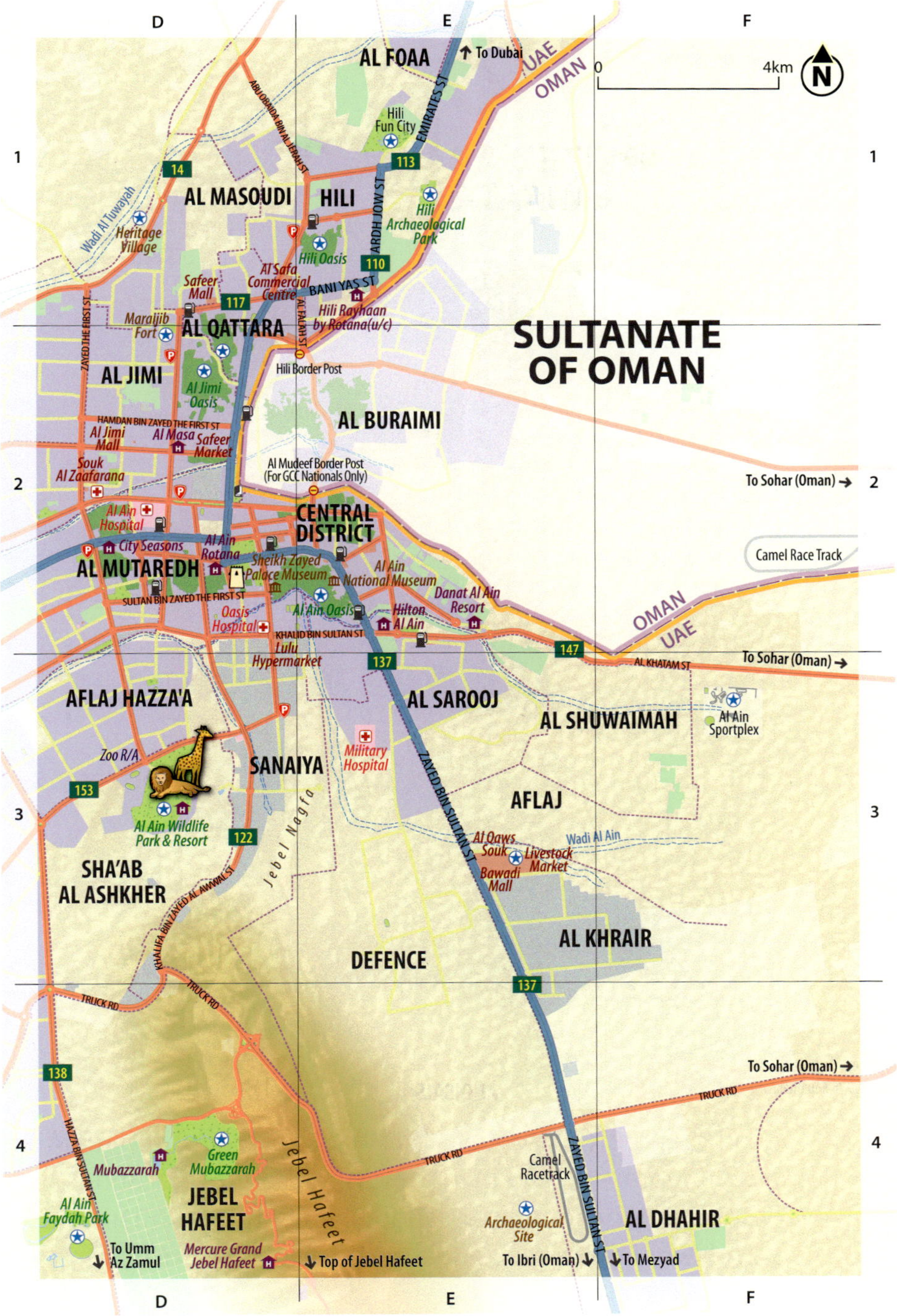

D
E
F
1
2
3
4
AL FOAA
To Dubai
UAE
OMAN
0
4km
N
ABU OBAIDA BIN AL JERAH ST
EMIRATES ST
Hili Fun City
14
113
AL MASOUDI
HILI
ARDH JOW ST
Hili Archaeological Park
Wadi Al Tuwayah
Heritage Village
Hili Oasis
110
Al Safa Commercial Centre
BANI YAS ST
Safeer Mall
117
ZAYED THE FIRST ST
AL FALAH ST
Hili Rayhaan by Rotana(u/c)
Maraijib Fort
AL QATTARA
SULTANATE OF OMAN
AL JIMI
Hili Border Post
Al Jimi Oasis
AL BURAIMI
HAMDAN BIN ZAYED THE FIRST ST
Al Jimi Mall
Al Masa
Safeer Market
Souk Al Zaafarana
Al Mudeef Border Post (For GCC Nationals Only)
To Sohar (Oman)
Al Ain Hospital
CENTRAL DISTRICT
City Seasons
Al Ain Rotana
Camel Race Track
AL MUTAREDH
Sheikh Zayed Palace Museum
Al Ain National Museum
Danat Al Ain Resort
SULTAN BIN ZAYED THE FIRST ST
Oasis Hospital
Al Ain Oasis
Hilton Al Ain
OMAN
UAE
KHALID BIN SULTAN ST
Lulu Hypermarket
137
147
AL KHATAM ST
To Sohar (Oman)
AFLAJ HAZZA'A
AL SAROOJ
AL SHUWAIMAH
Al Ain Sportplex
Zoo R/A
SANAIYA
Military Hospital
ZAYED BIN SULTAN ST
153
AFLAJ
Al Ain Wildlife Park & Resort
122
Jebel Nagfa
Al Qaws Souk
Livestock Market
Wadi Al Ain
SHA'AB AL ASHKHER
KHALIFA BIN ZAYED AL AWWAL ST
Bawadi Mall
AL KHRAIR
DEFENCE
137
TRUCK RD
TRUCK RD
138
To Sohar (Oman)
TRUCK RD
HAZZA BIN ZAYED ST
Jebel Hafeet
Green Mubazzarah
Mubazzarah
TRUCK RD
Camel Racetrack
ZAYED BIN SULTAN ST
JEBEL HAFEET
Al Ain Faydah Park
Archaeological Site
AL DHAHIR
To Umm Az Zamul
Mercure Grand Jebel Hafeet
Top of Jebel Hafeet
To Ibri (Oman)
To Mezyad

EXPLORER

Abu Dhabi Explorer – 9th Edition
Lead editor Jo Iivonen
Editorial team Charlie Scott, Laura Coughlin, Matt Warnock
Freelance contributions by Bertie Boardman, Hannah Unwin, Jessica Fuller, Jo Simmonds, Sarah Widdup, Steven Tweddel, Vanessa Scott
Proofread by Max Tuttle, Yvette Camba
Data managed by Amapola Castillo, Anas Abdul Latheef, Derrick Pereira, Ingrid Cupido, Mimi Stankova
Designed by Ieyad Charaf, Jayde Fernandes, Pete Maloney, Shawn Zuzarte
Maps by Sunita Lakhiani, Zainudheen Madathil
Photographs by Pamela Grist, Pete Maloney, Victor Romero

Publishing
Founder & CEO Alistair MacKenzie
Associate Publisher Claire England

Editorial
Editors Jo Iivonen, Matt Warnock
Corporate Editor Charlie Scott
Web Editor Laura Coughlin
Production Coordinator Kathryn Calderon
Production Assistant Janette Tamayo
Senior Editorial Assistant Mimi Stankova
Editorial Assistants Amapola Castillo, Ingrid Cupido

Design & Photography
Creative Director Pete Maloney
Art Director Ieyad Charaf
Contract Publishing Manager Chris Goldstraw
Designer Michael Estrada
Junior Designer Didith Hapiz
Layout Manager Jayde Fernandes
Layout Designers Mansoor Ahmed, Shawn Zuzarte
Cartography Manager Zainudheen Madathil
Maps Administrator Ikumi Shimizu
Cartographers Dhanya Nellikunnummal, Noushad Madathil, Sunita Lakhiani
Image Editor Henry Hilos

Sales & Marketing
Group Media Sales Manager Peter Saxby
Media Sales Area Managers Bryan Anes, Laura Zuffa, Pouneh Hafizi, Sabrina Ahmed, Yasin Alves
Corporate Solutions Account Manager Vibeke Nurgberg
Marketing Manager Lindsay Main
Senior Marketing Executive Stuart L. Cunningham
Sales & Marketing Assistant Shedan Ebona
Group Retail Sales Manager Ivan Rodrigues
Retail Sales Coordinator Michelle Mascarenhas
Senior Retail Sales Merchandisers Ahmed Mainodin, Firos Khan
Retail Sales Merchandisers Johny Mathew, Shan Kumar
Retail Sales Drivers Shabsir Madathil, Najumudeen K.I.
Warehouse Assistant Mohamed Haji

Finance & Administration
Administration Manager Fiona Hepher
Accountant Cherry Enriquez
Accounts Assistant Melody Beato, Sunil Suvarna
Reception & Admin Assistant Marie Joy Abarquez
Public Relations Officer Rafi Jamal
Office Assistant Shafeer Ahamed

IT & Digital Solutions
Digital Solutions Manager Derrick Pereira
Senior IT Administrator R. Ajay
Web Developer Anas Abdul Latheef

Contact Us

General Enquiries
We'd love to hear your thoughts and answer any questions you have about this book or any other Explorer product. Contact us at **info@explorerpublishing.com**

Careers
If you fancy yourself as an Explorer, send your CV (stating the position you're interested in) to **jobs@explorerpublishing.com**

Contract Publishing
For enquiries about Explorer's Contract Publishing arm and design services contact **projects@explorerpublishing.com**

PR & Marketing
For PR and marketing enquiries contact **marketing@explorerpublishing.com**

Corporate Sales
For bulk sales and customisation options, for this book or any Explorer product, contact **sales@explorerpublishing.com**

Advertising & Sponsorship
For advertising and sponsorship, contact **sales@explorerpublishing.com**

Explorer Publishing & Distribution
PO Box 34275, Dubai, United Arab Emirates
www.explorerpublishing.com

Phone: +971 (0)4 340 8805
Fax: +971 (0)4 340 8806

Useful Numbers

Embassies & Consulates

Australia	02 401 7500
Bahrain	02 665 7500
Canada	02 694 0300
China	02 443 4276
Egypt	02 444 5566
Finland	02 632 8927
France	02 443 5100
Germany	02 644 6693
India	02 449 2700
Iran	02 444 7618
Ireland	02 495 8200
Italy	02 443 5622
Japan	02 443 5696
Jordan	02 444 7100
Kuwait	02 447 7146
Lebanon	02 449 2100
Malaysia	02 448 2775
The Netherlands	02 632 1920
Oman	02 446 3333
Pakistan	02 444 7800
Philippines	02 639 0006
Poland	02 446 5200
Qatar	02 449 3300
Russia	02 672 1797
Saudi Arabia	02 444 5700
South Africa	02 447 3446
Spain	02 626 9544
Sri Lanka	02 631 6444
Sweden	02 417 8800
Switzerland	02 627 4636
Syria	02 444 8768
Thailand	02 642 1772
UK	02 610 1100
USA	02 414 2200
Yemen	02 444 8457

A&E Departments

Al Ain Hospital	03 763 588
Al Mafraq Hospital	02 582 310
Al Noor Hospital	02 626 526
Al Rahba Hospital	02 506 410
Al Salama Hospital	02 671 122
Corniche Hospital	02 672 490
Emirates International Hospital	03 763 777
Hospital Franco-Emirien	02 626 572
Madinat Zayed Hospital	02 884 444
National Hospital	02 671 100
NMC Speciality Hospital	02 633 225
Oasis Hospital	03 722 125
Sheikh Khalifa Medical City	02 610 200
Tawam Hospital	03 767 744

Emergency Services

Abu Dhabi Police	999
Ambulance	998/999
Fire Department	997
AAA (Roadside Assistance)	800 8181

24 Hour Pharmacy

Sheikh Khalifa Medical City ER Pharmacy	02 819 2188
Lifeline Hospital Pharmacy	02 633 3340
Al Noor Hospital Pharmacy	02 613 9100
Al Ain Hospital Pharmacy	03 763 5888
Liwa Hospital Pharmacy	02 882 2204

Useful Numbers

Abu Dhabi Municipality	800 555
Directory Enquiries	181/199
ADWEC (Emergency)	991/992
UAE Country Code	+971
Abu Dhabi Airport Flight Enquiries	02 575 7500